EXAM PREP

MCSE 70-293

Planning and Maintaining a Microsoft® Windows Server™ 2003 Network Infrastructure

Will Schmied

MCSE 70-293 Exam Prep: Planning and Maintaining a Microsoft® Windows Server™ 2003 Network Infrastructure

International Standard Book Number: 0-7897-3650-0

Printed in the United States of America

First Printing: December 2006

This product is printed digitally on demand.

Trademarks

All terms mentioned in this book that are known to be trademarks or service marks have been appropriately capitalized. Que Publishing cannot attest to the accuracy of this information. Use of a term in this book should not be regarded as affecting the validity of any trademark or service mark.

Microsoft is a registered trademark of Microsoft Corporation.

Windows Server is a trademark of Microsoft Corporation.

Warning and Disclaimer

Every effort has been made to make this book as complete and as accurate as possible, but no warranty or fitness is implied. The information provided is on an "as is" basis. The authors and the publisher shall have neither liability nor responsibility to any person or entity with respect to any loss or damages arising from the information contained in this book or from the use of the CD or programs accompanying it.

Bulk Sales

Que Publishing offers excellent discounts on this book when ordered in quantity for bulk purchases or special sales. For more information, please contact

U.S. Corporate and Government Sales
1-800-382-3419
corpsales@pearsontechgroup.com

For sales outside the U.S., please contact

International Sales
international@pearsoned.com

Library of Congress Cataloging-in-Publication Data

Schmied, Will.

MCSE 70-293 exam prep : planning and maintaining a Microsoft Windows server 2003 network infrastructure / Will Schmied.

p. cm.

Includes index.

ISBN 0-7897-3650-0 (pbk.)

1. Electronic data processing personnel--Certification. 2. Microsoft software--Examinations--Study guides. 3. Microsoft Windows server. I. Title.

QA76.9.D343S32 2006

005.4'476--dc22

2006033871

PUBLISHER
Paul Boger

ACQUISITIONS EDITOR
Betsy Brown

DEVELOPMENT EDITOR
Allison Beaumont Johnson

MANAGING EDITOR
Patrick Kanouse

SENIOR PROJECT EDITOR
San Dee Phillips

COPY EDITOR
Krista Hansing

INDEXER
JBIndexing

PROOFREADER
Kathy Bidwell

TECHNICAL EDITOR
Marc Savage

PUBLISHING COORDINATOR
Vanessa Evans

COVER/INTERIOR DESIGNER
Gary Adair

PAGE LAYOUT
TnT Design, Inc.

Microsoft 70-293 Exam Objectives

Planning and Maintaining a Microsoft Windows Server 2003 Network Infrastructure

Exam Number: 70-293

Associated Certifications: MCP, MCSA on Windows Server 2003, MCSE on Windows Server 2003

Length: 40–45 questions, including simulations

Exam Description

The Implementing, Managing, and Maintaining a Microsoft Windows Server 2003 Network Infrastructure exam is one of three core exams required of candidates pursuing the Microsoft Certified Systems Administrator (MCSA) on Windows Server 2003, and one of six core exams required of candidates pursuing the Microsoft Certified Systems Engineer (MCSE) on Windows Server 2003. This exam tests typical topics related to basic networking and security that the candidate will encounter on the job. Each top-level exam objective is related to a job skill that the candidate is expected to have and demonstrate.

Exam Objectives

Exam 70-293 consists of the following six objectives, each with several subobjectives:

- Planning and Implementing Server Roles and Server Security
- Planning, Implementing, and Maintaining a Network Infrastructure
- Planning, Implementing, and Maintaining Routing and Remote Access
- Planning, Implementing, and Maintaining Server Availability
- Planning and Maintaining Network Security
- Planning, Implementing, and Maintaining Security Infrastructure

Before taking the exam, you should be proficient in the job skills represented by the following objectives and subobjectives.

Planning and Implementing Server Roles and Server Security

The Planning and Implementing Server Roles and Server Security objective is designed to make sure that you understand and thus can plan and implement secure servers based on their roles in the network. You need to understand the default security configuration of new computers, as well as how to incrementally tighten security to meet your needs. The objectives are as follows:

- Configure security for servers that are assigned specific roles. 310
- Plan a secure baseline installation. 292
    - Plan a strategy to enforce system default security settings on new systems. 292
    - Identify client operating system default security settings. 300
    - Identify all server operating system default security settings. 307
- Plan security for servers that are assigned specific roles. Roles might include domain controllers, web servers, database servers, and mail servers. 307
    - Deploy the security configuration for servers that are assigned specific roles. 325
    - Create custom security templates based on server roles. 325
- Evaluate and select the operating system to install on computers in an enterprise. 289
    - Identify the minimum configuration to satisfy security requirements. 307

Planning, Implementing, and Maintaining a Network Infrastructure

The Planning, Implementing, and Maintaining a Network Infrastructure objective is designed to make sure that

Continues on Following Page

you can adequately plan, implement, configure, and troubleshoot a complex network infrastructure consisting of multiple protocols, multiple name-resolution services, and the physical and logical placement of objects and resources. The objectives are as follows:

Planning, Implementing, and Maintaining Routing and Remote Access

The Planning, Implementing, and Maintaining Routing and Remote Access objective is designed to make sure that you can adequately plan, implement, configure, and troubleshoot a remote access and routing solution. The objectives are as follows:

Planning, Implementing, and Maintaining Server Availability

The Planning, Implementing, and Maintaining Server Availability objective is designed to make sure that you can adequately plan, implement, configure, and troubleshoot complex highly available solutions, including clustering and network load balancing. You also are expected to understand and be able to plan and manage disaster-recovery operations for your network, in addition to monitoring your network for signs of trouble using available monitoring and logging tools. The objectives are as follows:

- Identify system bottlenecks, including memory, processor, disk, and network-related bottlenecks. 551
  - Identify system bottlenecks by using System Monitor. 556
- Implement a cluster server. 636
  - Recover from cluster node failure. 647
- Manage network load balancing. Tools might include the Network Load Balancing Monitor Microsoft Management Console (MMC) snap-in and the WLBS cluster control utility. 650
- Plan a backup and recovery strategy. 571
  - Identify appropriate backup types. Methods include full, incremental, and differential. 573
  - Plan a backup strategy that uses volume shadow copy. 590
  - Plan system recovery that uses Automated System Recovery (ASR). 572

Planning and Maintaining Network Security

The Planning and Maintaining Network Security objective is designed to make sure that you can adequately plan, implement, configure, and troubleshoot complex network data security solutions that use the IP Security (IPSec) protocol. The objectives are as follows:

- Configure network protocol security. 361
  - Configure protocol security in a heterogeneous client computer environment. 361
  - Configure protocol security by using IPSec policies. 368
- Configure security for data transmission. 395
  - Configure IPSec policy settings. 368
- Plan for network protocol security. 395
  - Specify the required ports and protocols for specified services. 368
  - Plan an IPSec policy for secure network communications. 368
- Plan secure network administration methods. 421
  - Create a plan to offer Remote Assistance to client computers. 421
  - Plan for remote administration by using Terminal Services. 430
- Plan security for wireless networks. 434
- Plan security for data transmission. 361
  - Secure data transmission between client computers to meet security requirements. 361
  - Secure data transmission by using IPSec. 368
- Troubleshoot security for data transmission. Tools might include the IP Security Monitor MMC snap-in and the Resultant Set of Policy (RSoP) MMC snap-in. 395

Planning, Implementing, and Maintaining Security Infrastructure

The Planning, Implementing, and Maintaining Security Infrastructure objective is designed to make sure that you can adequately plan, implement, configure, and troubleshoot a complex Certificate Services infrastructure for your network. You also are expected to understand change- and configuration-management basics. Finally, you will be tested on basic security-management tools such as Microsoft Baseline Security Analyzer (MBSA) and Windows Server Update Services (WSUS). The objectives are as follows:

- Configure Active Directory directory service for certificate publication. 501
- Plan a public key infrastructure (PKI) that uses Certificate Services. 485
  - Identify the appropriate type of certificate authority to support certificate issuance requirements. 494
  - Plan the enrollment and distribution of certificates. 506
  - Plan for the use of smart cards for authentication. 515
- Plan a framework for planning and implementing security. 521
  - Plan for security monitoring. 528
  - Plan a change and configuration management framework for security. 531
- Plan a security update infrastructure. Tools might include Microsoft Baseline Security Analyzer and Microsoft Software Update Services. 521

Contents at a Glance

Table of Contents

About the Author

Will Schmied, BSET, MCSE, CWNA, TICSA, MCSA, Security+, Network+, A+, is a Senior Systems Administrator for a world-renowned children's research hospital. As a freelance writer, Will has worked with many publishers, including Microsoft and Pearson. Will has also worked directly with Microsoft in the MCSE exam-development process and is the founder of the popular Internet certification portal www.mcseworld.com.

Will holds a Bachelor's degree in mechanical engineering technology from Old Dominion University along with his various IT industry certifications. Before becoming a civilian, he served in the U.S. Navy for more than 12 years in the nuclear power field.

Will currently resides in northern Mississippi, with his wife Chris; their children, Christopher, Austin, Andrea, and Hannah; their dogs, Charlie and Jack; and their cats, Smokey, Evin, and Socks. When he's not busy working, you can find Will enjoying time with his family, taking in a hockey game, or vegetating in front of the Xbox 360.

About the Technical Editor

Marc Savage is a senior national technical advisor and technical trainer for Nexient. Combined with more than 11 years of experience in microcomputer training and systems development in the private, public, and nonprofit organization sectors, his professional expertise is focused particularly on providing companies with a clear vision and direction for Microsoft products. Marc currently holds the following certifications: MCT, MCSE, MCSA, CNE, A+, Network +, ITIL, and HDA. Over the past ten years Marc has worked on many titles for New Riders and Que Publishing.

When not in front of his computer, Marc spends his time with his lovely wife Lynne and two daughters Isabelle and Carolyne. He can be reached at msavage@nexientlearning.com.

Dedication

To my wonderful and very understanding family: Thank you for your support on all those late nights. You make projects like this book worth doing!

Acknowledgments

I would like to thank all of the outstanding staff at Que Publishing, especially Betsy Brown, who brought this project to life. Thanks to Marc Savage for providing key insight into the ways that we could make this book better than its predecessor and who helped get all the bits and bytes in the right order in such a timely fashion.

We Want to Hear from You!

As the reader of this book, *you* are our most important critic and commentator. We value your opinion and want to know what we're doing right, what we could do better, what areas you'd like to see us publish in, and any other words of wisdom you're willing to pass our way.

As publisher for Que Publishing, I welcome your comments. You can email or write me directly to let me know what you did or didn't like about this book—as well as what we can do to make our books better.

Please note that I cannot help you with technical problems related to the topic of this book. We do have a User Services group, however, where I will forward specific technical questions related to the book.

When you write, please be sure to include this book's title and author as well as your name, email address, and phone number. I will carefully review your comments and share them with the author and editors who worked on the book.

Email: scorehigher@pearsoned.com

Mail: Paul Boger
Publisher
Que Publishing
800 East 96th Street
Indianapolis, IN 46240 USA

Reader Services

Visit our website and register this book at www.examcram.com/register for convenient access to any updates, downloads, or errata that might be available for this book.

Introduction

MCSE 70-293 Exam Prep: Planning and Maintaining a Microsoft Windows Server 2003 Network Infrastructure is designed for advanced end users, technicians, system administrators, and systems engineers who are seeking to pass Exam 70-293, *Planning and Maintaining a Microsoft Windows Server 2003 Network Infrastructure*, in pursuit of a Microsoft Windows certification. Passing Exam 70-293 qualifies you as a Microsoft Certified Professional (MCP) and counts as core credit toward the Microsoft Certified Systems Administrator (MCSA) and Microsoft Certified Systems Engineer (MCSE) certifications.

This exam measures your ability to perform more advanced planning and implementation of security solutions, TCP/IP, DNS and WINS infrastructures, routing, remote access, highly available solutions through clustering and network load balancing, secure administration methods, secure data-transmission methods, and digital certificates. It is already assumed that you understand the basics of all these topics and all the supporting areas that would be required at this stage of your career and experience with Windows Server 2003.

Who Should Read This Book

This book is designed to help you meet your certification goals by preparing you for the *Planning and Maintaining a Microsoft Windows Server 2003 Network Infrastructure* exam (70-293). In a Windows Server 2003 network, the ability to plan, install, support, and troubleshoot the various networking components and services included with Windows Server 2003 is critical to an administrator's success. Windows Server 2003 tightly integrates services such as DHCP and DNS into the core operating systems as well as Active Directory, and requires that they be configured correctly to function. This exam touches on all the major networking components critical to a successful Windows Server 2003 implementation. Although volumes of information are available on the history, theory, and underlying applications related to the networking services provided by Windows Server 2003, this book does not cover these portions of the services in detail. The purpose of this book is to provide you with an introduction to these services in general, provide you with an in-depth look at the Windows Server 2003 implementations of these network services, and prepare you to take the exam.

One additional area that is key to all Windows exams is the emphasis on network security. Keeping in line with the Microsoft Trustworthy Computing initiatives, Microsoft is putting much greater emphasis on the security facets of all its Windows Server 2003 exams.

Recognizing that a great deal of information exists on these topics that this book cannot cover, each chapter in this book contains a section called "Suggested Readings and Resources" that provides you with recommended sources for filling in the blanks. So although you might not be an expert at planning and implementing complex, multiple-site DNS architectures to support Active Directory, by the time you complete this book, you will know how to start and how to avoid many common pitfalls you might otherwise fall into. Additional resources are presented so that you can further your understanding and take your skills to the next level.

One of the most common questions with any of the Microsoft certification tests is, "Do I need to take a class to pass this test?" Although the information you need to pass the exam is in this book, one thing that is difficult for any book to provide is hands-on experience with the product. If you can set up an environment that enables you to perform the exercises outlined in this book (hardware and software recommendations for this environment are included at the end of this introduction), you will be in good shape. You'll be in especially good shape if you have the opportunity to work with Windows Server 2003 in a production environment. To pass the exam, you do not need to take a class in addition to buying this book. However, depending on your personal study habits or learning style, you might benefit from taking a class in conjunction with studying from this book.

Microsoft specifies the following audience profile for this exam, which also summarizes the experience level that a typical MCSE candidate should possess:

- The MCSE on Windows Server 2003 credential is intended for IT professionals who work in the typically complex computing environment of medium to large companies.
- Candidates should have experience implementing and administering a network operating system in environments that have the following characteristics:
    - 250 to 5,000 or more users
    - Three or more physical locations
    - Three or more domain controllers
    - Network services and resources such as messaging, database, file and print, proxy server, firewall, Internet, intranet, remote access, and client computer management
    - Connectivity requirements such as connecting branch offices and individual users in remote locations to the corporate network and connecting corporate networks to the Internet
- In addition, candidates should have experience in the following areas:
    - Implementing and administering a desktop operating system
    - Designing a network infrastructure

How This Book Helps You

This book takes you on a self-guided tour of all the areas covered by Exam 70-293 and teaches you the specific skills you need to achieve MCSE certification. You'll also find helpful hints, tips, real-world examples, and exercises, as well as references to additional study materials. Specifically, this book is set up to help you in the following ways:

- **Organization**—This book is organized by individual exam objectives. Every objective you need to know for Exam 70-293 is covered in this book. We have attempted to present the objectives in an order that is as close as possible to how Microsoft would teach the information. However, we have not hesitated to reorganize where needed, to make the material as easy as possible for you to learn. We have also attempted to make the information accessible in the following ways:
  - The full list of exam topics and objectives is included in this introduction.
  - Each chapter begins with a list of the objectives covered in that chapter.
  - Each chapter also begins with an outline that provides an overview of the material and the page numbers where particular topics can be found.
  - The objectives are repeated where the material most directly relevant to it is covered (unless the whole chapter addresses a single objective).
- **Instructional features**—This book is designed to provide you with multiple ways to learn and reinforce the exam material. Following are some of the helpful methods:
  - **Exam alerts**—These provide specific exam-related advice. Such alerts might address what material is likely to be covered (or not covered) on the exam, how it is covered, or particular quirks of that exam.
  - **Review breaks and summaries**—Crucial information is summarized at various points in the book in lists or tables. Each chapter ends with a summary as well.
  - **Key terms**—A list of key terms from the chapter appears at the end of each chapter.
  - **Notes**—Notes contain various kinds of useful information, such as tips on technology or administrative practices, historical background on terms and technologies, and side commentary on industry issues.
  - **Warnings**—When using sophisticated information technology, the potential for mistakes always exists; catastrophes can even occur because of improper application of the technology. Warnings alert you to such potential problems.
  - **"In the Field" sidebars**—These relatively extensive discussions cover material that might not be directly relevant to the exam but that is useful as reference material or in everyday practice. "In the Field" sidebars might also provide useful background or contextual information that is necessary for understanding the larger topic under consideration.

- **Exercises**—Found at the end of the chapters in the "Apply Your Knowledge" section and in the "Challenge Exercises" found throughout the chapters, exercises are performance-based opportunities for you to learn and assess your knowledge.
- **"Step by Steps"**—These are hands-on tutorial instructions that walk you through tasks and functions that are relevant to the exam objectives.

- **Extensive practice test options**—The book provides numerous opportunities for you to assess your knowledge and practice for the exam. The practice options include the following:
  - **Review questions**—These open-ended questions appear in the "Apply Your Knowledge" section at the end of each chapter. They enable you to quickly assess your comprehension of what you just read in the chapter. Answers to the review questions are provided later in the section.
  - **Practice exam**—A practice exam is included in the "Final Review" section of the book. The "Final Review" section and the practice exam are discussed later in this Introduction.
- **"Final Review"**—This part of the book provides valuable tools for preparing for the exam.
  - **"Fast Facts"**—This condensed version of the information contained in the book is extremely useful for last-minute review.
  - **Practice exam**—A practice exam is included in this book. As much as possible, questions on this practice exam are written in styles similar to those used on the actual exam. Use the practice exam to assess your readiness for the real thing. Use the extensive answer explanations to improve your retention and understanding of the material.

The book includes several other features, such as a "Suggested Readings and Resources" section at the end of each chapter that directs you to additional information that can aid you in your exam preparation and your real-life work. Valuable appendixes are provided as well, including a glossary and a description of what is on the CD-ROM.

For more information about the exam or the certification process, contact Microsoft at 800-636-7544 or MCPHelp@microsoft.com, or visit www.microsoft.com/learning/.

Hardware and Software You Will Need

As a self-paced study guide, *MCSE 70-293 Exam Prep: Planning and Maintaining a Windows Server 2003 Network Infrastructure* is meant to help you understand concepts that must be refined through hands-on experience. To make the most of your studying, you need to have as much background on and experience with Windows Server 2003 as possible. The best way to do this is to combine studying with working on real networks, using the products on which you will be tested. This section describes the minimum computer requirements you need to enjoy a solid practice environment.

The minimum computer requirements to ensure that you can study everything on which you'll be tested are one or more workstations running Windows 2000 Professional or Windows XP Professional, and two or more servers running Windows Server 2003—all connected by a network. Many of these examples, exercises, and references refer to Internet websites, so an Internet-connected network is a benefit. Because we look at some of the higher-level capabilities of the Windows Server 2003 family, the minimum requirements listed are specific to Windows Server 2003 Enterprise Edition; it has all the features covered by this exam and the lowest minimum hardware requirements.

Windows 2000 Professional

If you are using Windows 2000 Professional on your client workstations, those workstations need to meet the following *minimum* requirements:

- Major hardware listed on the Hardware Compatibility List at www.microsoft.com/whdc/hcl/search.mspx
- 133MHz or higher Pentium (or compatible) CPU
- At least 64MB of RAM
- Hard drive of at least 2GB, with 650MB free space minimum
- CD-ROM or DVD drive
- 3.5-inch 1.44MB floppy drive (recommended)
- VGA or higher-resolution monitor and video adapter
- Keyboard and mouse
- Network adapter, for networking

Windows XP Professional

If you are using Windows XP Professional on your client workstations, those workstations must meet the following *minimum* requirements:

- Major hardware listed in the Windows Marketplace at www.windowsmarketplace.com/
- 300MHz or higher Pentium (or compatible) CPU recommended, minimum of 233MHz CPU required

- 128MB of RAM recommended, minimum of 64MB of RAM required
- Hard drive with at least 1.5GB of free space
- CD-ROM or DVD drive
- 3.5-inch 1.44MB floppy drive (recommended)
- Super VGA or higher-resolution monitor and video adapter
- Keyboard and mouse
- Network adapter, for networking

Windows Server 2003 Enterprise Edition

Windows Server 2003 computers need to meet the following minimum requirements. You should strive to exceed these requirements where possible, to provide for enhanced performance and stability:

- 733MHz or higher Pentium (or compatible) CPU recommended for Intel x86–based computers, minimum of 133MHz CPU required
- 256MB of RAM recommended, minimum of 128MB of RAM required
- Hard drive with at least 1.5GB of free space minimum for Intel x86–based computers
- CD-ROM or DVD drive
- 3.5-inch 1.44MB floppy drive (recommended)
- Super VGA or higher-resolution monitor and video adapter
- Keyboard and mouse
- Network adapter, for networking

You can more easily obtain access to the necessary computer hardware and software in a corporate business environment. Allocating enough time within the busy workday to complete a self-study program, however, can be difficult. Most of your study time will occur after normal working hours, away from the everyday interruptions and pressures of your regular job.

TIP

Free Is Good! Microsoft is constantly making more resources available to IT professionals for free, many of which will likely help you during your preparation for this exam and even afterward.

You can view several online demonstrations at http://www.microsoft.com/windowsserver2003/evaluation/demos/default.mspx.

You can use several virtual labs at http://www.microsoft.com/technet/traincert/virtuallab/windowsserver2003.mspx.

TechNET webcasts are a great way to get to know more about Windows: http://www.microsoft.com/technet/community/webcasts/default.mspx.

Microsoft Virtual PC and Virtual Server 2005 R2 are both completely free now and will be very useful if your hardware is powerful enough to run multiple Virtual Machines on. Check out Virtual PC at http://www.microsoft.com/windows/virtualpc/default.mspx and Virtual Server at http://www.microsoft.com/windowsserversystem/virtualserver/default.mspx.

Finally, you can even get a free 180-day trial version of Windows Server 2003 R2 Enterprise Edition (32 or 64 bit) to work with, from http://www.microsoft.com/windowsserver2003/evaluation/trial/default.mspx.

Take advantage of all of these free resources from Microsoft to further your certification and knowledge level!

Advice on Taking the Exam

Although this list is not all inclusive, here are a few bits of advice to keep in mind as you study and prepare for your 70-293 exam:

- Read all the material. Microsoft has been known to include on its exams material not expressly specified in the objectives. This book includes additional information not reflected in the objectives, in an effort to give you the best possible preparation for the examination—and for the real-world network experiences to come.
- Do the "Step by Steps" and complete the exercises in each chapter. They will help you gain experience in using the specified methodology or approach. All Microsoft exams are task and experienced based, and require you to have experience actually performing the tasks on which you will be tested.
- Use the review and exam questions to assess your knowledge. Don't just read the chapter content; use the questions to find out what you know and what you don't. If you are struggling at all, study some more, review, and then assess your knowledge again.
- Review the exam objectives. Develop your own questions and examples for each topic listed. If you can develop and answer several questions for each topic, you should not find it difficult to pass the exam.

- Find a study buddy. This might sound corny, but it works. You should find a coworker or friend who is also preparing for the exam and use that person to improve your knowledge. Quiz each other and assist each other with sections where you feel your knowledge is weak.

NOTE

Exam-Taking Advice—Although this book is designed to prepare you to take and pass Exam 70-293, there are no guarantees. Read this book, work through the questions and exercises, and, when you feel confident, take the practice exam and additional exams, using the *MeasureUp* software. That should tell you whether you are ready for the real thing.

When taking the actual certification exam, make sure you answer all the questions before your time limit expires. Do not spend too much time on any one question. If you are unsure about an answer, answer the question the best you can; then mark it for review for when you have finished the rest of the questions. However, this advice does not apply when you are taking an adaptive exam. In that case, take your time on each question; no opportunity exists to go back to a question.

Be sure to read each question carefully and read all the answers before you make a selection. A question might have an answer that is close, but one of the other answers might, in fact, be a better answer. If you select an answer before reading all the choices, you might miss the best answer.

Get a good night's sleep before the exam. If you don't know the exam information by the night before the exam, an all-night cram session will just make you tired when you are taking the exam. You need to be at your sharpest when you take this exam; don't handicap yourself with sleep deprivation.

Remember, the primary objective of this book is not the exam; it is to ensure that you understand the material. When you understand the material, passing the exam should be simple. Knowledge is a pyramid: To build upward, you need a solid foundation. This book and the MCP programs are designed to ensure that you have that solid foundation.

Good luck!

You need to determine whether you can apply the information you have learned by attempting to create examples and scenarios on your own. You should think about how or where you could apply the concepts you are learning. Again, you should write down this information to process the facts and concepts in an active fashion.

The hands-on nature of the exercises at the ends of the chapters provides further active-learning opportunities that will reinforce concepts as well.

Common-Sense Strategies

You should follow common-sense practices when studying: You should study when you are alert, reduce or eliminate distractions, and take breaks when you become fatigued.

Pretesting Yourself

Pretesting allows you to assess how well you are learning. One of the most important aspects of learning is what has been called *meta-learning*. Meta-learning has to do with realizing when you know something well or when you need to study some more. In other words, you recognize how well or how poorly you have learned the material you are studying.

For most people, this can be difficult to assess. Review questions, practice questions, and practice tests are useful, in that they reveal objectively what you have learned and what you have not learned. You should use this information to guide review and further studying. Developmental learning takes place as you cycle through studying, assessing how well you have learned, reviewing, and assessing again until you feel you are ready to take the exam.

You might have noticed the practice exam included in this book. You should use it as part of the learning process. The *MeasureUp* test-simulation software included on this book's CD-ROM also provides you with an excellent opportunity to assess your knowledge.

You should set a goal for your pretesting. A reasonable goal would be to score consistently in the 90% range.

See Appendix B, "MeasureUp's Product Features," for further explanation of the test-simulation software.

Exam Prep Tips

When you have mastered the subject matter, the final preparatory step is to understand how the exam will be presented. Make no mistake: A Microsoft Certified Professional (MCP) exam will challenge both your knowledge and your test-taking skills. The following sections describe the basics of exam design, the exam formats, and hints targeted to each of the exam formats.

The MCSE Exam

Every MCSE exam is released in one of two basic formats. What's being called *exam format* here is really little more than a combination of the overall exam structure and the presentation method for exam questions.

Each exam format uses the same types of questions. These types or styles of questions include multiple-rating (or scenario-based) questions, traditional multiple-choice questions, and simulation-based questions. It's important to understand the types of questions you will be asked and the actions required to properly answer them.

Understanding the exam formats is key to good preparation because the format determines the number of questions presented, the difficulty of those questions, and the amount of time allowed to complete the exam.

Exam Format

The basic format for the MCSE exam is the traditional fixed-form exam. As its name implies, the fixed-form exam presents a fixed set of questions during the exam session.

Fixed-Form

A fixed-form computerized exam is based on a fixed set of exam questions and is the most likely form you will encounter for Exam 70-293. The individual questions are presented in random order during a test session. If you take the same exam more than once, you won't necessarily see the exact same questions. The reason is that two or three final forms are typically assembled for every fixed-form exam Microsoft releases. They are usually labeled Forms A, B, and C.

The final forms of a fixed-form exam are identical in terms of content coverage, number of questions, and allotted time, but the questions are different. You might notice, however, that some of the same questions appear on—or, rather, are shared among—different final forms. When questions are shared among multiple final forms of an exam, the percentage of sharing is generally small. Many final forms share no questions, but some older exams could have a 10% to 15% duplication of exam questions on the final exam forms.

Fixed-form exams also have a fixed time limit in which you must complete the exam. The MeasureUp software on the CD-ROM that accompanies this book carries fixed-form exams.

Finally, the score you achieve on a fixed-form exam, which is always reported for MCSE exams on a scale of 0 to 1,000, is based on the number of questions you answer correctly. The exam's passing score is the same for all final forms of a given fixed-form exam.

The typical format for the fixed-form exam is as follows:

- 50–60 questions.
- 75–90 minute testing time.
- Question review is allowed, including the opportunity to change your answers.

New Question Types: Simulation Questions

A variety of question types can appear on MCSE exams. Examples of multiple-choice questions and scenario-based questions appear throughout this book and the MeasureUp software. Simulation-based questions are new to the MCSE exam series.

Simulation-based questions reproduce the look and feel of key Microsoft product features for the purpose of testing. The simulation software used in MCSE exams has been designed to look and act, as much as possible, just like the actual product. Consequently, answering simulation questions in an MCSE exam entails completing one or more tasks just as if you were using the product itself.

The format of a typical Microsoft simulation question consists of a brief scenario or problem statement along with one or more tasks that must be completed to solve the problem.

This advice sounds obvious, but your first step when you encounter a simulation is to carefully read the question. Do not go straight to the simulation application! You must assess the problem being presented and identify the conditions that make up the problem scenario. Note the tasks that must be performed or outcomes that must be achieved to answer the question and review any instructions on how to proceed.

The next step is to launch the simulator by using the button provided. After clicking the Show Simulation button, you will see a feature of the product presented in a dialog box. The simulation application will partially cover the question text on many test center machines. Feel free to reposition the simulation or move between the question text screen and the simulation by using hotkeys, using point-and-click navigation, or even clicking the simulation launch button again.

It is important to understand that your answer to the simulation question will not be recorded until you move on to the next exam question. This gives you the added ability to close and reopen the simulation application (using the launch button) on the same question without losing any partial answer you might have made.

The third step is to use the simulator as you would the actual product to solve the problem or perform the defined tasks. Again, the simulation software is designed to function, within reason, just as the product does. But don't expect the simulation to reproduce product behavior perfectly. Most important, do not allow yourself to become flustered if the simulation does not look or act exactly like the product.

Two final points will help you tackle simulation questions. First, respond only to what is being asked in the question; do not solve problems that you are not asked to solve. Second, accept what is being asked of you. You might not entirely agree with conditions in the problem statement, the quality of the desired solution, or the sufficiency of defined tasks to adequately solve the problem. Always remember that you are being tested on your ability to solve the problem as it is presented. If you make any changes beyond those required by the question, the item will be scored as wrong on an MCSE exam.

Putting It All Together

As you can see, Microsoft is making an effort to use question types that go beyond asking you to simply memorize facts. These question types force you to know how to accomplish tasks and understand concepts and relationships. You should study so that you can answer these types of questions rather than those that simply ask you to recall facts.

Given all the different pieces of information presented so far, the following sections present a set of tips that will help you successfully tackle the exam.

More Pre-Exam Preparation Tips

Generic exam-preparation advice is always useful. Tips include the following:

- Become familiar with the product. Hands-on experience is one of the keys to success on any MCP exam. Review the exercises and the Step by Steps in the book.
- Review the current exam-preparation guide on the Microsoft Training & Certification website. The documentation Microsoft makes available on the Web identifies the skills every exam is intended to test.
- Memorize foundational technical detail, but remember that MCP exams are generally heavier on problem solving and application of knowledge than on questions that require only rote memorization.
- Take any of the available practice tests. We recommend the one included in this book and the ones you can create by using the MeasureUp software on this book's CD-ROM. As a supplement to the material bound with this book, try the free practice tests available on the Microsoft MCP website.
- Look on the Microsoft MCSE website for samples and demonstration items. These items tend to be particularly valuable for one significant reason: They help you become familiar with any new testing technologies before you encounter them on an MCSE exam.

During the Exam Session

The following generic exam-taking advice that you've heard for years applies when you're taking an MCP exam:

- Take a deep breath and try to relax when you first sit down for your exam session. It is very important that you control the pressure you might (naturally) feel when taking exams.
- You will be provided scratch paper. Take a moment to write down any factual information and technical detail that you have committed to short-term memory.
- Carefully read all information and instruction screens. These displays have been put together to give you information relevant to the exam you are taking.

- Accept the nondisclosure agreement and preliminary survey as part of the examination process. Complete them accurately and quickly move on.
- Read the exam questions carefully. Reread each question to identify all relevant detail.
- In fixed-form exams, tackle the questions in the order in which they are presented. Skipping around won't build your confidence; the clock is always counting down.
- Don't rush, but also don't linger on difficult questions. The questions vary in degree of difficulty. Don't let yourself be flustered by a particularly difficult or wordy question.

Besides considering the basic preparation and test-taking advice presented so far, you need to consider the challenges presented by the different exam designs, as described in the following sections.

Tips for Fixed-Form Exams

Because a fixed-form exam consists of a fixed, finite set of questions, you should add these tips to your strategy for taking a fixed-form exam:

- Note the time allotted and the number of questions on the exam you are taking. Make a rough calculation of how many minutes you can spend on each question, and use this figure to pace yourself through the exam.
- Take advantage of the fact that you can return to and review skipped or previously answered questions. Record the questions you can't answer confidently on the scratch paper provided, noting the relative difficulty of each question. When you reach the end of the exam, return to the more difficult questions.
- If you have session time remaining after you complete all the questions (and if you aren't too fatigued!), review your answers. Pay particular attention to questions that seem to have a lot of detail or that require graphics.
- As for changing your answers, the general rule of thumb here is, *don't*! If you read the question carefully and completely and you felt like you knew the right answer, you probably did. Don't second-guess yourself. If, as you check your answers, one clearly stands out as incorrect, however, of course you should change it. But if you are at all unsure, go with your first impression.

Tips for Answering Simulation Questions

Following are tips for answering the simulation questions:

- Avoid changing any simulation settings that don't pertain directly to the problem solution. Solve the problem you are being asked to solve and nothing more.
- Assume default settings when related information has not been provided. If something has not been mentioned or defined, it is a noncritical detail that does not factor into the correct solution.

- Be sure your entries are syntactically correct, paying particular attention to your spelling. Enter relevant information just as the product would require it.
- Close all simulation application windows after completing the simulation tasks. The testing system software is designed to trap errors that could result when using the simulation application, but trust yourself over the testing software.
- If simulations are part of a fixed-form exam, you can return to skipped or previously answered questions and change your answer. However, if you choose to change your answer to a simulation question or even attempt to review the settings you've made in the simulation application, your previous response to that simulation question will be deleted.

Final Considerations

Finally, a number of changes in the MCP program affect how frequently you can repeat an exam and what you will see when you do:

- Microsoft has an exam retake policy. The rule is "two and two, then one and two." That is, you can attempt any exam twice with no restrictions on the time between attempts. But after the second attempt, you must wait 2 weeks before you can attempt that exam again. After that, you are required to wait 2 weeks between subsequent attempts. Plan to pass the exam in two attempts, or plan to increase your time horizon for receiving the MCP credential.
- New questions are always being seeded into the MCP exams. After performance data is gathered on new questions, the examiners replace older questions on all exam forms. This means that the questions appearing on exams regularly change.

These changes mean that the brute-force strategies for passing MCP exams have lost their viability. So if you don't pass an exam on the first or second attempt, it is likely that the exam's form could change significantly by the next time you take it. It could be updated from fixed-form to adaptive, or, even more likely, it could have a different set of questions or question types.

Microsoft's intention is not to make the exams more difficult by introducing unwanted change, but to create and maintain valid measures of the technical skills and knowledge associated with the different MCP credentials. Preparing for an MCP exam has always involved not only studying the subject matter, but also planning for the testing experience itself. With the continuing changes, this is now truer than ever.

Lastly, and most importantly, the more practice and configuration time you can get with Windows Server 2003 the better. Practice, practice, and more practice is going to go a long way toward getting you to your MCSE goal!

PART I

Exam Preparation

1

CHAPTER ONE

Planning, Implementing, and Troubleshooting a TCP/IP Network Infrastructure

Your network is the road by which your data travels from point to point. Quite simply, if your network is flawed or is not functioning properly, your day will be unhappy, at best. At worst, your network services will not function, and if the network is down, most applications and services you are trying to deliver will not be deliverable. Good network designs do not just happen, nor are they necessarily hard to implement. A thorough knowledge of the mechanics of Transmission Control Protocol/Internet Protocol (TCP/IP), Internet Protocol (IP) routing, IP subnetting, and Internet connectivity goes a long way toward creating and maintaining a network that not only works, but also can evolve and grow as business and user needs change and/or become more complex.

Objectives

Microsoft has defined the TCP/IP connectivity portion of the "Planning, Implementing, and Maintaining a Network Infrastructure" objectives as follows:

Plan a TCP/IP network infrastructure strategy.

- **Analyze IP addressing requirements.**
- **Plan an IP routing solution.**
- **Create an IP subnet scheme.**
- Good networks begin with good planning and good designs. To plan and design a good network, you need to understand the IP addressing and routing requirements of your organization. With this knowledge in mind, you can move forward and start planning the IP subnets you require. This creates a solid backbone from which the rest of your network will be built.

Plan and modify a network topology.

- **Plan the physical placement of network resources.**
- **Identify network protocols to be used.**
- As mentioned before, all networks should have a design and/or plan. A large part of that plan should address where to physically and logically place network resources (file servers, print servers, Internet access, and so on) and identify protocols that will be used to connect to and access these resources.

Plan an Internet connectivity strategy.

- Reliable, available Internet access has become a required commodity in the vast majority of networks today. E-mail, web browsing, and a plethora of other business functions need Internet access to function. Thus, not having Internet connectivity would likely become a big problem in a short amount of time. In this chapter, we cover the importance of planning an Internet connectivity strategy.

Plan network traffic monitoring. Tools might include Network Monitor and System Monitor.

- Networks have problems that at times are hard to solve or reproduce but that need to be solved nonetheless. Using tools such as Network Monitor and System Monitor helps you locate, identify, and troubleshoot issues, as well as monitor traffic traversing your local area network (LAN).

Troubleshoot connectivity to the Internet.

- **Diagnose and resolve issues related to Network Address Translation (NAT).**
- **Diagnose and resolve issues related to name-resolution cache information.**
- **Diagnose and resolve issues related to client configuration.**
- When you are connected to the Internet, you might encounter many problems. You must address issues with NAT planning and implementation, issues with the domain name system (DNS), and, of course, issues with clients trying to connect to and use the Internet.

Troubleshoot TCP/IP addressing.

- **Diagnose and resolve issues related to client computer configuration.**
- **Diagnose and resolve issues related to DHCP server address assignment.**
- All great network administrators need to know, understand, and embrace TCP/IP. This objective covers what you need to know abut TCP/IP from a client perspective. You need to know how to troubleshoot TCP/IP issues, as well as those issues resulting from problems with a Dynamic Host Configuration Protocol (DHCP) server.

Outline

Study Strategies

- Focus on the objectives. Make sure you understand what each objective is asking you to do or learn. Read over the objectives a few times and try to understand what they are asking for; then think about how to plan, design, and troubleshoot problems resulting from each one.
- Memorize all TCP/IP charts, numbering, and standards as they map to the objectives. For instance, if your knowledge of subnetting is weak, you will most likely want to mark this as a weak spot. Make sure you attack your weak spots and get these issues under your belt for this exam.
- Get your hands dirty. The "Step by Steps" throughout this book provide plenty of directions and exercises, but you should go beyond these examples and create some of your own. If you can, experiment with each of the objectives to see how they work and why you would use each one.

Introduction

In this chapter, we look at how to plan, implement, and maintain a Windows Server 2003 network infrastructure. Before we delve into the specifics of how to do this, we first introduce the "why." Why should you worry so much about your network infrastructure? The answer is simple: If you don't have a well-developed network infrastructure, the rest of your applications, services, and systems will fail. Don't believe it? Let's look at an example from a client with a poorly designed network infrastructure.

ABC Corporation has been in business for 10 years. It is the primary producer of widgets for the world. ABC Corp. needs to merge with three new companies by the end of the year to broaden its widget inventory. The four widget companies will form one network after the merger is complete. You are the senior systems administrator responsible for making this happen. The following are some of the issues you will most likely see:

- Wasteful IP numbering schemes
- Routing loops and problems with routing tables from improperly designed networks or networks connected improperly
- A need to connect internal DNS namespaces, WINS servers, and Active Directory
- A need to have e-mail systems work together
- A need to tie applications and databases together and make them accessible to all users in all plants

The whole point to this example is that without a "rock solid" network infrastructure, you are sure to see problem after problem arise from lack of planning and design. Some of the items listed here are common business solutions that your users will demand and expect. It's up to you to understand the infrastructure well enough that you can implement these solutions easily enough.

The goal of this chapter is not only to present you the information you need to pass this exam, but also to introduce you to the importance of actually doing this work for real. In addition, because everything else builds off the network infrastructure, this chapter provides the ideal starting point for your preparation for Exam 70-293.

Planning a TCP/IP Network Infrastructure Strategy

Planning a TCP/IP network infrastructure strategy is no simple task. Accomplishing this task can take many years of experience and good a understanding of the mechanics of TCP/IP. This makes TCP/IP one of the exam items that many candidates shy away from because this topic deals with numbers; you might have to do some basic math or understand many concepts just to complete one specific item or task. For example, let's look at a possible problem you might have to contend with.

Looking back at the scenario facing you as the senior systems administrator of ABC Corporation, you need to connect another network to your own and plan a way for the other network to communicate with you. By itself, this problem is not very difficult, but when looking at the topology map (and all the many individual objects that exist in most networks), as shown in Figure 1.1, you start to see multiple places where complexity begins to surfaces.

EXAM ALERT

Implementing Windows Server 2003 in a TCP/IP-based network For Exam 70-293, you are responsible for knowing how to implement Windows Server 2003 in a TCP/IP-based network and how to troubleshoot any issues that arise. If you know how a TCP/IP network is designed, how TCP/IP works, and how to troubleshoot it, you will have few problems with that portion of the exam, as well as real-word scenarios in which you have to implement this technology on the job.

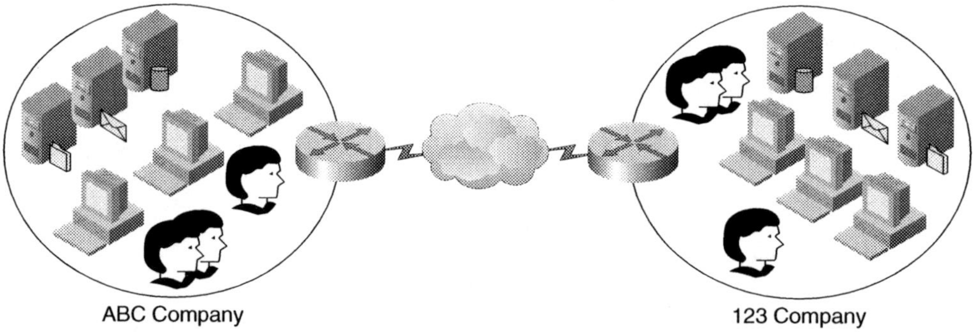

FIGURE 1.1 Viewing a TCP/IP infrastructure.

The true complexity surfaces when you start to examine the following issues:

1. How will the two domains work together?
2. Will DNS namespaces need to be connected?
3. Are any of the client computers Windows 9*x* legacy clients?
4. Will you need to implement WINS?
5. Does the company you are connecting to use DHCP, and what IP ranges does it have in its scopes?
6. Are the IP addresses and DHCP ranges duplicate to what you use in ABC Corporation?

7. How will you make the two routers communicate?
8. What wide area network (WAN) topology will you use between them?
9. What routing protocol will you use, or should you use static routes?
10. Are any firewalls, Access Control Lists (ACLs), or filtering devices present that could potentially block specific transmissions?

These questions are not meant to scare you; instead, they are meant to help you start thinking about the multitude of issues that surround the design and deployment of TCP/IP networks. Before we go any further, let's spend some time reviewing the fundamentals of TCP/IP.

TCP/IP Fundamentals

To successfully plan a TCP/IP-based network infrastructure strategy, you need to understand TCP/IP addressing and routing fundamentals. We examine these topics further in this section.

TCP/IP stands for *Transmission Control Protocol/Internet Protocol*, which is actually two separate protocols, one called TCP and the other called IP, within a "suite" of protocols that map to a model. Two models you have most likely heard of are the Open System Interface (OSI) model and the Department of Defense (DoD) model. This chapter does not contain a detailed explanation of these models because most of the information you need for the exam is not based on your memorizing the OSI model; however, you should understand it (if you don't already) before we cover the TCP/IP suite. You can find detailed information on the OSI model online at the Microsoft Technet website by examining Chapter 2 of *Microsoft Windows Server 2003 TCP/IP Fundamentals for Windows Server 2003*; the link is included in the "Suggested Readings and Resources" section at the end of this chapter.

TCP/IP maps to both the OSI and DoD models but actually maps more closely with the DoD model because the Department of Defense was the original creator and user of the protocol.

EXAM ALERT

Understanding the OSI and DoD models Although you are not expected to demonstrate master-level knowledge about the OSI or DoD models on your Exam 70-293, it is important to know that the OSI model is almost universally referenced in some way in any exam that deals with TCP/IP networking. As such, you should at least be familiar with it and know what layers make up the OSI model. Refer to Chapter 2 of the online book *TCP/IP Fundamentals for Windows Server 2003* for more detailed information about the OSI model, if you need a review.

The real importance of understanding the fundamentals of the OSI model becomes apparent when you try to troubleshoot TCP/IP base communications and services. Understanding what is happening at each layer makes it easier to determine where the fault might lie.

TCP/IP is the basic communication language or protocol of the Internet. Many other protocols are in use, some of which you might be familiar with, such as AppleTalk, IPX/SPX, or even SNA. TCP/IP has displaced all these protocols, however. Because most networks today are connected to the Internet somehow, using only TCP/IP on internal networks makes more sense.

You can see a good example of a TCP/IP-based network in Figure 1.2, which displays some of the TCP/IP concepts you will be working with both on this exam and during your day-to-day network administration.

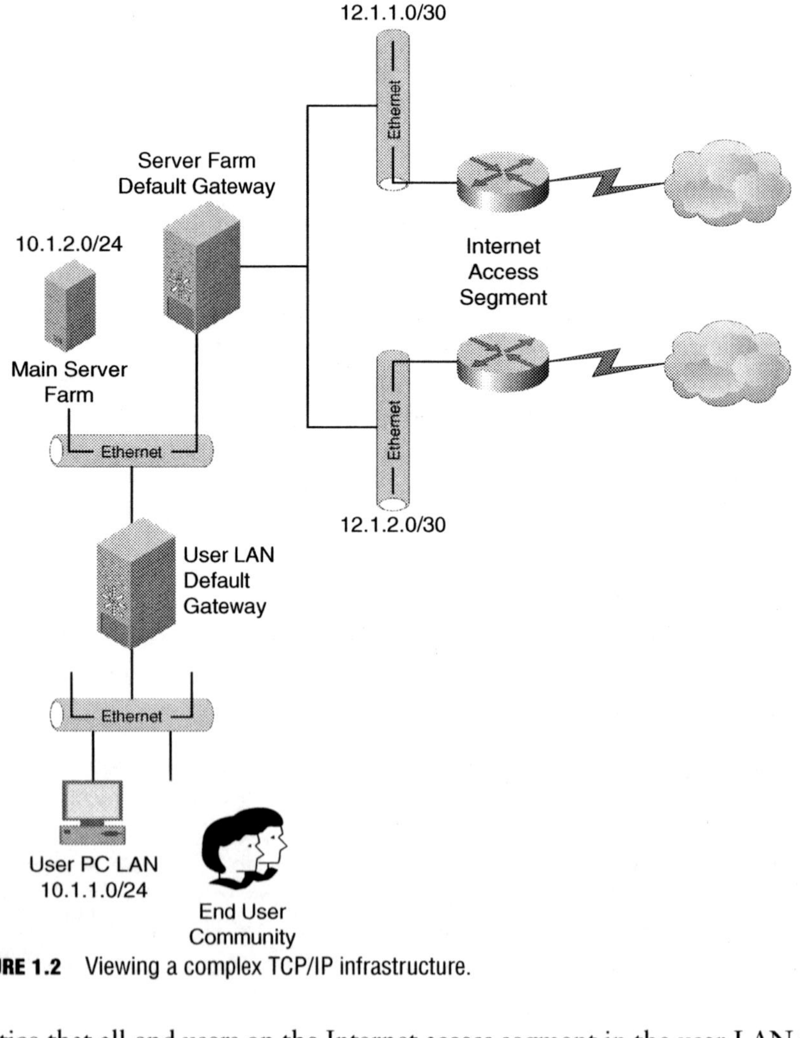

FIGURE 1.2 Viewing a complex TCP/IP infrastructure.

Notice that all end users on the Internet access segment in the user LAN in Figure 1.2 are on the 10.1.1.0/24 network, which is a privately addressed segment because you are using a 10.0.0.0 network address. This end-user segment accesses file, print, and application servers on the 10.1.2.0/24 segment.

A Layer 3 switch, which has a router built into the device, separates the user LAN from the server farm. The Layer 3 switch's IP address is 10.1.1.1, which makes it the default gateway for the user LAN.

Although a proxy server is not documented in the diagram, one is available in the server farm; it provides Internet access for the network users. This server has an IP address of 10.1.2.30. The proxy server points to a firewall and then out to the external routers on a publicly routable IP address segment.

To tie these two segments together, a PC on the user LAN would need to have an IP address on that segment that is in the same subnet (10.1.1.0) and a default gateway assignment of 10.1.1.1. If you need to access a server with an IP address of 10.1.2.30 (the proxy server for Internet access), the packets would be sent to the default gateway for processing.

You can run the `ipconfig /all` command to see how this configuration will look on the client end. The output is similar to the following:

```
C:\>ipconfig/all
Windows IP Configuration
        Host Name . . . . . . . . . . . . : AREA51A
        Primary Dns Suffix  . . . . . . . : corp.quepublishing.com
        Node Type . . . . . . . . . . . . : Hybrid
        IP Routing Enabled. . . . . . . . : No
        WINS Proxy Enabled. . . . . . . . : No
        DNS Suffix Search List. . . . . . : corp.quepublishing.com
                                            quepublishing.com
Ethernet adapter Local Area Connection:
        Connection-specific DNS Suffix  . : corp.quepublishing.com
        Description . . . . . . . . . . . : Intel(R) PRO/100 VE Network Connection
        Physical Address. . . . . . . . . : 00-12-3F-AE-23-1A
        DHCP Enabled. . . . . . . . . . . : Yes
        Autoconfiguration Enabled . . . . : Yes
        IP Address. . . . . . . . . . . . : 10.1.1.10
        Subnet Mask . . . . . . . . . . . : 255.255.255.0
        Default Gateway . . . . . . . . . : 10.1.1.1
        DHCP Server . . . . . . . . . . . : 10.1.1.12
        DNS Servers . . . . . . . . . . . : 10.1.1.15
                                            10.1.1.16
                                            10.1.1.17
        Lease Obtained. . . . . . . . . . : Tuesday, June 20, 2006 6:48:38 PM
        Lease Expires . . . . . . . . . . : Wednesday, June 28, 2006 6:48:38 PM
```

TIP

ipconfig output Make sure you know how to read the output of the `ipconfig` utility because it will be one of the most important tools you use when troubleshooting.

So now that you have viewed a common network setup, let's look at some relevant terminology:

- **IP address**—A 32-bit binary address that is used to identify a TCP/IP host's network and host ID.
- **Physical address (MAC address)**—A 48-bit alphanumeric number, such as 00-08-74-97-0B-26, that denotes the host's physical address. Also called a Media Access Control (MAC) address, the physical address is unique to the device to which it is assigned.
- **Network interface card (NIC)**—A device installed into a PC or other host device to allow it to have a MAC address and be assigned an IP address. This device connects you to the network.
- **Default gateway**—The configured router on a TCP/IP-enabled system that allows all packets destined for a remote network to be forwarded out of the local network.
- **Layer 3 switch (router)**—A Layer 3 switch is nothing more than a router and a switch integrated into the same chassis, which makes it faster, easier to manage, and more secure. In today's network infrastructures, the line separating switches, routers, and firewalls is becoming blurred because most of them are being integrated into one single device (chassis) that can perform all these tasks.
- **Subnet mask**—In TCP/IP, a mask that is used to determine what subnet an IP address belongs to. A subnet mask enables a host or router to determine which portion of an IP address is the network ID and which is the host ID. The host can then use this information to determine whether to send a packet to a host on the local network or to a router.
- **Public IP address**—An IP address for use on the Internet or a private network that must be assigned by an organization or Internet service provider (ISP) so that no duplicates will exist.
- **Private IP address**—An IP address range reserved for private (non-Internet-connected) networks. There are private address ranges in the Class A, Class B, and Class C address blocks.
- **Network Address Translation (NAT)**—A process by which private IP addresses are mapped to public IP addresses, and vice versa. The device that performs this translation keeps a table of which IP addresses given from the NAT pool map to the one that was distributed.
- **Proxy server**—A server-based application that serves as a go-between for the internal LAN clients and the public Internet. A proxy server also caches pages so that Internet response seems faster to internal clients.
- **Firewall**—A device that protects the internal network from the external Internet, WAN, business partner, or anything else you want to protect against.

EXAM ALERT

Unique IP addresses Duplicate IP addresses do not work. All IP addressing must be unique on each segment. If you have duplicates, your systems will know and give you error messages that duplicate addressing exists somewhere on your network.

So how exactly does IP work? In the following sections, we examine in more detail IP, IP addressing, ranges, classes, and other related terminology.

Internet Protocol Fundamentals

By now, you should have a good idea of what an IP network might look like; more important, you should know what to do with one come exam time. If not, fear not. As we progress through the rest of this chapter, we continue to lay out scenarios for you to enhance your understanding. Right now, however, we need to dig a little deeper into how IP addressing works so that you fully understand it.

NOTE

Using RFCs For detailed information on any protocol standard, you should become familiar with *Requests for Comments,* which are commonly called *RFCs*. They are the documents that depict a protocol's standards and fundamentals. Although their content is highly technical, they are the definitive information source on any protocol standard you need to research. For more information, check out the following RFCs:

Transmission Control Protocol (TCP) RFC: ftp.isi.edu/in-notes/std/std7.txt

Internet Protocol (IP) RFC: ftp.isi.edu/in-notes/std/std5.txt

The vast majority of production networks currently use IPv4, which stands for Internet Protocol version 4. More often than not, you don't even notice the v4 when discussing IP—and rightfully so. With the exception of the relatively new IPv6, which some networks are beginning to adopt, there is no other IP to talk about. In reality, you will not be tested on IPv6 on Exam 70-293, but you need to know of its existence because it is a standard part of the Windows Server 2003 networking suite.

IPv6 ... Coming Soon to a Network Near You!

It's no secret that we're running out of IP addresses under the current IPv4 addressing system. Under IPv4, IP addresses are 32-bit numbers consisting of four binary octets separated from each other by periods. For example, 11000000.10101000.00000000.10011010 is 192.168.0.154 in decimal notation. This way of providing IP addresses provides for 2^{32}, or 4,294,967,296, possible addresses, of which a small number are reserved for private networks and cannot be routed in the Internet.

The IPv6 addressing system aims to solve this problem by making use of 128-bit numbers to represent unique IP addresses. Using 128 bits gives you 2^{128}, or

(continues)

(continued)

340,282,366,920,938,463,463,374,607,431,768,211,456 (3.4×10^{38}) possible addresses. That is enough IP addresses to provide 655,570,793,348,866,943,898,599 (6.5×10^{23}) addresses for every square meter of the earth's surface. That *should* help solve the shortage of available public IP addresses. Of course, the true power of the IPv6 addressing system is that it allows multiple hierarchical levels of organization and flexibility in design, which is currently lacking from today's IPv4 Internet.

As you might suspect, a 128-bit IPv6 address looks different than what you are used to seeing in IPv4. An IPv6 address in binary form looks like this:

```
0010000111011010 0000000011010011 0000000000000000 0010111100111011
0000001010101010 0000000011111111 1111111000101000 1001110001011010
```

That translates into this in hexadecimal:

```
21DA:00D3:0000:2F3B:02AA:00FF:FE28:9C5A
```

The IPv6 protocol and addressing system should all but put an end to memorizing IP addresses! With the advent of the IPv6 protocol, IP classes and classless interdomain routing (CIDR) will be things of the past. The three commonly used private IP ranges (10.0.0.0/8, 172.16.0.0/12, and 192.168.0.0/16) will be replaced by one site-local address range (FEC0::/48). The familiar loopback address of 127.0.0.1 will be replaced by ::1.

In the interest of making things ever easier, you can use double colons (::) to represent contiguous strings of zero value. So the loopback address 0:0:0:0:0:0:0:1 becomes simply ::1. Of course, you can use double colons only once in an IPv6 IP address—for obvious reasons.

Additionally, you can use leading zero suppression to remove the leading zeros within an individual 16-bit string. Thus, 21DA:00D3:0000:2F3B:02AA:00FF:FE28:9C5A becomes 21DA:D3:0:2F3B:2AA:FF:FE28:9C5A. Of course, the drivers within the operating system and the infrastructure hardware devices (routers, switches, and so on) handle all these conversions automatically, invisible to you.

For more information on IPv6, visit the official IPv6 site, located at http://www.ietf.org/html.charters/ipv6-charter.html, or visit the Microsoft website on IPv6, located at http://www.microsoft.com/technet/itsolutions/network/ipv6/default.mspx.

With that brief detour into IPv6 out of the way, let's dig deeper into the mechanics of IP (IPv4, to be proper) and see how it all works together.

As we mentioned earlier, an IP address is a 32-bit number that denotes a node or host on a network. The number, which resembles 10.1.1.1/24, is a unique host on a single network. If you have two nodes, one numbered 10.1.1.1 and the other numbered 10.1.1.2, they can communicate if they are connected to the same network segment and no other outstanding issues stop communication.

An IP address is broken down into two specific parts: the network identifier and host identifier. Let's look at the following IP address to understand it better:

IP address: 10.1.1.1

Subnet mask: 255.255.255.0

You need to break down this number into binary bits to truly see what we mean by masking. First, consider the fact that you have a 32-bit address written in decimal format. If you want to see the subnet mask 255.255.255.0 in binary, you have to change the format from decimal to binary, or base 2, numbering, as follows:

255.255.255.0 = 11111111.11111111.11111111.00000000

Remember, binary uses only 1s and 0s, either on or off. No other numbers are used, so you can see how the network is masked. All 1s in the network portion denote the actual network you are working on. This leaves the host portion (the 0s at the end) available for assignment. This way, any device can know what network it's on—or, better, what subnet. Because we've used 24 1s here, we denote the IP address as 10.1.1.0/24. Using this form of notation is an easier way to show a subnet mask assignment. If you see /30, for example, the address appears like this in binary:

11111111.11111111.11111111.11111100

This concept can be confusing because, although you now have to perform an operation called *subnetting* on the exam, you need to know what network a host is on, and being able to see it in this format can help you pass this portion of the exam.

How did we get this subnet mask? Easy. First, you must understand what makes up a single octet. An octet is 8 bits out of 32 denoted and separated by a single period. Take one single octet and break it down as shown:

128	64	32	16	8	4	2	1

If you can duplicate this chart, then you can figure out a subnet mask. First, you have to know where this chart comes from. Remember how we described base 2 numbering as being 0s and 1s? We also use base 10 numbering, and to go from one to the other, you can use this chart. Remember, a single octet is broken down into 8 bits. Now, take this same chart and plug in the last octet that you don't know because you obviously know that the first three octets have all their bits turned on (1s) so they are all 255 in decimal.

128	64	32	16	8	4	2	1
1	1	1	1	1	1	0	0

Now, all you have to do is add the table elements, but to make your task even easier, you need to know that all the bits up to the last two should equal 255 because they were all turned on. So you can simply subtract the last 2 bits shown as 0s (which adds up to 3) from the number 255. This equals 252, which is a common subnet for a WAN link because you need only a network, a broadcast address, and two useable hosts on the subnet, one for each link from each router. Figure 1.3 illustrates this concept.

FIGURE 1.3 Viewing a point-to-point link.

So what exactly did we mean by a single network, a broadcast, and two useable nodes? When you subnet, you have to remember one major point: You always need a network address and a broadcast address for each subnet you create.

If any one thing is universally true when you are dealing with TCP/IP networks, it might be that each and every one is different from the next. Each network varies in size, complexity, and physical and logical layout—just to name a few key points of interest. So how will you go about planning a new TCP/IP network? What IP class will you choose to implement? How will you go about properly subnetting it? Will you use private or public IP addresses? You must consider all these questions—and more.

We start our examination of these questions by discussing public versus private IP addressing systems.

Public Versus Private IP Addressing

Public IP addressing uses three major spaces: Classes A, B, and C. There are also two more classes: Class D, which is used for multicast-based networks, and Class E, which is still experimental. Class A is typically used for very large networks, Class B is typically used for medium-sized networks, and Class C is typically used for networks that have no more than a couple hundred nodes. Public ranges run as shown in Table 1.1.

TABLE 1.1 Viewing IP Address Classes

Class	Range
Class A	1–126
Class B	128–191
Class C	192–223

EXAM ALERT

Loopback addressing The IP address 127.0.0.0 is reserved for loopback network and testing. 127.0.0.1 is also located in your HOSTS file, which enables you to test the IP connectivity of your own machine. If you use the command `ping localhost` (which is the hostname located in the HOSTS file), you can resolve to 127.0.0.1, and you should see a reply. This way, you know that TCP/IP is configured properly—at least, on your own system.

Although the private IP address ranges shown in Table 1.2 fall within the Class A, B, and C public IP addresses, note that private IP addresses are not routable on the Internet by design (and by default) and should never be seen outside an internal network.

TABLE 1.2 Viewing Private IP Classes

Class	Range
Class A	10.0.0.0–10.255.255.255
Class B	172.16.0.0–172.31.255.255
Class C	192.168.0.0–192.168.255.255

Now you are familiar with the IP address ranges that you will see in both public and private IP networks, but one question remains: Why do we have "private IP addresses"? IP addresses are a limited commodity—as difficult a concept as that might seem. Had ISPs and private organizations been allowed to use public IP addresses within their large internal networks, the number of useable IP addresses would have quickly vanished into nothing but a memory. Of course, you might argue that this is still a problem—hence the arrival of IPv6—and it is, to a certain extent. Private IP addressing has allowed us to avoid this problem until now, thus negating the need for a newer and better IP addressing system.

By assigning a single public IP address to a company, you can use multiple private IP addresses (tens, hundreds, thousands) internally without any problem, thanks to Network Address Translation (NAT). NAT provides a translation service allowing multiple private IP addresses to access Internet resources as if they indeed had a publicly routable IP address. This also helps explain why private IP addresses are not meant to be routable because it's entirely likely that IP address 192.168.0.100 (one of my internal network servers) is used several hundred thousand times in many other private IP networks.

So how does a device know on which class another device is numbered? The device (a router, for example) examines the first octet of the incoming packet and can determine from the first few bits of the packet what class the packet came from and is using. The first few bits of each IP address indicate which of the address class formats it is using. Table 1.3 shows the address structures.

If you have a Class A address, the first number is a 0, the network bits are at 7, and the local address makes up the corresponding 24 bits: 1 bit for the identifier, 7 for the network (8 in total), and 24 for host addressing. Table 1.3 shows all the identifiers used for Classes A, B, and C.

TABLE 1.3 Viewing Identifier List for Class A–C IP Addressing

Class	Identifier
Class A	0
Class B	10
Class C	110

You should now be familiar with the basic operation of IP. We can now begin to really get exam specific. Because we have already covered several of the terms and scenarios you are likely to see on the exam, we can cover each objective without having to go into very granular detail.

Analyzing IP Addressing Requirements

Objective

Plan a TCP/IP network infrastructure strategy.

- Analyze IP addressing requirements.
- Create an IP subnet scheme.

In this section, we look at what you need to know to analyze IP addressing requirements and how to plan a TCP/IP-based network strategy. If you think about the exam objective, what comes to mind? This would be a scenario-based discussion, much like the ones we had earlier. For instance, if you were to analyze requirements for a network infrastructure, you would need to use every skill taught to you since starting this chapter. Let's look at a sample situation:

> You are the administrator of 300 Windows XP Professional workstations and a server farm consisting of 25 Windows Server 2003 systems. You need to develop an IP addressing scheme to assign IP addresses to all 300 Windows XP workstations and all 25 servers, set up Internet access, and set up business-to-business connections or remote sites.

Sounds like a lot of work, doesn't it? Handling this situation really isn't too bad, so let's break down what you might need to know:

1. You need to set up TCP/IP, so you start by picking an IP range that works for you. You might not have the flexibility of picking a brand new one (a network specialist within your group might assign it if you do not manage addresses), so let's say the corporate office assigns the two Class C addresses 10.10.1.0/24 and 10.10.2.0/24. This assignment gives you more than 500 addresses you can use.
2. Next, you need to set up a topology map like the one shown in Figure 1.4. Such a map will most likely be provided for you in the exam, but knowing how to create one solves two problems: passing the exam and working on the job. Remember, exam questions don't come up on the job; real-world experience does, so make this topology map as if you were going to see it in the actual question.
3. After laying out a map, you can assign the IP addresses. First, you need to assign IP addresses to the user LAN. Because they are all connected to the Layer 3 switch in the middle of the network topology map, you can assign a set of virtual LANs (VLANs). A VLAN is used to logically segment the network into different subnets for security and manageability. You can either use this approach or make a DHCP superscope of two subnets. Either way, make sure that you have enough IP addresses to provide to all your hosts. Take into account that you will most likely have closet switches, printers, or other devices that might also need to use an IP address.

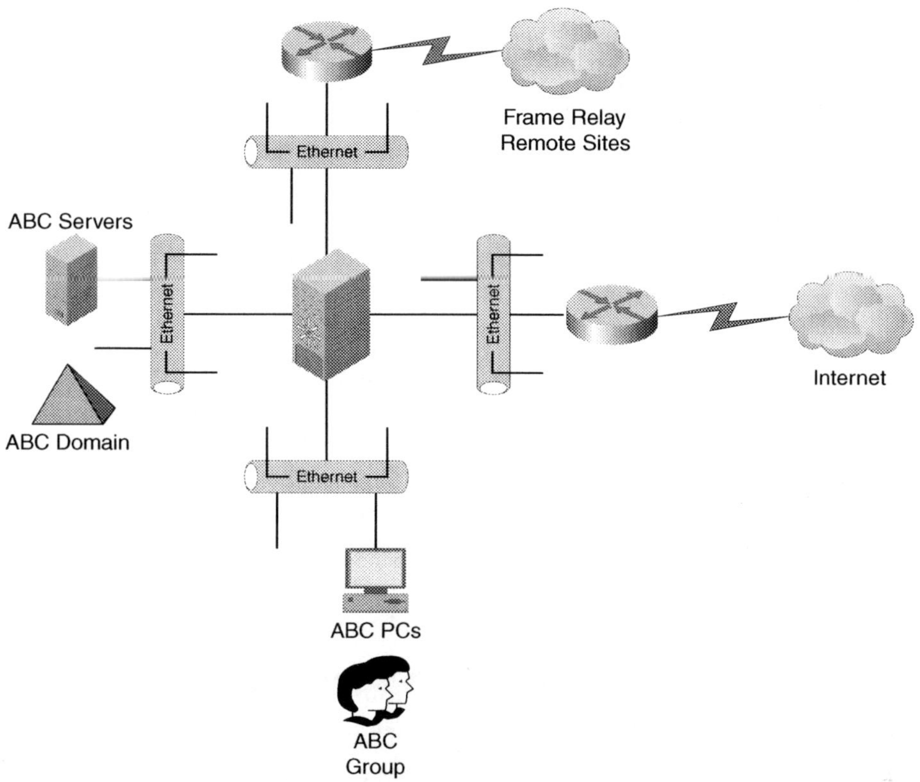

FIGURE 1.4 Planning a complex IP environment.

4. Make sure you have a default gateway. Because the Layer 3 switch is also a router, you can make it the default gateway for your network.
5. Next, you can assign IP addresses to your servers. You should assign static IP addresses to your servers, printers, and any other resource that will not change. Say you have a proxy server with an IP address of 10.10.1.40. If DHCP somehow gives it another IP address when its leases expires, you need to change all your client assignments. This is something you would never do, so make certain that you assign your resources static IPs.
6. Make sure that the Layer 3 switch has a route over to the Frame Relay network and the segment where your Internet access router is.
7. Finally, make sure that you have an IP helper address (better known as a DHCP relay agent) configured on your router because, by default, a router does not pass a broadcast across. Therefore, you would have to make sure that your users in the LAN can access and get DHCP addresses from the server farm where the server is located.

That's it! You have analyzed a problem and set up a basic IP addressing solution. Now you can get your network up and running.

Planning an IP Configuration Strategy

For the final step, you need to consider how you will lay out your IP configuration strategy. Because every computer on your network needs to be capable of connecting via an IP address, you must know how to get each one an IP address if you do not have addresses set statically. A DHCP server dynamically assigns addresses from a manually designated range of addresses called a *scope* that you predetermine when you deploy your DNS server. (We examine DHCP in great detail later in Chapter 3, "Planning, Implementing, and Troubleshooting DHCP.") Because we already discussed static assignments, let's look at one last option that you might come across and will most likely be tested on during Exam 70-293.

Automatic Private IP Addressing (APIPA) allows a workstation that cannot reach a DHCP server to assign its own IP address so that it can participate on a network. APIPA uses a range from 169.254.0.1 to 169.254.255.254. This is a great strategy if you do not have any other IP addresses on the network. This is true because the workstations can configure themselves, but most times, this strategy proves to be useless and only gives you a clue that, for some reason, this workstation cannot get an IP address from the DHCP server. In any case, make certain that you remember this range and what APIPA is used for.

EXAM ALERT

APIPA Automatic Private IP Addressing (APIPA) is a feature that allows DHCP clients to automatically configure themselves with an IP address and subnet mask when a DHCP server isn't available. The IP address range that APIPA uses is from 169.254.0.1 to 169.254.255.254. When the DHCP server is available, the client can switch back to DHCP.

Planning an IP Routing Solution

Objective

Plan a TCP/IP network infrastructure strategy.

- Plan an IP routing solution.

In this section, we analyze how to plan an IP routing solution. First, let's briefly review what *IP routing* is. A *router* is a device that looks at a packet that comes in one of its interfaces, analyzes the packet against its routing table (which can be dynamically or statically configured), and decides what segment of the network the packet needs to go to based on that table. In other words, if you have a router configured on your network (as your default gateway), and packets coming from the 10.10.1.0 segment need to get to 10.10.2.0, the router makes that decision. You can set up the router with static IP routes, which means that you hand-pick specific routes and enter them into the table manually, or you can have the router set up dynamically via a routing protocol such as *Routing Information Protocol (RIP)* or *Open Shortest Path First (OSPF)*. So before we get into specifics, let's look at what you can use as a router.

If you have a large environment or depend heavily on your routing infrastructure, you might opt to use a hardware routing device such as one from Cisco, Nortel, or 3Com. If you are interested in saving money and using a software-based router, Windows Server 2003 can provide such a tool. A software-based routing solution, such as one using the Routing and Remote Access Service (RRAS), can be ideal on a small, properly segmented network with relatively light traffic between subnets. This doesn't mean you should use one over the other; it just means you can select one based on preference or the best price solution after you have performed a cost analysis. Regardless, knowledge of general routing and routers is needed for Exam 70-293.

RRAS can provide a software-based router on top of Windows Server 2003. We examine how to use RRAS to configure routing in detail in Chapter 2, "Planning and Troubleshooting TCP/IP Routing."

Planning and Modifying a Network Topology

In this section, we cover ways to plan and modify a network topology. Why is this important? If you need to add on to or alter your network topology, you need to focus on the following areas before you do:

- You need to plan the physical placement of your network resources.
- You need to identify network protocols to be used.

Planning Physical Placement of Network Resources

Objective

Plan and modify a network topology.

- Plan the physical placement of network resources.

Now that you are familiar with how to plan a TCP/IP network, let's look at where you might want to place devices on a network. Before we get into the exact details you need to know, let's talk about why planning the placement is so important in the first place.

First, you should know how a network is laid out before you deploy it. You should know what you want a network to look like before you even contemplate ordering gear to populate it. This step is important because you must consider many factors before implementation:

- Do you want redundancy and high availability?
- Do you want security?

- Where will the application flows be generated from?
- How do you stop or contain bottlenecks from occurring?

Looking at these questions before you plan anything is critical because you might change your mind during the implementation. It is possible that before you are even done rolling it out, you will find something you would have done differently or better. Long story short, you need to plan physical placement of resources before you deploy them, and the best way to do this is to use a topology map.

Now you can answer the questions that you posed to yourself. Let's look at each of them in more detail.

- **Do you want redundancy and high availability?** When you design a network, you have to think about device failure. This chapter describes how to place network devices where they belong, as well as how to design them properly. If you consider all the situations that can happen on a network, you surely should consider some redundancy in your network solution. You should look at all points of failure; for example, if something fails, you could be down and off the network for several hours, so you must consider whether that's acceptable for your business. Always get management approval as well because the redundant hardware will cost extra. This extra expense, however, is worthwhile if you have to keep your network up and running all the time with minimal downtime. Examples of redundancy can be anything from redundant servers in a cluster or redundant routers for a default gateway, all the way to redundant power supplies in devices in case of failure. Today you can order just about anything redundant to provide greater resistance to failure.
- **Do you want security?** You have to plan your security infrastructure well in advance. The security infrastructure includes routers and switches, firewalls, proxy servers, even the Windows Server 2003 operating system you will deploy. Consider their placement in the network with an eye on security because where you place them (whether on a perimeter network or a VLAN) can actually increase or decrease the security on the network.
- **Where will the application flows be generated from?** You have to consider where you will place your resources on your network. If you have a file server, a print server, two domain controllers, a WINS server, a DNS server, and a DHCP server to populate your network, where does it make the most sense to locate them? In other words, you would want a server farm segment with a high-speed backbone (perhaps gigabit Ethernet) with high-speed connections to the Internet or remote sites. You would want to make sure that your user LAN segment is also capable of reaching this backbone with little trouble. (Later in the chapter, we describe network monitoring and ways you locate problems with this type of solution.)

- **How do you stop or contain bottlenecks from occurring?** You can follow the existing rules, one of which is called the 80/20 rule. In this rule, you make sure that 80% of your clients are closest to your network resources (such as e-mail, file and print, and so on) and only 20% of the other clients have to cross over a network router or other device to reach those resources. In other words, you must make sure that you design your network so that you have the fastest possible paths to all resources needed; if you do not, bottlenecks might occur.

Selecting Network Protocols

Objective

Plan and modify a network topology.

- Identify network protocols to be used.

Now that you know how to place devices on your network, let's look at what protocols to use. Besides TCP/IP, we mentioned other protocols earlier in this chapter. Here we discuss routing and routed protocols, and when or why to choose them. We also describe how to manage the protocols you are using, as well as why you might or might not want to use them.

When you want to plan for protocols besides TCP/IP (which we have covered throughout this chapter), you might need to consider the following protocols in your network infrastructure:

- IPX/SPX
- SNA
- NetBIOS/NetBEUI
- AppleTalk

We cover only these three because the point behind the whole objective is not to be an expert in any other protocol but TCP/IP, but to be able to recognize a need for other protocols in your network infrastructure, how to identify them, and how to plan for them. Whatever your situation, be sure to evaluate carefully the needs and requirements being presented to you—this will help you choose the correct protocols and implement them successfully in your environment.

IPX/SPX

IPX/SPX, which stands for *Internetwork Packet Exchange/Sequence Packet Exchange*, is similar to TCP/IP. You can think of IP mapping to IPX and TCP mapping to SPX. These protocols perform similar operations. IPX/SPX was originally created and used extensively by Novell with its NetWare platform of network operating systems. Although IPX/SPX was a good protocol,

TCP/IP became the protocol of the Internet. To avoid missing out on the Internet revolution, all vendors chose to develop TCP/IP into all their solutions moving forward, leaving in other protocols such as IPX/SPX only for backward compatibility. Novell NetWare version 5.0 was the first version to be shipped with a real version of TCP/IP, whereas the older versions of NetWare (versions 4.*x* and earlier) used add-on packs and NetWare IP (NWIP).

Because IPX/SPX was more readily adopted into the earlier network system platforms, Novell NetWare versions 4.*x* and earlier and some Novell Directory Services (NDS) functions did not work without IPX/SPX installed. Wherever you work in the field, you might run into older systems on a network running NetWare 4.x and earlier; therefore, IPX/SPX will be running as well. Consequently, you, the Microsoft Certified Professional, need to know how and when to deploy IPX/SPX into or out of your network, if necessary.

NOTE

NWLink NWLink is the Microsoft version of the IPX/SPX protocol.

SNA

Systems Network Architecture (SNA) is an old but still widely used protocol. Developed by IBM, SNA is a protocol suite that runs on most mainframes used today. Microsoft professionals who know only Microsoft might be shocked to learn that in today's networks they most likely will be confronted with some form of mainframe and might also be responsible for network connectivity to it.

SNA Server was an older Microsoft Backoffice product that helped Windows users connect to and print on an IBM mainframe via the SNA protocol. This solution has since been renamed Host Integration Server (HIS) 2004. Again, it is important that you understand that SNA might exist in your network, and that you need to know how to work with it.

NetBIOS

Another old protocol, the Network Basic Input/Output System (NetBIOS), is a session-layer communications service used by client and server applications in IBM-based Token Ring and PC LAN Ethernet-based networks. NetBIOS is really just a way for application programming interface–based communications to take place. This means that higher-level services can run over lower-level protocols such as IP. This process is known as *NetBIOS over TCP/IP (NBT)*. The NetBIOS service contains three main sections: the name, session, and datagram services.

Why do you need to know about such a protocol? You will be using NetBIOS names if you have older systems that rely on WINS. Older systems rely on NetBIOS, so until you can upgrade all your systems, you will have to use it.

AppleTalk

Used primarily in the past by older Apple Macintosh computers, the AppleTalk protocol may still be needed on your network, although all modern networks involving current Macintosh computers will likely be exclusively TCP/IP.

Planning for Network Traffic Monitoring

Objective

Plan network traffic monitoring. Tools might include Network Monitor and System Monitor.

For this objective, you need to look at a network with a critical eye toward packet-level analysis. Although you do not need to know all the details about packet-level analysis, you are responsible for knowing how to troubleshoot networks and systems with the tools that Microsoft provides with the base-level operating system. Windows Server 2003 provides both System Monitor and Network Monitor. System Monitor resides in the Performance Management console, and Network Monitor must be installed separately after a default installation. You can install Network Monitor from the Windows Components Wizard under the Network Management Tools group.

System Monitor helps you troubleshoot network issues, but few look to System Monitor for help. Why? People mainly do not know that some of the network-monitoring features are in it. For example, an MCP should know that System Monitor can monitor network card I/O, error packets, IP datagram error checking, and so on. You can use this tool to troubleshoot problems going in and going out of the network interface. This is a way for you to troubleshoot errors that might be coming from a bad NIC or from excessive broadcasts hitting your server. Having that many broadcasts hit your server could mean a network problem; you might need to replace a hub with a switch, for example. Either way, you can see why System Monitor is helpful.

Network Monitor, which comes with Windows Server 2003, is a protocol analyzer that enables you to "sniff" the network traffic traversing the network. This capability is important because, without a good picture of what is running through your network, you can't accurately talk about how to remove unneeded protocols, what protocols are creating problems, what protocols are incorrectly configured, or what network interface card repeatedly broadcasts packets because it has a hardware problem. All these issues, including an accurate statement of what your bandwidth utilization would be, are hidden from you without the use of Network Monitor.

One limitation of Network Monitor is that it captures and contains only traffic sent to and from the computer in which it is installed. If you need a more robust solution, you can use a third-party product such as Sniffer Pro or Ethereal. If you opt to move to a Microsoft solution, you must purchase Microsoft Systems Management Server (SMS), which can capture frames sent to or from any computer on which the Network Monitor driver is installed.

Using the Network Monitor

NOTE

Exam Overlap This topic has some overlap with a similar topic on Exam 70-291. So if it seems like you've seen this material previously, you probably have.

You can use Network Monitor to capture packets on a network. From these packets, you can troubleshoot network problems, discern how busy a network load is, and predict how the network will grow.

Network Monitor is made up of two primary components:

- **Network Monitor**—Network Monitor is the tool you use to capture packets sent to and from this server. The version of Network Monitor that is included with Windows Server 2003 records only packets sent to and from this server and the LAN.
- **Network Monitor driver**—The Network Monitor driver is installed automatically when you install Network Monitor on a server. However, you might want to install just the Network Monitor driver for remote computers to be monitored through the full version of Network Monitor that is included with Systems Management Server (SMS). If you install the Network Monitor driver on additional computers, you should make a point to install it only once per subnet.

EXAM ALERT

Beware the limitations of Network Monitor when taking this exam, be sure to remember the limitations of Network Monitor. Also, pay careful attention to where you opt to deploy the Network Monitor driver on other computers.

Installing Network Monitor

Network Monitor is not installed by default, but it's easy enough to add. Step by Step 1.1 walks you through the steps to install Network Monitor.

STEP BY STEP

1.1 Installing Network Monitor

1. Select Start, Settings, Control Panel, Add or Remove Programs.
2. Click the Add/Remove Windows Components button. The Windows Components Wizard dialog box opens, as shown in Figure 1.5.

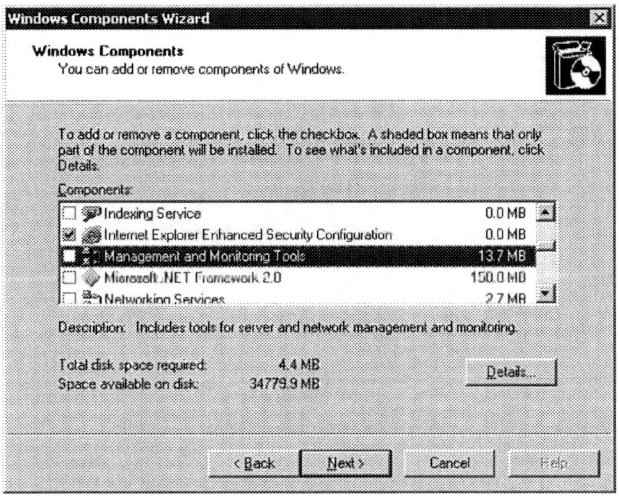

FIGURE 1.5 The Network Monitor components are listed under the Management and Monitoring group.

3. Scroll down the list and select Management and Monitoring Tools by double-clicking it. The Management and Monitoring Tools dialog box, shown in Figure 1.6, opens.

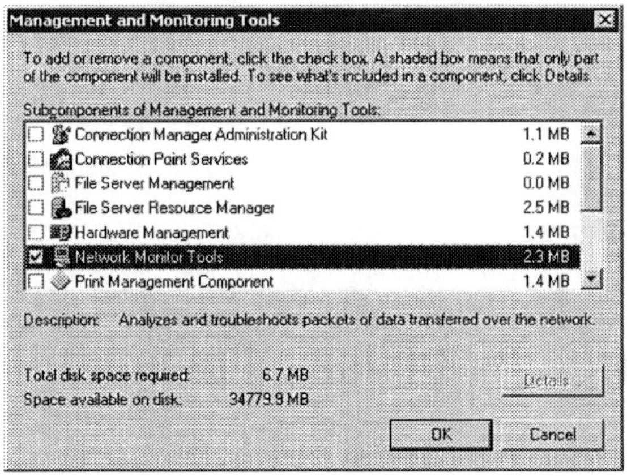

FIGURE 1.6 You can select the Network Monitor Tools option to install Network Monitor.

4. Select the Network Monitor Tools option in the subcomponents list, click OK, and then click Next.
5. If asked to do so, provide your Windows Server 2003 CD or type a path for accessing the setup files.
6. Click Finish when prompted to complete the Windows Components Wizard.

Installing the Network Monitor Driver

If you need to monitor a different subnet than the one on which you have installed Network Monitor or you need to support installation of SMS on a network, you need to add the Network Monitor driver. Step by Step 1.2 guides you through the process of adding only the driver.

STEP BY STEP

1.2 Adding the Network Monitor Driver

1. Open the Network Connections window by selecting Start, Settings, Network Connections.
2. Double-click the Local Area Connection icon to bring up the Local Area Connection Status dialog box.
3. Click the Properties button to open the Local Area Connection Properties dialog box.
4. On the General tab, click the Install button.
5. Choose Protocol from the list of available components and then click Add.
6. Select Network Monitor Driver and click OK. The necessary files are added.
7. If asked to do so, provide your Windows Server 2003 CD or type a path for accessing the setup files.

Using Network Monitor to Capture Data

Network Monitor, shown in Figure 1.7, captures frames, or packets, to and from the local computer and the network. Step by Step 1.3 walks you through the process of using Network Monitor and creating a simple capture. Later we go into greater detail on creating a capture filter through Network Monitor.

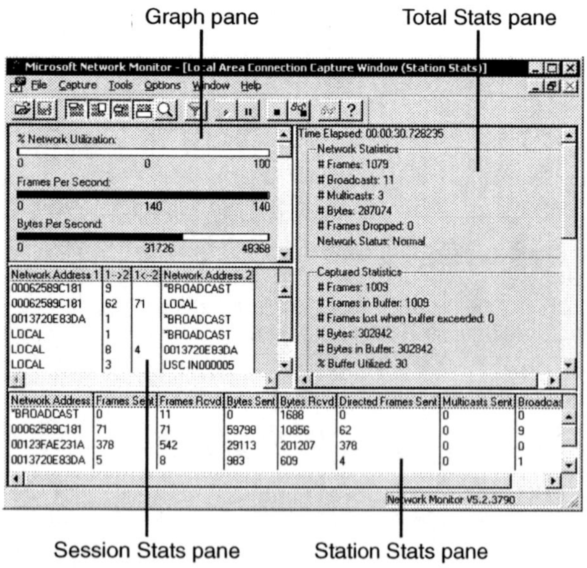

FIGURE 1.7 Network Monitor has four panes that display information about network traffic.

The four panes in Network Monitor report information about the current network activity or a captured file:

- **Graph pane**—The Graph pane reports percentages of activity, in bar chart format.

- **Session Stats pane**—The Session Stats pane reports individual statistics of client-to-server activity during a capture or live activity.
- **Station Stats pane**—The Station Stats pane reports information on each workstation's activity on a network. Keep in mind that this is actually activity between the specific workstation and the server on which Network Monitor is installed when using the Windows Server 2003 version of Network Monitor.
- **Total Stats pane**—The Total Stats pane reports the totals of the stats for all the other panes.

Now that you have seen how the captured data is displayed to you, you can create your first network capture, as outlined in Step by Step 1.3.

STEP BY STEP

1.3 Creating a Network Capture

1. Select Start, Programs, Administrative Tools, Network Monitor. The Network Monitor window opens. If you are prompted to do so, select the network to be monitored.
2. Select Capture, Start to begin the capture session. Network Monitor records activity to and from this computer. You can generate some activity by sending a `ping` command or browsing the Internet.
3. Select Capture, Stop and View to examine the results of the network data capture. Figure 1.8 shows an example of captured network data.

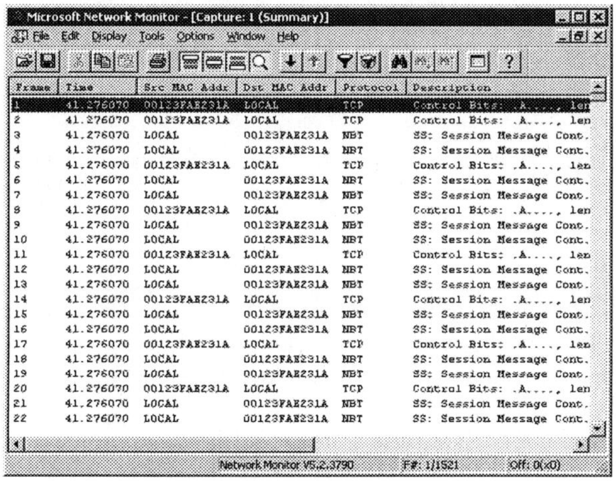

FIGURE 1.8 All network data that has been captured is listed sequentially.

4. Double-click any packet to examine it in greater detail, as shown in Figure 1.9. You can scroll through the list in the Summary pane and click any packet you want to examine in the Detail and Hex panes.

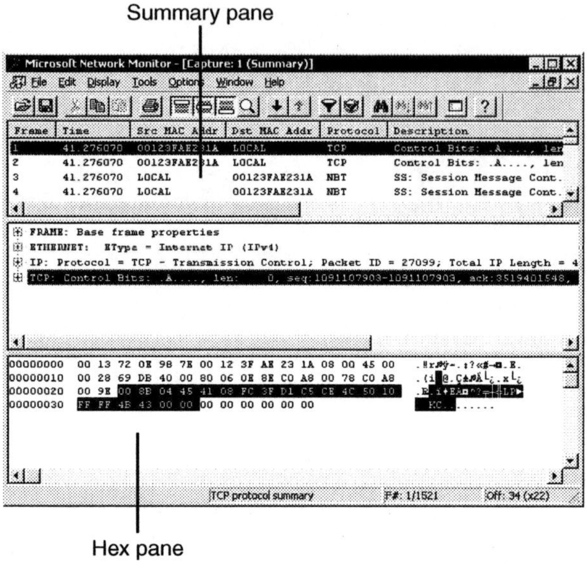

FIGURE 1.9 You can examine each packet captured during a network capture.

5. Close the Display window to return to the Network Statistics window.

Running Network Monitor from the Command Line

Like most other configuration and management tools in Windows Server 2003, you can run Network Monitor from the command line. This is a more difficult and advanced method of performing captures using Network Monitor, but it offers the advantage of letting you script commands to be executed on multiple computers with little effort. The basic syntax of using Network Monitor (`netmon`) from the command line is presented here and explained in more detail in Table 1.4:

```
start netmon [/net Number] [/capturefilter Path] [/displayfilter Path]
➥ [/buffersize Number]
➥ [/quickfilter {ATM | ETHERNET | IP | IPX | VINES | TOKENRING | FDDI},
➥ Address] [/quickfiltername FilterName] [/autostart] [/autostop]
```

TABLE 1.4 `netmon` Command-Line Switches

Switch	Description
`/net` *`Number`*	Enables you to specify the number of the network from which you want to capture data. You can specify any network segment that the computer is connected to.
`/capturefilter` *`Path`*	Enables you to specify a saved capture filter to be used. Can be abbreviated as `/cf` *`Path`*.
`/displayfilter` *`Path`*	Enables you to specify a display filter to be used. Can be abbreviated as `/df` *`Path`*.
`/buffersize` *`Number`*	Enables you to specify the size (in megabytes) of the capture buffer.

TABLE 1.4 *Continued*

Switch	Description
`/quickfilter {ATM	ETHERNET	IP	IPX	VINES	TOKENRING	FDDI}, Address`	Specifies that only frames of a particular type and from a particular address should be captured. You are allowed to specify up to three types at one time. Can be abbreviated as `/qf {ATM	ETHERNET	IP	IPX	VINES	TOKENRING	FDDI}, Address`.
`/quickfiltername` *`FilterName`*	Enables you to specify the name of the filter you use with the `/quickfilter` command. Can be abbreviated as `/qfn` *`FilterName`* and is not used if no `/quickfilter` options are specified.
`/autostart`	Instructs Network Monitor to begin capturing data at interface startup.
`/autostop`	Instructs Network Monitor to stop capturing data when the capture buffer is full.

Interpreting Captured Data

How you interpret captured data depends on the type of server you're working with. What is the server's role in the domain? Is it a domain controller (DC)? An application server? A file server? Each of these roles has different traffic patterns. You need a filter to get an accurate picture of the activity for a server.

Filters enable you to strip away packets that might not be relevant to the server, capture, or type of packets you're looking for. Within Network Monitor, you choose Capture, Filter to bring up the Capture Filter dialog box, shown in Figure 1.10. The Capture Filter dialog box enables you to do the following:

- **Specify capture filter protocols**—You can designate which protocols you want displayed in the capture. You complete the `SAP/ETYPE=` field by designating the protocol(s) you want displayed.
- **Specify address pairs**—You can choose up to three pairs of addresses that have sent and received packets from each other.
- **Specify frame data patterns to capture**—You can build your own variables to display captured data. You can display frames that contain a designated pattern.

Step by Step 1.4 walks you through the basic steps for configuring filtering for a capture before you actually start the capture. The advantage of using this method is that it cuts down on the amount of captured data. The disadvantage is that it captures only what you are filtering for.

STEP BY STEP

1.4 Configuring Capture Filters Before a Capture

1. Select Capture, Filter to open the Capture Filter dialog box, which is shown in Figure 1.10.

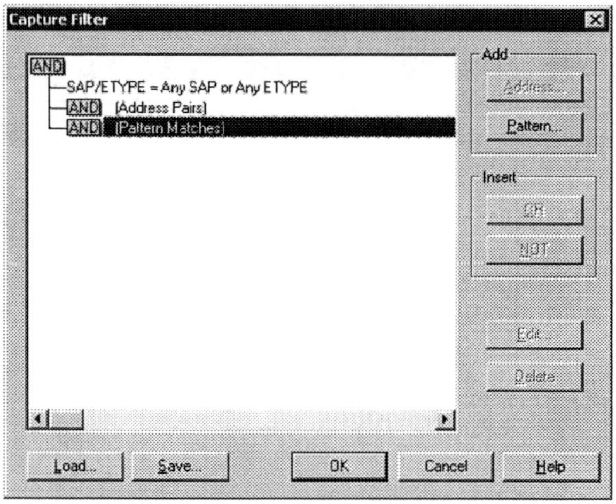

FIGURE 1.10 You can filter out unwanted packets by creating capture filters.

2. Click the `SAP/ETYPE=` line and then click the Edit button to open the Configure Filter SAPs and ETYPEs dialog box, shown in Figure 1.11. Typical options might include IP or NetWare. By default, all items are enabled. You might want to click Disable All and then enable the specific items you are looking for. When you are done, click OK.

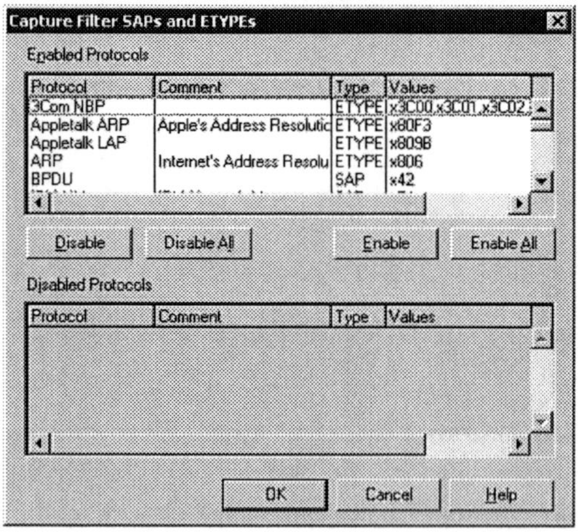

FIGURE 1.11 You start by configuring the SAPs and ETYPEs for which you want to see capture data.

3. If you want to specify any address pairs, do so by selecting the Address Pairs item and clicking the Address button to open the Address Expression dialog box, which is shown in Figure 1.12.
4. If you want to filter on data patterns, select the Pattern Matches item and click the Pattern button to open the Pattern Match dialog box, shown in Figure 1.13.

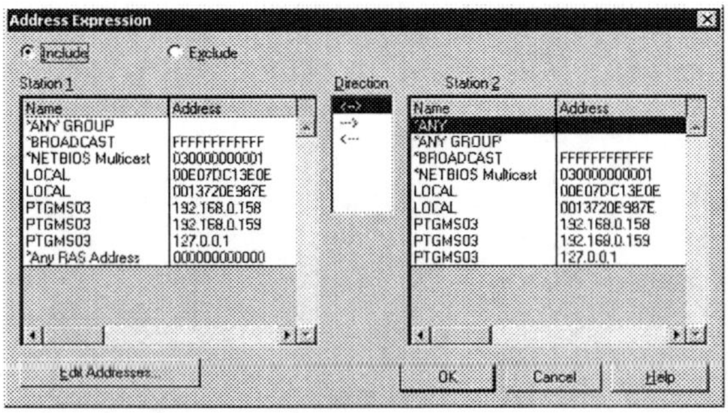

FIGURE 1.12 You can configure specific address pairs from which to examine data.

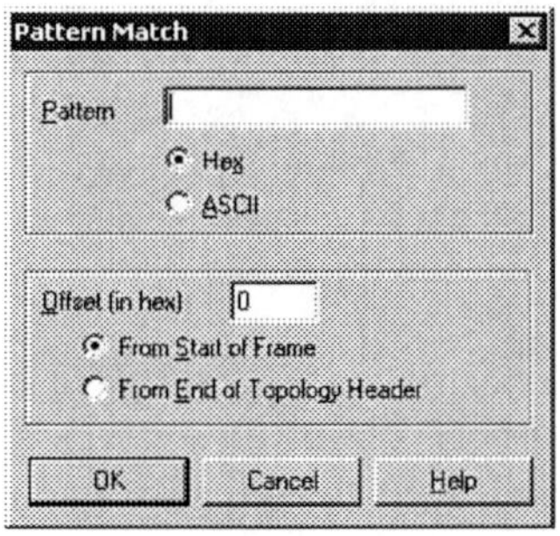

FIGURE 1.13 You can configure patterns to filter data by data patterns.

5. When you have configured the filters to your liking, click OK to close the Capture Filter dialog box. You can now perform a capture and get only the packets you are looking for.

Sometimes you might have already performed a capture and want to filter out specific data from it. You can do this by clicking the funnel icon or by selecting Display, Filter. In either case, the Display Filter dialog box opens, as shown in Figure 1.14.

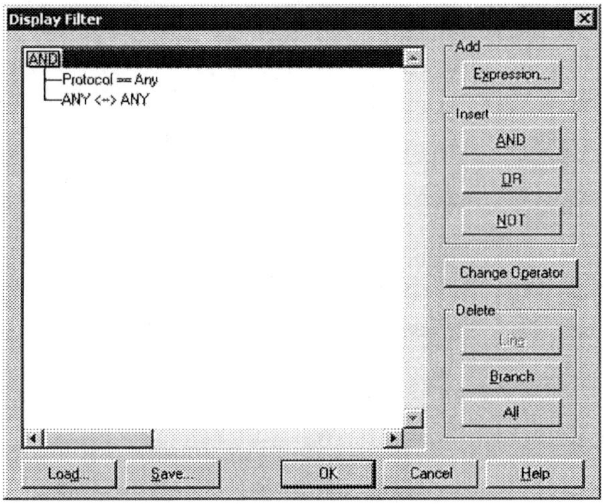

FIGURE 1.14 You can configure a filter for data that has already been captured.

By double-clicking the Protocol == Any item, you open the Expression dialog box, shown in Figure 1.15. You can use this dialog box to configure a filter; the most common filter is for a specific protocol type, such as ICMP.

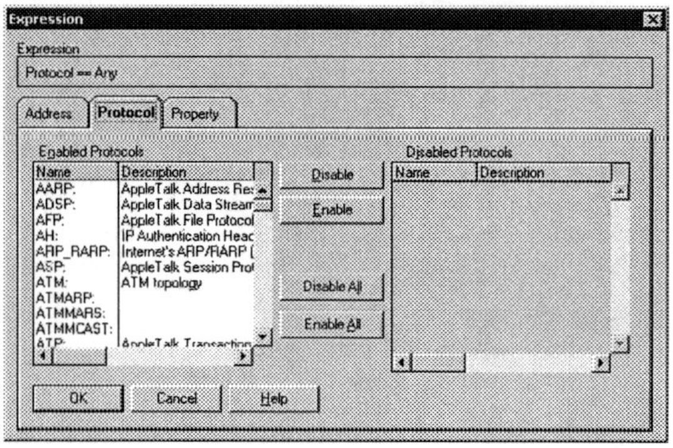

FIGURE 1.15 The Expression dialog box enables you to select how a filter should be constructed.

When you've determined the source of any problems with a network, you can begin to implement changes as required. Before you implement changes to a network, you should create a baseline. A *baseline* is a snapshot of how the network is operating under normal conditions.

After you create the baseline, you can make the desired changes and run the test again. After you run the test, you should ask yourself the following questions (among others):

- Did the changes help or hinder performance?
- If the changes hindered performance, have I configured all the options for this change properly? For example, have I configured bindings again?
- Has one area of network performance improved, such as logon times, but other areas of network performance worsened, such as communication between DCs?
- Is this network capacity more than 75%? If so, should I add a switch or router to break up the network?

After you've added and configured the changes to a network, you should create another baseline as a snapshot of the system after these changes. Over the next few days, weeks, and months, you should periodically run the same test again and compare the results you get with the baseline. This can help you predict how the network will be growing and what resources are using bandwidth.

Using System Monitor

Sometimes you might encounter network problems that Network Monitor doesn't help troubleshoot. Recall that the version of Network Monitor included in Windows Server 2003 can be used only to capture network traffic going to or from the server it is being run on. Although there are many very capable third-party network sniffers available for use, Exam 70-293 is not concerned with their usage. Therefore, for the exam, you need to know how to use System Monitor to monitor the statistics associated with network interfaces.

The following counters are listed under the Network Interface performance object:

- **Bytes Received/Sec**—This counter measures the rate at which bytes, including framing characters, are received over each network adapter. This counter is a subset of the Bytes Total/Sec counter.
- **Bytes Sent/Sec**—This counter measures the rate at which bytes, including framing characters, are sent over each network adapter. This counter is a subset of the Bytes Total/Sec counter.
- **Bytes Total/Sec**—This counter measures the rate at which bytes, including framing characters, are sent and received over each network adapter.
- **Current Bandwidth**—This counter measures an estimate of the current bandwidth of the network interface, in bits per second.
- **Output Queue Length**—This counter measures the length of the output packet queue (in packets). If this counter is greater than 2, there are delays, and you should find and eliminate the bottleneck, if possible.
- **Packets Outbound Discarded**—This counter measures the number of outbound packets that were chosen to be discarded even though no errors had been detected to prevent transmission. One possible reason for discarding packets is to free up buffer space.
- **Packets Outbound Errors**—This counter measures the number of outbound packets that could not be transmitted because of errors.
- **Packets Received Discarded**—This counter measures the number of inbound packets that were chosen to be discarded, even though no errors had been detected to prevent their delivery to a higher-layer protocol. One possible reason for discarding packets is to free up buffer space.
- **Packets Received Errors**—This counter measures the number of inbound packets that contained errors that prevented them from being deliverable to a higher-layer protocol.
- **Packets Received Non-Unicast/Sec**—This counter measures the rate at which non-Unicast packets are delivered to a higher-layer protocol.
- **Packets Received Unicast/Sec**—This counter measures the rate at which Unicast packets are delivered to a higher-layer protocol.
- **Packets Received Unknown**—This counter measures the number of packets received through the interface that were discarded because of an unknown or unsupported protocol.

- **Packets Received/Sec**—This counter measures the rate at which packets are received on the network interface.
- **Packets Sent Unicast/Sec**—This counter measures the rate at which packets are requested to be transmitted to subnet-Unicast addresses by higher-layer protocols.
- **Packets Sent/Sec**—This counter measures the rate at which packets are sent on the network interface.
- **Packets/Sec**—This counter measures the rate at which packets are sent and received on the network interface.

EXAM ALERT

Don't get tricked! When taking this exam, carefully read each question—especially those that deal with Performance Monitoring—to ensure that you select the correct answer. You might find several very similar answers being presented, but only one of them will be correct.

You can access System Monitor from the Administrative Tools folder by selecting Start, Programs, Administrative Tools, Performance. When it is initially opened, the Performance console looks as shown in Figure 1.16.

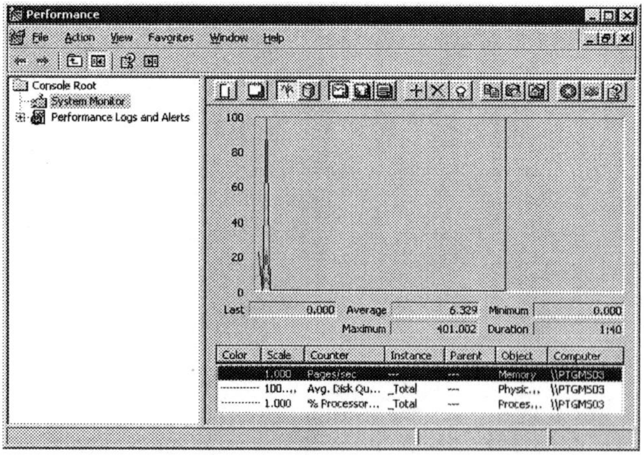

FIGURE 1.16 The Performance console in its default state monitors three basic items.

Monitoring Performance by Using the System Monitor

Configuring the Performance console to monitor and collect data about the network interface(s) in a server is a simple process, as described in Step by Step 1.5.

STEP BY STEP

1.5 Monitoring Network Adapter Statistics

1. Select Start, Program, Administrative Tools, Performance to open the Performance console.
2. Click System Monitor, as shown in Figure 1.16.
3. To add counter items to the System Monitor, click the + icon. The Add Counters dialog box, shown in Figure 1.17, opens, enabling you to begin adding counters.

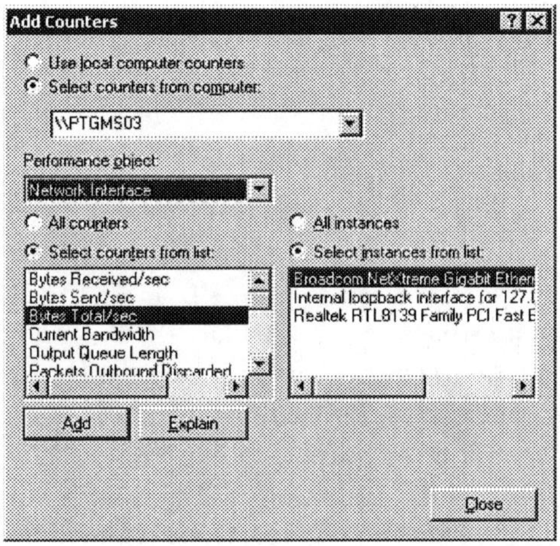

FIGURE 1.17 You can add counters to begin monitoring the network adapter statistics.

4. Select Network Interface from the Performance Object drop-down list box. The list of counters that relate to network interfaces and are available for selection appears. If you need to know what a counter means, select the counter and click the Explain button.
5. Be sure that you are adding counters for the correct network interface in your server and not for the loopback interface by selecting the Select Instances from This List option and then selecting the correct network interface (refer to Figure 1.17).
6. When you have decided what counter you want to monitor, click Add. You can add multiple counters either by selecting each counter and clicking Add or by holding down the Ctrl key while you select all the counters you want to monitor and then clicking Add.
7. Click Close when you are finished. Your counters are graphed like those shown in Figure 1.18.

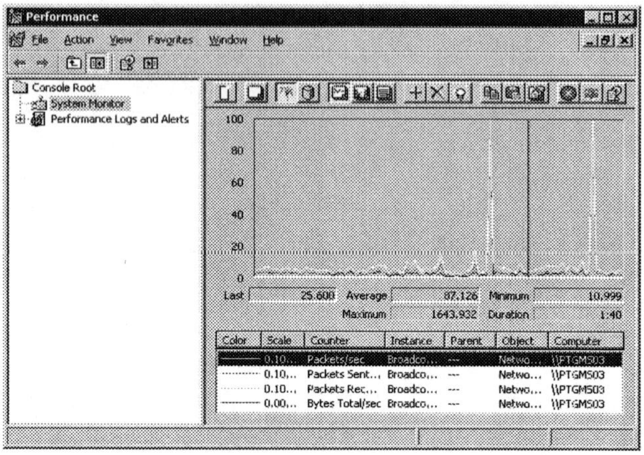

FIGURE 1.18 You can monitor the selected network interface statistics in real time.

Creating Baseline Counter Logs

Of course, monitoring the present operation and statistics of network interfaces will present you with only half of the picture. You need to create a baseline of the server performance that can be used to compare against the current performance statistics, to locate problematic areas. If you create baselines on servers, you will be able to compare the present-day performance to a known value. This can be very useful when you're performing troubleshooting, and it also aids when configurations are being modified. To create a baseline, you create a counter log from the Counter Logs option of the Performance Logs and Alerts node. Creation of a Counter Log is outlined in Step by Step 1.6.

STEP BY STEP

1.6 Creating and Using a Baseline Counter Log

1. Select Start, Program, Administrative Tools, Performance to open the Performance console.
2. Expand the Performance Logs and Alerts node and click the Counter Logs entry, as shown in Figure 1.19.

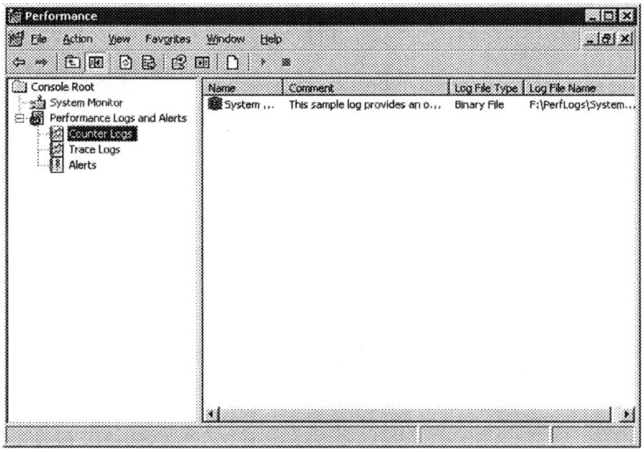

FIGURE 1.19 A counter log is created to keep baseline (historical) statistics about performance.

3. To add a new counter log, right-click the Counter Logs entry and select New Log Settings from the context menu.

4. Enter the name of the new counter log, as shown in Figure 1.20, and click OK. The Network Adapter Performance dialog box appears (see Figure 1.21).

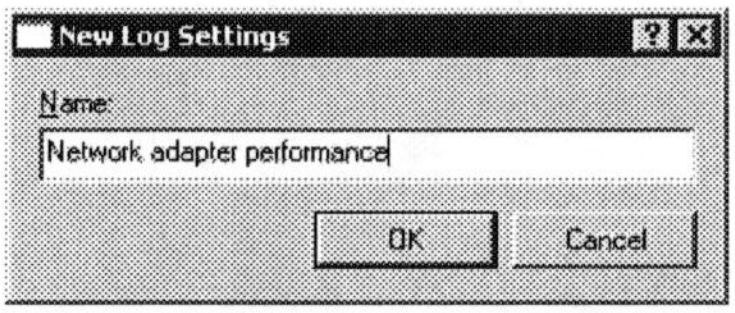

FIGURE 1.20 You should enter a descriptive name for the new counter log.

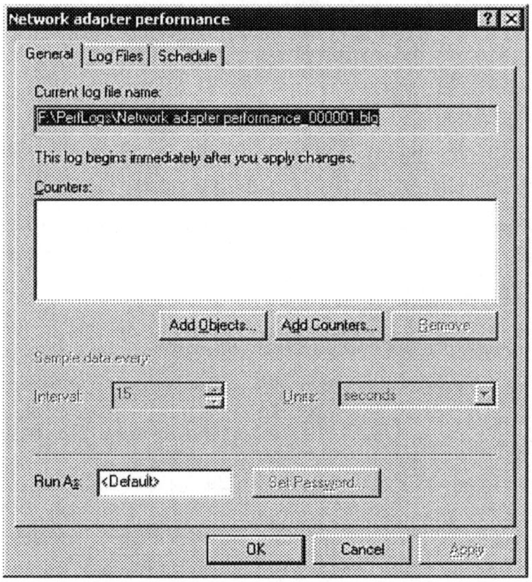

FIGURE 1.21 You must configure objects or counters on the new counter log before proceeding.

5. Configure new entire objects to be monitored by clicking the Add Objects button to open the Add Objects dialog box (see Figure 1.22). Alternatively, add individual counters by clicking the Add Counters button to open the Add Counters dialog box (see Figure 1.23). Add the objects or counters you want to the counter log.

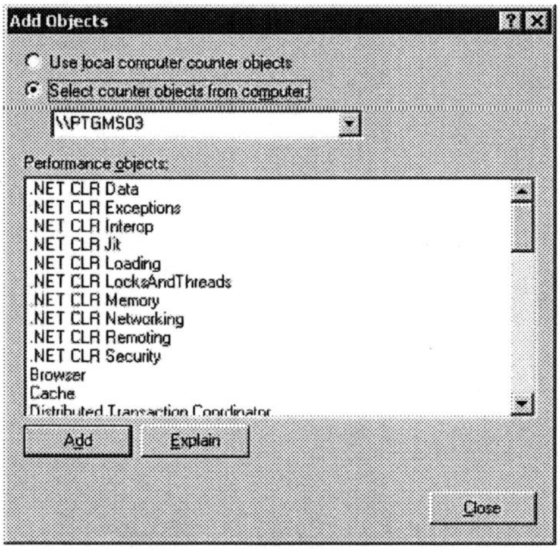

FIGURE 1.22 You can add entire objects to the counter log, if desired.

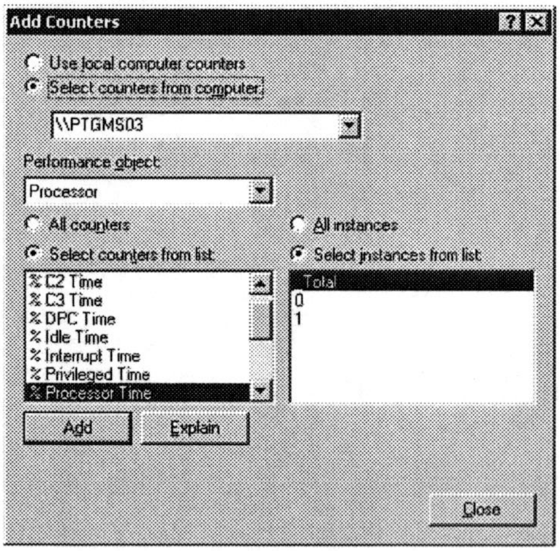

FIGURE 1.23 You can add specific individual counters to the counter log, if desired.

6. After you have added some objects or counters, you can configure the options for sampling interval. The default is every 15 seconds—meaning that while the counter log is running, data will be collected from the computers being monitored every 15 seconds. The sampling interval has a trade-off associated with it: Smaller intervals mean larger, more accurate log files; larger intervals result in smaller, less accurate log files. In addition, the smaller the sampling interval, the more resources performance monitoring consumes. You can also configure the account to be used to run the counter log.

7. On the Log Files tab of the Network Adapter Performance dialog box, shown in Figure 1.24, select the type of log file to be created, as well as the numbering system to be used. The default settings are Binary file and nnnnn. The available options are explained after this Step by Step in Tables 1.5 and 1.6. In addition, you can enter a comment that will help identify the counter log.

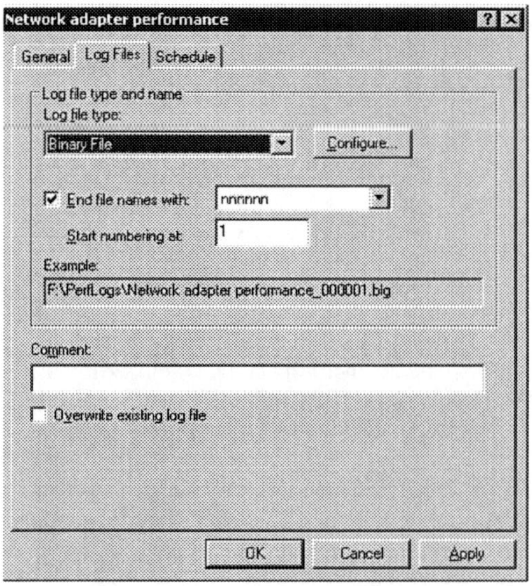

FIGURE 1.24 You can use the Log Files tab to configure how the log is to be saved.

8. Click the Configure button to open the Configure Log Files dialog box, shown in Figure 1.25. From here you can change the path of the log file and its maximum allowed size. Click OK after you make your changes.

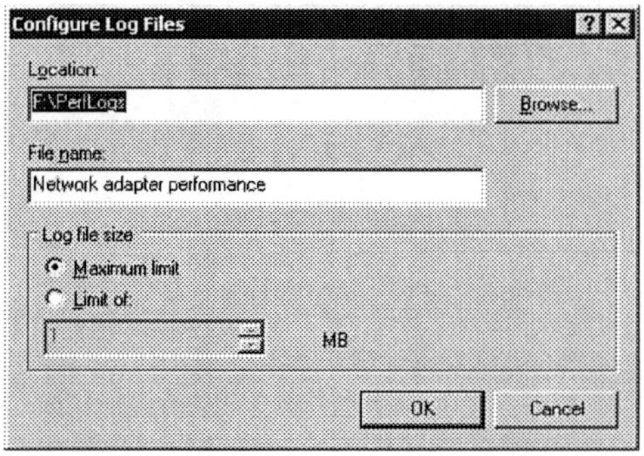

FIGURE 1.25 You can use the Configure Log Files dialog box to configure the maximum log file size as well as its path.

9. On the Schedule tab of the Network Adapter Performance dialog box, shown in Figure 1.26, you can configure how and when the counter log is to run. Typically, you will run it manually, although you might opt to have it run automatically at a configured time.

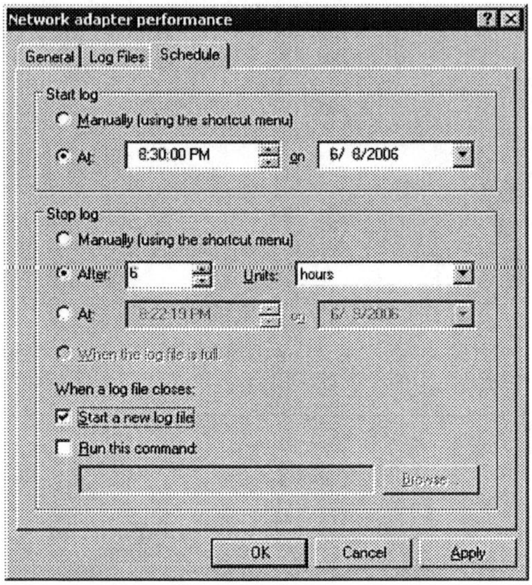

FIGURE 1.26 The counter log can be configured to start and stop automatically, if desired.

10. After you make all your configurations, click OK to save the counter log settings. Back at the Counter Logs node, seen previously in Figure 1.19, select the new counter log object and start it by clicking the start (right arrow) button in the menu. If you configured the counter log to start automatically, as seen in Figure 1.26, it will start at the configured time and run as configured, as seen in Figure 1.27.

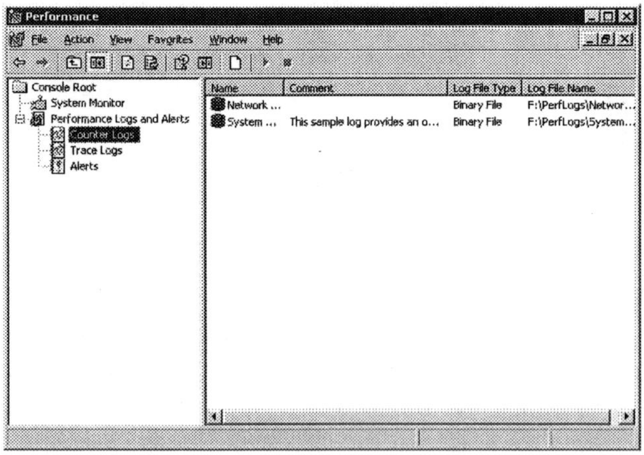

FIGURE 1.27 The counter log automatically starts if you configured it with a start time.

11. After the counter log has run for some time (or for its scheduled time), click the square stop icon to stop it.

12. Click the System Monitor node to switch back to System Monitor. Click the database icon to open a log file, as shown in Figure 1.28. The System Monitor Properties dialog box opens, showing the Source tab (see Figure 1.29).

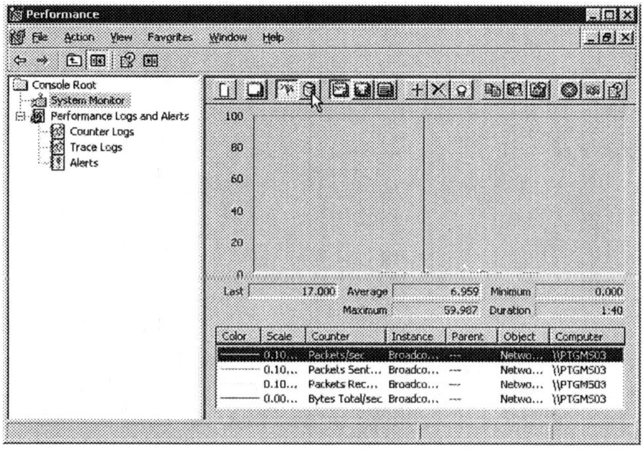

FIGURE 1.28 You need to load the counter log file into System Monitor to examine it.

13. Select the Log Files radio button and click the Add button to locate and add the counter log file.

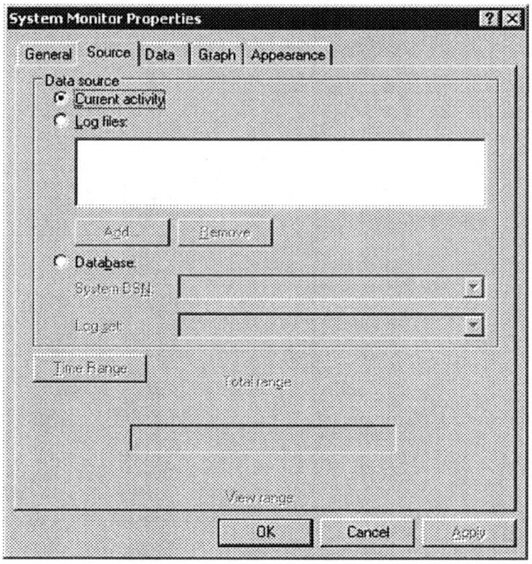

FIGURE 1.29 You can add one or more counter logs to the System Monitor.

14. Switch to the Data tab, shown in Figure 1.30, and ensure that all counters for which you are interested in seeing data are added. You will see data displayed only for counters that are selected here.

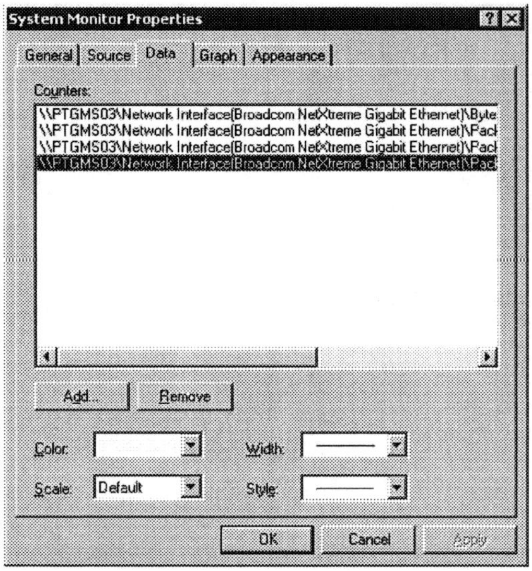

FIGURE 1.30 You need to ensure that all counters have been added for viewing.

15. The counter log data is displayed in System Monitor, as shown in Figure 1.31. If you need to display only a certain portion of the data, you can do so by configuring the Time Range option on the Source tab of the System Monitor Properties dialog box (refer to Figure 1.29).

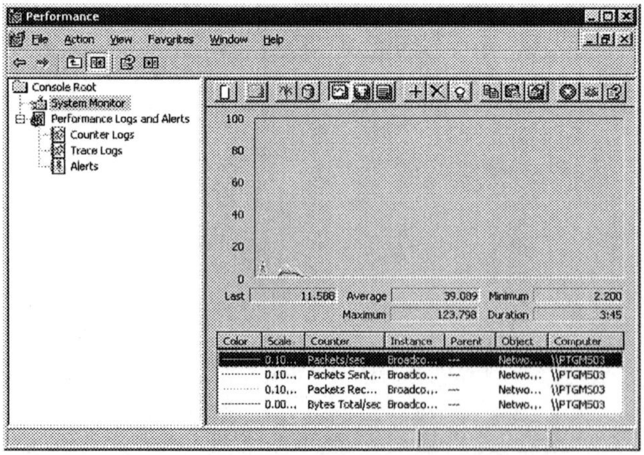

FIGURE 1.31 After you make the correct configurations, you can examine the historical counter log data.

Table 1.5 provides the counter log file format options available to you when creating a counter log.

TABLE 1.5 Counter Log File Format Options

Option	Description
Text File (Comma Delimited)	This option defines a comma-delimited log file (with a `.csv` extension).
Text File (Tab Delimited)	This option defines a tab-delimited log file (with a `.tsv` extension).
Binary File	This option defines a sequential, binary-format log file (with a `.blg` extension). You should use this file format if you want to be able to record data instances that are intermittent—that is, stopping and resuming after the log has begun running. Only binary file formats can accommodate instances that are not persistent throughout the duration of the log.
Binary Circular File	This option defines a circular, binary-format log file (with a `.blg` extension). You should use this file format to continuously record data to the same log file, overwriting previous records with new data when the file reaches its maximum size.

Table 1.6 illustrates the counter log numbering options available to you when creating a counter log.

TABLE 1.6 Counter Log Numbering Systems

System	Example
nnnnnn	`Network Adapter Performance_000007.blg`
mmddhh	`Network Adapter Performance_042011.blg`
mmddhhmm	`Network Adapter Performance_04201126.blg`
yyyyddd	`Network Adapter Performance_2003111.blg`
yyyymm	`Network Adapter Performance_200304.blg`
yyyymmdd	`Network Adapter Performance_20030420.blg`
yyyymmddhh	`Network Adapter Performance_2003042011.blg`

System Monitor Tips and Tricks

Microsoft provides some helpful tips and tricks that you should keep in mind when working with the Performance console to solve performance-related problems. Through careful analysis of data, you might be able to determine problems with the network that are not otherwise seen, such as excessive demands on resources that are resulting in bottlenecks—and, therefore, slowing network performance to the degree that users begin to notice that something is wrong.

EXAM ALERT

Saving Time by Saving Your Configuration No one wants to reinvent the wheel over and over. This holds true when you are configuring System Monitor with a set of counters. You can save a good amount of time and effort by setting up System Monitor with the counters and options you want on one server and then saving the configuration file and distributing that file to each of your other servers instead of re-creating the configuration each time.

The following are some of the most common causes of bottlenecks that you might encounter while troubleshooting your network:

- The current level of provided resources is inadequate, thus requiring additional or upgraded resources to be added to the network.
- The available resources are not be utilized evenly, thus requiring some form of load balancing to be implemented.
- An available resource is malfunctioning or stopped and needs to be repaired or restarted.
- An available resource is incorrectly configured, thus requiring a configuration correction.

When you have identified a problem, you should take care to avoid creating new problems while correcting the old one. You should make one change at a time to avoid masking the impact of changes. After each change, you should perform additional monitoring to determine the result and the effect of the change, and reevaluate the status and condition of the previously identified problem(s). In addition, you can compare the performance of applications that are run over the network to their performance when run locally to determine how the network is affecting performance.

The following are some basic network-configuration tips that you can check while troubleshooting and correcting network-related problems:

- As often as possible, ensure that resources are located on the same physical subnet as the users using the resource.
- Uninstall or unbind network protocols that are not in use.
- Configure the network protocol binding order to place the most commonly used protocols higher on the list.
- Use multiple network adapters in high-use servers to increase effective network throughput.

Challenge

You have been hired as a consultant to work for ABC Construction, Inc., because the company is having specific problems with its network. The problems range from clients timing out and loss of connectivity when trying to access network resources, to no connectivity to the network during peak hours. The network consists of four core switches, eight closets to connect the user segments consisting of four 24-port hubs each, and two redundant core routers.

Your task is to analyze the network, find the problems, and implement a solution that corrects the problems that ABC Construction, Inc., is experiencing.

Try to complete this exercise on your own by listing some of the tasks that you might want to perform on a sheet of paper. When you have completed the exercise, compare your results to those given here.

As a consultant going to ABC Construction, Inc., you immediately start to look at the network documentation and network topology maps. You need to make sure that there aren't any obvious errors in design (such as using stacked hubs in closets) and so on. It is your responsibility to check the network layout to see if there are any bottlenecks anywhere, choke points on the network, or mismatched bandwidth speeds going into critical areas. For example, you should make sure that you have a backbone segment with your critical servers that runs on Gigabit Ethernet and then move to the desktop users, most likely coming out of switch closets located around the building you are working in. These connections should run at a minimum of 100Mbps.

In today's networks, most businesses send around very large files, both video and voice, so you can't get away with using hubs running at 10Mbps anymore. The nature of a hub is to broadcast data out of every port, whereas a switch keeps a MAC-to-port memory map to keep the number of broadcasts to a minimum. Not using switches is a design flaw. Using hubs can cause massive collision counts, and if the collision counts are too high, your clients might experience timeouts, disconnects, or just bad performance.

In any case, by running a protocol analyzer on your network, you can find any excessive broadcasts, collisions, or extra protocols that are traversing the network. As a solution, you should run a protocol analyzer in the closet hubs, determine that traffic volume is way too high with collisions and broadcast traffic, and put in switches to control the traffic better. By doing so, you upgrade the network desktop users from 10Mbps to 100Mbps, a connection speed 10 times faster than they were using before. These changes might just solve all four network problems the company was experiencing.

Troubleshooting TCP/IP Addressing

For this objective, you are responsible for knowing how to troubleshoot basic client-based TCP/IP issues. This means that you must know all the things that can go wrong on a client workstation based on IP addressing and the ways to isolate these problems, as well as to resolve them. You have to know basic TCP/IP troubleshooting techniques, as well as ways to figure out whether the problem is DHCP based.

Troubleshooting Client Computers

Objective

Troubleshoot TCP/IP addressing.

- ▶ Diagnose and resolve issues related to client computer configuration.

When troubleshooting client-based TCP/IP problems, you really need to develop a good troubleshooting methodology; otherwise, you will just be wasting your time. You have to know what to check in what order, based on certain triggers you are looking for. For example, if a user tells you that she cannot log in to the network, that information is a trigger for a troubleshooting methodology. If the user cannot log on, you should then think about what the problem could be. Is only one user unable to log on, or are more users having the same problem? I usually ask this question first because if all the users are unable to log on, it's a big problem.

Assuming that only this user is unable to log on, you might be prompted to ask whether she keyed in the proper password, whether she had Caps Locks on, or whether she entered her password wrong a few times and locked herself out. If none of these is the case, your troubleshooting usually warrants a walk down to the user's desk for some investigation. From that trigger, you find out that not everyone has this problem; it is isolated to just this user. You also figure out that this is not a problem with a server; it is a problem with the client workstation. The user checked to make sure that she had the PC powered on and that she was, in fact, at the login screen and could not log in, even after checking to see whether she had used Caps Locks. Now you have a problem.

When you get to the user, you can try to repeat her steps first, then check her password again, and so on. When you move past these common problems, you can turn your attention to the network connection. You look at the back of the PC to check the link lights on the NIC and find that they are not on. You then check the cable plugged into the back of the PC, directly into the NIC. Finally, you move to the wall jack where the cable plugs into the wall to find it dislodged. Somehow it became unplugged. When you plug it back in and check the link lights on the NIC, the user is able to log on to the network a few seconds later.

The whole point behind this story is that a problem triggered a chain of responses from you to solve that problem.

Let's look at an IP-based issue now. If you have a server that cannot get on the network and you are able to isolate the problem to the bottom two layers (network access or physical and data link), your only other option is to start troubleshooting Layer 3. So how would you troubleshoot? First, look at any client that cannot access the network and for which you have isolated a Layer 3 problem. What would you do? You can use the `ping` command as follows from the workstation to see what the problem could be:

```
C:\> Ping 10.10.10.1 with 32 bytes of data:
Request timed out.
Request timed out.
Request timed out.
Request timed out.
Ping statistics for 10.10.10.1:
   Packets: Sent = 4, Received = 0, Lost = 4 <100% loss>,
Approximate round trip times in milli-seconds:
   Minimum = 0ms, Maximum = 0ms, Average= 0ms
```

Here, you can see the output of a simple `ping` command run to test the default gateway of a LAN. The `ping` tool is used to test IP connectivity to other hosts on the network. You use `ping` (which uses Internet Control Message Protocol, or ICMP, echo-based error reporting) to get an idea of what might be wrong. In this case, the `ping` to a default gateway timed out. You `ping` this device because you need to see whether the network has IP connectivity. As you can see from this output, it does not.

In the second example, shown here, you next `ping` another host on the network, which is a mainframe in the same VLAN. As you can see, the problem doesn't have anything to do with the workstation, which you might have assumed. The problem lies with the default gateway, which is bad. This result means something might be wrong with the router.

```
C:\> Ping 10.10.5.1 with 32 bytes of data:
Reply from 10.10.5.1: bytes=32 time=10ms TTL=255
Reply from 10.10.5.1: bytes=32 time=10ms TTL=255
Reply from 10.10.5.1: bytes=32 time=10ms TTL=255
Reply from 10.10.5.1: bytes=32 time=10ms TTL=255
Ping statistics for 10.10.5.1:
    Packets: Sent = 4, Received = 4, Lost = 0 (0% loss),
Approximate round trip times in milli-seconds:
    Minimum = 10ms, Maximum =  10ms, Average =  10ms
```

Are you beginning to understand how troubleshooting works? Problems can go many ways, so the best way to arm yourself is to understand not only the tool, but also the methodology behind it to isolate and resolve problems, and to identify the triggers you get from others that help you reduce your troubleshooting time.

You can, of course, use other tools, such as `ipconfig`. Typing this command at the command prompt provides a great deal of information, as you can see here:

```
C:\>ipconfig
Windows IP Configuration
Ethernet adapter Local Area Connection:
        Connection-specific DNS Suffix  . : corp.quepublishing.com
        IP Address. . . . . . . . . . . . : 192.168.0.121
        Subnet Mask . . . . . . . . . . . : 255.255.255.0
        Default Gateway . . . . . . . . . : 192.168.0.1
```

The `ipconfig` command returns your IP address, DNS domain, subnet mask, and default gateway. All this information is very important to troubleshooting client computers. If you do not see the proper information (such as an IP address of 0.0.0.0), you likely have some sort of problem.

EXAM ALERT

`ipconfig` questions Be prepared to look for questions with an `ipconfig` output like the example shown here. You might be shown an `ipconfig` screen with an IP address of 192.168.2.100 and a topology map that shows you trying to communicate on a subnet of 192.168.1.0. It should be obvious to you now that you are not able to communicate if you are not on the same subnet or there is a problem with a router connecting the subnets.

A host of switches can be used with the `ipconfig` command. Here, we cover only the `/all` switch. This switch, when used in conjunction with `ipconfig`, gives you even more TCP/IP-based information. We looked briefly at the use of this switch earlier in the chapter; remember that this switch provides more detailed information, such as DHCP, DNS, and WINS servers used, as well as your physical address and DHCP lease information. Understanding this command is important not only for the exam, but also for your job because you will be using it all the time. We cover the `ipconfig` command further in the following sections, where we cover more switches as they relate to DHCP and DNS.

Troubleshooting DHCP Server Issues

Objective

Troubleshoot TCP/IP addressing.

- Diagnose and resolve issues related to DHCP server address assignment.

Working through DHCP client-based issues is actually easy. The available scope either doles out an IP address to you or it doesn't. It's that easy. You know whether a client is configured to accept an IP address by using the `ipconfig /all` command. The results show a DHCP-enabled column with either Yes or No selected. If you see Yes and you don't have an IP address assigned, or you have an incorrect IP address assigned, you can try a few options. Always start with the easiest option first. You should consider `ipconfig` your tool of choice when trying to troubleshoot IP-based problems on clients and servers alike. When you want to troubleshoot a DHCP server issue, you can simply use the following two `ipconfig` switches:

```
ipconfig/ release
ipconfig/ renew
```

The `release` switch releases the IP address for the specified adapter; likewise, the `renew` switch asks the DHCP server to renew the lease and get your IP address back so you can participate on the network.

If you do not receive an answer from your DHCP server, you might have one of a few different problems. You might not have client connectivity, so you must make sure that you do. You cannot `ping` anything because you do not have an IP address, and you need that to communicate to the other host via ICMP. You can statically assign an IP to verify connectivity. You can also see whether you are on a segment with a DHCP server. If not, you might need an IP helper address assigned to the router; the helper agent is also known as a *DHCP relay agent*, which pushes the DHCP-based broadcasts over the router and points them to the DHCP server on the appropriate segment where it is located. If this relay agent is not configured, your client more than likely will not get a DHCP address. These are the most common issues you are likely to see on Exam 70-293 and also in production environments.

NOTE

More on DHCP We discuss DHCP in much more detail later in Chapter 3. The information in that chapter might be of some use to you in more advanced client-configuration troubleshooting situations.

Planning and Troubleshooting Internet Connectivity

In this section, we discuss your network infrastructure's Internet connectivity options, design issues, the reasons NAT is used, and the reasons the Internet and connectivity are so important. We also look at client-specific issues as well as issues relating to DNS. These are some of the more complicated issues to resolve, especially when you are dealing with NAT and DNS.

Planning Internet Connectivity

Objective

Plan an Internet connectivity strategy.

To connect your LAN to the Internet, you need to plan for the following issues:

- What type of connection do you want? What media, what technology?
- How much bandwidth do you need to provide?
- What hardware will you use?
- Will security be involved?

- Who provides DNS?
- Will you be doing Network Address Translation?
- Where does Windows Server 2003 fit into network connectivity?

These questions are often asked before a deployment because deploying an Internet connection strategy is easier if you plan for it. Not planning or making up the plan as you are deploying can lead to an unsecured connection with the wrong bandwidth, which causes nothing but problems. Let's look at each question in depth to plan your Internet connection strategy:

- **What type of connection do you want? What media, what technology?** You need to consider what type of connection to the Internet you will have installed because the type of Internet connection you select determines what the connection media will be (WISP, T1, DSL, cable, and so on), as well as what signaling method and what additional hardware (modem, router, CSU/DSU) you will need. Each connection type selected also dictates the bandwidth you will have available to you, in most instances. Therefore, you need to plan your Internet connection method well.
- **How much bandwidth do you need to provide?** You need to consider what type of traffic and how much of it will be traversing your Internet connection. Without applications to limit what can leave or enter your network via the Internet, outbound e-mail and Internet web browsing likely will consume most of your bandwidth.
- **What hardware will you use?** Will you use a Cisco router? A 3Com router? You need to know what to use for an Internet connection before you purchase the hardware because it is imperative that you plan the hardware around the connection type. You need specific interface types depending on what technology you select (T1, DSL, and so on), so you must make sure you plan your hardware accordingly.
- **Will security be involved?** Whether a firewall will be used dictates how you deploy your Internet connection. If you want to use a firewall, you must plan for it as well. If a firewall is used, you must plan what traffic you need to pass; otherwise, the firewall will block it out. For instance, if you were to use the Remote Desktop Protocol or Terminal Services over the Internet, you would need to configure the firewall to allow this traffic to pass.
- **Who provides DNS?** The domain name system is the lifeblood of the Internet. Without it, everyone would have to memorize IP addresses to get to everything they needed; instead, use easy-to-remember names such as quepublishing.com. Your ISP normally provides DNS, or you can move the DNS into your network (preferably on your demilitarized zone, DMZ) and have an internal namespace forward out to the public DNS servers. Either way, you need to consider this issue when deploying your Internet solution.

- **Will you be doing Network Address Translation?** NAT translates one set of IP addresses to another. If NAT is to be used, you must plan for it. Because setting up NAT is somewhat complex if you have never done it, you must make sure you properly plan what you need before you deploy it. For example, say you want to have a 10.1.1.0/24 LAN access the Internet via a translatable pool of addresses to the Internet via 12.1.1.1, 12.1.1.2, and 12.1.1.3. You must plan this configuration so you know what IP addresses you will need and how to deploy them so that they work.
- **Where does Windows Server 2003 fit into network connectivity?** Windows Server 2003 can be used as an Internet connection (via the Routing and Remote Access feature), but it is typically best practice in larger implementations that you purchase and use dedicated hardware devices for these types of roles. Hardware is available from many vendors, such as Cisco, 3Com, Blue Shield, and many others, depending on your specific needs.

Troubleshooting Client Configuration Issues

Objective

Troubleshoot connectivity to the Internet.

- Diagnose and resolve issues related to client configuration.

If you cannot connect to the Internet with a client PC, you have a few options to think about. First, you need to consider that the Internet might be inaccessible. Sometimes the line that supplies the traffic to and from your organization has problems with the ISP. Although such problems can be deemed inexcusable, you might see the line go down for maintenance or for an unpredicted outage.

As a client, you also might see that your IP address is not on the same subnet (if you have a static assignment on a laptop and move to another subnet) or your network connection is disconnected. Make sure that you know how to troubleshoot client issues for Exam 70-293.

NOTE

More on DHCP We discuss DHCP in much more detail later in Chapter 3. The information in that chapter might be of some use to you in more advanced client-configuration troubleshooting situations.

Troubleshooting DNS Issues

Objective

Troubleshoot connectivity to the Internet.

- Diagnose and resolve issues related to name-resolution cache information.

Here we discuss ways to troubleshoot DNS connectivity on a client workstation that is having problems with name resolution on a Windows network. You need to know how to diagnose and resolve problems related to name-resolution cache information. To do this, you need to know the `ipconfig` command, which was discussed previously. `ipconfig` has several switches associated with it, so if you are working from a Windows workstation and you cannot get a client to resolve names properly because the client-side DNS cache is either corrupted or not updated to a change already made on the DNS server, you can easily flush out that information by using one of the following commands:

EXAM ALERT

Know your commands Remember when you need to use each command because the test doesn't point you in the right direction. By understanding *and* memorizing these commands, you can effectively troubleshoot DNS on a client.

- `ipconfig /flushdns`—This command purges the DNS resolver cache.
- `ipconfig /displaydns`—This command displays the contents of the DNS resolver cache.
- `ipconfig /registerdns`—This command refreshes all DHCP leases and reregisters DNS names.

Everything you need to know is done at the command prompt.

NOTE

More on DNS We discuss DNS in much more detail later in Chapter 4, "Planning and Implementing a Name Resolution Infrastructure." The information in that chapter might be of some use to you in more advanced client-configuration troubleshooting situations.

Troubleshooting Network Address Translation (NAT) Issues

Objective

Troubleshoot connectivity to the Internet.

- Diagnose and resolve issues related to Network Address Translation (NAT).

We covered NAT in great detail throughout the chapter, so this section covers what you need to know about NAT for the exam. You need to be aware of the changes that have been made to the IPSec protocol and NAT in Windows Server 2003.

First, you need to understand why such changes were needed in the first place. NAT does not allow IPSec to work. IPSec is a security-based protocol that enables you to secure communications across your network. The problem is that the IPSec packet, by design, does not work well with NAT. Because NAT breaks down the packets to change the IP address, it also causes problems with the IPSec packet, which is essentially encrypted and cannot be changed. With Windows Server 2003, the biggest change is that IPSec and L2TP are both supported through NAT. Revised IPSec clients are available for Windows XP and 2000 Professional as well. Using Windows Server 2003 and NAT dramatically reduces problems with IPSec.

Chapter Summary

In this chapter, we described TCP/IP planning, design, and basic implementation. We also covered ways to troubleshoot TCP/IP. Now you can look at workstation problems with more confidence because you know how to `ping` devices on your network (and know what you are attempting to `ping`). You also know how to see whether you have an IP address or find what IP address you do have. You learned ways to plan a TCP/IP network, as well as the devices that populate a network.

Good networks begin with good planning and good designs. To plan and design a good network, you need to understand the IP addressing and routing requirements of your organization. With this knowledge in mind, you can move forward and start planning the IP subnets you need. This creates a solid backbone from which the rest of your network can be built. In this chapter, we looked at planning an IP-based network from many different angles. All networks should have a design and/or plan, and included in that plan should be information regarding where you would place your network resources (file, print, Internet access, and so on), as well as what protocols will be used to connect to and access such resources.

In all networks today, not connecting to the Internet would massively hamper a company's growth. E-mail, web browsing, and a plethora of other solutions need Internet access to function, so not having Internet connectivity would be a huge problem. In this chapter, we also covered the importance of planning an Internet connectivity strategy. We looked at strategy, planning, and design. Networks have problems that at times are hard to solve or reproduce but that need to be solved nonetheless. Using tools such as Network Monitor and System Monitor can help you find problems as well monitor traffic traversing your LAN. When your network is connected to the Internet, many things can happen. You might have problems with Network Address Translation planning and implementation, with DNS, and, of course, with clients trying to connect to and use the Internet.

All network administrators need to know, understand, and embrace TCP/IP. You need to know how to troubleshoot TCP/IP issues, as well as those issues resulting from problems with a DHCP server.

Key Terms

- Default gateway
- Firewall
- Layer 3 switch
- Network Address Translation (NAT)
- Network interface card (NIC)
- Physical address

- Public address
- Private address
- Proxy server
- Router
- Subnet mask
- TCP/IP

Apply Your Knowledge

In this chapter, you examined basic TCP/IP planning, design, and implementation. We also covered ways to troubleshoot TCP/IP in Windows Server 2003. In the following exercises, you practice some of the concepts and methods discussed in this chapter.

Exercises

1.1 Using `ping`

In this exercise, you learn how to use the `ping` utility. `Ping` can be used if you have a connectivity problem. In Exercise 1.2, we look at dealing with a connectivity issue and using `ping` to resolve it.

Estimated time: 5 minutes

1. You are the administrator for ABC, Inc. You are responsible for 30 Windows Server 2003 systems, 300 XP Professional clients, and all connecting network infrastructure. A client asks you to see why she can't connect to the network.
2. To perform this test, you can use the `ping` utility. Choose Start, Run. Type **CMD** in the Run dialog box and then press Enter. Type **`ping`** at the command prompt and enter the IP address of your default gateway.
3. You are able to successfully `ping` the router, so you are connected via IP.

1.2 Renew an IP Address

In this exercise, you learn how to renew an IP address from a DHCP server.

Estimated time: 5 minutes

1. You are the senior administrator for 123, Inc. You are responsible for 300 Windows Server 2003 systems, 2000 XP Professional clients, and all connecting network infrastructure. A client asks you why she can't access any network resources.

2. You try to `ping` the default gateway, and you receive hardware errors.
3. You use the `ipconfig` command and see that you have an IP address of 0.0.0.0.
4. You know that you have a DHCP server on your network, so you should have an IP address.
5. To get the IP address, choose Start, Run. Type **CMD** in the Run dialog box and then press Enter. Type **`ipconfig /renew`** to get a new IP address from the DHCP server.

1.3 Using `ipconfig`

In this exercise, you learn how to view all IP-related information associated with your workstation.

Estimated time: 5 minutes

1. You are the administrator for ABC, Inc. You are responsible for 30 Windows Server 2003 systems, 300 XP Professional clients, and all connecting network infrastructure. A client asks you to see why he cannot connect to the network.
2. You can't `ping` anything from the workstation.
3. You need to check whether you have an IP address assigned to the workstation.
4. To check the address, choose Start, Run. Type **CMD** in the Run dialog box and then press Enter. Type **`ipconfig /all`** and see whether you have an IP address assigned.

Review Questions

1. You have 20 network clients who cannot access any network resources. You try to `ping` the default gateway but cannot hit it; however, you are able to `ping` other devices on a different subnet. What could be the problem?
2. Several of your Windows XP Professional clients are having trouble connecting to an Internet website. You suspect that they have local DNS cache data that is preventing them from contacting the correct IP address. What can you do to quickly resolve this problem?
3. Four Windows workstations cannot access the network. You have DHCP enabled on the segment, and everyone else is okay. If nothing is wrong with the server, what could be the problem?
4. You are the senior administrator of your company. Your CIO cannot access the network. She checks to see whether the link lights are on and the cable is attached, and they are. What would be your next step to troubleshoot this problem?
5. One workstation cannot access the network. You want to run a simple test to see whether the workstation can communicate with other devices on the network. What utility could you use?

Exam Questions

1. As the lead systems administrator for the ABC, LLC, network, you are responsible for planning a TCP/IP network that is robust and functional. You have a total of 450 clients spread out over three

locations. You have 150 clients per location, and at one central location, you have approximately 25 servers. You are asked to select an IP addressing scheme that maps to your needs. Select the best option to subnet and IP address this network.

A. Use a Class A network of 10.1.1.0/8.

B. Use a Class B network of 172.16.0.0/16.

C. Use three Class C networks of 192.168.1.0/24, 192.168.2.0/24, and 192.168.3.0/24.

D. Use a single Class A subnetted network of 10.1.1.0/16.

2. Jake is the senior systems administrator for your organization. Jake is responsible for 200 Windows XP Professional clients and 15 Windows Server 2003 systems located on a network backbone running at 100Mbps. All 200 clients complain of slow response times on the network and have difficulty doing the simplest of tasks, such as browsing the Internet, especially during the midmorning and midafternoon periods of the day. The clients are running at 10Mbps. What can Jake do to increase the performance of his network? (Choose two answers.)

A. Upgrade the backbone to 1000Mbps.

B. Install hubs in the network closets to segment the network.

C. Upgrade the clients to 100Mbps.

D. Install a network monitor to adjust the network for better performance.

3. You are the systems administrator of the ABC Company, and you currently have a network client that cannot access the network. When you talk to the user on the phone, you find out that there is no break in the cable and the link lights on the NIC are operational. You then go down to the user's workstation to troubleshoot. Because you have determined that this is not a lower-layer problem, you are convinced it might be a IP-based problem. What two tools can you use to see whether this is a Layer 3 problem?

A. `ping` the default gateway.

B. Use `ipconfig` to see whether you have a valid IP address.

C. Use `ipconfig /release` to get a valid IP address.

D. Use `ipconfig /flushdns` to clear your cache because it could be corrupted.

4. Marshall is the systems administrator for QBC Corp. He runs a network of 20 Windows Server 2003 systems on a network backbone, as well as 200 Windows XP Professional clients. Marshall is worried about connectivity to the Internet. For some reason, none of the internal clients can resolve anything in the company's web browsers. Marshall runs some checks on the Internet connection, and it appears to be okay. He then runs some checks and finds out that if he enters the URL http://www.quepublishing.com in a browser, he cannot resolve this address, but if he enters the URL http://63.240.93.132, he can access the site. What could be the possible problem with the network?

A. Marshall is having a problem resolving DNS. He should check the DNS settings.

B. The network core switch is down. Marshall should check the device and reboot it.

C. A bad route in the Internet router keeps Marshall from getting on the Internet. He should add the correct route.

D. WINS is misconfigured. Marshall needs to reconfigure it and try again.

5. Pete is the systems administrator for RDT, Inc. He runs a network of 25 Windows Server 2003 systems on a network backbone, as well as 300 Windows XP Professional clients. Pete cannot get a server to connect to the network. He was given an IP address of 10.1.1.12/24 for the server. He has the server plugged into the network backbone (Gigabit Ethernet), which is on the 10.0.1.0/24 subnet. This subnet does not have a DHCP server located on it. What could be the problem?

A. Pete has the correct IP address, but the subnet mask is incorrect.

B. Pete has the correct IP address, but the DHCP server from another segment is interfering with his communications.

C. Pete has the wrong IP address; he needs one for that backbone segment.

D. Pete set up the wrong server and has a duplicate address on the network.

6. Sally is the senior systems administrator for Runners Corp. She runs a network of 20 Windows Server 2003 systems, as well as 250 Windows XP Professional clients. Sally is worried about a client that cannot connect to the network. She does not have an IP address assigned. Sally used `ipconfig` and found an IP address of 0.0.0.0. She knows that a DHCP server is present on the subnet in which she is located and that all lower-level troubleshooting has been performed, such as checking link lights and cable connectivity. What is the most likely solution to this problem?

A. Sally can issue the `ipconfig /renew` command to get a new IP address.

B. Sally can issue the `ipconfig /flushdns` command to get a new IP address.

C. Sally can issue the `ipconfig /dsiplayip` command to get a new IP address.

D. Sally can issue the `ipconfig /release` command to get a new IP address.

7. You are the systems administrator for IP Corp. The company has a network of 25 Windows Server 2003 systems on a network backbone, as well as 150 Windows XP Professional clients. You need to design a network with a new IP range given to you by your supervisor. You are given a range of 129.0.1.0/24 to use for your clients. What is the proper class that this IP address range falls into?

A. Class A

B. Class B

C. Class C

D. Class D

8. Marshall is the systems administrator for QBC Corp. He runs a network of 20 Windows Server 2003 systems on a network backbone, as well as 200 Windows XP Professional clients. Marshall is worried about a single PC that cannot connect to the network. Which would be the most logical troubleshooting step to start with?

- **A.** Marshall can use Network Monitor to see whether the network is congested.
- **B.** Marshall can use System Monitor to see whether the network interface card is defective.
- **C.** Marshall can `ping` localhost.
- **D.** Marshall can use the `ipconfig /ipinfo` command to see whether he has a valid IP address.

9. Pete is the systems administrator for RDT, Inc. He runs a network of 25 Windows Server 2003 systems on a network backbone, as well as 300 Windows XP Professional clients. Pete has been tasked with deploying an IP addressing solution to a remote network. He has to remain within the standards dictated by the networking group to use a private range within the private network. Which private range can he use within the network?

- **A.** Class A: 12.0.0.0–12.255.255.255
- **B.** Class B: 172.15.0.0–172.31.255.255
- **C.** Class C: 192.169.0.0–192.169.255.255
- **D.** Class A: 10.0.0.0–10.255.255.255

10. Sally is the senior systems administrator for Runners Corp. She runs a network of 20 Windows Server 2003 systems, as well as 250 Windows XP Professional clients. Sally has started to troubleshoot a workstation located on subnet 10.1.2.0/24. When Sally started to troubleshoot, she realized after running `ipconfig` that the workstation is not on the same subnet, which is keeping it from communicating. From running `ipconfig`, she finds an IP address of 169.254.0.1. What is the problem?

- **A.** The NIC failed, and this is the IP address given to show a NIC failure.
- **B.** There is nothing wrong; the workstation should communicate without error.
- **C.** The APIPA range 169.254.0.1 to 169.254.255.254 is being used probably because the DHCP server failed.
- **D.** The DHCP server is working fine but is doling out the wrong IP address scope.

11. A router on your network received packets from the LAN destined to remote networks. Your router will make a decision on what class a packet's source and destination IP addresses are from simply viewing the first few bits of the address. What prefix accurately shows a Class C network?

- **A.** 0
- **B.** 10
- **C.** 110
- **D.** 1110

12. Marshall is the network administrator for QBC Corp. He runs a network of 20 Windows Server 2003 systems on a network backbone, as well as 200 Windows XP Professional clients. Marshall is worried about whether to use static routes or dynamic routes in his routers. He wants to keep the router overhead low, and only one route (a default route) is needed. What course of action should Marshall take?

A. Marshall can use static routes but add a routing protocol as a backup.

B. Marshall can use the dynamic routing protocol OSPF.

C. Marshall can use a single static route.

D. Marshall can use Access Control Lists for reduced routing overhead.

13. Pete is the systems administrator for RDT, Inc. He runs a network of 25 Windows Server 2003 systems on a network backbone, as well as 300 Windows XP Professional clients. Pete is worried about configuring the right range of IP addresses for his network. Basically, he is given the choice to select a single Class C range from the private range of IP addresses. What range would fit this need?

A. Pete should assign a private range of 192.165.2.0/24 to the network segment.

B. Pete should assign a private range of 192.167.3.0/24 to the network segment.

C. Pete should assign a private range of 192.169.1.0/24 to the network segment.

D. Pete should assign a private range of 192.168.5.0/24 to the network segment.

14. Sally is the senior systems administrator for Runners Corp. She runs a network of 20 Windows Server 2003 systems, as well as 250 Windows XP Professional clients. Sally is asked to troubleshoot a server that cannot connect to the network. Starting from the most obvious to the most difficult, Sally begins to troubleshoot her server. Sally has isolated the issue to the NIC on the server. What troubleshooting technique makes the most sense to solve this problem?

A. The NIC has no link lights present.

B. `ipconfig` returns the "Hardware error" message.

C. `ping` returns the "Destination not found" message.

D. `ipconfig /renew` returns an "NIC failure" message.

15. You are the systems administrator for IP Corp. The company has a network of 25 Windows Server 2003 systems on a network backbone, as well as 300 Windows XP Professional clients. You need to test a workstation's capability to get, maintain, and then release an IP address. What two commands would you use to get and then give up an IP address on a host? (Choose only one answer.)

A. `ipconfig /off`, `ipconfig /on`

B. `ipconfig /release`, `ipconfig /renew`

C. `ipconfig /fluship`, `ipconfig /renewip`

D. `ipconfig /release`, `ipconfig /getip`

Answers to Review Questions

1. A switch on that segment is powered off or has failed. Because you can get to other areas of your network, there is a good chance that you have a simple hardware problem. For more information, see the section "Planning Physical Placement of Network Resources."

2. Use the `ipconfig /flushndns` command on the affected computers to purge the local DNS resolver cache and allow the computer to query a DNS server for the correct IP address. For more information, see the section "Troubleshooting DNS Issues."

3. The DHCP client leases might have expired on these four workstations, so use the `ipconfig /renew` command to get a new lease period. For more information, see the section "Troubleshooting TCP/IP Addressing."

4. Because you have link lights (Layer 2 is good), you would want to move to Layer 3 and see whether you have an IP address. Use the `ipconfig` command to see whether you have an IP address. For more information, see the section "Troubleshooting Client Computers."

5. You can use `ping` to test basic Layer 3 connectivity on the network. `ping` the default gateway, a server, or any other device you know is up and operational. For more information, see the section "Troubleshooting TCP/IP Addressing."

Answers to Exam Questions

1. **C.** You can solve this issue by using three Class C networks of 192.168.1.0/24, 192.168.2.0/24, and 192.168.3.0/24. For more information, see the section "Troubleshooting TCP/IP Addressing."

2. **A, C.** To get this network to operate faster and more effectively, Jake should upgrade the backbone to 1000Mbps and upgrade the clients to 100Mbps on the desktop. For more information, see the section "Planning Physical Placement of Network Resources."

3. **A, B.** To solve this problem, you can use two tools: the `ping` utility and `ipconfig`. `ping` the default gateway to test connectivity, and use `ipconfig` to see whether you have a valid IP address. For more information, see the section "Troubleshooting TCP/IP Addressing."

4. **A.** In this situation, Marshall is having a problem resolving DNS. He needs to check DNS settings and resolve any issues with them. For more information, see the section "Troubleshooting DNS Issues."

5. **C.** Pete has the wrong IP address; he needs one for that backbone segment. For more information, see the section "Analyzing IP Addressing Requirements."

6. **A.** Sally can issue the `ipconfig /renew` command to get a new IP address from the DHCP server. Basically, she needs to know that if she sees certain indicators that point to a lack of connectivity but can be solved by renewing an IP address, she needs to renew the lease on a system that might have been released after the time period. For more information, see the section "Troubleshooting DHCP Server Issues."

7. **B.** This IP address range falls into Class B. The Class B range is set from 128 to 191. For more information, see the section "Analyzing IP Addressing Requirements."

8. **C.** The IP address 127.0.0.0 is reserved for loopback networks and testing. 127.0.0.1 is also located in the HOSTS file, which allows Marshall to test the IP connectivity of his own machine. If he uses the command **`ping loopback`** (which is the hostname located in the HOSTS file), he can resolve to 127.0.0.1 and should see a reply. This way, Marshall knows that IP is configured properly—at least on his own system. For more information, see the section "Troubleshooting TCP/IP Addressing."

9. **D.** Class A falls between 10.0.0.0 and 10.255.255.255. Pete can use this entire Class A for internal network private IP addressing. Class B falls between 172.16.0.0 and 172.31.255.255, and Class C falls between 192.168.0.0 and 192.168.255.255. These numbering assignments are kept at www.iana.org. For more information, see the section "TCP/IP Fundamentals."

10. **C.** The APIPA range 169.254.0.1–169.254.255.254 is being used probably because the DHCP server failed. This happens when Sally has a client set to get an IP address from a DHCP server, but there is no DHCP server answering requests for service. For more information, see the section "Analyzing IP Addressing Requirements."

11. **C.** The prefix the router looks at would be the first few bits of the IP address, and this is how it knows the class. If you see a 0 as the first bit, it would be a Class A. If the first bit is a 1, it would be Class B. Class C would be 2 bits turned on, so the prefix would look like 110; thus, Answer C is correct. For more information, see the section "Planning an IP Routing Solution."

12. **C.** Marshall can use a single static route. The best option in this case is to use just a single route statement. Routing protocols are complex and offer significant overhead; they can also be a security risk in some instances. If Marshall needs only a single route, he should simply add that one route, not an entire protocol that would learn more routes than needed and advertise them unnecessarily. For more information, see the section "Planning an IP Routing Solution."

13. **D.** Pete should assign a private range of 192.168.5.0/24 to the network segment. The other answers are all in the public range of IP address assignments, so he should use the 192.168.01.0–192.168.255.255 range. Anything in this range is considered a private IP address. For more information, see the section "Analyzing IP Addressing Requirements."

14. **A.** In this situation, the NIC card has no link lights present, which indicates that there is a break somewhere on the network. All other answers given were Layer 3 issues dealing with IP addressing. Sally should always troubleshoot the lower layers first before moving up the model. For more information, see the section "Planning Physical Placement of Network Resources."

15. **B.** To solve this problem, you can use the `ipconfig/release` or `ipconfig/renew` commands to get a new IP address for use. For more information, see the section "Troubleshooting DHCP Server Issues."

Suggested Readings and Resources

1. Microsoft Corporation. *Microsoft Windows Server 2003 Resource Kit.* Redmond, WA: Microsoft Press, 2003. ISBN 0735614717.
2. Microsoft Corporation. *Microsoft Windows Server 2003 Deployment Kit.* Redmond, WA: Microsoft Press, 2003. ISBN 0735614865.
3. Davies, Joseph, and Thomas Lee. *Microsoft Windows Server 2003 TCP/IP Protocols and Services Technical Reference.* Redmond, WA: Microsoft Press, 2003. ISBN 0735612919.
4. "TCP/IP Fundamentals for Windows Server 2003." www.microsoft.com/technet/itsolutions/network/evaluate/technol/tcpipfund/tcpipfund.mspx.
5. Windows Server 2003 RFC Checklist at www.rfc-editor.org/rfc.html:
    - 768: User Datagram Protocol (UDP)
    - 783: Trivial File Transfer Protocol (TFTP)
    - 791: Internet Protocol (IP)
    - 792: Internet Control Message Protocol (ICMP)
    - 793: Transmission Control Protocol (TCP)
    - 826: Address Resolution Protocol (ARP)
    - 854: Telnet Protocol (TELNET)
    - 950: Internet Standard Subnetting Procedure
    - 959: File Transfer Protocol (FTP)
    - 1001, 1002: NetBIOS Service Protocols
    - 1065, 1035, 1123, 1886: Domain Name System (DNS)
    - 1256: ICMP Router Discovery Messages
    - 1518: Architecture for IP Address Allocation with CIDR
    - 1519: Classless Inter-Domain Routing (CIDR)
    - 1812: Requirements for IP Version 4 Routers
    - 2131: Dynamic Host Configuration Protocol
    - 2136: Dynamic Updates in the Domain Name System (DNS UPDATE)
    - 2581: TCP Congestion Control

CHAPTER TWO

Planning and Troubleshooting TCP/IP Routing

Objectives

Microsoft has defined the Routing portion of the "Planning, Implementing, and Maintaining Routing and Remote Access" objectives as follows:

Plan a routing strategy.

- **Identify routing protocols to use in a specified environment.**
- **Plan routing for IP multicast traffic.**
- Routing is the process of moving packets from one network to another. To do this efficiently, you must know how to plan a strategy that works for your business needs and ensure that it is implemented properly. You need to identify which routing strategy you might need (static versus dynamic routing) and what protocols you want to use. You also need to understand what multicast traffic is and how to plan routing for it.

Troubleshoot TCP/IP routing. Tools might include the `route`, `tracert`, `ping`, `pathping`, and `netsh` commands and Network Monitor.

- After your network infrastructure has been designed, planned, and implemented, you need to know how to troubleshoot it. Windows Server 2003 provides quite a few tools to help you troubleshoot, so you need to know how to use them not only to solve problems, but also to take Exam 70-293. Here, you learn how to use `route`, `tracert`, `ping`, `pathping`, `netsh`, and Network Monitor.

Outline

Study Strategies

- Focus on understanding what protocols are used for what solution. In other words, if you are asked to create a hub-and-spoke network with static routes on the spokes and a routing protocol in the core, which would you use? What routing protocol? If you are asked to make it secure, what would you use? These are the questions you need to know how to answer from a design and planning standpoint.
- Take some time to review network security planning. This exam focuses on security as well, so make sure you study not only how to plan a network infrastructure, but also how to secure your network infrastructure.
- Get your hands dirty. The Step by Steps throughout this book provide plenty of directions and exercises, but you should go beyond these examples and create some of your own. If you can, experiment with each of the objectives to see how they work and why you would use each one.

Introduction

In times gone by, it was considered safe practice to build a castle with a moat, a drawbridge, and very high walls to keep your enemies out. If business was to be done in your land, a visitor would have to enter the castle under guard, show or claim credentials or services, and then be allowed in to do business.

Things haven't changed much. In today's corporate network, the same basic procedures are still in place that were used in the past. The only real change is that networks are much more complex and at risk than any castle ever was. For this reason, as you plan and design your network, you must know how to analyze potential holes and pitfalls for security and implement a network security strategy to stop these potential problems. One of the key goals of this chapter is to do just that: to help you learn how to secure remote access to your network.

In the interconnected business environment of today, businesses cannot survive as isolated kingdoms. The trend is for companies to integrate with, merge with, and buy and sell each other. During any one of these processes, the likelihood that you will need to implement a secure remote-access solution is extremely high.

First, this chapter looks at how Microsoft provides Routing and Remote Access Service (RRAS) solutions. You also learn how to plan a routing strategy. *Routing* is the process of moving packets from one network to another. To route efficiently, you need to know how to properly configure RRAS for routing. To do this, you need to identify which routing strategy you might need (static versus dynamic routing) and what protocols you want to use. You also need to understand what multicast traffic is and how to plan routing for it.

As you might know, RRAS is good for more than just simple routing; its primary function is to provide remote-access connectivity for your network. Although this chapter focuses solely on the routing portion of RRAS, we examine the remote access portion later in Chapter 7, "Planning, Implementing, and Troubleshooting Secure Network Access."

Of course, planning, implementing, and securing do not constitute all of your work; you will undoubtedly spend some time troubleshooting your solution both during its implementation and after this point. Being able to identify the right troubleshooting tool for the job will make this process quicker and more efficient for you, thus bringing back critical business services to your network in a timely fashion. Some of the tools you need to become familiar with include the `route`, `tracert`, `ping`, `pathping`, and `netsh` commands and Network Monitor.

Planning a Routing Strategy

In this section, you discover how to plan a routing strategy. It is imperative that you first cover some basic material to be able to understand what you are planning and why you are planning it that way. As you are planning a routing strategy, you must also identify the routing protocols you will need to use in normal environments, as well as what protocols to implement while using multicast-based traffic.

What Is Routing?

Routing is the process of moving data from one network and to another network. If you recall, in Chapter 1, "Planning, Implementing, and Troubleshooting a TCP/IP Network Infrastructure," you learned the differences in subnets and how networks are identified by devices, such as by using the subnet mask. We also covered how a routing decision is made—for example, when a packet has a destination address that does not match the network it is currently on and needs to get to the network it is destined for. This is why you need a *default gateway*, which can be a router or a device acting as a router. The routing process truly takes place at the default gateway.

Chapter 1 also briefly covered the Open System Interconnect (OSI) and Department of Defense (DoD) models and TCP/IP. You learned how important these items are in today's network environment. You also learned about routing in general. Let's quickly review a simple network diagram showing one user accessing a single web server. In Figure 2.1, it is clear that a user is accessing a web page on a remote web server.

FIGURE 2.1 To get the web page the user requests, the traffic is routed between networks across the Internet.

Let's look at the details of the request in Figure 2.1. From this information, you can gain a fundamental understanding of routing and how data is routed from one network to another.

- First, the user on the PC LAN accesses a web page by opening his web browser (Internet Explorer) and entering the domain name or IP address of the server on which the page resides. In this case, that is http://12.1.2.2/index.htm.
- Next, the user's computer, which is on the 10.0.0.0/24 subnet, makes a request to a server on the 12.1.2.0/24 subnet. Because they are two different subnets, the packets need to be sent to the default gateway configured on the client LAN. The default gateway is set to 10.0.0.1, which is where routing takes place.
- The packets enter the router's Ethernet port, which is connected to the local area network (LAN). This interface (the one connected to the LAN) is nothing more than a network interface card (NIC) that gives access to and from the Ethernet-based network. After the packets enter the router, the router strips them down to look inside. This is done to view the destination address, which is 12.1.2.2 on the destination network of 12.1.2.0/24.

- Next, the router (10.0.0.1) looks in its routing table. A *routing table* is nothing more than a list of networks that the router will service. In this case, the router has been configured with a routing entry to do the following: If a packet comes from the LAN and is destined to go to the 12.1.2.0 network, it sends the traffic out interface 1. This interface is connected to the far-side router, which is labeled 12.1.2.1. As such, after the packets come in, they are forwarded to the 12.1.2.1 router, where the web server is located.
- After the 12.1.2.1 router receives the packets, it also looks inside the packets to see where the packets need to go. When the router opens and reads the packets, it sees that the packets are destined to go to the 12.1.2.0 network, and it is a host with an IP address of 12.1.2.2. What makes this process even easier is that a router also holds an Address Resolution Protocol (ARP) cache; as long as that router is up and directly connected to the same subnet as the web server, the packet will more than likely be sent directly to the web server.
- Finally, the web server receives the packets (which are a request to see a web page named index.htm) and answers that request by producing the web page to the remote client. The same process happens again, except in reverse order, to return the page to the requesting machine.

In Figure 2.2, the scenario has been expanded to show a routing environment over a larger network.

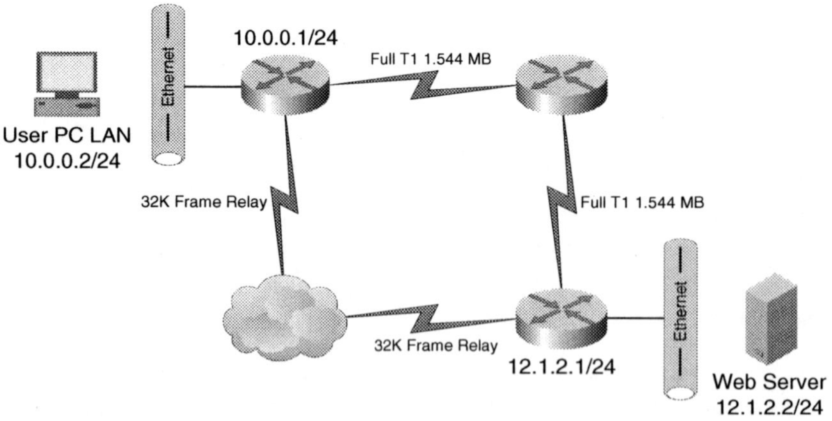

FIGURE 2.2 Complex routing environments offer multiple paths to the destination.

Based on the previous example, you should be somewhat familiar with the basic process of getting the packets from the source to the destination. Now, however, you have a problem because more than one router separates the two networks that need to interact. So how are the required routing decisions made in this situation?

As you can see, there is a one-hop connection via Frame Relay to the web server with 32KB of bandwidth. Also, you can see a two-hop connection from the client to the web server that is separated by two T1 lines. So, in general, where would the router send the traffic? Over the one-hop connection, which is technically shorter, or over the two-hop connection, which has much more bandwidth? A router also makes decisions that are very complex, including deciding what could be faster—a slower link over fewer hops or a multihop link that utilizes high-bandwidth links.

Static Versus Dynamic Routing

Now we look at what actually does the routing for you and what your involvement in the process is. For starters, routing is not as simple as it was made to sound. This process can become very complex and, without a proper design, could actually ruin your network. We describe the problems that can occur throughout the chapter, but you need to understand that you must plan your network for routing before you implement it. Major problems could arise if you don't plan. You should consider these planning questions:

- Will you use a static or dynamic routing environment, and why would you use one over the other?
- Which routing environment is more secure?

A *static routing* environment is one in which all routing entries in the routing table are entered manually. When static routing is used, the administrator responsible for the router must manually enter information into the router to allow it to perform its function. If you want the router to route packets intended for remote destinations, you need to configure its routing table so the router will forward the packets to the next hop along the path to their destination. This might be simply something such as "all traffic that is not addressed for the local subnet is to be forwarded out the router on Interface 1" or perhaps something more complex if the router has multiple interfaces connected to different networks.

A *dynamic routing* table is one that you create with a routing protocol such as *Routing Information Protocol (RIP)* or *Open Shortest Path First (OSPF)*, which we explore more shortly. When dynamic routing is used, the chosen routing protocol actually builds the routing table on the fly by "learning" about the routes that are available to it and maintaining an accurate status on these routes. If a route fails when dynamic routing is in use, all nearby routers adjust their routing tables to avoid sending packets along the failed route. Table 2.1 shows a simple example of a routing table.

TABLE 2.1 Sample Routing Table

Destination Network	Interface to Use	Number of Hops
172.16.0.0/16	Via 10.0.2.1	1 hop
10.0.0.0/8	Via 10.0.2.1	1 hop
12.1.2.0/24	Via 10.0.2.1	1 hop
0.0.0.0/0	Via 10.0.2.1	1 hop

The router keeps this table in memory so that when a packet comes in, it can look at the prefix (the first few bits), hop count, and destination network. It's that easy. A routing table tells packets where to go, and it can be created manually or dynamically.

Routing tables compute the next hop for a packet. You must remember that a routing table needs to have two fields to function: the *IP prefix* and the *next-hop address* (which must be a valid address). The routers the packet is leaving from and going to must be able to reach this valid address; you must be connected, or the route will not work. If you do not have a match (a packet comes in and does not have a routing table entry match), the packet is discarded and you will most likely get an *Internet Control Message Protocol (ICMP)* notification that the destination host was unreachable.

The following are some key points to consider about static versus dynamic routing:

- Static routing is tedious. You have to know exactly what you want to do because any mistake causes the router to not work properly, resulting in routing errors that can prevent network connectivity.
- You might want to implement static routing if you have only a few routes to maintain. Remember, each time a packet enters the router, the router needs to process it, so tables that are very long can cause the router to take longer to make a routing decision, which, in turn, could slow your network. When you use dynamic routing protocols, it is possible to have a router learn as many as hundreds of routes, depending on network size.
- Static routes are more secure because only a few required routes are in the table, so no one can see too much information. In this case, if the router is compromised by an attacker, that person cannot glean too much information from your compromised router. The attacker might know only a default route back to the core network, for example, whereas if the attacker compromised a core router with 300 networks in the table, he or she could map your whole network from that one router.
- Dynamic routing is easy to configure and, once configured, is easy to maintain. If changes are made to the network, more than likely, the routers will learn the changes and can quickly establish convergence on the network. *Convergence* occurs when all routers know all other routers on the network and the topology is accurate.

- Dynamic routing is becoming more secure as more routing protocols provide ways to encrypt and authenticate updates between peers. However, configuring dynamic routes requires the administrator to have a greater level of knowledge and experience than when configuring static routes.

One of the key elements required to design and implement efficient routing solutions is to understand the differences between your available options and then to implement the correct one. You might be wondering whether static and dynamic routing protocols can be used at the same time. The answer to that question is yes.

Distance Vector Versus Link State

Now that you understand dynamic and static routing, let's dig deeper into dynamic routing and the complexities it offers. You need to know this information for Exam 70-293 because Microsoft Windows Server 2003 enables you to configure either static or dynamic routing. If you choose dynamic, you have the option of using either a link-state dynamic routing protocol or a distance-vector dynamic routing protocol. You need to know the specifics of each and which one to select in a production environment.

Link State

Link-state protocols are highly functional routing protocols that allow routers to pass information efficiently. A link-state routing protocol ensures that each router on the network maintains a map of the network. You should also know that any network is prone to have a problem or failure occur at any time. Frame Relay links have problems, Telcos have problems, and all of them affect your networks. For example, assume that one of your T1 lines experiences a failure that separates two routers on a subnet across the Internet. Both would be able to (through the routing protocol) adjust for this loss of the link between them because that is what they are programmed to do. When your router link fails, it is programmed to sense the loss of carrier on the line and then, through the routing protocol, send updates to the other routers adjacent to them so that they all know that the link is down and the IP subnet where they are maintained is no longer available for destination packets on the wire.

When a network link changes state (up to down, or vice versa), a notification, called a *link state advertisement (LSA)*, is flooded throughout the network. Routers all over the network address this change and make sure that their routing tables are adjusted accordingly. Another configurable option of link-state protocols is that they can use something other than hop count to determine their path through the network. Link-state protocols can also determine that going over more routers might be quicker if the available bandwidth is higher instead of choosing the shortest path deemed solely on how many routers away the destination is.

Link-state protocols offer a number of advantages, especially when compared to the distance vector–based routing protocols:

- **Smaller routing tables**—Because the router maintains only a table of link states rather than a copy of every route on the network, it can maintain much smaller routing tables.
- **Highly scalable**—Link-state protocols are not limited to 15 hops as distance vector-based protocols are, so they can scale to much larger networks.
- **More efficient use of network bandwidth**—Because link-state information is not exchanged after the network has converged, routing updates do not consume precious bandwidth unless an outage forces the network to reconverge.
- **Faster convergence**—Link-state routing protocols converge faster than distance-vector protocols because updates are sent as soon as a change to the network occurs, instead of having to wait for the periodic update used with the distance-vector protocols.

One disadvantage of link-state protocols is that they are more complex to understand and configure than distance-vector protocols. They also require additional processing power on the router, due to the need to calculate the routing tree.

Distance Vector

Distance-vector protocols are easy to configure and maintain but are not as reliable or efficient as link-state protocols. Distance-vector protocols (such as RIP) allow for simple design and simple maintenance, but your bandwidth might suffer as a result.

Distance-vector routing protocols require that each router tell its neighbors what is in its routing table. This is done by sending the entire routing table when the router boots and then sending it again at scheduled intervals. Each router uses updates from its neighboring routers to update its own routing table based on the information it receives. Using the information from these updates, a router can build a network map in its routing table and determine hop counts (that is, the distance to any network) for each network entry in the routing table. Routing updates sent using a distance-vector routing protocol are unacknowledged and unsynchronized, which is one of the drawbacks of distance-vector protocols. Some other drawbacks of this type of routing protocol include the following:

- **High overhead**—Because every router on the network sends it entire routing table when it sends an update, distance-vector protocols produce very large routing tables. This adds overhead to the router memory needed to store these tables and the router processing power needed to maintain these tables. Large routing tables can also cause problems for an administrator who is trying to determine the source of a problem.
- **Not scalable**—Distance-vector networks are limited to 15 hops for any given route. In a large network (such as the Internet), it is very easy to have network segments that are greater than 15 hops away and that would be unreachable in a distance-vector network.
- **Network bandwidth intensive**—Distance-vector networks require that routers exchange their entire routing tables whenever they do updates. On a large network

with large routing tables, these routing updates can use significant amounts of bandwidth, especially across small WAN connections or demand-dial links.

- **Long convergence time**—*Convergence* is the amount of time it takes a routing algorithm to detect and route around a network failure. Distance-vector protocols typically have longer convergence times than link-state protocols.
- **Routing loops**—Distance-vector protocols can suffer from routing loop problems when there are multiple paths to a network. A routing loop occurs when the routing table creates a routing path that loops between routers. The packet is sent from router to router until its TTL is exceeded. Routing loops typically occur in poorly designed networks.
- **Count-to-infinity problems**—Count-to-infinity problems occur when there is a network outage and the routing algorithm cannot calculate a new router. One router broadcasts a route and increments the hop count for the router, and then a second router broadcasts the same route to the first router, also incrementing the hop count, and so on, until the route metric (that is, the hop count) reaches 16 and the route is discarded.

Distance-vector routing protocols have additional mechanisms that allow them to avoid the count-to-infinity problems and improve convergence:

- **Split horizon**—The split-horizon mechanism prevents routes from being broadcast out the interface from which they were received. Split horizon eliminates count-to-infinity problems and routing loops during convergence in single-path internetworks and reduces the chances of count-to-infinity problems occurring in multipath internetworks.
- **Split horizon with poison reverse**—The split horizon with poison reverse mechanism allows routes to be broadcast back to the interface from which they were received, but they are announced with a hop count of 16, which indicates that the network is unreachable (in other words, the route has been poisoned and is unusable through that interface). In a single-path internetwork, split horizon with poison reverse has no benefits in addition to those of split horizon. However, in a multipath internetwork, split horizon with poison reverse greatly reduces routing loops and count-to-infinity problems, which can still occur in a multipath internetwork because routes to networks can be learned from multiple sources.
- **Triggered updates**—Triggered updates allow a router to announce changes in metric values almost immediately rather than wait for the next periodic announcement. The trigger is a change to a metric in an entry in the routing table. For example, networks that become unavailable can be announced with a hop count of 16 through a triggered update. If triggered updates were sent by all routers immediately, each triggered update could cause a cascade of broadcast traffic across the IP internetwork. Triggered updates improve the convergence time of RIP internetworks, but at the expense of additional broadcast traffic as the triggered updates are propagated.

The main advantages of distance-vector routing are that it requires little maintenance and is easy to configure, making it popular in small network environments.

Planning the Correct Routing Protocol to Use

Objective:

Plan a routing strategy.

- Identify routing protocols to use in a specified environment.

With that lengthy but necessary routing introduction behind you, let's move forward now and examine the routing protocols available for use in Windows Server 2003. Windows Server 2003 provides three routing protocols to choose from: *RIP*, *RIPv2*, and *OSPF*. RIP and RIPv2 are distance vector based, and OSPF is link state based.

RIP

Although not commonly used as a protocol of choice for new network designs, the *Routing Information Protocol (RIP)* is still widely used throughout the world. The reason is that RIP was deployed widely in the past. RIP is not a proprietary protocol, either; it is universal to just about every router (or routing device) ever made, so your knowledge and understanding of RIP are critical. RIP is also part of just about every Windows-based server ever created. Consequently, you need to know about RIP—how to design it and how to troubleshoot problems that might occur when using it.

As mentioned previously, RIP is a distance-vector routing protocol. Remember that RIP is easy to configure and maintain, and should be used for smaller networks; it should not be used for very large enterprise deployments that span several routers. RIP is defined in Request for Comments (RFC) 1058 and updated by RFC 1388. To keep the amount of information you need to a minimum (you will be asked about RIP on Exam 70-293), we describe what you need to know for the exam here:

- RIP is limited to 15 router hops, with 16 hops being infinity. What does this mean? Picture a LAN with a PC that needs to communicate with a server on another LAN that is 15 routers away. The routers keep a list of which subnets are no more than 15 routers away, and if you try to expand the network past the 16th router, communications do not happen. Remember, you have a 15-hop maximum between networks, and the 16th is deemed infinity.
- RIPv1 has problems with subnetted networks. In Chapter 1, we briefly covered what subnetted networks would resemble in your design. RIP was created and deployed before networks were subnetted to the degree that they are today, and because they have no direct support for RIP, your networks cannot support it. It really comes down to the information that each router sends to each other and what that packet contains.

If the routing update does not contain a field in the packet to allow for subnetted networks, it does not carry over the information you might need it to. In other words, RIP is configured to look at the prefix of the IP address in the routing update and know whether it's either A, B, or C, and nothing more. If you subnet, your subnet will not be supported because RIP understands only that if a packet with an IP address of 10.0.0.1 comes in, it is automatically assigned a subnet of 255.0.0.0, even if you have it subnetted down to 255.255.255.0.

- RIP is bandwidth intensive, and although that isn't a problem on most networks, a smaller network with WAN links that are set small (such as Frame Relay links set with a 32KB committed information rate) could feel the effect of constant broadcasts every 30 seconds, especially if the routing table is large. If the routing table is too large, more than one update could be sent every 30 seconds, making it even more bandwidth intensive. By default, RIP broadcasts to its neighbors every 30 seconds lists of networks and subnets it can reach.
- RIP is not very secure. RIP contains no security features or configurable parameters to make it secure. Other protocols used today have configurable parameters to make them more secure; however, RIP does not contain any solution to make it secure by default.

NOTE

What's wrong with RIPv1? One of the largest drawbacks of RIPv1 is that it cannot support variable-length subnet masks (VLSMs). Chapter 1 covers the concepts of IP routing and subnetting in detail, but at this point, it is important that you understand that RIPv1 cannot understand any networks other than the standard Class A, Class B, or Class C networks defined by the TCP/IP RFCs. Supernetted and subnetted network routes are not broadcast by RIPv1.

In sum, RIP is a distance vector–based protocol that is available on Windows Server 2003 for configuration. It is easy to set up and configure for use but is limited in what it can do for you. For larger networks, therefore, using RIP would not be wise. In real-world production environments, you most likely will not use RIP in a new deployment, but because so much of it still exists today, you should know it and understand it well, especially for Exam 70-293.

Some of the most important features of troubleshooting RIP and the reasons it is so important to think about RIP's limitations when considering design are covered in the section "Other Problems with Routing," later in this chapter.

NOTE

RIP storms If you are working on a network that uses RIP, you might encounter RIP storms. A RIP storm occurs when there are so many RIP broadcasts on a subnet that no room is left on the network for data—the network space is all being used for RIP broadcasts. RIP storms occur more commonly with RIPv1 than with RIPv2, and they usually occur when the network is changing.

RIPv2

RIP was not the greatest protocol ever designed, but due to its ease of use, it was widely deployed and used. RIPv2, or RIP version 2, was created for RIP users to overcome problems with security. This version adds an option for authentication to the RIP packet, as well as support for subnetted networks. RIPv2 allows for variable-length subnetted networks to be passed through routing updates.

RIPv2 offers an opportunity for growth if a company feels either that it is either underskilled to deploy a routing protocol such as OSPF or that it will never grow to a larger company that could benefit more from a routing protocol like OSPF. RIPv2 is supported by Windows Server 2003 as well.

EXAM ALERT

Know the differences For Exam 70-293, make sure you are at least familiar with the major differences between RIP and RIPv2.

OSPF

Open Shortest Path First (OSPF) is a link state–based nonproprietary routing protocol. For today's networks growing in size and complexity, OSPF is a wise choice. It is configurable, scalable, and easy to troubleshoot. However, it is not easy to plan, design, and deploy. Understanding OSPF can take some time and effort because half of what you need to know is in the underlying terminology used to explain and use OSPF.

NOTE

OSPF and 64-bit versions of Windows Server 2003 OSPF is not available on 64-bit versions of Windows Server 2003.

For Exam 70-293, you need to know how to configure and use OSPF on a Windows Server 2003 system; more important, however, you need to know how to design it, know its nomenclature, and know when to use it. You can get a detailed explanation on OSPF by reading RFC 1247. OSPF Version 2 is documented in RFC 1583. As mentioned previously, OSPF is a link-state routing protocol with a complex set of options and features. So what is so great about OSPF that makes up for its high difficulty level in planning and design? Let's look at it further:

- OSPF is highly scalable. You will be hard pressed to build (or support) a network large enough to outdo OSPF. OSPF was designed to work in very large networks, and it works well at that. It does not have a hop count restriction as RIP does. With OSPF's use of areas and a subdivided domain, the design possibilities are almost seemingly infinite.
- With RIP, you cannot use subnetted networks; with OSPF, you can.

- With OSPF, your bandwidth is spared. With RIP, an entire routing table is broadcast from every router on the network every 30 seconds. With OSPF (in stable environments that do not suffer from many changes), packets (called hello packets) are sent out intermittently to verify links between adjacent routers. This way, less bandwidth is used, and a major update check is performed only every 30 minutes.

So now you can see where the trade-off comes in. If you want to use a more configurable and scalable protocol, you should use OSPF, but you need to remember that all its benefits equal added work on your part. You have to put more effort into the design, rollout, and maintenance of an OSPF network.

For Exam 70-293, you should also remember the disadvantages to using OSPF. It adds complexity, and its demands on memory and computation for the routers that use it can be devastating if you do not have the proper router hardware to maintain it.

What else do you need to know about OSPF? You should know how it is laid out in a design. OSPF divides the network (what it considers a routing domain) into areas. An *area* is a subdivision of the entire network and is given a label. *Area 0* (zero) is considered the backbone of an OSPF network. If your network is small enough, you can set up the entire network to use Area 0, which is very important. For example, if the network becomes more subdivided (say, you have three areas, including Area 0), you need to know that if all traffic must travel between areas, the packets are first routed to the backbone, or Area 0. When you plan a network this way, the design keeps subnets consolidated to areas, thus reducing the size of the link-state database that is updated on every router in an OSPF network. This keeps your OSPF network running optimally.

With OSPF, you also need to know which class of network you are using. There are three:

- **Point-to-point**—A WAN serial link connecting two routers on a single subnet can be considered a point-to-point link.

- **Multiaccess**—An Ethernet or Token Ring segment is a multiaccess link. Because the class is multiaccess (like Ethernet), you need to consider that each router on the connected network wants to know about it; it is not good for this to happen because not every router needs to form an adjacency with every other router. This would diminish the benefits of using a protocol such as OSPF. To avoid this problem, OSPF assigns a Designated Router (DR) to manage all the link state advertisements (LSAs) that are sent from router to router. Also, you need to know that a Backup DR (called the BDR), is selected from the available routers on the network to take over if the DR fails.

- **Nonbroadcast multiaccess (NBMA)**—A Frame Relay or X.25 cloud is classified as NBMA. Nonbroadcast multiaccess networks use DRs just like multiaccess, but you must remember that because broadcasts lack support on a Frame Relay network, for instance, you must manually configure each router with its neighbor. If you do not manually configure the routers, you suffer from loss of connectivity between the routers running OSPF.

TIP

Take it easy When designing, you can bypass the DR and NBMA network design by using a series of point-to-point links. They might be more intensive to configure, but they take the intricacies of DR election out of your equation.

Why is this information so important? Again, the focus of Exam 70-293 is planning and design. You must understand how a protocol works entirely before you plan to deploy it. You have to know its nuances, what makes it tick, and what makes it run under the hood. Understanding what kinds of networks can be connected to use OSPF is just as important as knowing how to configure and maintain it. If you do not design this protocol correctly, no matter how helpful it was programmed to be, you won't reap any benefits from it.

So now that you understand the link-state routing protocol OSPF, what do you need to remember for the exam? For Exam 70-293, you need to know the basic design features of OSPF. Most important, you need to remember the following points:

- OSPF sends hello packets to each adjacent router connected to the network. OSPF uses hello packets to verify that the network is always ready to work as advertised. These hellos are sent out every router interface every 10 seconds but are so small in size that they do not adversely affect your available bandwidth.
- Link-state advertisements provide other functionality, such as providing a solution for a scenario in which a router does not hear from its neighboring router for more than 40 seconds. The router then sends out LSAs marking the other router as down so that all the other routers can adjust their tables with the change.
- Hellos can be adjusted. A hello has a timer value that, when configured properly throughout the OSPF network, allows proper and accurate communications to take place. It is important to know that if a hello timer is misconfigured (not all timers are identical), problems can occur. Make sure that when you plan an OSPF network, you ensure that all the hello timers match. They must all be consistent across all routers on a network segment.
- Because LSAs age, it is important to get a refreshed routing table (or database) from a neighboring router, just in case anything has changed. If nothing has changed on a particular router for 30 minutes, the router flushes its information and seeks an updated database from its adjacent routers. This means that the network reconverges every 30 minutes—a far cry from the forced reconvergence in a RIP network every 30 seconds!

In sum, OSPF is a link state–based routing protocol that is difficult to plan, design, manage, and maintain, but is highly configurable and scalable, making it the best choice for large networks.

Now that you are familiar with RIP and OSPF, as well as what routing is and all the other details that surround it, let's discuss how to plan a routed environment, one of the objectives of Exam 70-293.

Planning a Routing Environment

Objective:

Plan a routing strategy.

Now that you are familiar with what routing is, how it is performed, what a router is, and what different protocols you can choose from, you need to know how to plan a routing environment. This section briefly covers what you can do to plan for your new routing environment. For starters, you can plan your network logically. This section briefly describes some of the more common routing topologies, such as *ring*, *mesh*, and *star*, so that you understand what they mean as they are mentioned in the book as well as on the exam.

The simplest routing topology to consider is the *ring*, which is also the least efficient and reliable of the common routing topologies. In the ring topology, shown in Figure 2.3, each site is connected to its two closest neighbors with a WAN link; thus, two WAN connections and two routers are needed at each site. The ring topology is fairly easy to install and configure but is less efficient than the next topology we will explore, the mesh, because no one site can communicate directly with any other site except its neighbor on either side.

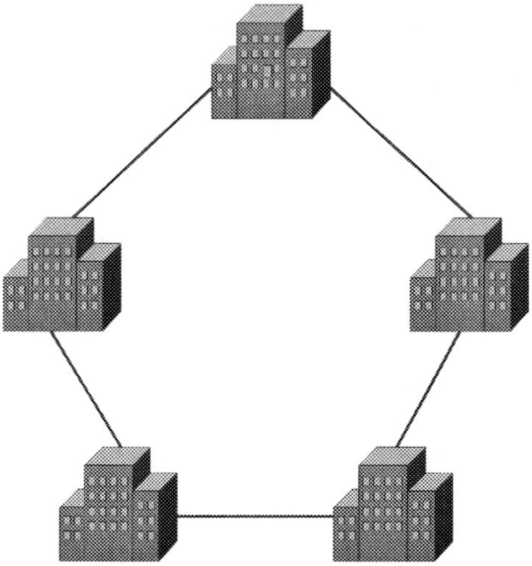

FIGURE 2.3 The ring topology is easy to implement and configure but is not efficient when compared to the mesh.

In a *mesh* topology, shown in Figure 2.4, every site in the network is connected to every other site in the network by a WAN link. This arrangement is costly because it uses a high number of links and might become difficult to manage as the number of sites—and, thus, the number of links—grows. The benefit of this arrangement is complete redundancy against failure. If you lose a link anywhere in the network, the entire network is always up, no matter what. The drawbacks are cost and maintainability.

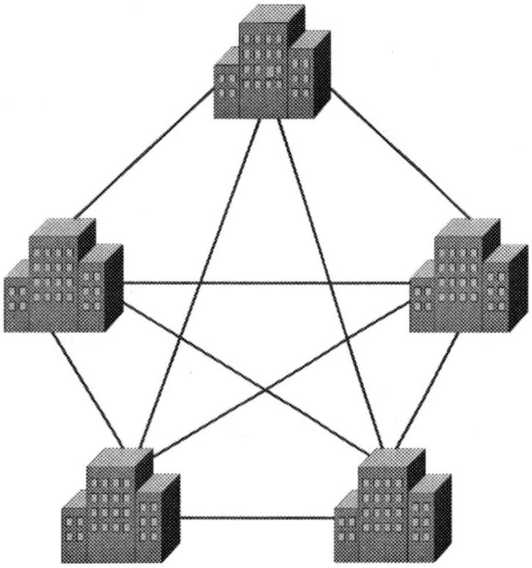

FIGURE 2.4 The mesh topology is expensive to implement and maintain, but it provides complete redundancy.

The last topology we examine here, the *star*, shown in Figure 2.5, is essentially a core location with remote sites linked to it. Remote sites are normally other business units, smaller locations, or business partners that need to access data from the core over the WAN. All communication from one remote site to another occurs via the core location. Having all resources centralized logically in a core location (such as the headquarters) makes the design easy to maintain from a routing perspective because every site, after it is connected, is only one hop away.

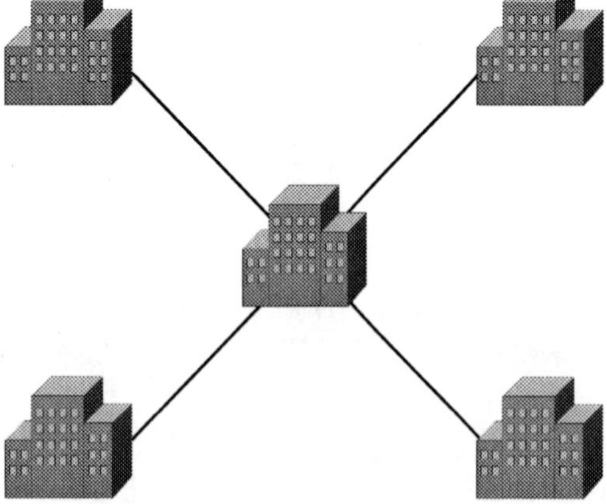

FIGURE 2.5 The star topology is very efficient and inexpensive to implement and maintain.

When planning a routing environment, other than planning for the topology you will use, you also must plan your routing protocols, which we discussed previously in great detail. Remember all this information not only for Exam 70-293, but also for all real-world production deployment scenarios.

CAUTION

Don't play with routing on a production network Working with any protocols on a live network is a very risky proposition; it should be avoided at all costs. At one company, an engineer was convinced he understood how routing worked, and he also believed he was a Windows expert.

During one of his experiments with routing on a Windows NT 4.0 server, this engineer bridged the corporate production network with a customer network in the same building. This was a very large customer network, and because this "expert" had routing enabled, he created a RIP storm that overwhelmed seven of the remote office routers, which promptly went into a constant reboot.

This is generally not considered an excellent career move in large companies. If you will experiment with routing, you should be sure to do it on an isolated network.

Windows Server 2003 Routing Solutions

As far back as Windows NT and its variations, you could always (and still can today) build a router out of a server. Remember that all routers do is connect networks. So if you have a switch with 10 PCs connected using the subnet 10.0.0.0/24 and another switch with another 10 PCs connected using the subnet 10.0.1.0/24, all you need to make them communicate is a router between the two switches. You can use either a router with two Ethernet interfaces or a Windows server with two NICs installed to connect the two subnets. You could conceivably connect the two subnets, turn on RIP, and be routing in no time.

Windows Server 2003 can act as a fully functional router using static routes or dynamic routing protocols, such as RIP (both versions) and OSPF. Would you use Windows Server 2003 for a router? Of course, you can; the only setback is that most routers today come with specialized hardware that allows them to contain telecom link–based interfaces such as ISDN, Serial, T1 lines, T3 lines, and so on. If you want to connect two or more Ethernet-based networks and route between them, you could set a Windows Server 2003 system to do that task, but can you connect to the Internet via a T1? Not so easily said and done. Remember, Windows Server 2003 is fully functional as a router, but you also need to remember its weaknesses for the exam.

Before you can configure RIP or OSPF routing to occur, you must enable the Routing and Remote Access Service (RRAS) on the server, as outlined in Step by Step 2.1.

EXAM ALERT

RRAS trickery On exam day, remember that RRAS is not something you must install separately in Windows Server 2003, like DNS or DHCP. RRAS is already installed by default and only needs to be configured to make it useful.

STEP BY STEP

2.1 Enabling Routing and Remote Access Services

1. Open the Routing and Remote Access console by choosing Start, Control Panel, Administrative Tools, Routing and Remote Access. By default, the local computer is listed as a server (see Figure 2.6). Notice the red arrow, indicating that the Routing and Remote Access Service is not presently enabled.

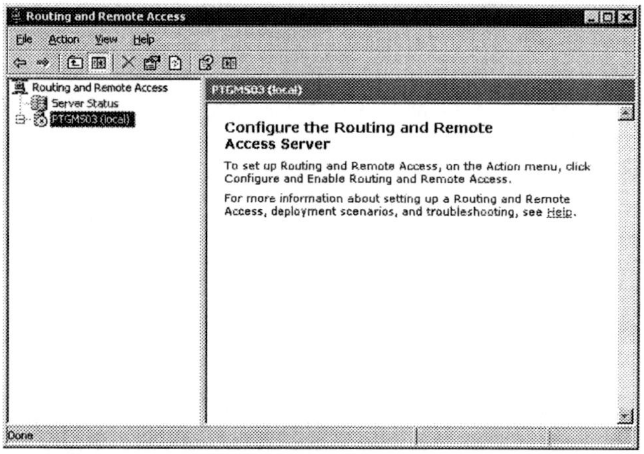

FIGURE 2.6 The Routing and Remote Access console is used to configure the Routing and Remote Access Service for a variety of functions, including acting as a router.

2. Right-click the server you want to configure and select Configure and Enable Routing and Remote Access. The Routing and Remote Access Server Setup Wizard starts.
3. Click Next to start configuring the Routing and Remote Access Service. The Configuration dialog box opens, as shown in Figure 2.7.
4. Select the Secure Connection Between Two Private Networks option and click Next to continue. The Demand-Dial Connections dialog box opens, as shown in Figure 2.8.
5. In the Demand-Dial Connections dialog box, select No and click Next to continue. The Completing the Routing and Remote Access Server Setup Wizard summary dialog box opens, as shown in Figure 2.9.

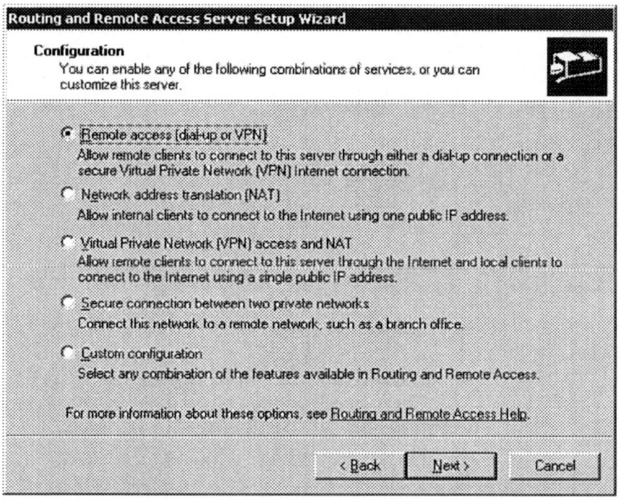

FIGURE 2.7 The Routing and Remote Access Server Setup Wizard includes the most common configuration options, to make the configuration process as easy as possible.

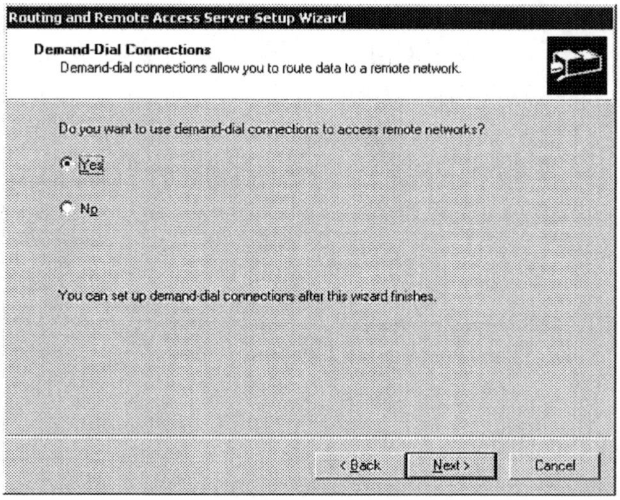

FIGURE 2.8 Demand-dial routing enables you to open connections between routers when traffic needs to pass through the router and disconnect connections when not needed.

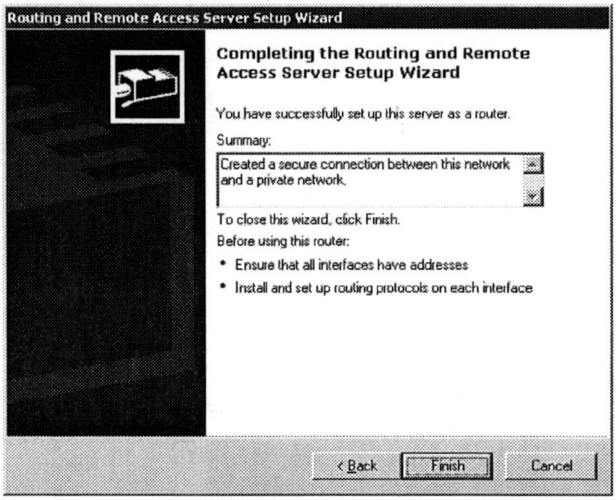

FIGURE 2.9 The last screen of the setup wizard summarizes the changes made, lists the next steps, and gives you one final opportunity to cancel the configuration changes.

6. Click Finish to complete the enabling of routing services.

With your Windows Server 2003 computer now enabled to provide routing, you must decide whether you will use static routing or dynamic routing.

Using the `route` Command to Configure Static Routes

The `route` command is primarily used to configure static routes within a network. It can also be used for troubleshooting by listing all the routes that this computer knows about.

The syntax of the `route` command is as follows:

```
route [-f] [-p] [command [destination] [mask subnetmask] [gateway]
➥ [metric costmetric]] [IF interface]
```

The `-f` parameter clears the routing tables of all entries. The `-p` parameter makes the route persistent. When a route is added to the router, by default, the entry is not kept across reboots of the system. The `-p` parameter ensures that the entry is maintained in the routing table across reboots of the system.

The following commands are used to specify what can be done with the `route` command:

- **`print`**—Prints the existing entries in the routing table
- **`add`**—Adds a new route to the routing table
- **`delete`**—Deletes an existing route from the routing table
- **`change`**—Modifies an existing route in the routing table

The destination parameter specifies the destination that you want to reach. The destination parameter can contain the following:

- Host address
- Subnet address
- Network address
- Default gateway

The `mask` parameter defines what portion of the destination address must match for that route to be used. When the mask is written in binary, a 1 is significant (must match) and a 0 need not match. For example, a 255.255.255.255 mask is used for a host entry. The mask of all 255s (all 1s) means that the destination address of the packet to be routed must exactly match the network address for this route to be used. For another example, the network address 157.57.8.0 has a netmask of 255.255.248.0. This netmask means the first two octets must match exactly, the first 5 bits of the third octet must match (248=11111000), and the last octet does not matter. Thus, any address of 157.57 and the third octet of 8 through 15 (15=00001111) will use this route.

The gateway parameter specifies where the packet needs to be sent. This can be the local network card or a router on the local subnet.

The `metric` parameter specifies a cost that is to be associated with that route. This cost is used in the decision of how packets should be routed. Packets are routed through the route that has the lowest cost.

The `interface` parameter, in a server with multiple network adapters, specifies which adapter (interface) is to be used for the specified route.

Step by Step 2.2 shows how to configure a static route for the network 10.100.10.0.

STEP BY STEP

2.2 Adding a Static Route to Windows Server 2003

1. Open the command prompt by choosing Start, Programs, Accessories, and selecting Command Prompt. The Command Prompt window opens.
2. Display the system's existing routing table by typing **`route print`** and pressing Enter. Make note of the routes listed now to check against the routes listed after you add the static route. You should see the following information (the output will vary from computer to computer, based on your computer's interfaces, network addresses, and existing routes):

```
IPv4 Route Table
===========================================================================
Interface List
0x1 ........................... MS TCP Loopback interface
0x10003 ...00 e0 7d c1 3e 0e ...... Realtek RTL8139 Family PCI Fast Ethernet NIC
0x10004 ...00 13 72 0e 98 7e ...... Broadcom NetXtreme Gigabit Ethernet
===========================================================================
===========================================================================
Active Routes:
Network Destination        Netmask          Gateway       Interface  Metric
          0.0.0.0          0.0.0.0      192.168.0.1   192.168.0.158     20
          0.0.0.0          0.0.0.0    192.168.0.158   192.168.0.159     20
        127.0.0.0        255.0.0.0        127.0.0.1       127.0.0.1      1
      192.168.0.0    255.255.255.0    192.168.0.158   192.168.0.158     20
      192.168.0.0    255.255.255.0    192.168.0.159   192.168.0.159     20
    192.168.0.158  255.255.255.255        127.0.0.1       127.0.0.1     20
    192.168.0.159  255.255.255.255        127.0.0.1       127.0.0.1     20
    192.168.0.255  255.255.255.255    192.168.0.158   192.168.0.158     20
    192.168.0.255  255.255.255.255    192.168.0.159   192.168.0.159     20
        224.0.0.0        240.0.0.0    192.168.0.158   192.168.0.158     20
        224.0.0.0        240.0.0.0    192.168.0.159   192.168.0.159     20
  255.255.255.255  255.255.255.255    192.168.0.158   192.168.0.158      1
  255.255.255.255  255.255.255.255    192.168.0.159   192.168.0.159      1
Default Gateway:       192.168.0.1
===========================================================================
Persistent Routes:
  None
```

3. Within the Command Prompt window, type the following command and press Enter:

```
Route Add 192.168.10.0 mask 255.255.255.0 192.168.0.158 metric 2
```

A successful entry returns you to the command prompt, with no message. If the entry addition is unsuccessful, you receive an error message.

4. To display the system's routing table with the newly added route, type **route print** and press Enter. This displays the following information (note the newly added route in boldface type):

```
IPv4 Route Table
===========================================================================
Interface List
0x1 ........................... MS TCP Loopback interface
0x10003 ...00 e0 7d c1 3e 0e ...... Realtek RTL8139 Family PCI Fast Ethernet NIC

0x10004 ...00 13 72 0e 98 7e ...... Broadcom NetXtreme Gigabit Ethernet
===========================================================================
===========================================================================
Active Routes:
Network Destination        Netmask          Gateway       Interface  Metric
          0.0.0.0          0.0.0.0      192.168.0.1   192.168.0.158     20
```

```
          0.0.0.0          0.0.0.0    192.168.0.158    192.168.0.159     20
        127.0.0.0        255.0.0.0        127.0.0.1        127.0.0.1      1
      192.168.0.0    255.255.255.0    192.168.0.158    192.168.0.158     20
      192.168.0.0    255.255.255.0    192.168.0.159    192.168.0.159     20
    192.168.0.158  255.255.255.255        127.0.0.1        127.0.0.1     20
    192.168.0.159  255.255.255.255        127.0.0.1        127.0.0.1     20
    192.168.0.255  255.255.255.255    192.168.0.158    192.168.0.158     20
    192.168.0.255  255.255.255.255    192.168.0.159    192.168.0.159     20
     192.168.10.0    255.255.255.0    192.168.0.158    192.168.0.158      2
        224.0.0.0        240.0.0.0    192.168.0.158    192.168.0.158     20
        224.0.0.0        240.0.0.0    192.168.0.159    192.168.0.159     20
  255.255.255.255  255.255.255.255    192.168.0.158    192.168.0.158      1
  255.255.255.255  255.255.255.255    192.168.0.159    192.168.0.159      1
Default Gateway:       192.168.0.1
===========================================================================
Persistent Routes:
  None
```

Implementing RIP Routing

As discussed earlier, static routing is not necessarily a viable solution in today's business network; thus, you should consider implementing one of the available dynamic routing protocols that Windows Server 2003 supports. Step by Step 2.3 shows how to enable RIPv2 for routing.

STEP BY STEP

2.3 Adding RIP to the Routing and Remote Access Service

1. Open the Routing and Remote Access console, shown in Figure 2.10, by choosing Start, Control Panel, Administrative Tools, Routing and Remote Access.

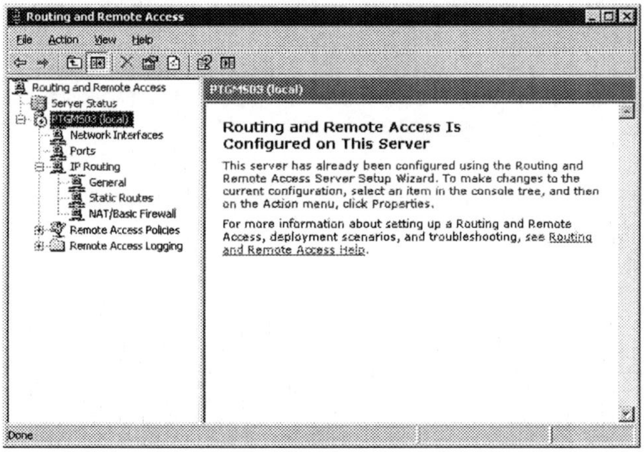

FIGURE 2.10 A server with an active Routing and Remote Access Service appears in the Routing and Remote Access console with a green up arrow.

2. In the left pane, expand the list under IP Routing and right-click General. From the context menu, select New Routing Protocol. The New Routing Protocol dialog box opens, as shown in Figure 2.11.

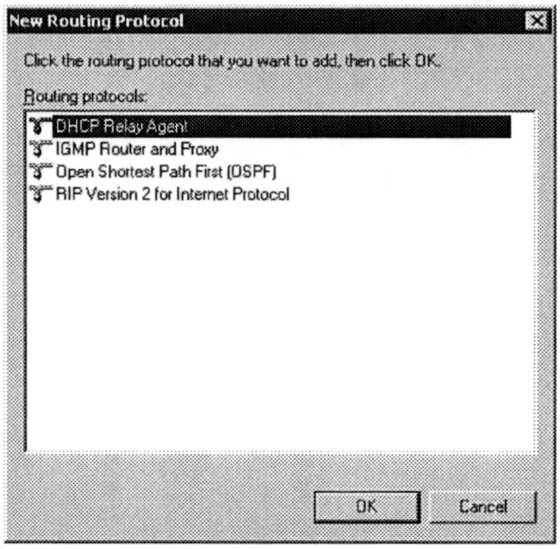

FIGURE 2.11 The New Routing Protocol Wizard can be used to add protocols to your Windows Server 2003 server.

3. Select RIP Version 2 for Internet Protocol and click OK. RIP then appears under the IP Routing entry, as shown in Figure 2.12. RIP is now installed on your Windows Server 2003 server.

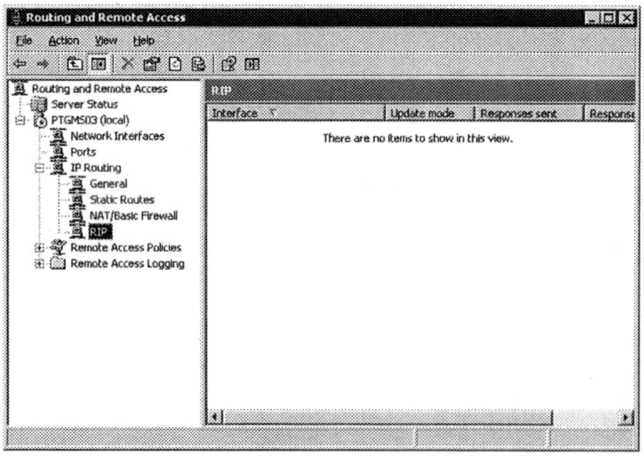

FIGURE 2.12 RIP appears under the IP Routing heading in the Routing and Remote Access console.

4. Right-click the RIP entry and select New Interface from the context menu. The New Interface for RIP Version 2 for Internet Protocol dialog box opens, as shown in Figure 2.13.

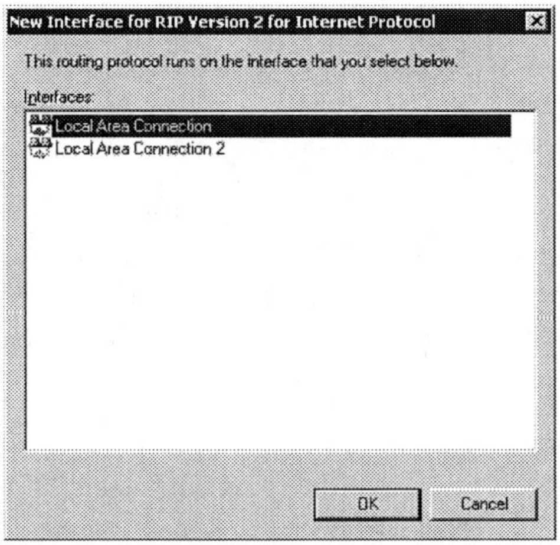

FIGURE 2.13 The first step in configuring RIP is to create a RIP interface.

5. Select the appropriate local area connection and click OK. The RIP Properties dialog box opens, as shown in Figure 2.14.

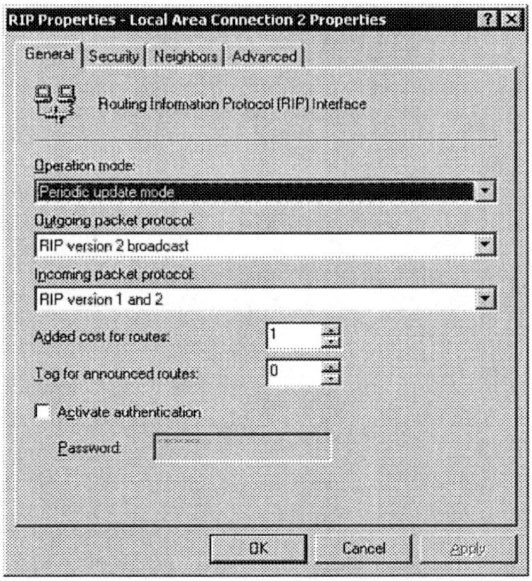

FIGURE 2.14 The RIP Properties dialog box enables you to configure the RIP protocol to work in your network environment.

6. On the General tab, under Outgoing Packet Protocol, select RIP Version 1 Broadcast. Under Incoming Packet Protocol, select RIP Version 1 and 2. Click OK to return to the Routing and Remote Access console and activate the changes. You have just configured the server to work with any legacy RIP version 1 routers that might still be on the network.

Implementing Silent RIP

RIP also has a feature known as *silent RIP* that allows a server running RRAS to build a routing table by listening to the RIP broadcasts on the network, but the host doesn't broadcast any updates to the network. A silent RIP router processes RIP announcements but does not announce its own routes.

NOTE

Using Silent RIP Silent RIP is typically used by hosts that will be acting as a gateway of any sort, but still need to have their routing tables updated.

To enable silent RIP on your Windows Server 2003 router, perform the steps outlined in Step by Step 2.4.

STEP BY STEP

2.4 Enabling Silent RIP on Windows Server 2003

1. Open the Routing and Remote Access console.
2. Expand the console tree and select RIP. The list of available interfaces running RIP appears in the right pane of the console, as shown in Figure 2.15.

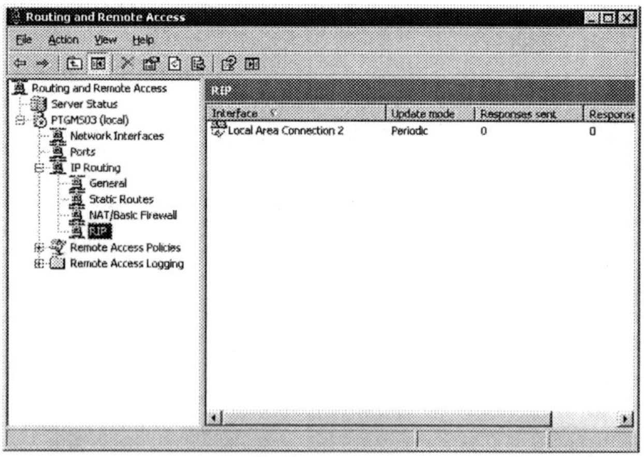

FIGURE 2.15 You can find the complete list of interfaces supporting a particular protocol by looking in the right pane of the console.

3. Right-click the interface that you want to configure for silent RIP mode and, from the context menu, select Properties. The Local Area Connection Properties dialog box opens, as shown in Figure 2.16.

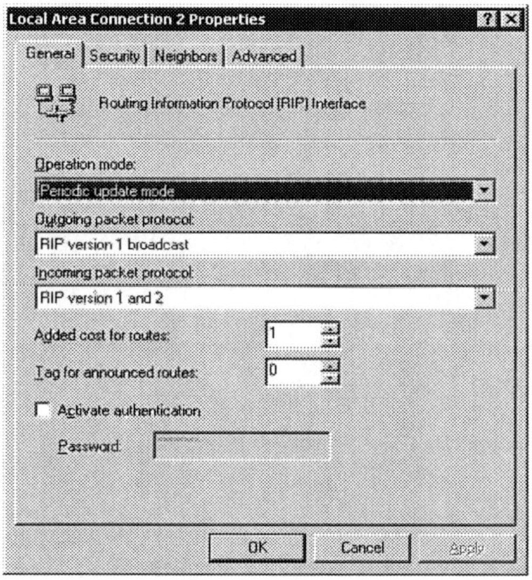

FIGURE 2.16 The Silent RIP setting can be found in the Outgoing Packet Protocol pull-down; the configuration is related to which routes are broadcast, not received.

4. On the General tab, under Outgoing Packet Protocol, select Silent RIP from the pull-down menu. Click OK to return to the Routing and Remote Access console and apply the changes.

Additional RIP Configuration Options

Before we move on to implementing and configuring the OSPF protocol, let's look at some of the other RIP settings you might need to set. Step by Step 2.5 shows how to set these options.

STEP BY STEP

2.5 Setting Additional RIP Configuration Options with Windows Server 2003

1. Open the Routing and Remote Access console.
2. Expand the console tree and select RIP. The list of available interfaces running RIP appears in the right pane of the console.
3. Right-click the interface that you want to configure and, from the context menu, select Properties. The Local Area Connection Properties dialog box opens.
4. As you saw in Step by Step 2.4, the General tab deals with the way routes are broadcast and received. Click the Security tab, shown in Figure 2.17. Look at how the RIP updates can be managed.
5. Click the Neighbors tab, shown in Figure 2.18. Review the settings that can be configured pertaining to how the router interacts with its RIP neighbors.

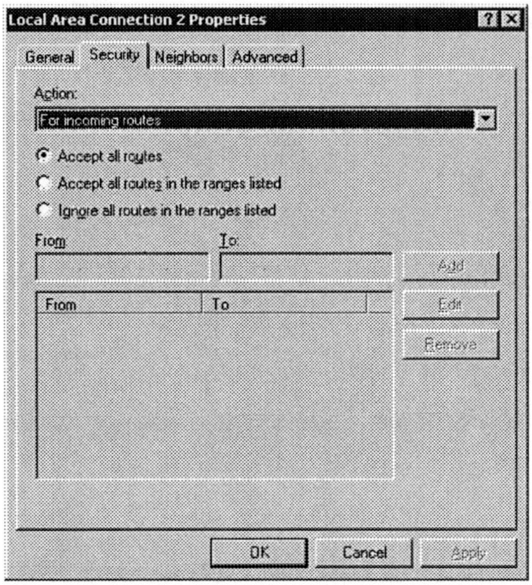

FIGURE 2.17 The Security tab enables you to restrict the networks that can send/receive RIP updates.

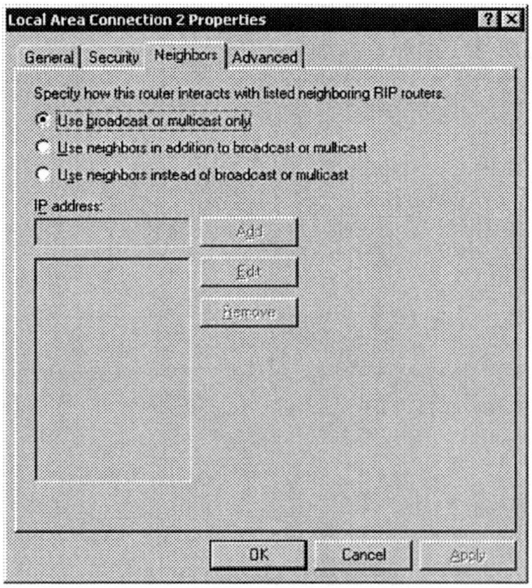

FIGURE 2.18 The Neighbors tab enables you to configure how RIP broadcasts are sent by your Windows Server 2003 router.

6. Click the Advanced tab, shown in Figure 2.19. The Advanced tab enables you to configure the more complex settings associated with RIP and the way Windows Server 2003 supports it. Click OK to return to the Routing and Remote Access console.

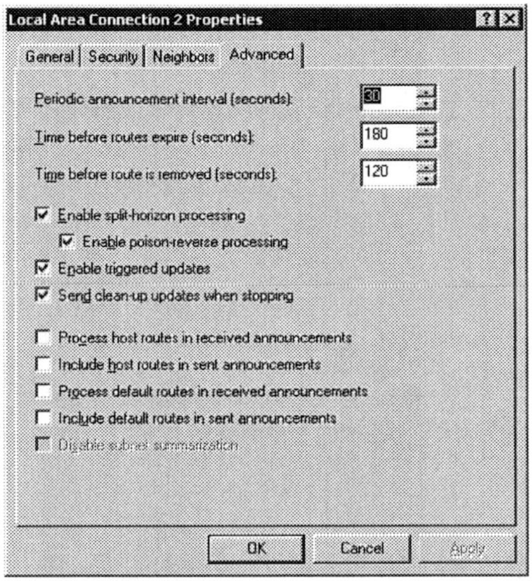

FIGURE 2.19 The Advanced tab enables you to configure advanced settings such as split horizon, poison reverse, and triggered updates.

Implementing OSPF Routing

If your network is growing or expected to grow, or you want to provide a more robust routing solution, you should consider implementing OSPF routing. Step by Step 2.6 outlines the process to configure OSPF routing on your Windows Server 2003 computer.

STEP BY STEP

2.6 Installing and Configuring OSPF on Windows Server 2003

1. Open the Routing and Remote Access console.
2. Expand the console tree and, under IP Routing, right-click General. From the context menu, select New Routing Protocol. The New Routing Protocol dialog box opens.
3. Select Open Shortest Path First and click OK to install it. It now appears under IP Routing in the Routing and Remote Access console, as shown in Figure 2.20.
4. Select the newly installed OSPF protocol and right-click. From the context menu, select New Interface. The New Interface for Open Shortest Path First (OSPF) dialog box opens, as shown in Figure 2.21.

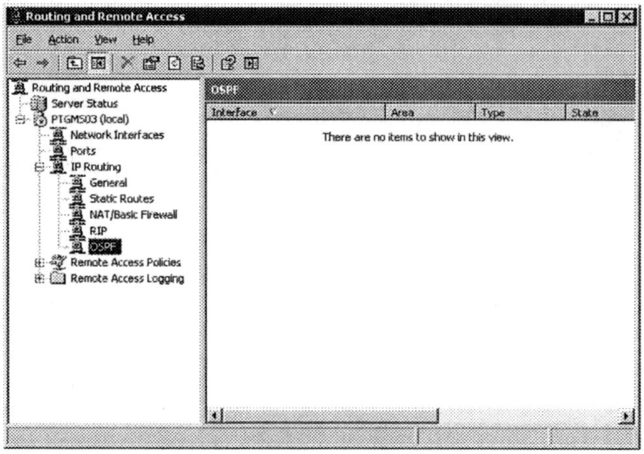

FIGURE 2.20 The OSPF protocol appears under the IP Routing node of the Routing and Remote Access console.

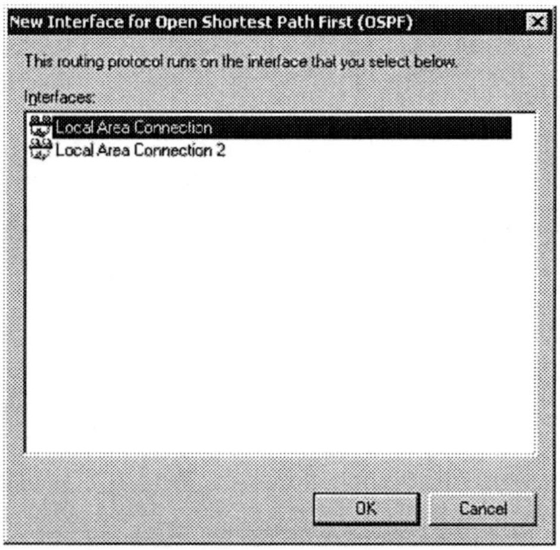

FIGURE 2.21 The OSPF protocol can be tied to a single interface or to multiple interfaces.

5. Select Local Area Connection and click OK. The OSPF Properties dialog box opens, as shown in Figure 2.22.
6. On the General tab, select the Enable OSPF for This Address option. In Area ID, click the ID of the area to which the interface belongs (for this exercise, it should be 0.0.0.0). In Router Priority, click the arrows to set the priority of the router over the interface to 1. In Cost, click the scroll arrows to set the cost of sending a packet over the interface to 2. In the Password text box, type a password. Under Network Type, set the type of OSPF interface as Broadcast. Click OK to complete the installation of the interface and return to the Routing and Remote Access console.

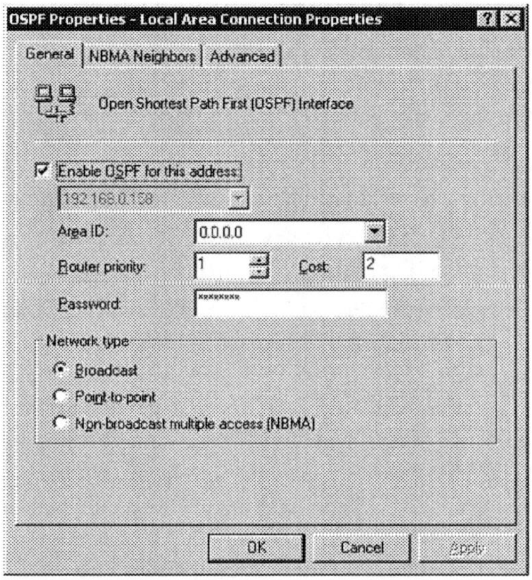

FIGURE 2.22 From the OSPF Properties dialog box, you can complete the configuration of the OSPF protocol.

EXAM ALERT

OSPF is a complex routing protocol If it seems as though OSPF is a really complex routing protocol, it is. Engineers who architect OSPF networks for large companies usually have extensive training and experience. For the exam, you should have a general understanding of the concepts associated with OSPF. You will not be asked to design a complex OSPF network as part of the exam.

Routing Hierarchies

Unlike RIP, OSPF operates within a hierarchy. The basic structure to this hierarchy includes areas, autonomous systems, and the OSPF backbone. The largest entity within the hierarchy is the autonomous system. An *autonomous system (AS)* is a collection of networks and routers under common administration, sharing a common routing protocol.

NOTE

When do I need more than one area? A good rule of thumb is to start creating a multiple-area OSPF network when you reach 50 routers. If you have 50 routers on your network, your network is probably complex enough to warrant creating additional areas.

Areas

An autonomous system can be further divided into *areas*. Each area is identified by an area ID. This identifier has no relation to an IP address or IP network ID, although it uses the same dotted-decimal formula. Area IDs are not used to reflect routing data and are actually convenient labels to simplify the management of the area. Although the area ID does not signify any IP routing information, if all the networks within an area correspond to a single subnetted network ID, the area ID can be set to the network ID. This can be convenient for administration of the areas. For example, if an area contains all the subnets of the IP network 10.1.0.0, the area ID can be set to 10.1.0.0. The reason for defining areas within an autonomous system is to reduce the size of a Link State Database.

NOTE

The Link State Database (LSDB) The LSDB provides the overall picture of networks in relation to routers within an area. The LSDB contains the collection of LSAs received from all routers in the same area. In an autonomous system with a large number of networks, each OSPF router must keep the LSA of every other router in its topological database.

To keep the size of LSDBs to a minimum, LSAs for an area's networks and routers are flooded within the area but not to routers outside the area. Each area becomes its own link-state domain with its own topological database.

Routers with multiple interfaces can participate in multiple areas. These routers, which are called *area border routers*, maintain separate LSDBs for each area. The routing tables within these routers are a combination of the routing table entries of all the SPF trees for each topological database, as well as static routes, Simple Network Management Protocol (SNMP) configured routes, and routes learned from other routing protocols. To reduce the number of entries in the routing table, the networks inside the area can be advertised outside the area using summary route advertisements. When you keep area topologies separate, OSPF passes less routing traffic than it would if the autonomous system were not partitioned.

The Default Route

Each area within an OSPF network can be configured with a default route. A *default route* has a destination address of 0.0.0.0 with a subnet mask of 0.0.0.0. The default route is used to route any packets that are destined for an address not explicitly listed in the routing table. Default routes are typically used to reduce the size of routing tables because they can be used to summarize all routes external to the area into a single route. Default routes typically point to the OSPF backbone.

OSPF Backbone

Every OSPF network must have at least one area. An OSPF network with more than one area must have a *backbone area* to interconnect all other areas within the network. The backbone area always has an area ID of 0.0.0.0 and acts as the hub for all the other areas on the network.

All other areas must communicate their routing information to the backbone area so that it can distribute the information to all other areas. Figure 2.23 shows an example of an internetwork with several areas and a backbone.

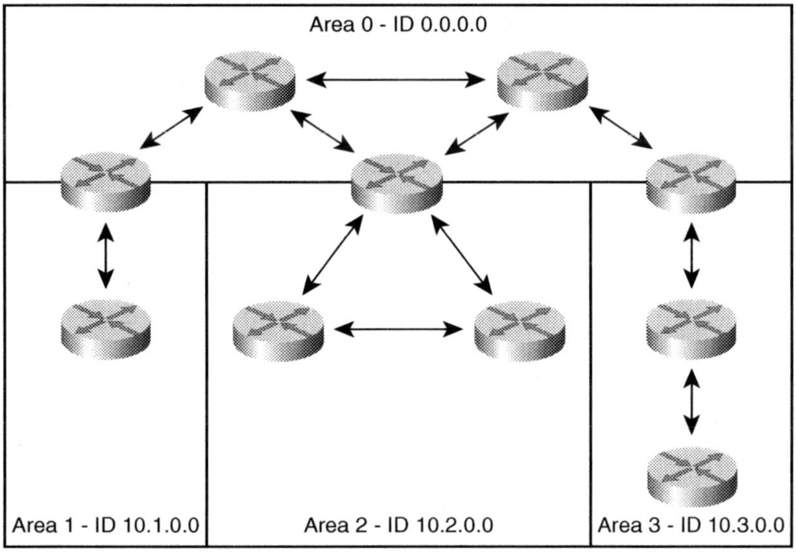

FIGURE 2.23 An OSPF network with multiple areas.

Backbone routers not only route host traffic between areas, but they can also provide summary routes within areas to other routers on the backbone. They, in turn, provide those summaries to the other routers within their areas. This configuration ensures that any host within an area can reach any host in another area. This capability ensures that no area's routing tables contain detailed information about another area's topology. This minimizes the size of routing tables and ensures that the backbone handles all interarea traffic.

Area Routing

Area partitioning creates the following two types of OSPF routing, depending on whether the source and destination are in the same area or in different areas:

- **Intra-area**—Intra-area routing occurs when the source and destination are in the same area. With intra-area routing, the source routes the packet to its default gateway (an internal area router). The internal area router then makes use of the explicit routes (as calculated by the SPF algorithm) maintained in the area routers and routes the packet through the appropriate interface to the destination internal area router. The destination internal area router then forwards the packet to the destination host.
- **Interarea**—Interarea routing occurs when the source and destination are in different areas. When routing between areas, the source routes the packet to its default gateway

(an internal area router); the area router then forwards the packet to an area border router using the shortest path. The area border router forwards the packets through backbone routers using the shortest path to the area border router for the destination host. The area border router for the destination host forwards the packets through internal area routers using the shortest path, until the packets reach their destination.

Step by Step 2.7 helps you create additional OSPF areas.

STEP BY STEP

2.7 Creating an OSPF Area with Windows Server 2003's Routing and Remote Access Service

1. Open the Routing and Remote Access console.
2. Expand the console tree and select IP Routing. In the details pane, right-click OSPF and select Properties from the context menu. The OSPF Properties dialog box opens.
3. Select the Areas tab.
4. Click Add to open the OSPF Area Configuration dialog box, shown in Figure 2.24.

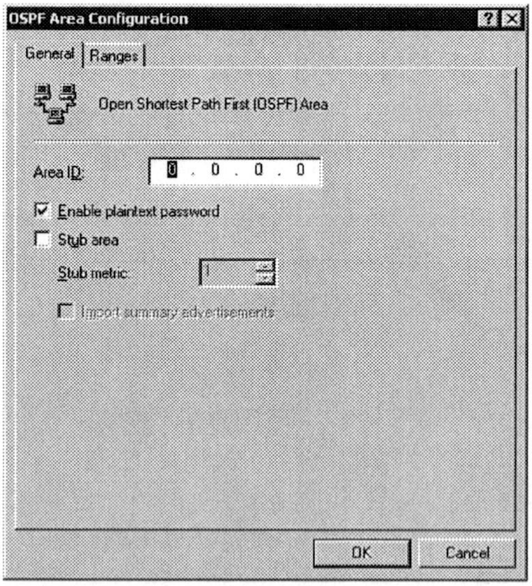

FIGURE 2.24 Be sure you know the network parameters and characteristics of your area before adding it to your OSPF network.

5. On the General tab, type a dotted-decimal number that identifies the area. To use a plain-text password, verify that the Enable Plaintext Password option is selected. To mark the area as a stub, select the Stub Area option. In Stub Metric, click the arrows to set the stub metric. To import routes of other areas into the stub area, select the Import Summary Advertisements option. Click OK twice to apply the changes and return to the Routing and Remote Access console.

NOTE

What is a stub area? A stub area is an OSPF area that doesn't advertise individual network routes from external areas. Instead, it relies on a default route (0.0.0.0 with a subnet mask of 0.0.0.0) to route all traffic out of the area. This is done to reduce the amount of memory required on the routers located in the stub area; they don't need to maintain a topology database.

Virtual Links

In rare cases, an area might not have direct physical access to the backbone. In this instance, you need to configure a connection from the new area to the backbone through a connection called a virtual link. A virtual link provides the disconnected area a logical path to the backbone. The virtual link has to be established between two area border routers that have a common area, with one area border router connected to the backbone. Virtual links are configured over a nonbackbone area known as a transit area.

Step by Step 2.8 shows how to configure a virtual link within RRAS. You need at least two OSPF areas to configure this interface.

STEP BY STEP

2.8 Configuring a Virtual Routing Link for Windows Server 2003

1. Open the Routing and Remote Access console.
2. Expand the console tree and select IP Routing. Right-click OSPF and select Properties from the context menu. The OSPF Properties dialog box opens.
3. Select the Virtual Interfaces tab.
4. On the Virtual Interfaces tab, click Add. In Transit Area ID, click the transit area over which you are connecting the virtual link. The OSPF Virtual Interface Configuration dialog box opens, as shown in Figure 2.25.
5. In Virtual Neighbor Router ID, type the OSPF router ID of the router at the other endpoint of the virtual link. In Transit Delay (Seconds), click the arrows to set the transit delay in seconds. In Retransmit Interval (Seconds), click the arrows to set the retransmit interval in seconds. In Hello Interval (Seconds), click the arrows to set the hello interval in seconds. In Dead Interval (Seconds), click the arrows to set the dead interval in seconds. Click OK to add the virtual interface, and click OK again to return to the Routing and Remote Access console.

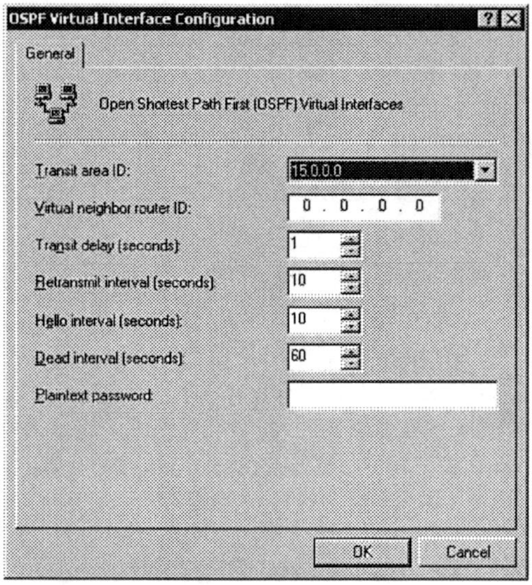

FIGURE 2.25 Be sure you know the network parameters and characteristics of your virtual link before configuring the virtual interface.

Autonomous System Routing

Routing does not occur only within areas using OSPF. When internetworks are connected to other internetworks that are under different administrative control, routing must be established. This type of routing between autonomous systems is established using external routes. Autonomous system border routers running OSPF learn about exterior routes through other routing protocols, such as Interior Gateway Routing Protocol (IGRP), RIP, or Border Gateway Protocol (BGP). Autonomous system border routers are similar to area border routers, except that they route between different autonomous systems.

TIP

Supported protocols Some of the more common border protocols such as Interior Gateway Routing Protocol or Border Gateway Protocol are not supported by Windows Server 2003. They are important to know as general information because they are commonly used in production networks, but they will not be on the exam.

By default, autonomous system border routers advertise all external routes within their autonomous system. This allows all areas and networks within areas to reach destination networks that might lie outside the autonomous system. As a network manager, you might find it necessary to restrict the external routes that are advertised within the autonomous system. Using Windows Server 2003 Router and Remote Access Services, you can configure the autonomous system border router to accept or ignore the routes of certain external sources, such as routing protocols (RIPv2) or other sources (static routes or Simple Network Management Protocol). You can also configure the autonomous system border router to accept or discard specific routes by configuring one or multiple (Destination, Network Mask) pairs. Step by Step 2.9 shows how to enable autonomous system border routing.

STEP BY STEP

2.9 Configuring Autonomous System Border Routing in Windows Server 2003's Routing and Remote Access Service

1. Open the Routing and Remote Access console.
2. Expand the console tree and select IP Routing. In the details pane, right-click OSPF and select Properties from the context menu. The OSPF Properties dialog box opens.
3. On the General tab, shown in Figure 2.26, click Enable Autonomous System Boundary Router.

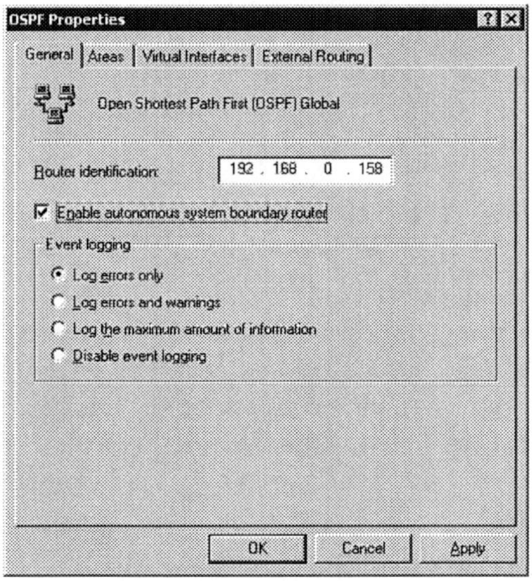

FIGURE 2.26 You need to enable the Autonomous System Boundary Router parameter to accept routing information from RIP.

4. Select the External Routing tab, shown in Figure 2.27, and click Accept Routes from All Route Sources Except Those Selected. If you want to exclude a specific route source, select it in the window below. You can also select Ignore Routes from All Route Sources Except Those Selected if you want to accept routes from only one or two sources.

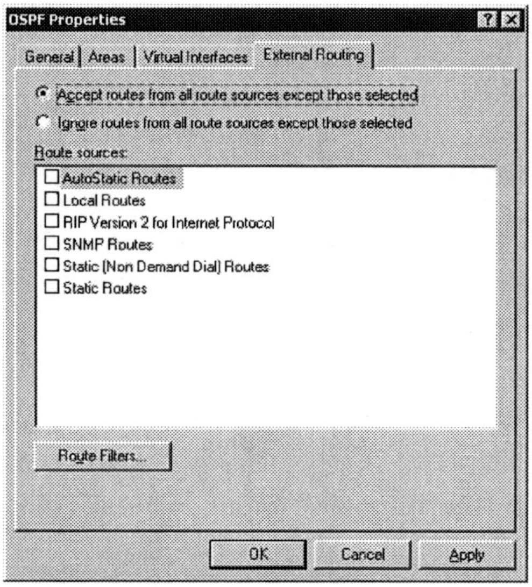

FIGURE 2.27 You have some granularity when configuring the sources your router will accept updates from.

5. Click OK to return to the Routing and Remote Access console and enable the OSPF boundary routing.

OSPF Operation

The SPF routing algorithm is the basis for OSPF operations. When an SPF router is powered up, it initializes its routing protocol data structures and then waits for indications from lower-layer protocols that its interfaces are functional.

After a router has verified that its interfaces are functioning, it uses the OSPF Hello protocol to acquire neighbors. *Neighbors* are routers that have interfaces sharing a common network. The router sends hello packets to its neighbors and receives their hello packets. In addition to identifying neighboring routers, hello packets act as keepalives to let routers know that other routers are still available.

Designated Routers

On multiaccess networks (that is, networks that support more than two routers), the Hello protocol elects a designated router and a backup designated router. Because the designated router is adjacent to all other routers, it acts as a hub for the distribution of link-state information, maintaining the synchronization of the topological database and controlling adjacencies between routers within the network. (The relationship between neighboring routers for the purposes of synchronizing the topological database is called an *adjacency*; adjacencies are discussed in more detail later in this chapter, in the section "Adjacencies.")

As an example of why a designated router is required, think about a broadcast network that has six OSPF routers. If you didn't control the adjacency behavior, each router could establish an adjacency with each of the other routers, for a total of 15 adjacency relationships. On a broadcast network with n routers, a total of $n \times (n-1)/2$ adjacencies would be formed. This could result in unneeded flooding traffic as routers attempt to synchronize with all their adjacent routers. Designated routers allow a reduction in network traffic and in the size of the topological database.

The designated router is elected via the Hello protocol. Hello packets are exchanged via IP multicast packets on each segment. The router with the highest OSPF priority on a segment becomes the designated router for that segment. In the case of a tie, the router with the highest router ID wins. The default for the interface OSPF priority is 1. A router priority of 0 means that the router cannot become a designated router.

In addition to electing a designated router, a backup designated router is elected for each multiaccess network, to prevent the loss in connectivity associated with the loss of a designated router. Like the designated router, the backup designated router is adjacent to all routers on the network. When the designated router fails, the backup designated router immediately becomes the designated router by sending LSAs to all its adjacent routers, announcing its new role. There is a very short period of time when transit traffic could be impaired as the backup designated router takes over the role of the designated router.

Like the designated router, the backup designated router is elected through the exchange of hello packets. Each hello packet contains a field for the backup designated router of the network. If the backup designated router is not specified, the router with the highest router priority that is not already the designated router becomes the backup designated router. If multiple routers have the highest router priority, the router with the highest router ID is elected the backup designated router.

Adjacencies

When the topological databases of two neighboring routers are synchronized, the routers are said to be *adjacent*. On multiaccess networks, the designated router determines which routers should become adjacent. Topological databases are synchronized between pairs of adjacent routers. Adjacencies control the distribution of routing protocol packets, which are sent and received only on adjacencies.

Adjacencies are first developed when an OSPF router initializes; it sends out a periodic OSPF hello packet. The OSPF hello packet contains configuration information such as the router's router ID and the list of neighboring routers for which the router has received hello packets. Initially, the neighbor list in the OSPF hello packet does not contain any neighbors.

The initializing OSPF router also listens for neighboring routers' hello packets. From the incoming hello packets, the initializing router determines the specific router or routers with which an adjacency is to be established. Adjacencies are formed with the designated router and backup designated router, which are identified in the incoming hello packets. Designated routers and backup designated routers were discussed in more detail earlier in this chapter, in the section "Designated Routers."

To begin the adjacency, the routers forming the adjacency describe the contents of their topological databases through a sequence of database-description packets. This is known as the *database exchange process*, during which the two neighboring routers form a master/slave relationship. The contents of each router's topological database are acknowledged by its neighboring router.

Each router compares its LSAs with the LSAs of its neighbor and notes which LSAs need to be requested from the neighbor to synchronize the topological database. The missing or more recent LSAs are then requested through link-state request packets. Link-state update packets are sent in response to the link-state request packets, and their receipt is acknowledged. When all link-state requests of both routers have been satisfied, the topological databases of the neighboring routers are fully synchronized and an adjacency is formed.

After an adjacency is formed, each neighboring router sends a periodic hello packet to inform its neighbor that the router is still active on the network. The lack of hello packets from a neighbor is used to detect a downed router.

If an event occurs such as a downed link or router, or the addition of a new network that changes the topological database of one router, the topological databases of adjacent routers are no longer synchronized. The router whose topological database has changed sends link-state update packets to its adjacent neighbor. The receipt of the link-state update packets is acknowledged. After the exchange, the topological databases of the adjacent routers are again synchronized.

Other Problems with Routing

Our last routing topic addresses problems that can occur and what the protocols themselves can do to fix those problems after they are configured. Here we cover hop count issues, split horizon and poison reverse, and convergence problems.

- **Hop count limit**—Hop count limitations restrict the network's scalability. This is a problem in design. If you have to keep building your network outward, and you suddenly can't route to a location or the network starts experiencing major routing problems, you might have surpassed the maximum hop count limit. RIP permits a maximum hop count of 15, whereas OSPF does not have this hop-count limitation. Remember that any packet traveling on a RIP network with a hop count greater than 15 hops is tagged as unreachable.
- **Split horizon**—Split horizon is a service that RIP performs to stop two node-routing loops; it should prevent routing loops between adjacent routers. Split horizon does not advertise routing information on the interface in which it was learned.
- **Poison reverse**—The Poison Reverse service tries to stop routing loops in the larger internetwork instead of just two nodes, as split horizon does. If a routing loop is occurring, poison reverse sends updates to adjacent routers to put that route (the one in question) in a hold-down state, which can be set by a timer. If these metrics are not fine-tuned, routing

loops can occur. In this case, poison reverse is activated and the network is put in a hold-down state. Depending on the timer, this problem could go on long enough to cause network timeouts that are experienced by the clients your network services.

- **Convergence issues**—If you have a problem with convergence, you need to analyze a topology map of your network as it currently operates and figure out where (and why) the network is having this problem. As stated previously, convergence occurs when all routers on the network know all other routers and the topology is accurate. If major activity occurs in your network so that it needs to constantly reconverge (perform updates and verify routing information), you might also experience problems in which routes are unknown and data cannot be accessed. In this case, you need to adjust your network settings or redesign the network so that it converges quickly or stays in a state of convergence longer. By using OSPF instead of RIP, you are already ahead of the game because RIP reconverges the entire network every 30 seconds, by default.

REVIEW BREAK

As a Microsoft Certified Professional, you must know how to design networks. No longer can you be a simple server jockey; now you need to know the connecting highway, which is the underlying network that allows your domain controllers to communicate with each other. You can't have WINS push/pull partners if you don't have a WAN. And when you have a WAN, you have routers, and when you have routers configured to use a dynamic routing protocol, you have either RIP or OSPF. So which do you choose? Because we discussed all the details of RIP and OSPF in the preceding sections, we provide a distilled list of OSPF versus RIP here. This information will help you decide which protocol you should use. You can consider this information a summary of what you have already read in this chapter.

RIP can no longer handle the growth of business as we know it today. No business today has boundaries. A business that currently (from a network view) has only one core network and 10 remote sites could easily be acquired by another company through a merger and become part of that company's network overnight. Because most large companies that acquire other smaller companies generally have large networks, it is safe to say that they use advanced routing protocols on their networks to handle their current size as well as their rapid growth. Your RIP-based network would be a thorn in their side, with route redistribution having to take place to communicate, or a complete network overhaul to take place to bring you into compliance with their network. RIP simply can't keep pace with businesses today; therefore, newly designed networks should not be configured to use RIP because RIP's lack of scalability does not match the nature of business.

If you decide to use RIP, you must consider that your network could never span any size larger than 15 hop counts. Remember that 16 is infinity.

Another vital flaw of RIPv1 is that it cannot use subnetted networks other than the default subnetted classes, which are 255.0.0.0, 255.255.0.0, and 255.255.255.0. Any other variable-length subnet will not work in a RIP environment, and in today's networks this is not something you can afford. Subnetting the private IP address ranges within your network allows a large number of hosts to be used. You should not waste a single host, and being able to efficiently subnet enables you to spare every single IP needed. RIP cannot route between links that are variably subnetted, so it is not wise to deploy RIP in any network you feel might grow to that size.

RIP is bandwidth intensive on networks that are built with very slow WAN links. This means that if you use very small circuit sizes (such as 32KB) per link, you more than likely will feel the effects of RIP on your wide area network. Remember that RIP tries to update its neighbors with its entire routing table every 30 seconds.

RIP is slower to converge than OSPF. This problem is felt only in very large networks because of the size it could span in router hops. If the network design is poorly laid out, you, as an end user, could experience timeouts on your PC if network convergence takes too long. Having this happen every time a Frame Relay link drops could prove annoying to everyone in your company. Very large networks using RIP and dealing with very slow convergence do not work well and might need a protocol such as OSPF to handle the distributed nature of the network it is made to manage. Remember that RIP should not be used on very large networks because everyone on the network will be affected if convergence becomes a problem.

RIP understands hop count only as a routable metric. If you want to get from one LAN to another over a few router hops, the shortest hop count from LAN 1 to LAN 2 will win. What happens if there is also another path to LAN 2? What if you have another path that consists of two router hops, both separated by a T1 link? This means that you would have 1.544MB of transfer on each link. Say that nothing else is utilizing this path. Now say the other one-hop path is an analog dial-up connection between two routers over 56Kbps. Which would be faster? Of course, the two T1 lines not being used would be the fastest option, but RIP believes the single-hop path is faster because it has a shorter path via hop counts, which, in this situation, is actually the slowest path RIP could choose. Through OSPF's configurable metrics, it would know the shortest path because it is smart enough (or configurable enough) to be able to know that the T1 link is, of course, the shortest path.

RIP also has a spin-off called RIP Version 2, or RIPv2 for short. If you are thinking of using RIPv2, you might want to consider using OSPF instead if your network will likely experience future growth. RIPv2 fixes the problems that RIP had—which are subnetted networks and authentication for security—but it still has slow convergence problems and a hop-count limitation.

OSPF is harder to plan, design, and implement, but once you do, you gain a world of flexibility and control not offered by protocols such as RIP. OSPF addresses all the problems that RIP experiences. OSPF can handle any kind of routed environment you can design because it was made to do so. If you are going to stay with a vendor-neutral routing protocol, all new networks designed and built today should use OSPF. It offers scalability and control over a corporation of just about any size.

OSPF provides the following great enhancements over RIP: no hop-count limitations; handling of variable-length subnetted networks; and the use of multicast packets (instead of broadcast packets) to give and send updates, which means less processing power used on routers not meant for the updates to process broadcast packets, which, in turn, eats CPU cycles for nothing. By using multicast packets, OSPF saves router CPU time. Bandwidth is also saved because routing updates are sent only as needed, not every 30 seconds. With OSPF, the network reconverges every 30 minutes, but that's to be expected and nowhere near as bandwidth-consuming as every 30 seconds with RIP.

With OSPF, you can set up areas. Area 0 is always the backbone, but as far as expansion, you can expand your network into other areas, such as Area 1, Area 2, and Area 3. You could configure all four areas as separate subnets and set up a logical definition of subnetted networks to limit the number of link-state updates needed per area. If you separate your network into areas, not every router needs to know what every other router does; if it did, a router 29 hops away would need to exchange a database with every other router on the network, and this would make convergence really slow. OSPF enables you to create areas so that such a problem never happens.

Planning Routing for IP Multicast Traffic

Objective:

Plan a routing strategy.

- Plan routing for IP multicast traffic.

This section covers IP multicast routing. We spend some time examining what multicast means and why knowing this information is important. To do that, we have to compare and contrast other forms of traffic traversing your LAN or WAN, which includes unicast, broadcast, and multicast.

- **Unicast**—When a single node on the network sends data to its destination node under one single packet, it knows where the destination node is and gets the data to it. Remember *uni* as being a single transmission.
- **Broadcast**—Broadcasting (think of the word *broad*) occurs when the destination is not known or cannot be found, and that node (which needs to find the destination node) sends out packets to all nodes on the network segment to see whether it can find its destination node. This process is conducive to increased traffic, collisions on hubbed networks, and so on. Broadcasts are at times a necessary evil, but most of the time you should prevent them from happening often or control their number. Basically, broadcast traffic adds overhead to your network (bandwidth utilization) and its devices (processing packets they don't need to look at).

- **Multicast**—Multicast is the happy medium but still can cause problems. A multicast transmission is based on a group. In simple terms, think of 20 nodes on a network, 5 of which need to communicate at all times and 15 of which do not need to ever know what the other 5 are doing. Say these nodes are OSPF routers. OSPF routers send updates to each other via a multicast, so you might ask, "What about devices that do not need to know this information?" If you use a multicast address, such as 224.0.0.5 (the all-OSPF routers multicast address) for OSPF-based networks, only those devices listen for transmissions from other nodes using this service. This reduces the problems caused by broadcast traffic and enables you to cause one sender to get information to multiple (group) nodes without that message going to every node on the network. Consequently, multicasting is good, but as with any other technology, it can cause problems as well or require an advanced level of administration to make it work properly. This section focuses on these issues and how they revolve around the Windows Server 2003 platform.

So now that you are familiar with the concept of multicast networks, let's consider the problems with routing such networks. Routing of multicast information is important, but first you should know why you need to route it.

Considering multicast routing is very important because your network must be capable of building packet-distribution trees that enable sources to send packets to all receivers. These trees ensure that each packet on the network exists one time only and is found only on a specific network. If this limitation did not exist, you would have problems with IP multicast routing. Also, multicast routing, which is the propagation of multicast listening information, is provided by multicast-routing protocols such as Distance Vector Multicast Routing Protocol (DVMRP) and Multicast Open Shortest Path First (MOSPF), which is an extension to OSPF that allows it to support IP multicasting. Such protocols ease manual configuration of VPN- and OSPF-based networks and are becoming the standard for these types of networks.

As a Windows Server 2003 administrator, you need to know this information. For example, if you set up a remote-access solution with Windows Server 2003 (such as a router), this router would need to know what to do with multicast traffic that approaches it. In other words, if you were to set up a Windows Server 2003 router on a multicast network, it could participate if configured properly.

TIP

Get more information For more information on this technology, you can visit the following RFCs:

- RFC 1075 defines the Distance Vector Multicast Routing Protocol (DVMRP).
- RFC 1584 defines the Multicast Open Shortest Path First (MOSPF) protocol.

Neither protocol is tested on Exam 70-293; this information is provided just so you know how to plan for such protocols in your environment.

The Windows Server 2003 family does not provide any multicast routing protocols like DVMRP. Other vendors, such as Cisco, are leaders in this arena. The purpose of Microsoft's product line is to conform with industry trends, vendor-neutral functionality, and so on; therefore, it is important for the server to at least be capable of "participating." How can it participate, then? It can use technologies to make sure that IP multicast routing does happen, even though it might not be directly responsible for routing of such information. Windows Server 2003 handles multicast traffic and its routing by forwarding this traffic. To do this, you can use the Internet Group Management Protocol (IGMP).

IGMP, which is described in RFC 2236, is an Internet protocol that allows nodes that are configured to use it to communicate as a group instead of individually. IGMP allows a node to report its multicast group membership (the group to which it is assigned) to adjacent routers. Multicasting allows a node to send data to multiple other nodes that have also identified themselves as being part of that group. This cuts down on broadcast traffic and bandwidth consumption.

Now that you know what IGMP does, let's look at the features you must plan and design into your infrastructure to work with Windows Server 2003, especially because it can't natively route multicast traffic based on the multicast routing protocol. If you run Windows Server 2003 in your environment to help with multicast traffic, you can set it up to use the IGMP routing protocol, IGMP router mode, and IGMP proxy mode to provide multicast forwarding in a single router-based network or when connecting a single router-based LAN to the Internet. This means that you can use a Windows Server 2003 system on your network to participate in multicast routing as a forwarding service.

With a service such as multicast forwarding, a router can forward multicast traffic to any network where nodes also configured to use the multicast service are listening. Only multicast-capable nodes can forward multicast traffic across an internetwork. A multicast-capable node must be able to send and receive multicast network traffic, as well as be able to register the multicast address that it and other routers are listening to. Again, Windows Server 2003 is capable of doing this.

EXAM ALERT

What are multicast packets? Multicast packets are IP-based packets. They must contain the right multicast address as the destination IP address. Remember the previous OSPF example in which the multicast address used to inform neighboring routers was 224.0.0.5. Only nodes listening for this destination address in the IP packet can receive multicast traffic.

Windows Server 2003 Multicast Specifics

Windows Server 2003 enables you to use TCP/IP (refer to Chapter 1); therefore, it can work with multicast traffic. Windows Server 2003 uses a multicast forwarding table to make decisions about where to forward its incoming multicast traffic, as well as to listen for IGMP report messages thus provided by the IGMP routing protocol on a single interface operating in IGMP router mode. You can plan to use the multicast routing protocol to propagate to other multicast-capable routers any information, such as multicast group listening information. Remember, though, RRAS does not provide a routing protocol for multicasting; it provides forwarding only.

EXAM ALERT

The IGMP routing protocol Do not be confused by the IGMP routing protocol provided by Windows Server 2003. This protocol is *not* a multicast routing protocol.

The Windows Server 2003 IGMP routing protocol is used for the maintenance of entries found in the multicast forwarding table on the router. When you add this component in RRAS, plan to configure them in one of two possible ways: IGMP router mode or IGMP proxy mode.

IGMP router mode enables you to set Windows Server 2003 to listen for IGMP Membership Report packets, as well as to track group membership.

IGMP proxy mode enables you to configure your router (you must have two or more interfaces or NICs) with different settings on different interfaces—one acting as a proxy multicast host that sends IGMP membership reports on one of its interfaces.

EXAM ALERT

The MBone The multicast-capable portion of the Internet is known as the Internet multicast backbone, or *MBone*. This is where all the multicast forwarding messages and reports go.

Challenge

You have been hired as a new senior systems engineer to work for ABC, Inc., the maker of the world's best widgets. Last week, a new segment was built onto the current LAN and connected via a Windows Server 2003 router. Now users on the new segment are experiencing timeouts when attempting to access resources on one of the older segments. Nobody can get to the other side of the network. Users on the older side of the LAN report no problems.

Through your discussions with various personnel within ABC, Inc., you've discovered the following problems:

- Timeouts are occurring on the LAN.
- Users cannot access resources.
- One side of the network cannot access the other side.
- The original side can access the other side.

(continues)

(continued)

Your task is to determine the problem with the network configuration and then provide a plan to correct it.

Try to complete this exercise on your own, listing your conclusions on a sheet of paper. When you have completed the exercise, compare your results to those given here.

As the new senior systems engineer, you need to analyze each problem one at a time and see whether they are all related. This step is important so that you do not waste a lot of time repeating yourself.

As you look at the problems, you realize that you can solve them all within the same device because the router is causing all the problems as a result of it being misconfigured. If you notice timeouts, that means users are complaining of no connectivity, and all the applications that they are trying to open are timing out because the servers they connect to cannot be reached. Because the resources are on the other segment across the router, you know the router is at fault if no one can pass traffic over it.

Next, you see that because one side of the network can access the other side, but not the other way around, this problem might indicate a missing route. As a sharp network engineer, you quickly open a command prompt on the server and type **`route print`**. This shows you that a route is missing its routing table. You figure out that a dynamic routing protocol is not being used, only static routes, and one route is missing. After adding the missing route, you discover that the timeout problems have disappeared and the remote hosts can now access their resources.

Troubleshooting TCP/IP Routing

Objective:

Troubleshoot TCP/IP routing. Tools might include the `route`, `tracert`, `ping`, `pathping`, and `netsh` commands and Network Monitor.

To conclude this chapter, we spend some time examining troubleshooting of TCP/IP routing. Knowing how to skillfully troubleshoot a routing problem is key to being able to administer a WAN. You have to know how to troubleshoot problems when they occur, and Windows Server 2003 provides several tools to help you do that.

Routing Troubleshooting Tools

Five commands and one utility are used here: `route`, `tracert`, `ping`, `pathping`, `netsh`, and the Network Monitor utility. Knowing when to use which one is the key to survival in this area of Exam 70-293. Let's start our discussion of these troubleshooting tools with the `route` command.

The `route` Command

As mentioned earlier, routers keep routing tables. If you are using static routes, you must manually edit your routing tables; the `route` command is the means by which you do this.

Although you can use the RRAS console to manipulate this data, nothing is faster or easier than using the `route` command. Within seconds, you can add a route in the routing table, adjust one, or take one out.

The `route` command is easy to manipulate. You use the `route` command, like most of the other commands we look at, from the command line. Entering the `route` command by itself provides you with a detailed description of its use. The syntax of the `route` command is as follows and is detailed in Table 2.2:

```
ROUTE [-f] [-p] [command] [destination] [MASK netmask] [gateway]
➥[METRIC metric] [IF interface]
```

TABLE 2.2 `route` Parameters

Parameter	Description
`-f`	Instructs the `route` command to clear the routing tables of all gateway entries.
`-p`	Specifies that a route being added is to be persistent and not dumped when the computer is restarted.
`command`	Specifies the action that is to be carried out. `print` prints a route. `add` adds a route. `delete` deletes a route. `change` changes an existing route.
`destination`	Specifies the host.
`MASK` *`netmask`*	Specifies a subnet mask value for the routing entry. If a value is not specified, the default of 255.255.255.255 is used.
`gateway`	Specifies a gateway.
`METRIC` *`metric`*	Specifies the metric (route cost of the destination).
`IF` *`interface`*	Specifies the interface number for the route.

You can use the `route print` command to display the routing table. You need to be familiar with its output. In the following output, you can see a standard routing table that consists of `route` statements with specific details in each route:

```
C:\>route print
IPv4 Route Table
===========================================================================
Interface List
0x1 ........................... MS TCP Loopback interface
0x10003 ...00 e0 7d c1 3e 0e ...... Realtek RTL8139 Family PCI Fast Ethernet NIC
0x10004 ...00 13 72 0e 98 7e ...... Broadcom NetXtreme Gigabit Ethernet
===========================================================================
===========================================================================
Active Routes:
Network Destination        Netmask          Gateway       Interface  Metric
          0.0.0.0          0.0.0.0      192.168.0.1    192.168.0.158      20
          0.0.0.0          0.0.0.0    192.168.0.158    192.168.0.159      20
```

```
        127.0.0.0        255.0.0.0        127.0.0.1        127.0.0.1      1
      192.168.0.0    255.255.255.0    192.168.0.158    192.168.0.158     20
      192.168.0.0    255.255.255.0    192.168.0.159    192.168.0.159     20
    192.168.0.158  255.255.255.255        127.0.0.1        127.0.0.1     20
    192.168.0.159  255.255.255.255        127.0.0.1        127.0.0.1     20
    192.168.0.255  255.255.255.255    192.168.0.158    192.168.0.158     20
    192.168.0.255  255.255.255.255    192.168.0.159    192.168.0.159     20
        224.0.0.0        240.0.0.0    192.168.0.158    192.168.0.158     20
        224.0.0.0        240.0.0.0    192.168.0.159    192.168.0.159     20
  255.255.255.255  255.255.255.255    192.168.0.158    192.168.0.158      1
  255.255.255.255  255.255.255.255    192.168.0.159    192.168.0.159      1
Default Gateway:       192.168.0.1
===========================================================================
Persistent Routes:
  None
```

Let's examine the first entry in the routing table to see how it is laid out:

```
          0.0.0.0          0.0.0.0      192.168.0.1    192.168.0.158     20
```

The first `0.0.0.0` is the destination, and the following `0.0.0.0` is the network subnet mask. In other words, say you need to move traffic from one network to another; to do so, you would specify the destination address with its proper subnet mask. You might want traffic from the 192.168.0.0 network to be able to get traffic across your router to the 192.168.1.0 network. This is done via a route. Here, all 0's in the destination and the netmask mean that this is a default route. A default route means that *any* destination network with *any* netmask can be sent out the other interface of your server, which should be the next hop. This is what the interface, as well as the gateway, is for. The gateway IP address, 192.168.0.1, specifies the forwarding or next-hop IP address over which the set of addresses defined by the network destination and subnet mask are reachable. A metric is a way to specify something specific for a route you enter. A route with the lowest metric is the one that is chosen, so if you have to weight routes with higher metrics to get them to be specified as first or last, this is how you do it. The interface is simply the interface index for the NIC over which the destination address can be reached.

The `tracert` Command

The `tracert` command is one of the most important routing troubleshooting commands around. Not knowing `tracert` (or `Traceroute` for UNIX and Cisco Systems) is not a good thing. The `tracert` command helps you find problem spots in a routed network. Consider Figure 2.28.

Where would you find the problem if you had one? Let's create a fictional problem that is very common on most production networks today. The clients on the 10.0.0.0 network routinely access the web server located at 12.1.2.2 with no problems. Today your clients suddenly can't get to this web server at 12.1.2.2. What do you do? Well, you can do many things, but by using `tracert`, you can trace a route from the 10.0.0.2 host to the 12.2.2.2 host, which is the web server, and see where the packets drop, if they do. Here is an example:

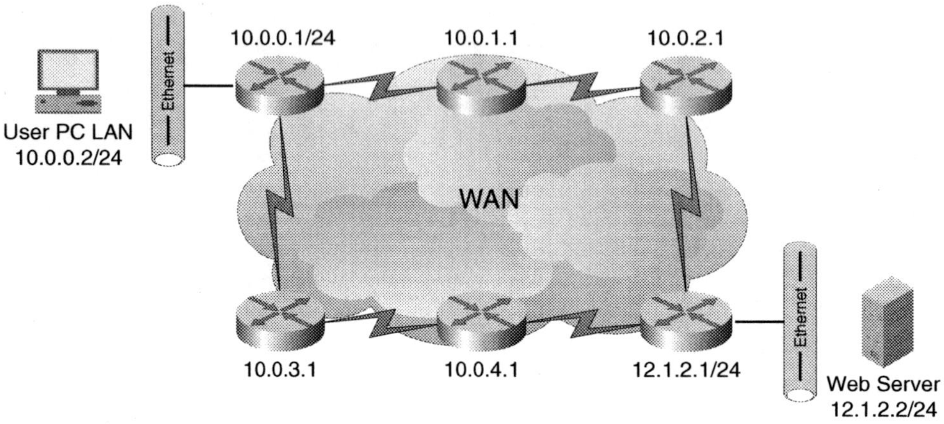

FIGURE 2.28 The `tracert` command will be useful in troubleshooting this complex routing environment.

```
C:\>tracert 12.1.2.2
Tracing route to 12.1.2.2 over a maximum of 30 hops
  1     10 ms     10 ms     10 ms  10.0.0.1
  2     10 ms     10 ms     10 ms  10.0.1.1
  3     40 ms     30 ms     40 ms  10.0.2.1
  4     40 ms     40 ms     40 ms  12.1.2.1
```

Now you can see how useful this command is. If the 10.0.2.1 router were down (nonfunctional), you would get a request timeout or unreachable ICMP–based error message so that you would know that you have a problem there.

Another useful function of the `tracert` command is to analyze traffic routes to determine whether the most economical route is being taken. This function is especially useful for troubleshooting and tuning private networks where you can make changes (or have changes made) on the routers of concern. Recall that RIP does not differentiate between a one-hop route using a 56Kbps link and a one-hop route using a full T1 link. The `tracert` command can be used to determine exactly how traffic is moving from one point to another and correct such problems.

As with most of the other commands we look at, you use the `tracert` command from the command line. Entering the `tracert` command by itself gives you a detailed description of its use. The syntax of the `tracert` command is as follows and is detailed in Table 2.3:

```
tracert [-d] [-h maximum_hops] [-j host-list] [-w timeout] [-R]
➥[-S srcaddr] [-4] [-6] target_name
```

TABLE 2.3 `tracert` Parameters

Parameter	Description
`-d`	Prevents tracert from resolving IP addresses of routers to host names, which increases the speed of the tracert because DNS name resolution is not required.
`-h` *`maximum_hops`*	Specifies the maximum number of router hops that will be taken to the destination host.
`-w` *`timeout`*	Specifies a timeout in milliseconds to wait for an ICMP Echo Reply or Time Exceeded message to be received. The default time is 4 seconds. If this time is exceeded, an asterisk (`*`) is returned instead of a time value.
`-R`	Specifies that the round-trip path is to be tested. The `-R` parameter is used only for IPv6.
`-S` *`srcaddr`*	Specifies the source address to start the tracert from. The `-S` parameter is used only for IPv6.
`-4`	Specifies that IPv4 is to be used, which is the default.
`-6`	Specifies that IPv6 is to be used.
`target_name`	Specifies the destination of the tracert.

The `tracert` command functions by sending ICMP Echo Request packets to the specified destination, similar to the `ping` command (discussed next), but with a key difference. For the first group of packets sent out, the TTL (Time to Live) is set to `1`. When the packets reach the first router, the router decrements the TTL by one, causing the TTL to be `0`. A TTL of `0` results in the router discarding the packets and sending back an error message to the originating system. This error message contains the IP address of the sending router, which is then displayed as the first line of the output. The process then continues, but with the next group of three packets having a TTL of `2`, thus allowing them to pass the first router, which decrements their TTL to `1`, and make their way to the second router. The second router decrements the TTL to `0`, and the process continues.

The `ping` Command

Using `ping` to test connections might become something you do every day for the rest of your IT career. No other tool is used as often or as frequently as `ping`. `ping`, which stands for Packet Internet Groper, is fueled by the ICMP protocol, just as `tracert` is. The same ICMP Echo type messages are used as well, so learning about `ping` is somewhat easier if you are already familiar with the basic operation of the `tracert` command.

The `ping` command is the basic test of network connectivity. But why would you need to use `ping`? Let's look at an example. You are the network administrator responsible for two servers that are located on opposite sides of a WAN link (hence, two or more routers). Today you have started to get complaints that nobody at the remote site can receive email. Because the email servers are on your side of the network, you are justifiably concerned about why nobody can get to that email. The first step in troubleshooting your problem lies with the `ping` command.

If you can ping the email server's IP address from your location, you have confidence that the problem is no longer apparent. But what if you cannot ping the server? Your next step is to ping each hop along the route from source to destination in an attempt to determine where the problem lies. There is an inherent limitation to the ping command, though: Even though you can ping a host or router, this does not guarantee that it is performing its intended function properly. Being able to successfully ping a host indicates that basic TCP/IP connectivity exists along the route, nothing more.

To ping a host, you can simply enter the ping command followed by an IP address or DNS host name, as shown here:

```
C:\>ping 10.0.0.1
Pinging 10.0.0.1 with 32 bytes of data:
Reply from 10.0.0.1: bytes=32 time=70ms TTL=124
Reply from 10.0.0.1: bytes=32 time=70ms TTL=124
Reply from 10.0.0.1: bytes=32 time=70ms TTL=124
Reply from 10.0.0.1: bytes=32 time=70ms TTL=124
Ping statistics for 10.0.0.1:
    Packets: Sent = 4, Received = 4, Lost = 0 (0% loss),
Approximate round trip times in milli-seconds:
    Minimum = 70ms, Maximum =  70ms, Average =  70ms
```

The following is the full syntax of the ping command:

```
ping [-t] [-a] [-n count] [-l size] [-f] [-i TTL] [-v TOS]
[-r count] [-s count] [{-j HostList | -k HostList}] [-w timeout]
```

Table 2.4 describes the switches used with the ping command.

TABLE 2.4 ping Parameters

Switch	Description
-t	Specifies that the ping command should continue sending echo request (ICMP) messages until manually interrupted. This is useful for establishing and monitoring a constant connection between two hosts.
-a	Specifies that reverse name resolution is to be performed on the destination IP address. (Chapter 3 discusses name resolution.)
-n *count*	Specifies how many echo request messages are to be sent to the destination computer. The default is 4.
-l *size*	Specifies the length of the data field on the echo request, up to a maximum of 65,527 bytes. The default is 32 bytes.
-f	Specifies that the echo request messages should not be fragmented by routers along their path. This setting can be used to troubleshoot Maximum Transmission Unit (MTU)–related problems.
-i *TTL*	Specifies the value of the Time to Live (TTL) field in the IP header for echo request messages sent. The default is the default TTL value for the host. The maximum TTL is 255.

TABLE 2.4 *Continued*

Switch	Description
`-v` *`TOS`*	Specifies the value for the Type of Service (TOS) field in the echo request. The default value is `0`, and valid values range from `0` to `255`.
`-r` *`count`*	Specifies that the Record Route option in the IP header is used to record the path taken by the echo request message and corresponding echo reply message. The count must between `1` and `9`.
`-s` *`count`*	Specifies that the Internet Timestamp option in the IP header is used to record the time of arrival for the echo request message and corresponding echo reply message for each hop. The count must be between `1` and `4`.
`-j` *`HostList`*	Specifies that the echo request messages use the Loose Source Route option in the IP header with the set of intermediate destinations specified in *`HostList`*. When you're using loose source routing, successive intermediate destinations can be separated by one or multiple routers. You can enter a maximum of nine addresses or host names in *`HostList`*.
`-k` *`HostList`*	Specifies that the echo request messages use the Strict Source Route option in the IP header with the set of intermediate destinations specified in *`HostList`*. When you're using strict source routing, the next intermediate destination must be directly reachable. You can enter a maximum of nine addresses or host names in *`HostList`*.
`-w` *`timeout`*	Specifies the amount of time, in milliseconds, to wait for the echo reply message to be received. The default timeout is 4,000 milliseconds (4 seconds).

NOTE

The story of `ping` If you want to read about the history of the `ping` command and learn some other interesting `ping`-related trivia, be sure to visit the page of the late Mike Muuss, creator of the `ping` application. You can find it at http://ftp.arl.mil/~mike/ping.html.

Although the `ping` command has many options available, you will most often find yourself using it as demonstrated previously, perhaps appending the `-t` and/or `-a` switches to it. This command provides a constant, verifiable connection and name resolution for your troubleshooting efforts.

The `pathping` Command

Testing routers by using `pathping` is outstanding if you want to use the best features of both `ping` and `tracert`, two tools you just learned about. Because of the similarities, you should already be familiar with what `pathping` can do for you. Not only does `pathping` use the best features of these tools, but it also has a set of excellent features of its own. First, the `pathping` command is a route-tracing tool used to troubleshoot remote problems. The `pathping` command sends packets over each hop to the destination over a very specific time, and then after the time has elapsed, `pathping` calculates a set of results based on it. This is how `pathping` gets very specific results. You can test connectivity, trace a path, and more. You can now see what links as well as routers are giving you problems.

The syntax of the `pathping` command is as follows and is detailed in Table 2.5:

```
pathping  [-g HostList] [-h MaximumHops] [-i IPAddress] [-n] [-p Period]
➥ [-q NumQueries] [-w Timeout] [-4 IPv4] [-6 IPv6] [TargetName]
```

TABLE 2.5 `pathping` Parameters

Parameter	Description
`-g` *`HostList`*	Specifies the that Echo Request messages are to use the Loose Source Route option in the IP header with the set of intermediate destinations specified in the *`HostList`*. Successive intermediate destinations can be separated by one or multiple routers. The *`HostList`* is a series of IP addresses (in dotted-decimal notation), separated by spaces.
`-h` *`MaximumHops`*	Specifies the maximum number of hops in the path to search for the target. The default is 30 hops.
`-i` *`IPAddress`*	Specifies the source address.
`-n`	Prevents `pathping` from resolving the IP addresses of intermediate routers to their names. This parameter speeds up the process.
`-p` *`Period`*	Specifies the number of milliseconds to wait between consecutive pings. The default is 250 milliseconds.
-q *`NumQueries`*	Specifies the number of Echo Request messages sent to each router in the path. The default is `100`.
`-w` *`Timeout`*	Specifies the number of milliseconds to wait for each reply. The default is 3,000 milliseconds.
`-4` *`IPv4`*	Specifies that `pathping` use IPv4 only.
`-6` *`IPv6`*	Specifies that `pathping` use IPv6 only.
`TargetName`	Specifies the destination, by either IP address or hostname.

So now that you know what `pathping` is, let's look at how to use it. To use `pathping`, you can open the command prompt and type **`pathping -n 10.0.0.1`**. Assuming that 10.0.0.1 is a valid host, you see the following output:

```
D:\>pathping -n 10.0.0.1
Tracing route to 10.0.0.1
over a maximum of 30 hops:
  0  172.16.2.1
  1  172.16.3,1
  2  192.168.2.1
  3  192.168.3.1

Computing statistics for 125 seconds...
```

```
            Source to Here   This Node/Link
Hop  RTT    Lost/Sent = Pct  Lost/Sent = Pct  Address
  0                                           172.16.2.1
                                0/ 100 =  0%   |
  1   41ms     0/ 100 =  0%     0/ 100 =  0%  172.16.3.1
                               13/ 100 = 13%   |
  2   22ms    16/ 100 = 16%     3/ 100 =  3%  192.168.2.1
                                0/ 100 =  0%   |
  3   24ms    13/ 100 = 13%     0/ 100 =  0%  192.168.3.1
                                0/ 100 =  0%   |
Trace complete.
```

The `pathping` output shows you not only what routes are experiencing packet loss, but also which routers are dropping packets. This information is valuable when you're trying to track down an Internet-related connectivity problem.

EXAM ALERT

Be aware of misleading results Sometimes what might appear to be a router failure might not be a router failure at all, but simply a firewall that is configured to block ICMP packets. You can test by trying to `ping` www.microsoft.com. Microsoft has been blocking ICMP packets for years now as a means of preventing denial-of-service (DoS) attacks on its networks.

The `netsh` Command

The `netsh` command is an advanced configuration and troubleshooting command that provides that capability to manage almost any networking-related component on your Windows Server 2003 computer, but requires you to have knowledge of the task you're trying to achieve. The `netsh` command can be used interactively or via scripting to manage the Windows Firewall, DHCP, WINS, network adapters, or IPSec (IP Security) settings, just to name a few of the things it can do.

Unlike the relatively easy-to-understand-and-use `ping` or `ipconfig` commands we examined earlier, `netsh` can seem significantly more complex to use because of its context-based operation. In other words, you don't simply append switches to the `netsh` command as you did previously with `ping` or `ipconfig`; you first must set the context that `netsh` operates in, such as *`interface`* to manage network adapters or *`firewall`* to manage the Windows Firewall.

Figure 2.29 demonstrates the context-based approach, as we've set the context to mange OSPF routing and then displayed the listing of available commands.

FIGURE 2.29 The `netsh` command can be used to manage almost any networking-related setting.

EXAM ALERT

Changes to `netsh` The `netsh` command has been enhanced in Windows Server 2003 to provide you a means of resetting the TCP/IP stack to its default values if the need arises. This replaces the capability in previous versions of Windows to remove and reinstall TCP/IP for troubleshooting. This advanced troubleshooting and repair action of `netsh` is also accessed from `netsh interface ip`.

The Network Monitor Utility

Network traffic is any activity to and from a host on a network. Any packet that leaves a network card, especially one that is routed, contributes to network traffic. The more hosts (or routers) there are on a network, the more services are added to a network; and the more of the network that is not segmented properly, the more network traffic that network has.

Why is the issue of network traffic so important? Too much network traffic, like rush-hour traffic, clogs the speed of the network, causes the network to become a bottleneck, and can ultimately cause the network to fail. As a rule, the more network services, shares, and resources that are added to a network, the more network traffic that is generated.

You can use Network Monitor to capture packets on a network. From these packets, you can troubleshoot network problems, discern how busy a network load is, and predict how the network will grow.

By now you should already be familiar with the basic operation of Network Monitor. If you need a review, look back at Chapter 1.

Troubleshooting RIP Environments

After RIP is configured within your environment, you might may be called on from time to time to troubleshoot issues that arise with routing. Although every problem is unique, Table 2.6 outlines some of the resolutions that might help when you're responding to issues within a RIP environment.

TABLE 2.6 RIP Problems, Potential Causes, and Possible Solutions

Problem	Cause/Solution
Routing tables have improper routing information in a mixed RIP network.	RIPv2 routers are configured to multicast announcements. Multicast RIPv1 and RIPv2 announcements are never received by RIPv1 routers. If you have a mixed environment of RIPv1 and RIPv2, you need to ensure that the routers configured with RIPv2 are using broadcast instead of multicast announcements.
Silent RIP hosts are not receiving routes.	RIPv2 routers are configured to multicast announcements. Silent RIP hosts never receive multicast announcements. If silent RIP hosts on a network are not receiving routes from the local RIP router, you need to verify the version of RIP supported by the silent RIP hosts. If it is the listening service in Windows NT 4.0 Service Pack 4 or Windows Server 2003, you must configure the RIP routers for RIPv1 or RIPv2 broadcasting.
RIP routers are not being updated with valid routes.	You might be deploying variable-length subnetting, disjointed subnets, or supernetting in a RIPv1 or mixed RIPv1-and-RIPv2 environment. You should not deploy variable-length subnetting, disjointed subnets, or supernetting in a RIPv1 or mixed RIPv1-and-RIPv2 environment because it is not supported.
Host or default routes are not being propagated.	By default, RIP is not configured to propagate host or default routes. If these need to be propagated, you should change the default settings on the Advanced tab of the Properties dialog box of a RIP interface.

Table 2.6 describes only some of the problems that can arise within a RIP environment. For further troubleshooting information, refer to Microsoft Technet or the Windows Server 2003 documentation.

Troubleshooting OSPF Environments

OSPF is a more complex protocol to understand than RIP. As such, there is more risk of problems arising because of the complexity of the protocol. Because OSPF is more hierarchical than other protocols, this offers an opportunity to help troubleshoot problems that can arise; you can isolate problems with a particular area or the interconnectivity between areas more easily. Table 2.7 outlines some of the problems you might face when troubleshooting OSPF.

TABLE 2.7 OSPF Problems, Potential Causes, and Possible Solutions

Problem	Cause/Solution
OSPF adjacency is not forming between two neighbors.	OSPF is not enabled on the interface. You should verify that OSPF is enabled on the interface on the network segment where an adjacency should form. By default, when you add an interface to the OSPF routing protocol, OSPF is disabled for the interface and must be manually enabled. If OSPF is enabled, you should try to `ping` the neighboring router to ensure basic IP and network connectivity. You can use the `tracert` command to trace the route to the neighboring router. No routers should exist between the neighboring routers.
A virtual link is not forming between two areas.	There could be a mismatched configuration of password, hello interval, or dead interval. You should verify that the virtual link neighbor routers are configured for the same password, hello interval, and dead interval. Another possible cause is that virtual link neighbors might be configured for the incorrect transit area ID. You should verify that both virtual link neighbors are configured for the same transit area ID and that they are configured to use the correct transit area.
Routing tables are not being updated with OSPF routes or improper OSPF routes are being received.	You might not be receiving summarized routes. If you are not receiving summarized OSPF routes for an area, you should verify that the area border routers for the area are configured with the proper destination/network mask pairs summarizing that area's routes. Another potential cause is that all area border routers are not connected to the backbone. You should verify that all area border routers are either physically connected to the backbone or logically connected to the backbone by using border routers, which are routers that connect two areas without going through the backbone.

Table 2.7 lists only some of the problems that can arise within an OSPF environment. For further troubleshooting information, refer to Microsoft TechNet or the Windows Server 2003 documentation.

Chapter Summary

In this chapter, you discovered the Routing and Remote Access capabilities of Windows Server 2003 and how to plan and design this feature into your network.

Understanding routing is critical because of its complexities and what Windows Server 2003 can do in the routing arena, using either a static router or a dynamic routing protocol. In this chapter, you also learned how to plan either type of protocol in any environment. You learned about RIP, RIPv2, and OSPF, examining how each operates and looking at their strengths and weaknesses.

This chapter described both Version 1 and Version 2 of RIP, along with specific features such as silent RIP. Features of the RIP protocol were related to the fundamental discussion of routing covered earlier in the chapter, such as distance vector and split horizon. A discussion of how RIP functions within a network environment was provided, along with a Step by Step for implementing RIP using the RRAS features of Windows Server 2003.

The second routing protocol discussed was the OSPF protocol. The chapter also described the features of OSPF and how they differ from RIP. The chapter then described the components and processes that make up the OSPF routing protocol. A discussion of how OSPF functions within a network environment was provided, along with a Step by Step for implementing OSPF using the RRAS features of Windows Server 2003 Advanced Server.

Finally, the chapter provided an overview of some of the tools for working with routing and diagnosing problems with routing. A discussion of the `route`, `ping`, `tracert`, `pathping`, and `netsh` commands and an overview of Network Monitor were provided. These tools will help you diagnose problems. In addition to an overview of the tools used, the chapter provided a brief discussion of problems that might arise with the different routing protocols and what can be done to resolve these problems. By no means was this discussion comprehensive, but it did provide insight into some of the different things to check, in case problems arise.

Key Terms

- Distance vector
- IGMP
- IGMP Proxy mode
- IGMP Routing mode
- Link state
- LSA
- Multicast

- `netsh`
- OSPF
- `ping`
- RIP
- RIP Version 2
- `route`
- Routing
- RRAS
- TCP/IP
- `tracert`

Apply Your Knowledge

In this chapter, you have examined implementing, configuring, and troubleshooting routing in Windows Server 2003. In the following exercises, you practice some of the concepts and methods discussed in this chapter.

Exercises

2.1 Enabling Routing and Remote Access

In this exercise, you enable and perform basic configuration on the Routing and Remote Access Service.

Estimated time: 15 minutes

1. Open the Routing and Remote Access console by choosing Start, Control Panel, Administrative Tools, Routing and Remote Access. By default, the local computer is listed as a server.
2. Right-click the server you want to configure and select Configure and Enable Routing and Remote Access. The Routing and Remote Access Server Setup Wizard starts.
3. Click Next to start configuring the Routing and Remote Access Service. The Configuration dialog box opens.
4. Select the Secure Connection Between Two Private Networks option and click Next to continue. The Demand-Dial Connections dialog box opens.
5. In the Demand-Dial Connections dialog box, select No and click Next to continue. The Completing the Routing and Remote Access Server Setup Wizard summary dialog box opens.
6. Click Finish to complete the enabling of routing services.

2.2 Adding a Static Route to the Existing Routing Table

This exercise explores using the `route` command to add a static route to an existing routing table. This method provides a way for you to add static routes to routing configurations.

Estimated time: 10 minutes

1. From the command prompt, enter route ADD 157.0.0.0 MASK 255.0.0.0 157.55.80.1 METRIC 3 IF 2.
2. Type **`route print`** to examine the new route in the routing table.

2.3 Adding RIP to the Routing and Remote Access Service

In this exercise, you add RIP as a dynamic routing protocol for use on your Windows Server 2003 RRAS computer.

Estimated time: 15 minutes

1. Open the Routing and Remote Access console.
2. In the left pane, expand the list under IP Routing and right-click General. From the context menu, select New Routing Protocol. The New Routing Protocol dialog box opens.
3. Select RIP Version 2 for Internet Protocol and click OK. RIP appears under the IP Routing entry. RIP is now installed on your Windows Server 2003 server.
4. Right-click the RIP entry and select New Interface from the context menu. The New Interface for RIP Version 2 for Internet Protocol dialog box opens.
5. Select the appropriate local area connection and click OK. The RIP Properties dialog box opens.
6. On the General tab, in Outgoing Packet Protocol, select RIP Version 1 Broadcast. In Incoming Packet Protocol, select RIP Version 1 and 2. Click OK to return to the Routing and Remote Access console and activate the changes.

2.4 Implementing Silent RIP

In this exercise, you implement silent RIP on your Windows Server 2003 RRAS computer.

Estimated time: 15 minutes

1. Open the Routing and Remote Access console.
2. Expand the console tree and select RIP. The list of available interfaces running RIP appears in the right pane of the console.
3. Right-click the interface that you want to configure for silent RIP mode, and from the context menu, select Properties. The Local Area Connection Properties dialog box opens.
4. On the General tab, in Outgoing Packet Protocol, select Silent RIP from the pull-down menu. Click OK to return to the Routing and Remote Access console and apply the changes.

2.5 Adding OSPF to the Routing and Remote Access Service

In this exercise, you add OSPF as a dynamic routing protocol for use on your Windows Server 2003 RRAS computer.

Estimated time: 15 minutes

1. Open the Routing and Remote Access console.
2. Expand the console tree and, under IP Routing, right-click General. From the context menu, select New Routing Protocol. The New Routing Protocol dialog box opens.
3. Select Open Shortest Path First and click OK to install it. It now appears under IP Routing in the Routing and Remote Access console.
4. Select the newly installed OSPF protocol and right-click. From the context menu, select New Interface. The New Interface for Open Shortest Path First (OSPF) dialog box opens.
5. Select Local Area Connection and click OK. The OSPF Properties dialog box opens.
6. On the General tab, select the Enable OSPF for This Address option. In Area ID, click the ID of the area to which the interface belongs (for this exercise, it should be 0.0.0.0). In Router Priority, click the arrows to set the priority of the router over the interface to 1. In Cost, click the scroll arrows to set the cost of sending a packet over the interface to 2. In Password, type a password. Under Network Type, set the type of OSPF interface as Broadcast. Click OK to complete the installation of the interface and return to the Routing and Remote Access console.

Review Questions

1. What is one reason link-state protocols are more efficient than distance-vector algorithms?
2. Several of your Windows 2000 Professional clients cannot access a server on a remote network segment that is separated by two routers. What can you do to test to see where the problem is occurring?
3. What ID is reserved for the OSPF backbone?
4. You are running three Windows Server 2003 computers in a network that needs to participate in multicast routing. You cannot add a multicast routing protocol to your server, but you are able to add a forwarding protocol. If you needed to add a routing protocol for multicast, what protocol would you recommend using?
5. You are a systems administrator responsible for deploying Windows Server 2003 in your network. You need a routing solution (in the form of a protocol) that will allow for massive scalability, that is dynamic in nature, and that will be scalable past 20 router hops. What routing protocol would you choose?

Exam Questions

1. As the lead administrator for the ABC LLC network, you are responsible for planning a TCP/IP network that is robust and functional. You have a total of 450 clients spread out over three locations. You have 150 clients per location, and at one central location, you have approximately 25 servers. You are asked to deploy a routing solution using Windows Server 2003. Your requirements are to give two different subnetted segments access to each other using Windows Server 2003. You would like to use a routing solution that is simple and that will forward traffic from one location to another without keeping too many unneeded routes in the table. Which of the following options represents the best choice?

   ❍ **A.** RIP

   ❍ **B.** OSPF

   ❍ **C.** IGMP

   ❍ **D.** Static routes

2. Marshall is the network administrator for QBC Corp. He runs a network of 20 Windows Server 2003 systems on a network backbone, as well as 200 Windows XP Professional clients. Marshall is worried about connectivity to the corporate network, which extensively uses multicasting for video services. He is asked to deploy a Windows Server 2003 solution so that it can participate in the multicast routing function. Which of the following options represents the best choice?

   ❍ **A.** IGMP routing mode

   ❍ **B.** DVMRP route static

   ❍ **C.** Static IP routes

   ❍ **D.** OSPF

3. Jake is the senior network administrator for your organization. He is responsible for 200 Windows XP Professional clients and 15 Windows Server 2003 systems located on a network backbone running at 100 Mbps. Jake needs to build a Windows Server 2003 system into a router connecting four subnets, and he needs to participate in a Cisco Router environment running the Enhanced Interior Gateway Routing Protocol (EIGRP) protocol. What can Jake configure on the Windows Server 2003 system to get it to pass routing updates from the Cisco routers to the four subnets connected?

   ❍ **A.** RIP

   ❍ **B.** OSPF

   ❍ **C.** EIGRP

   ❍ **D.** Jake can't use EIGRP

4. You are the network administrator of the ABC Company, and you currently have a network client that cannot access network resources that are on a separate subnet across the WAN. When you talk to the user on the phone, you find out that there is no break in the cable and the link lights on the NIC are operational. You then try to `ping` the default gateway router, and you get a response that the router is up and functional. What would be the next option you can try to find out where the breakdown in communication is coming from?

❍ **A.** `Ping` the next-hop router.

❍ **B.** Run `tracert` to the default gateway.

❍ **C.** Use `netsh` at the `routing>` prompt and type **`TEST`**.

❍ **D.** Run `pathping` to the default gateway.

5. Pete is the systems administrator for RDT, Inc. He runs a network of 25 Windows Server 2003 systems on a network backbone, as well as 300 Windows XP Professional clients. Pete needs to set up a Windows Server 2003 router with multicast forwarding capabilities. He has a specific requirement to configure the router with different settings on different interfaces. To do this, Pete must configure the router in which mode?

❍ **A.** IGMP Router mode

❍ **B.** IGMP Proxy mode

❍ **C.** IGMP Cancel mode

❍ **D.** IGMP Split mode

6. You are the network administrator of the Genie in a Bottle screensaver company. The company has a large corporate network that is using OSPF as the routing protocol. The company was just acquired by a competitor that is also using OSPF to route within its network. You are charged with bringing the two networks together, and you establish a virtual link with the other network. However, the virtual link is not forming. What could be the problem? (Choose all that apply.)

❍ **A.** The router on the other side has been set up to filter routes, so the virtual link will take time to be established.

❍ **B.** The password for each of the two routers is different.

❍ **C.** The router interfaces on each router are set to different connection speeds.

❍ **D.** The router is configured with a hello interval that is different from the other router's.

7. You are the lead network engineer for White Clouds Airlines. The company has 55 offices, located throughout the United States, all connected to the corporate WAN with a mixture of hardware routers and Windows Server 2003 servers running RRAS for routing. The network is configured to use a mix of RIPv1 and RIPv2. You notice that routing tables have improper routing information. Which of the following is the most likely cause of this problem?

❍ **A.** RIPv2 routers are configured to multicast announcements. Multicast RIPv1 and RIPv2 announcements are never received by RIPv1 routers.

❍ **B.** RIPv2 routers are configured to multicast announcements. Multicast announcements are never received by RIPv1 hosts.

❍ **C.** By default, RIP is not configured to propagate host or default routes.

❍ **D.** On a network of this size, you must use OSPF to ensure that hardware and software routers have the correct routing table information.

8. Pete is the systems administrator for RDT, Inc. He runs a network of 25 Windows Server 2003 systems on a network backbone, as well as 300 Windows XP Professional clients. Pete needs to work on testing a router that is 16 hops away. Pete's network runs the Routing Information Protocol (RIP). Every time Pete tries to get to and connect to the router, he times out and can't connect to it. What could be the problem?

❍ **A.** The router can't be reached because it is more than 12 hops away; RIP can handle only a 12-hop count limit.

❍ **B.** The router can't be reached because it is more than 13 hops away; RIP can handle only a 13-hop count limit.

❍ **C.** The router can't be reached because it is more than 14 hops away; RIP can handle only a 14-hop count limit.

❍ **D.** The router can't be reached because it is more than 15 hops away; RIP can handle only a 15-hop count limit.

9. You are the LAN administrator for Gonzo Candy, a lollipop manufacturer. You have three office locations, each with its own Windows Server 2003 servers. Each office has a local LAN that is very stable, and the company has no plans to add locations for the next three years. There are plans to network the three locations by using the existing Windows Server 2003 servers and ISDN lines. You have been asked to design a solution that will have the lowest impact on the servers, with no requirements for redundancy or failover. What routing method should you select?

❍ **A.** Static routes

❍ **B.** RIP

❍ **C.** OSPF

❍ **D.** BGP

10. Jason is the network administrator for QBC Corp. He runs a network of 20 Windows Server 2003 systems on a network backbone, as well as 200 Windows XP Professional clients. Jason has a PC on a remote network segment that is separated by two routers. Users are complaining of slow connections and time-out errors when attempting to connect to this remote PC. Jason needs to see where the trouble might be occurring on the network and also needs to find out why people are complaining of timed-out sessions on their applications. There must be a bandwidth problem as well. Which tool should he use to troubleshoot and resolve this problem?

- A. `tracert`
- B. `pathping`
- C. `ping`
- D. `route`

11. You are the lead administrator for Red Rabbit Motors, a chain of car dealerships. Red Rabbit has 14 locations and is using OSPF as part of its WAN implementation. You are training a new WAN engineer on supporting the WAN, and she asks for the correct name of the area with an ID of 0.0.0.0. What do you call this area?

    - A. The AS
    - B. The LSDB
    - C. The OSPF backbone
    - D. The root area
    - E. The default route

12. You are a system administrator for Belmont Technical College, which has a campus network that is very large and growing. You are in the process of reengineering the network, and you remove some segments from the overall network topology. Your network makes use of RIP to route information throughout the infrastructure. Users indicate that they cannot reach some segments on the network. As you investigate the problem, you determine that some of the routers do not have any information about other routers in the network. What could be the problem? (Choose all that apply.)

    - A. RIP is not propagating information.
    - B. RIP cannot support more than 15 hops.
    - C. RIP is suffering from a count-to-infinity problem.
    - D. The routers that are not reachable are not functioning properly.

13. You are the network administrator of Bombastic Publishing, a medium-size publishing company. You are receiving calls from people at the help desk, indicating that they cannot get access to the server. You check into it and determine that you cannot `ping` the server across the router. You check the router, and the services seem as though they are started and running fine. You would now like to check the routing tables. Which utilities can you use to determine what the routing tables contain? (Choose all that apply.)

    - A. The Routing and Remote Access console
    - B. The `route` command
    - C. The `tracert` command
    - D. The `arp` command

14. You are the network administrator for QBC Corp. The company has a network of 25 Windows Server 2003 systems on a network backbone, as well as 300 Windows XP Professional clients. You need to reset the IP address of your router quickly from the command line. Which utility should you use?

    ❍ **A.** `ping`

    ❍ **B.** `tracert`

    ❍ **C.** `route`

    ❍ **D.** `netsh`

Answers to Review Questions

1. A link-state routing protocol is generally more efficient than a distance-vector protocol. The fact that LSAs contain only information about the neighbors of a particular router leads to smaller routing tables. For large networks, the LSAs contain only neighbor information; therefore, the impact on the network is much less than it would be on a network using a distance-vector routing protocol. With a distance-vector routing protocol, all the routes in a routing table are propagated, resulting in more bandwidth use than with link-state protocols. In addition, because link-state information is not exchanged after the network has converged, it does not have the impact on the network that distance-vector routing does. By default, distance-vector routing broadcasts its information on a periodic basis, whether the information is required or not. For more information, see the section "Distance Vector Versus Link State."

2. If you are not able to access a segment that is separated from you by two routers or more, you can easily see where the breakdown in communications is occurring by using `tracert`. You can also use `ping` or `pathping` for diagnostics, but `tracert` enables you to trace the route to the destination to see where the break in communication might be. For more information, see the section "Troubleshooting TCP/IP Routing."

3. An OSPF backbone has a reserved area ID of 0.0.0.0. An OSPF backbone is responsible for distributing routing information between areas. At least one backbone exists per OSPF internetwork. It consists of all area border routers, networks that are not in any one area, and their attached routers. The backbone has to be at the center of all areas within the AS. That is, all areas have to be physically connected to the backbone. This is because OSPF expects all areas to inject routing information into the backbone; in turn, the backbone will disseminate that information into other areas. For more information, see the section "Implementing OSPF Routing."

4. If you want to participate in multicast routing, you can add the IGMP routing protocol to your Windows Server 2003 system in Routing and Remote Access. For more information, see the section "Planning Routing for IP Multicast Traffic."

5. You should deploy Open Shortest Path First (OSPF), a link state–based dynamic routing protocol that you can install and use on Windows Server 2003. You use this protocol if you want to be able to scale the network up, as well as to go beyond the 15-hop count limit that RIP imposes. For more information, see the section "OSPF."

Answers to Exam Questions

1. **D.** RIP and OSPF are routing protocols and IGMP is a multicast protocol, so answers A, B, and C are incorrect. For more information, see the section "RIP."

2. **A.** IGMP routing mode is not a multicast routing protocol, but a forwarding-based multicast protocol. DVMRP is a multicast routing protocol; static IP routes will do nothing for multicast forwarding; and OSPF is a dynamic routing protocol, not a multicast-based protocol, although it sends its updates via multicast. Therefore, answers B, C, and D are incorrect. For more information, see the section "Planning Routing for IP Multicast Traffic."

3. **D.** RIP and OSPF will not work because all routing protocols must be redistributed via another routing protocol or must be identical. EIGRP is not an option either because it is vendor specific and does not work with Microsoft Windows Server 2003. Therefore, answers A, B, and C are incorrect. For more information, see the section "Planning a Routing Environment."

4. **A.** Running `tracert` to the Default gateway will not give you the desired result; thus, answer B is incorrect. Using `netsh` at the `routing>` prompt and typing **`TEST`** will not work because it is really an invalid command; thus, answer C is incorrect. Running `pathping` to the default gateway also will not provide the desired result; thus, answer D is incorrect. For more information, see the section "The `ping` Command."

5. **B.** Although IGMP Router mode is a valid Windows Server 2003 router mode for forwarding multicast traffic, it is not the correct mode to solve the solution; thus, answer A is incorrect. IGMP Cancel mode and IGMP Split mode are not valid modes; thus, answers C and D are incorrect. For more information, see the section "Planning Routing for IP Multicast Traffic."

6. **B**, **D**. To establish a virtual link between the two organizations, it is necessary to ensure that the password, the hello interval, and the dead interval are configured to be the same. If they are not configured this way, the virtual link will have trouble being established. For more information, see the section "Planning the Correct Routing Protocol to Use."

7. **A.** RIPv1 will never receive multicast announcements from RIPv2 routers. If you have a mixed environment of RIPv1 and RIPv2, you need to ensure that the routers configured with RIPv2 are using broadcast instead of multicast announcements. For more information, see the section "Troubleshooting RIP Environments."

8. **D.** The router can't be reached because it is more than 15 hops away, and RIP can handle only a 15-hop count limit. All the other answers have the wrong hop count. For more information, see the section "RIP."

9. **A**. Because you are working with a small, static network and you are tasked with using the solution that has the lowest impact on resources, using static routes is the correct solution. For more information, see the section "Planning a Routing Environment."

10. **B.** The `pathping`, `tracert`, and `route` commands are all valid troubleshooting tools, but `pathping` solves the problem the best. For more information, see the section "The `pathping` Command."

11. **C**. The area with the ID 0.0.0.0 is the OSPF backbone. For more information, see the section "OSPF."

12. **B**, **C**. In this scenario, segments are being removed from the overall network; nothing is noted about routers or segments being added. This indicates that the problem could indeed be a count-to-infinity problem; therefore, answer C is correct. Because infinity is 15 hops, answer B is also correct. For more information, see the section "Planning the Correct Routing Protocol to Use."

13. **A**, **B**. The two utilities that can be used to check routing tables are the RRAS administration tool and the `route` command. You use the `print` option to display the existing routes. The `tracert` command is used to determine reachability through the network. The `arp` command is used to display the IP–to–physical address table. For more information, see the section "The `route` Command."

14. **D**. You can use `netsh` to add an IP interface and a wealth of other solutions right from the command line. This way, you can quickly change many things on your system. `ping`, `tracert`, and `route` are all incorrect tool options; thus, answers A, B, and C are incorrect. For more information, see the section "The `netsh` Command."

Suggested Readings and Resources

1. Microsoft Corporation. *Microsoft Windows Server 2003 Resource Kit.* Redmond, WA: Microsoft Press, 2003.

2. Microsoft Corporation. *Microsoft Windows Server 2003 Deployment Kit.* Redmond, WA: Microsoft Press, 2003.

3. Davies, Joseph, and Thomas Lee. *Microsoft Windows Server 2003 TCP/IP Protocols and Services Technical Reference.* Redmond, WA: Microsoft Press, 2003.

4. Doyle, Jeff. *Routing TCP/IP Volume I (CCIE Professional Development)*. Indianapolis: Cisco Press, 1998.

5. Thomas, Tom M. *OSPF Network Design Solutions*. Indianapolis: Cisco Press, 2003.

6. Moy, John T. *OSPF Complete Implementation*. Boston: Addison-Wesley, 2000.

7. Windows Server 2003 RFC Checklist at www.rfc-editor.org/rfc.html:

    - RIP RFC 1058
    - RIP (Updated) RFC 1388
    - OSPF RFC 1247
    - OSPF Version 2 RFC 1583
    - DVMRP RFC 1075
    - MOSPF RFC 1584
    - IGMP RFC 2236

CHAPTER THREE

Planning, Implementing, and Troubleshooting DHCP

The Dynamic Host Configuration Protocol (DHCP) is one of those services that has proven itself as a valued solution on TCP/IP networks of all sizes and complexities. With the advent of DHCP, gone are the days administrators previously faced of manually providing and tracking IP addresses for hundreds or thousands (or even hundreds of thousands) of network clients. This chapter examines the DHCP service and how it is planned for and implemented in a Windows Server 2003 environment.

Although no exam objectives are directly addressed in this chapter, we felt the material presented here was still relevant enough to warrant coverage. Additionally, it's not out of the realm of possibilities that you will need to understand the information presented here on test day (and after) as you carry out your day-to-day administrative activities. Please do take the time to read through this chapter, as you stand a good chance of having at least one question on your exam that deals directly or indirectly with the planning, implementation, or troubleshooting of the DHCP service.

Outline

Introduction

TCP/IP is the de facto standard for computer networking and appears to have no challengers in the networking protocol arena. If you are going to work with Windows Server 2003, you should expect to work with TCP/IP. One of the keys to successfully working with TCP/IP is understanding the concept of TCP/IP addresses. The designers of TCP/IP wanted an identification scheme that was independent of any one computer or network equipment design, so they established a scheme of IP addresses.

If you've ever surfed the web, you have probably seen IP addresses (numbers such as 192.168.144.77). As you administer TCP/IP on a network, a considerable part of your time will be devoted to IP address assignment because IP addresses don't just magically get assigned to network hosts—they have to be provided through manual configuration or some other means. When a computer is added to a network, it needs an IP address to communicate on that network. When the computer moves to a new location, it likely will need a new IP address. If you are just starting out managing a large TCP/IP network, you might find the notion of managing all those addresses a bit daunting. If you move a DNS server to a new subnet, you might have to reconfigure every client computer. If you move a client computer to a new subnet, you might have to update its IP address. This does not endear you to road warriors who travel among several offices, especially those who are regional managers. If you manually manage IP addresses, almost any change to the network will require a visit to one or more computers to update TCP/IP configurations—not a happy prospect. Fortunately, the people who brought us DNS to replace the `hosts` file also came up with a solution to this dilemma.

DHCP was the Internet community's answer to dynamically distributing IP addresses. DHCP is open and standards-based, as defined by the Internet Engineering Task Force (IETF) in their Requests for Comments (RFCs) 2131 and 2132. (The IETF is the main standards organization for the Internet.) This chapter examines the basics of DHCP as it applies to you, the systems administrator, and how you can use it to make your life and your network better.

Understanding DHCP

Public IP addresses are registered with the Internet Assigned Numbers Authority (IANA) so that IANA can keep track of IP addresses that are being used on the Internet. In some cases, a network is not connected to the Internet and does not need to use registered public IP addresses. In other cases, the network is connected to the Internet with special hardware and software that can be configured to allow the network to use private addresses in conjunction with address translation, commonly referred to as Network Address Translation (NAT). By using NAT, you can (in simple terms) place an entire private network behind a single public IP address. As an example, the organization I work for has more than 5,000 hosts on its internal network. When I or anyone else visits a website on the Internet, we all appear to be coming from a single IP address. That's NAT in action!

NOTE

What are RFCs? RFCs are used to propose changes to existing standards and to help create new standards that specify the way the Internet and IP behave. If an RFC can garner enough interest, it might eventually become a standard. Topics of RFCs range from File Transfer Protocol (FTP; originally RFC 0114 but updated by RFC 0141, RFC 0172, and RFC 0171) to the *Hitchhiker's Guide to the Internet* (RFC 1118). The first RFC was posted in 1969 by Steve Crocker, and the topic of that document was host software. You can find listings of all the RFCs at a number of sites throughout the Internet. One place is www.rfc-editor.org.

Quite often, systems administrators use private (unregistered) addresses on their internal networks to ensure that there are enough readily available addresses for all users. This model works great on a network that is not tied directly to the Internet. However, with the shortage of Class A and Class B (and even Class C) IP addresses, some environments use small pools of registered addresses to service larger numbers of DHCP clients; the idea is that not every client computer needs access simultaneously. These environments require aggressive leasing policies to ensure that everyone can get an address.

In addition to IP addresses, DHCP can provide gateway addresses, DNS server addresses, and Windows Internet Name Service (WINS) server addresses—in essence, everything the client computer needs to participate in the network. This means that all available IP addresses can be stored in a central database, along with associated configuration information such as the subnet masks, gateways, and addresses of DNS servers.

DHCP

DHCP provides the mechanism for dynamically distributing IP addresses on a network—but it doesn't happen magically. Here's how a client computer gets an address:

1. After bootup, the client computer broadcasts a `DHCPDISCOVER` message that is intended for the DHCP server(s) on the network. If a router sits between the DHCP server and the client, it needs to be configured with the IP address of the DHCP server and also be configured to forward BOOTP. BOOTP is discussed in the next section, "BOOTP."
2. Each DHCP server that receives the `DHCPDISCOVER` message responds with a DHCP offer message. That message includes an IP address that is appropriate for the subnet where the client computer is attached. The DHCP server determines the appropriate address by looking at the source subnet for the broadcast `DHCPDISCOVER` message.
3. The client computer considers the offer messages and selects one (usually the first offer it receives). It sends a request (`DHCPREQUEST`) to use the address to the DHCP server that originated the offer. If there are multiple DHCP servers, they need to be carefully configured. It is easy to inadvertently configure servers and end up with them conflicting, so if you have multiple DHCP servers on a network, they should not be capable of

offering duplicate IP addresses. Because DHCP servers do not communicate with one another, they have no way of telling whether another DHCP server has already issued an address.

4. The DHCP server acknowledges the request and grants the client computer a lease to use the address.
5. The client computer uses the IP address to bind to the network. If the IP address is associated with any configuration parameters, the parameters are incorporated into the client computer's TCP/IP configuration.
6. For the first renewal of the IP address, when 50% of the configured lease time has elapsed, the client sends another `DHCPREQUEST` message to the DHCP server that granted its lease, asking to renew and extend its current lease. All subsequent lease renewal is at 75%.
7. If the DHCP server is reachable, it responds with a `DHCPACK` message to the client, renewing and extending the DHCP lease as requested.
8. If the DHCP server is not reachable, the client continues trying to reach it until 87.5% of the lease time has elapsed. At this point, the client attempts to renew its lease with any DHCP server that responds. If this is unsuccessful, the client starts the process of acquiring a new DHCP lease.

TIP

DHCP solitude Be sure to remember that DHCP servers do not communicate with one another; therefore, they have no way of telling whether another DHCP server has already issued an address. For this reason, you will never create identical DHCP scopes on multiple DHCP servers.

The first step of this process indicates that DHCP clients request their addresses by using broadcast messages. If you are familiar with routing, particularly TCP/IP routing, you are probably familiar with the fact that one of the benefits of routing is that the router segregates broadcast domains. In other words, broadcasts do not generally cross routers. Does that mean that DHCP works only on the local segment and you need 50 DHCP servers for 50 subnets? No, that is not the case—not if you configure your routers or other Windows Server 2003 computers to act as DHCP relay agents.

Configuring a router or server as a DHCP relay agent causes it to begin using BOOTP. BOOTP was the precursor to DHCP, and it was the first protocol used to assign IP addresses dynamically. BOOTP was specially designed to pass across a router, and it continues to be used to allow DHCP broadcasts to propagate across routers. You'll learn about the installation and configuration of DHCP relay agents later in this chapter, in the section "Configuring and Implementing a DHCP Relay Agent."

BOOTP

Before we discuss installing and configuring the DHCP service in Windows Server 2003, a brief discussion about BOOTP is necessary. A number of DHCP's features had their beginnings in BOOTP. BOOTP was originally designed in 1985 by Bill Croft and John Gilmore to automate the configuration of network devices. To use BOOTP, the systems administrator must create a table with a list of client computers, their IP addresses, and their network configurations. When a client computer comes on to the network, it broadcasts a request that the BOOTP server receives. The BOOTP server looks up the client computer in the table and responds with the configuration information stored in the table, allowing the client computer to communicate on the network.

Because BOOTP worked well, it was used extensively in the early 1990s in conjunction with diskless workstations. (A BOOTP chip was a common option on a network interface card [NIC], and many networks thrived on BOOTP.) The downside of BOOTP was that it provided only the configuration information entered in the table. The administrator still needed to configure the table. The limitations of BOOTP effectively prevented any automation of these tasks, so it was eventually replaced with DHCP. BOOTP and DHCP packets look virtually identical, and DHCP even takes advantage of the BOOTP forwarder functionality of many routers and switches. DHCP offers the automation features BOOTP lacked.

Now that we've completed the history lesson, you should have a pretty good understanding of the theory of DHCP. Before moving on to the workings of DHCP in Windows Server 2003, let's examine the new DHCP features that Windows Server 2003 provides.

What's New with Windows Server 2003 DHCP

DHCP is not a new service in Windows Server 2003, but it has undergone some changes from both Windows 2000 and Windows NT 4.0. The following list summarizes some of the major changes in DHCP in Windows Server 2003, as compared to Windows 2000 Server and Windows NT 4.0:

- **DHCP integration in DNS**—Windows Server 2003 DHCP servers can trigger dynamic updates in the DNS database for all clients to which it leases IP addresses. Windows 2000 and newer clients can automatically update their DNS records if they are authorized to do so. Legacy clients can have their records updated by the DHCP server if it is authorized to do so.

- **Rogue DHCP server detection**—Unauthorized, or *rogue*, DHCP servers can cause a wide variety of problems, including denial of service (DoS) to clients. To prevent such problems, Windows Server 2003 provides for authorizing DHCP servers and detecting and shutting down unauthorized servers. Active Directory is required for the detection of rogue DHCP servers to occur.

- **Superscope and multicast scope support**—Superscopes enable you to group several standard DHCP scopes into a single administrative group without causing any service disruption to network clients. Multicast scopes enable you to lease Class D IP addresses to clients for participation in multicast transmissions, such as streaming video and audio transmissions. Multicast scopes are discussed in more detail in the section "Understanding Multicasting and Multicast Scopes," later in this chapter.
- **Local security groups for DHCP management**—Two new local administrative security groups are created when the DHCP service is installed: DHCP Users and DHCP Administrators. The DHCP Users group can be used to provide read-only console access to the server to enable group members to view but not modify DHCP data. The DHCP Administrators group provides full administrative control of the DHCP service without granting its members full administrative control over the entire server.
- **Improved monitoring and reporting**—DHCP is a critical network service that must be kept running. The key to discovering problems early is monitoring, so Windows Server 2003 provides a full set of performance-monitoring counters that can be used to monitor DHCP server performance.
- **Custom DHCP option classes**—User- and vendor-specified option classes can be used to distribute specific options to the clients that need them. For example, you can use option classes to distribute a specific default gateway or parent domain name to one group of computers on a network.
- **In-console backup and restore**—For the first time ever, Windows Server 2003 provides the administrator with the capability to perform DHCP scope backups and restorations from within the DHCP console itself.

Now that we've briefly examined the improvements made in the DHCP service in Windows Server 2003, we need to spend some time examining four of the more basic parts of planning for a new DHCP implementation.

Planning for DHCP

Unless you want to go back to manually assigning and tracking IP addresses for all clients on your network, DHCP is going to be a very important network service for you. As such, it requires some time spent evaluating the needs of the current and future environment you support. When properly planned and implemented up front, DHCP typically continues to function as intended for many years into the future.

Planning a DHCP Infrastructure Type

Before you can get down to the task of planning how many DHCP servers you'll need, where you'll put them, or how you'll configure the scopes and options, you need to first understand what type of network infrastructure you have and how DHCP will fit into it. In general, organizations make use of three basic types of network infrastructures: centralized, distributed, and mixed. Your DHCP design also typically makes use of one of these three models.

Centralized Infrastructures

The most common model used today is the centralized infrastructure model. In this model, your DHCP servers (along with most other network services) are located in a central location. Clients at remote locations or on other subnets (or other broadcast domains) need to use a DHCP relay agent to contact a DHCP server. Almost all modern routers in use today can be configured as a DHCP relay agent, thus passing the DHCP broadcast traffic from the remote subnet to the subnet where the DHCP servers are located.

As an example, an organization I've had experience with has multiple subnets configured for their campus, one for each building where clients are located. These subnets were implemented through VLANs, and all of the VLANs were trunked together to form a single broadcast domain. Because no routers are required to pass traffic from one subnet (VLAN) to another, no DHCP relay agents are required anywhere on the network. In this example, the organization has two DHCP servers configured in their data centers to provide DHCP for the entire network.

Distributed Infrastructures

In the distribution infrastructure model, each subnet (or VLAN) has its own DHCP server located locally. This model does have the advantage of keeping DHCP traffic off WAN links, which are almost always slower and less reliable than a LAN. Of course, the disadvantage to this distributed infrastructure is that you must have many more DHCP servers on your network, so you have more areas of concern to manage and monitor.

As an example, another organization I've had experience with also has multiple subnets configured on their network through VLANs, but their network is very distributed and each VLAN maps directly to a single remote location. Each remote site has a WAN link for access to the main location, and each location has a router and switch (or multiple switches) at that location to support local and remote traffic. In this scenario, the local core switches themselves provide DHCP service to the site instead of using Windows Server 2003 DHCP servers, so the extra cost of using this model is fairly low. Your experiences with distributed infrastructures might be very different, however.

Mixed Infrastructures

As you might have guessed, a mixed infrastructure combines features of the centralized and distributed infrastructure models. Using the mixed infrastructure model, you can plan for DHCP server placement on a location-by-location basis that makes the most sense for each location. When using the mixed infrastructure model, you will likely still have two or more DHCP servers in your central data center, but you'll also have one or more DHCP servers locally in remote locations where you have large client populations, for example.

Planning a DHCP Server Placement Strategy

You've probably heard before that you should use either the 70/30 or the 80/20 rule when planning and implementing DHCP on your network. But what exactly do these rules mean? Is it even correct to assume that using one of these rules is always the correct answer? As you no doubt know by now, there are no absolutes in network design—only best practices that have typically been proven to yield consistently high quality results when implemented properly. As such, you cannot just blindly follow either the 70/30 or the 80/20 rule in your DHCP design. In this section, we examine some items you'll want to consider when planning the placement of DHCP servers on your network.

The DHCP Rules

The real question you have to answer before deciding on a DHCP server rule is whether you will have multiple DHCP servers on multiple subnets. If so, you should consider using either the 70/30 or the 80/20 rule. These rules break up your DHCP scope ranges so that 70% (or 80%) of the available IP addresses in a scope range are configured on the DHCP server on the local subnet, with the remaining 30% (or 20%) of the available IP addresses in a scope range configured on a DHCP server located on a different subnet. Different subnets are typically broken up by switches or routers, and each subnet is a single broadcast domain, so this design strategy works well. DHCP is a broadcast-based system; by default, clients will find the DHCP server on their local subnet and obtain a lease, if available, from that local DHCP server.

On the other hand, if you will be placing your DHCP servers on the same subnet, you will want to follow the 50/50 rule, with each DHCP server containing half of the available IP addresses in the scope range. This model also works well in large organizations that have multiple VLANs and use VLAN trunking and a subnet mask that creates a single large broadcast domain. Although this is not a common design on the network side, when it is done properly, it can work well. When using the 50/50 rule for DHCP servers, you typically have more IP addresses available within your organization than are needed; either DHCP server will be capable of servicing the entire organization if the other fails.

The rules we've discussed here seem to imply using only two DHCP servers, which, in most organizations is adequate, but you can extend this logic to four, six, eight, or more DHCP servers. It's obviously easier to work with DHCP servers in pairs of two, but you should use the number that is best for your organization.

Creating Standby Servers

If you choose to follow one of the rules we discussed previously—80/20, 70/30 or 50/50—you might not need to worry about having a standby server configured. If you use a single DHCP server for your organization, you should seriously consider configuring and implementing a hot standby DHCP server. This standby DHCP server should be installed and configured identically to your production DHCP server, including all scopes and options, but will not provide DHCP leases until you manually configure it to do so.

You can either configure and enable all scopes and options but not authorize the DHCP server in Active Directory, or authorize the DHCP server in Active Directory but not enable any scopes to stage the standby server for when it is needed. As a practical matter, it is simpler (and quicker) to have all the scopes configured and enabled, but have the server itself not authorized in Active Directory. Note that although a standby server ensures that you can continue to provide DHCP if the primary DHCP server becomes unavailable, this is a manual method that requires an administrator to enable the standby DHCP server to function and provide leases to clients. For that reason, you should consider the standby server model as a nonpreferred one and instead use multiple DHCP servers to provide services, as discussed previously.

Clustering DHCP Servers

DHCP in Windows Server 2003 is a clustering-aware application; therefore, you can implement and configure DHCP servers in a cluster arrangement for maximum fault tolerance and failover. When you implement DHCP in a cluster, you do not need to use the 70/30 or 80/20 rules. In this implementation, you can opt to use the 50/50 rule for maximum fault tolerance or just place the entire scope range on a single DHCP virtual server. Clustering, which is discussed in more detail in Chapter 10, "Planning, Implementing, and Maintaining Highly Available Servers," does have some very high hardware and software resource requirements, however, so it is not the right or best solution for every organization.

Planning for DHCP Reservations

Although it is perfectly acceptable—and preferred—for most client workstations to use DHCP and get a randomly assigned IP address, sometimes you will want to use DHCP to assign the same IP address to a specific network object every time. Enter the DHCP reservation. A DHCP reservation is configured in a specific DHCP zone by entering the MAC address of network adapter installed in the client (printer, workstation, network hardware) that you want to have the same DHCP assigned IP address every time. Using reservations allows the client to be configured for DHCP, but still get a static IP address and other information being passed by the DHCP server as part of that scope where the reservation was configured.

Although it sounds like you might want to use DHCP reservations for every client on your network that requires a static IP address, this is not always the case. It's still best practice to always assign a static IP address to any Windows server that will be providing a network service such as DNS, WINS, DHCP, Exchange, SQL or Active Directory. In fact, services such as DNS and DHCP will actually "complain" about the network adapters installed in the server being configured for DHCP and not having a static network address. Most organizations that actually make use of DHCP reservations tend to use them for workstations that need the same IP address all the time or for printers on the network. In reality, most organizations still configure networked printers with a static IP address.

Planning for DHCP Options

A DHCP scope is not just a range of IP addresses that can be handed out to requesting clients—it's also a full suite of TCP/IP configuration information that the clients need to communicate effectively on the network. When you create your DHCP scopes, you can configure common DHCP scope options—be sure that you do, or your clients will likely not be able to communicate effectively.

Table 3.1 presents some of the most commonly used DHCP scope options configured.

TABLE 3.1 Common DHCP Scope Options

Code	Option Name	Option Description
3	Router	Specifies a list of IP addresses for routers on the client's subnet
4	Time Server	Specifies a list of RFC 868 time servers available to the client
6	DNS Servers	Specifies a list of DNS servers available to the client
15	DNS Domain Name	Specifies the domain name that the client should use when resolving host names via DNS
27	All Subnets Are Local	Specifies whether the client can assume that all subnets of the IP network to which the client is connected use the same MTU as the subnet of the network to which the client is directly connected
28	Broadcast Address	Specifies the broadcast address in use on the client's subnet
44	WINS/NBNS Servers	Specifies a list of RFC 1001/1002 NBNS servers, listed in order of preference
46	WINS/NBT Node Type	Allows NetBT clients, which can be configured as described in RFC 1001/1002

DHCP has a provision for configuring manufacturer-specific DHCP options. You can select these options by opening the DHCP management console and selecting the scope for which to configure options, as described later in Step by Step 3.3. Selecting the Advanced tab enables you to select Microsoft Options from the drop-down list in the Vendor Class window. Table 3.2 shows the manufacturer options that Microsoft defines.

TABLE 3.2 Microsoft-Specific DHCP Options

Code	Option Name	Description
1	Microsoft Disable NetBIOS	This option can be used to selectively enable or disable NetBT for DHCP-enabled computers running Windows.
2	Microsoft Release DHCP Lease on Shutdown	This option can be used to control whether DHCP-enabled computers running Windows send a release for their current DHCP lease to the DHCP server when shutdown occurs.
3	Microsoft Default Router Metric Base	This value is a specified router metric base to be used for all default gateway routes.

You can configure DHCP options at four different levels for each DHCP server:

- **Server options**—These are DHCP options that are applied, by default, to all scopes on the DHCP server.
- **Scope options**—These are DHCP options that are applied only to the specific scope on the DHCP server. When a scope option conflicts with a server option, the scope option wins and that value is made a part of the scope. If the conflicting scope option is later removed, the server option once again becomes effective in the scope.
- **Class options**—These are DHCP options that are applied only to clients identified as members of specified user or vendor classes.
- **Reservation options**—These are DHCP options that are applied only to a single specific computer.

Now that we've done some initial planning for an implementation of the DHCP service in Windows Server 2003, we can talk about installing and implementing it on the network. After DHCP is installed and configured, we'll take some time to examine how it can be secured and also how you'll go about troubleshooting it.

Installing and Implementing DHCP

The first question many managers ask when presented with a request to install Windows Server 2003 DHCP is this: "Can't we just use our existing DHCP?" The answer to this question is both yes and no. If you are maintaining a legacy domain and WINS network, Windows Server 2003 can receive DHCP information from any DHCP server with which Windows NT 4.0 or Windows 2000 Server works. However, if you want to take advantage of the features of Active Directory and possibly migrate away from the legacy WINS architecture, you need the Windows Server 2003 DHCP service.

The following sections discuss how to install and configure DHCP for a network.

Installing the DHCP Server Service

When you install Windows Server 2003, you can install DHCP as one of the optional services. To prepare for Exam 70-293, you need to know how to install DHCP on an existing server that does not already have DHCP installed.

NOTE

A DHCP server cannot also be a DHCP client If you currently have a server configured as a DHCP client, the DHCP installation prompts you to enter a static IP address for the server.

Before you install DHCP, you must configure the server with a static IP address. When the DHCP server's network adapter is configured with a static IP address, you can install the DHCP service on the server. To install the DHCP service on your server, perform the steps described in Step by Step 3.1.

STEP BY STEP

3.1 Installing the DHCP Service

1. Select Start, Settings, Control Panel, Add or Remove Programs.
2. On the Add or Remove Programs page, click Add/Remove Windows Components to open the Windows Components Wizard.
3. Select Networking Services, as shown in Figure 3.1.

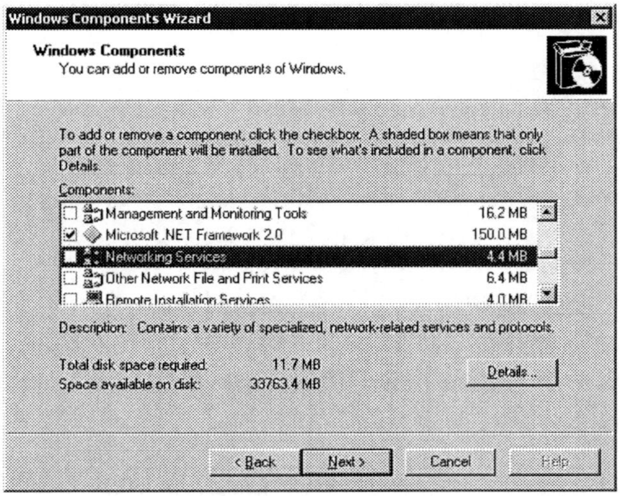

FIGURE 3.1 DHCP is located in the Networking Services group in the Windows Components Wizard.

4. Click the Details button to open the Networking Services window, shown in Figure 3.2.
5. Select Dynamic Host Configuration Protocol (DHCP) and click OK.

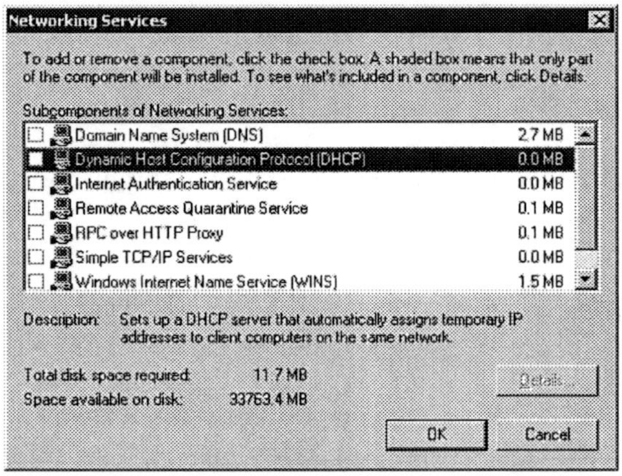

FIGURE 3.2 You select the Dynamic Host Configuration Protocol (DHCP) option to install the DHCP server.

6. Back in the Windows Components Wizard page, click Next to begin the installation.
7. If you are prompted to supply the location of your Windows Server 2003 CD-ROM or installation files, provide the correct location. Windows installs the DHCP service files on your computer.
8. When prompted that installation is complete, click Finish to close the Windows Components Wizard.

After you've installed the DHCP service, you need to begin configuring the DHCP server so that it can service network clients. Before you can begin the configuration process, you need to understand the types of DHCP scopes in Windows Server 2003.

Understanding DHCP Scopes

A *scope* is a range of IP addresses that are available for dynamic assignment to hosts on a given subnet. The scope for a particular subnet is determined by the network address of the broadcast DHCP request. In addition to address information, a scope can include a set of configuration parameters to be assigned to client computers when the address is assigned. This list of configuration parameters can include DNS servers, WINS servers, default gateways, the subnet mask, a NetBIOS scope ID, IP routing information, and WINS proxy information.

You should make the scope as large as you can. Later in the scope-creation process, you can exclude addresses and define reservations for particular addresses that exist within the scope.

NOTE

At least one scope After you install the DHCP service, you must define at least one scope on the server. Otherwise, the service will not respond to DHCP requests.

Understanding DHCP Superscopes

The *superscope* type of scope was introduced to the Windows NT product family with Service Pack 2 for Windows NT 4.0. A superscope enables you to support a supernetted or multinetted network with a Windows Server 2003 DHCP server.

A supernetted network is a network that has multiple network addresses or subnets running on the same segment. This configuration is common in a network environment with more than 254 hosts on a subnet and in an environment in which certain hosts need to be isolated from the rest of the logical network for security or routing reasons. Superscopes support a local multinet or a multinet that is located across a router and configured to use the BOOTP forwarder service.

Understanding Multicasting and Multicast Scopes

Multicasting is the act of transmitting a message to a select group of recipients. This is in contrast to the concept of a *broadcast*, in which traffic is sent to every host on the network, or a *unicast*, in which the connection is a one-to-one relationship and there is only one recipient of the data.

Let's look at an example using an email message. If you send an email message to your manager, that email is a unicast message. If you send an email message to every user on the system, you have sent a broadcast. If you send an email message to a mailing list, you have sent a multicast message, which falls between a unicast message and a broadcast message. Teleconferencing and videoconferencing use the concept of multicasting, as does broadcast audio, in which the connection is from one source computer to a selected group of destination computers. At this time, only a few applications take advantage of multicasting, but with the growing popularity of multicast applications, we might see more multicast applications in the future.

The following are a few terms you need to understand before we discuss the Windows Server 2003 multicast capabilities:

- **Multicast DHCP (MDHCP)**—An extension to the DHCP standard that supports dynamic assignment and configuration of IP multicast addresses on TCP/IP–based networks.
- **Multicast forwarding table**—The table used by an IP router to forward IP multicast traffic. An entry in the IP multicast forwarding table consists of the multicast group address, the source IP address, a list of interfaces to which the traffic is forwarded (that is, the *next-hop interfaces*), and the single interface on which the traffic must be received to be forwarded (that is, the *previous-hop interface*).
- **Multicast group**—A group of member TCP/IP hosts configured to listen for and receive datagrams sent to a specified destination IP address. The destination address for the group is a shared IP address in the Class D address range (224.0.0.0 to 2239.255.255.255).
- **Multicast scope**—A scope of IP multicast addresses in the range 239.0.0.0 to 239.254.255.255. Multicast addresses in this range can be prevented from propagating in either direction (send or receive) through the scope-based multicast boundaries.

Windows Server 2003 makes use of the concept of a multicast scope. The DHCP service has been extended to allow the assignment of multicast addresses in addition to unicast (single-computer) addresses. A proposed IETF standard (RFC 2730, "Multicast Address Dynamic Client Allocation Protocol [MADCAP]") defines multicast address allocation. MADCAP (also known as MDHCP in Microsoft lingo) would enable administrators to dynamically allocate multicast addresses to be assigned in the same fashion as unicast addresses. The Windows Server 2003 DHCP multicasting capability also supports *dynamic membership*, which allows individual computers to join or leave a multicast group at any time. This is similar to registering to receive an Internet broadcast or joining and leaving an email mailing list. Group membership is not limited by size, and computers are not restricted to membership in any single group.

How do client computers join and leave a multicast group? The answer is via MDHCP and the MDHCP application programming interface (API). Client computers using MDHCP must be configured to use the MDHCP API. MDHCP assists in simplifying and automating configuration of multicast groups on a network, but it is not required for the operation of multicast groups or for the DHCP service. Multicast scopes provide only address configuration and do not support or use other DHCP-assignable options. MDHCP address configuration for client computers should be done independently of how the client computers are configured to receive their primary IP addresses. Computers using either static or dynamic configuration through a DHCP server can also be MDHCP clients.

TIP

Class D IP addresses for the multicast scope Remember that, along with a primary IP address, a computer receives a multicast address, which is for multicasts only and uses the Class D IP addresses specified in the multicast scope. Multicast addresses are not used for regular network traffic such as web traffic or other IP-based applications.

Now that you know the different types of scopes supported in Windows Server 2003, you can move forward to creating scopes on a DHCP server.

Creating a DHCP Scope

Now that you are familiar with the different types of scopes, you can create one. To create a standard DHCP scope, you perform the steps described in Step by Step 3.2.

TIP

Preparing before performing Before you actually start to create a DHCP scope, you should ensure that you have gathered all the required information. You typically need the starting and ending IP addresses, the subnet mask, the DNS server IP address, and the gateway IP addresses.

STEP BY STEP

3.2 Creating a DHCP Scope

1. Open the DHCP console by selecting Start, Programs, Administrative Tools, DHCP.
2. Right-click the DHCP server and select New Scope from the context menu.
3. Click Next to dismiss the opening page of the New Scope Wizard.
4. On the first page of the wizard, the Scope Name page, enter a name and description for the new scope, as shown in Figure 3.3. You should make this name something that will enable you to easily identify this scope if you have multiple scopes on the DHCP server. When you're done entering the information, click Next to continue.

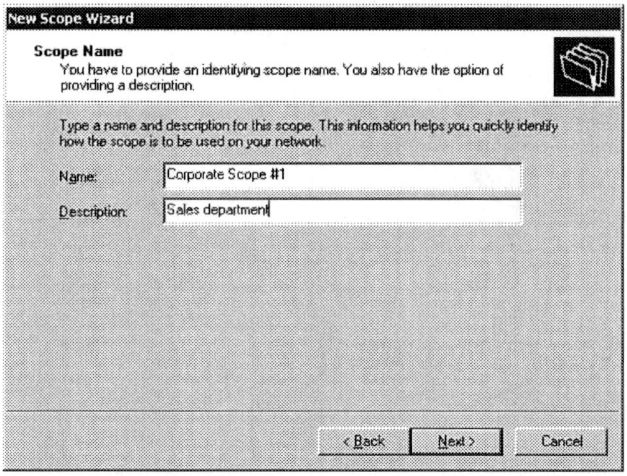

FIGURE 3.3 You should enter an intuitive name and description for the new scope.

5. On the next page of the wizard, the IP Address Range page, enter the IP address range and subnet mask that you need for the network, as shown in Figure 3.4. You can define the subnet mask by using the standard octet method (for example, 255.255.255.0) or by using the more router-centric mask length field (for example, 24 bits). When you're done entering the information, click Next to continue.
6. On the next page of the wizard, the Add Exclusions page (see Figure 3.5), you can configure a range of IP addresses that will not be leased to client computers. These are typically addresses assigned to application servers, routers, printers, or other infrastructure equipment that requires static addresses. You can have multiple excluded IP addresses or ranges for each scope. When you're done entering the information, click Next to continue.

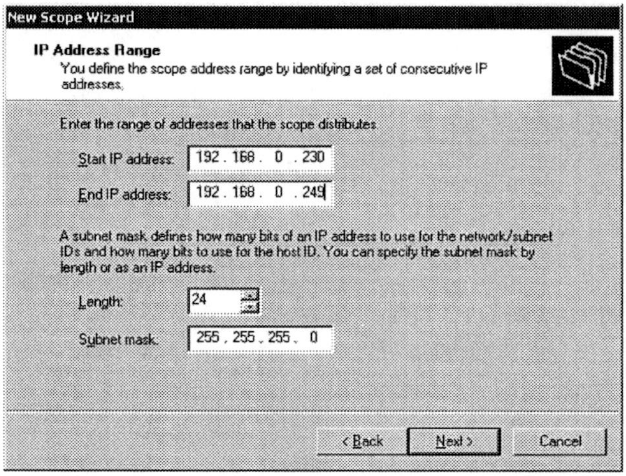

FIGURE 3.4 Configuring the IP address range and subnet mask information defines the scope boundaries.

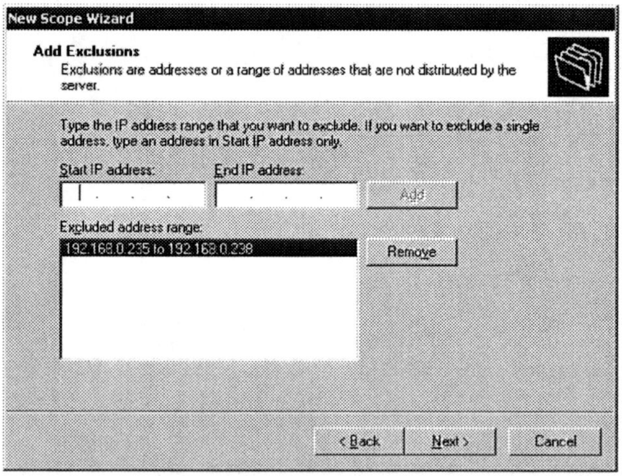

FIGURE 3.5 Configuring IP address exclusions enables you to prevent addresses within the scope from being leased.

7. On the next page of the wizard, the Lease Duration page, you can configure the amount of time for which a DHCP lease is valid, as shown in Figure 3.6. The default setting is 8 days and can be changed to any value between 1 minute and almost 1,000 days (999 days, 23 hours, 59 seconds, to be exact). For the average network, the default setting of 8 days is sufficient. In a network that has a large number of computers connecting at various locations, such as portable computers on wireless connections, you might want to reduce the lease duration. Conversely, in a network with clients that do not change location, you might consider increasing the lease duration to cut down on DHCP traffic on the network. When you're done entering the information, click Next to continue.

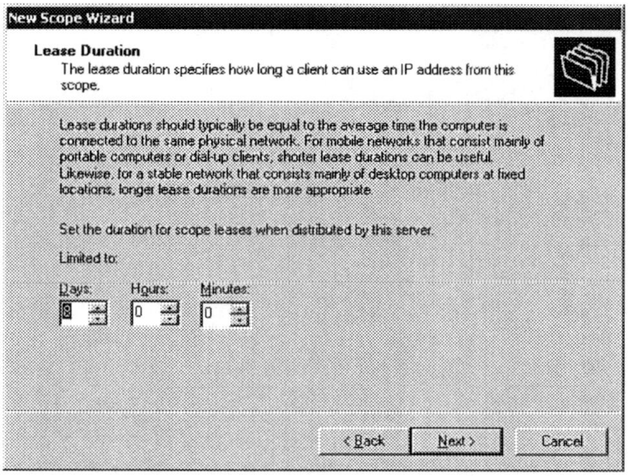

FIGURE 3.6 You should configure the lease duration that seems appropriate for the network.

8. On the next page of the wizard, the Configure DHCP Options page, you have the choice to configure additional options for your scope now or later. It is usually best to configure these options at the time of scope configuration, so you should do that now. Select Yes, I Want to Configure These Options Now and click Next to continue.

9. On the next page of the wizard, the Router (Default Gateway) page, enter the default gateway for the network or the subnet that the scope serves, as shown in Figure 3.7. When you're done entering the information, click Next to continue.

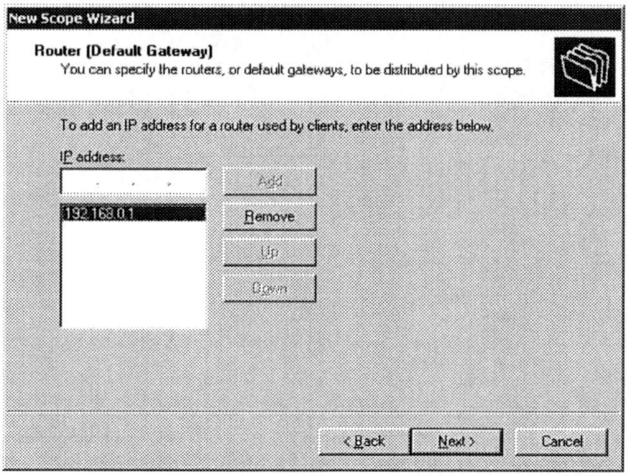

FIGURE 3.7 If you configure multiple gateways, you need to ensure that you place them in preferred order from top to bottom.

10. On the next page of the wizard, the Domain Name and DNS Servers page, configure the parent domain that all DHCP clients should be made part of, as well as any number of DNS servers you require, as shown in Figure 3.8. It is recommended that you enter at least two DNS servers for your clients to use. If you need to resolve a server name to an IP address, you can enter the server's name and then click the Resolve button. When you're done entering the information, click Next to continue.

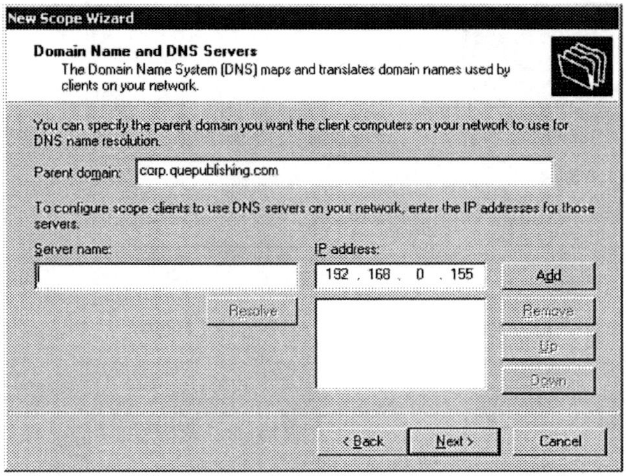

FIGURE 3.8 If you configure multiple DNS servers, you should ensure that you place them in preferred order from top to bottom.

11. On the next page of the wizard, the WINS Servers page, enter the IP addresses of the network's WINS servers, as shown in Figure 3.9. WINS servers are used to convert NetBIOS names to IP addresses for legacy clients on the network. As on the Domain Name and DNS Servers page, you can use the Resolve button to resolve a host name to an address. If a network is purely Windows 2000 or better, you do not need to have a WINS server on the network because Windows 2000, Windows XP, and Windows Server 2003 use DNS by default for all name resolutions. If you need WINS servers on a network, it is recommended that you enter at least two of them here. When you're done entering the information, click Next to complete the scope-creation process.

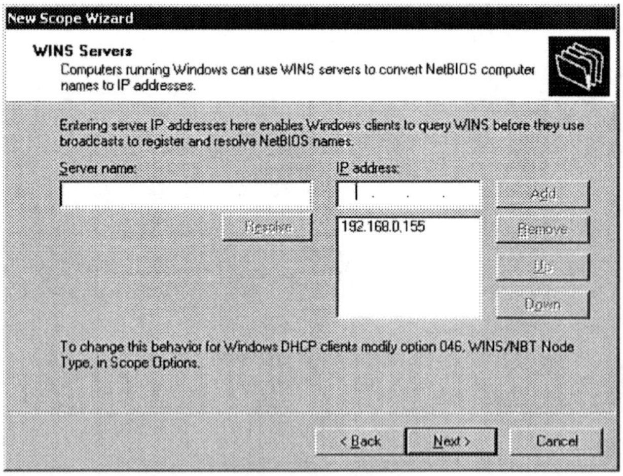

FIGURE 3.9 WINS servers are not required for networks that use only Windows 2000, Windows XP, or Windows Server 2003 computers.

12. On the next page of the wizard, the Activate Scope page (see Figure 3.10), you have the option to active the configured scope now or later. In most cases, you want to activate the scope right away. Select Yes, I Want to Activate This Scope Now and click Next to activate the configured scope.

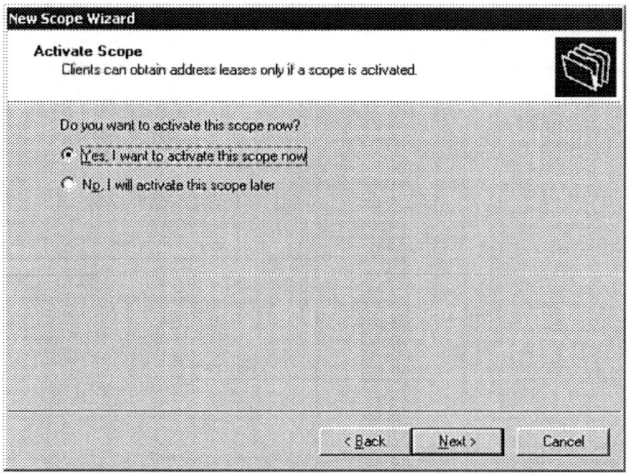

FIGURE 3.10 You typically want to activate the scope immediately after configuring it.

13. Click Finish to close the New Scope Wizard. Note that the DHCP won't issue any IP address from your new scope unless it has already been authorized in Active Directory. We discuss this a bit later in this chapter.

NOTE

Configuring scope ranges Common practice when configuring a new DHCP scope is to configure it and leave out enough addresses to cover all servers and other infrastructure devices that require statically assigned IP information without needing all the other options provided in a DHCP scope, such as DNS servers, WINS servers, and default gateways. For example, you might configure a scope of 192.168.0.10 to 192.168.0.200, with the remaining IP addresses available for servers, routers, switches, and other infrastructure equipment on that subnet. This practice keeps you from forgetting a configured reservation and ending up with duplicate IP addresses.

TIP

When to use the New Multicast Scope option Creating a new scope and creating a new multicast scope are two different tasks. If you get a question on the exam regarding the procedure for creating a multicast scope, remember that you need to start the process by selecting New Multicast Scope, not New Scope.

Configuring Scope Properties

After you've created a scope, you might want to modify its properties. To modify a scope's properties, you perform the steps described in Step by Step 3.3.

NOTE

Changing scope properties It's worth pointing out that you cannot change every option a scope has. For example, if you need to change the subnet mask that DHCP clients are receiving as part of their DHCP lease, you need to create a new DHCP scope reflecting this change and then remove the existing DHCP scope. Clients will then get the new information when they renew their lease the next time.

STEP BY STEP

3.3 Configuring a DHCP Scope's Properties

1. Right-click the scope and select Properties from the context menu.
2. The Properties dialog box opens, as shown in Figure 3.11.

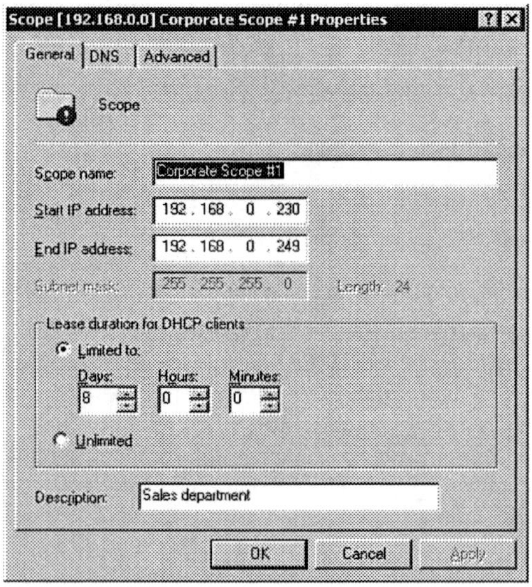

FIGURE 3.11 You can use the Scope Properties dialog box to change scope properties after you create a scope.

3. On the General tab, change the scope name, IP address range, lease duration, and scope description, if you want to.
4. If you want to change the options on the DNS tab, do so now. The options on the DNS tab are discussed later in this chapter, in the section "Configuring DHCP for DNS Integration."
5. On the Advanced tab, select options related to BOOTP clients, as shown in Figure 3.12. If you have BOOTP clients on your network, select either the BOOTP Only option or the Both option, depending on your network configuration. The default setting is DHCP Only. Click OK to close the Scope Properties dialog box after you make your changes.

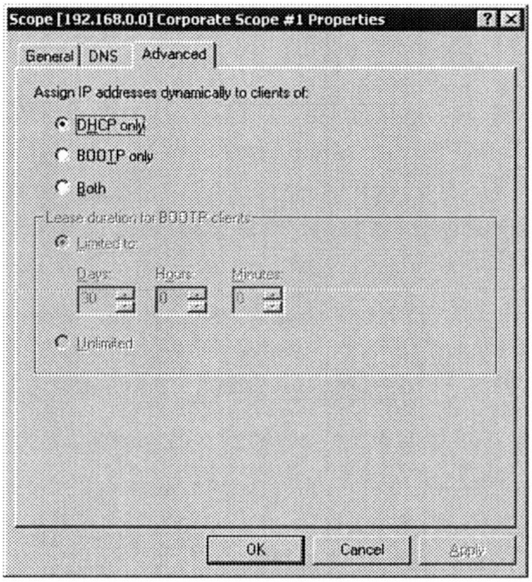

FIGURE 3.12 You can configure the scope to service BOOTP clients on the Advanced tab of the Scope Properties dialog box.

6. To view the address pool and configured exclusion ranges, click the Address Pool node of the DHCP console, as shown in Figure 3.13.

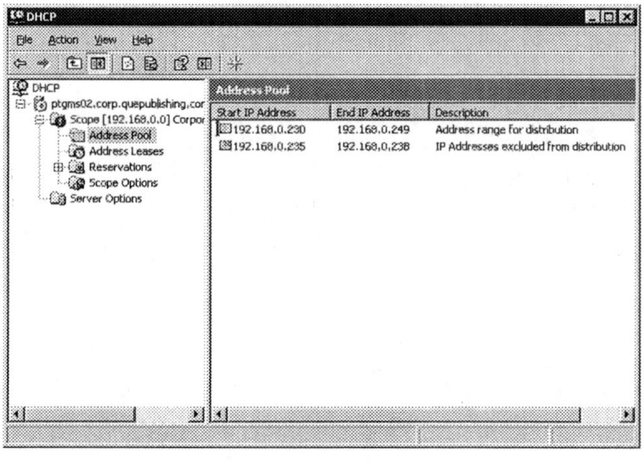

FIGURE 3.13 You can quickly view all configured scope ranges and exclusion ranges from the Address Pool node.

7. To add a new exclusion range, right-click Address Pool and select New Exclusion Range from the context menu. The Add Exclusion window appears (see Figure 3.14). Click Add after you enter your new exclusion range.

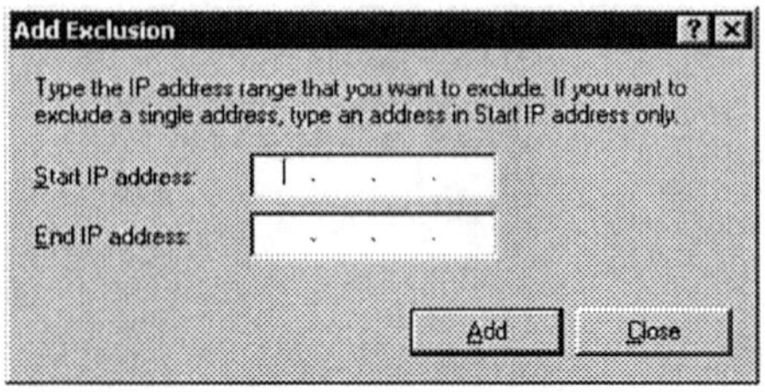

FIGURE 3.14 You can add a new exclusion range to a configured DHCP scope by using the Add Exclusion dialog box.

8. To view the addresses that have been leased, click the Address Leases node, as shown in Figure 3.15. (Of course, no leases are shown here until you authorize the DHCP server, as discussed later in this chapter, in the section "Authorizing a DHCP Server in Active Directory.")

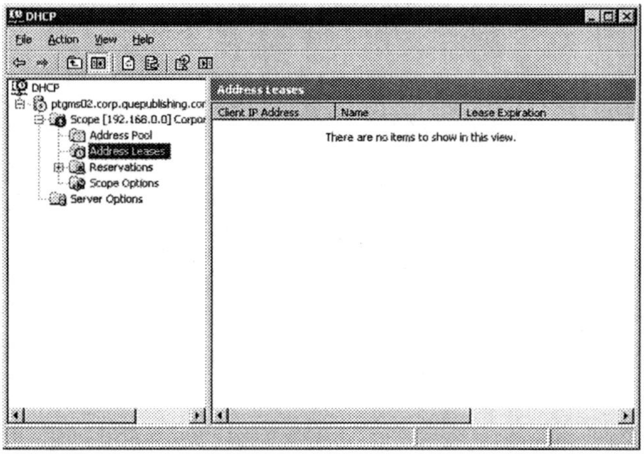

FIGURE 3.15 You can view all active scope leases from the Address Leases node.

9. If you want to manually revoke an active client lease, right-click it in the right pane of the Address Leases node and select Delete from the context menu.
10. To view the configured reservations, click the Reservations node of the DHCP console.
11. You can configure a new address reservation by right-clicking Reservations and selecting New Reservation from the context menu. You can configure a reservation for any device for which you want to have a DHCP-assigned IP address that never expires. Configure the reservation as shown in Figure 3.16 and click Add to add it. Click Close to close the New Reservation input box when you're done configuring reservations for this scope. After you've configured a reservation, you can see it in the Reservations node of the DHCP console, as shown in Figure 3.17.
12. You can view existing scope options by clicking the Scope Options node, as shown in Figure 3.18.
13. To configure a new scope option, right-click the Scope Options node and select Configure Options from the context menu. Configure the options in the Scope Options window (see Figure 3.19). Table 3.1 listed the common DHCP options available for configuration. Table 3.2 listed the Microsoft-specific DHCP options that are available for configuration.

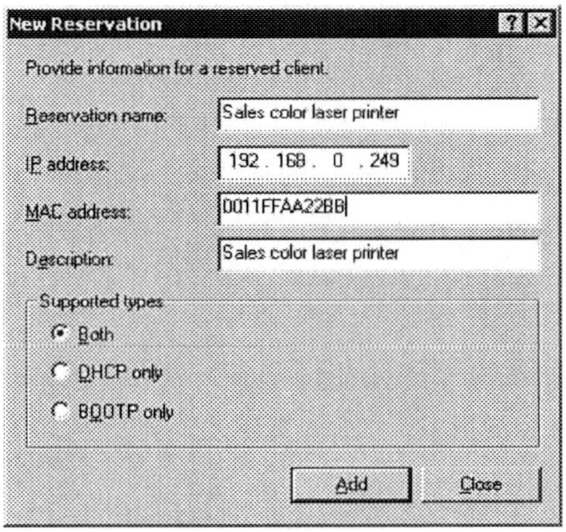

FIGURE 3.16 You can configure a new DHCP reservation, which is typically done for printers and other static infrastructure devices.

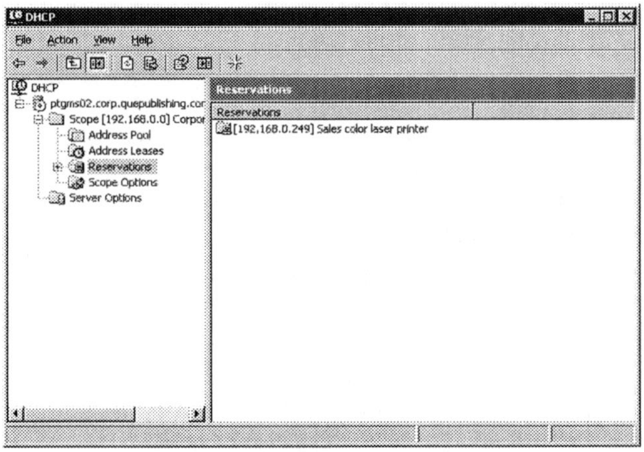

FIGURE 3.17 You can view all scope reservations from the Reservations node.

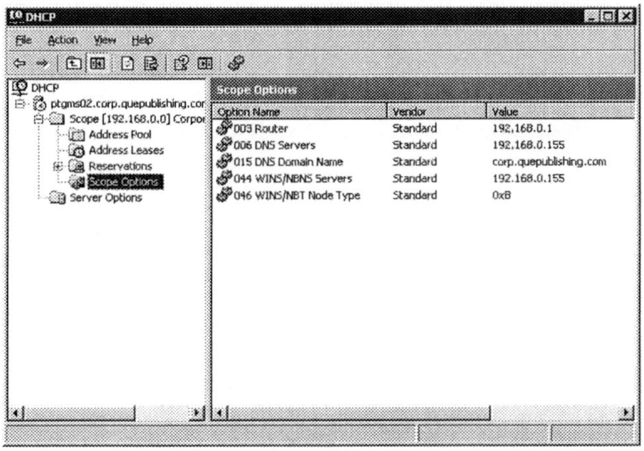

FIGURE 3.18 The Scope Options node lists all currently configured scope options.

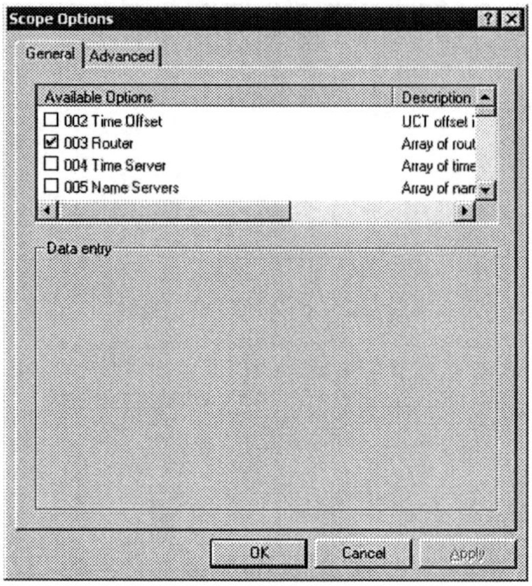

FIGURE 3.19 You can configure extra scope options from the Scope Options dialog box.

TIP

Configuring server options You can configure server-wide DHCP options as mentioned in Step by Step 3.3. To configure server DHCP options that apply to all scopes on the DHCP server, right-click the Server Options node in the DHCP console and select Configure Options from the context menu.

Authorizing a DHCP Server in Active Directory

For security reasons, a new DHCP server must be authorized in Active Directory before it can assign IP addresses by an administrator with Enterprise Admin credentials. This prevents unauthorized DHCP servers from running on the network. One of the nastiest things a troublemaker can do is put up a rogue DHCP server and have it issue addresses that conflict with infrastructure devices' addresses. The nice thing about this feature is that if you are running Windows 2000 or better client computers and they are using Active Directory, the computers will not accept DHCP addresses from an unauthorized server. To authorize a DHCP server in Active Directory, you perform the steps described in Step by Step 3.4.

STEP BY STEP

3.4 Authorizing a DHCP Server in Active Directory

1. Open the DHCP console by selecting Start, Programs, Administrative Tools, DHCP.
2. Right-click the DHCP server and select Authorize from the context menu.

3. The authorization process might take some time, depending on network conditions. Refresh the DHCP console by pressing F5. You should see the window shown in Figure 3.20. When authorization is complete, the status is shown as Active and the server is ready to issue addresses when it receives DHCP requests. Note also that the status arrow on the server itself is now pointing up instead of down, as before.

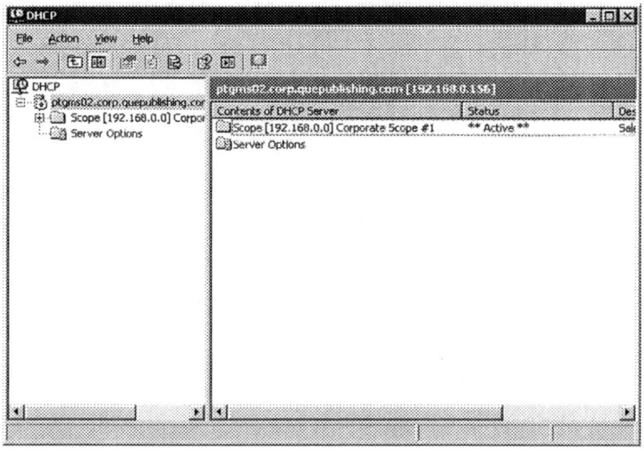

FIGURE 3.20 When a DHCP server is authorized, DHCP server scope information appears in the right pane of the DHCP console window.

Windows Server 2003 and Windows 2000 Server DHCP servers that are not authorized do not provide DHCP services to network clients. These unauthorized servers also check every 5 minutes to see if their authorization status has changed, thus allowing them to begin servicing clients.

You have now installed, configured, and authorized a Windows Server 2003 DHCP server. We next examine configuring DHCP for DNS integration.

Configuring DHCP for DNS Integration

One of the keys to effectively implementing an Active Directory environment is the capability for Windows 2000 and Windows XP workstations using DHCP to be automatically registered in DNS. You can set the following settings for DNS integration (see Step by Step 3.5):

- **Dynamically Update DNS A and PTR Records Only If Requested by the DHCP Clients**—This is the default behavior of the Windows Server 2003 DHCP server. It causes the DHCP server to register and update client information with the authoritative DNS server of the zone in which the DHCP server is located, according to the DHCP client's request. The DHCP client can request the way in which the DHCP server performs updates of its host (A) and pointer (PTR) resource records. If possible, the DHCP server accommodates the client's request for handling updates to its name and IP address information in DNS. This selection requires you to select the Enable Dynamic DNS Updates According to the Settings Below option.

- **Always Dynamically Update DNS A and PTR Records**—When this option is selected, the DHCP server always updates the client's fully qualified domain name (FQDN), IP address, and both A and PTR resource records, regardless of whether the client has requested to perform its own updates. This selection requires you to select the Enable Dynamic DNS Updates According to the Settings Below.
- **Discard A and PTR Records When Lease Is Deleted**—This option, which is selected by default, instructs the DHCP server to cause the DNS server to delete the client's A and PTR records when the lease has expired or otherwise has been deleted. This selection requires you to select the Enable Dynamic DNS Updates According to the Settings Below option.
- **Dynamically Update DNS A and PTR Records for DHCP Clients That Do Not Request Automatic Updates**—This option allows legacy clients, such as Windows NT 4.0 and Windows 9x clients, to participate in DNS dynamic updates. This selection requires you to select the Enable Dynamic DNS Updates According to the Settings Below option.

NOTE

New Group Policy object options Although it is beyond the scope of Exam 70-293, you can also configure the DNS options discussed here from Group Policy. The options are located in Computer Configuration, Administrative Templates, Network, DNS Client node.

Because the DHCP server controls DNS dynamic updating, you need to perform all the applicable DNS configuration from the DHCP console. The DHCP server automatically updates any DNS server configured as part of the server's TCP/IP network properties. It is important to be sure that the primary DNS server is configured as one of the DNS servers because any updates sent to it are propagated to the rest of the DNS servers for that domain. However, the DNS server in question must support DDNS. The Windows Server 2003 DNS server supports these updates, as do a number of other DNS servers.

To configure a DHCP server for DNS integration, you perform the steps described in Step by Step 3.5.

STEP BY STEP

3.5 Configuring DHCP for DNS Integration

1. Open the DHCP console by selecting Start, Programs, Administrative Tools, DHCP.
2. Right-click the DHCP server and select Properties from the context menu. Select the DNS tab of the DHCP Server Properties dialog box, shown in Figure 3.21.

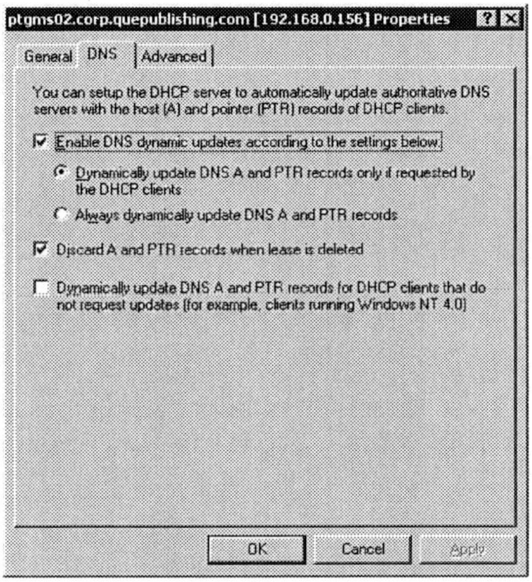

FIGURE 3.21 You can configure DDNS options on the DNS tab.

3. To enable DHCP integration with DNS, ensure that the Enable Dynamic DNS Updates According to the Settings Below check box is selected.
4. Select to have the DHCP server update A and PTR records when requested or to always update A and PTR records.
5. To help keep the DNS database clean and consistent, allow the DHCP server to cause expired leases to lead to A and PTR record deletion.
6. If there are legacy clients on the network, ensure that dynamic updating is configured for them.
7. If you are using secure dynamic updates, consider configuring a dedicated network user account for dynamic updating. You can enter the account credentials by switching to the Advanced tab of the DHCP Server Properties dialog box, as shown in Figure 3.22.
8. Click the Credentials button to open the DNS Dynamic Update Credentials window, as shown in Figure 3.23.
9. Enter the domain user account name, domain, and password in the DNS Dynamic Update Credentials dialog box. Click OK to accept the credentials or Cancel to avoid entering credentials at this time.
10. Click OK to close the DHCP Server Properties dialog box.

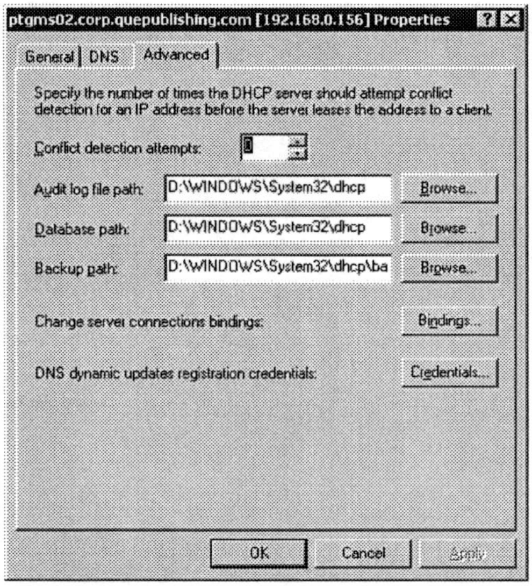

FIGURE 3.22 Click the Credentials button to enter the account username and password for DDNS.

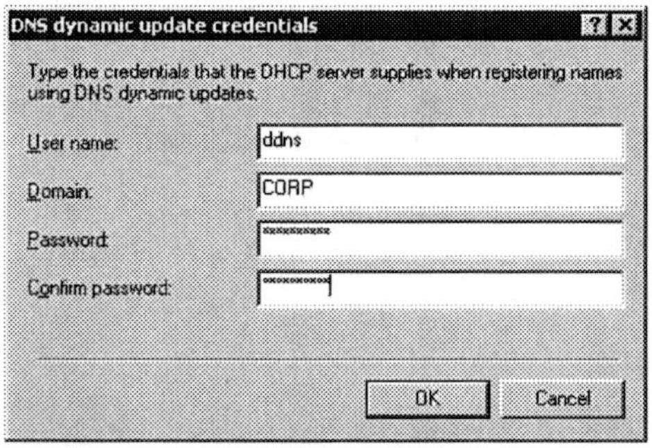

FIGURE 3.23 Enter the dynamic updates account credentials in the DNS Dynamic Update Credentials dialog box.

DHCP option code 81 is required to make dynamic updates work. Let's look at two examples that explain the basic dynamic update process.

The first example looks at a Windows 2000 Professional client computer that has requested a DHCP lease from a Windows Server 2003 DHCP server configured with the default options:

1. During the DHCP lease-negotiation process, the Windows 2000 Professional client sends a DHCPREQUEST message. By default, the client includes DHCP option 81 in this message, informing the DHCP server that it is requesting that the DHCP server register its PTR record in DNS. The client is responsible for registering its A record on its own.

2. The DHCP server replies with a `DHCPACK` message, granting the requested DHCP lease. This message includes DHCP option 81. With the default DHCP server settings, the DHCP server informs the client that it will register the PTR record and that the client is responsible for registering the A record in DNS.
3. The client registers its A record, and the DHCP server registers the client's PTR record in DNS.

The second example looks at a Windows NT 4.0 Workstation client computer that has requested a DHCP lease from a Windows Server 2003 DHCP server configured with the default options:

1. During the DHCP lease-negotiation process, the Windows NT 4.0 Workstation client sends a `DHCPREQUEST` message. DHCP option 81 is not included in this message.
2. The server returns a `DHCPACK` message to the client, granting its DHCP lease request.
3. The DHCP server updates the DNS server with the client's A and PTR records.

TIP

DHCP and DNS It is important to remember that Windows 2000 and Windows XP client computers update the A records in DNS without any assistance from the DHCP server. The only client computers for which DHCP updates DNS are older legacy clients.

CAUTION

DDNS updates and domain controllers To perform DDNS updates, you should not configure the DHCP service on a computer that is also a domain controller. If a DHCP server exists on a domain controller, the DHCP server has full control over all DNS objects stored in Active Directory because the account under which it is running (the domain controller computer account) has this privilege. This creates a security risk that should be avoided. You should not install the DHCP server service that is configured to perform DDNS updates on a domain controller; instead, you should install it on a member server if you're performing DDNS updates.

As an alternative, you can use a new feature in Windows Server 2003 DHCP. This feature enables you to create a dedicated domain user account that all DHCP servers will use when performing DDNS updates.

Configuring and Implementing a DHCP Relay Agent

Today most networks that use DHCP are routed. As discussed previously, DHCP messages are broadcast messages. By default, nearly all routers do not pass broadcast traffic, in the interest of reducing overall network traffic levels. Fortunately, you can get around this design limitation by configuring a DHCP relay agent to pass BOOTP messages across routers.

You can set up a DHCP relay agent in three basic configurations. The first involves entering the IP address or addresses of the DHCP server(s) into the router itself, instructing it to pass DHCP messages to a specified IP address for action. The second method involves using the Windows Server 2003 Routing and Remote Access Service (RRAS) component as a router (in place of a hardware-based router) and configuring the DHCP relay agent within it. The third solution, and the one that we examine in this section, uses a Windows Server 2003 computer located on a subnet without a DHCP server to act as a DHCP relay agent. This option requires RRAS components, but it does not involve creating or configuring a router, as the second solution would. What's important to understand is that the server providing the DHCP relay agent service does not have to be dedicated to that purpose; it could be a file server, a print server, or any other type of Windows Server 2003 (or Windows 2000 Server) server on that subnet. Figure 3.24 shows how this arrangement would look on a network.

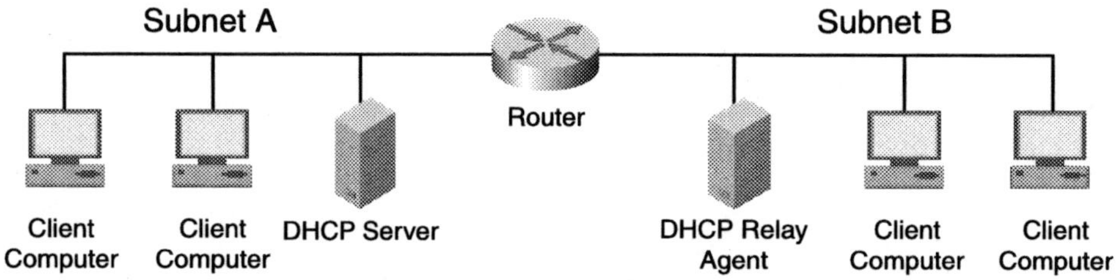

FIGURE 3.24 The DHCP relay agent allows clients on the other side of a router to communicate with the DHCP server.

TIP

DHCP relay agent Recall that the DHCP relay agent is needed only to help pass DHCP traffic across a router that otherwise could not pass that traffic. As such, the server acting as the relay agent is not the same server providing DHCP and is located on the subnet on the *other side* of the router in question. Referring back to Figure 3.24, the DHCP server is located on subnet A, whereas the DHCP relay agent is located on subnet B.

In Step by Step 3.6, you enable the DHCP relay agent on a Windows Server 2003 computer. This exercise assumes that you have not previously configured and enabled RRAS on the computer.

STEP BY STEP

3.6 Configuring a DHCP Relay Agent

1. Select Start, Programs, Administrative Tools, Routing and Remote Access to open the Routing and Remote Access console, shown in Figure 3.25. (If you've previously configured and enabled RRAS, you can skip to Step 7.)

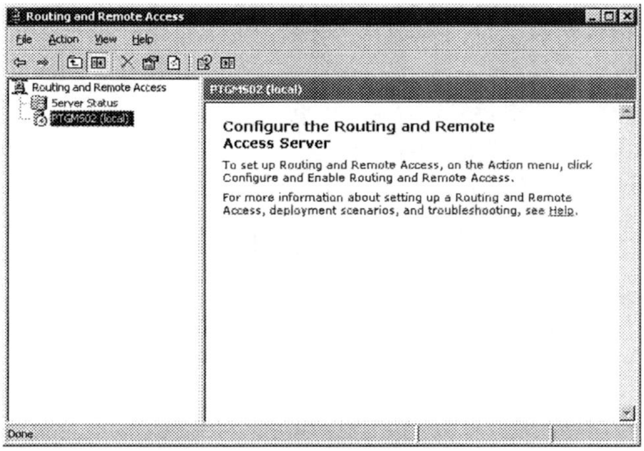

FIGURE 3.25 The Routing and Remote Access console is initially empty.

2. Right-click the server name and select Configure and Enable Routing and Remote Access from the context menu. The Routing and Remote Access Server Setup Wizard appears. Click Next to dismiss the opening page.

3. On the Configuration page of the wizard, shown in Figure 3.26, select the Custom Configuration option and click Next to continue.

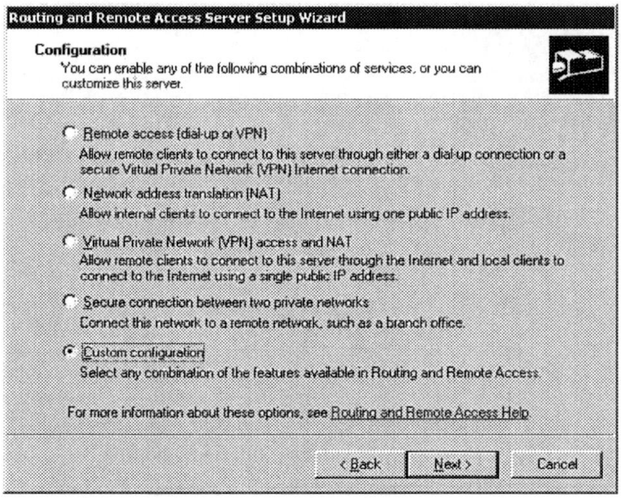

FIGURE 3.26 You need to specify a custom configuration to perform basic DHCP relay agent setup.

4. On the Custom Configuration page of the wizard, shown in Figure 3.27, select the LAN Routing option and click Next to continue.

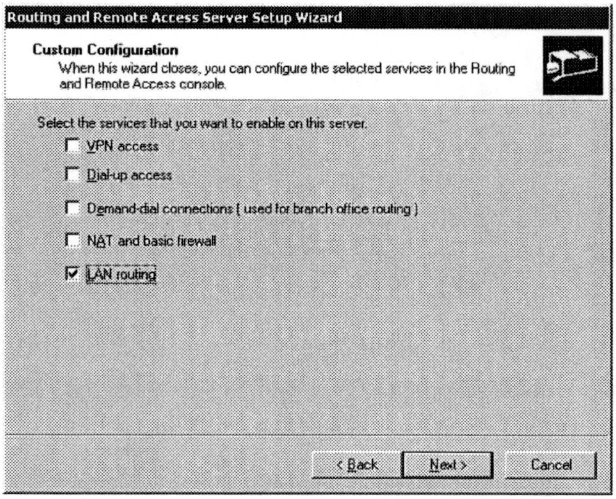

FIGURE 3.27 The LAN Routing option is the bare minimum you need to support later installation of the DHCP relay agent.

5. When the summary page is displayed, review your selections and click Finish to continue.
6. You are prompted to start RRAS. Click Yes to start the service.
7. Back at the Routing and Remote Access console, expand the following nodes: Routing and Remote Access, *ServerName*, IP Routing, and General, as shown in Figure 3.28.

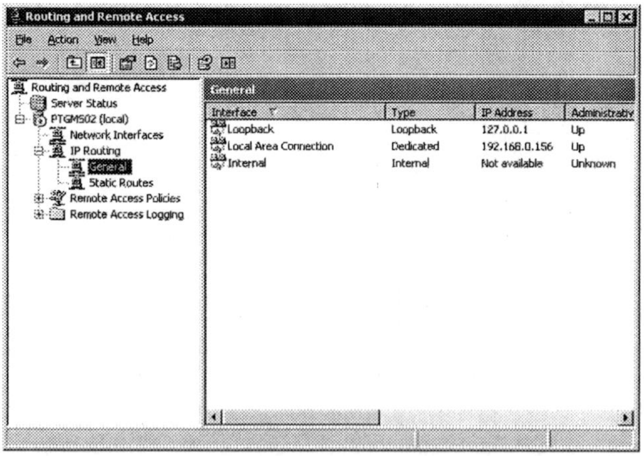

FIGURE 3.28 You need to add the DHCP relay agent from the General node.

8. Right-click the General node and select New Routing Protocol from the context menu. This opens the New Routing Protocol dialog box.
9. From the New Routing Protocol dialog box, shown in Figure 3.29, select DHCP Relay Agent. Click OK to confirm your configuration.

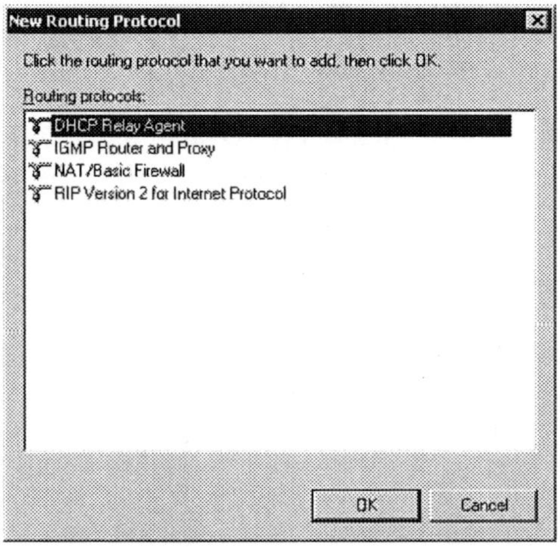

FIGURE 3.29 You can add the DHCP relay agent in addition to standard IP routing protocols.

10. To select a network interface for the DHCP relay agent to run on, right-click the DHCP Relay Agent node in the RRAS console and select New Interface from the context menu.

11. On the New Interface for DHCP Relay Agent page, shown in Figure 3.30, select the network interface that you want to be available for the DHCP relay agent. Click OK to continue. The DHCP Relay Properties dialog box, shown in Figure 3.31, opens.

FIGURE 3.30 Select one or more installed network adapters for use by the DHCP relay agent.

12. In the DHCP Relay Properties dialog box, configure the required values for hop-count threshold and boot threshold. The default value for each of them is 4. Click OK to confirm your settings.

13. The last configuration you need to perform is to assign the DHCP server IP addresses to which the DHCP relay agent forwards DHCP messages. Right-click the DHCP Relay Agent node in the RRAS console and select Properties to open the DHCP Relay Agent Properties dialog box, shown in Figure 3.32. Enter one or more remote DHCP servers in the list and click OK to confirm your settings.

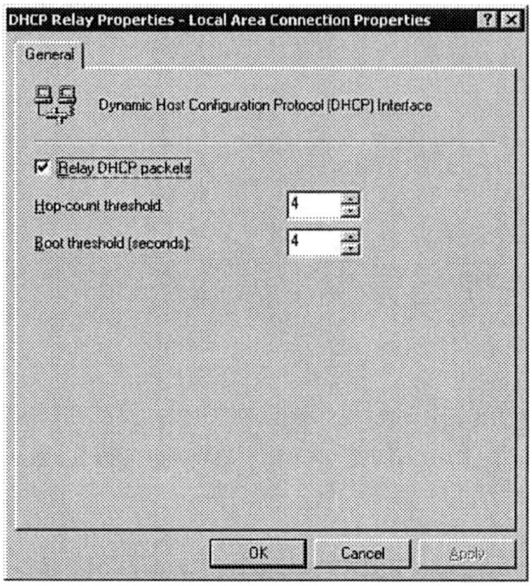

FIGURE 3.31 You need to configure the maximum hop count and length of delay time for the DHCP relay agent.

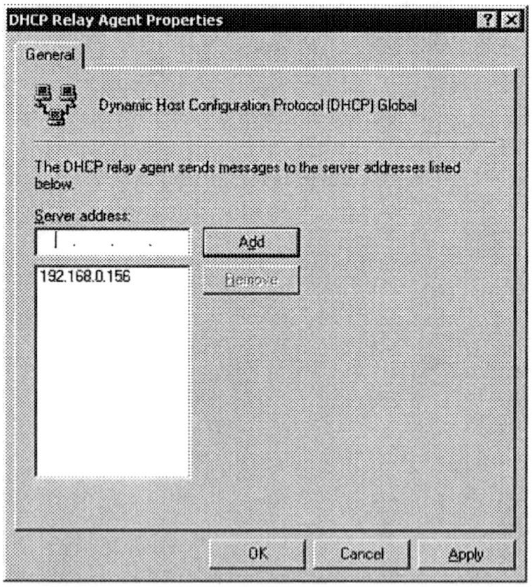

FIGURE 3.32 Provide one or more remote DHCP servers to which the DHCP relay agent can forward DHCP messages.

TIP

DHCP relay agent options The Hop-Count Threshold option enables you to configure a value for the maximum number of DHCP relay agents that are allowed to handle DHCP-relayed traffic. The maximum value is 16 hops, meaning that you can have only 16 DHCP relay agents (typically on different connected subnets) between a client and a DHCP server.

The Boot Threshold option enables you to specify how long the DHCP relay agent waits before forwarding DHCP messages. By configuring DHCP relay agents with different values, you can establish one that should respond first and then one or more DHCP relay agents that should forward DHCP messages, if required.

Configuring Security for DHCP

Although no administrative tasks outwardly appear to help secure your DHCP infrastructure, you can follow some best practices and take other actions to provide a more secure (and, thus, more reliable) DHCP implementation in your environment. We briefly examine them here:

- **Use the 80/20, 70/30, or 50/50 address-allocation rule**—By using one of these configurations, you can ensure that leases will still be made available to clients requesting them if a single server is under a DoS attack or otherwise becomes unavailable.
- **Create and use DHCP server clusters**—By enabling a DHCP server cluster, you remove a single server as a single point of failure (SPOF). By having two (or more) servers in a cluster acting as a single DHCP entity, a failure of a single server (or multiple servers, depending on your configuration) will not result in a failure to provide leases to clients.
- **Examine the DHCP audit logs regularly**—Ensure that audit logging is enabled, as shown in Figure 3.33. The audit logs are stored in the location defined on the Advanced tab, which was shown in Figure 3.22. The location is `%systemroot%\system32\dhcp\` by default.
- **Harden servers**—You can get detailed information and assistance on hardening Windows Server 2003 servers from the "Windows Server 2003 Security Guide."

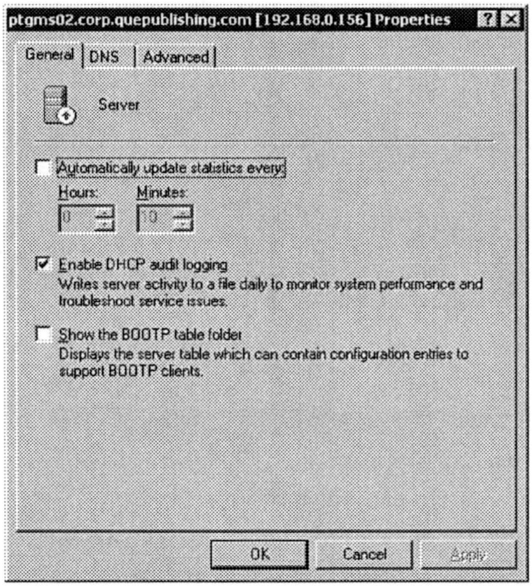

FIGURE 3.33 DHCP audit logging is enabled from the General tab of the DHCP server Properties dialog box.

Troubleshooting DHCP

Although DHCP is typically one of the easiest of the common network services to configure and maintain, from time to time, you might encounter problems. More often than not, the DHCP-related problems that arise stem from a misconfiguration in a scope, unauthorized DHCP servers on the network, or network connectivity problems. You might also find information that has changed in some way, but the change has not been reflected in your DHCP configuration, as in the case of DHCP reservations (which are tied to MAC addresses) or a DHCP server's IP address change. The following sections examine some troubleshooting tasks you can do to quickly determine the cause of DHCP woes and get this vital network service back into proper operation.

Troubleshooting DHCP Server Authorization Problems

As discussed previously, one of the first indicators you might see of an unauthorized or rogue DHCP server is an unexpected increase in the number of `DHCPNACK` messages. You can monitor this statistic over time by using the Performance console. The Performance console includes several counter objects that you can use to monitor and troubleshoot your DHCP server:

- **Acks/Sec**—This counter monitors the number of `DHCPACK` messages sent per second by the DHCP server to client computers. The DHCP server uses the `DHCPACK` messages to acknowledge requests for an address. An increase in this number indicates that a large number of client computers are probably trying to renew their leases with the DHCP server. This could be because of a short lease time configuration or because a number of new computers are entering the network.
- **Active Queue Length**—This counter monitors the current length of the internal message queue of the DHCP server. This number represents the number of unprocessed messages received by the server. A large number here could indicate an unusually large amount of network traffic or a heavy load on the server.
- **Conflict Check Queue Length**—This counter monitors the current length of the conflict check queue for the DHCP server. Before a Windows Server 2003 DHCP server issues an address, it checks whether any IP address conflicts exist. The conflict check queue holds the messages not responded to while the DHCP server performs address conflict detection. A large value here could indicate heavy lease traffic at the server. You might also want to check the Conflict Detection Attempts parameter, which could be set too high.
- **Declines/Sec**—This counter monitors the number of `DHCPDECLINE` messages that the DHCP server receives per second from client computers. This counter indicates that the DHCP client computer has declined the IP address issued by the server. You see this number rise when client computers start having address conflict problems, and it could indicate a network problem, computers with static addresses also being part of a scope, or a rogue DHCP server on the network.
- **Discovers/Sec**—This counter monitors the number of `DHCPDISCOVER` messages received per second by the server. The `DHCPDISCOVER` message is the initial request a client computer sends when it first enters the network and looks for a DHCP server to issue an address. A sudden increase in this counter could indicate that a large number of client computers are attempting to initialize and obtain an IP address lease from the server at the same time. You might see this first thing in the morning, when users power on their PCs, or after a power failure, when all the PCs might be powered on at about the same time.
- **Duplicates Dropped/Sec**—This counter monitors the number of duplicate packets per second dropped by the DHCP server. Duplicate packets on a network are never a good sign, and they can indicate that DHCP clients are timing out before the server can respond. This can be caused by client computers timing out too fast or the server not responding quickly enough.
- **Informs/Sec**—This counter monitors the number of `DHCPINFORM` messages received per second by the DHCP server. `DHCPINFORM` messages are used when the DHCP server queries the directory service for the enterprise root and when dynamic updates are being done on behalf of client computers by the DNS server. This is part of the DDNS integration, and an unusual increase in this number could indicate a large number of addresses being issued.

- **Milliseconds Per Packet (Avg)**—This counter monitors the average time, in milliseconds, the DHCP server takes to process each packet it receives. This is a very subjective number that depends on the server configuration; therefore, having a baseline for this number is a good idea. A sudden increase in this counter could indicate a disk problem or an increased load on the server.
- **Nacks/Sec**—This counter monitors the number of DHCP negative acknowledgment (`DHCPNACK`) messages sent per second by the DHCP server to client computers. A `DHCPNACK` message indicates that the server cannot fulfill the DHCP request. A very high value for this counter could indicate a network problem or a misconfiguration of client computers or the server. Watch for a deactivated scope as a possible culprit.
- **Offers/Sec**—This counter monitors the number of `DHCPOFFER` messages that the DHCP server sends per second to client computers. A `DHCPOFFER` message is the message the server returns to the client computer after the client computer sends a `DHCPDISCOVER` message, and it indicates that the server is offering to issue an address to that client computer. A sudden increase in this value could indicate heavy traffic or a heavy load on the server.
- **Packets Expired/Sec**—This counter monitors the number of packets per second that expire and are dropped by the DHCP server. This situation is caused by a packet remaining in the server's internal message queue too long. A large number for this counter indicates that the server either is taking too long to process some packets or is causing other packets to wait in queue, or that the traffic on the network is too heavy for the DHCP server to handle. It is important to note that high numbers for this counter can indicate pure network traffic problems and not necessarily DHCP-related problems.
- **Packets Received/Sec**—This counter monitors the number of message packets received per second by the DHCP server. A large number indicates heavy DHCP message traffic to the server. These message packets might be requests for addresses, renewals, or releases.
- **Releases/Sec**—This counter monitors the number of `DHCPRELEASE` messages that the DHCP server receives per second from client computers. A `DHCPRELEASE` message is sent only when the client computer manually releases an address, such as when the `ipconfig /release` command is used or the Release All button in the `winipcfg` utility is used at the client computer. Because most users do not manually release their addresses, this number should be low in all but the most unusual network environments.
- **Requests/Sec**—This counter monitors the number of `DHCPREQUEST` messages that the DHCP server receives per second from client computers. These messages are the requests that the client computer sends to request an IP address after it has found a server that can issue addresses. An increase in this number indicates that a large number of client computers are probably trying to renew their leases with the DHCP server. This could be caused by a short lease time configuration or by a number of new computers entering the network.

Configuring the Performance console to monitor and collect data about a DHCP server is a simple process, as outlined in Step by Step 3.7.

STEP BY STEP

3.7 Monitoring DHCP Performance

1. Select Start, Program, Administrative Tools, Performance to open the Performance console.
2. Click System Monitor, as shown in Figure 3.34.

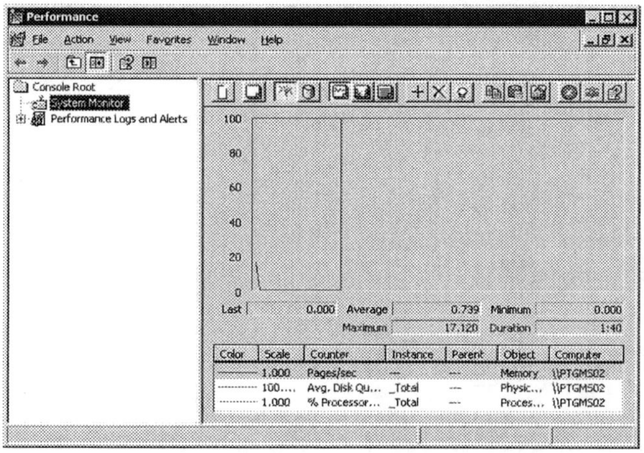

FIGURE 3.34 You can view server performance statistics by using the Performance console.

3. To create an entry in System Monitor, click the + icon. The Add Counters dialog box shown in Figure 3.35 opens, enabling you to begin adding counters.

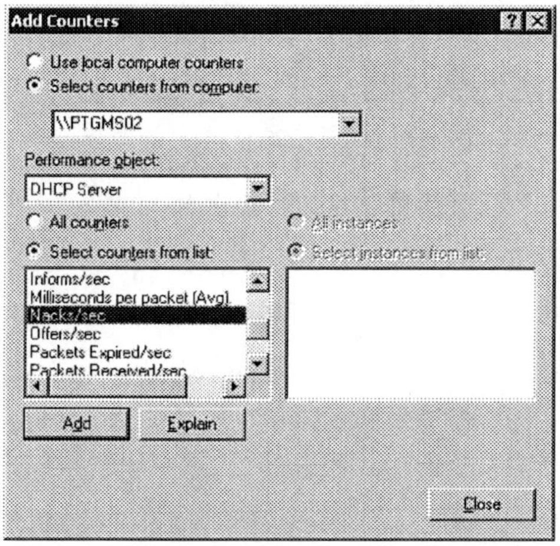

FIGURE 3.35 You can add counters to begin monitoring DHCP server statistics.

4. Select the DHCP Server performance object in the Performance object drop-down list box. You then see the list of counters available for selection that relate to the DHCP service. If you need to know what a counter means, select the counter and click the Explain button.

5. When you have decided what counter you want to monitor, click Add. You can add multiple counters either by selecting each counter and clicking Add or by holding down the Ctrl key while you select all the counters you want to monitor and then clicking Add. Click Close when you are finished. Your counters are graphed like those shown in Figure 3.36.

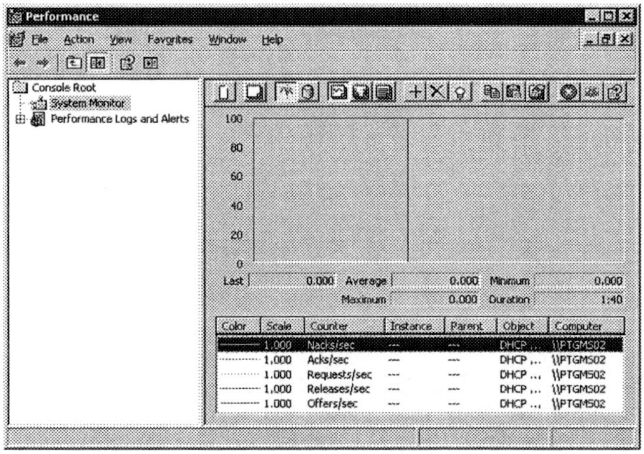

FIGURE 3.36 You can monitor DHCP server statistics in real time.

NOTE

Creating server baselines If you create baselines on servers, you can compare the performance at any given time to a known value. This can be very useful in performing troubleshooting, and it also helps when configurations are being modified. To create a baseline, you create a counter log from the Counter Logs option of the Performance Logs and Alerts node, shown in Figure 3.35. The configuration and use of a counter log is nearly identical to the creation and use of System Monitor, as described in Step by Step 3.7.

If you notice a trend of higher-than-normal DHCPNACK messages, you need to determine the source. The most common cause is a rogue DHCP server that has been set up on the network. You can also examine the DHCP lease properties of clients to determine whether any of them have different information than what you have configured in your DHCP scopes.

It's important to remember that Windows 2000 and Windows XP clients in an Active Directory environment that are configured to use DHCP do not accept leases from unauthorized DHCP servers. Older clients accept these leases and can contribute to the number of DHCPNACK messages when they attempt to renew their DHCP leases.

You can also examine the DHCP server daily audit logs, located in the `%systemroot%\sysytem32\dhcp` folder, to look for rogue-detection events. The DHCP audit logs are discussed in the next section.

Using the DHCP Logs

The DHCP server daily audit logs are often overlooked as a valuable source of information. You have learned how to enable the audit logs; now let's look at what they contain. Unlike the logs the Windows 2000 Server DHCP service produces, the Windows Server 2003 daily audit logs are natively in text format; you open them simply by double-clicking them. A sample of what you might expect to find in a log is displayed here:

```
ID,Date,Time,Description,IP Address,Host Name,MAC Address
00,04/27/06,20:08:38,Started,,,,
55,04/27/06,20:08:39,Authorized(servicing),,lab1.area51partners.com,,
24,04/27/06,20:44:10,Database Cleanup Begin,,,,
25,04/27/06,20:44:10,0 leases expired and 0 leases deleted,,,,
25,04/27/06,20:44:10,0 leases expired and 0 leases deleted,,,,
24,04/27/06,21:44:12,Database Cleanup Begin,,,,
25,04/27/06,21:44:12,0 leases expired and 0 leases deleted,,,,
25,04/27/06,21:44:12,0 leases expired and 0 leases deleted,,,,
11,04/27/06,19:39:46,Renew,192.168.0.231,
    xpclient01.corp.quepublishing.com,00E07DC13E70,
31,04/27/06,19:39:46,DNS Update Failed,
    192.168.0.231,xpclient01.corp.quepublishing.com,-1,
10,04/27/06,19:43:07,Assign,192.168.0.230,
    iMac01.corp.quepublishing.com,00306509D772,
30,04/27/06,19:44:14,DNS Update Request,192.168.0.231,
    xpclient01.corp.quepublishing.com,,
31,04/27/06,19:44:14,DNS Update Failed,192.168.0.231,
    xpclient01.corp.quepublishing.com,-1,
30,04/27/06,19:47:03,DNS Update Request,192.168.0.231,
    xpclient01.corp.quepublishing.com,,
11,04/27/06,19:47:03,Renew,192.168.0.231,
    xpclient01.corp.quepublishing.com,00E07DC13E70,
30,04/27/06,19:47:03,DNS Update Request,
    192.168.0.231,xpclient01.corp.quepublishing.com,,
11,04/27/06,19:47:03,Renew,192.168.0.231,
    xpclient01.corp.quepublishing.com,00E07DC13E70,
32,04/27/06,19:47:03,DNS Update Successful,192.168.0.231,
    xpclient01.corp.quepublishing.com,,
32,04/27/06,19:47:03,DNS Update Successful,192.168.0.231,
    xpclient01.corp.quepublishing.com,,
```

As you can see from this example, the DHCP server cleans up the database hourly. You can also see that two clients requested leases. One of them, an Apple iMac, requested and was assigned the IP address 192.168.0.230, with no further actions. Another client, a Windows XP Professional computer, requested and received the IP address 192.168.0.231, with several failed DNS updates (evidenced by ID 31). After the DNS dynamic update account was properly configured, the DHCP server was able to make the DNS dynamic updates and generate an ID of 32. Table 3.3 explains the ID codes used in the DHCP daily audit logs.

TABLE 3.3 The DHCP Daily Audit Log ID Codes

ID	Description
00	The log was started.
01	The log was stopped.
02	The log was temporarily paused due to low disk space.
10	A new IP address was leased to a client.
11	A client renewed a lease.
12	A client released a lease.
13	An IP address was found to be in use on the network.
14	A lease request could not be satisfied because the scope's address pool was exhausted.
15	A lease was denied.
16	A lease was deleted.
17	A lease was expired.
20	A BOOTP address was leased to a client.
21	A dynamic BOOTP address was leased to a client.
22	A BOOTP request could not be satisfied because the scope's address pool for BOOTP was exhausted.
23	A BOOTP IP address was deleted after a check was made to see that it was not in use.
24	The IP address cleanup operation has begun.
25	IP address cleanup statistics are provided.
30	A DNS update request to the named DNS server was made.
31	The DNS update failed.
32	The DNS update was successful.
50+	These IDs are used for Rogue Server Detection information.

In addition to the DHCP daily audit logs, events related to the DHCP service are generated and placed in the system log, as shown in Figure 3.37.

As you can see in Figure 3.38, a DHCP server on the network has not been authorized in Active Directory. The system log contains many useful log events about all aspects of a server, and this is an area you should review often.

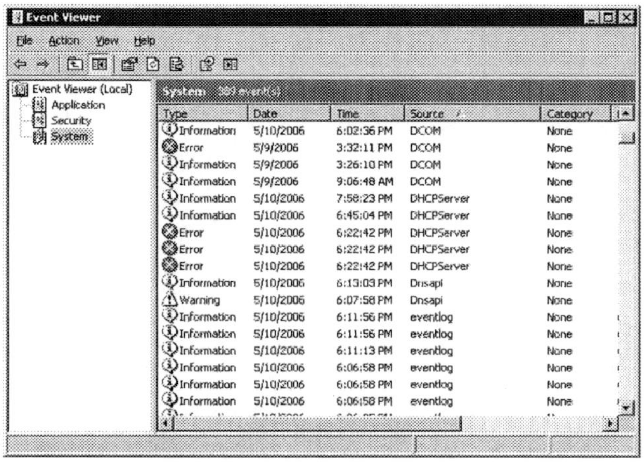

FIGURE 3.37 The system log contains events related to the DHCP service.

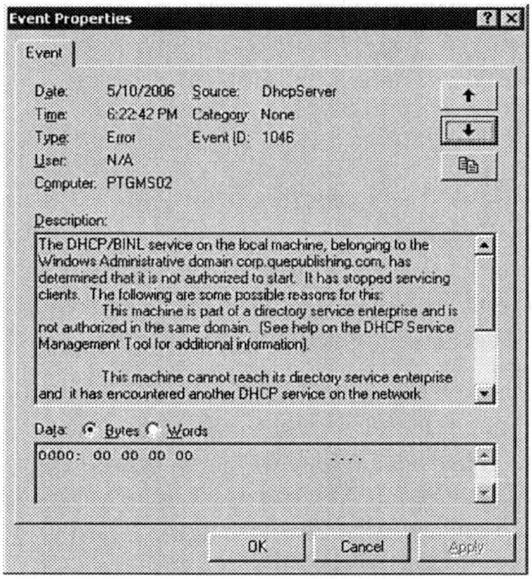

FIGURE 3.38 An unauthorized DHCP server cannot start the DHCP service.

Troubleshooting DHCP Reservations

For the most part, the only problem that prevents a DHCP reservation from functioning properly is a misconfigured MAC address. If you have a misconfigured DHCP reservation, it should show up in the Address Leases node of your DHCP server with the status Reservation (Inactive). Reservations that are configured properly show the status Reservation (Active). If you look back at Figure 3.16, you'll see that the reservation we created had a bad MAC address and, thus, was the cause of the problem in Figure 3.39.

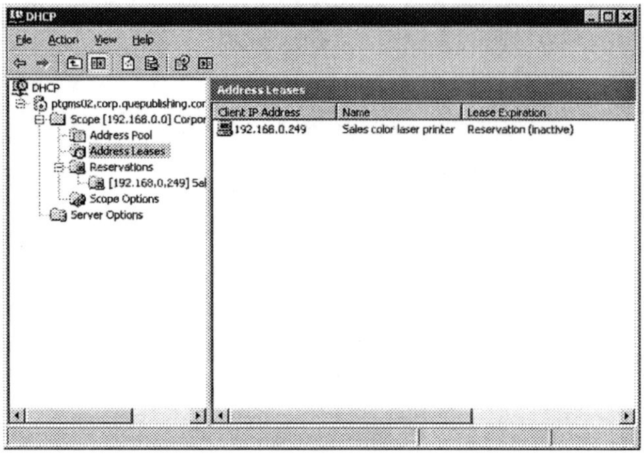

FIGURE 3.39 A DHCP reservation that is not active usually indicates a misconfiguration.

To verify that a reservation is configured properly, you can compare the MAC address of the component that is to have a reserved DHCP address (a print server, for example) to the MAC address entered in the reservation Properties dialog box. The vast majority of the time, this will reveal the source of the problem.

Troubleshooting the DHCP Relay Agent

The DHCP relay agent, like a DHCP reservation, typically doesn't present a problem. However, in some cases, relay services are not being provided to network clients. Some of the most common problems that you might encounter with the DHCP relay agent include the following:

- The network interface on the DHCP relay agent server that is connected to the subnet where the DHCP clients are located has not been selected for use with the DHCP relay agent. You can verify whether the interface has been added or add it from the DHCP Relay Agent node of the DHCP console. You should also verify that the Relay DHCP Packets check box is selected on all adapters that have been selected for use.

- An incorrectly entered DHCP server IP address on the DHCP Relay Agent Properties dialog box (refer back to Figure 3.32) prevents the successful relay of packets. You can verify and correct this problem from the properties dialog box of the DHCP Relay Agent node of the DHCP console.

- Remote DHCP servers might not be reachable because of network or server problems. In this case, you need to troubleshoot basic network connectivity, as discussed in Chapter 1, "Planning, Implementing, and Troubleshooting a TCP/IP Network Infrastructure". You should troubleshoot the server status as discussed in this chapter.

- DHCP traffic might be being filtered. In this case, you need to ensure that no IP filters exist for UDP ports 67 and 68 at any point between the DHCP servers and the remote DHCP clients.

Chapter Summary

In this chapter, we've examined how to implement, manage, and troubleshoot DHCP in Windows Server 2003. Some points of interest to take away from this chapter include the following:

- Windows Server 2003 DHCP supports three types of scopes: standard scopes, superscopes, and multicast scopes. A superscope is a grouping of one or more standard DHCP scopes, whereas a multicast scope is used for special Class D IP addresses for multicasting to clients.
- DHCP servers must be authorized in Active Directory to service clients. Windows Server 2003 DHCP servers that have not been authorized cannot offer leases to DHCP clients.
- DHCP can be integrated with DNS to provide dynamic updating of DNS A and PTR records for DHCP clients. This keeps the DNS database accurate and up-to-date as DHCP assigns leases to client computers.
- You can perform monitoring and troubleshooting on a DHCP server by using the DHCP counters in the Performance console.

Key Terms

- BOOTP
- DHCP
- DHCP client
- DHCP reservation
- DHCP server
- DNS
- Exclusion
- Lease
- Multicast scope
- Registered IP address
- RFCs
- Scope
- Supernetted network
- Superscope
- TCP/IP
- Unicast address

Apply Your Knowledge

In this chapter, you learned what DHCP is and how it works to make IP address assignment easier, quicker, and more accurate. In the following exercises, you will practice some of the concepts and methods discussed in this chapter.

Exercises

3.1 Creating a DHCP Scope

This exercise guides you through the process of creating a standard DHCP scope. This exercise requires you to have a Windows Server 2003 computer with the DHCP service installed.

Estimated time: 20 minutes

1. Open the DHCP console by selecting Start, Programs, Administrative Tools, DHCP.
2. Right-click the DHCP server and select New Scope from the context menu.
3. Click Next to dismiss the opening page of the New Scope Wizard.
4. On the Scope Name page, enter the name **SCOPE1** and an appropriate description for the new scope. Click Next to continue.
5. On the IP Address Range page, enter the IP address range **10.0.0.2**–**10.0.0.100**, and the subnet mask **255.255.255.0**. Click Next to continue.
6. On the Add Exclusions page, enter the IP address ranges **10.0.0.5**–**10.0.0.10** and **10.0.0.15**–**10.0.0.20** as exclusions. Click Next to continue.
7. On the Lease Duration page, you can leave the default setting of 8 days. Click Next to continue.
8. Select to configure advanced options and click Next to continue.
9. On the Router (Default Gateway) page, enter the default gateway IP address **10.0.0.1**. Click Next to continue.
10. On the Domain Name and DNS Servers page, enter the IP addresses **10.0.0.250** and **10.0.0.251** for the DNS servers. Specify the parent domain as **testlab.local**. Click Next to continue.
11. On the WINS Servers page, enter the IP addresses of the WINS servers if you have legacy clients that still need WINS services. Enter the IP addresses **10.0.0.250** and **10.0.0.251** for the WINS servers. Click Next to continue.
12. Opt to activate the scope now and click Finish to complete the wizard.

3.2 Creating a Superscope

This exercise shows you how to manage multiple scopes by creating a superscope. You must have completed Exercise 3.1 for this exercise to work.

Estimated time: 20 minutes

1. Open the DHCP console by selecting Start, Programs, Administrative Tools, DHCP.
2. Right-click the DHCP server and select New Scope from the context menu.
3. Create a second scope, using the IP address range 10.0.0.102 to 10.0.0.200, using the same default gateway, DNS servers, and WINS servers as detailed in Exercise 3.1, with no exclusions. Name the scope **SCOPE2**.
4. Right-click the DHCP server and select New Superscope from the context menu.
5. Click Next to dismiss the opening page of the New Superscope Wizard.
6. On the Superscope Name page, enter **SUPERSCOPE1** and click Next to continue.
7. On the Select Scopes page, select SCOPE1 and SCOPE2 by holding down the Ctrl key and clicking both scopes. Click Next to continue.
8. Verify your configuration on the Completing the New Superscope Wizard page. Click Next to complete the superscope-creation process.
9. The Completing the New Superscope Wizard dialog box summarizes the selections you made throughout the wizard. Click Finish to create the superscope.

3.3 Configuring a DHCP Relay Agent

This exercise walks you through the process of creating and configuring a DHCP relay agent for a network.

Estimated time: 15 minutes

1. Open the Routing and Remote Access console.
2. Expand the console nodes so that you can access the IP Routing, General node.
3. Right-click the General node and select New Routing Protocol.
4. Select the DHCP relay agent.
5. Right-click the DHCP Relay Agent node and select New Interface from the context menu to select the interface to be used for the DHCP relay agent.
6. Configure your required values for hop-count threshold and boot threshold.
7. Right-click the DHCP Relay Agent node and select Properties. Enter one or more remote DHCP servers in the list and click OK to confirm your settings.

3.4 Authorizing a DHCP Server in Active Directory

This exercise walks you through authorizing a DHCP server in Active Directory. This exercise requires that you have an Active Directory environment with an installed DHCP server.

Estimated time: 5 minutes

1. Open the DHCP console by selecting Start, Programs, Administrative Tools, DHCP.
2. Right-click the DHCP server and select Authorize from the context menu.
3. The authorization process might take some time, depending on network conditions. Refresh the DHCP console by pressing F5. The DHCP server status is shown as Active when the authorization is complete. The server is then ready to issue addresses when it receives DHCP requests.

3.5 Configuring DHCP for DNS Integration

This exercise walks you through configuring a DHCP server for DNS integration. This exercise requires that you have an Active Directory environment with an installed DHCP server and DNS server. To complete this exercise, you must have completed Exercise 3.4.

Estimated time: 15 minutes

1. Open the DHCP console by selecting Start, Programs, Administrative Tools, DHCP.
2. Right-click the DHCP server and select Properties from the context menu. Switch to the DNS tab of the DHCP Server Properties dialog box.
3. To enable DHCP integration with DNS, ensure that the Enable Dynamic DNS Updates According to the Settings Below check box is selected.
4. Select either to have the DHCP server update A and PTR records when requested or to always update A and PTR records.
5. To help keep your DNS database clean and consistent, you should allow the DHCP server to cause expired leases to lead to A and PTR record deletion.
6. If you have legacy clients on the network, ensure that dynamic updating is configured for them as well.
7. If you are using secure dynamic updates, you should consider configuring a dedicated network user account for the dynamic updating. You can enter the account credentials by switching to the Advanced tab.
8. Click the Credentials button on the Advanced tab to open the DNS Dynamic Update Credentials dialog box.
9. Enter the domain user account name, domain, and password.

Review Questions

1. You are the systems administrator for Exponent Mathematicians, and you have been asked to implement DHCP on a multinetted network segment. What should you do to ensure that you do this successfully?

2. You are the administrator of the DHCP server for the Get Bux pawn shop chain. You are getting complaints from users that they keep getting address-conflict messages when they turn on their computers. What DHCP counter might help you identify the problem?

3. You are the administrator for Fly Away Travel. When administering Fly Away's DHCP server, you notice that the number of DHCP requests is very high for the number of users on the network. Where is the first place you should look for a server-related problem?

4. You're the administrator of the DHCP server for Little Faith Enterprises. You notice that the DHCP server is running sluggishly during peak hours. When you check the Performance utility, you notice that the DHCP Conflict Check Queue Length counter is very high. What could be causing the DHCP server to be running slowly?

5. You're the administrator of the DHCP server for Little Faith Enterprises. You have just installed the DHCP service and created your first scope by using the New Scope Wizard. You are trying to provide DHCP addresses to a group of users that are two router hops away. What do you still need to do?

Exam Questions

1. You are the systems administrator for Wild Widgets, Inc. You are training a new employee on the use of the DHCP service in Windows Server 2003. She asks you how the client computer requests and receives an address from the server. Which of the following answers is correct?

   ❍ **A.** The client computer broadcasts a `DHCPDISCOVER` message. The DHCP server offers an IP address. The client computer accepts the address and uses it to communicate on the network.

   ❍ **B.** The client computer broadcasts a `DHCPDISCOVER` message. The DHCP server offers an IP address. The client computer accepts the address and sends a request to use that address back to the DHCP server. The client computer uses the address to communicate on the network.

   ❍ **C.** The client computer broadcasts a `DHCPDISCOVER` message. The DHCP server offers an IP address. The client computer accepts the address and sends a request to use that address back to the DHCP server. The DHCP server acknowledges the request and grants the client computer a lease to use the address. The client computer uses the address to connect to the network.

   ❍ **D.** The client computer broadcasts a `DHCPDISCOVER` message. The DHCP server offers an IP address. The client computer accepts the address and sends a request to use that address back to the DHCP server. The DHCP server acknowledges the request and grants the client computer a lease to use the address. The client computer responds with an acknowledgment of the lease and uses the address to connect to the network.

2. You are the system administrator for Phil's Phill-up Stations, a chain of gas stations. As part of the network, you maintain a Windows Server 2003 DHCP server to dynamically assign addresses. You have three superscopes set up, and within each superscope are four scopes. One day, you start experiencing problems with one of the scopes issuing bad addresses. You check the server and suspect that there is a database problem. How can you verify that the database is intact?

 ❍ **A.** Open the DHCP console. Select the scope in question and select Action, Reconcile Scope.

 ❍ **B.** Open the DHCP console. Select the superscope that contains the scope in question and then select Action, Reconcile All Scopes.

 ❍ **C.** Open the DHCP console. Select the DHCP server that contains the scope in question and then select Action, Reconcile All Scopes.

 ❍ **D.** Open the DHCP console. Select the DHCP server that contains the scope in question and then select Action, Reconcile DHCP Database.

3. You are the LAN administrator for Get Stuffed Taxidermy, and you are responsible for maintaining the company's Windows Server 2003 DHCP server. While doing your daily system checks, you notice that the number of `DHCPDISCOVER` packets spiked at 9:00 this morning. What could cause the Discovers/Sec counter to spike at 9:00 a.m.?

 ❍ **A.** A network problem

 ❍ **B.** The DHCP service being restarted

 ❍ **C.** A large number of computers entering the network at approximately the same time

 ❍ **D.** A rogue DHCP server issuing duplicate addresses

4. You are the systems administrator for Hank's Harmonicas, Ltd. Your Active Directory–based network consists of all Windows Server 2003 server computers and Windows 98, Windows 2000 Professional, and Windows XP Professional client computers. This morning, one of the users of a Windows 98 computer called you and said that she could no longer connect to network resources. Upon further investigation, you discover that several other Windows 98 clients are experiencing the same problem. You determine that the cause of the problem is an incorrectly configured DHCP lease. What is the most likely reason that only your Windows 98 clients are exhibiting this problem?

 ❍ **A.** The DHCP service in Windows 98 is not as stable as that in Windows 2000 or Windows XP, and this sometimes results in corrupted lease information.

 ❍ **B.** An unauthorized DHCP server has been set up on the network.

 ❍ **C.** A misconfigured DHCP server has been set up on the network.

 ❍ **D.** The Windows 98 clients were unable to renew their DHCP lease and have thus assumed APIPA IP addresses instead.

5. You are the lead systems administrator for Little Faith Enterprises, and a customer has asked you to install the DHCP service on her Windows Server 2003 computer, get one scope configured, and issue addresses. What minimum steps do you need to take to accomplish this?

   ❍ **A.** Install the DHCP service from the Windows Components Wizard. After the service is installed, authorize it in Active Directory. Next, create the scope. Finally, configure the DNS integration.

   ❍ **B.** Install the DHCP service from the Windows Components Wizard. After the service is installed, create the scope and then configure the DNS integration.

   ❍ **C.** Install the DHCP service from the Windows Components Wizard. After the service is installed, create the scope. Create a superscope and add the scope to it. Authorize the server in Active Directory.

   ❍ **D.** Install the DHCP service from the Windows Components Wizard. After the service is installed, create the scope. Authorize the server in Active Directory.

6. You are the systems administrator for the Hittem Boxing Glove Corporation. The corporation is running a routed network with a centrally located Windows Server 2003 DHCP server. The server is capable of issuing addresses to users on the local segment, but it cannot issue addresses to any of the sites that are across a router. What is the most probable cause of this problem?

   ❍ **A.** The DHCP forwarder service is not enabled on the DHCP server.

   ❍ **B.** The BOOTP forwarder service is not enabled on the DHCP server.

   ❍ **C.** The DHCP forwarder service is not enabled on the routers.

   ❍ **D.** The BOOTP forwarder service is not enabled on the routers.

7. You manage the Windows Server 2003 DHCP servers for the Really Big Screwdriver Corporation. You are running in a purely Windows Server 2003 environment with all Windows XP Professional clients, and you need to make sure that workstations are registered properly in DNS for Active Directory integration. How should you configure DNS integration?

   ❍ **A.** Set DNS integration to automatically update DHCP client information in DNS.

   ❍ **B.** Set DNS integration to discard A and PTR records when a lease is deleted.

   ❍ **C.** Set DNS integration to enable updates for DNS clients that do not support dynamic updates.

   ❍ **D.** Set DNS integration to enable DNS keepalives.

8. You are the systems administrator for UR Write publishing, a bookseller. Your Windows Server 2003 DHCP server issues a block of 40 addresses to 120 salespeople on the Sales network. These users are frequently in and out of the office, so no more than 40 users are ever on the network at one time. What do you need to do to ensure that users get addresses when needed?

   ❍ **A.** Set the DHCP lease duration to 60 minutes.

   ❍ **B.** Set the DHCP lease duration to 5 days.

❍ **C.** Configure a reservation for each user.

❍ **D.** Configure an exclusion for each user.

9. You are the distributed computing administrator for Talk to Me Telephone. The company has Windows Server 2003 installed, with the DHCP service running. Mixed in with the DHCP client computers, the company still has some old workstations on the network with BOOTP chips on their Ethernet cards. You need to add support for BOOTP for these computers. How do you ensure that support?

❍ **A.** Add the BOOTP service to the server.

❍ **B.** In the Advanced tab of the scope Properties dialog box, configure the server to issue addresses to BOOTP clients.

❍ **C.** In the Advanced tab of the server Properties dialog box, configure the server to issue addresses to both DHCP and BOOTP clients.

❍ **D.** In the Advanced tab of the scope Properties dialog box, configure the server to issue addresses to both DHCP and BOOTP clients.

10. You manage the Windows Server 2003 DHCP servers for the Really Big Hammer Corporation. It is a mixed environment, with Windows 2000, Windows XP, and Windows 98 workstations. You need to make sure workstations are registered properly in DNS for Active Directory integration. What do you need to do?

❍ **A.** Set DNS integration to automatically update DHCP client information in DNS.

❍ **B.** Set DNS integration to discard A and PTR records when a lease is deleted.

❍ **C.** Set DNS integration to enable updates for DNS clients that do not request dynamic updates.

❍ **D.** Set DNS integration to enable DNS keepalives.

11. You are the systems administrator for BT Editing Unlimited. You have a 50-host network and are running a Windows Server 2003 DHCP server to assign IP addresses. You also have five IP-based printers with static IP addresses. Your assistant administrator has been working on the DHCP server and has made some changes. Now your users cannot print to one of the printers. What is most likely the problem?

❍ **A.** The scope from which the printers were receiving their IP addresses has been deleted.

❍ **B.** The existing scope has been modified so that it overlaps the addresses reserved for the printers.

❍ **C.** The existing scope has been modified so that it overlaps the addresses reserved for the printers, and a workstation has been assigned the same address as one of the printers.

❍ **D.** The DHCP service was inadvertently stopped.

12. You are the systems administrator for the Little Faith Department Store. You are responsible for maintaining the company's Windows Server 2003 DHCP server. The company recently added a new router and routed a segment to the network. Now that segment must be added to the DHCP server. The address of the router port is 10.10.25.1, and the router is subnetted with a Class C subnet mask. You need to provide 40 addresses, starting at 10.10.25.20. What needs to occur for you to get DHCP working on that segment?

❍ **A.** You need to install and configure an additional DHCP server on that segment to provide DHCP services.

❍ **B.** You need to add to the DHCP server a scope that contains the addresses from 10.10.25.20 through 10.10.25.59. The scope needs a subnet mask of 255.255.255.0. You need to configure the BOOTP forwarder for the new segment's router, using the address of the DHCP server. You need to activate the scope.

❍ **C.** You need to add to the DHCP server a scope that contains the addresses from 10.10.25.20 through 10.10.25.60. The scope needs a subnet mask of 255.255.255.0. You need to configure the BOOTP forwarder for the new segment's router, using the address of the DHCP server. You need to activate the scope.

❍ **D.** You need to add to the DHCP server a scope that contains the addresses from 10.10.25.20 through 10.10.25.60. The scope needs a subnet mask of 255.255.255.0. You need to configure the BOOTP forwarder for the new segment's router, using the address of the DHCP server. You do not need to activate the scope because that happens automatically when the scope is created.

13. You are the network manager for IntCo Manufacturing. You are running in a mixed environment, and you are using a Windows Server 2003 DHCP service to support three network segments. Your client computers consist of Windows 2000 Professional, Windows NT Workstation, and Windows 98 SE workstations. What do you need to do to ensure that all the client computers can receive DHCP addresses?

❍ **A.** Configure a scope for each network segment. Configure each client computer to receive IP addresses dynamically. Configure the DHCP service for backward compatibility.

❍ **B.** Configure a scope for each network segment. Configure each client computer to receive IP addresses dynamically. For the Windows NT Workstation client computers, ensure that the DHCP update from Service Pack 6 has been installed.

❍ **C.** Configure a scope for each network segment. Configure each client computer to receive IP addresses dynamically. Configure the DHCP service for mixed mode.

❍ **D.** Configure a scope for each network segment. Configure each client computer to receive IP addresses dynamically.

14. You are the systems administrator for BT Editing, and you are running a purely Windows Server 2003 network, using Active Directory and the Windows Server 2003 DHCP service. A user in another department has installed a DHCP server on a UNIX server. How do you prevent your client computers from receiving DHCP addresses from that server?

❍ **A.** Disable the unauthorized server in Active Directory.

❍ **B.** Make sure all your domain client computers are running Windows 2000 or higher.

❍ **C.** Reconfigure BOOTP on the router.

❍ **D.** Go to each client computer and enter the address of the production DHCP server in the Internet Protocol (TCP/IP) Properties dialog box.

15. You are the systems administrator for Area 51 Partners, a consulting firm that is not involved in any way, shape, or form with alien activity in Nevada. You have a customer who would like to ensure that only authorized DHCP servers can make dynamic updates to the DNS database. What will you configure for the customer to make this happen? (Choose all that apply.)

❍ **A.** Create a new domain user account called `DNSDYNUPD`.

❍ **B.** Enter the credentials for the `DNSDYNUPD` account in the scope options for your DHCP server.

❍ **C.** Enter the credentials for the `DNSDYNUPD` account in the DNS Dynamic Update Credentials dialog box for your DHCP server.

❍ **D.** Add the `DNSDYNUPD` account to the Enterprise Administrators group.

Answers to Review Questions

1. To successfully implement DHCP in a multinetted environment, you should consider using a superscope to ease the management of the scopes for each of the multinetted networks. For more information, see the section "Understanding DHCP Superscopes."

2. You should check the Declines/Sec counter in the Performance console for the DHCP object. The number of `DHCPDECLINE` messages received per second by the DHCP server from client computers can be used to see whether the DHCP client computer has declined the IP address issued by the server. You see this number rise when client computers start having address conflict problems, and it could indicate a network problem, computers with static addresses also being part of a scope, or a rogue DHCP server being on the network. For more information, see the section "Troubleshooting DHCP Server Authorization Problems."

3. You should check the length of the DHCP lease. If the lease has been set to a very short duration, client computers would need to request addresses frequently. For more information, see the section "Creating a DHCP Scope."

4. Either a lot of DHCP requests are occurring during peak hours or the Conflict Detection Attempts parameter is set too high. If that parameter is enabled, the Windows Server 2003 DHCP service issues an address and checks whether any IP address conflicts exist. This can put a lot of additional overhead on the server and drive up the DHCP conflict check queue length. For more information, see the section "Troubleshooting DHCP Server Authorization Problems."

5. First, you need to authorize the DHCP server in Active Directory. The DHCP server cannot provide addresses until that occurs. You also need to configure the BOOTP forwarder on any routers between the DHCP server and the client workstations so that the routers know where to forward DHCP messages. For more information, see the section "Authorizing a DHCP Server in Active Directory."

Answers to Exam Questions

1. **C**. The client computer cannot use the address until the DHCP server grants the lease. After the DHCP server acknowledges the DHCP request and grants the lease, the client computer can use the address. Before a client computer can actually use an offered address, it must request to do so and receive an acknowledgment from the offering DHCP server; thus, answers A, B, and D are incorrect. No additional step is required in the process. For more information, see the section "DHCP."

2. **C**. You need to reconcile all the scopes on the server. Answer A is almost correct because you can reconcile a single scope, but the correct command is Reconcile, not Reconcile Scope. You cannot reconcile scopes at the superscope level, as stated in answer B. The command in answer D does not exist.

3. **C**. The `DHCPDISCOVER` packet is sent when a computer first requests an address. The most likely reason for the Discovers/Sec counter to spike would be a large number of concurrent requests occurring, which could happen when a large number of client workstations request addresses at the same time. A network problem would have the opposite effect because no `DHCPDISCOVER` packets would reach the server; thus, answer A is incorrect. A DHCP service restart or a rogue DHCP server couldn't affect the number of `DHCPDISCOVER` packets because the packets are generated by client PCs; thus, answers B and D are incorrect. For more information, see the section "Troubleshooting DHCP Server Authorization Problems."

4. **B**. In this scenario, the most likely cause for the problem is that an unauthorized DHCP server has been set up on the network. Windows 2000 and Windows XP clients in an Active Directory domain do not take DHCP leases from DHCP servers that have not been authorized in Active Directory. The DHCP service in Windows 98 would not likely cause this sort of problem; thus, answer A is incorrect. A misconfigured DHCP server that was authorized would give bad DHCP lease information to all clients, not just to Windows 98 clients; thus, answer C is incorrect. In addition, if clients were unable to reach a DHCP server, the Windows 2000 and Windows XP clients would also assign themselves APIPA IP addresses; thus, answer D is incorrect. For more information, see the section "Troubleshooting DHCP Server Authorization Problems."

5. **D**. If the task is to install the DHCP service and get it issuing addresses, you do not need to configure DNS, but you do need to authorize the server in Active Directory; thus, answers A and B are incorrect. Even though you learned how to create a superscope in this chapter, you do not need a superscope for the server to function; thus, answer C is incorrect.

6. **D**. To issue addresses using DHCP across a router, the router needs to have the BOOTP forwarder service enabled and configured; thus, answer C is incorrect. DHCP relay is configured on a router or a Windows Server 2003 computer running Routing and Remote Access; thus, answer A is incorrect. There is no such thing as the BOOTP forwarder server; thus, answer B is incorrect. For more information, see the section “Configuring and Implementing a DHCP Relay Agent.”

7. **A**. In a purely Windows 2000, Windows XP, and Windows Server 2003 environment, you need to configure DHCP to automatically update DNS to ensure that the client computers appear on the network correctly. Setting the DNS integration to discard lookups after a lease is deleted also works with a purely Windows 2000 network, but it has nothing to do with the computers registering properly; thus, answer B is incorrect. Windows 2000, Windows XP, and Windows Server 2003 all support dynamic updates; thus, answer C is incorrect. Keepalives are associated with HTTP sessions, not DNS; thus, answer D is incorrect. For more information, see the section “Configuring DHCP for DNS Integration.”

8. **A**. To ensure that addresses are available, the DHCP lease needs to be set to a short interval; thus, answer B is incorrect. Reservations won’t help since you have too few leases already; thus, answer C incorrect. There was no mention of a need for exclusions and, thus, no need to configure them; therefore, answer D is incorrect. For more information, see the section “Creating a DHCP Scope.”

9. **D**. You need to configure the scope to issue addresses to both DHCP and BOOTP clients; thus, answers A, B, and C are incorrect. For more information, see the section “Creating a DHCP Scope.”

10. **C**. Because the non–Windows 2000 (or non–Windows XP) machines lack the capability to directly update the DNS server themselves, you need the DHCP server to make the updates to DNS. Using DNS integration to enable updates for DNS client computers that do not support dynamic updates enables the DHCP server to perform this service. The options mentioned in answers A and B do not exist; thus, they are incorrect. Keepalives are associated with HTTP sessions, not DNS; thus, answer D is incorrect. For more information, see the section “Configuring DHCP for DNS Integration.”

11. **C**. The address from the printer has probably been issued to another computer. Because the printers use static addresses, the only change to the DHCP server that could have affected printing would be another host having the same address. Deleting the scope would cause problems, but not likely right away; thus, answer A is incorrect. Answer B is close, but just creating an overlapping scope is not a problem until the overlapping addresses are assigned. As with deleting the scope, stopping the DHCP service would causes problems, but not unless a client needed a new address; thus, answer D is incorrect.

12. **B**. A single DHCP server can serve multiple segments, so you do not need an additional server. To get 40 addresses, the range must be from 10.10.25.20 to 10.10.25.59, which is an inclusive range. Also, the last step of the New Scope Wizard is to authorize the new scope. The actions listed in answer A are not enough to perform the required task; thus, answer A is incorrect. Answers C and D each provide 41 addresses; in addition, answer D has you not activating the scope, which you must do to use the scope. Therefore, answers C are D are incorrect.

13. **D**. You do not need to make any special configurations to the DHCP service; it can communicate with non–Windows 2000 or non–Windows XP client computers without problems. Thus, answers A and C are incorrect. You also do not need to update any of the client computers. Windows NT and Windows 98 are capable of using DHCP without needing updates applied; thus, answer B is incorrect. You just need to configure the appropriate scope and configure the client computers to use that scope.

14. **B**. Because a UNIX server cannot be enabled in Active Directory, Windows 2000 (and Windows XP) client computers do not accept DHCP addresses from the server. Answer A is not correct because you cannot disable a server that isn't joined to the Active Directory domain. Changing the BOOTP configuration on the router might prevent remote users from receiving addresses, but local users would still be vulnerable; thus, answer C is incorrect. In answer D, there is nowhere to enter the address of the DHCP server. For more information, see the section "Authorizing a DHCP Server in Active Directory."

15. **A, C**. Windows Server 2003 enables you to use a preconfigured domain user account to perform DNS dynamic updates. This ensures that only authorized DHCP servers are performing dynamic updates and that all DHCP servers can update and modify DNS entries. In addition, this prevents problems previously associated with allowing a DHCP server running on a domain controller to perform DNS dynamic updates. The best course of action is to create a dedicated domain user account for this purpose. The account information to be used for dynamic updates is configured at the server level; thus, answer B is incorrect. The account used for dynamic updates does not need to be a member of the Enterprise Administrators group; thus, answer D is incorrect. For more information, see the section "Configuring DHCP for DNS Integration."

Suggested Readings and Resources

1. Davies, Joseph, and Thomas Lee. *Microsoft Windows Server 2003 TCP/IP Protocols and Services Technical Reference*. Redmond, WA: Microsoft Press, 2003.

2. Stevens, W. Richard. *TCP/IP Illustrated, Volume 1: The Protocols*. Boston: Addison-Wesley, 1994.

3. "Deploying Network Services." http://technet2.microsoft.com/WindowsServer/en/Library/119050c9-7c4d-4cbf-8f38-97c45e4d01ef1033.mspx.

4. "Technical Overview of Windows Server 2003 Networking and Communications." www.microsoft.com/windowsserver2003/techinfo/overview/netcomm.mspx.

5. "Windows Server 2003 Reviewer's Guide." www.microsoft.com/windowsserver2003/techinfo/overview/reviewersguide.mspx.

6. "Dynamic Host Configuration Protocol (DHCP) Operations Topics." http://technet2.microsoft.com/windowsserver/en/operations/dhcp.mspx.

7. "Windows Server 2003 Security Guide." www.microsoft.com/technet/security/prodtech/windowsserver2003/W2003HG/SGCH00.mspx.

4

CHAPTER FOUR

Planning and Implementing a Name Resolution Infrastructure

In today's well-connected network-centric world, name resolution is a critical component of any Windows Server 2003 network. The domain name system (DNS) is often considered one of the "critical" core network services—and rightfully so. The Windows Internet Naming Service (WINS) has fallen out of favor with the move away from the Network Basic Input/Output System (NetBIOS) and NetBIOS Extended User Interface (NetBEUI), but it is still lingering in the background for many administrators who are faced with maintaining a heterogeneous network environment. Despite the fact that Windows Server 2003 (and Windows 2000 Server, for that matter) runs on Transmission Control Protocol/Internet Protocol (TCP/IP) through and through, many networks still must support legacy Windows 9*x* and NT clients; thus, WINS still has a small place in Windows Server 2003 and, therefore, in this MCSE exam.

Objectives

Microsoft has defined the name resolution portion of the "Planning, Implementing, and Maintaining a Network Infrastructure" objectives as follows:

Plan a host name resolution strategy.

- **Plan a DNS namespace design.**
- **Plan zone replication requirements.**
- **Plan a forwarding configuration.**
- **Plan for DNS security.**
- **Examine the interoperability of DNS with third-party DNS solutions.**
- DNS is king when it comes to name resolution in Windows Server 2003 networks. Proper planning is essential to implementing a functional DNS environment for your network. Planning for DNS involves many different processes and steps, however, and you must be aware of them all to be able to create the correct DNS infrastructure you require.

Plan a NetBIOS name resolution strategy.

- **Plan a WINS replication strategy.**
- **Plan NetBIOS name resolution by using the LMHOSTS file.**
- Even though Microsoft has officially moved away from WINS as the primary name resolution, it still exists to provide backward compatibility with legacy clients, such as Windows 98 and Windows NT 4.0 computers. You need to have a basic understanding of how WINS is configured to provide name resolution for your legacy clients—and do well on the exam.

Troubleshoot host name resolution.

- **Diagnose and resolve issues related to DNS services.**
- **Diagnose and resolve issues related to client computer configuration.**
- DNS is one of those core network services that works right almost all the time. However, when the day comes that "DNS is broken," you will most certainly hear about it. In addition to the complaints your users will undoubtedly flood you with, your network might well come to a screeching halt because Active Directory is absolutely dependent on a functional DNS infrastructure. Being able to quickly identify and correct DNS-related problems is an essential part of your duties as the network administrator.

Outline

Study Strategies

- Be sure that you have a thorough understanding of the WINS service and NetBIOS name resolution. Although this is a legacy Microsoft protocol, it is still required in many environments, and Microsoft wants to be absolutely sure you understand how it works.
- Review the use of the monitoring tools and the different parameters of WINS that can be monitored. In its exams, Microsoft has focused a great deal of attention on the monitoring and troubleshooting of the different services, including the WINS service.
- Get your hands dirty. The Step by Steps throughout this book provide plenty of directions and exercises, but you should go beyond these examples and create some of your own. If you can, experiment with each of the objectives to see how they work and why you would use each one.

Introduction

Just 10 years ago, TCP/IP was not the king when it came to network communications protocols. Windows NT 3.51 relied on the venerable NetBIOS Extended User Interface (NetBEUI) protocol by default, and NetWare servers could be counted on to understand only IPX/SPX. With the recent widespread adoption of the Internet by the masses, TCP/IP slowly started to creep into private networks of all sizes and purposes. Administrators and network designers began to see the power and flexibility that TCP/IP offered them, and Microsoft and Novell took note of the shift. It wasn't long before all operating systems provided support for TCP/IP, but it still was not the networking protocol of choice. With the introduction of Windows 2000, Microsoft made TCP/IP and the domain name system (DNS) integral parts of Windows Active Directory networks.

Introduction to DNS

You probably use DNS every day, whether or not you are familiar with the underlying mechanism. Domain names are easy to use and remember. The ease with which you can access a website using domain names (such as www.microsoft.com or www.quepublishing.com) is a built-in simplicity that comes with a price: The DNS namespace is complex. DNS names are created as part of a hierarchical database that functions much like the directories in a file system. Hierarchies are powerful database structures because they can store tremendous amounts of data while making it easy to search for specific bits of information. Before examining the specifics of the DNS namespace hierarchy, let's review some rules about hierarchies in general.

Hierarchies

Before getting into the details of a hierarchy, we should review some terms:

- **Tree**—This is a type of data structure with each element attached to one or more elements directly beneath it. In the case of DNS, this structure is often called an inverted tree because it is generally drawn with the root at the top of the tree.
- **Top-level domain (TLD)**—TLD refers to the suffix attached to Internet domain names. There is a limited number of predefined suffixes, and each one represents a top-level domain. The more popular TLDs include `.COM`, `.EDU`, `.GOV`, `.MIL`, `.NET`, and `.ORG`.
- **Node**—A node is a point at which two or more lines in the tree intersect. In the case of DNS, a node can represent a TLD, a subdomain, or an actual network node (host).
- **Fully qualified domain name (FQDN)**—A domain name that includes all domains between the host and the root of DNS is an FQDN. For example, www.microsoft.com is an FQDN.

- **Leaf**—A leaf is an item at the bottom of a hierarchical tree structure, and it does not contain any other objects.
- **Zone**—A DNS zone is a logical grouping of host names within DNS. For example, `quepublishing.com` is considered the forward lookup zone for Que Publishing. It is the place where the information about the Que Publishing hosts is contained within DNS.

In DNS, containers called domains hold the information. The hierarchy starts with a root container, called the *root domain*. The root domain doesn't have a name, so it is typically represented by a single period, as shown in Figure 4.1. The root domain contains pointers to all TLDs, which are directly below the root domain. These domains are also sometimes called *first-level domains*. Lower-level domains are second-level, third-level, and so on. Every domain name has a suffix that indicates which TLD domain it belongs to. There is only a limited number of such domains as defined by Request for Comment (RFC) 1591. Following are some of the more common TLDs:

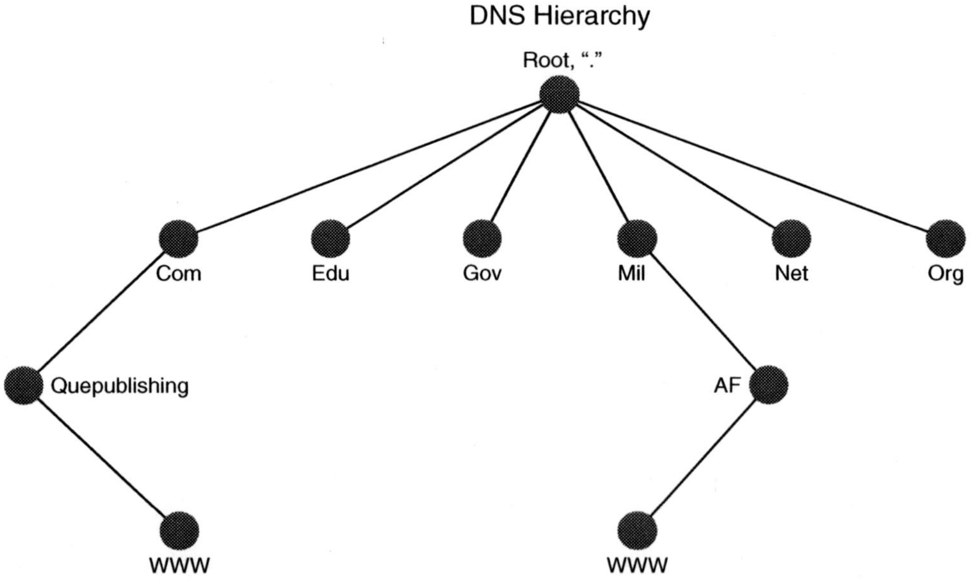

FIGURE 4.1 This portion of the DNS hierarchy shows the location of two domains in the DNS database in relation to the rest of the DNS database.

- **.COM**—Intended for commercial entities, but it has become the overwhelming favorite top-level domain (example: `area51partners.com`)
- **.EDU**—Intended for higher-education institutions, such as four-year colleges and universities (example: `berkeley.edu`)

- **.GOV**—Intended for use by agencies of the U.S. federal government (example: `whitehouse.gov`)
- **.MIL**—Intended for use by agencies of the U.S. military (example: `af.mil`)
- **.NET**—Intended for use by network providers and organizations dedicated to the Internet, such as Internet service providers (example: `ibm.net`)
- **.ORG**—Intended for nonprofit or noncommercial establishments, such as professional groups, charities, and other such organizations (example: `npr.org`)

NOTE

DNS country codes Two-letter country-code TLDs also exist for nearly all countries on the planet. Examples include `.US` for the United States, `.CA` for Canada, `.JP` for Japan, and `.UK` for the United Kingdom. New TLDs are constantly being added to meet the requirements for new domain names on the Internet. Recent additions include `.BIZ` and `.INFO`, among others.

Fully Qualified Domain Names (FQDNs)

As we have discussed, DNS is used to translate a host name to an IP address. The FQDN name typically looks something like the following:

```
mail01.na.quepublishing.com
```

This is known as the host's fully qualified domain name (FQDN) because it lists the host's precise location in the DNS hierarchy. The DNS name in the example represents the host `mail01` in the subdomain `na` (a commonly used geographical reference for North America), which is in the subdomain `quepublishing` (this is frequently the name of the company or organization that has registered the domain), which is in the TLD `.com`.

EXAM ALERT

Fully qualified domain names Make sure you have a good understanding of what an FQDN is and how it is represented.

What's New with Windows Server 2003 DNS

DNS is certainly not a new service in Windows Server 2003, but it has undergone some changes from both Windows 2000 and Windows NT 4.0. The following list summarizes some of the major changes in DHCP in Windows Server 2003 from Windows 2000 Server and Windows NT 4.0:

- **Integrated zones**—With the Windows Server 2003 DNS server service, you can integrate DNS into Active Directory, and resource records are stored in Active Directory and can be updated by any DC running DNS. This integration is a proprietary feature of the Windows Server DNS, but it can yield a much more secure, robust, and fault-tolerant implementation than standard DNS.
- **Incremental zone transfers**—The standard model for DNS zone transfers is to transfer the entire zone whenever an update is made. Transferring entire zones is very inefficient. Windows Server 2003 DNS allows secondary servers to request incremental updates, which contain only changes that have occurred since the last transfer. Incremental zone transfers are commonly abbreviates as IXFR.
- **Secure DNS updates**—Changes to records in a zone can be restricted to those coming only from trusted sources.
- **DNS/DHCP integration**—The power of DDNS lies in its integration of DHCP with DNS. Any Windows Server 2003 DHCP client computer is automatically added to the DNS table at the time that its IP address is issued.
- **Support for stub zones**—A stub zone contains only those resource records that are necessary to identify the authoritative DNS servers for that zone.
- **Conditional forwarding**—Conditional forwarding allows administrators to direct DNS requests to other DNS servers based on domain. Previous versions of Microsoft DNS would support only one forwarder, so if forwarding was enabled, all requests would be sent to a single server. Conditional forwarding is used frequently when you want requests made to the internal network to be forwarded to a master DNS server that stores internal DNS zones, but you want to have resolution requests that are made to Internet domains sent to the Internet by using the standard resolution process.
- **Enhanced debug logging**—The Windows Server 2003 DNS service offers extremely detailed debug logging for advanced DNS troubleshooting.
- **DNS security (DNSSEC) extensions**—In keeping with Microsoft's secure computing initiatives, Windows Server 2003 DNS provides basic support for the DNSSEC extensions defined in RFC 2535.
- **Additional round-robin DNS capabilities**—Round-robining of all resource record types is supported under Windows Server 2003 DNS.
- **Support for application directory partitions**—An application directory partition stores dynamic, application-specific data. An application directory partition can store any type of object except security principals and is not replicated to the global catalog. Replication of application directory partitions can be tightly controlled, and application directory partitions can be replicated only to a Windows Server 2003 DC.

EXAM ALERT

Active Directory relies on DNS Because Active Directory relies completely on DNS for name resolution and the Active Directory structure is also modeled on DNS, you can expect DNS to make a very good topic for exam questions.

Planning a DNS Namespace Design

Objective:

Plan a host name resolution strategy.

- Plan a DNS namespace design.

TIP

Know DNS? The following discussion about DNS assumes that you are already familiar with installing the DNS service and performing basic management and configuration tasks. If you need a review, see Chapter 3, "Implementing and Managing DNS," of *MCSA/MCSE 70-291 Exam Prep: Implementing, Managing, and Maintaining a Windows Server 2003 Network Infrastructure* (Que Publishing, 2006; ISBN 0-7897-3649-7), by Will Schmied.

Up to this point in our discussion about DNS, we have looked at only the historical and design aspects of DNS—and for good reason. Only by understanding how DNS was created and designed can you effectively plan and implement a DNS design in a Windows Server 2003 Active Directory domain. Because DNS permeates Windows Server 2003, you should deliberately and carefully plan your DNS namespace *before* you ever perform the first installation of Windows Server 2003 on a computer.

The following list represents some questions you should ask yourself when planning your namespace needs:

- **Is your DNS namespace to be used for internal purposes only?** If so, you can use characters that are not typically used in DNS names, such as those outside the RFC 1123 standards. An example might be `bigcorp.local`.
- **Is your DNS namespace to be used on the Internet as well?** If you are currently using a corporate DNS namespace on the Internet or think that you might at any point in the future, you should register your own domain name and conform to Internet naming standards.
- **Will you be implementing Active Directory?** The design and implementation of Active Directory on your network play a critical role in determining how domains should be created and nested within each other.

You have the following three basic options to consider when planning the DNS namespace you will be using:

- **Use an existing DNS namespace**—This option uses the same namespace for both the internal (corporate network) and external (Internet) portions of your network. If your domain name is `bigcorp.com`, you would use it for both internal and external use. Although this method is the easiest and provides simple access to both internal and external resources, it poses additional administrative requirements because an administrator must ensure that the appropriate records are being stored on the internal and external DNS servers as a security precaution.
- **Use a delegated DNS namespace**—This option uses a delegated domain of the public namespace. If your domain name is `bigcorp.com`, you might consider using `corp.bigcorp.com` for the internal namespace. When you use this option, the `corp.bigcorp.com` domain becomes the root of the Active Directory forest and domain structure. Internal clients should be allowed to resolve external namespace addresses; however, external clients should not. Using a delegated DNS namespace provides a namespace that is easy to understand and remember, and that fits in nicely with the existing registered domain name. All internal domain data is isolated in the domain or domain tree, thus requiring its own DNS server for the delegated internal domain. The downside to delegated namespaces is that this adds length to the total FQDN.
- **Use a unique DNS namespace**—This option uses a completely separate but related domain name for your internal namespace. As an example, if you are using `bigcorp.com` for your external namespace, you might use `bigcorp.net` for your internal namespace. This configuration provides the advantage of improving security by isolating the two namespaces from each other. Additionally, the administrative burden is relatively low because zone transfers do not need to be performed between the two namespaces, and the existing DNS namespace remains unchanged. In addition, this option prevents internal resources from being exposed directly to the Internet.

Consider the following example of a fictitious company that is in the planning stages of a major worldwide network reorganization and upgrade to Windows Server 2003 Active Directory. Gidget's Widgets, Inc., is a major manufacturer of household goods and already owns the `gidgets.com` domain name for its Internet website. Gidget's makes everything from bath towels to kitchen sinks. Gidget's corporate headquarters are located in the United States, with regional field offices in Canada, Mexico, England, Germany, India, Japan, and Australia. Gidget's corporate structure has the following major departments: Executive, Administrative, Engineering, Manufacturing, Facilities, Sales, Legal, and Information Services. Within each department are one or more individual divisions. How would you go about designing a DNS namespace for the Gidget's Widgets internal network?

You have several options; let's assume for the sake of argument that you will first create a delegated domain named `corp` to serve as the root of the internal network and also as the Active Directory root. Starting with the `corp.gidgets.com` domain, you could create fourth-level domains by country code. Within these domains, you could create fifth-level domains, as required, for each of the major departments. You might end up with a configuration that looks something like that shown in Figure 4.2.

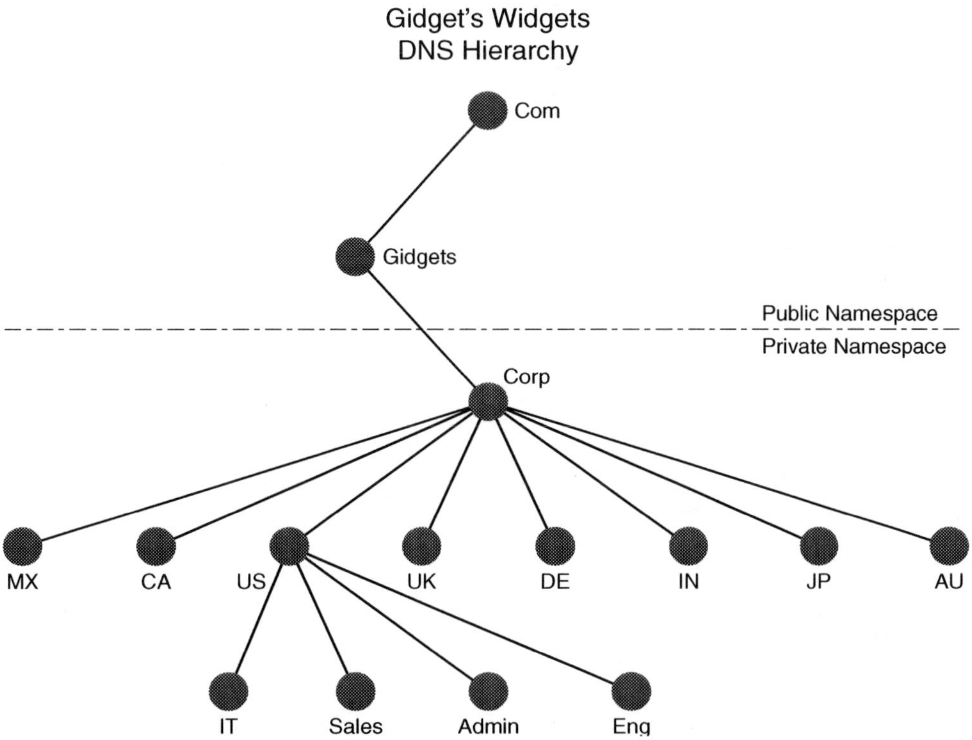

FIGURE 4.2 Gidget's network has been nicely organized by using countries as fourth-level domains and major departments as fifth-level domains.

If you were a network administrator in the United States working from a computer called `greenguy42`, your FQDN would be `greenguy42.it.us.corp.gidgets.com`. Of course, you could also design the DNS namespace using continents instead of countries, if desired. When creating DNS namespaces that are several levels deep, as in the example in Figure 4.2, you must keep in mind some general DNS restrictions, as outlined in Table 4.1.

EXAM ALERT

Designing the DNS hierarchy Several of the examples presented in this chapter do not represent "best design practices," in that they have many levels of depth. This is done for illustrative purposes to help you gain a better understanding of how DNS works. In reality, you might want to consider placing resources within Organizational Units instead of fifth-level domains and below. Having too many levels in your domain architecture can lead to slower authentication, among other issues.

TABLE 4.1 DNS Name Restrictions

Restriction	Standard DNS	DNS in Windows Server 2003 (and Windows 2000)
Characters	Supports RFC 1123, which permits *A* to *Z*, *a* to *z*, 0 to 9, and the hyphen (-).	Supports several different configurations: RFC 1123 standard, as well as support for RFCs 2181 and the character set specified in RFC 2044.
FQDN length	Permits 63 bytes per label and 255 bytes for an FQDN.	Permits 63 bytes per label and 255 bytes for an FQDN. Domain controllers are limited to 155 bytes for an FQDN.

No matter what design you settle on, you must (in most cases) get it right the first time. Redesigning a DNS namespace is a difficult and time-consuming task after the fact, at best. In addition, failing to properly design the namespace for Active Directory compatibility can lead to functionality problems in the future.

After you've planned your namespace, you're ready to get down to business and start working out the finer points of your DNS implementation. The next thing you need to plan for is the types of zones you will be using. But what exactly is a zone?

Planning DNS Zone Requirements

Objective:

Plan a host name resolution strategy.

- Plan zone replication requirements.

You can easily get lost in the maze of acronyms and buzzwords surrounding DNS, especially if you are having a conversation with someone who has been working with IP networking and DNS for a while. You have a standard primary server for each zone, which might also be a domain, unless it's a reverse-lookup zone; then you have zone transfers happening when you least expect it. To the uninitiated, this discussion can sound alarmingly like some arcane networking ritual, paying homage to the DNS deities.

Working with DNS is not nearly as bad as it sounds. But before we get any deeper into the Windows Server 2003 DNS infrastructure, we must discuss what exactly is meant when we refer to a *DNS zone*. First, although it is typically abbreviated in the world of DNS, a zone is actually a *zone of authority*, which means that it contains the complete information on some part of a domain namespace. In other words, it is a subset or root of that portion of namespace. The nameserver is considered to have authority for that zone, and it can respond to any requests for name resolution from that zone. So when you look at the DNS name www.quepublishing.com, `quepublishing.com` is a DNS zone within the `.com` hierarchy. The www denotes the DNS record of a host contained within the `quepublishing.com` zone.

This conceptual representation of a zone also has a physical counterpart: All the information relating to a particular zone is stored in a physical file known as the *zone database file*—or, more commonly, the *zone file*—which can be found at `%systemroot%\system32\dns` for zones that are not stored in Active Directory. Windows Server 2003 supports the following types of zones:

- **Standard primary**—A standard primary zone holds a master copy of a zone and can replicate it to all configured secondary zones in standard text format. Any changes that must be made to the zone are made on the copy stored on the primary.
- **Standard secondary**—A standard secondary zone holds a read-only copy of the zone information in standard text format. Secondary zones are created to increase performance and resilience of the DNS configuration. Information is transferred from the primary zone to the secondary zones.
- **Active Directory–integrated**—Active Directory–integrated zones are available only on Windows 2000 Server and Windows Server 2003 DNS servers in an Active Directory domain. The zone information is contained within the Active Directory database and is replicated using Active Directory replication. Active Directory–integrated zones provide an increased level of replication flexibility as well as security. Active Directory–integrated zones also operate in a multimaster arrangement because they are hosted within Active Directory itself; this way, any DNS server (domain controller) hosting the Active Directory–integrated zone can update the zone data.
- **Stub**—Microsoft has introduced support for stub zones for the first time in Windows Server 2003. A stub zone contains only those resource records that are necessary to identify the authoritative DNS servers for that zone. Those resource records include Name Server (NS), Start of Authority (SOA), and possibly glue host (A) records. (Glue host records provide A record pointers to ensure that the master zone has the correct nameserver information for the stub zone.) Stub zones are best used to replace standard secondary zones in a multi-domain Active Directory forest. In the past, secondary zones were created in other domains that for a domain's Active Directory DNS zone. This method is both administratively burdensome and also error prone. By using Active Directory integrated stub zones (that are replicated throughout the forest), you can eliminate entirely the need to create secondary zones in all Active Directory integrated DNS implementation.

NOTE

"What's the difference between a zone and a domain?" Although the two terms can seem as if they are used interchangeably, there is a difference. A DNS domain is a segment of the DNS namespace. A zone, on the other hand, can contain multiple contiguous domains.

For example, `quepublishing.com` is a DNS domain. It contains all the information for that specific portion of the DNS namespace. `sales.quepublishing.com` is another example of a domain, which is contiguous with the `quepublishing.com` domain; in other words, the two domains "touch." So, if you were to create a DNS forward-lookup zone on your DNS server, it could contain records for both domains. Zones allow for the logical grouping and management of domains and resource records on your DNS servers.

Although determining the zone type might not seem to be an important part of planning your DNS solution, nothing could be further from the truth. The type of DNS zone that you implement ultimately determines the placement of the DNS servers in your network. In addition, the type of DNS zone that you create will, in part, affect the construction of the network and the interoperability with other DNS servers, such as UNIX Berkeley Internet Name Domain (BIND) servers.

When you are using a standard primary/standard secondary DNS zone implementation, the following points are of concern:

- A single DNS server is the master, holding the only writeable copy of the DNS zone file.
- Zone transfers can be conducted using either incremental or full-zone transfer.
- This implementation is fully compatible with BIND DNS servers by using the standard DNS zone-transfer methods in place.

NOTE

Integrating Active Directory with BIND If you'll be using BIND as your DNS source for an Active Directory implementation, be sure that it at least meets the minimum required version. BIND version 8.2.2 patch 7 (and newer) offer full support for SRV records (per RFC 2782) and Dynamic DNS (per RFC 2136).

When you are using an Active Directory–integrated DNS zone implementation, the following points are of concern:

- A multimaster arrangement allows any DNS server to make updates to the zone file.
- Zone data is replicated with Active Directory data.
- Increased security is provided on the zone file.
- Redundancy is provided for DNS dynamic update.
- The administrator can adjust replication scope. Additionally, the zone file can be replicated to a standard secondary DNS server—a common practice for DNS servers placed on screened subnets.
- This implementation appears to be a standard primary zone to a BIND DNS server, thus allowing the use of BIND DNS servers as standard secondary zone servers.

Table 4.2 provides a comparison of Active Directory–integrated zones and standard DNS zones.

TABLE 4.2 DNS Zone Type Comparison

DNS Feature	Standard DNS Zones	Active Directory Integrated DNS Zones
Complies with Internet Engineering Task Force (IETF) specifications	Yes	Yes
Uses Active Directory for replication	No	Yes
Increases availability by providing a multimaster arrangement	No	Yes
Allows for zone updates after the failure of a single DNS server	No	Yes
Supports incremental zone transfers	Yes	Yes

Regardless of whether you create standard or Active Directory–integrated DNS zones, you should be aware of the benefits of also using standard secondary zones. The following list presents some of the benefits you can realize by placing secondary zones on your network:

- The addition of standard secondary zone servers increases the redundancy of the zone by proving name resolution even if the primary zone server is unresponsive.
- When remote locations are connected to the core network over WAN links, secondary zone servers can greatly reduce costs and network traffic. By placing standard secondary zones in these remote locations or in locations with a high number of clients, you can improve overall network performance.
- Standard secondary zone servers reduce the load on the primary servers by distributing name-resolution requests among more DNS servers.

NOTE

Keeping zones safe If you are using standard zones or a secondary zone within an Active Directory–integrated zone implementation, you must ensure that you configure your DNS servers to perform zone transfers only with those servers you trust.

At this point, you have a fair amount of information in hand to start planning your DNS zone requirements. Depending on what types of zones you implement, your zones will use either transfers or replication. Zone transfers occur in standard zones, whereas zone replication occurs in Active Directory–integrated zones.

Unlike WINS, which allows for a push/pull arrangement, zone transfers always originate with the secondary server polling the primary zone at the configured interval. It does so by checking the zone version number on the primary server to see whether it has changed in comparison to the version number on the secondary server. As changes are made to the zone file, the zone version number is incremented. When the zone version number on the primary server has been incremented, a zone transfer is required and will be performed. If the secondary zone supports incremental zone transfers (which Windows Server 2003 does), the secondary zone pulls (from the primary zone) only the changes made to resource records for each incremental zone version—meaning that a resource record could potentially be updated one or more times in a single zone transfer. When you use incremental zone transfers, network traffic is reduced and zone transfer speed is increased.

EXAM ALERT

Zone transfer types Windows Server 2003 supports two zone transfer types for standard zones: *full-zone transfers* and *incremental zone transfers*. You might also see these transfers abbreviated as *AXFR* and *IXFR*, respectively. A full-zone transfer causes the entire zone data file to be transferred, which is a large user of both bandwidth and time. When performing zone transfers to Windows NT 4.0 DNS servers, AXFR will always be used.

Active Directory–integrated DNS zones replicate data among all domain controllers, allowing any domain controller that has the DNS service installed to modify the zone file and replicate the changes to the rest of the domain controllers that are running the DNS service. Replication occurs on a per-property basis, meaning that only the relevant changes will be replicated. Active Directory–integrated zones replicate only the final result of multiple changes to a resource record, unlike standard zones, which transfer the changes to a resource record that occurred in each zone version number.

With your namespace and zone type plans complete, you must next evaluate the need for forwarder and slave DNS servers. That is the topic of the next section.

Planning DNS Forwarding Requirements

Objective:

Plan a host name resolution strategy.

- Plan a forwarding configuration.

Before a discussion of forwarding and slave DNS servers can be undertaken, some general knowledge of how DNS clients query a DNS server to resolve IP addresses is of some use.

In a TCP/IP network, a *DNS resolver* is any system that has been configured with one or more DNS server IP addresses and that performs queries against these DNS servers. The DNS resolver is part of the DNS Client service, which is automatically installed when Windows is installed. The resolver can request one of two types of queries from a DNS server: recursive or iterative.

A *recursive query* is a DNS query that is sent to a DNS server from a DNS resolver asking the DNS server to provide a complete answer to the query, or an error stating that it cannot provide the information. If the DNS server is also configured as a forwarder, the query can be forwarded directly to another DNS server. If the query is for a name outside the local DNS server's zone of authority, it performs an iterative query against a root DNS server, which then responds with the IP address of the DNS server whose zone of authority includes the desired IP top-level domain. Additional iterative queries are then performed until the name is resolved into its IP address or an error is produced.

An *iterative query* is a DNS query that a DNS server sends to another DNS server in an effort to perform name resolution. Consider the example of a workstation (DNS resolver) in the `bigcorp.com` domain that wants to communicate with a web server located in the `smallcorp.com` domain. Figure 4.3 illustrates the process by which the IP address for www.smallcorp.com will be resolved to its IP address. Recall that www is a typical alias for a web server or bank of clustered web servers.

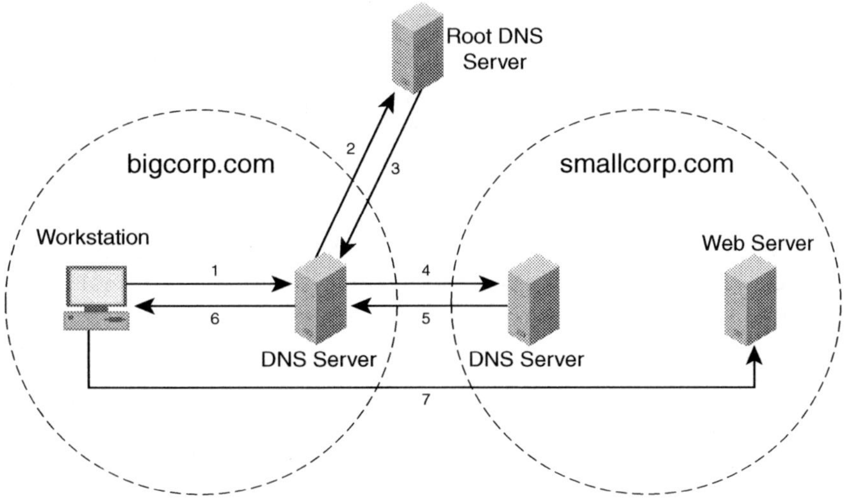

FIGURE 4.3 The initial recursive query results in several iterative queries in an effort to resolve the name to an IP address.

The process illustrated in Figure 4.3 follows these basic steps:

1. The DNS resolver (the local workstation) sends a recursive query to its local DNS server requesting the IP address of www.smallcorp.com.
2. The local DNS server, which is also configured as a forwarder, does not have information about www.smallcorp.com in its zone of authority and thus issues an iterative query to a root DNS server for the IP address of www.smallcorp.com.
3. The root DNS server does not have the requested information about the IP address of www.smallcorp.com, but it does know the IP address of a nameserver for the `smallcorp.com` zone. It provides this information back to the requesting DNS server.

4. The local DNS server next issues an iterative query to the DNS server for the `smallcorp.com` zone asking it for the IP address of www.smallcorp.com.
5. The `smallcorp.com` DNS server is authoritative for that zone, so it provides the requested IP address back to the local DNS server for www.smallcorp.com.
6. The local DNS server next passes the IP address of www.smallcorp.com back to the requesting workstation.
7. The client can now make a connection to www.smallcorp.com.

So with the discussion of how DNS queries are performed and resolved under your belt, you can begin to plan for configuration and use of DNS forwarders on the network.

A *DNS forwarder* is a DNS server that accepts forwarded recursive lookups from another DNS server and then resolves the request for that DNS server. This capability can be useful if you do not have local copies of your internal DNS zone and want to have your local DNS server forward DNS queries to a central DNS server that is authoritative for your internal DNS zone. Caching-only servers make good DNS forwarders. If the DNS forwarder does not receive a valid resolution from the server that it forwards the request to, it attempts to resolve the client request itself.

A *DNS slave server* is a DNS forwarder server that does not try to resolve a resolution request if it doesn't receive a valid response to its forwarded DNS request. You typically see this type of DNS server implemented in conjunction with a secure Internet connection.

A new feature in Windows Server 2003, *conditional forwarding*, enables administrators to direct DNS requests to other DNS servers based on domain. Previous versions of Microsoft DNS supported only one forwarder, so if forwarding were enabled, all requests would be sent to a single server. This feature is used frequently when you want requests made to the internal network to be forwarded to a master DNS server that stores internal DNS zones, but have resolution requests that are made to Internet domains be sent to the Internet using the standard resolution process.

EXAM ALERT

Know conditional forwarding Because enabling conditional forwarding is a new capability with Windows Server 2003's DNS service, you need to be familiar with how it works and when you might need to use it.

Figure 4.4 shows the Forwarders tab of the DNS server Properties dialog box.

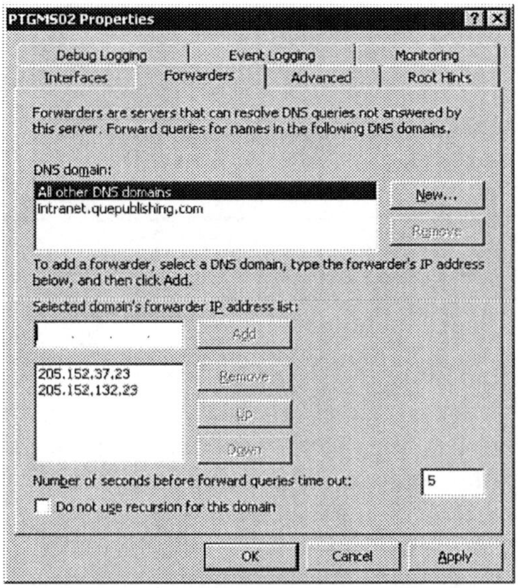

FIGURE 4.4 On the Forwarders tab, you can configure where this server will send DNS requests if another DNS server will be supplying some or all of the DNS resolution for that server.

Say that you have a single internal domain called `corp.quepublishing.com`. By default, all queries to hosts in that domain will be answered by your DNS servers (as configured on the client), as they always have been. However, the Windows Server 2003 DNS service enables you to configure forwarding for a single domain, a group of domains, or all domains selectively. Earlier versions of the Windows DNS service supported only forwarding of all domains; it was an all-or-nothing proposition. The functionality of being able to divide forwarding among multiple servers while still resolving some domains locally is known as *conditional forwarding*. Figure 4.5 shows the different IP address that has been configured for conditional forwarding to a different internal domain than the one our clients are located in.

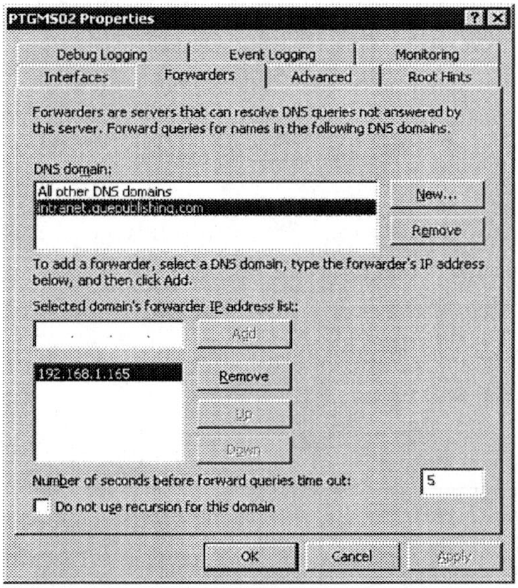

FIGURE 4.5 Conditional forwarding enables you to configure specific DNS servers by domain.

NOTE

Don't disable recursion If you disable recursion in the DNS server properties, you cannot use a forwarder. Forwarding DNS requests requires that the DNS server be capable of making recursive queries. You'll only need to disable recursion if you do not want name resolution requests being forwarded to another server, such as in isolated networks.

A common implementation of DNS forwarders in a Windows Server 2003 network has one specific DNS server being allowed to make queries to DNS servers outside the firewall. This implementation allows the firewall to be configured to allow DNS traffic only from this specific DNS server to leave the protected network, and allows only valid replies back to the DNS server to enter the protected network. Through this approach, all other DNS traffic—both inbound and outbound—can be dropped at the firewall, adding to the overall security of the network and the DNS service. Figure 4.6 illustrates this concept.

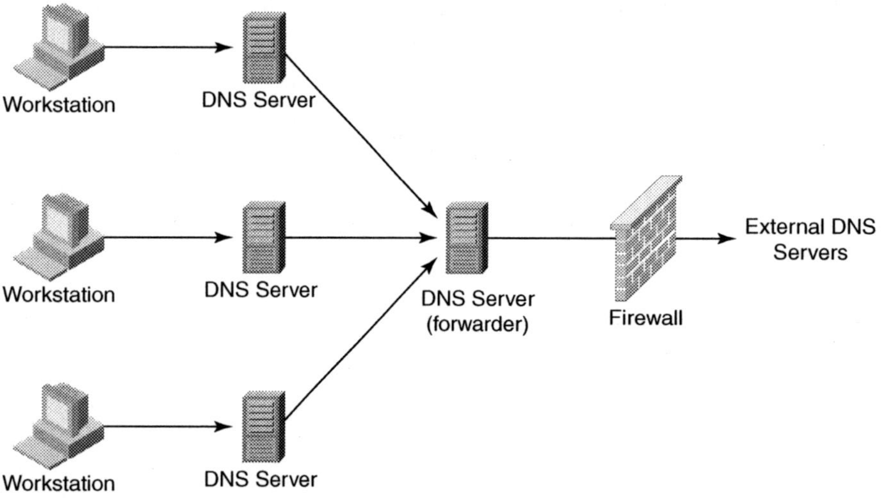

FIGURE 4.6 DNS forwarders can be implemented to control DNS traffic into and out of the protected network.

Forwarders can be used to ensure that DNS queries have the best possible chance of being answered with the requested information. As you have seen, they also can be implemented to increase security of the DNS service on your network. With security in mind, we examine other ways you can configure additional security to your DNS servers.

Configuring DNS Security

Objective:

Plan a host name resolution strategy.

- Plan for DNS security.

With the majority of your planning already accomplished, you now need to plan the security of the DNS service. Providing security for DNS is not a task that you can accomplish by performing one action or by configuring one item. DNS is a dynamic service that, by its very nature, must be capable of interacting with network clients on several different levels. Not only must clients be capable of retrieving information from a DNS server through queries, but authorized clients must also be capable of having their resource records entered or updated when they acquire a Dynamic Host Configuration Protocol (DHCP) lease on the network. Thus, DNS security is a multifaceted area that takes some preplanning to implement properly.

Configuring DNS security can be broken into the following seven general areas of concern:

- Dynamic updates
- Zone transfer security
- Securing of the cache against pollution
- DNS Security (DNSSEC)
- Integration of Active Directory and DNS
- Active Directory DNS permissions
- Other DNS security configuration items

Each of these concerns is addressed in the sections that follow.

Dynamic Updates

Dynamic updates occur when a DHCP server or a DNS client computer automatically updates the applicable DNS resource records when a DHCP lease is granted (or expires). Three types of dynamic updates exist in Windows Server 2003, each with its own security specifics.

Secure dynamic updates are available when Active Directory–integrated zones are in use. Using secure dynamic updates, the DNS zone information is stored in Active Directory and thus is protected using Active Directory security features. When a zone has been created as or converted to an Active Directory–integrated zone, Access Control List (ACL) entries can be used to specify which users, computers, and groups can make changes to a zone or a specific record.

Dynamic updates from DHCP can be configured to allow only specific DHCP servers to update DNS zone entries. The configuration takes place on the DHCP server by configuring it with the DNS zone that is responsible for automatically updating. It takes place on the DNS server by configuring it with the DHCP servers that are to be the only authorized computers to update the DNS entries. Dynamic updates from DHCP are best implemented when the DHCP client computers are not Windows 2000 or later—such as when the client computers are Windows 98 computers. You also can implement dynamic updates from DHCP if you determine that managing individual NTFS permissions for users, computers, and groups to update their respective DNS entries becomes an administrative burden. Finally, dynamic updates from DHCP can overcome the security risks that could potentially come from allowing unauthorized computers to impersonate authorized computers and populate the DNS zone file with bad information.

DNS client dynamic updates are performed by clients running Windows 2000 or later. When these client computers start, their DNS client service automatically connects to the DNS server and registers the DNS client with the DNS server. Allowing DNS clients to perform dynamic updates is the least preferred method of dynamic updating and is hampered by manageability issues and potential security problems. You should typically plan to have DNS clients perform dynamic updates only when the computer has a static IP address and the assignment of the required permissions is manageable.

By default, dynamic updates are not enabled for standard zones, thus providing increased security by preventing an attacker from updating DNS zone information with bad entries. This setting is the most secure, but it offers the least functionality because all dynamic updates are disabled in this configuration. Dynamic updates are required for Active Directory–integrated zones and should be configured to allow secure dynamic updates or dynamic updates from DHCP instead of DNS client dynamic updates wherever possible, to increase security of the DNS zone data.

Zone Transfer Security

You can use several methods to increase the security of zone transfers—and thus increase the security of your DNS servers overall. If attackers cannot capture your zone data from a zone transfer—once a very common method of gathering information about a domain (called *footprinting*)—they will not be able to easily determine the makeup of your network. In addition, zone transfer security prevents the injection of unauthorized data into the zone files through zone transfer from an unauthorized DNS server.

By default, Windows Server 2003 DNS performs zone transfers only with the DNS servers that are listed in a zone's name server (NS) resource records. Even though this configuration is fairly secure, you should consider changing this setting to allow zone transfers to be carried out only with specific IP addresses that you have explicitly configured. Figure 4.7 shows how you might make this configuration for a DNS server. Although you are still subject to IP address spoofing with this option configured, you have taken one more step toward a more secure DNS implementation. The task of identifying and defeating spoofed IP addresses lies at your perimeter security devices: firewalls, screening routers, and proxy servers.

NOTE

Securing zone transfers Although you can perform this configuration on Active Directory–integrated zones (which we discuss a bit later), you typically specify DNS servers for zone transfers only when you're working with standard DNS zones. In the Active Directory–integrated zone model, only authorized DNS servers get the zone by default (which are the domain controllers in the domain or forest that you configure the zone to replicate to).

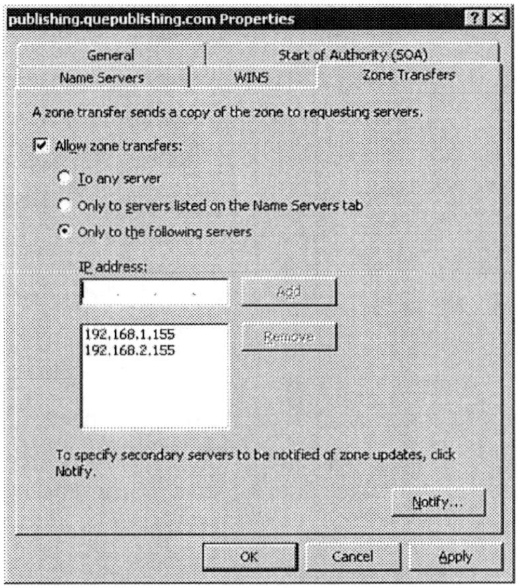

FIGURE 4.7 You can configure which DNS servers participate in zone transfers.

As shown in Figure 4.7, you have the following options available to configure:

- **Allow Zone Transfers**—If this option is unchecked, the options below it become unavailable and no zone transfers are allowed for the server. Turning off zone transfers (for standard zones) is useful only when no other DNS servers exist that would need a zone transfer, which is typically an unlikely scenario. By default, Active Directory–integrated zones do not allow zone transfer because the zone data is replicated by Active Directory itself and is not stored in a flat text file.
- **To Any Server**—The least secure option available allows any server that requests a zone transfer of your zone file to have it.
- **Only to Servers Listed on the Name Servers Tab**—The default option selected allows zone transfers with the authoritative name servers that you configured on the Name Servers tab.
- **Only to the Following Servers**—This option enables you to explicitly specify which servers (by IP address) are allowed to perform zone transfers with this zone.

If you must perform zone transfers across an untrusted network, you should consider implementing and using a VPN tunnel between the two DNS servers. Encrypted zone information traveling inside the tunnel is safe from prying eyes, thus providing an uncompromised zone transfer. When using a VPN tunnel for zone-transfer data, you should use the strongest possible level of encryption and authentication supported by both sides of the tunnel.

Your last (and definitely the best) option to secure zone data is to use only Active Directory–integrated zones. Because the DNS zone data is stored in Active Directory, it is inherently more secure. When Active Directory–integrated zones are in use, only Active Directory–integrated DNS servers participate in zone replication. In addition, all DNS servers hosting Active Directory–integrated zones must be registered with Active Directory. All replication traffic between Active Directory–integrated DNS servers is also encrypted, further adding to the level of security provided.

Securing the Cache Against Pollution

By default, Windows Server 2003 DNS is configured to prevent unrequested resource records from being added to the DNS zone data, thus increasing zone security. From the Advanced tab of the DNS server Properties dialog box (see Figure 4.8), you can see the Secure Cache Against Pollution option, which is checked by default.

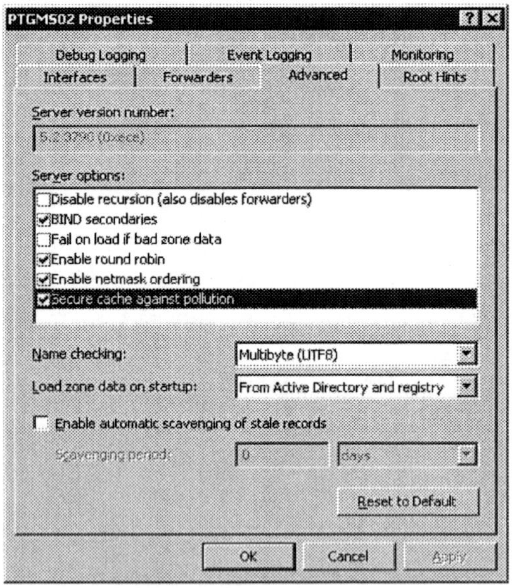

FIGURE 4.8 The Secure Cache Against Pollution option prevents unrequested resource records from being added to the zone data.

By default, Windows Server 2003 DNS servers use a secure response option that eliminates the addition of unrelated resource records that are included in a referral answer to the cache. The server typically caches any names in referral answers, thus expediting the resolution of subsequent DNS queries. However, when this feature is in use, the server can determine whether the referred name is polluting or insecure and discard it. The server thus determines whether to cache the name offered in the referral, depending on whether it is part of the exact DNS domain tree for which the original name query was made. As an example, a query made for `sales.bigcorp.com` with a referral answer of `smallcorp.net` would not be cached.

DNS Security (DNSSEC)

RFC 2535 provides for DNS Security (DNSSEC), a public key infrastructure (PKI)–based system in which authentication and data integrity can be provided to DNS resolvers. Digital signatures are used and encrypted with private keys. These digital signatures can then be authenticated by DNSSEC-aware resolvers by using the corresponding public key. The required digital signature and public keys are added to the DNS zone in the form of resource records.

The public key is stored in the KEY RR (Resource Record), and the digital signature is stored in the SIG RR. The KEY RR must be supplied to the DNS resolver before it can successfully authenticate the SIG RR. DNSSEC also introduces one additional RR, the NXT RR, which is used to cryptographically ensure the resolver that a particular RR does not exist in the zone.

DNSSEC is only partially supported in Windows Server 2003 DNS, providing basic support as specified in RFC 2535. A Windows Server 2003 DNS server could, therefore, operate as a secondary to a BIND server that fully supports DNSSEC. The support is partial because DNS in Windows Server 2003 does not provide any means of signing or verifying the digital signatures. In addition, the Windows Server 2003 DNS resolver does not validate any of the DNSSEC data that is returned as a result of queries.

Integrating Active Directory and DNS

Throughout this chapter, we've been working with standard DNS zones on a Windows Server 2003 member server—a server that is not a Domain Controller. Although there is nothing wrong (at a basic level) with this configuration and implementation of the Windows Server 2003 DNS service, to fully use the power and flexibility, you'll want to be using Active Directory–integrated DNS. Not only does Active Directory–integrated DNS offer several performance enhancements, but it is also inherently more secure. Recall that the Security tab in the server Properties dialog box is unavailable for standard DNS servers; it is available only when DNS is running on a Domain Controller. Likewise, the Security tab in the zone Properties dialog box is available only when a zone is configured as Active Directory–integrated and running on a Domain Controller. Additionally, only when using Active Directory–integrated zones can you configure secure dynamic updates.

EXAM ALERT

Securely implementing DNS using Windows Server 2003 Active Directory is more secure than a flat file, and updates and zone transfers occur as part of Active Directory replication activities, which are encrypted. As a result, an Active Directory–integrated zone is the most secure DNS implementation possible.

The DNS and Active Directory Relationship

To this point, we've discussed planning for DNS in detail, including how to integrate DNS into Active Directory. As you've no doubt noticed, DNS is an important network service. As you've also likely noticed by now, Active Directory is the heart and soul of a Windows Server 2003 network infrastructure. So it only stands to reason that Active Directory absolutely cannot function without a reliable and functional DNS implementation in place.

Here are some key points that emphasize the importance of DNS to Active Directory:

- Without a properly working DNS infrastructure, Domain Controllers cannot replicate information about the domain among themselves.
- Without a properly working DNS infrastructure, Windows 2000 and Windows XP client computers experience very long logon times or possibly cannot log on at all.
- Without a properly working DNS infrastructure, Exchange Server 2003 and Exchange 2000 Server cannot work, and servers typically fail to start critical services properly.

Of course, the list goes on, but the failures mentioned are some of the more important ones—ones that will likely bring your Active Directory domain to its knees. In short, without DNS, you don't have an Active Directory implementation.

EXAM ALERT

About secure dynamic updates When you enable secure dynamic updates on an Active Directory–integrated DNS zone, this creates a situation in which there can be only owner for a resource record, and only that one owner can update that resource record. Obviously, this is an unacceptable and impossible condition when you might have multiple DHCP servers trying to register host (A) records on behalf of clients that cannot perform the action themselves and, thus, the DHCP server registering the record becomes the owner.

Without some other provision in place, only that same DHCP server could ever update the record, and problems would soon ensue in your DNS zones. To avoid this problem, all authorized DHCP servers should be added to the `DnsUpdateProxy` security group. The servers that are a member of this special security group are blocked from recording ownership on any resource records they create or update in DNS, thus allowing any other DHCP server to make changes to that record.

You should realize, however, that enforcing only secure dynamic updates decreases the security offered because no owner is specified for these records. Windows 2000 and Windows XP client computers do not cause this problem because they can register their own A records without assistance from the DHCP server. As a new feature, you can expect to see a question relating to the `DnsUpdateProxy` security group on your Exam 70-293.

Active Directory DNS Permissions

If the zone is integrated with Active Directory, the Discretionary Access Control List (DACL) for the zone can be used to configure the permissions for the users and groups that can change or control the data in the DNS zone. Table 4.3 lists the default group and user permissions for Active Directory–integrated DNS zones.

TABLE 4.3 Default Group and User Permissions on Active Directory–Integrated DNS Zones

Group or User	Permissions
Administrators	Allow: Read, Write, Create All Child Objects, Special Permissions
Authenticated Users	Allow: Create All Child Objects
Creator Owner	Allow: Special Permissions
DnsAdmins	Allow: Full Control, Read, Write, Create All Child Objects, Delete Child Objects, Special Permissions
Domain Admins	Allow: Full Control, Read, Write, Create All Child Objects, Delete Child Objects
Enterprise Admins	Allow: Full Control, Read, Write, Create All Child Objects, Delete Child Objects
Enterprise Domain Controllers	Allow: Full Control, Read, Write, Create All Child Objects, Delete Child Objects, Special Permissions
Everyone	Allow: Read, Special Permissions
Pre-Windows 2000 Compatible Access	Allow: Special Permissions
System	Allow: Full Control, Read, Write, Create All Child Objects, Delete Child Objects

You can modify these default values to suit your particular needs, as shown in Figure 4.9.

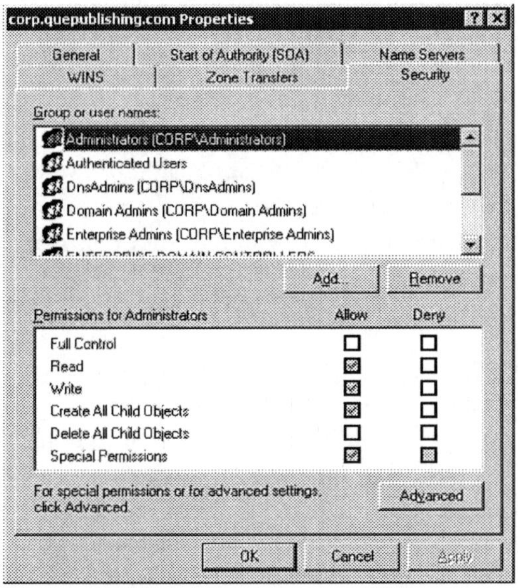

FIGURE 4.9 You can configure security via the DACL on Active Directory–integrated zones.

NOTE

The Security tab The Security tab is not available for configuration on DNS servers that are not installed on a Domain Controller.

Other DNS Security Configuration Items

Although we've discussed some very good ways to secure DNS, even more advanced configuration changes can be made in the interest of further securing the server. Although this is not a complete listing of items by any means, the following list presents some of the more common items that you can work with to increase security:

- **Network interfaces**—If your DNS server has multiple network interfaces, the DNS service listens for and responds to name-resolution queries on all of them by default. You can add some security to your DNS server installation by configuring it so that it listens only on the IP address that DNS clients will be using to contact it.
- **Disabling recursion**—Recursion is enabled by default in Windows Server 2003 DNS, which allows the DNS server to perform recursive queries to other DNS servers on behalf of its DNS clients and other DNS servers that have forwarded queries to it for resolution. If a DNS server is not intended to perform recursive queries, you should disable them to prevent recursion from being used as an attack vector on the DNS server.
- **Removing root hints**—If you have configured an internal DNS root in your DNS infrastructure, configure the root hints on all of your other internal DNS servers to point to only your internal DNS root server. By removing the capability for the other DNS servers to contact root servers on the Internet, you remove the capability to accidentally disclose your private internal information on the Internet.
- **Use a private DNS namespace**—If your network clients will never need to communicate with the Internet, you can use a private DNS namespace, such as `quepublishing.corp`, along with an internal root DNS server and applicable firewall configuration to prevent DNS-related traffic from ever leaving your organization. You should note that simply by using a private DNS namespace, you have not eliminated the capability to communicate with the Internet.
- **Use a split DNS namespace**—If your network clients will need to communicate with the Internet, consider using a split DNS namespace. In this model, the Internet namespace might be something such as `quepublishing.com`, and the internal namespace might be `corp.quepublishing.com`. Each section of the DNS namespace should be hosted on separate DNS servers located on the applicable side of your corporate firewall. Requests made by clients internally should be forwarded to your external DNS servers if the internal DNS servers cannot provide the requested query answer. This would be accomplished by configuring your internal DNS servers to forward requests only to your external DNS servers. Additionally, you should configure your external DNS servers to forward only requests to your ISP's trusted DNS servers.
- **Use firewall rules**—You can configure and implement a firewall rule on your packet-filtering firewall separating your internal network from the Internet to allow only TCP and UDP traffic on port 53 between your internal and external DNS servers.

- **Harden servers**—You can get detailed information and assistance on hardening Windows Server 2003 servers from the "Windows Server 2003 Security Guide."

CAUTION

Recursion and forwarding If you disable recursion by selecting Do Not Use Recursion for This Domain in the DNS server Properties dialog box, you will not be able to use a forwarder. Forwarding DNS requests requires that the DNS server be capable of making recursive queries.

Integrating with Third-Party DNS Solutions

Objective:

Plan a host name resolution strategy.

- Examine the interoperability of DNS with third-party DNS solutions.

It's a fact of life that many organizations already have existing DNS solutions, such as UNIX BIND, in place. In some cases, these existing BIND servers might not meet the DNS requirements of Active Directory. Table 4.4 outlines the features of some of the more common versions of BIND in use.

TABLE 4.4 Features of Various BIND Versions

BIND Version	Features
4.9.4	Support for fast zone transfers
4.9.6	Support for service (SRV) resource records
8.1.2	Support for dynamic DNS (DDNS)
8.2.1	Support for incremental zone transfer (IXFR) between DNS servers
8.2.2 (patch 7)	Full support for all Active Directory features

If you are faced with a situation in which you are dealing with other DNS systems, you have two basic choices of implementation:

- Upgrade existing DNS systems to meet the DNS requirements of Active Directory. For BIND, Version 8.1.2 and later are sufficient.
- Migrate existing DNS zones to Windows Server 2003 DNS.

Although it is recommended that you use only Windows Server 2003 DNS servers to ensure full support for Active Directory, you can use any DNS system that meets the following specifications:

- Support for SRV resource records
- Dynamic updates per RFC 2136

Although support for dynamic updates is highly recommended, it is not mandatory. Support for SRV resource records is mandatory, however, because they are required to provide DNS support to Active Directory.

If you have UNIX BIND servers in your DNS infrastructure, you should consider placing them as secondaries instead of primaries. By default, Windows Server 2003 DNS servers use a fast zone-transfer format whereby compression is used and multiple records can be sent in a single TCP message. BIND versions 4.9.4 and later support fast zone transfers. If you are using an earlier version of BIND or another third-party DNS system that does not support fast zone transfers, you must disable fast zone transfers. When you select the BIND Secondaries option (see Figure 4.10), fast zone transfers are disabled for that server.

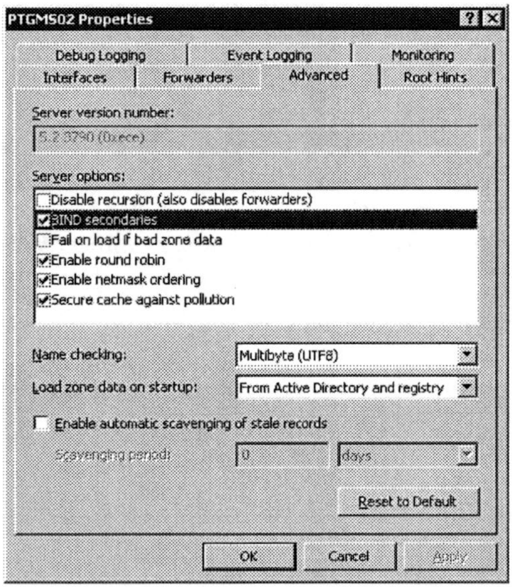

FIGURE 4.10 The BIND Secondaries option prevents fast zone transfers from occurring.

With the DNS service installed at a basic level, let's take a look at configuring DNS zones so that the new server can perform name resolution.

Introduction to WINS

If you are at all familiar with Windows NT 4.0 networks, you are undoubtedly familiar with the intricacies of a WINS infrastructure. You might also be wondering why Microsoft didn't get rid of WINS in Windows Server 2003. Well, the good news is that, with Windows Server 2003, WINS is used for backward compatibility only. Windows Server 2003 Active Directory networks do not need WINS at all.

So that means we don't need to talk about WINS, right? Sorry, but you don't get off that easily. Until your network is 100% Windows 2000 or later, you still need WINS to provide backward compatibility for legacy Windows operating systems, particularly with your NT domains. With that in mind, let's talk about what WINS is and how it works.

EXAM ALERT

"I don't need WINS" This statement is accurate only if the client computer is running DNS. Don't make the mistake of assuming that DNS is implied when you get WINS questions.

In the Internet-centric environment that most companies are designing and maintaining, TCP/IP has become the ubiquitous networking protocol. For old-time UNIX users, using TCP/IP is a good thing. TCP/IP came out of the UNIX arena and has been the native protocol for UNIX systems since the late 1980s.

Microsoft, on the other hand, started with a different protocol as its LAN Manager operating system's native protocol—NetBIOS Extended User Interface (NetBEUI). NetBEUI was a pretty good protocol for small networks; it required no configuration and didn't require complex addressing like TCP/IP does. However, NetBEUI cannot handle routing and does not perform well in large environments. Microsoft needed to add TCP/IP support.

When Microsoft began to add TCP/IP support to its LAN server products, the company ran into a little problem. The naming system used on Microsoft networks at that time would not function on routed TCP/IP networks. Microsoft LAN Manager computers used the computer's NetBIOS names for identification. Although this makes maintaining the network very simple for an administrator—because servers are automatically advertised on the network by name—this naming system was a problem with TCP/IP.

NetBIOS has a design limitation that shows up in routed networks because NetBIOS relies heavily on broadcast messages to advertise servers and their shared resources. *Broadcast messages* are messages that are received by every computer on a network segment rather than by a specific computer. This paradigm is useable on smaller networks but can add overwhelming amounts of broadcast traffic on an enterprise network. If you have ever suffered from a broadcast storm on your network, you are familiar with the issue. To confine the impact of broadcast messages on a TCP/IP network, IP routers do not forward broadcast messages. Unlike the Microsoft NWLink protocol for IPX compatibility, which Microsoft wrote to support broadcasts, TCP/IP conforms to very strict standards. To function in a TCP/IP environment, Microsoft's TCP/IP implementation had to conform to the standard. Therefore, Microsoft had to find a way to make NetBIOS naming work in a standard TCP/IP network.

Microsoft's first solution, introduced in its older LAN Manager server, was to use a LAN Manager `HOSTS` (`LMHOSTS`) file on each computer on the network. Similar to the `HOSTS` file used before DNS was available, `LMHOSTS` consists of records matching NetBIOS names to IP addresses. When a computer couldn't find a particular NetBIOS computer on the local network, it would consult its `LMHOSTS` file to see whether the computer could be found elsewhere.

An `LMHOSTS` file is a text file that must be edited manually. After creating a master `LMHOSTS` file, an administrator must copy the file to every computer on the network. Every time a computer was installed or removed, the master `LMHOSTS` file had to be updated and redistributed. The architects of TCP/IP faced a similar issue with `HOSTS` files before the DNS specification was written.

WINS and DNS Integration

Although it would be nice if you no longer had to support WINS clients, this is not always the case—thus the reason Microsoft still provides a very robust and powerful WINS server in Windows Server 2003. What's more, DNS and WINS can be integrated to provide a more complete name-resolution solution for all clients on your network.

You can configure a DNS server to query a WINS server by configuring a DNS zone setting. This is helpful when some of the clients you support require NetBIOS name resolution, such as legacy Windows 9*x* clients, or cannot register themselves with DNS. In effect, you are providing a means for DNS clients to look up WINS client names and IP addresses without needing to contact the WINS server directly. This is accomplished by adding a WINS lookup record to the authoritative zone. After it is configured, the DNS server queries a WINS server for every request made to it for which it does not have a valid record. If the requested name is located on the WINS server, the information is returned to the requesting client via the DNS server. The process is invisible to all clients. Note that you can configure this for both forward- and reverse-lookup zones.

If you have a mixture of Windows and third-party DNS servers in your organization, you will run into problems if you attempt to replicate WINS lookup records to these third-party DNS servers. Only Microsoft DNS servers support WINS lookup records; thus, zone transfers to third-party DNS servers will fail. In this situation, you should use WINS referral to create and delegate a special "WINS zone" that refers queries to WINS when needed. This zone does not perform any registrations or updates. Clients need to be configured to append this additional WINS referral zone to their queries for unqualified names, thus allowing clients to query both WINS and DNS as required. You also need to ensure that this WINS referral zone is not configured to transfer to any third-party DNS servers.

Microsoft also needed a dynamic name service that would keep itself current on computers on the network—a name service that could work in routed TCP/IP environments. Microsoft's answer was WINS. Four elements can be found in a WINS network:

- **WINS servers**—When WINS client computers enter the network, they contact a WINS server using a directed message. The client computer registers its name with the WINS server and uses the WINS server to resolve NetBIOS names to IP addresses.
- **WINS client computers**—WINS client computers use H-node to communicate with WINS. Windows 2000, Windows NT, Windows 95 and 98, and Windows for Workgroups computers can be WINS client computers.

- **Non-WINS client computers**—Older Microsoft network client computers that can't use P-node can still benefit from WINS. Their broadcast messages are intercepted by WINS proxy computers that act as intermediaries between the B-node client computers and WINS servers. MS-DOS and Windows 3.1 client computers function as non-WINS clients.
- **WINS proxies**—Windows NT, Windows 95 and 98, and Windows for Workgroups client computers can function as WINS proxies. They intercept B-node broadcasts on their local subnet and communicate with a WINS server on behalf of the B-node client computer.

WINS servers can replicate their databases so that each WINS server can provide name resolution for the entire network. Whenever possible, it is desirable to have at least two WINS servers. This way, name resolution can take place when one name server is down. Also, administrators can distribute WINS activity across multiple servers to balance the processing loads. WINS server addresses are one of the configuration settings that can be issued with DHCP.

What's New in Windows Server 2003 WINS

If you're moving from a Windows NT 4.0–based WINS implementation, some great changes are in store for you in Windows Server 2003. The following improvements have been made to WINS since Windows 2000 Server:

- **Record filtering**—Using improved filtering and search functions, you can quickly locate records by showing only the records that fit the specified criteria. This capability can be useful when you are managing larger WINS databases. You can now specify multiple criteria to perform advanced searches. Also, you can combine filters for customized results. The available filters include record owner, record type, NetBIOS name, and IP address (with or without the subnet mask). Finally, because the results of the query are stored in the local NetBIOS cache on your computer, the performance of subsequent queries and name lookups is improved.
- **Specified replication partners**—You can define a list of WINS servers that are allowed to be the source of incoming WINS records during pull replication events. You can opt to block specific WINS servers from replicating with your WINS servers. Alternatively, you can opt to allow a specific list of WINS servers to perform replication, blocking all other WINS servers from replicating with your WINS servers.

The following improvements were also made to WINS in Windows 2000 Server and are carried over into the WINS implementation in Windows Server 2003:

- **Command-line management**—You can use the `netsh` command with the WINS context to manage WINS servers from the command line and to use batch files.
- **Persistent connections**—Each WINS server can be configured to maintain a persistent connection with one or more of its replication partners. This configuration increases replication speed and eliminates network overhead associated with building and tearing down connections for replication.
- **Manual tombstoning**—Records can be marked for deletion (tombstoning). This tombstoned state is replicated to all WINS servers, preventing an active copy of the record on a different WINS server from being propagated.
- **Improved management**—The WINS console is Microsoft Management Console based and can be added to customized MMCs, resulting in a user-friendly, powerful, and customized management interface.
- **Dynamic record deletion and multiselect**—Using the WINS console, you can easily manage the WINS database. You can point, click, and delete one or more WINS static or dynamic entries.
- **Record verification**—Record verification performs a comparison of the IP address returned by a NetBIOS query of different WINS servers. This feature helps check the consistency of names stored and replicated on your WINS servers.
- **Version number validation**—Version number validation examines the owner address–to–version number mapping tables. This feature helps check the consistency of names stored and replicated on your WINS servers.
- **Export function**—The WINS database can be exported to a comma-delimited text file for importation into Excel or another application for offline analysis.
- **Increased fault tolerance**—Windows 98 and later clients can specify up to 12 WINS servers per interface, up from the previous limit of 2. These extra WINS servers can be queried if the primary and secondary WINS servers do not respond.
- **Dynamic renewal**—WINS clients are no longer required to restart after renewing their NetBIOS name registration.
- **`Nbtstat -RR` option**—The `Nbtstat -RR` option provides the capability to release and renew the NetBIOS name registration.
- **WINS Users group**—A special local group, WINS Users, is created when WINS is installed; this group provides read-only use of the WINS console. Members of this group can view but not change information and properties of the WINS servers.

Planning for WINS Replication

Objective:

Plan a NetBIOS name resolution strategy.

- Plan a WINS replication strategy.

NOTE

Know WINS?—The following discussion about WINS assumes that you are already familiar with installing the WINS service and performing basic management and configuration tasks. If you need a review, see Chapter 4 of *MCSA/MCSE 70-291 Exam Prep: Implementing, Managing, and Maintaining a Windows Server 2003 Network Infrastructure* (Que Publishing, 2006; ISBN 0-7897-3649-7), by Will Schmied.

In most environments that rely on WINS for name resolution for legacy systems, it is important to ensure that more than one WINS server exists so that you provide redundancy and availability. To ensure that each server has a current copy of the database, it is important to configure replication between your WINS servers. Let's quickly look at the different types of replication you can configure for the WINS service:

- **Pull replication**—In pull replication, your server pulls the database from the replication partner. A pull replication is time based and occurs at the time you have configured. You can decide whether to establish a persistent connection for replication, and you can set the start time and interval for replication.
- **Push replication**—In push replication, your server pushes its database to the replication partner. A push replication is event driven, and the number of database updates determines when the event occurs. You can decide whether to use a persistent connection for push activities, and you can set the number of changes in version ID before replication.
- **Replication partner type**—The partner type can be push, pull, or push/pull, depending on your requirements. (In push/pull replication, database replication can occur using either method—push or pull.)

EXAM ALERT

WINS replication Recall that one of the improvements in WINS since Windows NT 4.0 is the capability to maintain a persistent connection with one or more of the replication partners, enabling real-time replication. Because this is one of the new features of the WINS service, you will probably find it on the exam. Microsoft is more likely to test your familiarity with new features of the service than your understanding of the general WINS functionality because WINS has been part of the Windows server operating systems since its inception.

Before you actually start configuring replication on your WINS servers, however, you should take some time to carefully design and plan your WINS replication strategy. With our introduction to WINS and WINS replication types out of the way, we can move forward and examine the common areas of concern when planning for WINS replication.

Planning Replication Partners

When planning for your WINS replication partners, you are trying to accurately determine which server or servers a WINS server will need to replicate with. Another important question that you must answer, however, is how replication partners will discover each other.

For example, if yours is a small network, you might consider allowing your WINS servers to automatically configure their replication partners. When you opt to use automatic partner configuration, new WINS servers are "discovered" when they first join your network and are added as replication partners to your existing WINS servers. However, this approach comes at the tradeoff of knowing exactly how and to where your WINS servers are replicating their information. When configured for automatic partner configuration, a WINS server will announce that it is present on your network by multicasting to the IP address of 224.0.1.24, which is reserved strictly for use by WINS. These multicasts do add extra network traffic to the network, however, and thus are best used only in smaller networks with only a few WINS servers installed. When a new WINS server is discovered, the existing WINS server configures it as a push/pull partner with pull replication configured to occur at two-hour intervals with the existing WINS server.

Alternatively, and more commonly, you will manually configure your replication partners. In this way, you can control exactly how, when, and to where your WINS servers will replicate. If you need to configure WINS replication to occur with an untrusted domain, you need to perform that task manually as well.

Planning Replication Type and Path

When you will have multiple WINS servers on your network, you will face the question of how they should replicate among themselves and what path replication should follow. Sometimes you might want every WINS server on your network to have information about every address in use on your network. In this case, you might opt for a hub-and-spoke arrangement using push/pull configuration on all servers, as shown in Figure 4.11.

Alternatively, you might have good reason to not have a hub-and-spoke arrangement. Perhaps you have a WAN link separating offices that contain WINS servers; you most likely don't want every WINS server at each location trying to perform push/pull replication with every other WINS server at each location—the example shown in Figure 4.11 most likely isn't a good solution for you. In this, you might plan to arrange your WINS servers like that seen in Figure 4.12, which draws from the same design principal used for DNS forwarding servers and Active Directory/Exchange bridgeheads.

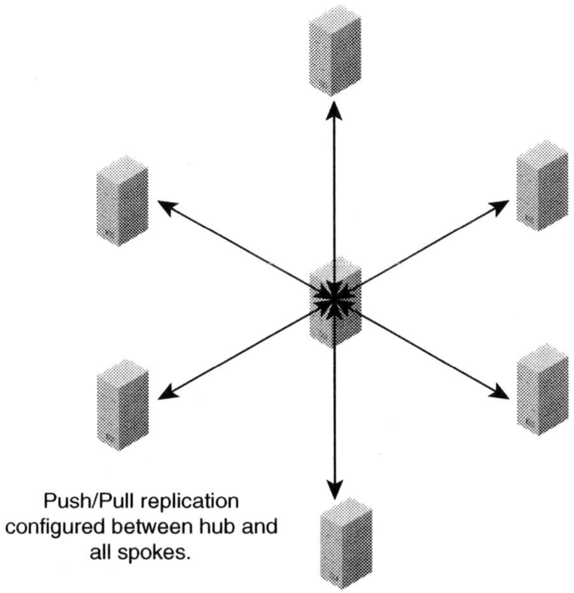

FIGURE 4.11 A push/pull hub-and-spoke design ensures that all servers contain the same information.

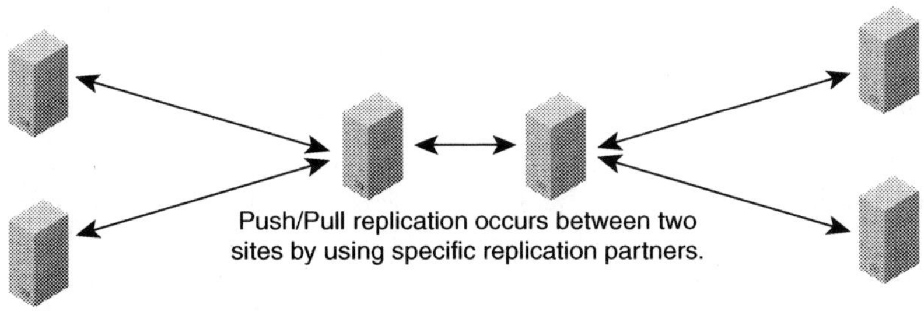

FIGURE 4.12 Sometimes WINS replication must be controlled tightly.

Other times you don't want to perform push/pull replication if you want certain servers to know only information pertinent to their part of the network and other servers to know information about the entire network. Figure 4.13 illustrates this example.

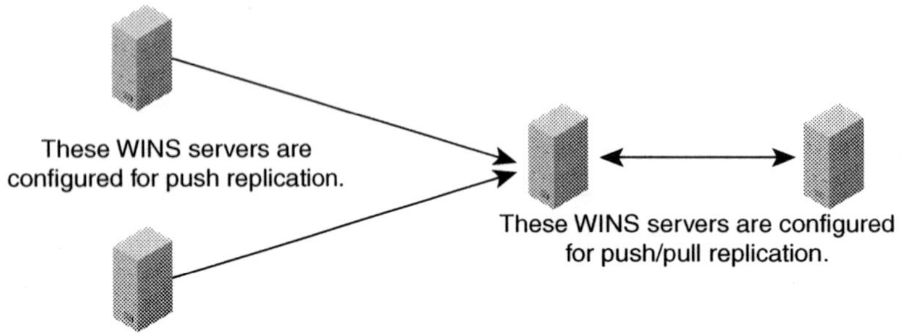

FIGURE 4.13 You can configure replication to control how much information a WINS server has.

Convergence time is the amount of time it takes for a new entry in the WINS database of a WINS server to be replicated to every other WINS server that has a replication path with that server. When planning your WINS replication solution, you need to pay careful attention to how your replication type and path impacts your convergence time.

Planning Replication for LANs and WANs

When planning your WINS replication strategy, the placement of WINS servers in relation to your WAN and LAN arrangement is of key concern. It's expected that servers on the same LAN segment or separated only by routers or switches within a larger LAN will typically have fast, reliable connectivity between themselves. The same cannot always be said for WINS servers that are separated from other WINS servers by one or more WAN links.

With the higher bandwidth available on a LAN, you might want to configure WINS replication between partners on a LAN to occur more frequently. Conversely, you will likely want to configure replication that occurs on a WAN link to occur less frequently. You can control how often replication occurs by changing the value of the Number of Changes in Version ID Before Replication for push partners. It is perfectly acceptable for this value to be lower on WINS servers replicating across the LAN and higher for those replicating across a WAN link. For pull partners, you can consider changing the value of the Replication Interval setting high for WAN replication and lower for LAN replication. Bear in mind, however, that any changes you make in this regard will have a direct impact on your convergence time. In addition, even when replication occurs across the same LAN segment, too much replication is almost always going to be a bad thing because of the marked increase in network traffic. Take care to balance your needs with the needs of other clients and applications on the network.

Planning Server Placement

The last area you'll commonly need to take into consideration when planning your WINS replication infrastructure is where your users are located. It makes little sense to place three WINS servers in a branch office of 145 users, while at the same time placing only one WINS server in the corporate headquarters, which has more than 2,000 users.

WINS servers can typically handle up to 10,000 clients each, although you will find that your actual numbers will vary with the hardware configuration of your WINS servers. So in this example, you could theoretically get away with only one WINS server for the entire company. Doing so, however, would undoubtedly set you up for failure in the future when that single WINS server became unavailable for any reason. Furthermore, one is good, two is better when it comes to infrastructure servers. In the previous example, you might consider placing two WINS servers in the corporate office for redundancy and a third server in the branch office to cut down on resolution requests across the WAN link.

With your planning out of the way, we now move forward into actually configuring WINS replication between servers, to ensure that you've seen it before test day.

Enabling and Configuring WINS Replication

To enable WINS replication, complete Step by Step 4.1.

STEP BY STEP

4.1 Enabling WINS Replication

1. Open the WINS manager by selecting Start, Programs, Administrative Tools, WINS.
2. In the right pane, right-click Replication Partners and select New Replication Partner. The New Replication Partner dialog box opens and asks you to enter the address of another WINS server, as shown in Figure 4.14. This can be either the server name or the IP address. If the server name can't be resolved, you are prompted to enter the address of the server.

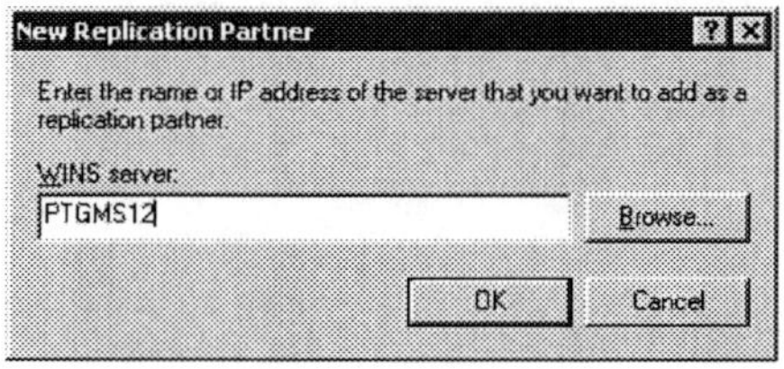

FIGURE 4.14 The replication partner can be listed by name or address.

3. Enter the name of the server and click OK.
4. Click Replication Partners in the left pane. You should see your new replication partner in the right pane, as shown in Figure 4.15.

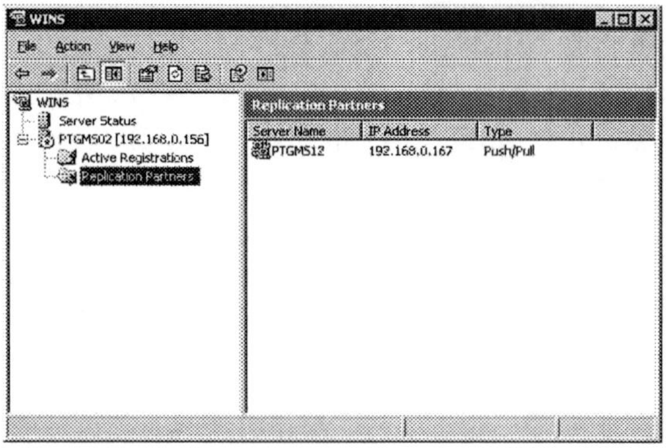

FIGURE 4.15 After the replication partner has been created, it is listed in the Replication Partners pane of WINS manager.

5. Right-click the newly created replication partner and select Properties. This opens the Replication Partner Properties dialog box, which shows only the name and address of the replication partner.
6. Click the Advanced tab, shown in Figure 4.16. On this tab, you can configure the replication properties for the replication partner. Select the appropriate type for your environment.

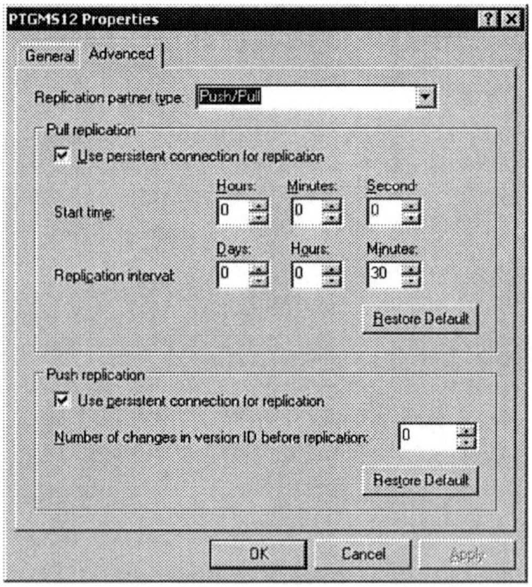

FIGURE 4.16 The Advanced tab enables you to customize the WINS replication setting to meet your network's requirements.

7. Click OK when the settings meet your requirements.

You have now configured replication with a WINS replication partner. Now let's look at the global replication properties.

Configuring WINS Replication

To review the global replication properties, open the WINS manager application as described in the first part of Step by Step 4.1 and select the Replication Partners folder in the left pane. Right-click and select Properties from the context menu. This opens the Replication Partners Properties dialog box to the General tab, as shown in Figure 4.17.

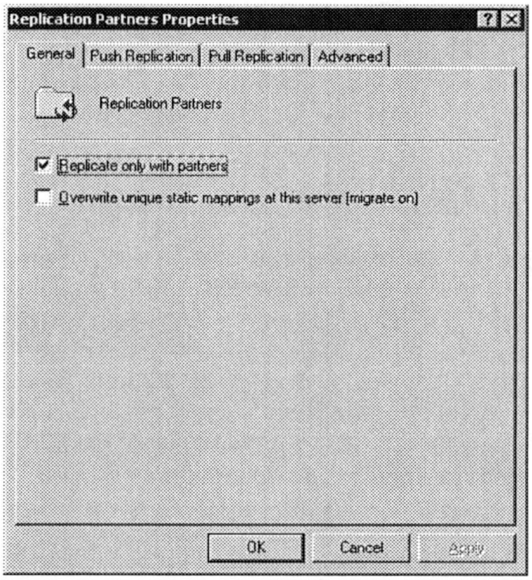

FIGURE 4.17 The General tab provides basic replication-configuration options.

The General Tab

The options on the General tab are pretty basic in nature, compared to many others. From here, you can opt to restrict replication to only the replication partners you've previously specified by leaving the default selection in place for the Replicate Only with Partners option. In addition, you can enable the Overwrite Unique Static Mappings option to enable the WINS server to overwrite static mappings in the database currently with dynamic WINS mappings during replication. As with static IP addresses and static DNS records, static WINS mappings can become a burden to manage efficiently and accurately, and thus should be avoided in most cases.

NOTE

It takes two to replicate Remember that you must configure both partners in a replication relationship to replicate with each other; otherwise, replication does not occur.

The Push Replication Tab

The Push Replication tab, shown in Figure 4.18, provides configurable options that govern how push replication behaves for your WINS server.

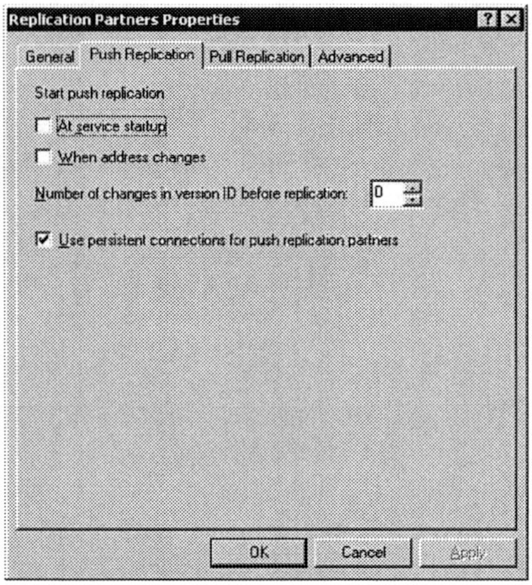

FIGURE 4.18 The Push Replication tab provides options that enable you to configure how WINS push replication behaves.

Options available for configuration include those to start a push replication at server startup or when an address changes in a mapping in the database. By configuring a value in the Number of Changes in Version ID field, you are specifying how many updates can be made in the WINS database before push partners are informed of the changes. The last option on the Push Replication tab allows you to enable persistent connections, which is typically advisable as long as the replication partners support them.

The Pull Replication Tab

The Pull Replication tab, shown in Figure 4.19, provides configurable options that govern how pull replication behaves for your WINS server.

The options on the Pull Replication tab are fairly straightforward and pertain to how pull replication should occur for this server. In most cases, you can leave the default entries for Start Time and Replication interval as is—doing do will result in a replication schedule that starts push replication every 30 minutes. The Number of Retries option enables you to specify how many failed attempts the server will make to replicate with a partner before giving up. Additionally, you can configure the server to push replicate at startup and use persistent connections with replication partners; both of these options are defaults and should typically stay selected.

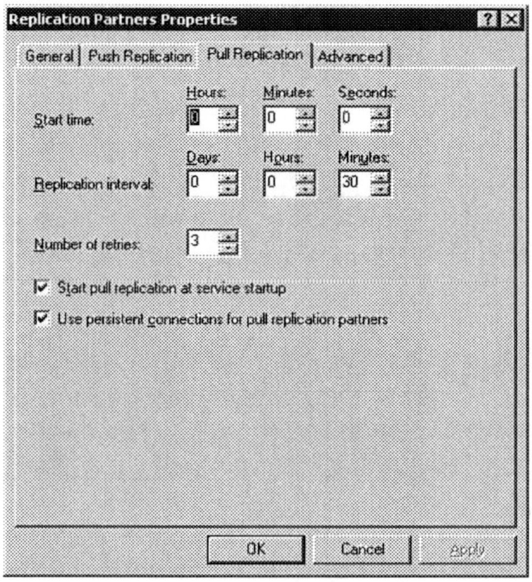

FIGURE 4.19 The Pull Replication tab provides options that enable you to configure how WINS pull replication behaves.

The Advanced Tab

The Advanced tab, shown in Figure 4.20, provides configurable options that govern how pull replication behaves for your WINS server.

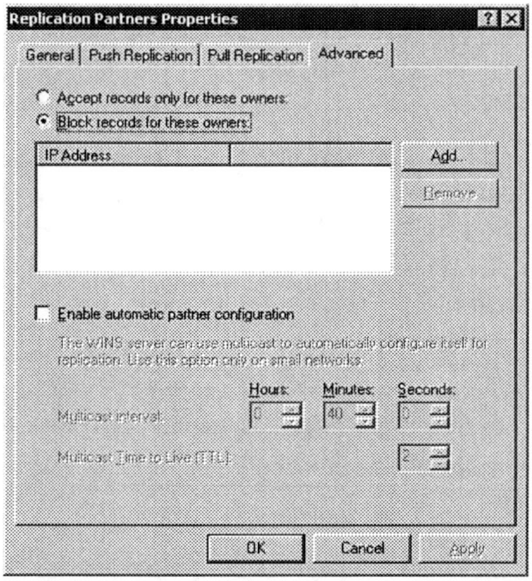

FIGURE 4.20 The Advanced tab provides you with the rest of the replication options available to configure.

The options found on the Advanced tab are usually a collection of what didn't fit anywhere else, and that's the case with those found here. You have the option to configure a list of servers that will be the only ones you accept new WINS records from, or the option to configure a list of servers that you will block acceptance of new records from. This can be helpful in larger enterprises where there might be unknown WINS servers and you want to absolutely limit replication to only the servers you know and identify here.

Conversely, you have the option to allow the WINS server to automatically discover and configure replication partners through a scheduled multicast message. Typically, you'll not want to configure the autodiscovery settings, though, because this will lead to some amount of loss of administrative control over how replication is configured and occurs for your WINS servers.

EXAM ALERT

Global replication settings Because we just finished discussing how to configure replication partners, these parameters should look familiar. However, in this section, the changes apply to any replication partners created after the modifications are made; they are not applied to existing replication partners.

You have now successfully configured the replication partner parameters. Let's take a quick look at implementing NetBIOS name resolution.

Implementing NetBIOS Name Resolution

Objective:

Plan a NetBIOS name resolution strategy.

- Plan NetBIOS name resolution by using the LMHOSTS file.

Microsoft TCP/IP uses NetBIOS over TCP/IP (NetBT) as specified in RFC 1001 and 1002 to support the NetBIOS client and server programs in the local area network (LAN) and wide area network (WAN) environments. Before we look at the specifics of NetBIOS name resolution, let's briefly review how computers communicate on the network. This review should help you understand how the different NetBIOS modes work and why some are preferable to others.

Computers can use two ways to communicate on a network:

- Through broadcast messages, which every computer receives
- Through directed messages, which are sent to a specific computer

EXAM ALERT

Microsoft does test on backward compatibility Don't be fooled. Just because WINS is a legacy technology doesn't mean it won't be tested on the exam. Microsoft recognizes the importance of backward compatibility, and as a result, you can expect to see questions on WINS for this exam. If you have not worked with it in a legacy environment, make sure you understand how WINS works.

Whenever possible, communicating through directed messages is preferable. This approach cuts down on the amount of network traffic and ensures that only the affected hosts receive the message. It also ensures that the messages propagate across routers. So Microsoft needed to make sure that WINS communicated primarily with directed messages. The company accomplished this by allowing several types of NetBIOS naming methods. These naming methods are commonly called node types. A node is simply a device on a network. Every computer on a Microsoft computer is configured as one of four node types. The node type determines whether the computer will learn names through broadcast messages, directed messages, or some combination of broadcast and directed messages. Before you can work with WINS, you need to know what the node types are and when they are used:

- **B-node (broadcast node)**—This node relies exclusively on broadcast messages and is the oldest NetBIOS name-resolution mode. A host needing to resolve a name request sends a message to every host within earshot, requesting the address associated with a host name. B-node has two shortcomings: Broadcast traffic is undesirable and becomes a significant user of network bandwidths, and TCP/IP routers don't forward broadcast messages, which restricts B-node operation to a single network segment.
- **P-node (point-to-point node)**—This node relies on WINS servers for NetBIOS name resolution. Client computers register themselves with a WINS server when they come on the network. They then contact the WINS server with NetBIOS name-resolution requests. WINS servers communicate using directed messages, which can cross routers, so P-node can operate on large networks. Unfortunately, if the WINS server is unavailable, or if a node isn't configured to contact a WINS server, P-node name resolution fails.
- **M-node (modified node)**—This hybrid mode first attempts to resolve NetBIOS names using the B-node mechanism. If that fails, an attempt is made to use P-node name resolution. M-node was the first hybrid mode put into operation, but it has the disadvantage of favoring B-node operation, which is associated with high levels of broadcast traffic.
- **H-node (hybrid node)**—This hybrid mode favors the use of WINS for NetBIOS name resolution. When a computer needs to resolve a NetBIOS name, it first attempts to use P-node resolution to resolve a name via WINS. Only if WINS resolution fails does the host resort to B-node to resolve the name via broadcasts. Because it typically results in the best network utilization, H-node is the default mode of operation for Microsoft TCP/IP client computers configured to use WINS for name resolution. Microsoft recommends leaving TCP/IP client computers in the default H-node configuration.

NOTE

DHCP supplied node types You can configure the node type through a DHCP option if you so desire. DHCP is discussed in detail in Chapter 3, "Planning, Implementing, and Troubleshooting DHCP."

The time might come when you need to understand exactly how WINS resolves a name. (Because H-node is not only the default but is also the recommended configuration, we restrict our discussion to the H-node name resolution.) When a WINS client computer configured for hybrid node needs to resolve a host name, it goes through the following series of steps:

1. The WINS client computer checks its NetBIOS name cache. If the name is found, that name is returned.
2. The client queries the WINS server. If the name is found, that name is returned.
3. The client issues a broadcast to find the host on the local network. If the name is found, that name is returned.
4. The client looks for the `LMHOSTS` file to check for an entry. If the name is found, that name is returned.
5. The client looks for the `HOST` file to check for an entry. If the name is found, that name is returned.
6. The client queries the DNS server for the entry. If the name is found, that name is returned.
7. If all these methods fail, the WINS client computer issues an error message saying that it cannot communicate with the host.

Although networks can be organized using a mixture of node types, Microsoft recommends against doing so. B-node client computers ignore P-node-directed messages, and P-node client computers ignore B-node broadcasts. Therefore, it is conceivable that two client computers could separately be established with the same NetBIOS name. If WINS is enabled on a Windows 2000 or XP computer, the system uses H-node by default. Without WINS, the system uses B-node by default. Non-WINS client computers can access WINS through a WINS proxy, which is a WINS-enabled computer that listens to name-query broadcasts and then queries the WINS server on behalf of the requesting client computer.

EXAM ALERT

Registering with WINS When your Windows client computer enters the network, it registers with WINS so that other Microsoft client computers can resolve its name to an address. For the exam, you should be aware that although a WINS proxy server can be used to resolve names for hosts that have registered with WINS, it cannot be used to register with WINS. You need access to the WINS server to successfully register.

Another point that many people have a misconception about is how clients actually contact the WINS server. Unlike DHCP clients, WINS clients cannot locate a WINS server through broadcasts. A WINS server IP address needs to be provided to a client ahead of time either though DHCP or by manual configuration.

The actual configuration of a computer to use `LMHOSTS` for NetBIOS name resolution is not done by using the WINS console or a Group Policy Object, as you might expect. You must actually configure it computer by computer by setting the options available to you on the WINS tab of the Advanced TCP/IP Settings dialog box, shown in Figure 4.21.

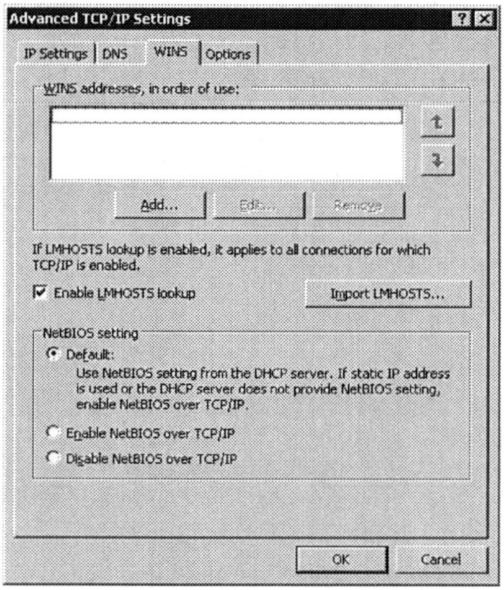

FIGURE 4.21 On the WINS tab of the Advanced TCP/IP Settings dialog box, you can configure the network connection to use an `LMHOSTS` file.

You have the following options available to you to allow the use of the `LMHOSTS` file on the local computer:

- **Enable `LMHOSTS` lookup**—This option, which is selected by default, specifies that an `LMHOSTS` file is to be used to resolve NetBIOS host names to an IP address.
- **Default**—This option, which is selected by default, specifies that this network connection is to obtain the NetBIOS over TCP/IP (NetBT) setting from the Windows DHCP server that granted its lease.
- **Enable NetBIOS over TCP/IP**—This option specifies that this network connection is to use NetBT and WINS.
- **Disable NetBIOS over TCP/IP**—This option specifies that this network connection is not to use NetBT and WINS.

`LMHOSTS` files typically contain entries similar to the following ones, which are examples given in the default `LMHOSTS` file located in the `%systemroot%\System32\Drivers\Etc` folder:

```
102.54.94.97     rhino
102.54.94.123    popular
102.54.94.117    localsrv
```

Each entry maps a NetBIOS name to an IP address for hosts that are not located on the local subnet, thus allowing legacy clients to locate other legacy clients on the network.

Challenge

Rick's Rockets is a leading manufacturer of toy rocket kits. Rick's currently owns the ricksrocketsna.com domain name and uses its ISP to host its web, FTP, and email services through that domain name. Rick's current internal network is extremely decentralized and disorganized, and is actually still functioning as a Windows 2000 workgroup. All workstations are Windows 2000 Professional, and all servers are Windows 2000 Advanced Server.

You have been hired by Rick, the CEO of Rick's Rockets, to plan and implement a completely new network infrastructure to include an internal DNS namespace to support the rollout of Windows Server 2003 and Active Directory. Rick's Rockets will not be purchasing any additional publicly accessible domain names. Rick's will be upgrading its Windows 2000 Advanced Server licenses to Windows Server 2003 Enterprise Edition licenses to support the new network plan.

Roger, the CIO of Rick's Rockets, has informed you that he wants the new internal DNS namespace to be easy for users to remember but to provide complete isolation from the external DNS namespace. Internal clients should be allowed to resolve IP addresses for external resources, but external clients should not be able to resolve IP addresses for internal resources. All clients should automatically update their IP addresses in DNS, and DNS should accept updates only from authorized clients to increase security of the internal DNS servers. The internal DNS servers should not be capable of resolving external IP addresses directly but should provide forwarding to the external DNS servers maintained by Rick's ISP.

Through your discussions with various personnel within Rick's Rockets, you've discovered that these items need to be addressed:

- You need to plan a new DNS namespace that meets the requirements outlined by the CEO and CIO.
- You need to use a delegated namespace to provide the required results.
- Secure dynamic updates in an Active Directory–integrated zone are required to provide the DNS data protection required yet still allow clients to update their IP address information in DNS.
- Conditional forwarding must be configured to forward all name-resolution requests for the `ricksrocketsna.com` domain to the external DNS servers provided by the ISP.

Your task is to determine the problem with the network configuration and then provide a plan to correct it.

Try to complete this exercise on your own, listing your conclusions on a sheet of paper. When you have completed the exercise, compare your results to those given here.

You propose to create a delegated namespace, such as `corp.ricksrocketsna.com`, for the internal network. It will provide an easy-to-remember namespace for users while still isolating the internal network from the external network.

If you create Active Directory–integrated zones using secure dynamic updates, all Windows 2000 workstation clients will be capable of automatically updating their DNS information after receiving a DHCP lease. Secure dynamic updates also prevent unauthorized clients from polluting the DNS data with bad information.

By configuring conditional forwarding for the ricksrocketsna.com zone, you can ensure that all name-resolution requests are performed as quickly as possible for your clients without having to host the zone on your internal DNS servers.

Integrating DNS and WINS

If you have to provide WINS name resolution in your network, you're going to want to ensure that it is available to DNS for name resolution. By selecting the Use WINS Forward Lookup option for forward-lookup zones (see Figure 4.22) or the Use WINS-R Lookup Option for reverse-lookup zones (see Figure 4.23), you can configure the DNS server to look up host names or IP addresses in WINS that it cannot otherwise resolve.

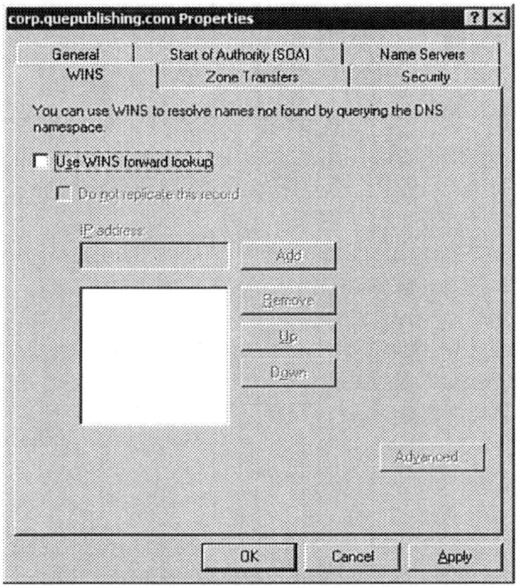

FIGURE 4.22 You can configure DNS forward-lookup zones to use WINS from the WINS tab of the zone properties dialog box.

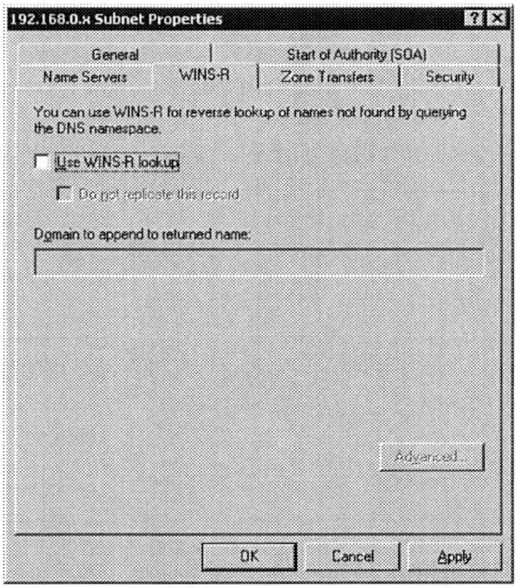

FIGURE 4.23 You can configure DNS reverse lookup zones to use WINS from the WINS-R tab of the zone properties dialog box.

Troubleshooting Name-Resolution Problems

Objective:

Troubleshoot host name resolution.

- Diagnose and resolve issues related to DNS services.
- Diagnose and resolve issues related to client computer configuration.

Troubleshooting name resolution is a sometimes tricky art that you might need to master. Fortunately, Windows Server 2003 provides a wealth of tools that you can use to quickly determine and correct the cause of the problems at hand. You have five basic tools at your disposal when it comes to troubleshooting name-resolution issues:

- `ipconfig`
- `ping`
- `nbtstat`
- `tracert`
- `pathping`
- `nslookup`
- `netsh`

We briefly examine the use of each of these tools in the following sections.

ipconfig

The first—and easiest—step in troubleshooting any TCP/IP–related network problem is to gather information about the computer on which the problem is occurring or has been reported. The `ipconfig` command makes this process easy. To get a complete report of the computer's IP configuration properties, enter the **`ipconfig/all`** command at the command line. A typical output might look something like that shown here:

```
c:\>ipconfig/all

Windows IP Configuration
   Host Name . . . . . . . . . . . . : PTGMS02
   Primary Dns Suffix  . . . . . . . : corp.quepublishing.com
   Node Type . . . . . . . . . . . . : Unknown
   IP Routing Enabled. . . . . . . . : No
   WINS Proxy Enabled. . . . . . . . : Yes
   DNS Suffix Search List. . . . . . : corp.quepublishing.com
                                       quepublishing.com
```

```
Ethernet adapter Local Area Connection 3:
   Connection-specific DNS Suffix  . : corp.quepublishing.com
   Description . . . . . . . . . . . : Realtek RTL8139 Family PCI Fast Ethernet
NIC
   Physical Address. . . . . . . . . : 00-E0-7D-C1-3E-0E
   DHCP Enabled. . . . . . . . . . . : Yes
   Autoconfiguration Enabled . . . . : Yes
   IP Address. . . . . . . . . . . . : 192.168.0.123
   Subnet Mask . . . . . . . . . . . : 255.255.255.0
   Default Gateway . . . . . . . . . : 192.168.0.1
   DHCP Server . . . . . . . . . . . : 192.168.0.1
   DNS Servers . . . . . . . . . . . : 205.152.37.23
                                       205.152.132.23
                                       192.168.1.254
   Lease Obtained. . . . . . . . . . : Wednesday, July 05, 2006 5:40:09 PM
   Lease Expires . . . . . . . . . . : Wednesday, July 05, 2006 11:40:09 PM

Ethernet adapter Local Area Connection:
   Connection-specific DNS Suffix  . : corp.quepublishing.com
   Description . . . . . . . . . . . : Broadcom NetXtreme Gigabit Ethernet
   Physical Address. . . . . . . . . : 00-13-72-0E-98-7E
   DHCP Enabled. . . . . . . . . . . : No
   IP Address. . . . . . . . . . . . : 192.168.0.156
   Subnet Mask . . . . . . . . . . . : 255.255.255.0
   Default Gateway . . . . . . . . . : 192.168.0.1
   DNS Servers . . . . . . . . . . . : 192.168.0.155
                                       205.152.37.23
   Primary WINS Server . . . . . . . : 192.168.0.156
   NetBIOS over Tcpip. . . . . . . . : Disabled
```

You can learn several key pieces of information about your computer's network connections just from examining the output of the `ipconfig/all` command, including whether DHCP is enabled for the adapter, the IP address assigned, the default gateway (always a prime concern when problems arise with computers on different subnets), and other critical information, including the IP addresses for the DNS servers in use by the network connection. All this information can be used to identify where the problem lies by determining simply "what doesn't look right." Usually, the problem jumps right out at you when you start to look around for it.

You also can use the `ipconfig` command to display and purge the contents of the local DNS resolver cache, as shown in the following output:

```
c:\>ipconfig/displaydns

Windows IP Configuration
    1.0.0.127.in-addr.arpa
    ----------------------------------------
    Record Name . . . . . : 1.0.0.127.in-addr.arpa.
    Record Type . . . . . : 12
    Time To Live  . . . . : 596820
```

```
    Data Length . . . . . : 8
    Section . . . . . . . : Answer
    PTR Record  . . . . . : localhost

    ptgdc01.corp.quepublishing.com
    ----------------------------------------
    Record Name . . . . . : ptgdc01.corp.quepublishing.com
    Record Type . . . . . : 1
    Time To Live  . . . . : 495
    Data Length . . . . . : 4
    Section . . . . . . . : Answer
    A (Host) Record . . . : 192.168.0.155

    ptgdc01
    ----------------------------------------
    Record Name . . . . . : ptgdc01.corp.quepublishing.com
    Record Type . . . . . : 1
    Time To Live  . . . . : 495
    Data Length . . . . . : 4
    Section . . . . . . . : Answer
    A (Host) Record . . . : 192.168.0.155

    localhost
    ----------------------------------------
    Record Name . . . . . : localhost
    Record Type . . . . . : 1
    Time To Live  . . . . : 596820
    Data Length . . . . . : 4
    Section . . . . . . . : Answer
    A (Host) Record . . . : 127.0.0.1

c:\>ipconfig/flushdns

Windows IP Configuration
Successfully flushed the DNS Resolver Cache.

c:\>ipconfig/displaydns

Windows IP Configuration
    1.0.0.127.in-addr.arpa
    ----------------------------------------
    Record Name . . . . . : 1.0.0.127.in-addr.arpa.
    Record Type . . . . . : 12
    Time To Live  . . . . : 596758
    Data Length . . . . . : 8
    Section . . . . . . . : Answer
    PTR Record  . . . . . : localhost

    localhost
    ----------------------------------------
```

```
Record Name . . . . . : localhost
Record Type . . . . . : 1
Time To Live  . . . . : 596758
Data Length . . . . . : 4
Section . . . . . . . : Answer
A (Host) Record . . . : 127.0.0.1
```

This command can be helpful when the local DNS cache is corrupt or contains invalid information. This cache will rebuild itself over time as the computer queries DNS servers.

ping

The `ping` command is practically as old as TCP/IP networking itself. You can use the `ping` command to test basic network connectivity between two computers, over local and remote networks. The basic syntax of the `ping` command looks something like `ping` *`computerIP`* or `ping` *`HostName`*. This command causes Windows to send four special Internet Control Message Protocol (ICMP) packets to the remote computer that are then returned to the local computer. You can instruct Windows to send a continuous stream of `ping` packets by using the `ping -t` command. Using the `ping -a` command specifies that name resolution is to be performed during the `ping` process. Refer to Chapter 2, "Planning and Troubleshooting TCP/IP Routing," for a full discussion on using `ping`.

nbtstat

NBT stands for NetBIOS over TCP/IP. Thus, `nbtstat` gives you statistics for NetBIOS over TCP/IP. The utility is used to determine which NetBIOS names the machine has cached and to which IP addresses those names have been resolved. You need to be aware of the options for using `nbtstat`, as outlined in Table 4.5.

TABLE 4.5 The `nbtstat` Command Switches

Switch	Description
-a	Displays the name table of a remote machine given its name.
-A	Displays the name table of a remote machine given its IP address.
-c	Displays the cache of NetBIOS names held by the local machine. This is useful for determining which names the local client has requested recently and how they were resolved. Figure 4.23 shows the results of an `NBTSTAT -c`.
-n	Displays a list of local NetBIOS names.
-r	Displays a list of names that have been resolved by broadcast and via WINS.
-R	Purges and reloads the remote cache name table.
-s	Displays a sessions table, showing the name of remote machines.
-S	Displays a session's table, showing only IP addresses for remote machines.
-RR	Performs a release and refresh by sending name-release packets to WINS and then starting a refresh.

EXAM ALERT

nbtstat The exam expects you to know these three basic options (but not whether the uppercase or lowercase version is necessary). You should know how to retrieve the NetBIOS names from an IP address, retrieve the cache, and show current sessions.

You can use several different switches with `nbtstat` to determine how it returns information to you. Using the `nbtstat -n` command returns the local NetBIOS name table, as shown here:

```
C:\>nbtstat -n
Local Area Connection 3:
Node IpAddress: [192.168.0.156] Scope Id: []
                NetBIOS Local Name Table
       Name               Type         Status
    ---------------------------------------------
    PTGMS02        <00>  UNIQUE      Registered
    PTGMS02        <20>  UNIQUE      Registered
    CORP           <00>  GROUP       Registered
    CORP           <1E>  GROUP       Registered
```

If you need to list the contents of the NetBIOS name cache, use the `nbtstat -c` command to produce the following output:

```
C:\>nbtstat -c
Local Area Connection:
Node IpAddress: [192.168.0.156] Scope Id: []
                  NetBIOS Remote Cache Name Table
        Name              Type       Host Address    Life [sec]
    ------------------------------------------------------------
    PTGDC01.CORP.QU<45>  UNIQUE          192.168.0.155       595
```

To examine the NetBIOS name table of a remote computer, use the `nbtstat -a` *`RemoteComputerName`* command to produce the following output:

```
C:\>nbtstat -a ptgdc01
Local Area Connection:
Node IpAddress: [192.168.0.156] Scope Id: []
           NetBIOS Remote Machine Name Table
       Name               Type         Status
    ---------------------------------------------
    PTGDC01        <00>  UNIQUE      Registered
    CORP           <1C>  GROUP       Registered
    CORP           <00>  GROUP       Registered
    PTGDC01        <20>  UNIQUE      Registered
    CORP           <1B>  UNIQUE      Registered
    CORP           <1E>  GROUP       Registered
    CORP           <1D>  UNIQUE      Registered
    ..__MSBROWSE__.<01>  GROUP       Registered
    MAC Address = 00-13-72-0E-83-DA
```

To display a listing of client and server connections, use the `nbtstat -s` command to produce the following output:

```
C:\>nbtstat -s
Local Area Connection:
Node IpAddress: [192.168.0.156] Scope Id: []
                     NetBIOS Connection Table
    Local Name       State       In/Out  Remote Host      Input   Output
    ---------------------------------------------------------------------
    PTGMS02 <00>     Connected   Out     PTGDC01<20>      97MB    92MB
```

You can also clear the contents of the cache and reload it from the `LMHOSTS` file by using the `nbtstat -R` command. You must use an uppercase `R` in this command. To release and subsequently refresh name records on a WINS server, issue the `nbtstat -RR` command.

tracert

`tracert` is another of the old standby tools that network administrations have grown to love over time. `tracert` routes tracing from the source to the destination, showing all intermediate hops (routers) that are used to forward and deliver the packets to their destination. In addition, `tracert` calculates how long each hop takes. Refer to Chapter 2 for a full discussion on using `tracert`.

pathping

The `pathping` command is a new tool first introduced in Windows 2000 that combines the capabilities of `ping` and `tracert` into one tool. `pathping` is used to gather information about network latency and network loss at the intermediate hops between the source and destination. It accomplishes this by sending multiple ICMP messages to each router between the source and destination over a period of time and then computing results based on the packets returned from each router. `pathping` can thus be used to quickly determine the operational status of each router or subnet the packets must cross. Refer to Chapter 2 for a full discussion on using `pathping`.

nslookup

The `nslookup` command can be used to look up and display information for troubleshooting DNS issues. `nslookup`, however, is not a simple tool that you can jump right into with a fair amount of DNS knowledge. Unlike other troubleshooting tools, `nslookup` has an interactive and noninteractive usage mode—much the same as the `netsh` command.

When looking up a single item, you are better off using the noninteractive mode by issuing a command similar to the following:

```
nslookup quepublishing.com 192.168.0.155
```

In this example, the first parameter specifies the DNS name or IP address of the computer you want to look up, and the second parameter specifies the DNS name or IP address of the DNS server you want to use. If you do not specify a DNS server, the default DNS server for the requesting computer is used. This sample `nslookup` query might return a result such as this:

```
C:\>nslookup quepublishing.com 192.168.0.155
Server:  ptgdc01.corp.quepublishing.com
Address:  192.168.0.155

Non-authoritative answer:
Name:    quepublishing.com
Address:  63.240.93.132
```

If you need to look up multiple pieces of information or more complex information, such as information about specific resource records contained in a zone, you need to use `nslookup` in interactive mode. You can see how interactive mode can be used to gain more advanced information, such as the list of all name servers (NS resource record) and mail exchangers (MX resource record) for the `microsoft.com` zone.

```
C:\>nslookup
Default Server:  ptgdc01.corp.quepublishing.com
Address:  192.168.0.155

> server 205.152.37.23
Default Server:  dns.asm.bellsouth.net
Address:  205.152.37.23

> set type=ns
> microsoft.com
Server:  dns.asm.bellsouth.net
Address:  205.152.37.23

Non-authoritative answer:
microsoft.com   nameserver = ns3.msft.net
microsoft.com   nameserver = ns4.msft.net
microsoft.com   nameserver = ns5.msft.net
microsoft.com   nameserver = ns1.msft.net
microsoft.com   nameserver = ns2.msft.net

> set type=mx
> microsoft.com
Server:  dns.asm.bellsouth.net
Address:  205.152.37.23

Non-authoritative answer:
microsoft.com   MX preference = 10, mail exchanger = mailc.microsoft.com
microsoft.com   MX preference = 10, mail exchanger = maila.microsoft.com
microsoft.com   MX preference = 10, mail exchanger = mailb.microsoft.com
```

The `Non-authoritative answer` label indicates that this information was retrieved from the selected DNS server's local cache and was not directly queried as a result of the `nslookup` query.

You can exit interactive mode at any time by typing **`exit`**.

The `nslookup` command has an extremely large feature set, too large to do justice to it here in this space. You can get more information on the full use and functionality of `nslookup` at www.microsoft.com/technet/prodtechnol/windowsserver2003/proddocs/standard/nslookup.asp.

netsh

The netsh command is an advanced configuration and troubleshooting command that provides that ability to manage almost any networking related component on your Windows Server 2003 computer, but requires you to have knowledge of the task you're trying to achieve. The `netsh` command can be used interactively or via scripting to manage the Windows Firewall, DHCP, WINS, network adapters or IPSec (IP Security) settings, just to name a few of the things it can do.

Unlike the relatively easy to understand and use `ping` or `ipconfig` commands we examined earlier, `netsh` can seem significantly more complex to use due to its context based operation. In other words, you don't simply append switches to the `netsh` command as you've seen previously with ping or ipconfig, you first must set the context that `netsh` operates in, such as *interface* to manage network adapters or *firewall* to manage the Windows Firewall.

You can find more information about the `netsh` command by searching for "netsh" at technet.microsoft.com or by using the built-in help functionality of the `netsh` command itself.

Chapter Summary

In the TCP/IP network of today's connected world, DNS is no longer a nicety; it's a requirement. Originally created to replace the antiquated and difficult-to-maintain `HOSTS` file, the domain name system (DNS) has quickly seen its popularity rise as TCP/IP has become the king of all networking protocols. Microsoft has led the charge to make TCP/IP and DNS the de facto standards for all networks, small and large.

Because DNS is so critical to a Windows Server 2003 network, it is important that you prepare adequately before implementing your DNS solution. Only through proper planning can you be reasonably well assured of not having any problems down the road. The first decision you need to make is what your DNS namespace will look like. You need to choose from using an existing, delegated, or unique namespace.

After choosing your namespace, you can determine what types of zones you will require, as well as how you will configure forwarding to occur. Of course, you will also want to look into securing your DNS infrastructure from attack and compromise. By choosing an Active Directory–integrated zone, you can ease administrative burden and increase DNS security.

If you have other DNS systems in use on your network, you need to decide what their role is to be in your Windows Server 2003 network. Will you upgrade these servers to a newer version that is compatible with and supports the DNS requirements of Windows Server 2003? If not, you should consider migrating their DNS zones over to your Windows Server 2003 DNS servers and then retiring these legacy DNS servers or making them secondaries for improved redundancy.

Although Windows Server 2003 networks do not normally require WINS, WINS is still very much alive and available for use to ensure that legacy Windows clients can actively participate in newer networks that use the more robust DNS for name resolution. You should have a good understanding of the basics of WINS, including the `LMHOSTS` file, and how to maintain and monitor WINS. WINS servers do not perform zone transfers, as do standard DNS zones; they replicate—the same term used for Active Directory–integrated DNS zones. You must be able to configure and manage WINS replication if your network is distributed over more than one site or has more than one WINS server.

When something goes awry with a TCP/IP configuration, you need to be able to determine the cause and required corrective action. Windows Server 2003 (and Windows XP) provides a suite of tools that you can use to troubleshoot TCP/IP configuration. You will most commonly find yourself relying on the `ipconfig`, `ping`, `nbtstat`, `tracert`, `pathping`, and `nslookup` command-line tools.

Key Terms

- Active Directory
- Active Directory–integrated zone
- B-node
- Conditional forwarding
- Discretionary Access Control List (DACL)
- Domain name service (DNS)
- Dynamic Host Configuration Protocol (DHCP)
- DNS client dynamic update
- DNS forwarder
- DNS resolver
- DNS Security (DNSSEC)
- DNS slave server
- Dynamic updates from DHCP
- Fully qualified domain name (FQDN)
- H-node
- Internet Control Message Protocol (ICMP)
- `ipconfig`
- Iterative query
- LAN Manager `HOSTS` (`LMHOSTS`)
- Leaf
- M-node
- `nbtstat`
- NetBIOS
- `pathping`
- `ping`
- P-node
- Pull replication

- Push replication
- Push/pull replication
- Recursive query
- Replication partner
- Secure dynamic update
- Standard primary zone
- Standard secondary zone
- Stub zone
- Top-level domain (TLD)
- `tracert`
- Transmission Control Protocol/Internet Protocol (TCP/IP)
- Tree
- Windows Internet Naming Service (WINS)
- Zone
- Zone transfer

Apply Your Knowledge

In this chapter, you have examined name resolution in Windows Server 2003. In the following exercises, you practice some of the concepts and methods discussed in this chapter.

Exercises

4.1 Testing TCP/IP

This exercise guides you through the process of retrieving IP address information. Then you use a few command-line entries to test the configuration and connectivity of the IP address.

Estimated time: 10 minutes

1. Select Start, Run. Then type **CMD** and press Enter.
2. At the command prompt, type the command **`ipconfig`** and press Enter. What is your IP address? What is your subnet mask? Can you determine the IP address of the DNS server?

3. Enter **`ipconfig/all`**. What additional information can you now see?
4. Enter **`ping 127.0.0.1`**. This is a special loopback test that tells you whether your network interface card is dead, just playing sick, or, you hope, just fine.
5. Enter **`ping`** ***`XX`***, where *XX* is your favorite website.
6. If you have another computer on this network, `ping` the IP address of that computer.
7. `ping` the name of the computer.
8. Did all your communications occur successfully? If not, you might need to perform some additional investigation and troubleshooting to determine where your problem lies. Note that more publicly accessible networks (such as `microsoft.com`) now actively drop ICMP packets, thus preventing the `ping` command from working properly.

4.2 Configuring a Replication Partner

In this exercise, you configure a replication partner.

Estimated time: 10 minutes

1. Open the WINS console by clicking Start, Programs, Administrative Tools, WINS.
2. In the right pane, right-click Replication Partners and select New Replication Partner. The New Replication Partner dialog box opens and asks you to enter the address of another WINS server. You can enter either the server name or the IP address. If the server name cannot be resolved, you are prompted to enter the address of the server.
3. Enter the name or IP address of the server and click OK.
4. Click Replication Partners in the left pane of the WINS console. You should see your new replication partner in the right pane.
5. Right-click the newly created replication partner. Then select Properties from the context menu to open the Replication Partner Properties dialog box.
6. Click the Advanced tab. On this tab, you can configure the replication properties for the replication partner. You can choose from Push/Pull (the default), Push, or Pull. You can also specify the options to control how and when the replication is to occur.
7. Click OK when the settings meet your requirements.

4.3 Performing a Manual Push Replication

In this exercise, you manually perform a push replication.

Estimated time: 10 minutes

1. Open the WINS console by clicking Start, Programs, Administrative Tools, WINS.
2. Right-click WINS Server and select Start Push Replication.

3. Enter the DNS name or IP address of the other WINS server and click OK.
4. Select Start for This Partner Only as the replication method. You can select Propagate to All Partners as the other method. Click OK. You receive a message that the replication request has been queued.
5. Check the event log for the status of the request and to see when it is completed.

4.4 Performing a Manual Pull Replication

In this exercise, you manually perform a pull replication.

Estimated time: 10 minutes

1. Open the WINS console by clicking Start, Programs, Administrative Tools, WINS.
2. Right-click the WINS Server and select Start Pull Replication.
3. Enter the DNS name or IP address of the other WINS server and click OK.
4. When asked to confirm the request, click Yes. You receive a message stating that the replication request has been queued.
5. Check the event log for the status of the request and to see when it is completed.

Review Questions

1. You need to determine whether one of the routers between your network and your partner's network is dropping packets. What command-line utility can you use to make this determination?
2. You are planning a new Windows Server 2003 Active Directory network for your organization. The organization currently uses three UNIX BIND DNS servers. What minimum version of BIND do you need to have to support Active Directory?
3. You have been directed to create a new DNS namespace for your company. The namespace must be as short as possible and be easily accessible from inside and outside your organization. The namespace will be used within a screened subnet to host a publicly accessible e-commerce application. What type of namespace should you implement?
4. You are considering setting up WINS for your network. You feel that you need a better understanding of how NetBIOS works and how the different node types work. What are the four NetBIOS node types, and how do they work?
5. What is the major difference between push replication and pull replication?

Exam Questions

1. You are currently planning the DNS namespace for a new Windows Server 2003 deployment. The namespace will be used only for the internal network. There will be a separate public network located in a DMZ with a different DNS namespace. Which of the following DNS namespaces would be acceptable on the internal network but not on the public network? (Choose all that apply.)

   ❍ **A.** `bigcorp.com`

   ❍ **B.** `bigcorp.corp`

   ❍ **C.** `bigcorp.local`

   ❍ **D.** `corp.bigcorp.com`

   ❍ **E.** `local.bigcorp.com`

2. You are the systems administrator for Rick's Rockets, a leading aerospace manufacturing corporation. You have several dozen legacy clients on your network that require WINS to be available. You are configuring a new Windows Server 2003 computer to act as a WINS server for your network. You also have one existing Windows 2000 Server computer providing WINS services. You want replication to occur after a certain number of changes have occurred. What configuration do you need to make?

   ❍ **A.** Configure a push partner on the Advanced tab of your WINS server properties page.

   ❍ **B.** Configure a pull partner on the Advanced tab of your WINS server properties page.

   ❍ **C.** Configure a push partner on the Settings tab of your WINS server properties page.

   ❍ **D.** Configure a pull partner on the Settings tab of your WINS server properties page.

3. You are a consultant who has been hired by Carmen's Clown College, Inc. You have been given the task of designing a delegated DNS namespace for Carmen's new Windows Server 2003 network. Carmen's already owns the `clowncollege.com` domain, and its ISP is hosting its website. Which of the following options represents a valid delegated DNS namespace?

   ❍ **A.** `clowncollege.net`

   ❍ **B.** `corp.clowncollege.com`

   ❍ **C.** `clowncollege.corp.com`

   ❍ **D.** `clowncollege.com.corp`

4. You are the systems administrator for a five-location pet-food manufacturer. You have WINS servers at all five locations, and you would like them to replicate with each other automatically. What should you do?

   ❍ **A.** Configure each WINS server as a replication partner. In Replication Partner properties, select Replicate with All Partners.

- ❍ **B.** Configure each WINS server as a replication partner. In Replication Partner properties, select Replicate Only with Partners.
- ❍ **C.** In Replication Partner properties, deselect Replicate Only with Partners. The server automatically replicates with any WINS servers.
- ❍ **D.** Install WINS. Any WINS servers on the network automatically replicate.

5. You are interviewing Chris, a candidate for an assistant administrator position in your company. When you ask her what a standard secondary zone is, what answer should she tell you?

- ❍ **A.** A zone that holds a writeable copy of the zone data and that can transfer it to all configured servers
- ❍ **B.** A zone that holds a read-only copy of the zone data
- ❍ **C.** A zone that has its zone data held within Active Directory
- ❍ **D.** A zone that contains only resource records necessary to identify the authoritative DNS servers for a zone

6. You are the systems administrator for Blue Sky Air, and you are training another administrator to assist with maintaining the network. She is having a hard time understanding the different NetBIOS node types, especially what type the Windows 2000 Professional and Windows XP Professional computers use. What is the default node type for these computers?

- ❍ **A.** H-node
- ❍ **B.** M-node
- ❍ **C.** P-node
- ❍ **D.** B-node

7. You are a senior consultant for Legacy Systems, Inc., a leading consultancy that helps organizations integrate their existing networks with newer technologies, such as Windows Server 2003. You are currently trying to get the existing BIND DNS implementation working with the newer Windows Server 2003 DNS service. Eventually, you will be able to migrate the existing BIND DNS zones to Windows Server 2003, but the customer wants this to occur over a six-month period, to prepare for any troubles. There are several different BIND servers, all of different versions. You are not sure what the version is on each of them. What setting can you change in the Windows Server 2003 DNS configuration to ensure that zone transfers succeed between the Windows Server 2003 DNS servers and the BIND servers?

- ❍ **A.** BIND Secondaries
- ❍ **B.** Enable Round-Robin
- ❍ **C.** Enable Netmask Ordering
- ❍ **D.** Secure Cache Against Pollution

8. You are the systems administrator for Widgets and Things, Inc. You are installing a WINS server on your Windows Server 2003 server. Your end users are all using DHCP. What is the best way to configure the workstations to use the WINS server?

❍ **A.** Make sure the WINS server is installed on a domain controller. WINS resolution will happen automatically.

❍ **B.** Modify the DHCP scope options for the WINS server to include the address of the new WINS server.

❍ **C.** Open the Network applet and open the TCP/IP properties. On the WINS tab, modify the TCP/IP properties to point to the WINS server. Repeat this procedure for each machine.

❍ **D.** Update the `LMHOSTS` file to include the address of the new WINS server.

9. A client computer that makes a DNS query to a DNS server for name resolution of a remote host is referred to as what?

❍ **A.** A recursive query

❍ **B.** An iterative query

❍ **C.** A DNS resolver

❍ **D.** A DNS forwarder

10. The WINS service was created to replace what?

❍ **A.** The domain name service

❍ **B.** The `HOSTS` file

❍ **C.** The `LMHOSTS` file

❍ **D.** The `WINS` file

11. You are a senior consultant for Legacy Systems, Inc., a leading consultancy that helps organizations integrate their existing networks with newer technologies, such as Windows Server 2003. You are currently trying to get the existing BIND DNS implementation working with the newer Windows Server 2003 DNS service. Eventually, you will be able to migrate the existing BIND DNS zones to Windows Server 2003, but the customer wants this to occur over a six-month period, to prepare for any troubles. There are several different BIND servers, all of different versions. You are not sure what the version is on each of them. What is the minimum version of BIND that you will require on these BIND servers to ensure that they meet the DNS requirements of Active Directory?

❍ **A.** 4.9.4

❍ **B.** 4.9.6

❍ **C.** 8.1.2

❍ **D.** 8.2.1

12. You are the WAN administrator for the Women's Place clothing store. You have six satellite locations all connected with low-bandwidth WAN links. Each location has its own WINS server for name resolution and will need to be replicated to. What is the best configuration for the WINS replication from the corporate WINS server to those in the field?

❍ **A.** Configure a pull replication from the remote servers to the central server and schedule it to occur whenever 100 entries have been added to the table.

❍ **B.** Configure a push replication from the remote servers to the central server and schedule it to occur whenever 100 entries have been added to the table.

❍ **C.** Configure a pull replication from the central server to the remote servers and schedule it to occur whenever 100 entries have been added to the table.

❍ **D.** Configure a push replication from the central server to the remote servers and schedule it to occur whenever 100 entries have been added to the table.

13. By default, with what DNS servers will a Windows Server 2003 DNS server perform zone transfers?

❍ **A.** Only those servers listed on the Zone Transfers tab of the zone properties dialog box

❍ **B.** Only those servers listed on the Name Servers tab of the zone properties dialog box

❍ **C.** All servers listed on the Name Servers and Zone Transfers tabs of the zone properties dialog box

❍ **D.** All servers not listed on the Name Servers and Zone Transfers tabs of the zone properties dialog box

14. You are troubleshooting network connectivity between two computers on a routed IP network. What command can you use to send a continuous flow of ICMP echo request packets to the destination IP address?

❍ **A.** `ping -a`

❍ **B.** `ping -t`

❍ **C.** `ping -l`

❍ **D.** `ping -f`

15. You are configuring your Windows Server 2003 DNS servers for increased security. You are concerned about the possibility of queries' responses containing resource records that are not pertinent to the original queries. What option can you select that will prevent this from occurring by allowing the DNS server to not cache a resource record if it is not part of the exact DNS domain tree for which the original query was made?

❍ **A.** BIND Secondaries

❍ **B.** Enable Round-Robin

❍ **C.** Enable Netmask Ordering

❍ **D.** Secure Cache Against Pollution

Answers to Review Questions

1. The `pathping` command combines the functionality of the `ping` and `tracert` commands and enables you to quickly determine which routers or subnets are dropping packets. For more information, see the section "`pathping`."

2. The BIND servers need to be at Version 4.9.6 (support for SRV resource records). For more information, see the section "Integrating with Third-Party DNS Solutions."

3. You should implement a unique DNS namespace. This option uses a completely separate but related domain name for your internal namespace. As an example, if you are using `bigcorp.com` for your external namespace, you might use `bigcorp.net` for your internal namespace. This configuration provides the advantage of improving security by isolating the two namespaces from each other. For more information, see the section "Planning a DNS Namespace Design."

4. The main differentiator among the four node types is the methods they use for name resolution (broadcast vs. direct connection). The four types are as follows:

   B-node (broadcast node), which relies exclusively on broadcast messages and is the oldest NetBIOS name-resolution mode. A host needing to resolve a name request sends a message to every host within earshot, requesting the address associated with a host name. B-node has two shortcomings: Broadcast traffic is undesirable and becomes a significant user of network bandwidths, and TCP/IP routers don't forward broadcast messages, which restricts B-node operation to a single network segment.

   P-node (point-to-point node), which relies on WINS servers for NetBIOS name resolution. Client computers register themselves with a WINS server when they come on the network. They then contact the WINS server with NetBIOS name-resolution requests. WINS servers communicate using directed messages, which can cross routers, so P-node can operate on large networks. Unfortunately, if the WINS server is unavailable or if a node isn't configured to contact a WINS server, P-node name resolution fails.

   M-node (modified node) is a hybrid mode that first attempts to resolve NetBIOS names using the B-node mechanism. If that fails, an attempt is made to use P-node name resolution. M-node was the first hybrid mode put into operation, but it has the disadvantage of favoring B-node operation, which is associated with high levels of broadcast traffic.

   H-node (hybrid node) is also a hybrid mode that favors the use of WINS for NetBIOS name resolution. When a computer needs to resolve a NetBIOS name, it first attempts to use P-node resolution to resolve a name via WINS. Only if WINS resolution fails does the host resort to B-node to resolve the name via broadcasts. Because it typically results in the best network utilization, H-node is the default mode of operation for Microsoft TCP/IP networks configured to use WINS for name resolution. Microsoft recommends leaving TCP/IP client computers in the default H-node configuration. For more information, see the section "Implementing NetBIOS Name Resolution."

5. The main difference between push and pull replication (besides the direction the database is replicated) is the trigger for the event. In the case of a push replication, the trigger is event based. When a specified number of changes are made to the database, the replication is triggered. A pull replication is triggered by the time configured for the replication. This is user configured. For more information, see the section "Planning for WINS Replication."

Answers to Exam Questions

1. **B, C.** The `bigcorp.corp` and `bigcorp.local` namespaces are not allowable public DNS namespaces, per RFC 1123. However, they are perfectly acceptable for an internal namespace. Answers A, D, and E represent valid external (public) namespaces and could thus be used internally or externally. Only answers B and C represent namespaces that are valid only on an internal network. For more information, see the section "Planning a DNS Namespace Design."

2. **A.** If you want your WINS server to send notification to replication partners that a number of changes have happened on your WINS server, you need to select the Push option for the WINS server. For more information, see the section "Planning for WINS Replication."

3. **B.** The `corp.clowncollege.com` namespace represents a delegated DNS namespace. `corp.clowncollege.com` would thus become the root of the Active Directory forest and domain structure. Internal network clients should be allowed to resolve both internal and external domain names; however, external (Internet) clients should not be allowed to resolve internal host names. The namespace `clowncollege.net` represents a unique namespace; thus, answer A is incorrect. The namespaces `clowncollege.corp.com` and `clowncollege.com.corp` are not delegated namespaces of the `clowncollege.com` namespace; thus, answers C and D are incorrect. For more information, see the section "Planning a DNS Namespace Design."

4. **B.** After the WINS servers have been configured as replication partners, they replicate with each other based on the replication configuration. For more information, see the section "Planning for WINS Replication."

5. **B.** A standard secondary zone holds a read-only copy of the zone information in standard text format. Secondary zones are created to increase performance and resilience of the DNS configuration. Information is transferred from the primary zone to the secondary zones. A master zone is one that holds the only writeable copy of the zone data; thus, answer A is incorrect. An Active Directory–integrated zone operates in multimaster mode, whereby all name servers can make changes to the zone data; thus, answer C is incorrect. A stub zone contains only the resource records necessary to identify the authoritative DNS servers for a zone; thus, answer D is incorrect. For more information, see the section "Planning DNS Zone Requirements."

6. **A.** Windows 2000 Professional and Windows XP Professional computers use H-node (hybrid) for NetBIOS name resolution. This node type favors the WINS server for name resolution but attempts to resolve the name by broadcast if the WINS server is unavailable. For more information, see the section "Implementing NetBIOS Name Resolution."

7. **A.** By selecting the BIND Secondaries option, you disable fast zone transfers and ensure that zone transfers are compatible and can succeed with older DNS implementations that do not support fast zone transfers. BIND Version 4.9.4 and later do support fast zone transfers. Selecting the Enable Round-Robin option configures the DNS server to use a round-robin rotation to rotate and reorder resource records if multiple records exist; thus, answer B is incorrect. The Enable Netmask Ordering option configures the DNS server to reorder its host records in the response it sends to a query based on the IP address of the DNS resolver from which the query came; thus, answer C is incorrect. The Secure Cache Against Pollution option configures the DNS server to prevent the addition of resource records that are unrelated to the original query; thus, answer D is incorrect. For more information, see the section "Integrating with Third-Party DNS Solutions."

8. **B.** Because this is a DHCP environment, just add/update the WINS option for the DHCP scope. Answer C might work, but it is much more labor intensive than the one-time scope update. For more information, see the section "Planning for WINS Replication."

9. **C.** A DNS resolver is any system that has been configured with the IP addresses of one or more DNS servers and that performs name-resolution queries against these servers. Recursive and iterative represent the types of name-resolution queries that are performed. A recursive query is a DNS query that is sent to a DNS server from a DNS resolver asking the DNS server to provide a complete answer to the query, or an error stating that it cannot provide the information; thus, answer A is incorrect. An iterative query is a DNS query that is sent by a DNS server to another DNS server in an effort to perform name resolution; thus, answer B is incorrect. A DNS forwarder is a DNS server that has received a forwarded name-resolution request from another DNS server; thus, answer D is incorrect. For more information, see the section "Planning DNS Forwarding Requirements."

10. **C.** WINS is a dynamic replacement for the `LMHOSTS` file. For more information, see the section "Introduction to WINS."

11. **C.** BIND 8.1.2 meets all the DNS requirements to support Active Directory by adding support for dynamic DNS. BIND 4.9.4 introduces support for fast zone transfers and does not meet the requirements for Active Directory; thus, answer A is incorrect. BIND 4.9.6 introduces support for SRV resource records but does not meet all the requirements for Active Directory; thus, answer B is incorrect. BIND 8.2.1 introduces support for incremental zone transfers—although this is not a requirement for Active Directory; thus, answer D is also incorrect. For more information, see the section "Integrating with Third-Party DNS Solutions."

12. **D.** For this question, keep two components in mind: the trigger (when a certain number of entries are added, this is the least bandwidth-intensive mechanism) and the direction the information must travel. Answer D is the only one with the right combination of these factors. For more information, see the section "Planning for WINS Replication."

13. **B.** By default, Windows Server 2003 DNS servers perform zone transfers only with the DNS servers that are listed on the Name Servers tab of the zone properties dialog box; thus, answers A, C, and D are incorrect. All DNS servers that are considered to be authoritative for the DNS zone are listed on the Name Servers tab. Although this configuration is fairly secure, you can make it more secure by explicitly configuring DNS servers by IP address on the Zone Transfers tab for which you want to allow zone transfers to occur. For more information, see the section "Zone Transfer Security."

14. **B.** By issuing the `ping -t` command, you can send a continuous stream of ICMP echo request packets to the destination IP address. You can stop the stream of packets by pressing the Ctrl+C key combination. For more information, see the section "`ping`."

15. **D.** DNS servers typically cache any names in referral answers, thus expediting the speed of resolving subsequent DNS queries. However, when this feature is in use, the server can determine whether the referred name is polluting or insecure and discard it. The server thus determines whether to cache the name offered in the referral, depending on whether it is part of the exact DNS domain tree for which the original name query was made.

Suggested Readings and Resources

1. Microsoft Corporation. *Microsoft Windows Server 2003 Resource Kit*. Redmond, WA: Microsoft Press, 2003.
2. Microsoft Corporation. *Microsoft Windows Server 2003 Deployment Kit*. Redmond, WA: Microsoft Press, 2003.
3. Davies, Joseph, and Thomas Lee. *Microsoft Windows Server 2003 TCP/IP Protocols and Services Technical Reference*. Redmond, WA: Microsoft Press, 2003.
4. "Deploying Network Services." http://technet2.microsoft.com/WindowsServer/en/Library/119050c9-7c4d-4cbf-8f38-97c45e4d01ef1033.mspx.
5. "Technical Overview of Windows Server 2003 Networking and Communications." www.microsoft.com/windowsserver2003/techinfo/overview/netcomm.mspx.
6. "Windows Server 2003 Reviewer's Guide." www.microsoft.com/windowsserver2003/techinfo/overview/reviewersguide.mspx.
7. Windows Server 2003 Online documentation: "Network Services." www.microsoft.com/technet/prodtechnol/windowsserver2003/proddocs/entserver/sag_NPStopnode.asp.

CHAPTER FIVE

5

Planning and Implementing Server Roles and Server Security

Now that we've looked at the networking aspects of Exam 70-293, we're going to shift gears and move to security. Security is now front and center in Windows Server 2003, permeating it from front to back, top to bottom. Thus, it is only fitting that we discuss security and server roles before moving on any further into this book.

Objectives

Microsoft defines the "Planning and Implementing Server Roles and Server Security" objectives as follows:

Configure security for servers that are assigned specific roles.

- The key to configuring and implementing role-based server security is to recognize the different levels at which security must be implemented. Servers should be grouped in Organizational Units (OU) by role for the purpose of applying security settings to them in an administratively efficient manner.

Plan a secure baseline installation.

- **Plan a strategy to enforce system default security settings on new systems.**
- **Identify client operating system default security settings.**
- **Identify all server operating system default security settings.**
- Windows Server 2003 is the most secure network operating system out of the box ever produced by Microsoft. While planning and implementing your overall network security plan, you need to be able to identify and, if necessary, enforce the default security settings on servers and client computers.

Plan security for servers that are assigned specific roles. Roles might include domain controllers, web servers, database servers, and mail servers.

- **Deploy the security configuration for servers that are assigned specific roles.**
- **Create custom security templates based on server roles.**
- Not all servers are created alike; this simple fact has been proven repeatedly to administrators who got caught with their proverbial pants down. To effectively secure servers with varying roles, you need to identify the threats and vulnerabilities that each server faces.

Evaluate and select the operating system to install on computers in an enterprise.

- **Identify the minimum configuration to satisfy security requirements.**
- A default, out-of-the-box installation of Windows Server 2003 might not be the best choice for your particular security requirements. Being able to identify the best operating system and the optimal security configuration for that operating system is an important part of your overall network security plan.

Outline

Study Strategies

- Become familiar with the topics presented in this chapter, including security templates, Group Policy, and hierarchical organizational systems. All these topics will be important as you plan and implement a security solution for your network.
- Understand the strengths and weaknesses of the different security-configuration tools available to you. Each has a specific purpose and can be used to secure your network.
- Get your hands dirty. The Step by Steps throughout this book provide plenty of directions and exercises, but you should go beyond these examples and create some of your own. If you can, experiment with each of the objectives to see how they work and why you would use each one.

Introduction

Windows Server 2003 is inherently more secure right out of the box than any previous version of Windows to come before it. The Trustworthy Computing campaign that Microsoft is leading has shown itself directly in the intrinsic security of Windows Server 2003. Although this version is overall more secure than its predecessors, that does not relieve you of the responsibility to evaluate, plan, and implement additional, custom security measures for your Windows Server 2003 network.

Whatever security plan you ultimately design and implement, you are best served by implementing *role-based security*. Role-based security is implemented by using a layered approach to security; the most general security settings are applied at the highest level and become increasingly restrictive as you go deeper into the organizational structure of the domain. Through the use of the preconfigured security templates included with Windows Server 2003, combined with careful planning and attentive administration of the network, you will be able to implement a role-based security solution.

Windows Server 2003 comes with a complete set of preconfigured security templates that you can use to quickly apply standardized security settings to a single computer, an Organizational Unit (OU), or a domain, if desired. In addition to these preconfigured security templates, Microsoft has made available additional security templates that can be used to enforce very specific security settings on Windows Server 2003 computers, depending on their assigned role. Throughout this chapter, we examine the various ways that security templates can be configured and implemented to apply to both default and customized security solutions in your Windows Server 2003 network.

Implementing Enterprise Security

If any one thing can be said about Windows Server 2003, it might be that Windows Server 2003 depends on Active Directory through and through. Active Directory permeates every part of an enterprise Windows Server 2003 network and is the conduit through which the network functions efficiently and securely. Although this is not a text on Active Directory design and implementation, nor is it designed to ready you for Exam 70-294, "Planning, Implementing, and Maintaining a Microsoft Windows Server 2003 Active Directory Infrastructure," you will become acutely aware throughout this chapter of how important a good Active Directory design and implementation are to your Windows Server 2003 network security plan.

Because Active Directory is so important to effectively planning and implementing a solid security plan in Windows Server 2003 networks, it is critical that you understand how to effectively organize your Active Directory structure to achieve the best results, both from a security standpoint and from an administrative one. When Windows 2000 was introduced, many network administrators mistakenly believed that the domain was a security boundary. This is simply not the case. The only absolute security boundary is that of the forest itself. In any forest environment, there exist ways for trusted administrators to acquire more privileges than they should have and abuse the power that has been granted to them.

Unfortunately, the reality is that the single-forest arrangement with a single domain model is typically the best overall way to design, implement, and manage the vast majority of Windows Server 2003 networks—including those that you will most likely be working on. With that in mind, you must plan for security from the beginning of your design.

OUs, sometimes thought of as nothing more than an organizational tool to "clean" up the visual appearance of Active Directory, are actually among your most powerful tools for planning, implementing, and maintaining a secure network environment. OUs offer an easy way to segment users and other security principals—specifically, computers in this instance—for the purpose of creating and enforcing administrative boundaries. Nesting OUs within each other, each with its own specific Group Policy Object (GPO), enables you to piece together the overall security solution for your network. Figure 5.1 illustrates this principle.

With this brief introduction to the way you might create a layered security solution, let's now move forward and start examining the tools available to you. The first step in implementing role-based security is to implement a *baseline configuration*. Before you can implement this baseline configuration, however, you must be aware of the default security settings that Windows gives you to start the process. This is the topic of the next section.

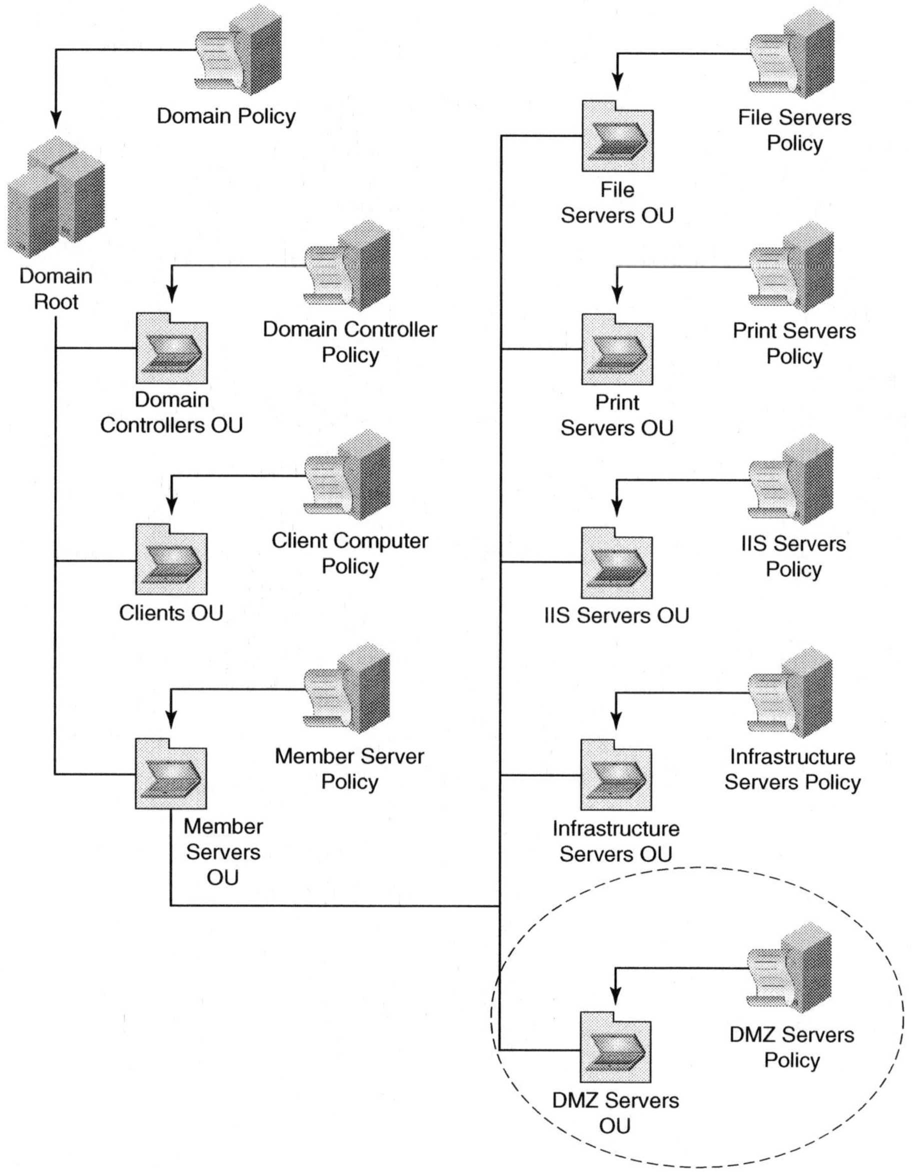

FIGURE 5.1 By nesting Organizational Units, you can create segmented and secure networks.

Planning Secure Baseline Installations

Objective:

Plan a secure baseline installation.

- Plan a strategy to enforce system default security settings on new systems.
- Identify client operating system default security settings.
- Identify all server operating system default security settings.

Security doesn't just happen; it requires careful planning, meticulous attention to detail, and persistence. We've already talked a bit about the inherent security of Windows Server 2003 right out of the box, but what about client operating systems? Are they to be thought of as less secure? The answer: yes and no. Ultimately, the security of your servers and clients is what you make of it. To make them secure, you need a baseline—a starting point. Where you know where you are starting from, you can better see where you are going. To that end, we examine the default security settings of Windows Server 2003 after a clean installation of a member server, and the default security settings of Windows XP Professional after a clean installation. By default, these security settings are applied to every clean installation that is performed. By ensuring that only authorized personnel perform operating system installations in a prescribed and consistent manner, you can ensure that these settings are applied uniformly across all new installations.

Identifying Windows Server 2003 Default Security Settings

The security you get out of Windows Server 2003 depends in part on how it is installed. Clean installations of Windows Server 2003 automatically receive the complete set of default configuration settings and thus are more secure (by default) than an upgrade installation. A computer that is upgraded to Windows Server 2003 is likely to inherit security settings that were present in the previous installation. This problem becomes even more acute when Windows NT 4.0 is upgraded to Windows Server 2003 because of the differences in the way Windows NT 4.0 handles the Registry and file system Discretionary Access Control Lists (DACLs).

You might be tempted to assume that by applying the default security template, `Setup security.inf`, to a computer, you can easily reset it to the security settings and it would have after a clean installation. This assumption is not always correct. The default security template is automatically created during the installation of Windows Server 2003 on a computer. It represents the current security configuration at that time: either new settings for a clean installation or the resulting settings after an upgrade installation. This security template cannot accurately be used to ensure that security settings are uniform unless the same type of installation is being performed on the same type of hardware. However, as discussed in more detail in the next section of this chapter, this security template can be used to reset the computer to a known state. This capability becomes important over time as you need to enforce security settings on computers that might have experienced some changes.

You can identify the default security settings on a newly installed Windows Server 2003 Service Pack 1 (SP1) member server through a variety of different means, such as the Local Group Policy console, the Local Security Policy console, or the Resultant Set of Policy (RSoP) snap-in. Although the default security settings can be identified easily enough, they are presented in Table 5.1 for your reference.

TIP

For a complete rundown on the security settings you can expect to find in Windows Server 2003 and Windows XP Professional in several different configurations, download "Threats and Countermeasures: Security Settings in Windows Server 2003 and Windows XP" from http://go.microsoft.com/fwlink/?LinkId=15160.

TABLE 5.1 Windows Server 2003 SP1 Member Server Default Security Settings

Group Policy Node/Policy Item	Default Member Server Setting
Windows Settings\Security Settings\Account Policies	
Enforce password history	24 passwords remembered
Maximum password age	42 days
Minimum password age	1 days
Minimum password length	7 characters
Passwords must meet complexity requirements	Enabled
Store password using reversible encryption for all users in the domain	Disabled
Windows Settings\Security Settings\Account Lockout Policy	
Account lockout duration	Not defined
Account lockout threshold	0 invalid login attempts
Reset account lockout counter after	Not defined
Windows Settings\Security Settings\Kerberos Policy	
Enforce user logon restrictions	Not applicable
Maximum lifetime for service ticket	Not applicable
Maximum lifetime for user ticket	Not applicable
Maximum lifetime for user ticket renewal	Not applicable
Maximum tolerance for computer clock synchronization	Not applicable
Windows Settings\Local Policies\Audit Policy	
Audit account logon events	Success
Audit account management	No auditing

(continues)

TABLE 5.1 *Continued*

Group Policy Node/Policy Item	Default Member Server Setting
Windows Settings\Local Policies\Audit Policy	
Audit directory service access	No auditing
Audit logon events	Success
Audit object access	No auditing
Audit policy change	No auditing
Audit privilege use	No auditing
Audit process tracking	No auditing
Audit system events	No auditing
Windows Settings\Local Policies\User Rights Assignment	
Access this computer from the network	Backup Operators, Power Users, Users, Administrators, Everyone
Act as part of the operating system	Not defined
Add workstations to domain	Not defined
Adjust memory quotas for a process	Administrators, NETWORK SERVICE, LOCAL SERVICE
Allow logon locally	Backup Operators, Power Users, Users, Administrators
Allow logon through Terminal Services	Remote Desktop Users, Administrators
Back up files and directories	Backup Operators, Administrators
Bypass traverse checking	Backup Operators, Power Users, Users, Administrators, Everyone
Change the system time	Power Users, Administrators
Create a pagefile	Administrators
Create a token object	Not defined
Create global objects	SERVICE, Administrators
Create permanent shared objects	Not defined
Debug programs (SeDebugPrivilege)	Administrators
Deny access to this computer from the network	SUPPORT_388945a0
Deny logon as a batch job	Not defined
Deny logon as a service	Not defined
Deny logon locally	SUPPORT_388945a0
Deny logon through Terminal Services	Not defined
Enable computer and user accounts to be trusted for delegation	Not defined
Force shutdown from a remote system	Administrators

TABLE 5.1 *Continued*

Group Policy Node/Policy Item	Default Member Server Setting
Windows Settings\Local Policies\User Rights Assignment	
Generate security audits	NETWORK SERVICE, LOCAL SERVICE
Impersonate a client after authentication	SERVICE, Administrators
Increase scheduling priority	Administrators
Load and unload device drivers	Administrators
Lock pages in memory	Not defined
Log on as a batch job	SUPPORT_388945a0, LOCAL SERVICE
Log on as a service	NETWORK SERVICE
Manage auditing and security log	Administrators
Modify firmware environment values	Administrators
Perform volume-maintenance tasks	Administrators
Profile single process	Power Users, Administrators
Profile system performance	Administrators
Remove computer from docking station	Power Users, Administrators
Replace a process-level token	NETWORK SERVICE, LOCAL SERVICE
Restore files and directories	Backup Operators, Administrators
Shut down the system	Backup Operators, Power Users, Administrators
Synchronize directory service data	Not defined
Take ownership of files or other objects	Administrators
Windows Settings\Local Policies\Security Options	
Accounts: Administrator account status	Enabled
Accounts: Guest account status	Disabled
Accounts: Limit local account use of blank passwords to console logon only	Enabled
Accounts: Rename administrator account	Administrator
Accounts: Rename guest account	Guest
Audit: Audit the access of global system objects	Disabled
Audit: Audit the use of Backup and Restore privilege	Disabled
Audit: Shut down system immediately if unable to log security audits	Disabled

(continues)

TABLE 5.1 *Continued*

Group Policy Node/Policy Item	Default Member Server Setting
Windows Settings\Local Policies\Security Options	
DCOM: Machine access restrictions in Security Descript or Definition Language (SDDL)	Not defined
DCOM: Machine access restrictions in Security Descript or Definition Language (SDDL)	Not defined
Devices: Allow undock without having to log on	Enabled
Devices: Allowed to format and eject removable media	Administrators
Devices: Prevent users from installing printer drivers	Enabled
Devices: Restrict CD-ROM access to locally logged-on user only	Disabled
Devices: Restrict floppy access to locally logged-on user only	Disabled
Devices: Unsigned driver installation behavior	Warn but allow installation
Domain controller: Allow server operators to schedule tasks	Not defined
Domain controller: LDAP server signing requirements	Not defined
Domain controller: Refuse machine account password changes	Not defined
Domain member: Digitally encrypt or sign secure-channel data (always)	Enabled
Domain member: Digitally encrypt secure-channel data (when possible)	Enabled
Domain member: Digitally sign secure-channel data (when possible)	Enabled
Domain member: Disable machine account password changes	Disabled
Domain member: Maximum machine account password age	30 days
Domain member: Require strong (Windows 2000 or later) session key	Disabled
Interactive logon: Display user information when the session is locked	Not defined
Interactive logon: Do not display last username	Disabled
Interactive logon: Do not require Ctrl+Alt+Del	Disabled
Interactive logon: Message text for users attempting to log on	Not defined
Interactive logon: Message title for users attempting to log on	Not defined
Interactive logon: Number of previous logons to cache (in case domain controller is not available)	10 logons
Interactive logon: Prompt user to change password before expiration	14 days
Interactive logon: Require Domain Controller authentication to unlock workstation	Disabled
Interactive logon: Require smart card	Disabled
Interactive logon: Smart card removal behavior	No action
Microsoft network client: Digitally sign communications (always)	Disabled
Microsoft network client: Digitally sign communications (if server agrees)	Enabled

TABLE 5.1 *Continued*

Group Policy Node/Policy Item	Default Member Server Setting
Windows Settings\Local Policies\Security Options	
Microsoft network client: Send unencrypted password to third-party SMB servers	Disabled
Microsoft network server: Amount of idle time required before suspending session	15 minutes
Microsoft network server: Digitally sign communications (always)	Enabled
Microsoft network server: Digitally sign communications (if client agrees)	Enabled
Microsoft network server: Disconnect clients when logon hours expire	Enabled
MSS: Enable automatic logon	Disabled
MSS: Allow Windows to automatically restart after a system crash	Enabled
MSS: Enable administrative shares	Enabled
MSS: IP source-routing protection level	Medium, source-routed packets are ignored when IP forwarding is enabled
MSS: Prevent the dial-up password from being saved	Disabled
MSS: Allow automatic detection of dead network gateways	Disabled
MSS: Allow ICMP redirects to override OSPF-generated routes	Enabled
MSS: Hide computer from the browse list	Disabled
MSS: How often keep-alive packets are sent, in milliseconds	7,200,000
MSS: Enable `NoDefaultExempt` for IPSec Filtering	Enabled
MSS: Disable autorun for all drives	Disabled
MSS: Allow the computer to ignore NetBIOS name-release requests except from WINS servers	Enabled
MSS: Enable the computer to stop generating 8.3-style filenames	Disabled
MSS: Allow IRDP to detect and configure default gateway addresses	Disabled
MSS: Enable safe DLL search mode	Enabled
MSS: The time in seconds before the screen saver grace period expires	5
MSS: Syn attack protection level	Enabled
MSS: SYN-ACK retransmissions when a connection request is not acknowledged	3 and 6 seconds, half-open connections dropped after 21 seconds
MSS: How many times unacknowledged data is retransmitted	5
MSS: Percentage threshold for the security event log at which the system will generate a warning	0 (not configured)
(ActiveX Signed Controls) `RunInvalidSignatures`	Not defined
(RPC Endpoint Mapper) `EnableAuthEpResolution`	Not defined

(continues)

TABLE 5.1 *Continued*

Group Policy Node/Policy Item	Default Member Server Setting
Windows Settings\Local Policies\Security Options	
(RPC Endpoint Mapper) `RestrictRemoteClients`	Not defined
(WebDAV Redirector) `DisableBasicOverClearChannel`	Not defined
(WebDAV Redirector) `UseBasicAuth`	Not defined
Network access: Allow anonymous SID/name translation	Disabled
Network access: Do not allow anonymous enumeration of SAM accounts	Enabled
Network access: Do not allow anonymous enumeration of SAM accounts and shares	Disabled
Network access: Do not allow storage of credentials or .NET passports for network authentication	Disabled
Network access: Let Everyone permissions apply to anonymous users	Disabled
Network access: Named pipes that can be accessed anonymously	COMNAP, COMNODE, SQL\QUERY, SPOOLSS, EPMAPPER, LOCATOR, TrkWks, TrkSvr
Network access: Remotely accessible Registry paths	*Too numerous to list*
Network access: Remotely accessible Registry paths and subpaths	*Too numerous to list*
Network access: Restrict anonymous access to named pipes and shares	Enabled
Network access: Shares that can be accessed anonymously	COMCFG,DFS$
Network access: Sharing and security model for local accounts	Classic—local users authenticate as themselves
Network security: Do not store LAN Manager hash value on next password change	Disabled
Network security: Force logoff when logon hours expire	Disabled
Network security: LAN Manager authentication level	Send NTLM response only
Network security: LDAP client signing requirements	Negotiate signing
Network security: Minimum session security for NTLM SSP-based (including secure RPC) clients	No minimum
Network security: Minimum session security for NTLM SSP-based (including secure RPC) servers	No minimum
Recovery console: Allow automatic administrative logon	Disabled
Recovery console: Allow floppy copy and access to all drives and all folders	Disabled
Shutdown: Allow system to be shut down without having to log on	Disabled
Shutdown: Clear virtual memory pagefile	Disabled
System cryptography: Force strong key protection for user keys stored on the computer	Not defined

TABLE 5.1 *Continued*

Group Policy Node/Policy Item	Default Member Server Setting
Windows Settings\Local Policies\Security Options	
System cryptography: Use FIPS-compliant algorithms for encryption, hashing, and signing	Disabled
System objects: Default owner for objects created by members of the Administrators group	Administrators group
System objects: Require case insensitivity for non-Windows subsystems	Enabled
System objects: Strengthen default permissions of internal system objects (e.g. Symbolic Links)	Enabled
System settings: Optional subsystems	Posix
System Settings: Use certificate rules on Windows executables for software-restriction policies	Disabled
Windows Settings\Event Log\Settings for Event Logs	
Maximum application log size	16,384KB
Maximum security log size	16,384KB
Maximum system log size	16,384KB
Restrict guest access to application log	Enabled
Restrict guest access to security log	Enabled
Restrict guest access to system log	Enabled
Retain application log	Not defined
Retain security log	Not defined
Retain system log	Not defined
Retention method for application log	Overwrite as needed
Retention method for security log	Overwrite as needed
Retention method for system log	Overwrite as needed

NOTE

File system, Registry, and services Information about the default settings of the file system, the Registry, and services is not provided because of the large number of possible configurations of the hardware and operating system.

Of course, the defaults listed in Table 5.1 can and will change depending on the final role of the server. The Default Domain Policy will be applied to all member servers in the domain, modifying the defaults previously listed. Servers that are promoted to domain controller status will also be subjected to the additional configuration in the default Domain Controller policy. The installation and configuration of various network services and applications might also lead to additional security configuration modifications. Recall, as you saw in Figure 5.1, that the final configuration of a computer is the cumulative total of all policies applied to it at all levels, unless they have been blocked.

Identifying Windows XP Professional Default Security Settings

You can identify the default security settings on a newly installed Windows XP Professional workstation through a variety of different means, such as the Local Group Policy console, the Local Security Policy console, or the Resultant Set of Policy (RSoP) snap-in. Although the default security settings can be identified easily enough, they are presented in Table 5.2 for your reference.

TABLE 5.2 Windows XP Professional SP2 Default Security Settings

Group Policy Node/Policy Item	Domain Member Effective Default Setting
Windows Settings\Security Settings\Account Policies	
Enforce password history	0 passwords remembered
Maximum password age	42 days
Minimum password age	0 days
Minimum password length	0 characters
Passwords must meet complexity requirements	Disabled
Store password using reversible encryption for all users in the domain	Disabled
Windows Settings\Security Settings\Account Lockout Policy	
Account lockout duration	Not applicable
Account lockout threshold	0 invalid login attempts
Reset account lockout counter after	Not applicable
Windows Settings\Security Settings\Kerberos Policy	
Enforce user logon restrictions	Not applicable
Maximum lifetime for service ticket	Not applicable
Maximum lifetime for user ticket	Not applicable
Maximum lifetime for user ticket renewal	Not applicable
Maximum tolerance for computer clock synchronization	Not applicable
Windows Settings\Local Policies\Audit Policy	
Audit account-logon events	No auditing
Audit account management	No auditing
Audit directory service access	No auditing

TABLE 5.2 *Continued*

Group Policy Node/Policy Item	Domain Member Effective Default Setting
Windows Settings\Local Policies\Audit Policy	
Audit logon events	No auditing
Audit object access	No auditing
Audit policy change	No auditing
Audit privilege use	No auditing
Audit process tracking	No auditing
Audit system events	No auditing
Windows Settings\Local Policies\User Rights Assignment	
Access this computer from the network	Everyone, Administrators, Users, Power Users, Backup Operators
Act as part of the operating system	Not defined
Add workstations to domain	Not defined
Adjust memory quotas for a process	LOCAL SERVICE, NETWORK SERVICE, Administrators
Allow logon through Terminal Services	Administrators, Remote Desktop Users
Back up files and directories	Administrators, Backup Operators
Bypass traverse checking	Everyone, Administrators, Users, Power Users, Backup Operators
Change the system time	Administrators, Power Users
Create a pagefile	Administrators
Create a token object	Not defined
Create global objects	Not applicable
Create permanent shared objects	Not defined
Debug programs	Administrators
Deny access to this computer from the network	Support_*xxxxxxxx*, Guest
Deny logon as a batch job	Not defined
Deny logon as a service	Not defined
Deny logon locally	Support_*xxxxxxxx*, Guest
Deny logon through Terminal Services	Not defined
Enable computer and user accounts to be trusted for delegation	Not defined

(continues)

TABLE 5.2 *Continued*

Group Policy Node/Policy Item	Domain Member Effective Default Setting
Windows Settings\Local Policies\User Rights Assignment	
Force shutdown from a remote system	Administrators
Generate security audits	LOCAL SERVICE, NETWORK SERVICE
Increase scheduling priority	Administrators
Load and unload device drivers	Administrators
Lock pages in memory	Not defined
Log on as a batch job	Support_*xxxxxxxx*
Log on as a service	NETWORK SERVICE
Log on locally	Administrators, Users, Power Users, Backup Operators
Manage auditing and security log	Administrators
Modify firmware environment values	Administrators
Perform volume-maintenance tasks	Administrators
Profile single process	Administrators, Power Users
Profile system performance	Administrators
Remove computer from docking station	Administrators, Power Users
Replace a process-level token	LOCAL SERVICE, NETWORK SERVICE
Restore files and directories	Administrators, Backup Operators
Shut down the system	Administrators, Power Users, Backup Operators, Users
Synchronize directory service data	Not defined
Take ownership of files or other objects	Administrators
Windows Settings\Local Policies\Security Options	
Accounts: Administrator account status	Enabled
Accounts: Guest account status	Disabled
Accounts: Limit local account use of blank passwords to console logon only	Enabled
Accounts: Rename administrator account	Administrator
Accounts: Rename guest account	Guest
Audit: Audit the access of global system objects	Disabled
Audit: Audit the use of Backup and Restore privilege	Disabled
Audit: Shut down system immediately if unable to log security audits	Disabled

TABLE 5.2 *Continued*

Group Policy Node/Policy Item	Domain Member Effective Default Setting
Windows Settings\Local Policies\Security Options	
DCOM: Machine access restrictions in Security Descriptor Definition Language (SDDL)	Not defined
DCOM: Machine launch restrictions in Security Descriptor Definition Language (SDDL)	Not defined
Devices: Allow undock without having to log on	Enabled
Devices: Allowed to format and eject removable media	Administrators
Devices: Prevent users from installing printer drivers	Disabled
Devices: Restrict CD-ROM access to locally logged-on user only	Disabled
Devices: Restrict floppy access to locally logged-on user only	Disabled
Devices: Unsigned driver installation behavior	Warn but allow installation
Domain controller: Allow server operators to schedule tasks	Not defined
Domain controller: LDAP server signing requirements	Not defined
Domain controller: Refuse machine account password changes	Not defined
Domain member: Digitally encrypt or sign secure channel data (always)	Enabled
Domain member: Digitally encrypt secure channel data (when possible)	Enabled
Domain member: Digitally sign secure channel data (when possible)	Enabled
Domain member: Disable machine account password changes	Disabled
Domain member: Maximum machine account password age	30 days
Domain member: Require strong (Windows 2000 or later) session key	Disabled
Interactive logon: Do not display last username	Disabled
Interactive logon: Do not require Ctrl+Alt+Del	Not defined
Interactive logon: Message text for users attempting to log on	Not defined
Interactive logon: Message title for users attempting to log on	Not defined
Interactive logon: Number of previous logons to cache (in case domain controller is not available)	10 logons
Interactive logon: Prompt user to change password before expiration	14 days
Interactive logon: Require Domain Controller authentication to unlock workstation	Disabled
Interactive logon: Smart card removal behavior	No Action
Microsoft network client: Digitally sign communications (always)	Disabled
Microsoft network client: Digitally sign communications (if server agrees)	Enabled
Microsoft network client: Send unencrypted password to third-party SMB servers	Disabled

(continues)

TABLE 5.2 *Continued*

Group Policy Node/Policy Item	Domain Member Effective Default Setting
Windows Settings\Local Policies\Security Options	
Microsoft network server: Amount of idle time required before suspending session	15 minutes
Microsoft network server: Digitally sign communications (always)	Disabled
Microsoft network server: Digitally sign communications (if client agrees)	Disabled
Microsoft network server: Disconnect clients when logon hours expire	Enabled
MSS: Enable automatic logon	Disabled
MSS: Allow Windows to automatically restart after a system crash	Enabled
MSS: Enable administrative shares	Enabled
MSS: IP source-routing protection level	Medium, source-routed packets are ignored when IP forwarding is enabled
MSS: Prevent the dial-up password from being saved	Disabled
MSS: Allow automatic detection of dead network gateways	Enabled
MSS: Allow ICMP redirects to override OSPF-generated routes	Enabled
MSS: Hide computer from the browse list	Disabled
MSS: How often keep-alive packets are sent, in milliseconds	7,200,000
MSS: Enable NoDefaultExempt for IPSec Filtering	Enabled
MSS: Disable autorun for all drives	Disabled
MSS: Allow the computer to ignore NetBIOS name-release requests except from WINS servers	Enabled
MSS: Enable the computer to stop generating 8.3-style filenames	Disabled
MSS: Allow IRDP to detect and configure default gateway addresses (could lead to DoS)	2 (enable only if DHCP sends the Perform Router Discovery option)
MSS: Enable safe DLL search mode	Disabled
MSS: The time in seconds before the screen saver grace period expires	5
MSS: Syn attack protection level	Disabled
MSS: SYN-ACK retransmissions when a connection request is not acknowledged	3 and 6 seconds, half-open connections dropped after 21 seconds
MSS: How many times unacknowledged data is retransmitted	5
MSS: Percentage threshold for the security event log at which the system will generate a warning	0 (not configured)

TABLE 5.2 *Continued*

Group Policy Node/Policy Item	Domain Member Effective Default Setting
Windows Settings\Local Policies\Security Options	
(ActiveX signed controls) `RunInvalidSignatures`	Disabled
(RPC Endpoint Mapper) `EnableAuthEpResolution`	Disabled
(RPC Endpoint Mapper) Restrict remote clients	1
(Security Center) `AntiVirusDisableNotify`	0
(Security Center) `FirewallDisableNotify`	0
(Security Center) `UpdatesDisableNotify`	0
(`StorageDevicePolicies`) `WriteProtect`	0
Network access: Allow anonymous SID/name translation	Disabled
Network access: Do not allow anonymous enumeration of SAM accounts	Enabled
Network access: Do not allow anonymous enumeration of SAM accounts and shares	Disabled
Network access: Do not allow storage of credentials or .NET Passports for network authentication	Disabled
Network access: Let Everyone permissions apply to anonymous users	Disabled
Network access: Named pipes that can be accessed anonymously	COMNAP, COMNODE, SQL\QUERY, SPOOLSS, EPMAPPER, LOCATOR, TrkWks, TrkSvr
Network access: Remotely accessible Registry paths	Too numerous to list
Network access: Shares that can be accessed anonymously	COMCFG,DFS$
Network access: Sharing and security model for local accounts	Guest only—local users authenticate as Guest
Network security: Do not store LAN Manager hash value on next password change	Disabled
Network security: Force logoff when logon hours expire	Disabled
Network security: LAN Manager authentication level responses	Send LM and NTLM
Network security: LDAP client signing requirements	Negotiate signing
Network security: Minimum session security for NTLM SSP-based (including secure RPC) clients	No minimum
Network security: Minimum session security for NTLM SSP-based (including secure RPC) servers	No minimum
Recovery console: Allow automatic administrative logon	Disabled
Recovery console: Allow floppy copy and access to all drives and all folders	Disabled

(continues)

TABLE 5.2 *Continued*

Group Policy Node/Policy Item	Domain Member Effective Default Setting
Windows Settings\Local Policies\Security Options	
Shutdown: Allow system to be shut down without having to log on	Enabled
Shutdown: Clear virtual memory pagefile	Disabled
System cryptography: Use FIPS-compliant algorithms for encryption, hashing, and signing	Disabled
System objects: Default owner for objects created by members of the Administrators group	Object creator
System objects: Require case insensitivity for non-Windows subsystems	Enabled
System objects: Strengthen default permissions of internal system objects (e.g. Symbolic Links)	Enabled
Windows Settings\Event Log\Settings for Event Logs	
Maximum application log size	512KB
Maximum security log size	512KB
Maximum system log size	512KB
Restrict guest access to application log	Enabled
Restrict guest access to security log	Enabled
Restrict guest access to system log	Enabled
Retain application log	7 days
Retain security log	7 days
Retain system log	7 days
Retention method for application log	Overwrite events as needed
Retention method for security log	Overwrite events as needed
Retention method for system log	Overwrite events as needed

Of course, the defaults listed in Table 5.2 can and will change, depending on the final role of the workstation. You will likely apply custom policies on your network, modifying the defaults previously listed. The installation and configuration of various network services and applications can also lead to additional security configuration modifications. Recall, as you saw in Figure 5.1, that the final configuration of a computer is the cumulative total of all policies applied to it at all levels, unless they have been blocked.

Selecting Secure Operating Systems

Objective:

Evaluate and select the operating system to install on computers in an enterprise.

- Identify the minimum configuration to satisfy security requirements.

The enterprise operating systems of choice these days are Windows 2000, Windows XP Professional, and Windows Server 2003. Your choice depends on several factors, including budgetary issues, licensing, and specific role requirements.

You should be aware of potential problems with legacy clients, such as Windows 95 and Windows NT 4.0, in newer Windows Active Directory domains. These legacy clients cannot participate fully in the Active Directory domain environment because they cannot use Group Policy Objects; you need to implement security settings on these computers through System Policies or direct editing of the Registry. Also, these legacy computers might not be capable of communicating with Windows Server 2003 Domain Controllers because of the increased level of security of domain controller communications through server message block (SMB) signing.

If your budget allows it, you will be best served by installing all Windows Server 2003 SP1 or R2 servers and all Windows XP Professional SP2 workstations. This combination provides the greatest amount of security configuration capability, including newer items such as wireless networking security, 802.1x configuration, and software-restriction policies. Also, the improved Certificate Services in Windows Server 2003 was designed to be used with Windows XP Professional clients.

Planning and Implementing Role-Based Security Using Security Templates

As discussed in the beginning of this chapter, security is best achieved through careful planning and attentive administration. Realizing that you, as a systems administrator, might not have the time or detailed knowledge required to create complex security policies on your own, Microsoft has given you a leg up on the bad guys by providing several preconfigured security templates with Windows Server 2003. You can use these preconfigured security templates to quickly and easily implement security settings on servers and workstations. You can think of them in one of two ways: as a starting point from which to make your own customized security template or as a solution in and of themselves. Neither thought is more correct than the other.

In addition to the preconfigured security templates provided within Windows Server 2003, Microsoft has done security-minded network administrators everywhere a favor by providing additional role-based security templates in the Windows Server 2003 Security Guide, a free download that you can acquire from http://go.microsoft.com/fwlink/?LinkId=14845. We discuss these role-based security templates later in this chapter.

In simple terms, a security template is little more than a specially formatted flat text file that can be read by the Security Configuration Manager tools. These preconfigured templates have an `.inf` extension and can be located in the %systemroot%\security\templates folder on your Windows Server 2003 computer. You can use the Security Configuration and Analysis console, the `secedit.exe` tool, or the Local Security Policy console to apply these templates to a local computer. You can apply templates to an OU or domain by importing them into the Security Settings section of the applicable Group Policy using the Group Policy Editor. You also can use these preconfigured templates as a baseline to compare an unknown system against a known set of configuration settings by using the Security Configuration and Analysis console or the `secedit.exe` tool.

We examine the security templates included with Windows Server 2003 in the next section and then move forward into how they are configured and used after that.

Introducing the Windows Server 2003 Security Templates

Table 5.3 details the preconfigured security templates that ship with Windows Server 2003.

TABLE 5.3 The Preconfigured Security Templates in Windows Server 2003

Template (Filename)	Description
Default (`Setup security.inf`)	This template is created during the installation of Windows on the computer. This template varies from one computer to the next, depending on whether the installation was performed as a clean installation or an upgrade. `Setup security.inf` represents the default security settings that a computer started out with and thus can be used to reset portions of security as required. This template can be applied to both workstations and member servers, but not to domain controllers (DCs), and it should never be applied via Group Policy; the large amount of data it contains could result in performance degradations.
Default DC (`DC security.inf`)	This template is automatically created when a member server is promoted to a DC. It represents the file, Registry, and system service default security settings for that DC and can be used later to reset those areas to their default configurations.
Compatible (`compatws.inf`)	The Compatible workstation/member server template provides a means of allowing members of the Users group to run applications that do not conform to the Windows Logo Program for Windows 2000 and above. Applications that were written for Windows NT 4.0 do not use the same security model that Windows 2000 and above applications use. In most cases, applications that do conform to the Windows Logo Program can be successfully run by members of the Users group without any

TABLE 5.3 *Continued*

Template (Filename)	Description
	further modifications required. For applications that do not conform, you have two basic choices: You can make the users members of the Power Users group or relax the default permissions of the Users group. The Compatible template solves this problem by changing the default file and Registry permissions that are granted to the Users group to allow them to run most applications that are not part of the Windows Logo Program. As a side effect of applying this template, all users are removed from the Power Users group because the basic assumption is that the template is being applied to prevent the need for that group. This template should not be applied to DCs, so you need to be sure not to import it into the Default Domain Policy or the Default Domain Controller Policy.
Secure (`securews.inf`, `securedc.inf`)	The Secure templates are the first ones to actually begin the process of locking down the computer to which they are applied. Two different Secure templates exist: `securews.inf`, which is for workstations and member servers, and `securedc.inf`, which is for DCs only. The Secure templates prevent the usage of the LAN Manager (LM) authentication protocol. Windows 9*x* clients need to have Active Directory Client Extensions installed so that NT LAN Manager Version 2 (NTLMv2) will allow them to communicate with Windows 2000 and above clients and servers using these templates. These templates also impose additional restrictions on anonymous users, such as preventing them from enumerating account and share information. The secure templates also enable Server Message Block (SMB) signing on the server side. By default, SMB signing is enabled on client computers. If you apply this template, SMB packet signing will always be negotiated between clients and servers.
Highly Secure (`hisecws.inf`, `hisecdc.inf`)	The Highly Secure templates impose further restrictions on computers they are applied to. Whereas the Secure templates require at least NTLM authentication, the Highly Secure templates require NTLMv2 authentication. The Secure templates enable SMB packet signing, and the Highly Secure templates also require SMB packet signing. In addition to the various extra security restrictions that are imposed by the Highly Secure templates, these templates make several changes to group membership and the login process. All members of the Power Users group are removed from this group. In addition, only members of the Domain Admins group and the local administrative account are allowed

(continues)

TABLE 5.3 *Continued*

Template (Filename)	Description
	to be members of the local Administrators group. When the Highly Secure templates are used, it is assumed that only Windows Logo Program–compliant applications are in use. Therefore, no provision is in place for users to use non-compliant applications because the Compatible template is not needed and the Power Users group has no members. Members of the Users group can use applications that are Windows Logo Program compliant. In addition, members of the Administrators group can use any application they want.
System Root (`rootsec.inf`)	This template defines the root permissions for the root of the system volume. If these permissions are changed, they can be reapplied by using this template. In addition, you can modify this template to apply the same permissions to other volumes. Explicitly configured permissions are not overwritten on child objects when you use this template.
No Terminal Server Use SID (`notssid.inf`)	This template is used on servers that are not running Terminal Services to remove all unnecessary Terminal Services security identifiers (SIDs) from the file system and Registry. However, this does not increase the security of the server.
Internet Explorer SACL (`iesacls.inf`)	This template is used to enable auditing on registry keys that are used by Internet Explorer. By default, the keys in question are set to allow the built-in Everyone group Full Control. By enabling this auditing, changes can be tracked should users (or the applications they use within Internet Explorer) attempt to modify the settings of any of these keys.

CAUTION

Templates are incremental All the preconfigured security templates are incremental, meaning that they have been designed to be applied to computers that are using the default security settings. These templates do not implement the default security settings before applying their security settings.

Using the Security Configuration Manager Tools

Objective:

Plan security for servers that are assigned specific roles. Roles might include domain controllers, web servers, database servers, and mail servers.

- Deploy the security configuration for servers that are assigned specific roles.
- Create custom security templates based on server roles.

Now that you've seen the security templates available for your use, let's take a brief look at the tools available to you for the design, testing, and implementation of these (and other) security templates. The Security Configuration Manager is not one console or tool, per se, but instead is actually a collection of tools and utilities that you can use to implement security solutions across your network.

The components of the Security Configuration Manager include these:

- The Security Configuration and Analysis snap-in
- The Security Templates snap-in
- Group Policy security extensions
- The `secedit.exe` command

Each of these tools is examined in the following sections as it relates to implementing security solutions using the preconfigured security templates that are supplied in Windows Server 2003. At this point, you need to construct a customized Microsoft Management Console (MMC) that you can use to work with these security templates, as outlined in Step by Step 5.1.

STEP BY STEP

5.1 Creating a Customized Security Console

1. Open an empty MMC shell by selecting Start, Run and entering **mmc** in the Open field. Click OK. An empty MMC shell appears, as shown in Figure 5.2.

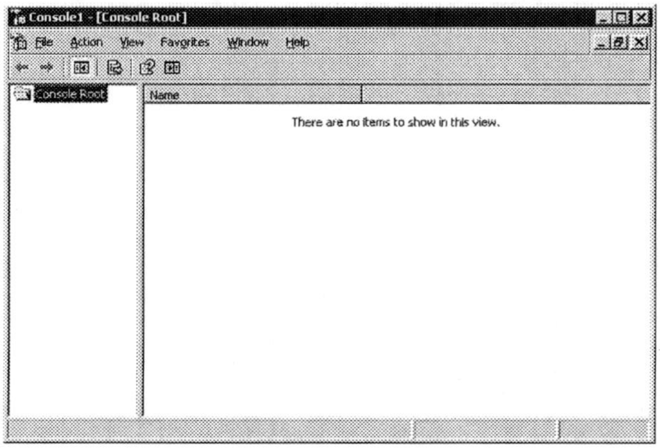

FIGURE 5.2 Starting with an empty MMC shell, you can build any number of customized configuration and management consoles.

2. Select File, Add/Remove Snap-In to open the Add/Remove Snap-in dialog box. Click Add to open the Add Standalone Snap-in dialog box, shown in Figure 5.3.

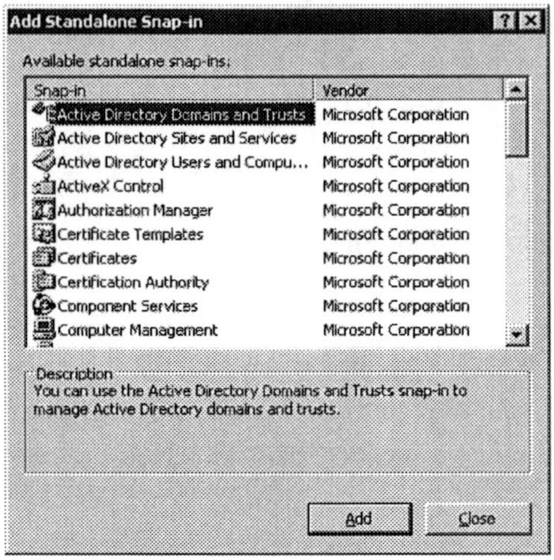

FIGURE 5.3 You can add a number of snap-ins from here.

3. Scroll down the Snap-In list and select the Security Configuration and Analysis and Security Templates snap-ins by double-clicking each of them.
4. Click Close and then click OK to return to the MMC console (see Figure 5.4).

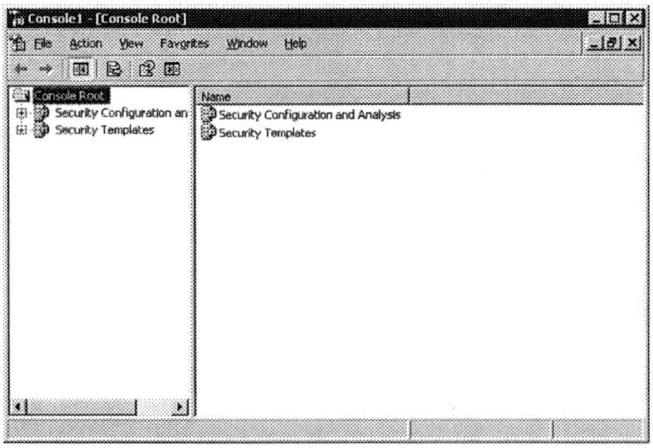

FIGURE 5.4 The customized console is not as empty as it was.

5. Save the console by selecting File, Save. A standard Save dialog box appears. Specify the filename and location to save the console to. By default, the console is saved in the Administrative Tools folder of the currently logged-in user.

Armed with a custom security console, let's move forward and examine how the tools are put to work.

The Security Configuration and Analysis Snap-in

The Security Configuration and Analysis snap-in is an important tool in an administrator's security template toolbox. By using the Security Configuration and Analysis snap-in, you can create, configure, test, and implement security template settings for a local computer. Therein lies its one real weakness: It can be used to work with only the settings of a local computer. However, you can find ways to get around this limitation by using the other tools that are at your disposal, including `secedit.exe` and the security extensions to Group Policy, both of which are discussed later in this chapter.

The Security Configuration and Analysis snap-in can be used in two basic modes, as its name suggests—configuration and analysis—although not necessarily in that order. When you're using the Security Configuration and Analysis snap-in to analyze the current system security configuration, no changes are ever made to the computer being analyzed. The administrator simply selects a security template to compare the computer against (either a preconfigured template or a custom-created template). The settings from the template are loaded into a database and then compared to the settings currently implemented on the computer. It is possible to import multiple templates into this database, thus merging their settings into one conglomerate database. In addition, you can specify that existing database settings are to be cleared before another template is imported into the database. When the desired security templates have been loaded into the database, any number of analysis actions can be performed, both by the Security Configuration and Analysis snap-in and by the `secedit.exe` command, as discussed later in this chapter.

After the database has been populated and an analysis scan has been initiated, the Security Configuration and Analysis snap-in examines each configurable Group Policy option and then reports back to you with the results of the analysis scan. Each setting is marked with an icon that denotes one of several possible outcomes, such as that the settings are the same, the settings are different, or the settings do not apply. Table 5.4 outlines the possible icons that you might see and what they indicate.

TABLE 5.4 The Preconfigured Security Template Icons in Windows Server 2003

Icon	Description
Red X	The item is defined in the analysis database and on the computer but does not match the currently configured setting.
Green check mark	The item is defined in the analysis database and on the computer and matches the currently configured setting.
Question mark	The item is not defined in the analysis database and was not examined on the computer.
Exclamation point	The item is defined in the analysis database but not on the computer.
No special icon	The item is not defined in the analysis database or the computer.

The best way to begin to understand the Security Configuration and Analysis snap-in is to work with it. Step by Step 5.2 presents the process of comparing the security configuration of a Windows Server 2003 member server to that of the `securews.inf` template.

NOTE

Not all computers are created equal It is expected that not every computer will have the same security settings initially. Your results when performing this process might vary, depending on the initial state of the computer being used for the analysis.

STEP BY STEP

5.2 Using the Security Configuration and Analysis Snap-In to Analyze Settings

1. From the customized security console you created in Step by Step 5.1, select the Security Configuration and Analysis node. Notice that the Security Configuration and Analysis snap-in actually provides you with some instructions on how to proceed.
2. Right-click the Security Configuration and Analysis node and select Open Database from the context menu. The Open Database window appears, as shown in Figure 5.5.

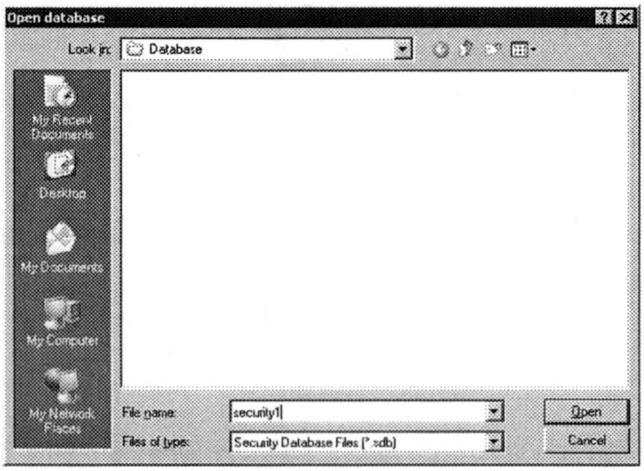

FIGURE 5.5 You can either load an existing database or create a new one.

3. Because you do not have an existing database, create a new one by entering the name **`security1`** into the Filename field and click Open to open it.
4. On the Import Template page, shown in Figure 5.6, select the security template you are loading into the database. In this exercise, you should use the `securews.inf` template. If this is an existing database that you want to clear, be sure to select the Clear This Database Before Importing option. Click Open after you make your selections. The Security Configuration and Analysis snap-in appears again.
5. To perform the analysis operation, right-click the Security Configuration and Analysis node and select Analyze Computer Now to start the analysis. The Perform Analysis dialog box appears.
6. Provide a pathname and a filename for an error log. In most cases, the default pathname and filename, as shown in Figure 5.7, are suitable, but you can change this as required. Click OK to start the analysis process.

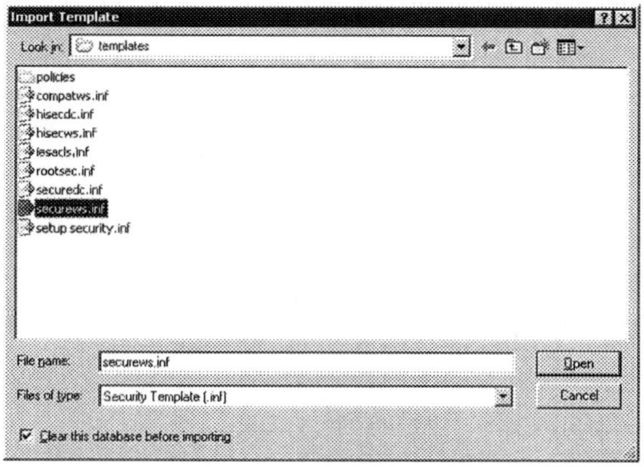

FIGURE 5.6 You need to select a template to load into the database.

FIGURE 5.7 The error log is used to keep track of any errors encountered during the analysis process.

7. You will briefly see the Analyzing System Security dialog box. When the analysis is complete, you are returned to the Security Configuration and Analysis snap-in, except that now it has been populated and looks similar to what you might expect to see in the Group Policy Editor, as shown in Figure 5.8.

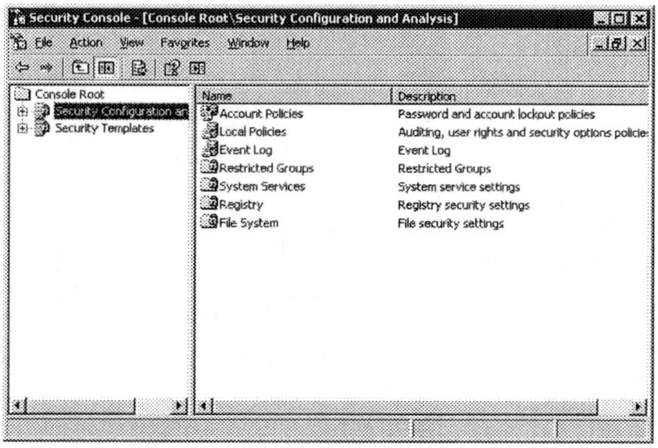

FIGURE 5.8 The analysis output resembles the information shown in the Group Policy Editor.

8. Open the Account Policies, Password Policy node, shown in Figure 5.9. You can see that some items are not in agreement between the database settings and the computer settings.

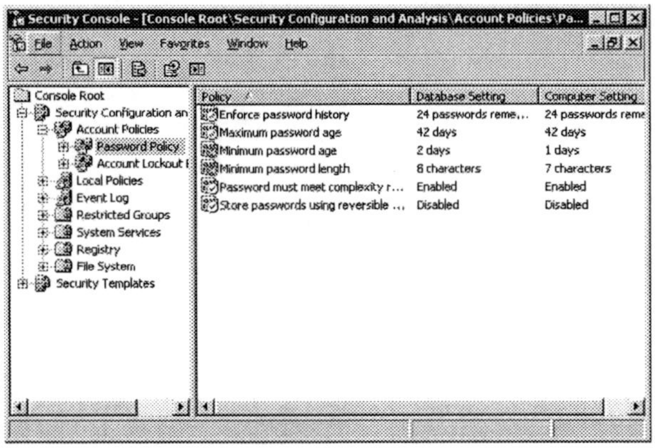

FIGURE 5.9 You can quickly determine the status of the computer against the settings of the security template.

As shown in Figure 5.8, you can analyze and configure several areas by using the Security Configuration and Analysis snap-in:

- **Account Policies**—This node contains items that control user accounts. In Windows NT 4.0, these items are managed from the User Manager for Domains. It has two subnodes: the Password Policy node and the Account Lockout Policy node. The Password Policy node deals with account password–related items, such as minimum length and maximum age. The Account Lockout Policy node contains options for configuring account lockout durations and lockout reset options.
- **Local Policies**—This node contains policies that are applied to the local machine. It has three subnodes: Audit Policy, User Rights Assignment, and Security Options. The Audit Policy node is pretty self-explanatory; it offers options for configuring and implementing various auditing options. The User Rights Assignment node contains miscellaneous options that deal with user rights, such as the capability to log in to a computer across the network. The Security Options node contains many other options—such as the option to set a login banner or allow the system to be shut down without being logged in first—that previously could be edited only in the Windows NT 4.0 Registry or by using System Policies.
- **Event Log**—This node contains options that enable you to configure the behavior and security of the event log. In this node, for example, you can include maximum log sizes and disallow guest access to the event logs.
- **Restricted Groups**—This node enables you to permanently configure which users are allowed to be members of specific groups. For example, company policy might provide the capability to perform server backups to a specific group of administrators. If another user who is not otherwise authorized with these privileges is added to this group and not removed after he or she has performed the intended function, you have created a security problem because the user has more rights than normally authorized. By using the Restricted Groups node, you can reset group membership to the intended membership.

- **System Services**—This node enables you to configure the behavior and security assignments associated with all system services running on the computer. Options include defining that a service is to start automatically or be disabled. In addition, you can configure the user accounts that are to have access to each service.
- **Registry**—This node enables you to configure access restrictions that specify who is allowed to configure or change individual Registry keys or entire hives. This option does not give you the means to create or modify Registry keys, however; you must still do that by using the Registry Editor.
- **File System**—This node enables you to set folder and file NTFS permissions. This is especially handy if you need to reset the permissions on a large number of folders or files.

When a security settings analysis is completed and you have examined the results, you can begin the process of determining what changes need to be made. You can configure your changes directly in the database by using the Security Configuration and Analysis snap-in, or you can create or edit a security template by using the Security Templates snap-in, as discussed in the next section. When you use the Security Configuration and Analysis snap-in to make changes, your changes reside only in the database until you do one of two things: export the database to a security template file or apply the database settings to the computer. When you work with the Security Templates snap-in, you actually make changes to the template directly and need to save it when you're finished. The end result is the same, no matter which way you go about it.

NOTE

Working with templates If you should find yourself working with one of the preconfigured security templates and wanting to make changes, stop! Before making any changes to any of the preconfigured templates, be sure to save a copy of the template using a different name and then make your changes to the copy. By following this process, you'll always be sure to have your pristine preconfigured templates intact and available for later usage.

The second part of the Security Configuration and Analysis snap-in is the configuration—applying the settings contained in the database to the local computer. Before you apply the settings to the computer, you should complete the analysis as detailed in Step by Step 5.2. When this is done and you are happy with the configuration (or have edited the configuration to suit your needs), you can apply the settings by right-clicking the Security Configuration and Analysis node and selecting Configure Computer Now from the context menu. You are again asked for the pathname and filename of the error log. After you provide this information, the settings in the database are applied to the computer. Running the analysis again confirms this by showing that all items are now in agreement.

EXAM ALERT

For the local computer only Remember that the Security Configuration and Analysis snap-in can be used to apply the settings to only the local computer. You need to export the database to a security template if you want to apply the settings to another computer or to a larger scope of computers, such as a domain or an OU. You can use the Group Policy editor or the Group Policy Management Console to apply security templates via Group Policy Objects.

As mentioned previously, if you need to get the database settings out and into the form of a security template, you simply right-click the Security Configuration and Analysis node and select Export Template from the context menu. The Export Template To window appears, as shown in Figure 5.10, prompting you to enter the path and filename of the security template. You should be sure to use a unique name—in other words, do not save over one of the preconfigured security templates because you might need it again in the future.

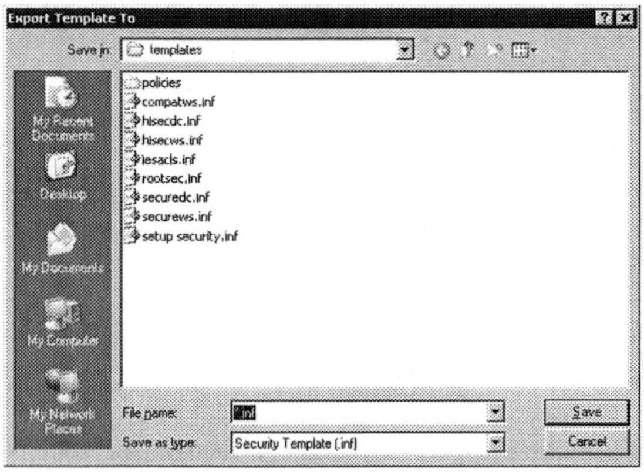

FIGURE 5.10 Be sure to specify a unique name for an exported template, to avoid overwriting a preconfigured security template.

The Security Templates Snap-In

The Security Templates snap-in, shown in Figure 5.11, might at first seem to have no real purpose. However, this is not the case. You can use this snap-in to modify existing templates or create new ones from scratch without the danger or possibility of accidentally applying the template to the computer or Group Policy Object (GPO).

To customize an existing template, you simply begin making changes to it to suit your requirements. When you are done, you should save it with a new name by right-clicking on it and selecting Save As from the context menu. The standard Save dialog box that enables you to specify the path and filename of the template appears.

To start with a completely empty template—in which no settings are preconfigured—you can do so by right-clicking the template location node (where the template file system path is displayed on the left side of the console) and selecting New Template from the context menu.

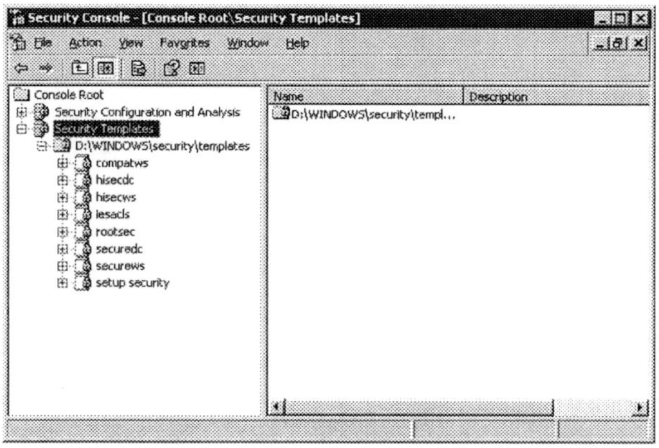

FIGURE 5.11 The Security Templates snap-in enables you to work with existing and new templates.

Group Policy Security Extensions

Applying a security template to a local computer by using the Security Configuration and Analysis snap-in is certainly not the only way to apply a security template. Imagine the amount of time and effort involved in applying a security template locally at each computer using the Security Configuration and Analysis snap-in. As difficult and time consuming as that evolution would be, try to imagine doing it to several different types of computers, such as DCs, member servers, and client workstations. You would have the added hassle of trying to remember which template goes on what computer.

NOTE

Editing Group Policy Objects In this chapter, we show how Group Policy Objects are accessed and edited using the default out-of-the box configuration of Windows Server 2003. For all practical purposes, it is recommended that you download and install the Group Policy Management Console (GPMC) for enhanced Group Policy control and visibility. Find out more information about the GPMC at www.microsoft.com/windowsserver2003/gpmc/gpmcintro.mspx.

Fortunately, you can easily and quickly import security templates into GPOs by using the Group Policy Editor. Step by Step 5.3 outlines this process.

STEP BY STEP

5.3 Importing a Security Template into a GPO

1. Open the Active Directory Users and Computers console by selecting Start, Programs, Administrative Tools, Active Directory Users and Computers.
2. Locate the domain or OU to which you want to apply the security template. In this example, we are applying the `securews.inf` template to the CORP OU.

3. Right-click the CORP OU and select Properties from the context menu. The Sales Properties dialog box appears. Switch to the Group Policy tab, shown in Figure 5.12.

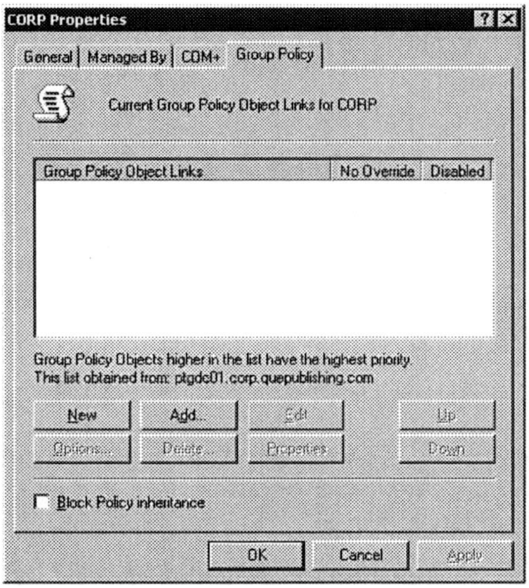

FIGURE 5.12 You need to create a new GPO if no GPOs exist already.

4. To create a new GPO, click the New button. Supply a name for the new GPO and press Enter.

5. Click the Edit button to open the Group Policy Editor for the selected GPO.

6. Expand the nodes as follows: Computer Configuration, Windows Settings, Security Settings. You should be looking at something like that shown in Figure 5.13.

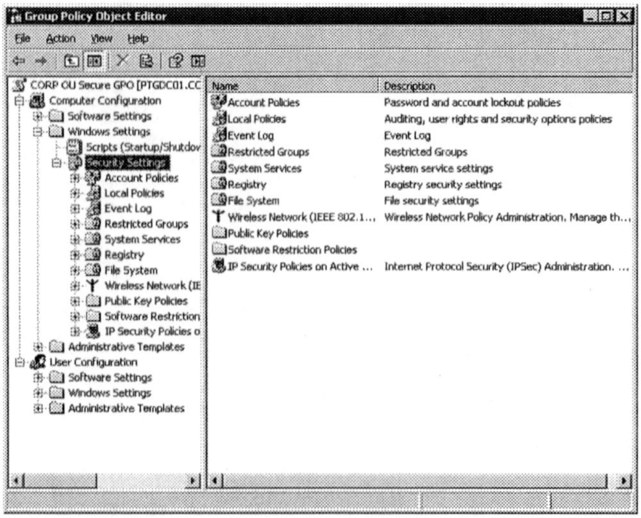

FIGURE 5.13 You can import a security template from the Security Settings node.

7. Right-click the Security Settings node and select Import Policy from the context menu. The Import Policy From dialog box, shown in Figure 5.14, appears, providing a list of the preconfigured security templates. You can navigate to another location if required to use a custom-created security template.

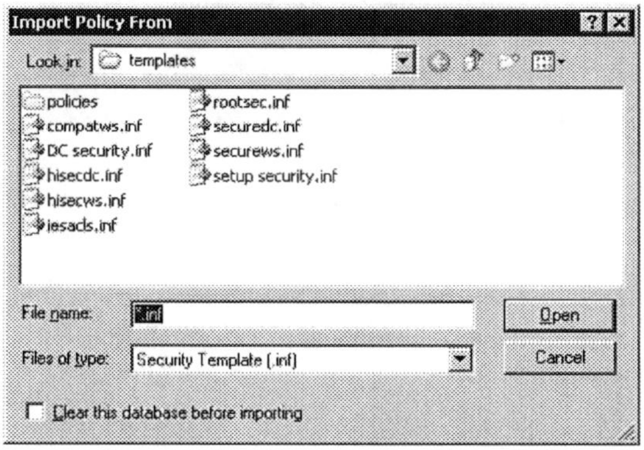

FIGURE 5.14 You need to select the security template that you want to import into the GPO.

8. Select the desired policy and click the Open button. The settings configured in the template are now applied to the GPO and will be applied during the next Group Policy refresh cycle.

Note that you can also perform this evolution at the domain level to apply security settings to all computers within the domain. As a general rule, you should apply the most generic settings at the domain level and then apply at the OU level specific settings that pertain to the computers in that OU.

secedit.exe

EXAM ALERT

`secedit.exe` Pay special attention to the usage and uses of the `secedit.exe` command. It's been known to show on exam day more often than people expect!

We have spent a good amount of time so far in this chapter examining the ways you can work with security templates by using the Windows GUI. What about configuring security from the command line? As you might have guessed, there is a command-line alternative to the Security Configuration and Analysis snap-in, and it comes in the form of the `secedit.exe` command.

You can use `secedit.exe` to perform the same functions as the Security Configuration and Analysis snap-in, plus a couple additional functions not found in the snap-in. The `secedit.exe` command has the top-level options available for use as detailed in Table 5.5.

TABLE 5.5 The `secedit.exe` Options

Icon	Description
`/analyze`	Enables you to analyze the security settings of a computer by comparing them against the baseline settings in a database. This will be useful in situations where you need to ensure that the security settings on a computer are in fact what they should be.
`/configure`	Enables you to configure the security settings of the local computer by applying the settings contained in a database.
`/export`	Enables you to export the settings configured in a database to a security template `.inf` file.
`/import`	Enables you import the settings configured in a security template `.inf` file into a database. If you will be applying multiple security templates to a database, you should use this option before performing the analysis or configuration.
`/validate`	Validates the syntax of a security template to ensure that it is correct before you import the template into a database for analysis or configuration.
`/GenerateRollback`	Enables you to create a rollback template that can be used to reset the security configuration to the values it had before the security template was applied.

Of the available options, you will most often make use of the `/analyze` and `/configure` switches. Examples and explanations of their use are provided here.

To analyze the current security configuration of the local computer, you issue the `secedit.exe` command with the following syntax:

```
secedit /analyze /db FileName /cfg FileName /overwrite /log FileName
 /quiet
```

EXAM ALERT

Viewing the results of a security analysis You need to view the results of a security analysis in the Security Configuration and Analysis snap-in by opening the database created during the analysis. At first, it might seem as if running the analysis from the command line and then viewing the results in the GUI is counterproductive. In reality, the opposite is the case. Say you run `secedit.exe` from a script on multiple computers. You can then view the databases, one for each computer, in the GUI at your leisure to determine what changes need to be made to the security settings on the computers. You can use the `%computername%` variable when creating the database and log files to create one set of results for each computer being scanned.

Table 5.6 explains the `secedit /analyze` parameters in detail.

TABLE 5.6 The `secedit /analyze` Parameters

Parameter	Description
`/db FileName`	Specifies the pathname and filename of the database to be used to perform the analysis.
`/cfg FileName`	Specifies the pathname and filename of the security template that is to be imported into the database before the analysis is performed.
`/overwrite`	Specifies that the database is to be emptied before the security template is imported.
`/log FileName`	Specifies the pathname and filename of the file that is used to log the status of the analysis process. By default, a log named `scesrv.log` is created in the `%windir%\security\logs` directory.
`/quiet`	Specifies that the analysis process should take place without further onscreen comments.

For example, suppose that you want to analyze the settings on a computer compared to the settings contained in the `securews.inf` template. You could issue the following command to perform this function:

```
secedit /analyze /db d:\sectest\test1.sdb
/cfg d:\WINDOWS\security\templates\securews.inf /log d:\sectest\test1.log
```

If all went well, you would see something like what is shown in Figure 5.15.

FIGURE 5.15 You can quickly perform an analysis from the command line by using the `secedit.exe` command.

To configure the current security configuration of the local computer, you would issue the `secedit.exe` command with the following syntax:

```
secedit /configure /db FileName /cfg FileName /overwrite
/areas Area1 Area2 ... /log FileName /quiet
```

Table 5.7 explains the `secedit /configure` parameters in detail.

TABLE 5.7 The `secedit /configure` Parameters

Parameter	Description
`/db FileName`	Specifies the pathname and filename of the database to be used to perform the configuration.
`/cfg FileName`	Specifies the pathname and filename of the security template that is to be imported into the database before the configuration is performed.
`/overwrite`	Specifies that the database is to be emptied before the security template is imported.
`/areas`	Specifies the security areas that are to be applied to the system. By default, when this parameter is not specified, all security areas are applied to the computer. These are the available options: ▶ **GROUP_MGMT**—The Restricted Group settings ▶ **USER_RIGHTS**—The User Rights Assignment settings ▶ **REGKEYS**—The Registry permissions settings ▶ **FILESTORE**—The File System permissions settings ▶ **SERVICES**—The System Service settings
`/log FileName`	Specifies the pathname and filename of the file that is used to log the status of the analysis process. By default, a log named `scesrv.log` is created in the `%windir%\security\logs` directory.
`/quiet`	Specifies that the configuration process should take place without further onscreen comments.

For example, suppose that you want to configure the settings on a computer with the settings in the `securews.inf` template. You could issue the following command to perform this function:

```
secedit /configure /db d:\sectest\test1.sdb
/cfg D:\WINDOWS\security\templates\securews.inf /log d:\sectest\test1.log
```

Challenge

You are a network security consultant who has been hired by the ACME Rocket Company to work with its in-house systems administrators to plan, develop, and implement a hierarchical role-based server security plan.

When you meet with the company president, he gives you the following information: "I want you to help our administrators get a solid security plan in place for the network. After talking with the CIO, we both agree that the best way to implement security for our network is to assign servers specific tasks and secure them appropriately."

The CIO has the following additional information for you: "We are going to use a role-based approach to secure our network's servers. Each server will be assigned one specific role that will not change. We are implementing a completely new network using all Windows Server 2003 servers and all Windows XP Professional client workstations. We will have only one forest and one domain; all segmentation will need to be accomplished within this domain."

(continues)

(continued)

ACME Rockets has the following types of servers planned for its new network: domain controllers, file servers, print servers, IIS intranet servers, and FTP servers that will be located in the DMZ.

Through your discussions with various personnel within ACME Rockets, you've determined that the following are the main focus points:

- Security will be implemented in a hierarchical fashion using role-based security templates.
- Only one forest and one domain will be created. OUs will thus be used to segment the specific server roles.
- The FTP servers located in the DMZ will require extra security measures because they are susceptible to more types of attacks.
- A more secure initial security plan can be implemented because there are no legacy clients to be supported.

Your task is to plan and help implement the desired security configuration for ACME Rocket's servers.

Try to complete this exercise on your own, listing your conclusions on a sheet of paper. When you have completed the exercise, compare your results to those given here.

By default, all domain controllers are automatically placed in the Domain Controllers OU. Also, all client workstations, by default, are placed in the Computers OU. You need to create an OU called Member Servers and then create additional OUs inside it for the file servers, print servers, and intranet IIS servers. Finally, you need to create an OU in the domain root for the DMZ FTP servers.

You next need to develop a Domain Baseline Security Policy that will be applied to the domain root itself. This security policy will be applied to all computers in the domain. Next, you should apply a Domain Controller Specific Security Policy that hardens your domain controllers. You should then apply a Member Server Baseline Security Policy to the Member Server OU that hardens all member servers. Finally, you should develop and apply a High Security Policy to the DMZ server OU.

Using Role-Based Security Templates and the Security Configuration Wizard

Objective:

Configure security for servers that are assigned specific roles.

Plan security for servers that are assigned specific roles. Roles might include domain controllers, web servers, database servers, and mail servers.

- Deploy the security configuration for servers that are assigned specific roles.
- Create custom security templates based on server roles.

Now that you have seen the preconfigured security templates provided with Windows Server 2003 and also the tools of the Security Configuration Manager, you are ready to move forward and implement role-based security solutions for your network. Looking back again at Figure 5.1, you can see how security policies are applied at several nested levels in the sample network.

Referring specifically to servers, you thus apply security policies (via security templates and GPOs) at the three following hierarchical levels:

- **Domain**—The most common security requirements, such as password and account lockout policies, are applied at the domain level. These policies are applied to all computers—servers and workstations alike—within the domain.
- **Baseline**—This policy contains security configuration items that apply to all member servers, such as auditing policies and user rights assignments. In the example shown in Figure 5.1, baseline policies are applied through the Domain Controller Policy, Client Computer Policy, and Member Server Policy.
- **Role specific**—To address the specific security needs of each specific server role, member servers are divided into role-based groups using OUs and have specific individual security policies applied to them. In the example shown in Figure 5.1, the role-specific policies are applied through the File Servers Policy, Print Servers Policy, and so on.

As you can see, the first step in successfully establishing role-based security is dividing computers by role. When that task has been accomplished, the Domain and Baseline Policies must be implemented by importing them into the applicable Group Policy Objects. Because these security templates are incremental in nature, you are expected to have applied these higher-level policies before attempting to subsequently apply the role-specific security policy. Also, to achieve the best results from a role-based security plan, your member servers should be performing only one specific function, such as print server, file server, IIS server, and so on. When member servers perform multiple functions, the level of complexity increases rapidly in regard to managing, maintaining, and securing them.

As discussed earlier in this chapter, the Windows Server 2003 Security Guide (located at http://go.microsoft.com/fwlink/?LinkId=14845) contains several excellent security templates that can be used to quickly and uniformly create a role-based security solution for your Windows Server 2003 network. This guide actually includes the following three sets of security templates:

- **Legacy Client**—The least secure environment, these security polices are designed for networks using Windows Server 2003 or Windows 2000 Server domain controllers and member servers. Clients run Windows 98 or Windows NT 4.0, Windows 2000, or Windows XP Professional.

- **Enterprise Client**—A fairly secure environment in which the network uses Windows Server 2003 domain or Windows 2000 Server controllers and member servers. Clients run Windows 2000 or Windows XP Professional.
- **Specialized Security—Limited Functionality**—An extremely secure environment in which the network uses Windows Server 2003 or Windows 2000 Server domain controllers and member servers. Clients run Windows 2000 or Windows XP Professional. Because of the extremely restrictive settings contained in these security policies, many applications might fail to function properly. Network usability declines, and management of workstations and servers becomes very difficult.

Table 5.8 outlines the typical Windows Server 2003 server roles and the security templates supplied for each of these respective roles.

EXAM ALERT

Test before deployment Although Microsoft thoroughly tested the default security templates provided with Windows Server 2003 and the additional security templates provided in the Windows Server 2003 Security Guide in a lab environment, this does not alleviate you of the same responsibility. It is nothing short of foolish to blindly apply any security template to a production environment without thorough testing and evaluation in a lab environment that closely mimics your actual production network.

TABLE 5.8 The Windows Server 2003 Server Roles

Server Role	Security Template
Domain Controller	`EC-Domain Controller.inf`
Member servers	`EC- Member Server Baseline.inf` (applied to all member servers)
Certificate Services servers	`EC-CA Server.inf`
File servers	`EC-File Server.inf`
Infrastructure servers (DHCP, WINS)	`EC-Infrastructure Server.inf`
Internet Authentication Server (IAS) servers	`EC-IAS Server.inf`
Internet Information Services (IIS) servers	`EC-IIS Server.inf`
Print servers	`EC-Print Server.inf`
Bastion hosts (DMZ servers)	`SSLF-Bastion Host.inf`

NOTE

No DNS server security? Notice that DNS servers are not listed anywhere among the possible Windows Server 2003 server roles. The reason is that, in the most secure environment, all domain controllers are also DNS servers, thus providing for the best security and replication possible.

The specifics associated with the security settings applied to each server role are far too numerous to lend themselves to discussion here; however, as you might expect, they are specifically crafted for each role. These security templates can be applied using the Security Configuration Wizard (discussed next), or by the methods we've already seen using the tools in the Security Configuration Manager set.

The Security Configuration Wizard

The Security Configuration Wizard is a new, more advanced security-hardening tool for Windows Server 2003 SP1 and Windows Server 2003 R2. If you have servers running these latest versions of Windows Server 2003, the SCW is worth taking a look at.

By default, the *Security Configuration Wizard* is not installed on your Windows Server 2003 computer. Before you can work with it, you need to install it as detailed in Step by Step 5.4.

STEP BY STEP

5.4 Installing the Security Configuration Wizard

1. Log on to Windows Server 2003 using the Administrator account or another account that has administrator privileges.

2. Open the Control Panel and then open the Add/Remove Programs applet. The Add or Remove Programs dialog box appears, as shown in Figure 5.16.

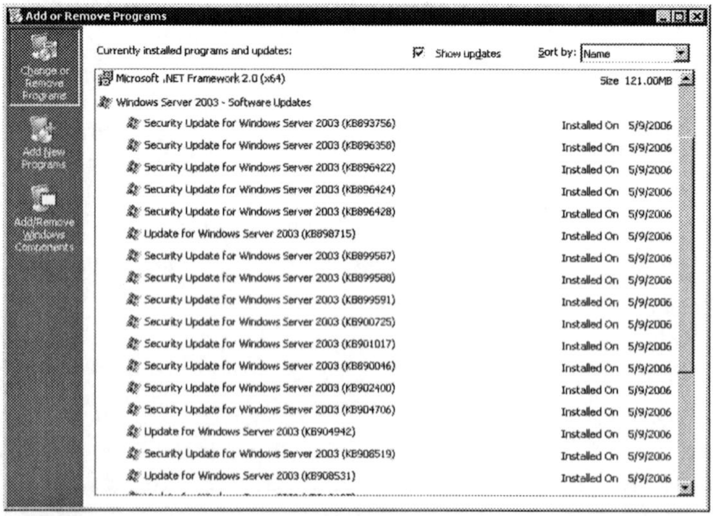

FIGURE 5.16 The Add or Remove Programs dialog box provides useful information about installed applications, including application size and, in some cases, the frequency of use of an installed application.

3. Click Add/Remove Windows Components on the left side of the Add or Remove Programs dialog box. The Windows Components Wizard dialog box appears, as shown in Figure 5.17.

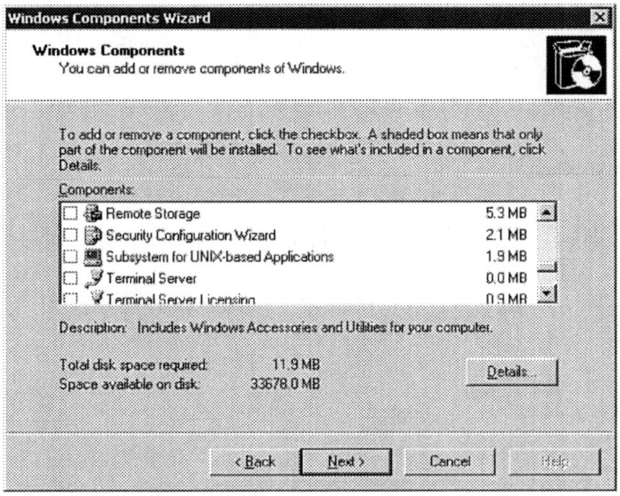

FIGURE 5.17 The Windows Components Wizard enables you to install, remove, or configure the various components of Windows Server 2003.

4. Select the Security Configuration Wizard option and click OK.
5. On the next screen that appears, click Next to complete the installation. The Windows Component Wizard prompts you for the Windows Server 2003 CD-ROM if it needs to copy files.
6. When the wizard is finished, it displays a summary window of the changes to be made. Click Finish to complete the installation.

EXAM ALERT

The Security Configuration Wizard The Security Configuration Wizard is a new tool added to Windows Server 2003 with Service Pack 1. If your servers are Service Pack 1 or Windows Server 2003 R2, the SCW is available for you. As a new tool (and a security-related one, at that), you should expect that it could make an appearance on your Exam 70-293, even though it is not explicitly mentioned in the exam objectives.

Using the Security Configuration Wizard

Now that you have installed the Security Configuration Wizard on your server, we examine its usage in this section. Step by Step 5.5 details the steps to be followed to use the SCW to create a new policy.

STEP BY STEP

5.5 Using the Security Configuration Wizard to Create a Policy

1. Select Start, Control Panel, Administrative Tools, Security Configuration Wizard. The Welcome to the Security Configuration Wizard screen appears, as shown in Figure 5.18. After reading the information presented, click Next to continue.

FIGURE 5.18 This welcome screen presents some important and useful information.

2. On the Configuration Action page, shown in Figure 5.19, you need to tell the SCW what to do. For this exercise, we want to create a new security policy. After making your selection, click Next to continue.

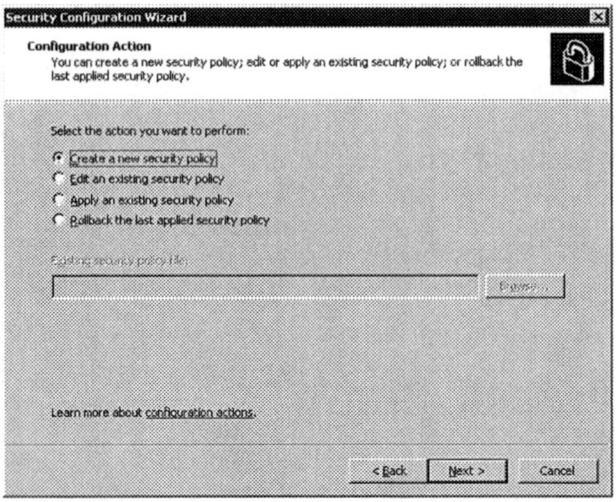

FIGURE 5.19 The Configure Action page enables you to tell the SCW what to do.

3. On the Select Server page, shown in Figure 5.20, you select a server that will serve as the baseline by which the security policy is created. By default, the server the SCW is being run on is populated for you. After making your selection, click Next to continue.

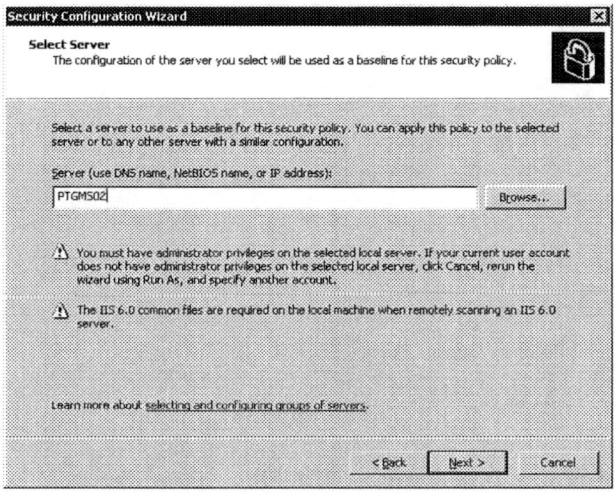

FIGURE 5.20 You need to specify a server to act as the baseline.

4. On the Processing Security Configuration Database page, shown in Figure 5.21, the configuration is processed briefly before you can click Next to continue. When the processing is complete, click Next to continue. If you want to examine the Security Configuration Database first, you can click the View Configuration Database button before clicking Next.

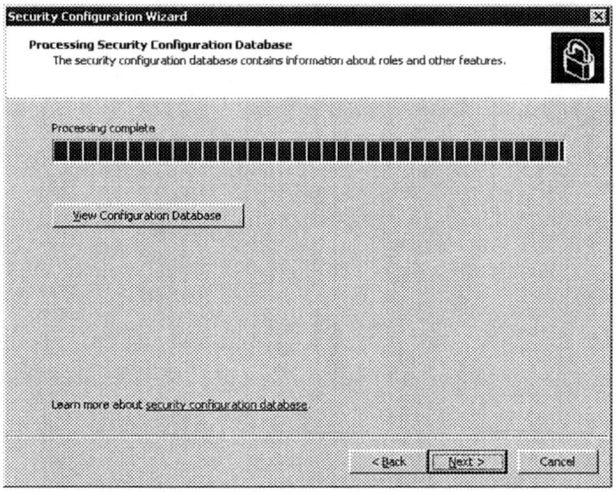

FIGURE 5.21 The SCW analyzes and processes the security configuration.

5. The Security Configuration Wizard now moves to the next phase of the configuration process. On the Role-Based Service Configuration page, shown in Figure 5.22, you again are presented with critical information. After reading the information, click Next to continue on with the Security Configuration Wizard.

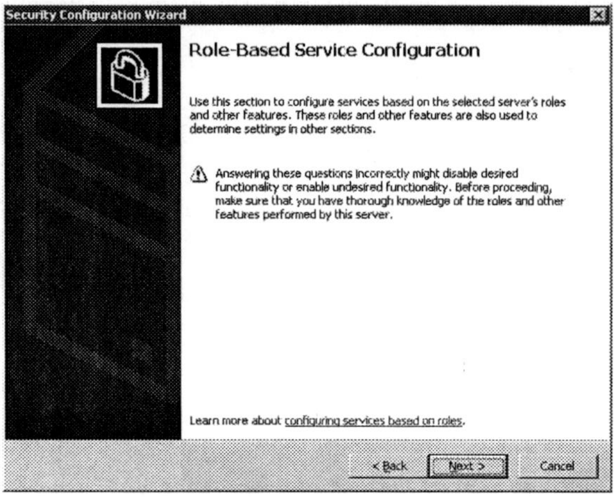

FIGURE 5.22 More critical information is presented to you before continuing.

6. On the Select Server Roles page, shown in Figure 5.23, you view the currently installed and roles the server has. Clicking the View drop-down changes the view so that you can examine all roles, uninstalled roles, installed roles (but not necessarily active), and selected roles (installed and active). Clicking the arrow next to a role opens a small informational box below the role. If you want to add or remove a role, which configures the ports and services but does not actually install any required files, you can do so. Click Next to continue after making any changes (typically none if the server is already configured correctly beforehand).

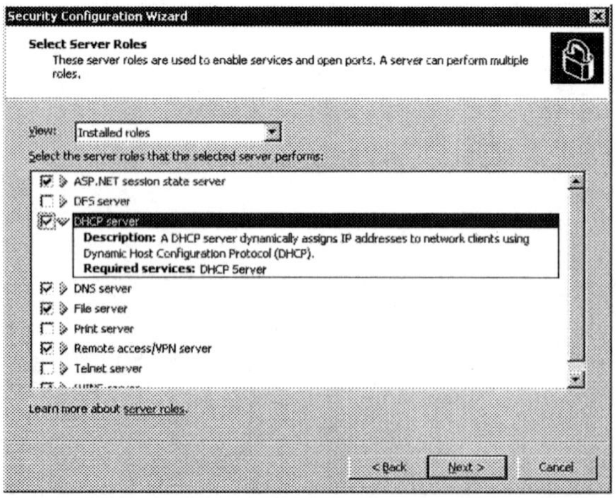

FIGURE 5.23 The SCW displays the current roles the server is fulfilling and enables you to change them.

7. On the Select Client Features page, shown in Figure 5.24, you can view the currently installed client features the server has. The View drop-down works the same as on the Select Server Roles page to change the features list. Click Next to continue after making any changes (typically none if the server is already configured correctly beforehand).

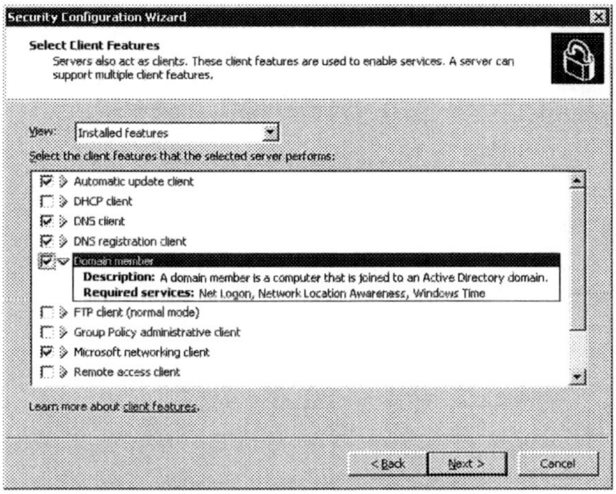

FIGURE 5.24 The SCW displays the current client features the server is using and enables you to change them.

8. On the Select Administration and Other Options page, shown in Figure 5.25, you can really get granular (and, thus, dangerous) with the configuration changes you can make with servers. Note the option selected in Figure 5.25. If you need to make any changes, do so, but be sure to understand the implications the changes might have. Click Next to continue.

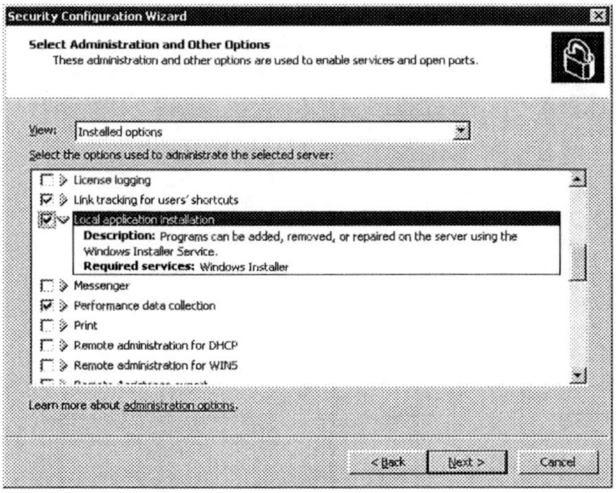

FIGURE 5.25 The SCW enables you to make very granular and otherwise difficult changes to the security posture of a server.

9. On the Select Additional Services page, shown in Figure 5.26, you are presented with any additional services the SCW encountered during its analysis. Click Next to continue after making any changes (typically none if the server is already configured correctly beforehand).

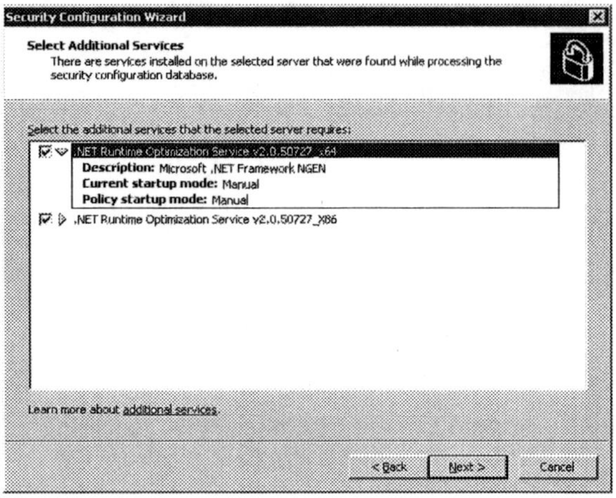

FIGURE 5.26 The SCW alerts you to any other services it found during the analysis.

10. On the Handling Unspecified Services page, shown in Figure 5.27, the SCW asks you what to do if it finds services on the target server that were not on the baseline server. In most cases, it's usually safer to leave the default selection of Do Not Change the Startup Mode of the Service as your selection. If you know for a fact that you want to have unspecified services disabled and are willing to take that risk, select that option. After making your choice, click Next to continue.

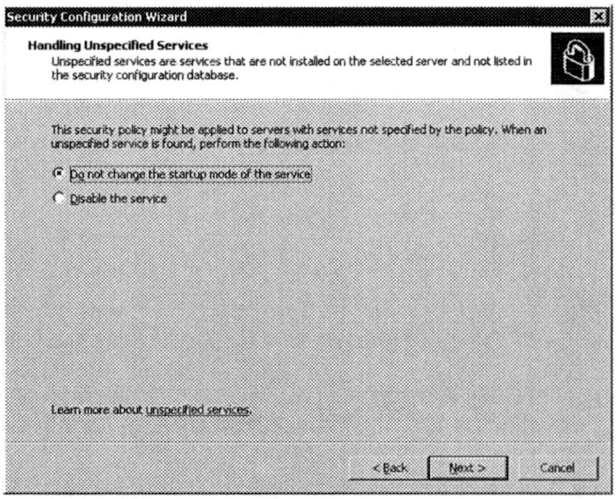

FIGURE 5.27 The SCW wants to know what to do about unspecified services it finds.

11. On the Confirm Service Changes page, shown in Figure 5.28, you are given a last look at how the server services will be modified by the creation and implementation of the policy. If you need to make changes, you need to go back to the applicable page of the wizard. When you're ready to continue, click Next.

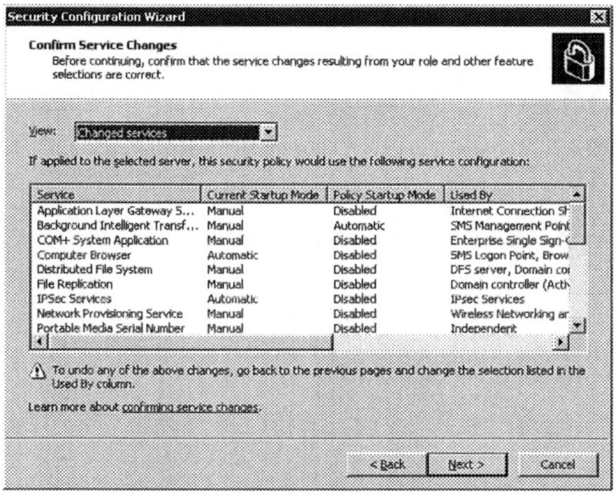

FIGURE 5.28 The SCW shows you all the service changes that it will make as a result of the newly created policy.

12. The Security Configuration Wizard now moves to the next phase of the configuration process. On the Network Security page, shown in Figure 5.29, you are again given important information to read. You can opt to skip the Network Security portion of the wizard by leaving the Skip This Section option selected and clicking Next. If you want to continue on to the Network Security portion of the SCW, unselect the Skip option and click Next.

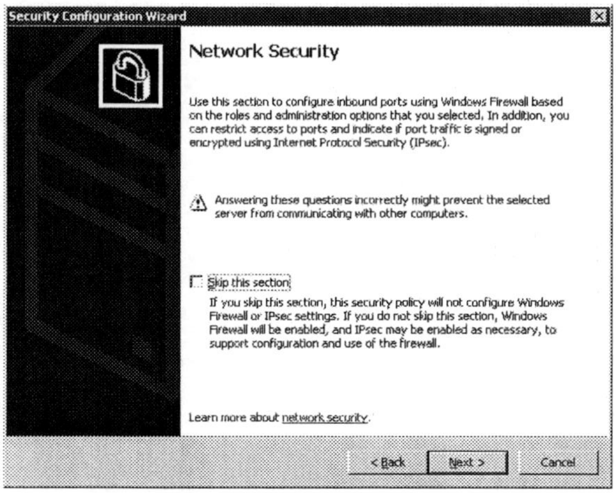

FIGURE 5.29 The SCW now moves into the Network Security portion of the policy creation.

NOTE

No security for RRAS and VPN servers The Security Configuration Wizard does not process the Network Security section on servers that are configured with Routing and Remote Access. You are forced to skip ahead to the next section of the wizard, the Registry Settings section.

13. On the Open Ports and Approve Applications page, show in Figure 5.30, you have the option to open or close ports in the policy. Click Next to continue after making any changes (typically none if the server is already configured correctly beforehand).

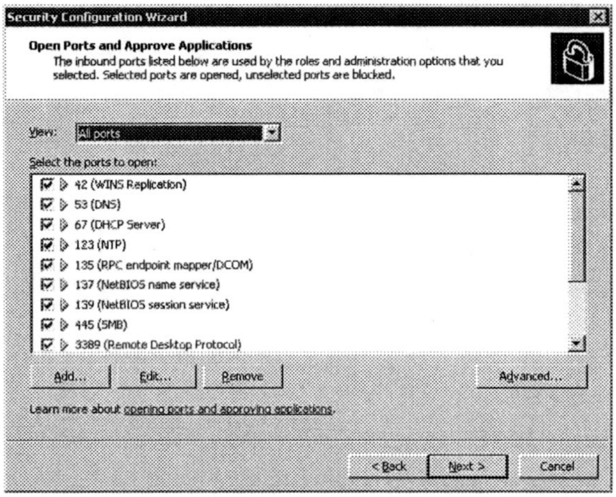

FIGURE 5.30 The SCW enables you to configure which ports will and will not be opened as part of the policy. This is another area that can get you intro trouble if not done carefully.

14. On the Confirm Port Configuration page, shown in Figure 5.31, you are presented with a summary of what the SCW will do to the ports on the server as part of the policy. If you need to make a change, click Back; otherwise, click Next to continue to the next part of the wizard.

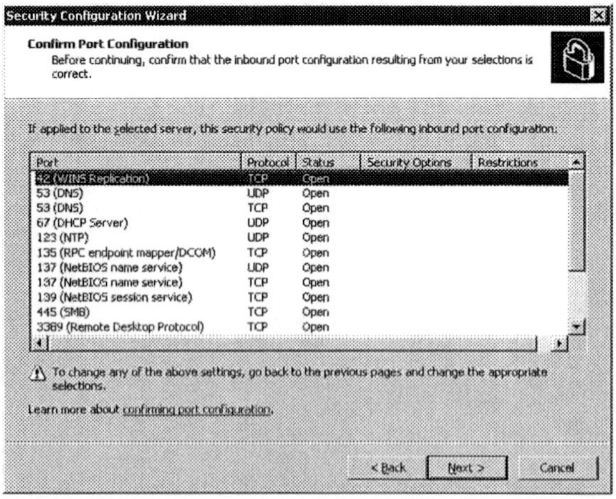

FIGURE 5.31 The SCW summarizes the port changes that it will make as part of the policy.

15. The Security Configuration Wizard now moves to the next phase of the configuration process. On the Registry Settings page, shown in Figure 5.32, you are again given important information to read. You can opt to skip the Registry Settings portion of the wizard by leaving the Skip This Section option selected and clicking Next. If you want to continue on to the Registry Settings portion of the SCW, unselect the Skip option and click Next.

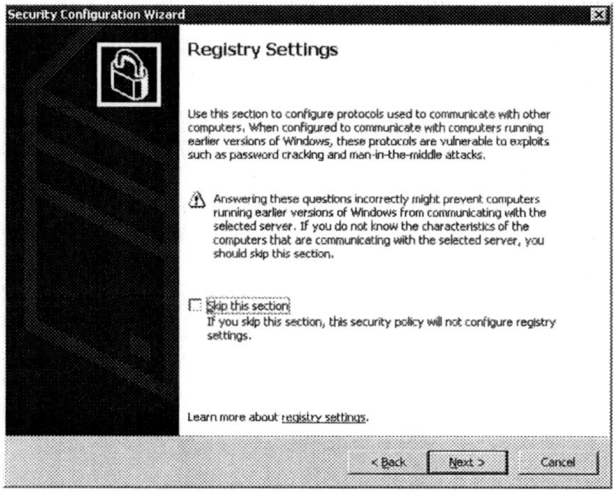

FIGURE 5.32 The SCW now moves into the Registry Settings portion of the policy creation.

CAUTION

Beware the Registry It is my personal belief that the upcoming Registry Settings section of the Security Configuration Wizard is the one that is likely to be least understood and, therefore the most difficult to make sound decisions about the options presented. Tread carefully and make sure you understand the options presented. Of course, the SCW is always ready to help you understand what you're about to configure by providing a helpful informational link on each page.

16. On the Require SMB Security Signatures page, shown in Figure 5.33, you are asked to make two choices about how to enable and configure SMB signing. Click Next to continue after making your choices.

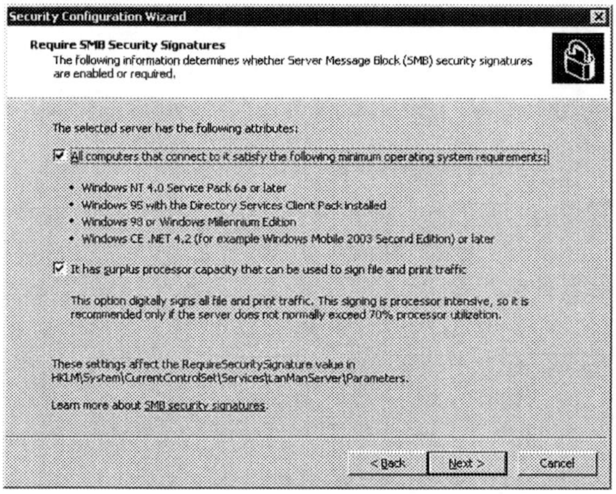

FIGURE 5.33 SMB signing will strengthen network communications security on your network.

17. On the Outbound Authentication Methods page, seen in Figure 5.34, you are asked to make choices about how the server to be configured with the policy will be allowed to authenticate with remote servers. Note that the default select of Domain Accounts provides the highest level of authentication security. Click Next to continue after making your choices.

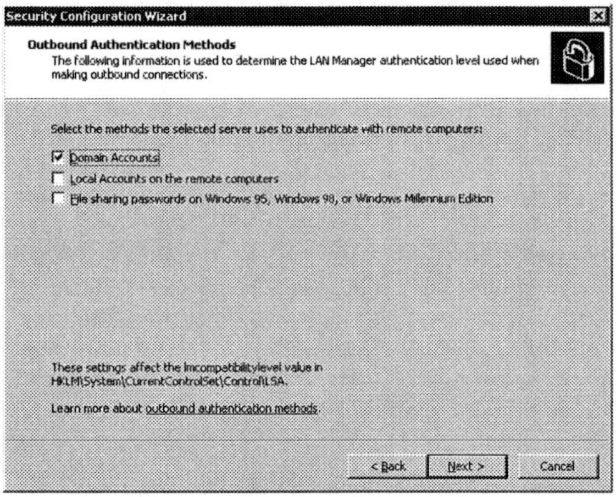

FIGURE 5.34 Typically, for maximum security, you should allow only Domain Accounts authentication for the server.

18. On the outbound authentication using the Domain Accounts page, shown in Figure 5.35, you are presented with two options that describe the Domain Controllers in your environment. By default, only the first option is selected. However, the second option should be selected in an Active Directory domain because time synchronization from the server configured as the time master should keep all computers within 5 minutes of each other. Click Next to continue after making your choices.

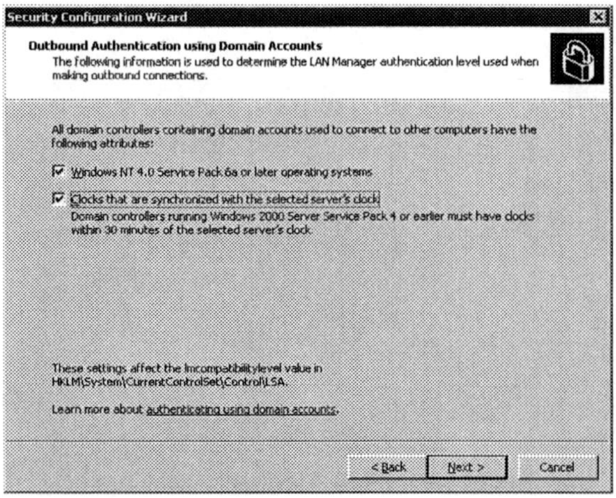

FIGURE 5.35 For maximum security, make sure that all computers are synchronized with the server's clock.

19. On the Inbound Authentication Methods page, shown in Figure 5.36, both options are selected by default. For maximum security, you will want to unselect both options. However, before implementing this policy on a server, make sure you understand the implications of requiring NTLMv2 authentication. Click Next to continue after making your choices.

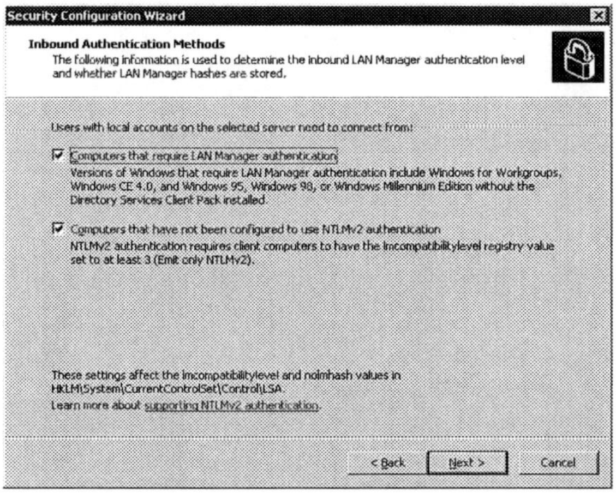

FIGURE 5.36 The SCW enables you to configure how secure inbound authentication should be.

20. On the Registry Settings Summary page, seen in Figure 5.37, you are presented with a summary of what the SCW will do to the Registry on the server as part of the policy. If you need to make a change, click Back; otherwise, click Next to continue to the next part of the wizard.

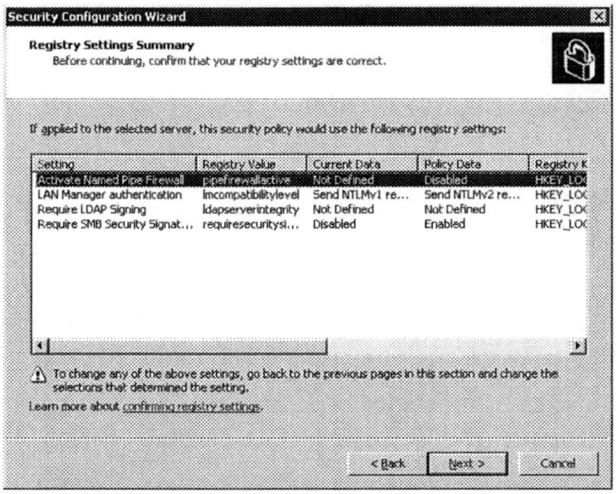

FIGURE 5.37 The SCW gives you a chance to see how the Registry will be modified as a result of the policy being created.

21. The Security Configuration Wizard now moves to the next phase of the configuration process. On the Audit Policy page, shown in Figure 5.38, you are again given important information to read. You can opt to skip the Audit Policy portion of the wizard by leaving the Skip This Section option selected and clicking Next. If you want to continue on to the Audit Policy portion of the SCW, unselect the Skip option and click Next.

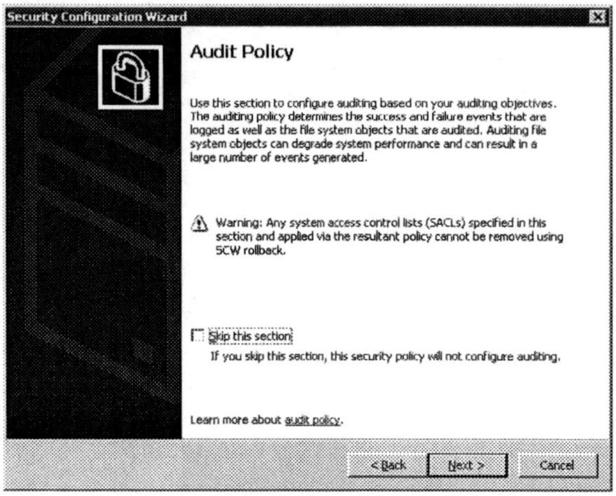

FIGURE 5.38 The SCW now moves into the Audit Policy portion of the policy creation.

22. On the System Audit Policy page, shown in Figure 5.39, you are asked to decide what type of auditing you will configure. The default selection is to audit successful activities, but for maximum auditing (which will fill your security log even faster), you can opt for the Audit Successful and Unsuccessful Activities option. Click Next to continue after making your choice.

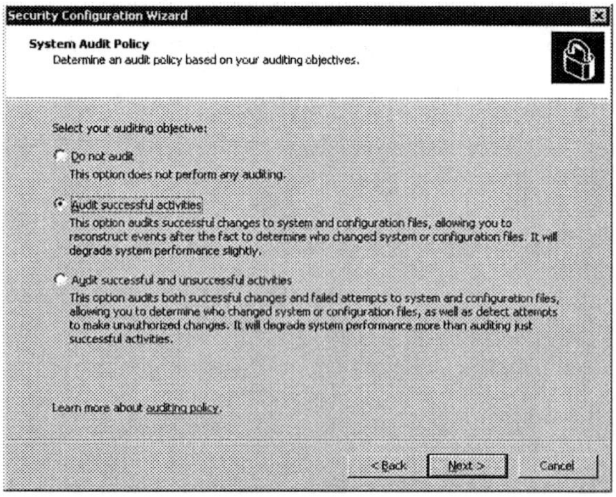

FIGURE 5.39 The SCW helps you configure auditing via the policy being created.

23. On the Audit Policy Summary page, shown in Figure 5.40, you are presented with a summary of your auditing choices. Note that even though we selected to audit success events only on the previous page, the SCW has implemented a best practice for us and enabled both success and failure auditing for key security events. If you need to make a change, click Back; otherwise, click Next to continue to the next part of the wizard.

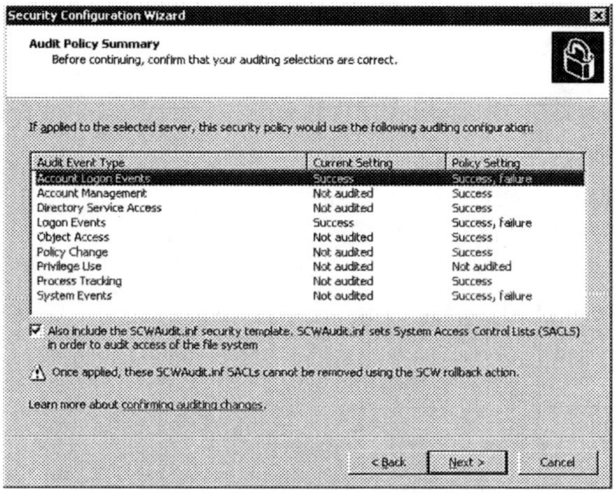

FIGURE 5.40 The SCW shows you what the auditing policy will be like after the policy is applied.

24. The Save Security Policy page now appears. There are no configuration choices to make on this page. Click Next to dismiss it and continue.

25. On the Security Policy Filename page, shown in Figure 5.41, you are asked to enter a filename for the policy and also a useful description. Note that the path is provided by default; however, in a larger environment, you might consider saving the policies to a central share so that multiple administrators can use them.

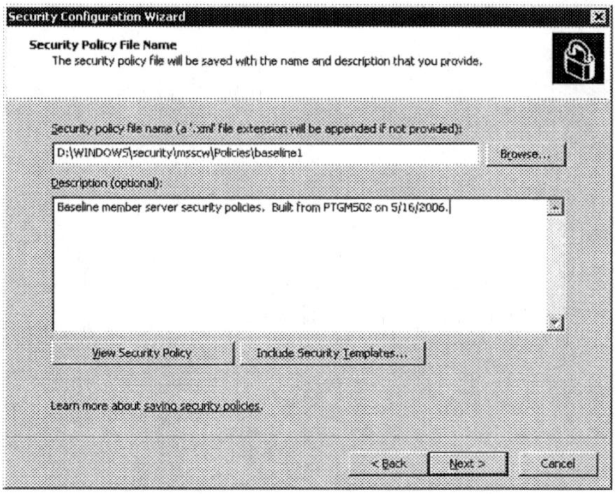

FIGURE 5.41 Finally … you get to save the policy.

26. If you want to examine the complete policy and its settings, click the View Security Policy button to SCW Viewer, shown in Figure 5.42. Otherwise, click Next to continue.

27. You are prompted with a warning dialog, seen in Figure 5.43. Click OK to acknowledge the warning and continue.

28. On the Apply Security Policy page, shown in Figure 5.44, you will be asked to make one last decision. Select Apply Later option and click Next.

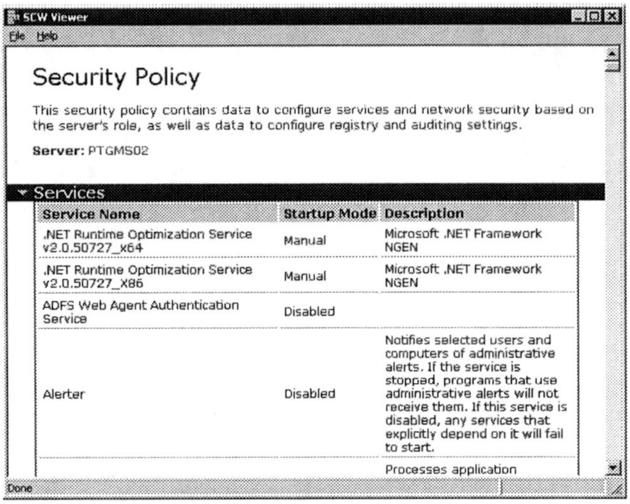

FIGURE 5.42 The SCW Viewer enables you to get an all-at-once look at the policy you've just created.

FIGURE 5.43 A server needs to be restarted after applying the settings in an SCW policy.

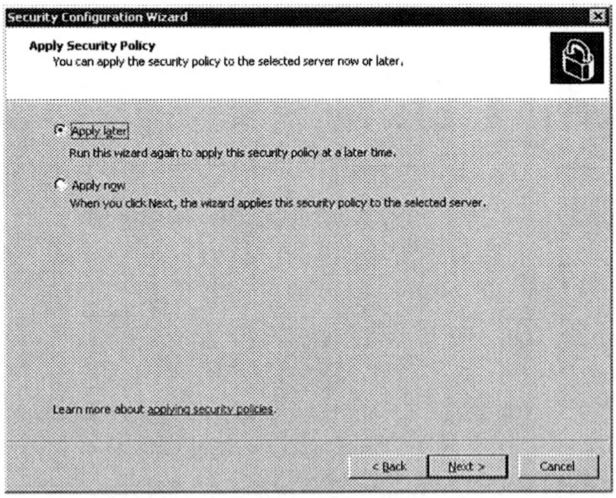

FIGURE 5.44 Save the policy for application later.

29. The Completing the Security Configuration Wizard page appears, signaling the end of the policy-creation process. Click Finish to close the Security Configuration Wizard.

Now that the Security Configuration Wizard has been used to create a policy, you can use the SCW on other servers to implement that policy. Alternatively, you can use the SCW to implement policies on remote servers if the SCW is already installed on that server and you have administrative credentials to that server. Step by Step 5.6 details the steps to be followed to use the SCW to implement an existing policy—such as one that you've created previously or one that you've downloaded in the Windows Server 2003 Security Guide.

STEP BY STEP

5.6 Using the Security Configuration Wizard to Implement a Policy

1. Select Start, Control Panel, Administrative Tools, Security Configuration Wizard. The Welcome to the Security Configuration Wizard screen appears. After reading the information presented, click Next to continue.
2. On the Configuration Action page, shown in Figure 5.45, you need to tell the SCW what to do. For this exercise, we want to apply an existing security policy. If you need to locate the policy, click the Browse button to open the Open dialog box seen in Figure 5.46. After making your selection, click Next to continue.

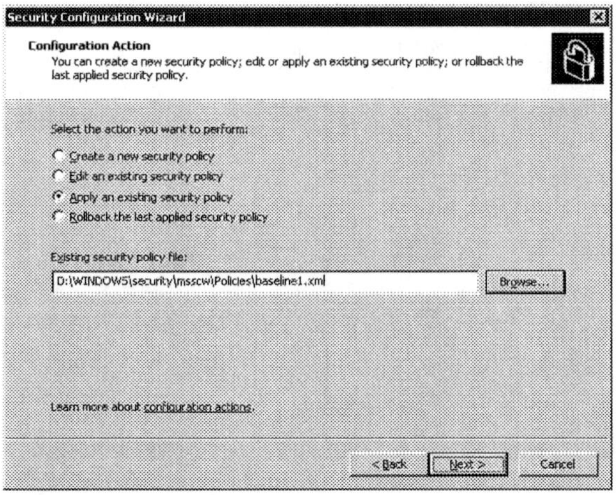

FIGURE 5.45 The Configure Action page enables you to tell the SCW what to do.

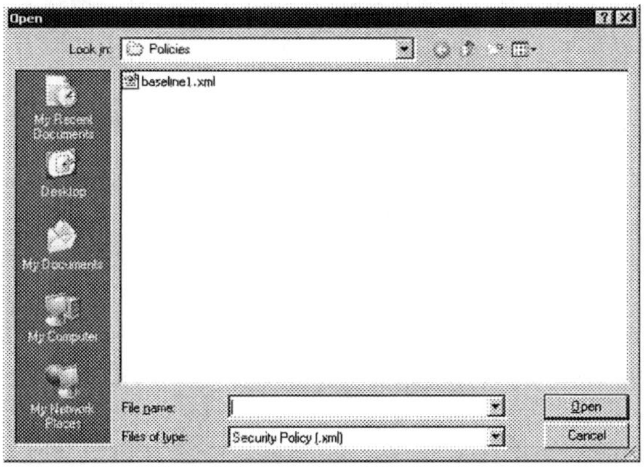

FIGURE 5.46 The Open dialog box helps you find the policy to be applied.

3. On the Select Server page, shown in Figure 5.47, you select a server that will serve as the baseline by which the security policy is created. By default, the server the SCW is being run on will be populated for you. Enter the server name and server credentials, as shown in Figure 5.48 if implementing the policy on a remote server. After making your selection, click Next to continue.

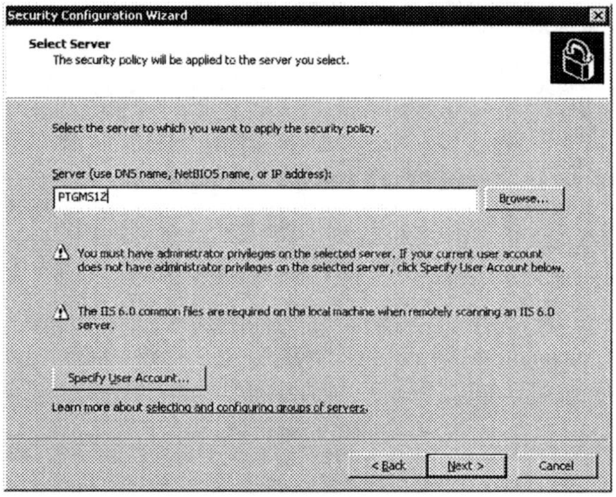

FIGURE 5.47 You need to tell the SCW which server to implement the policy on.

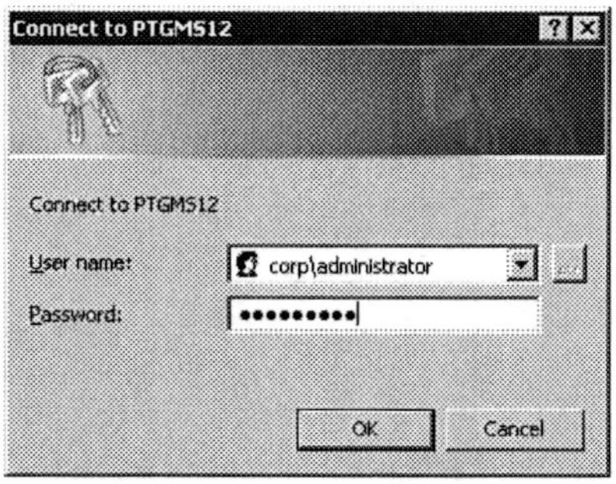

FIGURE 5.48 For remote servers, you need to provide credentials.

4. On the Apply Security Policy page, shown in Figure 5.49, you have a final chance to review the policy being applied by clicking the View Security Policy button (seen previously in Figure 5.42). When you are ready to implement the policy, click Next.
5. The Applying Security Policy page appears. When the processing is complete, you can click the Next button to continue.
6. On the Completing the Security Configuration Wizard page, click Finish to close the Security Configuration Wizard.

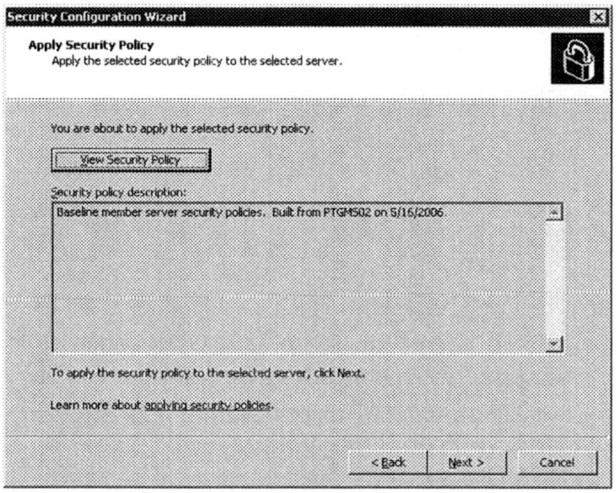

FIGURE 5.49 You have one last chance to avoid implementing the policy if you change your mind.

Chapter Summary

"Quality is job one" was a common expression used by a major automotive manufacturer in years past. You can now say that, when it comes to Windows Server 2003 networks, at least, security is job one. In this chapter, we only scratched the surface of the security pool. Security is a very deep and often misunderstood part of network administration—and one that you cannot afford to overlook.

Every security plan must have a starting point. By making use of the preconfigured security templates supplied with Windows Server 2003 and the additional security templates included in the Windows Server 2003 Security Guide, you can quickly and efficiently implement role-based security in your network. By configuring and testing security templates in the Security Configuration and Analysis snap-in, you can avoid mistakenly applying them to a large group of computers via Group Policy until you are ready to do so. When you are happy with your security templates, you can quickly apply them to your computers by importing them into Group Policy objects at the applicable levels within your network's organization. Because security templates are incremental, you can apply general settings at the domain root level and increase the security configuration as you navigate deeper into the network.

Additionally, we examined the Security Configuration Wizard, new in Windows Server 2003 Service Pack 1 and Windows Server 2003 R2. This wizard enables to you create and implement advanced security policies that can be all encompassing and that include every part of a server's configuration.

EXAM ALERT

SCW revisited You will likely not be required to demonstrate any advanced knowledge of the SCW on your Exam 70-293 exam, but don't let that stop you from getting to know what it is and how it works.

Key Terms

- Active Directory
- Baseline
- Compatible security template
- Default DC security template
- Default security template
- Discretionary Access Control List
- Domain
- Forest

- Group Policy Editor
- GPO
- Highly Secure security template
- Organizational Unit
- Resultant Set of Policy
- Role-based security
- `secedit.exe`
- Secure security template
- Security Configuration and Analysis snap-in
- Security template
- Security Templates snap-in

Apply Your Knowledge

In this chapter, you learned about getting and keeping your Windows Server 2003 network secure by using security templates and security-management tools. In the following exercises, you practice some of the concepts and methods discussed in this chapter.

Exercises

5.1 Analyzing a Local Computer's Security Settings

In this exercise, you use the Security Configuration and Analysis snap-in to perform an analysis of the local computer's security.

Estimated time: 20 minutes

1. Open your custom security console or create one that contains the Security Configuration and Analysis snap-in.
2. Right-click the Security Configuration and Analysis node, and select Open Database from the context menu.
3. Create a new database by entering the name **`securitydb`**.
4. Select the security template you are loading into the database for this exercise.
5. Right-click the Security Configuration and Analysis node, and select Analyze Computer Now to start the analysis.

6. Provide an error log name and pathname and click OK to start the analysis process. When the analysis is complete, you are returned to the Security Configuration and Analysis snap-in.
7. Compare the database settings to those of the local computer. How are they different? How are they the same? What do you need to change to implement the required security?

5.2 Importing a Security Template into Group Policy

In this exercise, you import a security template into a Group Policy Object.

Estimated time: 15 minutes

1. Open the Active Directory Users and Computers console.
2. Locate the domain or OU to which you want to apply the security template.
3. Right-click the appropriate OU or domain and select Properties from the context menu. The Properties dialog box appears. Select the Group Policy tab.
4. To create a new GPO, click the New button. Supply a name for the new GPO and press Enter.
5. Click the Edit button to open the Group Policy Editor for the selected GPO.
6. Expand the nodes as follows: Computer Configuration, Windows Settings, Security Settings. Right-click the Security Settings node and select Import Policy from the context menu.
7. Select the template to be imported.

Review Questions

1. You are trying to explain to your CIO why using security templates to configure security is a better idea than directly configuring a GPO. What are some reasons that you might present to him to support your position?
2. You have just completed an analysis of one of your Windows Server 2003 computers using the `secedit.exe` command. How can you now most easily view the analysis output produced?
3. Security templates in Windows Server 2003 have what file extension?

Exam Questions

1. You are the administrator of a Windows Server 2003 Active Directory network. Your network consists of 1,500 Windows XP Professional client computers spread out over 15 OUs with approximately 100 computers each. Your network also has 300 Windows Server 2003 servers fulfilling various roles, including domain controllers, file servers, print servers, IIS servers, and Certificate Services servers. You have just finished creating a customized security template that specifies the Account Policy and auditing settings that are required by your organization's corporate policy for specific departments. What is the best way for you to apply this template to only the Sales, Marketing, Production, and Engineering OUs?

- ❍ **A.** Import the security template at the domain level into a GPO.
- ❍ **B.** Import the security template into each required OU by using a GPO.
- ❍ **C.** Script the `secedit.exe` command to apply the security template to the required computers.
- ❍ **D.** Manually apply the security template to each of the computers.

2. You are the systems administrator for Just Right Tops, LLC. Your network consists of three geographically distant sites that function as three different domains. No site has a direct link to any other site. You have recently completed the creation of two custom security templates that are to be applied to all computers in all three sites of your company network. How can you most easily deploy these security templates at all three sites?

- ❍ **A.** Create and configure a new domain controller for each remote site. Apply the security templates to the domain controllers. Place a new domain controller in each site and allow Active Directory to replicate.
- ❍ **B.** Export the security templates into `.inf` files by using the Security Configuration and Analysis snap-in. Deliver the security templates to the remote location and import them into the appropriate GPOs.
- ❍ **C.** Establish connectivity among all sites and force the remote site domain controllers to perform replication with the local site domain controllers after implementing the new security templates.
- ❍ **D.** Re-create the security templates at each remote site and then import them into the appropriate GPOs.

3. You are the systems administrator of the Gidget's Widgets, LLC, corporate network. You have instructed Andrea, your assistant administrator, to configure file access auditing for all files in the `CorpDocs` folder on your file server. In which node of the Group Policy Editor will Andrea find the auditing options?

- ❍ **A.** Account Policies
- ❍ **B.** Local Policies
- ❍ **C.** Restricted Groups
- ❍ **D.** File System

4. You are the systems administrator for Sunbrew Dairy Farms, Inc. You are currently interviewing a candidate for the position of assistant network administrator. You have asked Christopher, the candidate, what the `secedit.exe` command can be used for. Which of the following answers that Christopher gives you are correct? (Choose all that apply.)

- ❍ **A.** `secedit.exe` can be used to analyze the current security settings.
- ❍ **B.** `secedit.exe` can be used to apply new security settings to a computer.

- ❍ **C.** `secedit.exe` can be used to apply new security settings to a GPO.
- ❍ **D.** `secedit.exe` can be scripted, allowing it to be run on many computers across the entire network.

5. You are interviewing Austin for the position of assistant network security administrator. When you ask him what the best uses for an Organizational Unit are, what correct answers do you expect to hear from him? (Choose two correct answers.)

- ❍ **A.** OUs can be used to group together objects for simplified network administration.
- ❍ **B.** OUs can be used to create child domains within the DNS namespace.
- ❍ **C.** OUs can be used to create child domains within the Active Directory forest environment.
- ❍ **D.** OUs can be used to apply role-specific settings to groups of like objects.

6. In a Windows Server 2003 Active Directory environment, what constitutes the security boundary?

- ❍ **A.** The domain
- ❍ **B.** The Organizational Unit
- ❍ **C.** The forest
- ❍ **D.** The security principal

7. Austin is the systems administrator for the Eternal Light Group, LLC. He is attempting to perform an analysis of a computer by using the Security Configuration and Analysis snap-in. What is the correct order of performance of the following steps? (Delete any steps that are not needed.)

1. Select the security template to be used in the analysis.
2. Right-click Security Configuration and Analysis, and then select Analyze Computer Now.
3. Select the log file to be used in the analysis.
4. Right-click Security Configuration and Analysis and then select Open Database.
5. Right-click Security Configuration and Analysis and then select Configure Computer Now.
6. Select the database to be used in the analysis.

- ❍ **A.** 2, 1, 3, 4, 6, 5
- ❍ **B.** 4, 1, 6, 2, 5, 3
- ❍ **C.** 4, 6, 1, 2, 3
- ❍ **D.** 2, 6, 1, 3, 4

8. You have just completed an analysis of a computer by using the Security Configuration and Analysis snap-in. When you examine the results, you notice several items that have red circle with white X icons next to them. What do they indicate?

- ❍ **A.** The item is not defined in the analysis database and was not examined on the computer.
- ❍ **B.** The item is defined in the analysis database and on the computer, and it matches the currently configured setting.
- ❍ **C.** The item is defined in the analysis database but not on the computer.
- ❍ **D.** The item is defined in the analysis database and on the computer, but it does not match the currently configured setting.

9. You are the systems administrator for Gidget's Widgets, LLC. You are trying to explain to one of your assistant administrators, Hannah, how the `secedit.exe` command can be used to apply security templates to computers. Which of the following additional switches do you need to make sure she uses with the `secedit /configure` command? (Choose all that apply.)

- ❍ **A.** `/analyze`
- ❍ **B.** `/db`
- ❍ **C.** `/log`
- ❍ **D.** `/cfg`

10. Chris is creating a security plan for her network that will be using a role-based approach. If her domain has the following types of servers, how many different security policies should she plan to use?

- ▶ Domain Controllers
- ▶ File servers
- ▶ Print servers
- ▶ IIS servers
- ▶ DHCP servers

- ❍ **A.** 5
- ❍ **B.** 6
- ❍ **C.** 7
- ❍ **D.** 8

11. Chris is creating a security plan for her network that will be using a role-based approach. What is the first step in implementing a role-based security configuration for her Active Directory network?

- ❍ **A.** Implementing a Domain Baseline Security Policy
- ❍ **B.** Implementing a Domain Controller Baseline Security Policy
- ❍ **C.** Implementing a Member Server Baseline Security Policy
- ❍ **D.** Implementing role-specific security policies for her different member servers

12. Christopher is preparing to implement a role-based security solution on his Windows Server 2003 Active Directory network. However, he does not know the starting configuration of his workstation clients. He proposes that he will just apply the `Setup Security.inf` security template located on each computer to that computer to restore the settings to a known state, with all settings being the same across all client workstations. What is wrong with his proposal?

❍ **A.** The `Setup Security.inf` security template is found only on domain controllers.

❍ **B.** The `Setup Security.inf` security template is specific to the computer and can vary from one computer to the next.

❍ **C.** The `Setup Security.inf` security template is found only on computers that are upgraded from a previous operating system.

❍ **D.** The `Setup Security.inf` security template cannot actually be used to apply security settings to a computer; it is only a record of the initial security configuration the computer had.

13. Where can you find the preconfigured security templates that are installed with Windows Server 2003?

❍ **A.** `%systemroot%\templates`

❍ **B.** `%systemroot%\security\templates`

❍ **C.** `%systemroot%\security\`

❍ **D.** `%systemroot%\security\default\templates`

14. What limitation of the Security Configuration and Analysis snap-in can you get around by using Group Policy Objects?

❍ **A.** Security Configuration and Analysis cannot be used to implement security policies on a computer.

❍ **B.** Security Configuration and Analysis cannot be used to implement security policies at the domain level.

❍ **C.** Security Configuration and Analysis cannot be used to determine the current security configuration of a computer.

❍ **D.** Security Configuration and Analysis has no command-line equivalent.

15. Christopher is preparing to use the `secedit.exe` command to analyze the security on one of his member servers. If Christopher is using the secure workstation security template as his comparison point and needs to ensure that the analysis database is clear before importing the security template, which of the following choices represents the correct command that Christopher should enter to perform the analysis?

❍ **A.** `secedit /analyze /overwrite /db c:\sectst\`
`➥sectst1.sdb /cfg C:\WINDOWS\security`
`➥ \templates\securedc.inf /log c:\sectst\`
`➥ sectst1.log`

❍ **B.** `secedit /configure /db c:\sectst\sectst1.sdb /cfg`
`➥ C:\WINDOWS\security\templates\securedc.inf`
`➥ /log c:\sectst\sectst1.log`

❍ **C.** `secedit /analyze /db c:\sectst\sectst1.sdb /`
`➥ cfg C:\WINDOWS\security\templates`
`➥ \securews.inf /log c:\sectst\sectst1.log`

❍ **D.** `secedit /analyze /overwrite /db c:\sectst`
`➥ \sectst1.sdb /cfg C:\WINDOWS\security`
`➥ \templates\securews.inf /log c:\sectst`
`➥ \sectst1.log`

Answers to Review Questions

1. By using security templates, you can perform configuration and testing on a computer that will not result in changes being applied across the network until they are ready. In addition, by using a security template, you are in effect using a script: You can ensure that all changes will be identical to all computers they are applied to, even if they are in different OUs or domains. For more information, see the section "Introducing the Windows Server 2003 Security Templates."

2. Although `secedit.exe` enables you to analyze and configure computers throughout the network from the command line, you cannot easily view the analysis reports created from it except through Security Configuration and Analysis. Although you can view the log file in a text editor, such as Notepad, accurately determining the results of the analysis is not easy. For more information, see the section "The Security Configuration and Analysis Snap-in."

3. Security templates are flat text files that have the `.inf` file extension. For more information, see the section "Introducing the Windows Server 2003 Security Templates."

Answers to Exam Questions

1. **B.** The best way to apply the settings to only computers that require them is to import the template into a GPO associated with each OU that requires the settings. Importing the security template into the domain-level GPO would apply the settings to all computers in the domain, most likely with unwanted side effects. For more information, see the section "Group Policy Security Extensions."

2. **B.** Because you created custom security templates using the Security Configuration and Analysis snap-in, you can simply export them into `.inf` files and transfer them to the remote sites via any available means. When they are at the remote sites, the security templates can be imported to the appropriate GPOs, thus placing them into effect. For more information, see the section "Group Policy Security Extensions."

3. **B.** The Local Policies node of the Group Policy Editor contains three subnodes: Audit Policy, User Rights Assignment, and Security Options. Andrea will find the auditing items she needs to configure in the Audit Policy subnode. For more information, see the section "The Security Configuration and Analysis Snap-in."

4. **A, B, D.** The `secedit.exe` command can be used to analyze a computer, configure a computer, export a computer's security settings to a template, import the settings from a template, validate the context of a template, and create a rollback template. Because `secedit.exe` is a command-line tool, you can script it and use it on many computers across an entire network. For more information, see the section "`secedit.exe`."

5. **A, D.** Organizational Units can be used—very efficiently, in fact—to group objects that are similar in nature, for easier administration. In addition, you can apply security and other configuration settings to an OU to quickly have these settings applied to the objects within the OU itself. OUs should not be thought of as just containers to hold objects for the sake of better organizing Active Directory from a visual standpoint; they are actually very powerful administrative tools when properly used. Permissions to perform administrative functions can be assigned through delegation to nonadministrators at the OU level as well, further enhancing the administrative benefit of OUs. For more information, see the section "Implementing Enterprise Security."

6. **C.** Contrary to popular belief in the past, the forest is the only absolute security boundary in a Windows Server 2003 Active Directory domain. Domains are only administrative boundaries: A user with Domain Admin credentials in one domain could possibly gain domain administrative credentials in other domains through unscrupulous actions. For more information, see the section "Implementing Enterprise Security."

7. **C.** The correct steps to be used to perform an analysis of a computer with the Security Configuration and Analysis snap-in are as follows: Select Open Database, select the database, select the security template, select Analyze Computer, and select the log file. For more information, see the section "The Security Configuration and Analysis Snap-in."

8. **D.** A red circle with a white X icon next to an item in the Security Configuration and Analysis snap-in results indicates that the item is present in both the database and the computer but does not match the currently configured setting. For more information, see the section "The Security Configuration and Analysis Snap-in."

9. **B, C, D.** The `/db` switch specifies the pathname and filename of the database to be used, the `/log` switch specifies the pathname and filename of the error log to be used during the process, and the `/cfg` switch specifies the pathname and filename of the security template to be loaded into the database. For more information, see the section "`secedit.exe`."

10. **C.** Chris should be using seven different security policies, as follows: Domain Baseline Policy, Domain Controllers OU Policy, Member Servers OU Baseline Policy, File Servers OU Policy, Print Servers OU Policy, IIS Servers OU Policy, and DHCP Servers OU Policy. Each type of server has specific security requirements that necessitate different security policies. The domain itself needs a Baseline Security Policy that takes care of things such as password and account lockout policies. Also, the Member Servers OU needs a Baseline Security Policy to configure items that apply to all member servers, such as auditing and user rights assignments. For more information, see the section "Using Role-Based Security Templates and the Security Configuration Wizard."

11. **A.** The first step to successfully implementing a role-based security solution is to create the baseline—the starting point. Thus, Chris needs to implement a Domain Baseline Security Policy before she moves on. For more information, see the section "Implementing Enterprise Security."

12. **B.** Christopher's mistake is that he proposes to use the `Setup Security.inf` security template located on each client workstation to apply the same settings across all his workstations. The `Setup Security.inf` security template is created during the installation of Windows on the computer—either clean or upgrade—and varies from one computer to the next. For more information, see the section "Introducing the Windows Server 2003 Security Templates."

13. **B.** The preconfigured security templates that install with Windows Server 2003 can be found in the `%systemroot%\security\templates` directory. Typically, this is `C:\WINDOWS\security\templates`. For more information, see the section "Planning and Implementing Role-Based Security Using Security Templates."

14. **B.** The only real failing in Security Configuration and Analysis is that it cannot be used to analyze or configure security on anything other than the local computer. It does not have the capability to be targeted at a remote computer like some of the other MMC snap-ins. For more information, see the section "The Security Configuration and Analysis Snap-in."

15. **D.** Only option D meets all the specified requirements that Christopher has for performing this analysis: He must use the secure template for a member server (`securews.inf`), and he must ensure that the database is cleared before importing the security template. Answer C appears to meet these requirements but does not provide for clearing the database before importing the security template. For more information, see the section "`secedit.exe`."

Suggested Readings and Resources

1. Windows Server 2003 Security Guide. http://go.microsoft.com/fwlink/?LinkId=14845.

2. Threats and Countermeasures: Security Settings in Windows Server 2003 and Window XP. http://go.microsoft.com/fwlink/?LinkId=15159.

3. "Security Configuration Manager." http://technet2.microsoft.com/WindowsServer/en/library/74d8fed6-cf2f-4ba4-94f3-fc95bad914b01033.mspx.

4. Security Configuration Wizard for Windows Server 2003. www.microsoft.com/windowsserver2003/technologies/security/configwiz/default.mspx.

6

CHAPTER SIX

Planning, Implementing, and Troubleshooting Network Security Using IPSec

Planning and implementing network security methods does not end after you've implemented the security solutions discussed in Chapter 5, "Planning and Implementing Server Roles and Server Security." You still must ensure that a handful of other issues are taken care of before your network is to be considered secure. *Secure*, however, is a relative term and one that is defined by the business and organizational requirements in place in your organization.

Objectives

Microsoft defines the IPSec portion of the "Planning, Implementing, and Maintaining Routing and Remote Access" objective and the "Planning and Maintaining Network Security" objective as follows:

Configure network protocol security.

- **Configure protocol security in a heterogeneous client computer environment.**
- **Configure protocol security by using IPSec policies.**

Configure security for data transmission.

- **Configure IPSec policy settings.**

Plan security for data transmission.

- **Secure data transmission between client computers to meet security requirements.**
- **Secure data transmission by using IPSec.**

Plan for network protocol security.

- **Specify the required ports and protocols for specified services.**
- **Plan an IPSec policy for secure network communications.**
- IP Security (IPSec) is the de facto standard for security network transmissions in both heterogeneous and homogenous network environments. IPSec can be used to provide secure network connections, both internal to your network and external to your network. IPSec operates in two modes, transport and tunnel, depending on where the endpoints in a communication lie in relation to each other. IPSec is fully supported in Windows Server 2003, and three preconfigured IPSec policies are supplied to get you going quickly. It is important for you to understand not only how to implement and configure IPSec for this exam, but also for you to secure your network.

Troubleshoot security for data transmission. Tools might include the IP Security Monitor MMC snap-in and the Resultant Set of Policy (RSoP) MMC snap-in.

- Unfortunately, nothing works right all the time; IPSec is no exception. Using improperly configured IPSec policies is a quick way to bring all normal network traffic to a screeching halt. Windows Server 2003 provides the IP Security Monitor and the Resultant Set of Policy snap-in to monitor and troubleshoot IPSec-related traffic issues.

Outline

Study Strategies

- Carefully work your way through the material discussing the component parts of an IPSec policy. Practice creating and implementing an IPSec policy between two computers on your network.
- Get your hands dirty. The Step by Steps throughout this book provide plenty of directions and exercises, but go beyond these examples and create some of your own. If you can, experiment with each of the objectives to see how they work and why you would use each one.

Introduction

Although we examined the basics of network security in Chapter 5, we have much more to talk about in regard to securing your network; that is the topic of this chapter. This chapter, however, is not the end-all when it comes to security or securing your Windows Server 2003 network. Many volumes have been written on this topic, but we seek to examine only a sampling of the overall subject area in this chapter that is directly related to the objectives for this exam.

Planning Security for Data Transmission

Objective:

Plan security for data transmission.

- Secure data transmission between client computers to meet security requirements.
- Secure data transmission by using IPSec.

IP Security (IPSec) is a framework of open standards for ensuring private, secure communications over IP networks. This protocol is rapidly becoming the underlying framework for secure communications using VPNs and will likely replace Point-to-Point Tunneling Protocol (PPTP) as Microsoft's VPN protocol of choice. IPSec takes advantage of many of the most popular encryption protocols in use today. For more information on encryption protocols, see Chapter 4, "Planning and Implementing a Name Resolution Infrastructure." IPSec is based on an end-to-end security model, which means that the only computers that must know about IPSec are the sending and receiving computers. The packets travel the network without being affected by any of the intervening network devices. Each IPSec device handles its own security and functions with the assumption that the transport medium is not secure. The Internet is an excellent example of a transport medium that is not secure.

The Microsoft Windows Server 2003 implementation of IPSec is based on standards developed by the Internet Engineering Task Force (IETF) IPSec working group. However, it is important to note that Microsoft uses two implementations of IPSec: the IETF version, also known as Pure IPSec Tunnel mode, or just tunnel mode; and the Microsoft variant on IPSec, which Microsoft calls L2TP/IPSec mode, or transport mode. An IPSec VPN configured to use transport mode secures an existing IP packet from source to destination, using the encryption and authentication methods discussed later in this section. Tunnel mode puts an existing IP packet inside a new IP packet that is sent to a tunnel endpoint in the IPSec format. Both transport and tunnel mode can be encapsulated in Encapsulating Security Protocol (ESP) or Authentication Header (AH) headers. The original IETF Request for Comments (RFC 2401, www.ietf.org/rfc/rfc2401.txt) IPSec tunnel protocol specifications did not include mechanisms suitable for remote-access VPN clients, instead focusing on site-to-site VPN implementations.

For that reason, Microsoft's implementation of tunnel mode relies on the use of the L2TP protocol developed jointly with Cisco to provide this additional packet format. (An introduction to the components of IPSec comes later in this chapter.) It is worth noting that a new RFC (RFC 3193, www.ietf.org/rfc/rfc3193.txt) introduced in late 2001 discusses using L2TP with IPSec.

NOTE

Protecting VPN connections By default, client remote-access VPN connections are protected using an automatically generated IPSec policy that uses IPSec transport mode (not tunnel mode) when the L2TP tunnel type is selected. You will probably see this configuration in almost every production implementation of a Windows Server 2003 IPSec implementation. To enable this configuration, configure the Routing and Remote Access Service for L2TP VPN connectivity, as described in Chapter 7, "Planning, Implementing, and Troubleshooting Secure Network Access."

EXAM ALERT

Understand IPSec The exam includes questions and scenarios on IPSec. Although you don't need to memorize the minutiae surrounding the encryption protocols IPSec uses, you should be familiar with what the components of IPSec are, how to implement an IPSec tunnel, and especially how to work with IPSec policies.

Understanding the Architecture and Components of IPSec

Let's look at the underlying architecture and components of the IPSec protocol. IPSec provides data- and identity-protection services for each IP packet by adding a security protocol header to each IP packet. This header is made up of several components, each with its own function.

Authentication Header (AH)

The IPSec Authentication Header (AH) provides three services as part of the IPSec protocol. First (as its name might suggest), AH authenticates the entire packet. Second, it ensures data integrity. Third, it prevents any replaying of the packet by a third party who might be trying to penetrate the IPSec tunnel. One service AH doesn't provide is payload encryption. AH protects your data from modification, but an attacker who is snooping the network would still be able to read the data. To prevent the modification of the data, AH uses two hashing algorithms to "sign" the packet for integrity:

- The Message Digest 5 (MD5) algorithm applies the hashing function to the data in four passes.
- The Secure Hash Algorithm (SHA1) is closely modeled after MD5. SHA uses 79 32-bit constants during the computation of the hash value, which results in a 160-bit key. Because SHA has a longer key length, it is considered more secure than MD5.

AH uses an IP protocol decimal ID of 51 to identify itself in the IP header. The AH header contains the following fields:

- **Next Header**—This field identifies the next header that uses the IP protocol ID.
- **Length**—This field indicates the length of the AH header.
- **Security Parameters Index (SPI)**—Used in combination with the destination address and the security protocol (AH or ESP), the SPI is used by the receiver to identify the cryptographic keys and procedures to be used to decode the packet.
- **Sequence Number**—This field provides the antireplay functionality of AH. The sequence number is an incrementally increasing number (starting from 0) that is never allowed to cycle and that indicates the packet number. The machine receiving the packet checks this field to verify that the packet has not been received already. If a packet with this number has already been received, the packet is rejected.
- **Authentication Data**—This field contains the Integrity Check Value (ICV) used to verify the integrity of the message. (This is the hash value mentioned previously.) The receiver calculates the hash value and checks it against the ICV to verify packet integrity.

An IP packet that has AH applied in transfer mode is modified with the AH header between the IP header and the TCP header, as shown in Figure 6.1.

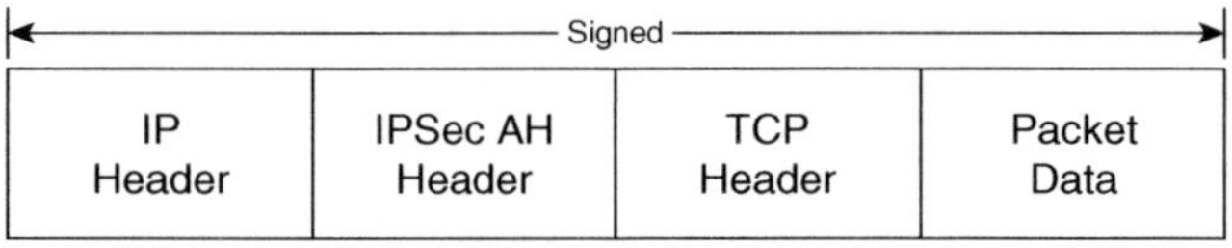

FIGURE 6.1 An IP packet with the AH header inserted in transfer mode.

AH can be used alone or in combination with the ESP protocol, which is discussed next.

Encapsulating Security Protocol (ESP)

Encapsulating Security Protocol (ESP) provides confidentiality in addition to authentication, integrity, and antireplay. This portion of the IPSec protocol encrypts the data contents of the packet. The format of the ESP varies, depending on the type and mode of encryption being used. ESP can be used alone, in combination with AH, or using Microsoft's implementation, nested within the L2TP.

ESP appears in the IP header with an IP protocol decimal ID of 50. The ESP header contains the following fields:

- **SPI**—The receiver uses the SPI, in combination with the destination address and the security protocol (AH or ESP), to identify the cryptographic keys and procedures to be used to decode the packet.

- **Sequence Number**—This field provides the antireplay functionality of ESP. The sequence number is an incrementally increasing number (starting from 0) that is never allowed to cycle and indicates the packet number. The machine receiving the packet checks this field to verify that the packet has not been received already. If a packet with this number has already been received, the packet is rejected.

NOTE

Replaying: Why is it bad? You might have noticed that replaying has been included several times as part of the discussion of IPSec. Replaying is a somewhat obscure method for obtaining access to a system. A replay attack occurs when packets are intercepted by an unauthorized party, stored, and later retransmitted in an effort to trick one or both sides of the transmission into thinking that it is a valid communication. A replay attack becomes an issue because TCP/IP protocols such as Network File System (NFS) have no mechanisms to determine whether a packet is being replayed—even after several hours. Fortunately, the antireplay mechanisms in IPSec make a replay attack a virtual impossibility.

The ESP trailer contains the following fields:

- **Padding**—Specifies 0 to 255 bytes used for 32-bit alignment and with the block size of the block cipher.
- **Padding Length**—Indicates the length of the Padding field in bytes.
- **Next Header**—Identifies the makeup of the payload, such as TCP or UDP.

The ESP Authentication Trailer contains one field: Authentication Data. This field contains the Integrity Check Value (ICV) and a media access control (MAC) used to verify the sender's identity and ensure message integrity.

ESP is inserted after the IP header and before an upper-layer protocol, such as TCP, UDP, or ICMP, or before any other IPSec headers (such as AH) that have already been inserted. Everything following ESP (the upper-layer protocol, the data, and the ESP trailer) is encrypted, as shown in Figure 6.2. The IP header is not signed and, therefore, not necessarily protected from modification unless tunneling mode is active, as shown in Figure 6.3.

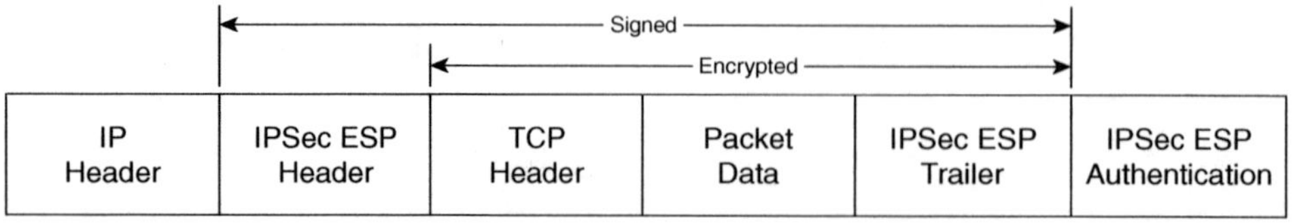

FIGURE 6.2 An IP packet with the ESP header inserted in transfer mode.

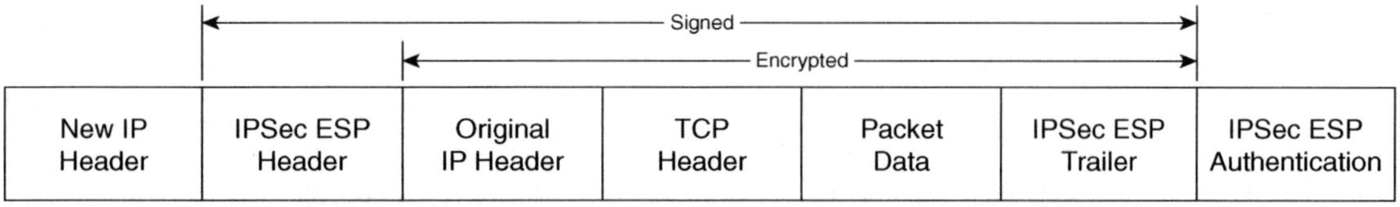

FIGURE 6.3 An IP packet with the ESP header inserted in tunnel mode; the original IP header is now encrypted.

The final piece of the IPSec protocol is the authentication and key-exchange mechanism. Authentication and key exchange are accomplished using a pair of protocols.

Internet Security Key Association Key Management Protocol (ISAKMP/Oakley)

ISAKMP/Oakley (also known as ISAKMP/IKE, for Internet Key Exchange) provides the mechanism that allows disparate VPN servers to share encryption key information and make the IPSec protocol practical in today's environment. Before secured data can be exchanged between VPN servers, a contract between the two computers must be established. In this contract, called SA, both computers agree on how to exchange and protect information. In other words, the two servers (or the server and client computer) need to agree on how to encrypt and decrypt the data to be sent.

To enable this process, the IPSec protocol uses a standard process to build this contract between the two computers. This process combines the ISAKMP and Oakley key-generation protocols. ISAKMP provides the centralized security-association management, whereas Oakley actually generates and manages the encryption keys used to secure the information.

IKE actually performs a two-phase operation to establish the secure communication channel. In each phase, confidentiality and authentication are ensured by the use of encryption and authentication algorithms that the computers negotiating agree upon. In the first phase (also known as main mode), the two computers establish a secure, authenticated channel called the Phase I (Main Mode) SA. The IKE provides identity protection during this phase. In the first phase (also known as quick mode), the two computers establish the rules for communication called the Phase II (Quick Mode) SA. During the second phase, a new shared key is created for use. When the Phase II SA is in place, IPSec secured communications can occur.

The final piece of this puzzle that needs to be covered is Microsoft's IPSec/L2TP implementation, which adds an additional tunneling protocol to the IPSec implementation.

L2TP and IPSec

The major difference between the ESP tunnel and L2TP is that the L2TP tunnel performs at Layer 2 of the OSI model, the data link layer. This way, L2TP can tunnel additional protocols, such as IPX or NetBEUI. IPSec's ESP tunneling protocol tunnels only the TCP/IP protocol, based on the standard. When L2TP and IPSec are used in combination to provide a secured tunnel, the original packet header is used to carry the packet's source and final destination, whereas the tunnel packet's IP header might contain the address of an IPSec gateway. The L2TP header carries the information needed to route the packet over the network. The Point-to-Point Protocol (PPP) header within the encapsulated packet identifies the protocol of the original packet. In other words, when using L2TP to transfer data, IPSec is used to secure the tunnel. L2TP encapsulates the packet in a PPP frame. The PPP frame is then added to a UDP-type frame assigned to port 1701. UDP, which is part of the TCP/IP suite, qualifies for IPSec to secure the contents; thus, the contents of L2TP are secure, regardless of the originating protocol and/or data type.

One additional benefit of the L2TP method is that you have a choice of additional encryption algorithms for securing the data.

What's New with Windows Server 2003 IPSec

The following new features are supported in the Windows Server 2003 IPSec implementation:

- IPSec in Windows Server 2003 now supports User Datagram Protocol (UDP) encapsulation of IPSec packets to allow Internet Key Exchange (IKE) and Encapsulating Security Protocol (ESP) traffic to pass through a Network Address Translation (NAT) device—something not previously possible in Windows 2000. It is now possible for Windows 2000 and Windows XP clients to establish IPSec connections with a Windows Server 2003 server that is located behind one or more NAT devices.
- The IP Security Monitor is now implemented as an MMC snap-in instead of a standalone executable as in Windows 2000. Also, you can now monitor information about local and remote computers, as well as several other enhancements.
- IPSec now supports the use of a 2,048-bit Diffie-Hellman key exchange. As a result, the secret key resulting from the Diffie-Hellman exchange has greater strength. This results in a longer key length, which increases the difficulty an attacker faces when trying to determine a secret key.
- You can administer and control IPSec from the command line with new extensions to the `netsh` command. Using the `netsh ipsec` context, you can configure static or dynamic IPSec main mode settings, quick mode settings, rules, and configuration parameters. The `netsh ipsec` context replaces the `Ipsecpol.exe` tool that was provided with the Windows 2000 Server Resource Kit.
- IPSec now provides stateful filtering of network traffic during computer startup. Any outbound traffic initiated by the computer upon startup is permitted, as is any inbound reply traffic. Dynamic Host Configuration Protocol (DHCP) is exempt from this new protection provided by IPSec and is thus allowed during startup. You can also specify other types of traffic you want to exempt. Computer startup security can be configured only by using the `netsh` command with the `ipsec` context.

- Windows Server 2003 Enterprise Edition and Windows Server 2003 Datacenter Server Edition provide improved support for integration of IPSec with network load balancing. This allows a group of NLB servers to better provide highly available IPSec-based VPN services to clients. NLB can now accurately track IPSec-secured sessions, and the IPSec Internet Key Exchange (IKE) protocol can now detect when an IPSec-secured session is being established with a cluster server and quickly recover from a failover.
- IPSec provides an extension to the Resultant Set of Policy (RSoP) snap-in (another new addition to Windows Server 2003) that can be used to view IPSec policy assignments of computers or other Active Directory objects.

EXAM ALERT

netsh and IPSec Microsoft seems to really like the `netsh` command. Don't forget that it now can be used to manage IPSec!

The following are the standard features of the Windows Server 2003 IPSec implementation:

- IPSec in Windows Server 2003 is policy based. It cannot be configured without an IPSec policy being in place, allowing an administrator to more easily apply settings to groups of objects such as computers or users.
- IPSec on Windows Server 2003 can use Kerberos v5, a digital certificate, or a shared secret (string) for user authentication.
- IPSec mutually authenticates computers before any data is exchanged.
- IPSec establishes a security association (SA) between the two host computers involved in the data transfer. An SA is the collection of a policy and keys, which define the rules for security settings.
- IPSec encrypts data using Data Encryption Standard (DES) or Triple DES (3DES).
- IPSec uses the MD5 or SHA1 algorithm for data hashing.
- IPSec is invisible to users. IPSec operates at the network level of the Open System Interface (OSI) model; therefore, users and applications do not directly interact with the protocol. After an IPSec tunnel has been created, users can connect to applications and services as if they were on the local network and not on the other side of a public network.

IPSec operates at the network layer; therefore, it is invisible to applications and computers. An understanding of the following features, however, will help you troubleshoot problems that might arise in connectivity:

- IPSec policies are part of Group Policy, both locally and within Active Directory. This built-in feature allows changes and management to be centralized. Settings for IPSec are enforced on the computer as the policy is enforced.
- The Internet Security Key Association Key Management Protocol (ISAKMP) monitors the negotiations between the hosts and provides the keys to use with security algorithms.
- The installed IPSec driver secures traffic between the two hosts.

Now that you have a basic introduction to the benefits and background of the IPSec protocol, you are ready to look at working with IPSec.

Configuring and Implementing IPSec

Objective:

Plan for network protocol security.

- Specify the required ports and protocols for specified services.
- Plan an IPSec policy for secure network communications.

Objective:

Configure network protocol security.

- Configure protocol security in a heterogeneous client computer environment.
- Configure protocol security by using IPSec policies.

Objective:

Configure security for data transmission.

- Configure IPSec policy settings.

Before enabling IPSec on your local computer or domain, you should configure IPSec through policies. An IPSec policy is a set of rules that define how and when communication is secured between two endpoints. This is done through the configuration of various rules. Each rule contains a collection of actions and filters that begin when they encounter endpoints that match.

Policies enable you to quickly and easily configure IPSec based on the settings required within your organization. Windows Server 2003 comes with the following three preconfigured IPSec policies, which might or might not meet your needs:

- **Client (Respond Only)**—This policy requires IPSec-provided security only when another computer requests it. This policy allows the computer to attempt unsecured communications first and switch to IPSec-secured communications if requested. This policy contains the default response rule, which creates dynamic IPSec filters for inbound and outbound traffic based on the requested protocol and port traffic for the communication that is being secured. This policy, which can be used on workstations and servers alike, provides the minimum amount of IPSec security.
- **Server (Request Security)**—This policy requests security from the other computer and allows unsecured communication with non-IPSec-aware computers. The computer accepts inbound unsecured traffic but always attempts to secure further communications by requesting IPSec security from the sending computer. If the other computer is not IPSec enabled, the entire communication is allowed to be unsecured. This policy, which can be used on workstations and servers alike, provides a medium level of IPSec security.
- **Secure Server (Require Security)**—This policy is implemented on computers that require highly secure communications, such as servers transmitting sensitive data. The filters in this policy require all outbound communication to be secured, allowing only the initial inbound communication request to be unsecured. This policy has a rule to require security for all IP traffic, a rule to permit ICMP traffic, and the default response rule to respond to requests for security from other computers. This policy, typically used only on servers, provides the highest level of IPSec security on a network. This policy can also be used on workstation computers, if you want. Non-IPSec-enabled computers cannot establish any communications with computers using this policy.

You can opt to either use one of the preconfigured policies that comes with Windows Server 2003 or create your own policy. You can also modify the preconfigured policies to suit your needs, if you want. Before we can go any further into our discussion about IPSec, we need to create the tools that enable us to manage IPSec on a local computer. Step by Step 6.1 helps you to create your own IPSec management console.

STEP BY STEP

6.1 Creating the IPSec Management Console

1. Open a blank MMC by clicking Start, Run. Then type **mmc** to open a blank MMC, as shown in Figure 6.4.
2. In your new console, click the File menu and select Add/Remove Snap-in. The Add/Remove Snap-in dialog box opens, as shown in Figure 6.5.
3. Click the Add button to open the Add Standalone Snap-in dialog box, shown in Figure 6.6.

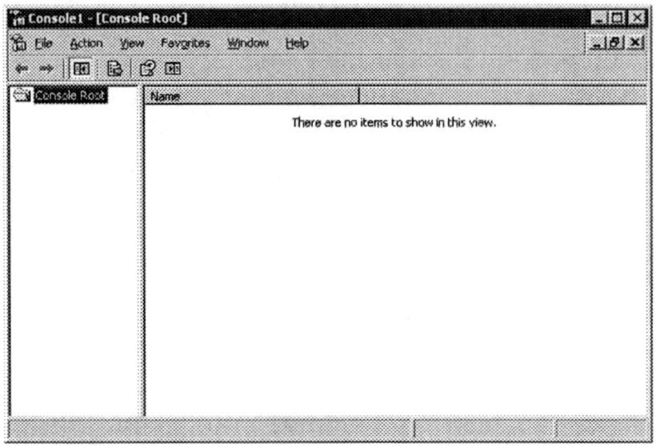

FIGURE 6.4 The MMC provides a powerful, flexible framework from which to manage Windows Server 2003.

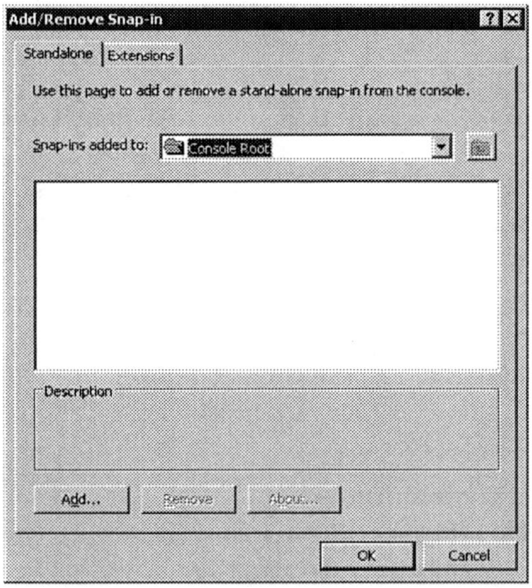

FIGURE 6.5 You can add snap-ins to your console to customize its management features.

4. Scroll down the list, select IP Security Monitor, and click the Add button.

5. Select IP Security Policy Management and click the Add button. You are prompted to choose the scope that the snap-in will manage, as shown in Figure 6.7.

6. For this example, choose Local Computer from the Select Computer or Domain page. Notice that you have the option to select the Active Directory domain that this computer is part of, another Active Directory domain, or another computer. Click Finish to complete the addition of the IP Security Policy Management snap-in to your console.

7. Click Close on the Add Standalone Snap-in dialog box.

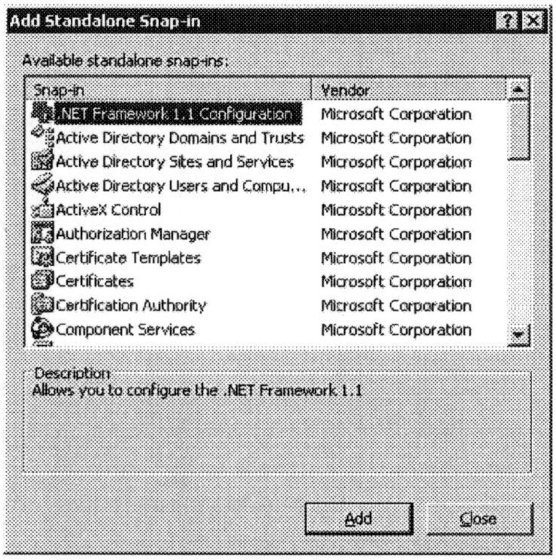

FIGURE 6.6 Windows Server 2003 comes with several dozen snap-ins you can choose from.

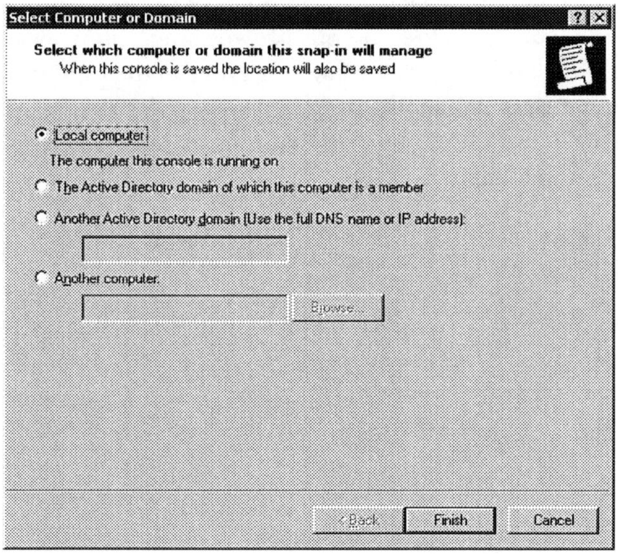

FIGURE 6.7 Many MMC snap-ins can be targeted at several different levels of management.

8. Click OK on the Add/Remove Snap-in dialog box. Figure 6.8 shows your completed IPSec management console.

9. Save your newly created console by clicking File, Save. Enter a suitable name, such as **`Local IPSec Management Console`**, and click Save. By default, the console is saved in the Administrative Tools folder of the currently logged-in user.

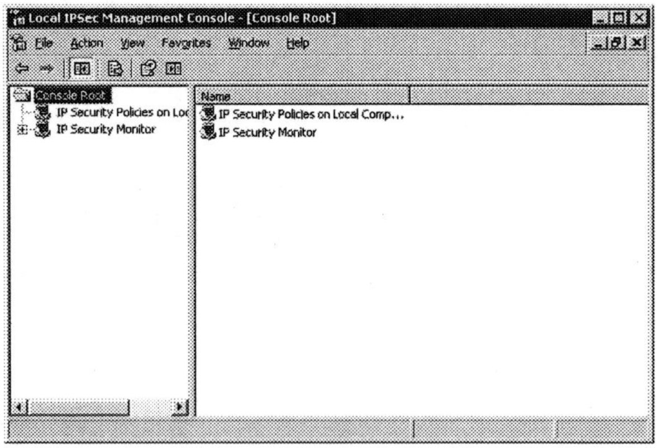

FIGURE 6.8 Your completed IPSec management console contains the tools you need to manage and monitor IP Security.

Armed with your newly created IPSec management console, you can now get to work configuring and managing IPSec. At this point, you might want to do one of two things: implement a preconfigured IPSec policy or create one of your own. We explore the latter in the next Step by Step. You can accomplish the former by right-clicking the desired policy in the right pane of the console window, as seen in Figure 6.9, and selecting Assign from the context menu. Note that you can have only one IPSec policy assigned at a time.

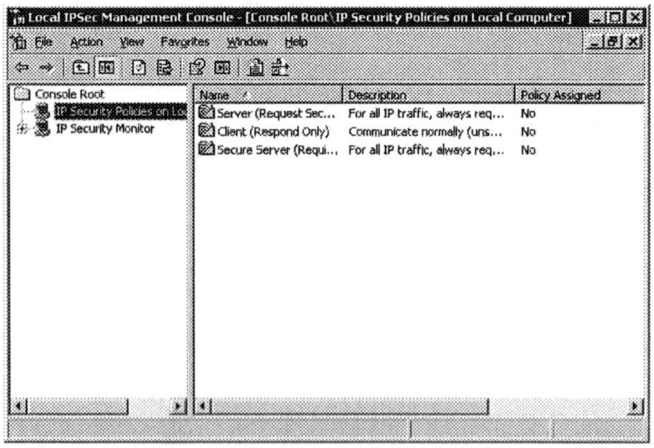

FIGURE 6.9 Assigning an IPSec policy to the local computer is a quick task.

You can verify that the policy is now assigned to the computer by examining the Active Policy node of the IP Security Monitor, shown in Figure 6.10.

We examine the use of the IP Security Monitor console later in this chapter. For now, we need to look at the process to create a custom IPSec policy.

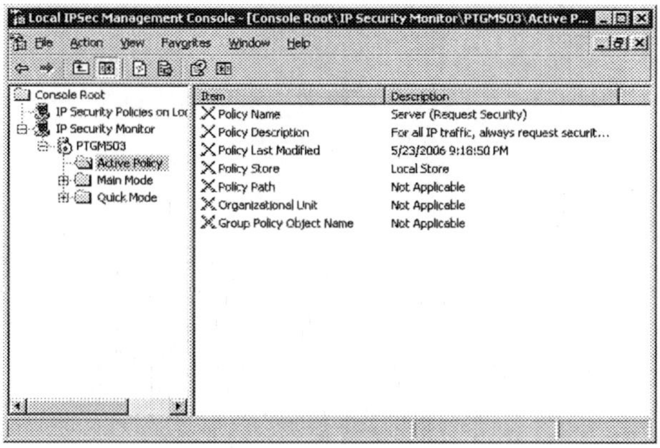

FIGURE 6.10 The IP Security Monitor can be used to display many bits of useful information about IPSec.

Understanding IPSec Policy Components

After you've decided to use IPSec on your network, you might realize that the preconfigured IPSec policies do not provide exactly the solution you are looking for. You can opt to either customize an existing policy or create a new one from scratch. I prefer to create policies from scratch to ensure that I have complete control over every piece of the puzzle, and that's exactly what IPSec can turn out to be if not treated with caution and respect—one large puzzle that you are left to piece together.

Before we start to actually create our own IPSec policy, let's take a few moments to examine the parts that make up an IPSec policy by dissecting the Secure Server (Require Security) policy. From within your IPSec management console, double-click this policy to open its Properties dialog box, as shown in Figure 6.11. It has two tabs: Rules and General. Let's look at the Rules tab first.

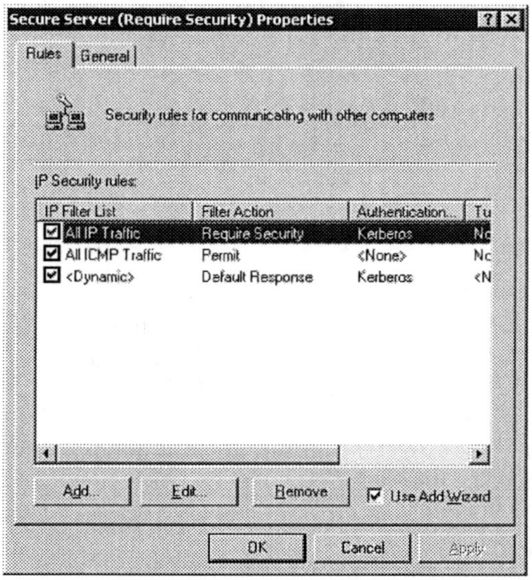

FIGURE 6.11 Examining the properties of a preconfigured IPSec policy can help you learn what makes up such a policy.

The Rules Tab

The IP Security Rules window lists all the IP Security Rules that are active for that policy. Selecting a rule and clicking the Edit button opens the Edit Rule Properties dialog box, shown in Figure 6.12. The five tabs on the Edit Rule Properties dialog box contain the configuration settings for this particular rule.

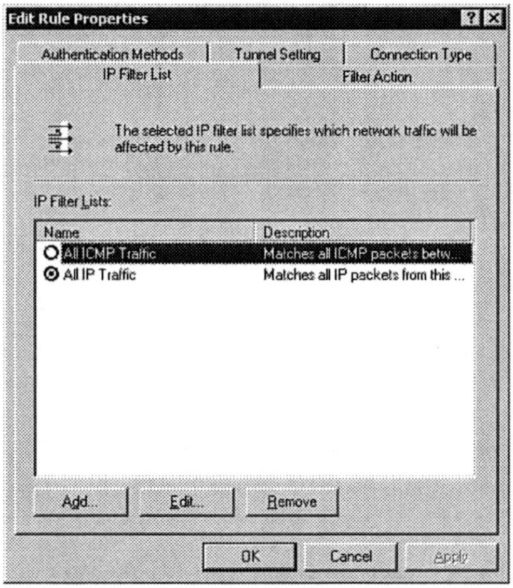

FIGURE 6.12 The IP Filter List tab of the Edit Rule Properties dialog box.

Edit Rule Properties: IP Filter List Tab

The IP Filter List tab shows all IP filters configured for the selected rule. An IP filter contains source and destination IP addresses that apply to this rule. These IP addresses can be those of an individual computer or that of a network subnet. If this tab identifies a network communication that has a participant listed in an IP filter, a particular filter action that is specific for that connection is applied. Selecting the All IP Traffic filter for editing opens the dialog box shown in Figure 6.13. From here, you can specify many items, including the source and destination IP addresses that this filter applies to.

Edit Rule Properties: Filter Actions Tab

The Filter Action tab of the Edit Rule Properties dialog box, shown in Figure 6.14, contains actions that specify the type of security and methods by which security is established.

Filter actions, seen in Figure 6.15, define the type of security and methods by which security is established. The default methods are Permit, Block, and Negotiate Security. The Permit option passes the traffic without the requirement for security. This action is appropriate if you never want to secure traffic to which a rule applies. The Block action silently blocks all traffic from computers specified in the IP filter list. The Negotiate Security action specifies that the computer is to use a list of security methods to negotiate the appropriate security for the communication.

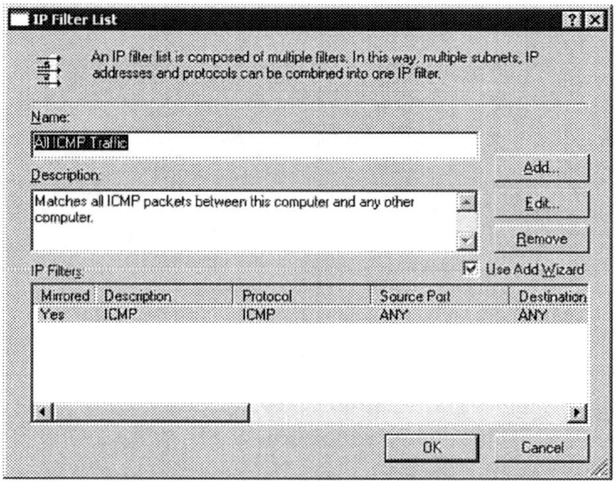

FIGURE 6.13 You can edit the filter properties to specify the source and destination computers that they apply to.

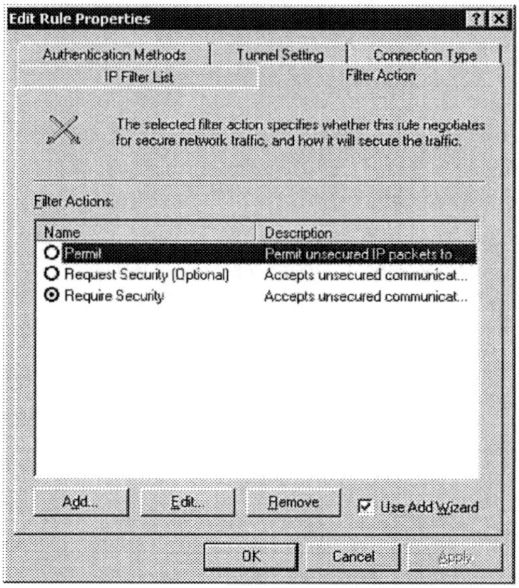

FIGURE 6.14 The Filter Action tab defines the types of security and methods by which security is established.

If the Negotiate Security action is selected, both computers must agree on the security parameters to be used, meaning that they both must support at least one common set of security parameters from those in the list. The list entries are processed in order of preference from top to bottom. The first security method shared by both computers is used.

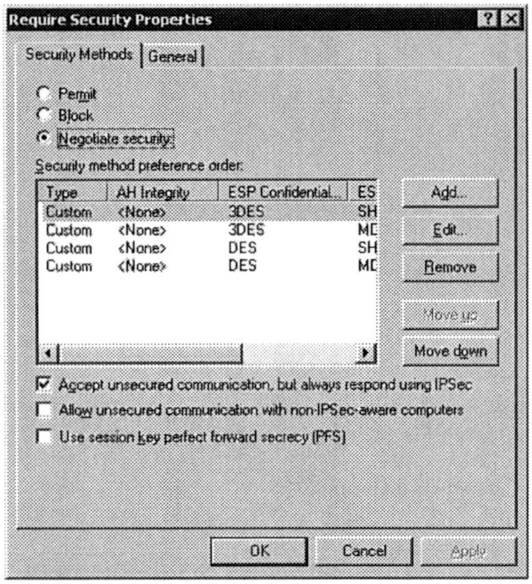

FIGURE 6.15 You can specify exactly what the computer will do when a filter action is processed.

Edit Rule Properties: Authentication Methods Tab

From the Authentication Methods tab, shown in Figure 6.16, you can configure what method will be used to authenticate both sides of the communication. You can choose from Kerberos (the default setting), a digital certificate, or a shared secret (string) that will be used to protect the key-exchange process. You can configure more than one method and also choose the order of precedence for your configured methods. Using the shared secret is not recommended because this static entry can be compromised.

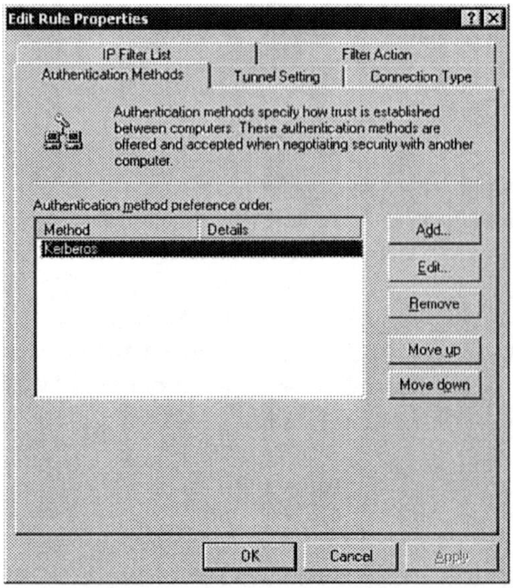

FIGURE 6.16 You can specify Kerberos, digital certificate, or shared secret as the authentication methods.

Edit Rule Properties: Tunnel Setting Tab

From the Tunnel Setting tab, shown in Figure 6.17, you can either have the rule apply to a tunnel by specifying an endpoint or not have it apply to a tunnel (transport mode).

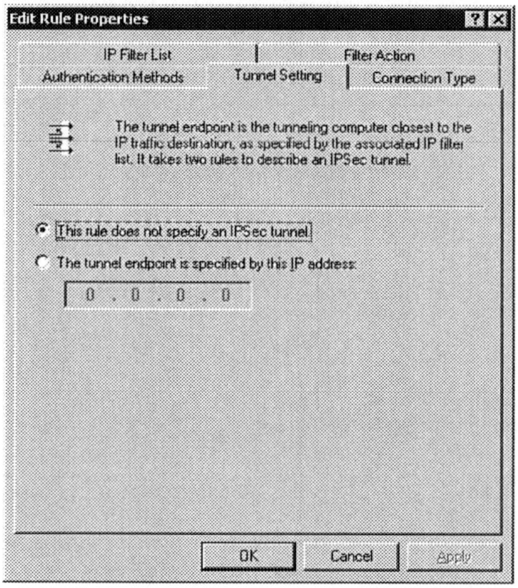

FIGURE 6.17 The Tunnel Setting tab enables you to configure a tunnel endpoint, if required.

Edit Rule Properties: Connection Type Tab

The Connection Type tab, shown in Figure 6.18, determines the types of connections for which the rule will be applied: LAN, Remote Access, or All Network Connections

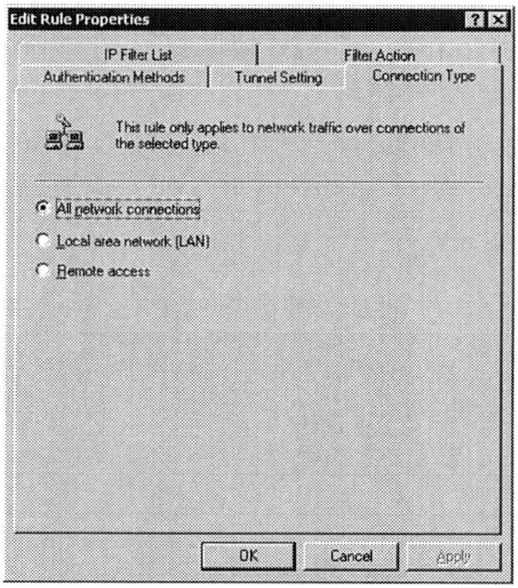

FIGURE 6.18 The Connection Type tab enables you to specify which connections the policy affects.

The General Tab

Whereas the Rules tab contains all the configuration settings that control how the policy behaves in regard to allowing or denying traffic to pass, the General tab, seen in Figure 6.19, contains the configuration settings that define how the IPSec policy, as a whole, behaves after it has been assigned.

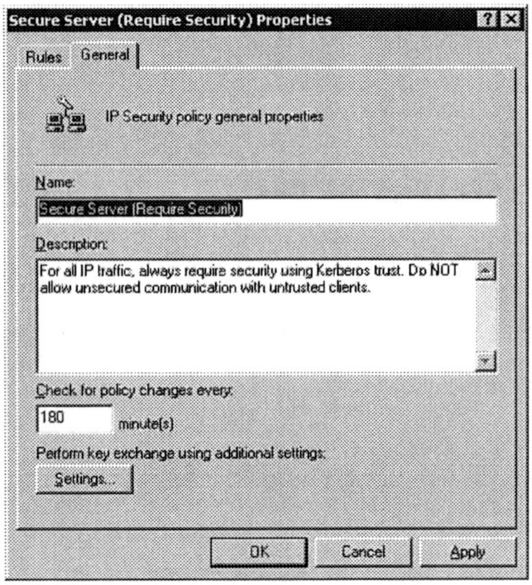

FIGURE 6.19 The General tab enables you to control the behavior of the IPSec policy itself.

On the General tab, you see some of the same basic items that you'll see on a lot of General tabs throughout Windows: the name and description of the policy. That's where the similarities end. You also have the options on the General tab to configure the interval at which the computer will check for updates and changes to the security policy. The default setting of 180 minutes is usually acceptable.

Clicking the Settings button at the bottom of the General tab opens the Key Exchange Settings dialog box, seen in Figure 6.20. In the Key Exchange Settings dialog box, you can configure for master key perfect forward secrecy, which improves security of the keying process. Additionally, you can change the defaults provided for key generation.

Clicking the Methods button on the Key Exchange Settings dialog box opens the Key Exchange Security Methods dialog box, seen in Figure 6.21. If you want to configure the methods used to protect the identities, you can accomplish that task from here. Note that, by default, the new 2,048-bit Diffie-Hellman key-exchange method is not used. You can select it by adding or editing a security method, as shown in Figure 6.22.

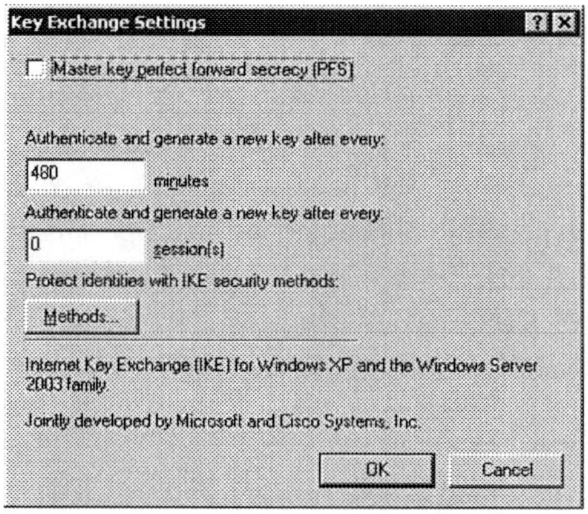

FIGURE 6.20 You can configure advanced IKE properties from the Key Exchange Settings dialog box.

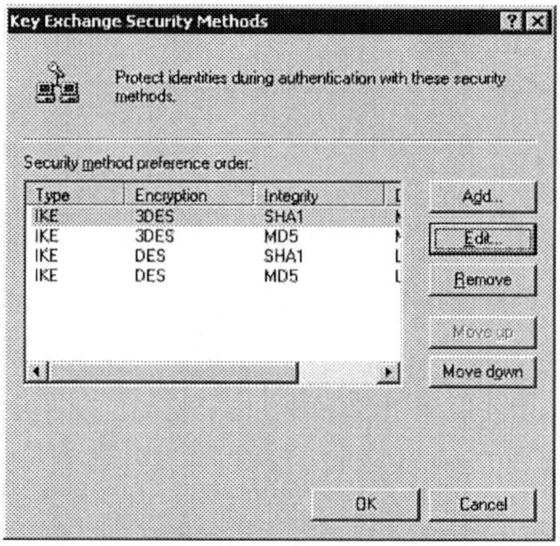

FIGURE 6.21 Customizing the key-exchange security methods can increase security.

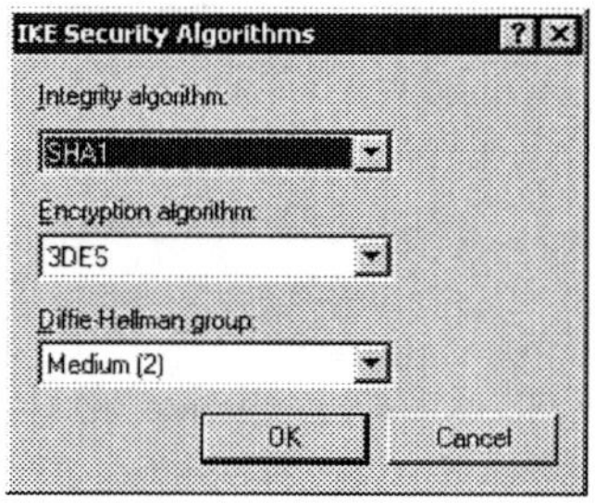

FIGURE 6.22 Using the new 2,048-bit Diffie-Hellman key-exchange method.

Ironically, the General tab has options that are so advanced for configuring an IPSec policy that it should instead be called the Advanced tab. Don't take these configuration settings for granted when creating a custom IPSec policy.

Creating Customized IPSec Policies

You can create two basic types of IPSec policies: those that specify a tunnel and those that do not specify a tunnel. Tunneling is commonly used in the creation of a VPN and is called tunnel mode. Not using a tunnel, called transport mode, is commonly used between subnets or computers on an intranet. Step by Step 6.2 shows how to create a new IPSec policy that operates in transport mode between two subnets (192.160.11.0 and 192.168.12.0) in the same intranet of the company Que Publishing. These two subnets represent the Accounting and Payroll departments, respectively, and they need to pass only secured traffic between their subnets.

STEP BY STEP

6.2 Creating a Custom Transfer Mode IPSec Policy

1. Open the IPSec management console that you created in Step by Step 6.1.
2. Right-click IP Security Policies and select Create IP Security Policy from the context menu.
3. Dismiss the opening page of the IP Security Policy Wizard by clicking Next.
4. In the IP Security Policy Name dialog box, enter a descriptive name for the new policy. For this example, use **`Accounting to Payroll Security Policy`**, as shown in Figure 6.23. Click Next after entering the required information.

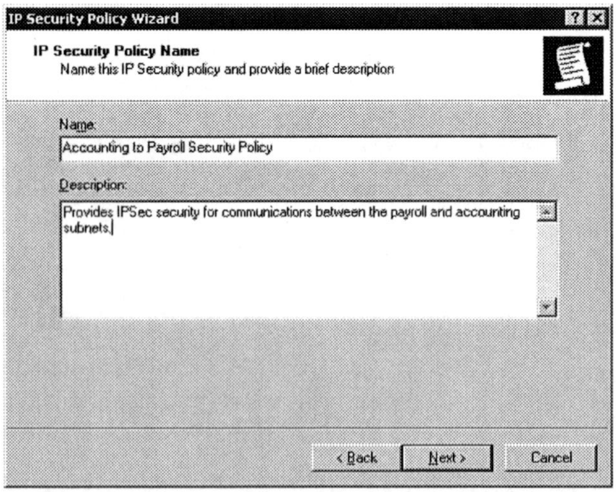

FIGURE 6.23 You should enter a policy name and description that will make sense later.

5. In the Requests for Secure Communication dialog box, shown in Figure 6.24, deselect Activate the Default Response Rule option. You will configure this policy entirely by yourself. Click Next to continue.

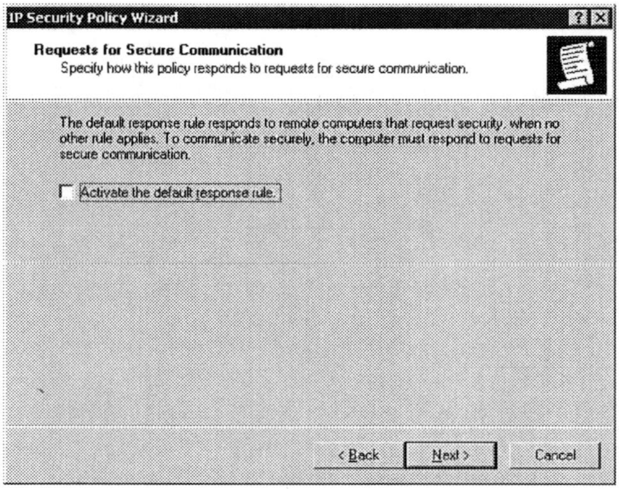

FIGURE 6.24 Removing the opportunity for unsecured communications to occur with the new rule.

6. You are now at the end of the wizard portion of the creation process. Ensure that the Edit Properties option is selected, as shown in Figure 6.25, and click Finish to begin editing the policy's properties.

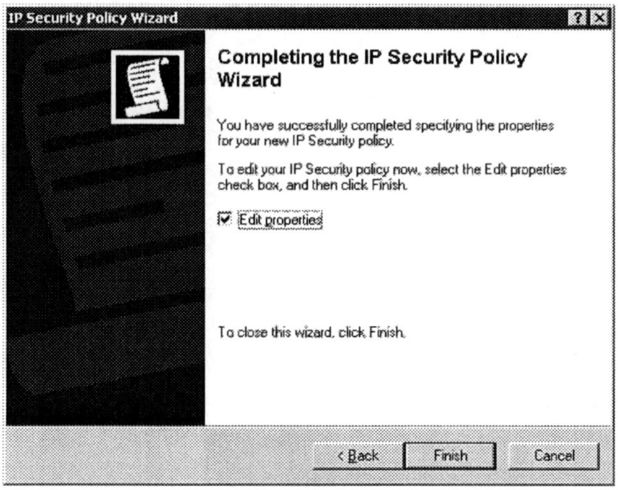

FIGURE 6.25 The completion of the wizard is not the completion of the policy-creation process.

7. The Accounting to Payroll Security Policy Properties dialog box opens, as shown in Figure 6.26.
8. On the Rules tab, ensure that the Use Add Wizard option is selected; then click the Add button to start the Security Rule Wizard to create a new filter list and action.
9. Click Next to dismiss the opening page of the Security Rule Wizard.
10. In the Tunnel Endpoint dialog box, shown in Figure 6.27, select This Rule Does Not Specify a Tunnel (recall that this IPSec policy is being created to secure communications between two subnets on the same intranet). Click Next to continue.

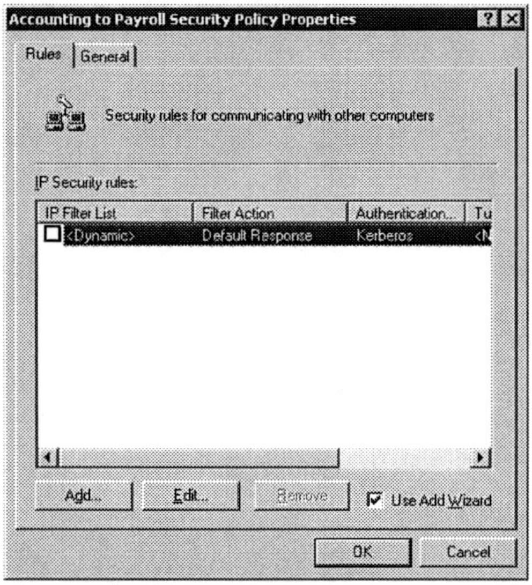

FIGURE 6.26 Your new IPSec policy requires some configuration to complete.

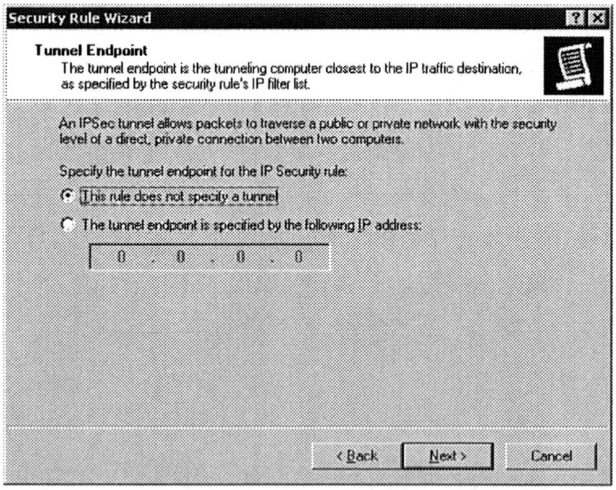

FIGURE 6.27 You can create a rule for either transport mode or tunnel mode.

11. In the Network Type dialog box, shown in Figure 6.28, select the network connections to which this rule applies. For this example, select All Network Connections and click Next to continue.
12. The IP Filter List dialog box, shown in Figure 6.29, shows that no IP filters are configured for this rule. Click the Add button to create a filter that meets your requirements.
13. From the IP Filter List dialog box, shown in Figure 6.30, you need to configure the IP filter properties for this rule. Enter a descriptive name such as **`Accounting to Payroll security`** in the name box and a description, if you like. Ensure that the Use Add Wizard option is selected, and click the Add button.

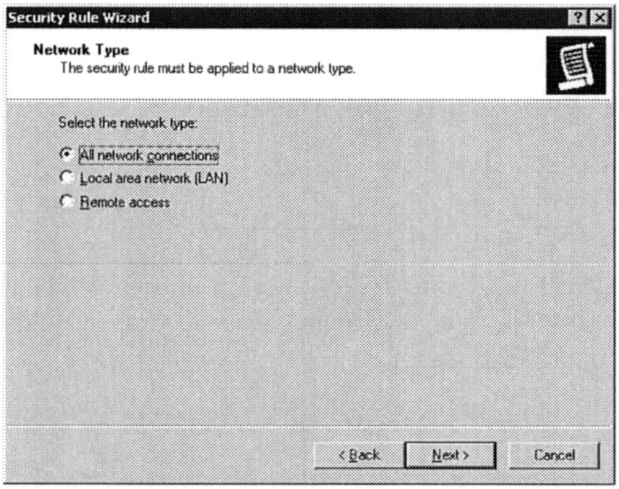

FIGURE 6.28 Selecting All Network Connections ensures that all communications by the server are secured using the new policy.

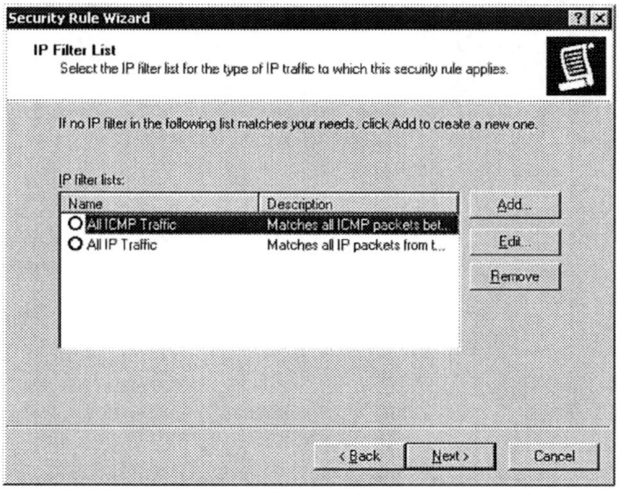

FIGURE 6.29 You must configure an IP filter for this rule to work properly.

14. The IP Filter Wizard opens to start the process of configuring the IP filter. Click Next to dismiss the opening page of the wizard.

15. In the IP Filter Description and Mirrored Property dialog box, shown in Figure 6.31, enter a description of the filter. Ensure that the Mirrored option is selected. This option allows the rule to automatically match packets with the exact opposite source and destination addresses to ensure that machines from the destination subnet are also included in the incoming filter. Click Next to continue.

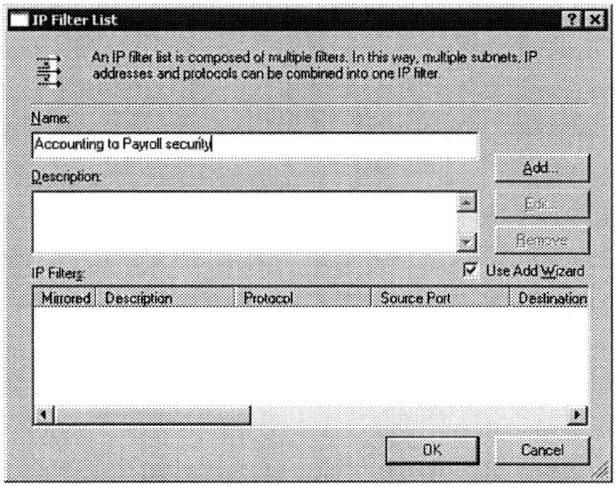

FIGURE 6.30 The process to configure an IP filter begins with the IP Filter List dialog box.

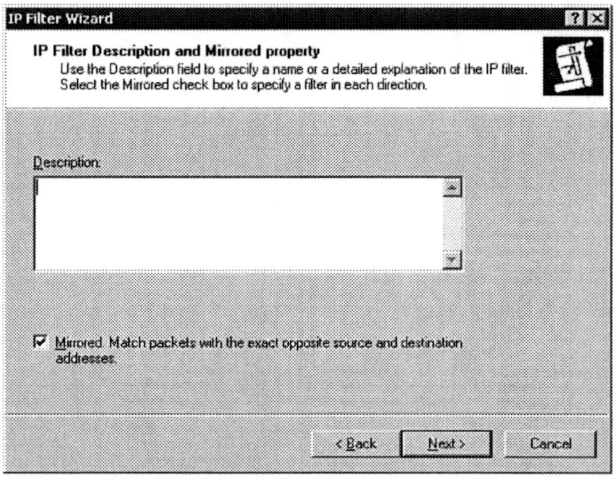

FIGURE 6.31 Allowing the IP filter to be mirrored saves you work.

16. In the IP Traffic Source dialog box, select the A Specific IP Subnet option and configure the IP address and subnet mask as required. Recall that we are creating a policy between the 192.168.11.0 and 192.168.12.0 subnets. Enter **`192.168.11.0`** and the subnet mask of **`255.255.255.0`**, as shown in Figure 6.32, and click Next to continue.

17. In the IP Traffic Destination dialog box, select the A Specific IP Subnet option and configure the IP address and subnet mask as required. Enter **`192.168.12.0`** and the subnet mask of **`255.255.255.0`**, as shown in Figure 6.33, and click Next to continue.

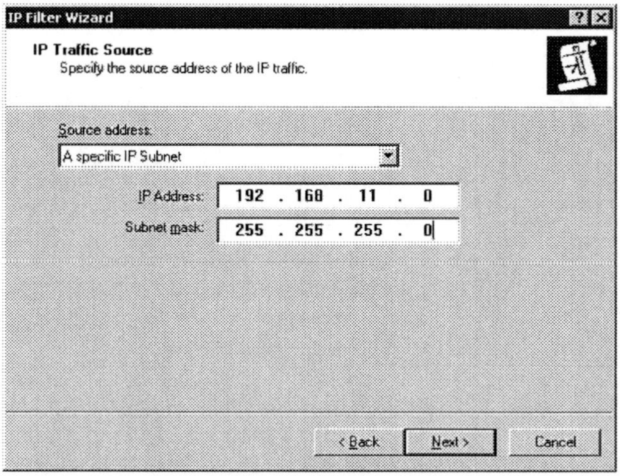

FIGURE 6.32 Be sure to specify the correct source address and subnet mask.

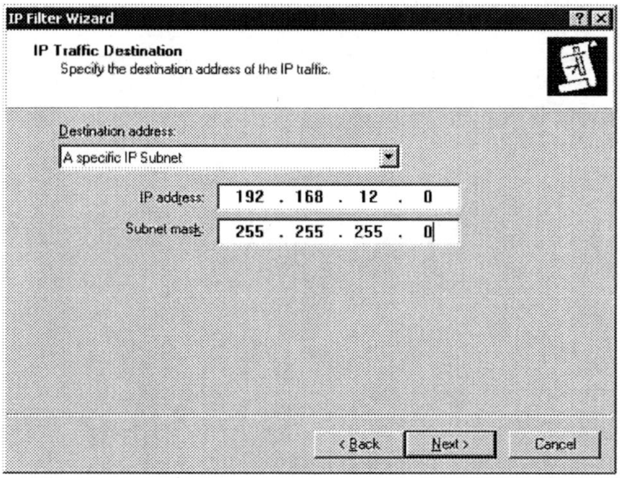

FIGURE 6.33 Be sure to specify the correct destination address and subnet mask also.

18. In the IP Protocol Type dialog box, shown in Figure 6.34, you can configure which IP protocol types you want to be included in the filter. We want the filter to apply to all types, so leave the default selection of Any and click Next to continue.

19. The Completing the IP Filter Wizard dialog box opens, as shown in Figure 6.35. Deselect the Edit Properties option and click Finish.

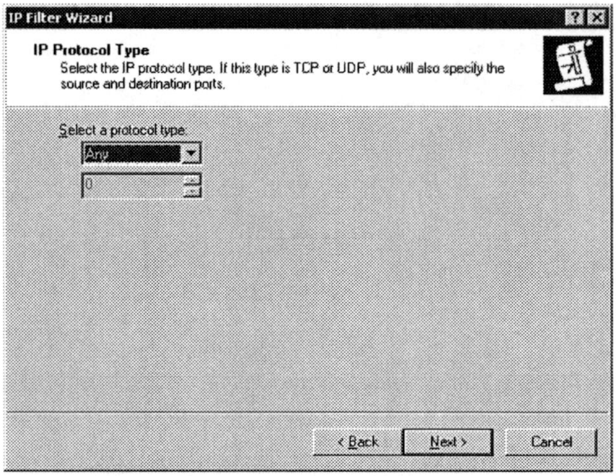

FIGURE 6.34 You can configure the filter to be very specific about what types of protocols it applies to.

FIGURE 6.35 The IP filter has been created, but much work still remains.

20. Back at the IP Filter List dialog box, shown in Figure 6.36, you can see your newly created IP filter. Click OK to close the filter and complete the creation process. If you click Cancel, your newly created filter will be lost, so be careful.

21. Select the Accounting to Payroll Security filter from the list in the IP Filter List dialog box, as shown in Figure 6.37, and click Next to continue with the Security Rule Wizard.

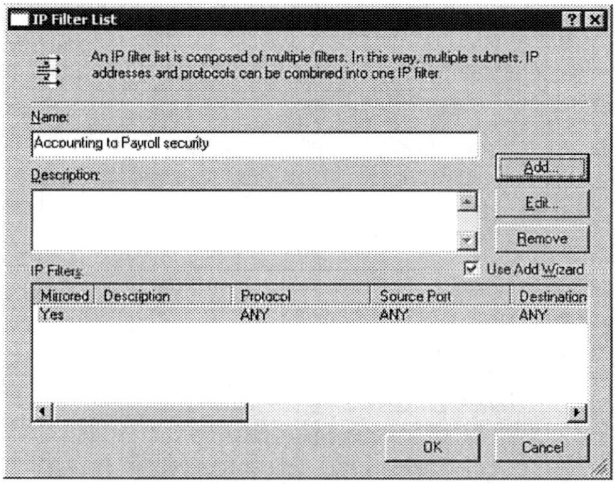

FIGURE 6.36 The new IP filter is listed on the IP Filter List dialog box.

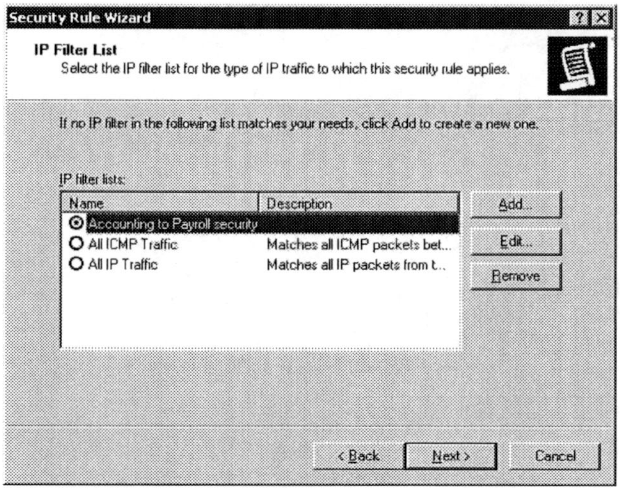

FIGURE 6.37 You need to select the filter for use after creating it.

22. In the Filter Action dialog box, shown in Figure 6.38, select a filter action. Ensure that the Use Add Wizard option is selected and click Add to start the Filter Action Wizard.
23. The Filter Action Wizard starts. Dismiss its opening dialog box by clicking Next.
24. In the Filter Action Name dialog box, enter a descriptive name and description for the filter. Click Next to continue.
25. In the Filter Action General Options dialog box, shown in Figure 6.39, select Negotiate Security and click Next to continue.

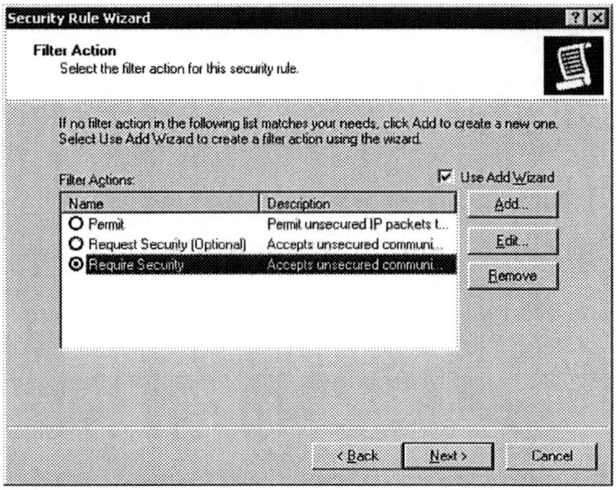

FIGURE 6.38 You now need to configure the action that the filter will take.

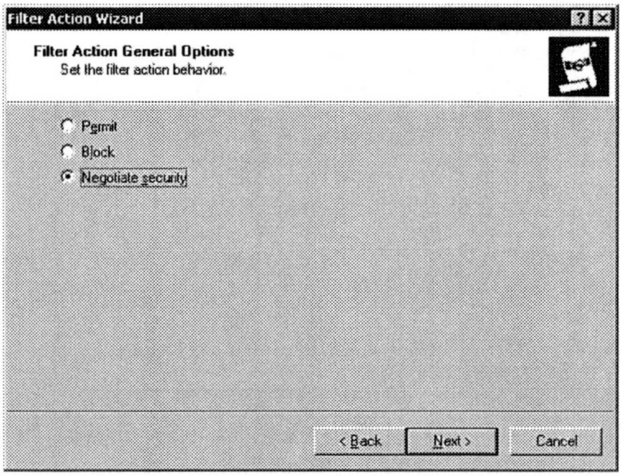

FIGURE 6.39 Instructing the filter action to negotiate security between communication computers.

26. In the Communicating with Computers That Do Not Support IPSec dialog box, shown in Figure 6.40, you are asked whether you want to allow unsecured communications. In this case, such communications are not allowed because all communications must be secured. Ensure that the Do Not Communicate with Computers That Do Not Support IPSec option is selected and click Next to continue.

27. In the IP Traffic Security dialog box, shown in Figure 6.41, select Custom to specify what security methods are to be used. Click Settings to edit the security settings.

28. The Custom Security Method Settings dialog box, shown in Figure 6.42, opens. From here, you can specify the settings you want. Ensure that both the AH and ESP check boxes are selected. Configure the desired integrity and encryption algorithms. Do not configure settings for the session key at this time. Click OK to accept your settings.

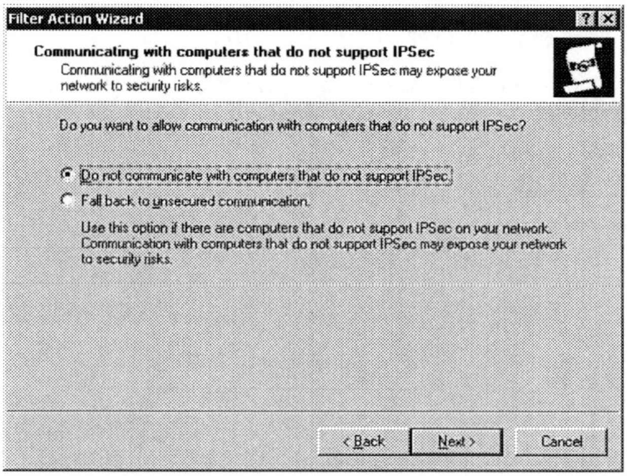

FIGURE 6.40 Ensure that you do not allow unsecured communications to occur.

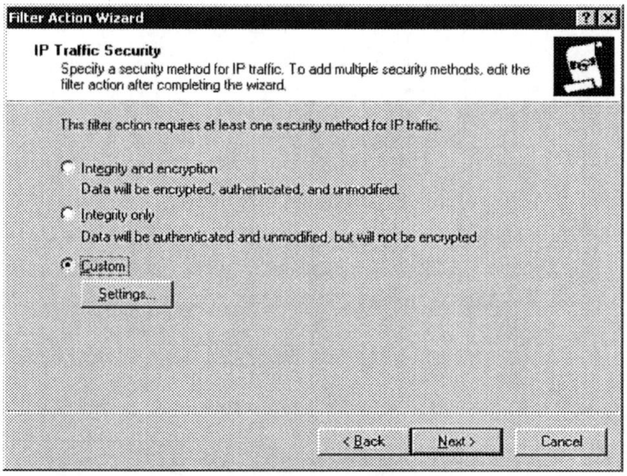

FIGURE 6.41 You can specify custom settings or use the standard settings provided.

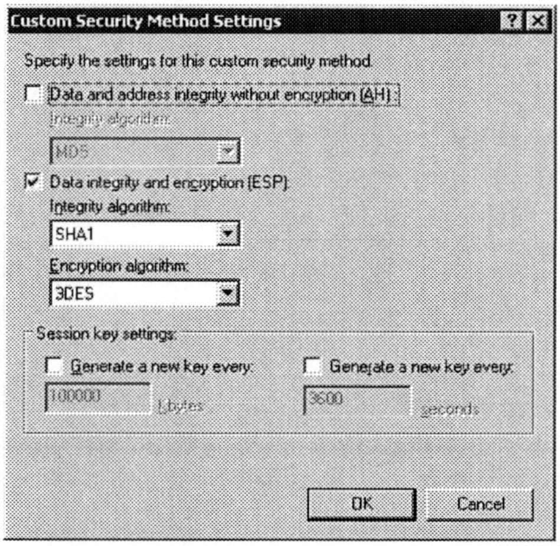

FIGURE 6.42 You can specify the encryption and integrity algorithms to be used in your filter action.

29. Back at the IP Traffic Security dialog box, click Next to continue.

30. In the Completing the IP Security Filter Action Wizard dialog box, shown in Figure 6.43, ensure that the Edit Properties option is selected and click Finish.

FIGURE 6.43 The Filter Action Wizard is completed, but the filter still requires a bit more configuration.

31. Back at the filter action Properties dialog box, shown in Figure 6.44, ensure that the Use Session Key Perfect Forward Secrecy (PFS) option is selected and click OK. Selecting session key PFS ensures that the master key keying material cannot be used to generate more than one session key, which adds both security and overhead to the connection. Do not click Cancel unless you want to scrap your newly configured filter action. Click OK.

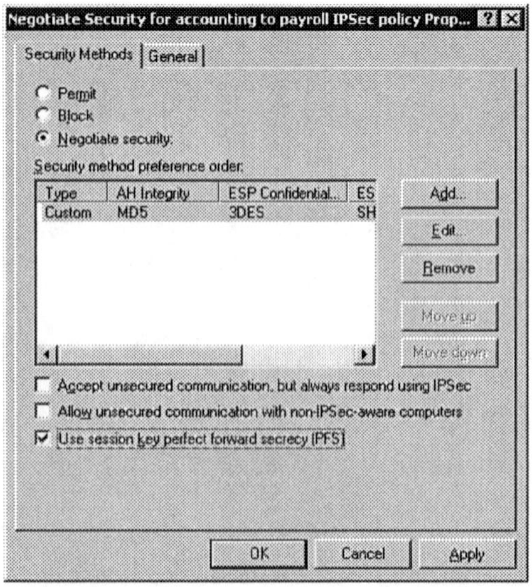

FIGURE 6.44 Selecting to use perfect forward secrecy to increase the security of the session key.

32. Back at the Filter Action dialog box, shown in Figure 6.45, select the newly created filter and click Next to continue.

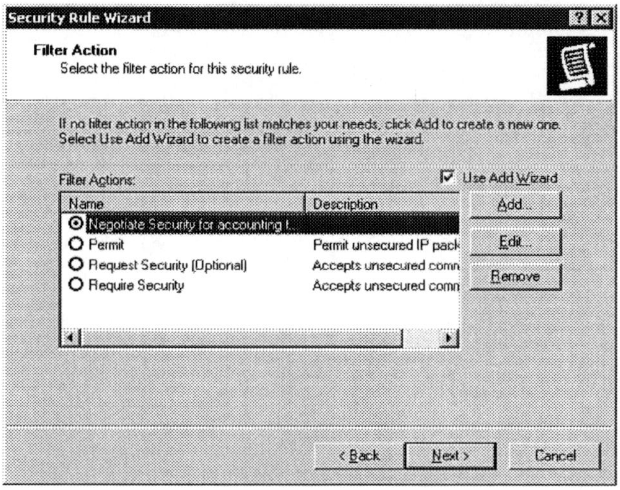

FIGURE 6.45 The filter action is configured, so it's time to move on.

33. In the Authentication Method dialog box, shown in Figure 6.46, select the primary authentication method this rule will use. The default selection of Kerberos v5 should be used in most cases. You can add authentication methods after the rule is configured. Click Next to continue.

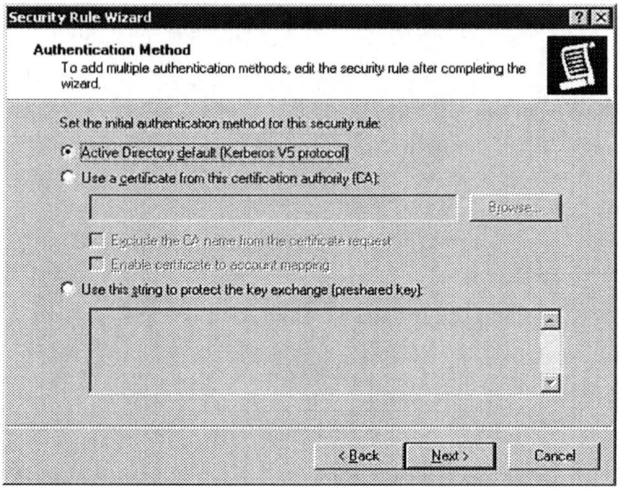

FIGURE 6.46 Specify the preferred authentication method; Kerberos v5 is preferred.

34. From the Completing the Security Rule Wizard dialog box, ensure that the Edit Properties option is deselected and click Finish to complete the rule-creation process.

35. Finally, you are back to the policy Properties dialog box. You still have some additional configuration that you can complete, however.

36. On the General tab, you can configure the interval at which the computer will check for updates and changes to the security policy, as shown in Figure 6.47. The default setting of 180 minutes is usually acceptable.

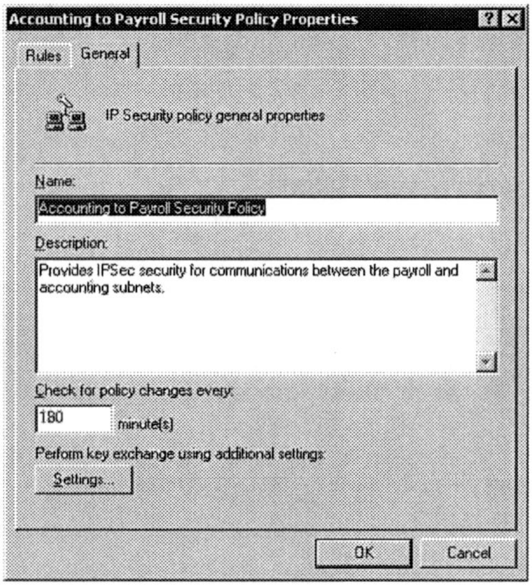

FIGURE 6.47 Configuring the policy update interval.

37. You can modify the settings used for the IKE process by clicking the Settings button at the bottom of the General tab.

38. In the Key Exchange Settings dialog box, shown in Figure 6.48, you can configure for master key perfect forward secrecy, which improves security of the keying process. Additionally, you can change the defaults provided for key generation.

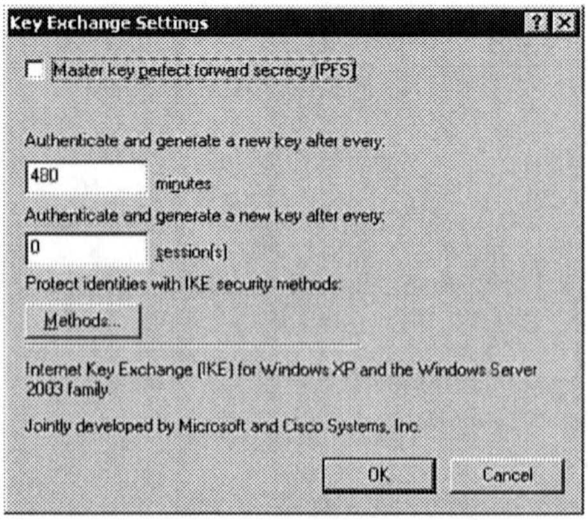

FIGURE 6.48 You can configure advanced IKE properties from the Key Exchange Settings dialog box.

39. If you want to configure the methods used to protect the identities, click the Methods button. The Key Exchange Security Methods dialog box opens, as shown in Figure 6.49. Note that, by default, the new 2,048-bit Diffie-Hellman key-exchange method is not used. You can select it by adding or editing a security method, as shown in Figure 6.50.

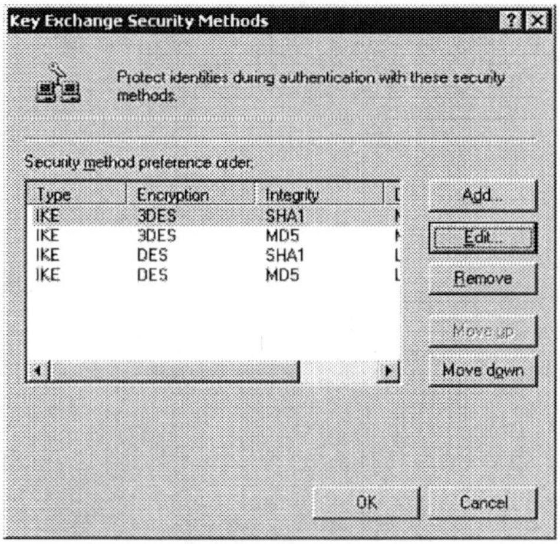

FIGURE 6.49 Customizing the key-exchange security methods can increase security.

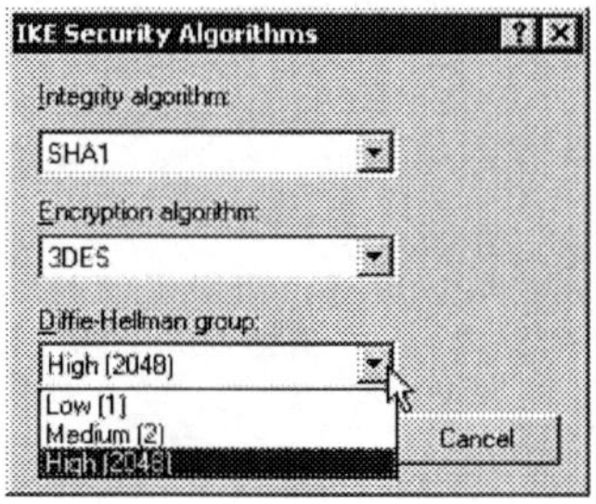

FIGURE 6.50 Using the new 2,048-bit Diffie-Hellman key-exchange method.

40. Click OK as required to return to the policy Properties dialog box.

41. Click OK to close the policy Properties dialog box. Your new IPSec policy is now configured and ready to use. Assign it as previously discussed at the end of the "Configuring and Implementing IPSec" section of this chapter.

IPSec can be deployed at any level within your organization. Thus far, we have examined it only from the point of view of a local computer. You can just as easily apply it via Group Policy using the Active Directory Users and Computers console, as shown in Figure 6.51.

With the task of implementing IPSec out of the way, you are now left to monitor and troubleshoot it, as we examine in the next section.

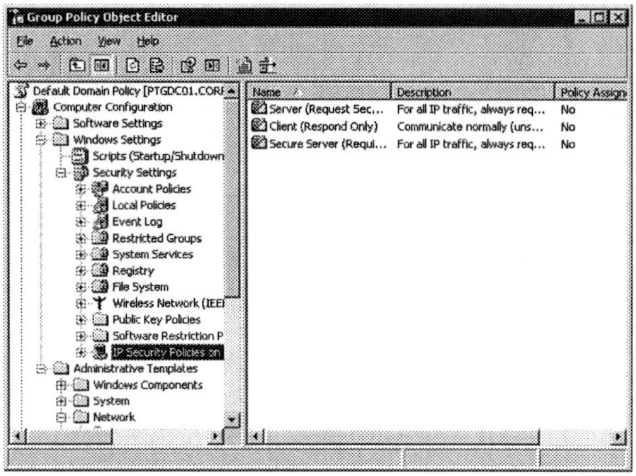

FIGURE 6.51 You can easily apply IPSec at the domain or OU level using Group Policy.

Challenge

You are the system and network administrator of Axioms Publishing, a small publishing company. The company is located in a single building in Memphis, Tennessee, with each department on its own IP subnet. From time to time, the marketing and sales departments need to share confidential information about forthcoming books and promotions. This information needs to be protected from other users accessing it while in transit across the network.

The information is question is stored on two different servers, a database server and a file server, both of which are running on Windows Server 2003. These two servers perform no other function but to store and serve up this confidential information. The servers are patched with the latest Service Pack and security updates, and have been hardened to disable unneeded services. These servers are located on a separate IP subnet all by themselves and are physically secured inside the company's data center. The servers are also located in their own OU, named Confidential Servers, within Active Directory.

The workstations that the marketing and sales department use to access these servers, however, are not special purpose and are used by their users for day-to-day tasks, such as email, browsing the Internet, and accessing files and databases on other servers in your network. All marketing and sales department workstations are located in their own OUs, named Marketing Computers and Sales Computers, respectively.

The CIO has asked you to ensure that these confidential resources can be securely accessed only by users in the sales and marketing departments. All other users in the company must not be able to connect to either of these servers.

Your task is to implement the required IPSec solution for Axioms Publishing.

Try to complete this exercise on your own, listing your conclusions on a sheet of paper. When you have completed the exercise, compare your results to those given here.

(continues)

(continued)

When you're implementing a very specific IPSec solution, as this scenario calls for, you want to first ensure that you understand the requirements and the scope for the solution. Because you've already got a good network and OU structure in place, you can simply build off that to implement your solution.

At first, you might be tempted to create and assign custom IPSec policies that secure all traffic between these networks. If the workstations the marketing and sales departments use had no other communications than with the subnet the servers were located on, you could rightfully do just that. However, because the workstations are general-purpose computers and need to communicate securely (via IPSec) only when they are accessing the two servers in question, a different approach is required.

You should first create and link a new Group Policy Object (GPO) to the Marketing Computers OU. In this new GPO, you should assign the Client (Respond Only) IPSec policy. This causes all computers in the OU to attempt unsecured communications first and switch to IPSec-secured communications if requested, as will be the case when the servers require IPSec-secure communications. You should next link this GPO to the Sales Computers OU as well, thus making sure that those computers will behave the same way in regard to IPSec usage.

The next task for you to perform is to create and link a new GPO to the Confidential Servers OU. In this new GPO, you should assign the Secure Server (Require Security) policy. This requires that all communications to and from the server are IPSec secured.

When these new Group Policy Objects are in place, you should start to see SAs forming and secure communications occurring between the servers and the workstations. The workstations should also be capable of successfully communicating to non-IPSec-secured computers and servers, both inside and outside your network.

Monitoring and Troubleshooting Network Protocol Security

Objective:

Troubleshoot security for data transmission. Tools might include the IP Security Monitor MMC snap-in and the Resultant Set of Policy (RSoP) MMC snap-in.

With the discussion of creating and implementing IPSec policies behind us, although at a rather simple level, it's time to move on and examine the monitoring and troubleshooting of IPSec on your network. In addition, Kerberos is the default user-authentication protocol in Windows Server 2003, and you will from time to time need to monitor and troubleshoot Kerberos as well.

EXAM ALERT

Know your IPSec! For this exam, even though the objectives don't really lend themselves to it, you must have a solid understanding of IPSec, the three default IPSec policies, and basic IPSec policy components. Be sure you understand the background of IPSec before you take this exam.

Monitoring IPSec

Going back to the customized IPSec management console that you created earlier in Step by Step 6.1, let's spend some time now with the IP Security Monitor snap-in, which is divided into three major areas: the Active Policy node, the Main Mode node, and the Quick Mode node. Figure 6.52 shows the Active Policy node. Table 6.1 explains each of the information items shown in the Active Policy node of the IP Security Monitor snap-in.

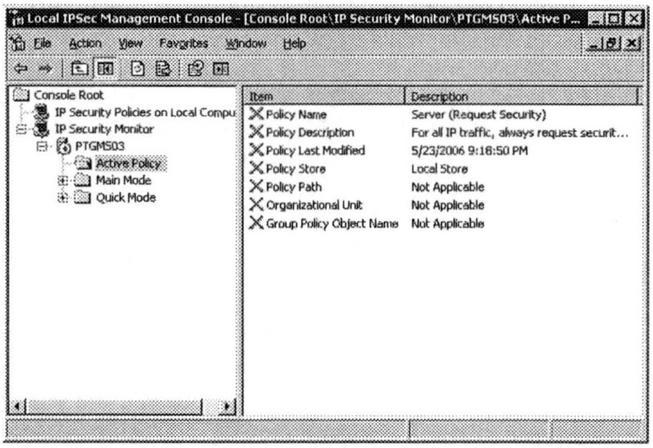

FIGURE 6.52 The Active Policy node statistics get you up to speed quickly on the currently assigned IPSec policy.

EXAM ALERT

Know the IPSec monitoring areas For this exam, make sure that you have a good understanding of what types of information you can find in each node of the IP Security Monitor.

TABLE 6.1 Active Policy Node Items

Item	Description
Policy Name	Specifies the name of the active IPSec policy.
Description	Describes the active IPSec policy.
Policy Last Modified	Provides the date and the time that the active IPSec policy was modified.
Policy Store	Provides the storage location for the active IPSec policy. For a local policy, it reads Local Store, and for a domain policy, it reads Domain Store.
Policy Path	Applies only to domain policies and provides the LDAP path to the active IPSec policy.
Organizational Unit	Applies only to domain policies and lists the organizational unit to which the GPO is applied.
Group Policy Object Name	Applies only to domain policies and lists the GPO to which the active IPSec policy is applied.

The Statistics folder in the Main Mode node, shown in Figure 6.53, provides information about the Phase I security associations (SAs), as detailed in Table 6.2. The remaining Main Mode folders all provide specific information about the IPSec policy currently in effect and thus will be empty when no policy is in effect.

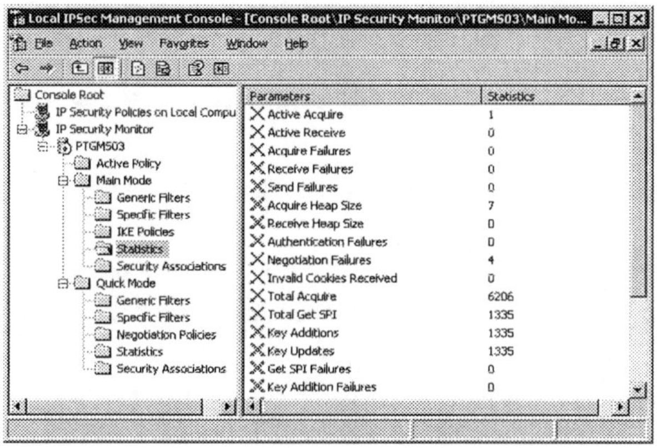

FIGURE 6.53 The Main Mode node Statistics folder displays information about the Phase I SAs.

TABLE 6.2 Main Mode (Internet Key Exchange) Statistics

Statistic	Description
Active Acquire	Specifies a request by the IPSec policy to have IKE perform a task. This number includes all outstanding and queued requests and is typically 1. Under heavy loading, this number increases.
Active Receive	Displays the number of IKE messages that have been received and are queued for processing.
Acquire Failures	Displays the number of times that an acquire has failed.
Receive Failures	Displays the number of times that errors have occurred in receiving IKE messages.
Send Failures	Displays the number of times that errors have occurred in sending IKE messages.
Acquire Heap Size	Displays the number of entries in the acquire heap, which stores active acquires. This number increases with heavy loading and decreases as the heap is cleared.
Receive Heap Size	Displays the number of entries in the IKE receive buffers for incoming IKE messages.
Authentication Failures	Displays the total number of identity authentication failures that have occurred during Main mode negotiation. This is a very useful indicator to determine whether the authentication methods match between two computers attempting communications.
Negotiation Failures	Displays the total number of negotiation failures that occurred during Main mode or Quick mode negotiation. This is a useful statistic to determine whether security and/or authentication methods match between two computers attempting communications.

(continues)

TABLE 6.2 *Continued*

Statistic	Description
Invalid Cookies Received	Specifies a value contained in a received IKE message that IKE uses to find the state of an active Main mode. If a cookie in a received IKE message cannot be matched with an active Main mode, it is invalid.
Total Acquire	Displays the total number of requests submitted by IKE to the IPSec driver to establish an SA for securing traffic.
Total Get SPI	Displays the total number of requests submitted by IKE to the IPSec driver to obtain a unique Security Parameters Index (SPI).
Key Additions	Displays the number of outbound Quick mode SAs that IKE adds to the IPSec driver.
Key Updates	Displays the number of inbound Quick mode SAs that IKE adds to the IPSec driver.
Get SPI Failures	Displays the number of failed requests that IKE has submitted to the IPSec driver to obtain a unique SPI.
Key Addition Failures	Displays the failed number of outbound Quick mode SA addition requests that IKE submitted to the IPSec driver.
Key Update Failures	Displays the failed number of inbound Quick mode SA addition requests that IKE submitted to the IPSec driver.
ISADB List Size	Displays the number of Main mode state entries, including negotiated Main modes, Main modes in progress, and Main modes that have failed and have not yet been deleted.
Connection List Size	Displays the number of Quick mode state entries. This number indicates the load placed on the computer.
IKE Main Mode	Displays the total number of successful SAs created during Main mode negotiations.
IKE Quick Mode	Displays the total number of successful SAs created during Quick mode negotiations. There are typically multiple Quick mode SAs created for each Main mode SA; thus, this value might not necessarily match that of the Main mode.
Soft Associations	Displays the total number of negotiations that resulted in the use of unsecured traffic (also known as *soft SAs*). Typically, this is an indication of SAs formed with computers that do not support IPSec or were not capable of negotiating successful IPSec connections. This can be an indication of mismatched security and authentication settings.
Invalid Packets Received	Displays the number of received IKE messages that were invalid. Most commonly, invalid IKE messages are a result of retransmitted IKE messages or unmatched shared keys between the communicating computers.

The Statistics folder in the Quick Mode node, shown in Figure 6.54, provides information about the Phase II SAs, as detailed in Table 6.3. The remaining Quick Mode folders all provide specific information about the IPSec policy currently in effect and thus are empty when no policy is in effect.

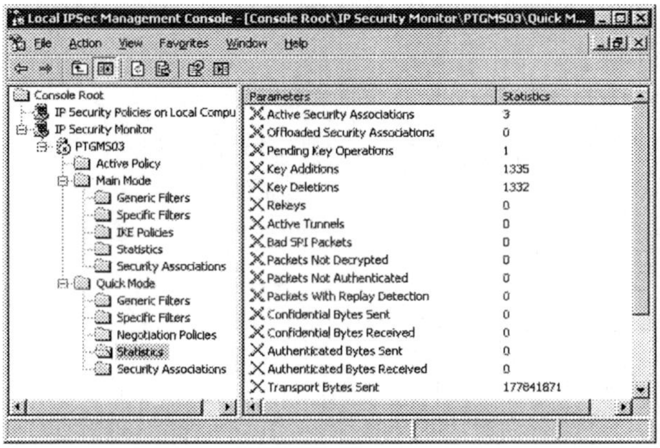

FIGURE 6.54 The Quick Mode node Statistics folder displays information about the Phase II SAs.

TABLE 6.3 Quick Mode (IPSec) Statistics

Statistic	Description
Active Security Associations	Displays the number of active IPSec SAs.
Offloaded Security Associations	Displays the number of active IPSec SAs that have been offloaded to hardware.
Pending Key Operations	Displays the number of IPSec key operations that are in progress.
Key Additions	Displays the total number of successful IPSec SA negotiations.
Key Deletions	Displays the number of key deletions for IPSec SAs.
Rekeys	Displays the number of rekey operations for IPSec SAs.
Active Tunnels	Displays the number of active IPSec tunnels.
Bad SPI Packets	Displays the total number of packets for which the SPI was incorrect. SPIs are used to match inbound packets with SAs. If the SPI is incorrect, the inbound SA might have expired. If rekeying intervals are set very short, this number is likely to increase very rapidly. Under normal conditions, a bad SPI packet does not mean that IPSec is failing because SAs expire normally.
Packets Not Decrypted	Displays the total number of packets that were not decrypted successfully. This might indicate that a packet has arrived for which the SA has previously expired. When the SA expires, the session key used to decrypt packets is removed. By itself, this does not indicate that IPSec is failing.
Packets Not Authenticated	Displays the total number of packets for which data could not be verified, meaning that the integrity hash verification failed. Most commonly, this is a result of an expired SA.
Packets with Replay Detection	Displays the total number of packets that contained a valid Sequence Number field.
Confidential Bytes Sent	Displays the total number of bytes sent using the ESP.
Confidential Bytes Received	Displays the total number of bytes received using the ESP.

(continues)

TABLE 6.3 *Continued*

Statistic	Description
Authenticated Bytes Sent	Displays the total number of bytes sent using the AH protocol.
Authenticated Bytes Received	Displays the total number of bytes received using the AH protocol.
Transport Bytes Sent	Displays the total number of bytes sent using IPSec transport mode.
Transport Bytes Received	Displays the total number of bytes received using IPSec transport mode.
Bytes Sent in Tunnels	Displays the total number of bytes sent using IPSec tunnel mode.
Bytes Received in Tunnels	Displays the total number of bytes received using IPSec tunnel mode.
Offloaded Bytes Sent	Displays the total number of bytes sent using hardware offload.
Offloaded Bytes Received	Displays the total number of bytes received using hardware offload.

Configuring the IP Security Monitor hasn't changed much since Windows 2000, except that the IP Security Monitor is now an MMC snap-in. You can open the IP Security Monitor properties for any server listed in the IP Security Monitor node by right-clicking it and selecting Properties from the context menu. The server Properties page opens, as shown in Figure 6.55. You have the option to change the refresh interval for the display of the IP Security Monitor statistics and to decide whether you want to enable DNS name resolution, which comes into play when you're examining the SAs that are formed.

EXAM ALERT

ipsecmon Don't forget that you can no longer start ipsecmon from the command line. ipsecmon is now available only via the MMC.

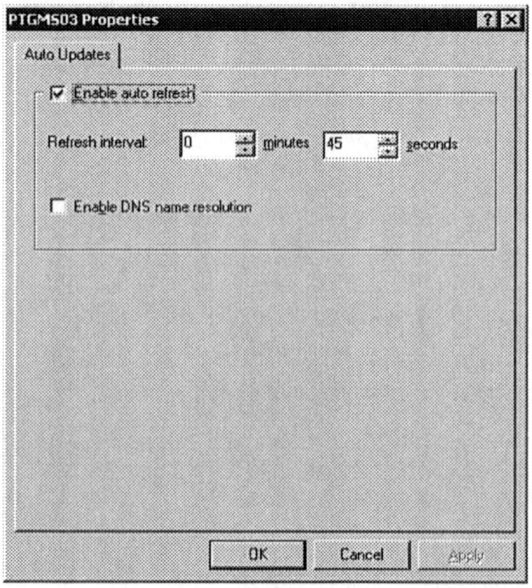

FIGURE 6.55 There's not much to configure for the IP Security Monitor's properties.

The Resultant Set of Policy (RSoP) MMC Snap-In

The Resultant Set of Policy (RSoP) snap-in can be added to a blank or custom MMC to provide a means for you to create queries that poll Group Policy at all levels and then report the results of the query. RSoP gathers this information from the Common Information Management Object Model (CIMOM) database (otherwise known as CIM-compliant object repository) through Windows Management Instrumentation (WMI).

Often when policies are applied on multiple levels, results can conflict. Using the RSoP snap-in can easily help you to determine where the problem lies and the precedence (processing order) of the policies involved. RSoP can be used in one of two modes:

- **Planning mode**—Enables you to simulate the effect of policy settings that you want to apply to a computer and user
- **Logging mode**—Enables you to determine the existing policy settings for a computer and user who is currently logged on

RSoP can be added to an MMC using the same basic process as discussed in Step by Step 6.1. After you have created the custom MMC, right-click the Resultant Set of Policy object and select Generate RSoP Data to start the Resultant Set of Policy Wizard. Run the query in logging mode by following the wizard through the required steps. When you are done running the query, you can examine the results, specifically for the IPSec policies.

General IPSec Troubleshooting

If you have problems with IPSec, you should first verify that any routers or firewalls that traffic might be passing through are configured to support IPSec traffic. You need to allow the following traffic:

- Protocol ID 50 and 51 or ESP and AH traffic
- UDP port 500 for IPSec-negotiation traffic

Some other basic problems and troubleshooting tips for them are outlined here:

- **You cannot establish any communications with a computer**—In this case, you should first verify that basic network connectivity exists between the computers in question by using the `ping` command. You should also ensure that all required network services, such as DHCP and DNS, are operating properly for both computers.
- **You cannot establish any communications with a computer**—This can result if a computer has been removed from the domain. Whatever the cause, it causes IPSec communications to fail.

- **Communications are occurring, but not as expected**—You need to ensure that you have the correct (and compatible) IPSec policies assigned on both computers.
- **No hard associations are being formed**—If there are currently soft associations in place, a hard association will not be formed. You need to completely stop all communications between the computers for approximately 5–10 minutes to allow the soft associations to time out. The easiest way to do this is to disable the network connection. After you have allowed the soft association to time out, you should check to see that a hard association has been formed. If a hard association still has not been formed, you need to examine the IPSec policy to verify that unsecured communications are not allowed.
- **IPSec communications are failing after you configure a digital certificate for authentication**—You must make sure that the required digital certificate is installed on the computers that are attempting to communicate by using that IPSec policy. This can also be a result of specifying an incorrect Certificate Authority (CA).
- **Some computers can create IPSec connections and some cannot**—This is most likely caused by not having the same IPSec policy applied to all the computers. If you are intentionally using different policies, you need to ensure that they share at least one common authentication and security method.

You should also be aware that IPSec-related problems can be found in the security log. You can view IKE events (negotiation success and failure) by enabling success and/or failure auditing for the Audit Logon Events audit policy for the domain or the local computer. The IKE event category is also used for the auditing of user logon events in other services as well, but you can disable this by editing the registry. For more information on configuring and implementing auditing, refer to Chapter 5.

When success and/or failure auditing for the Audit Logon Events audit policy is enabled, IPSec records the success and/or failure of each Main mode and Quick mode negotiation. The establishment and termination of each negotiation are logged as separate events for easier analysis and troubleshooting. Be aware, however, that when you enable audit logon events, the security log will likely quickly fill up with IKE events unless you opt to disable auditing of those events through Registry editing.

The Network Monitor included in Windows Server 2003 can also be used to view IPSec traffic between the computer it is installed on and other network computers. Network Monitor includes parsers for the ISAKMP (IKE), AH, and ESP protocols. The parsers for ESP can parse inside the ESP packet only if null encryption is being used and the full ESP packet is captured. Network Monitor cannot parse the encrypted portions of IPSec-secured ESP traffic when the encryption is being performed in Windows; however, if the encryption is being performed by an IPSec hardware offload network adapter, the ESP packets have already been decrypted when

Network Monitor captures them, and as a result, they can be parsed and interpreted into the upper-layer protocols. If you need to diagnose ESP Windows-encrypted communication (that is, software-encrypted communication), you must first disable ESP encryption and use ESP null encryption by changing the IPSec policy on each computer.

Monitoring and Troubleshooting Kerberos

Kerberos seems to pop up all over the place in Windows Server 2003. Kerberos is the default network authentication method for Windows Server 2003 networks. It can also be used as an IPSec authentication method. Although Kerberos is often thought of as a "set it and forget it" service, you might from time to time need to monitor and troubleshoot it.

Although no default tools are provided in Windows Server 2003 that enable you to monitor and manipulate Kerberos tickets, two *Windows Server 2003 Resource Kit* tools are available that you can use:

- **`kerbtray.exe`**—You can use the `kerbtray.exe` utility to view cached Kerberos tickets for the current computer from within the Windows GUI.
- **`klist.exe`**—The `klist.exe` utility is a command-line tool that is similar to `kerbtray.exe`. `klist.exe` enables you to view and delete cached Kerberos tickets.

You can download the *Resource Kit* tools from the Microsoft website, at www.microsoft.com/downloads, by searching for "Windows Server 2003 Resource Kit Tools."

The following sections examine the function and usage of these two tools.

kerbtray.exe

This `kerbtray.exe` tool is used to display the cached ticket information for a computer running the Microsoft implementation of the Kerberos version 5 protocol. After `kerbtray.exe` has been installed and executed, it sits (appropriately enough) in the tray area of the taskbar, as shown in Figure 6.56.

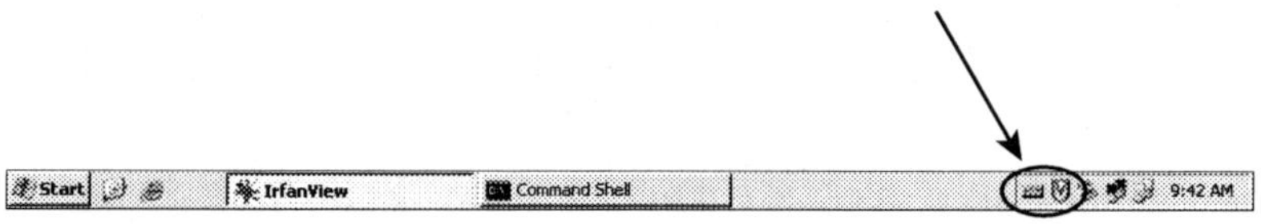

FIGURE 6.56 The `kerbtray.exe` icon waits in the tray area of the taskbar.

By moving the cursor over the `kerbtray.exe` icon, you can quickly see a display that lets you know how much time is left before the ticket-granting ticket (TGT) expires. In addition, this icon changes during the last hour before the local security authority (LSA) renews the ticket.

When you double-click the `kerbtray.exe` icon, the Kerberos Tickets dialog box opens, as shown in Figure 6.57, enabling you to quickly determine the cached ticket status.

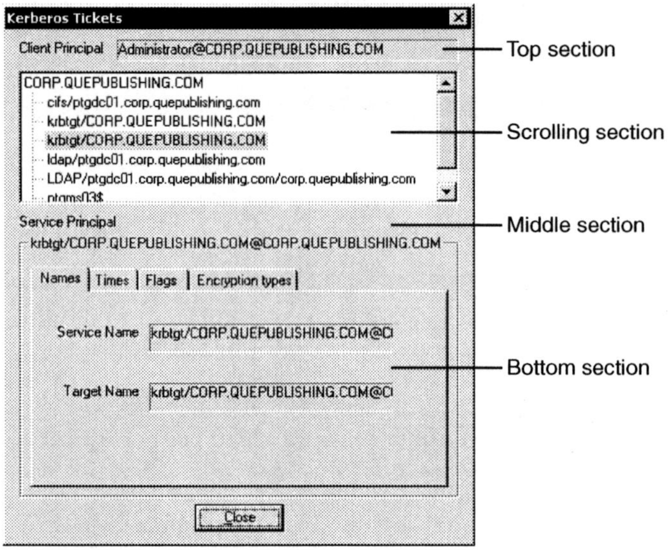

FIGURE 6.57 The Kerberos Tickets dialog box enables you to graphically view cached Kerberos tickets for the local computer.

The Kerberos Tickets dialog box consists of four informational areas:

- **Top section**—The top section provides the name of the Kerberos client principal that is associated with the Windows domain account.
- **Scrolling section**—The scrolling section lists the domains and tickets for all services that have been used since the user logon occurred. Selecting an item here causes its properties to display in the middle and bottom sections.
- **Middle section**—The middle section displays the service principal—the target principal for the selected ticket from the domain list.
- **Bottom section**—The bottom section provides a set of tabs (Names, Times, Flags, and Encryption Types) that provide attributes of the selected ticket in the scrolling section.

Table 6.4 details the information that you see on the tabs of the bottom section of the Kerberos Tickets dialog box.

TABLE 6.4 Options on the Kerberos Tickets Dialog Box Bottom Section Tabs

Option	Description
Names Tab	
Client Name	This is the requester of the ticket, which, in most cases, is the client's principal name.
Service Name	This is the canonical name of the account principal for the service, which is the same as the `samAccountName` property in the directory.
Target Name	This is the service name that the ticket was requested for.
Times Tab	
Start Time	This is the time that the ticket becomes valid.
End Time	This is the time when the ticket's validity ends.
Renew Until	This specifies the maximum lifetime of the ticket, if it is renewable.
Flags Tab	
Forwardable	When this option is set, it allows for authentication forwarding without requiring the user to enter a password again.
Forwarded	The ticket-granting service (TGS) sets this flag when a client presents a ticket with the Forwardable flag set and requests that it be set by specifying the Forwarded (KDC) option and supplying a set of addresses for the new ticket.
Proxiable	When this option is set, it allows a client to pass a proxy to a server to perform a remote request on its behalf.
Proxy	The TGS sets this flag on a ticket when the service issues a proxy ticket.
May Postdate	This flag can be set in a TGT to issue a postdated ticket based on the presented ticket.
Postdated	When this option is set, it indicates that a ticket has been postdated.
Invalid	When this option is set, it indicates that the ticket is not valid. For example, a post-dated ticket is typically issued in this form.
Initial	When this option is set, it indicates that the ticket was issued by using the authentication server AS protocol and was not issued based on a TGT.
Renewable	When this option is set, it allows the ticket holder to maintain a valid ticket for long periods of time.
HW Authenticated	This flag is used to provide additional information about the initial authentication, regardless of whether the current ticket was issued directly.
Preauthenticated	This flag is used to provide additional information about the initial authentication, regardless of whether the current ticket was issued directly.
OK as Delegate	When this option is set, it indicates that the server specified in the ticket has been determined by policy to be a suitable recipient of delegation.
Encryption Types Tab	
Ticket Encryption Type	This option specifies the encryption type that is used to encrypt the Kerberos ticket.
Key Encryption Type	This option specifies the encryption type that is used with the enclosed session key.

klist.exe

The `klist.exe` tool is run from the command line and provides similar functionality to that offered by `kerbtray.exe`. In addition, `klist.exe` enables you to purge cached tickets, if desired. The basic syntax of the `klist.exe` command is shown here:

```
klist [tickets | tgt | purge]
```

Table 6.5 details the functions of the `klist.exe` options.

TABLE 6.5 `klist.exe` Switches

Option	Description
`tickets`	The `tickets` option lists information about the current cached tickets of services that you have authenticated to since logging on.
`tgt`	The `tgt` option lists information about the initial Kerberos TGT.
`purge`	The `purge` option enables you to delete a specific ticket.

Table 6.6 explains the `tickets` and `tgt` switches in more detail.

CAUTION

Purging tickets When you purge a ticket, you destroy all tickets that have been cached. You should do this with extreme caution. Purging tickets often prevents you from being able to successfully authenticate to network resources. If this occurs, you need to log off and log on again to obtain new tickets—and this can be disastrous if you have files open for editing across the network.

TABLE 6.6 The `klist.exe tickets` and `tgt` Switches

Switch	Description
The `tickets` Switch	
`Server`	Lists the server and domain for the ticket.
`KerbTicket Encryption Type`	Lists the encryption type used to encrypt the Kerberos ticket.
`End Time`	Lists the time that the ticket becomes invalid.
`Renew Time`	Lists the maximum lifetime of the ticket, if it is renewable.
The `tgt` Switch	
`ServiceName`	Displays the service name for the TGT, which is `krbtgt`.
`TargetName`	Displays the name of the service for which the ticket was requested.
`FullServiceName`	Displays the canonical name of the account principal for the service.
`DomainName`	Displays the domain name of the service.
`TargetDomainName`	Displays the realm (domain) in which the ticket is good if the ticket is a cross-realm ticket.

TABLE 6.6 *Continued*

Switch	Description
The `tgt` Switch	
`AltTargetDomainName`	Displays the name supplied to the `InitializeSecurityContext` that generated the ticket—which is typically a service principal name.
`TicketFlags`	Displays the ticket flags set on the current ticket in hexadecimal. The `kerbtray.exe` tool displays these flags on the Flags tab.
`KeyExpirationTime`	Displays the expiration time from the KDC reply.
`Start time`	Displays the time when the ticket becomes valid.
`End Time`	Displays the time when the ticket becomes invalid.
`RenewUntil`	Displays the maximum lifetime of the ticket, if the ticket is renewable.
`TimeSkew`	Displays the reported time difference between the client computer and the server computer for a ticket.

The `klist.exe` tool can be used to monitor and troubleshoot Kerberos from the command line. Figure 6.58 presents an example of what the `klist tickets` command might return.

FIGURE 6.58 The `klist tickets` command displays information about all cached Kerberos tickets for the computer.

Chapter Summary

IPSec can be used to secure communications both on your intranet and between endpoints over the Internet. VPNs can be created using IPSec and L2TP to ensure authenticity, integrity, and confidentiality of data in transit. The IPSec implementation in Windows Server 2003 has received several improvements since Windows 2000, most notably the capability to pass through NAT devices. Also, the Diffie-Hellman key exchange has been increased to a maximum of 2048 bits to further increase the security of the secret key.

Key Terms

- Extensible Authentication Protocol (EAP)
- Internet Key Exchange (IKE)
- IPSec
- `kerbtray.exe`
- `klist.exe`
- Main mode
- MMC
- Packet
- Quick mode
- Transport mode
- Tunnel mode

Apply Your Knowledge

In this chapter, you have examined the basic planning, implementation, and troubleshooting of IPSec in Windows Server 2003. In the following exercises, you practice some of the concepts and methods discussed in this chapter.

Exercises

6.1 Creating an IPSec Management Console

In this exercise, you create a customized MMC console that can be used to implement, monitor, and troubleshoot IPSec.

Estimated time: 10 minutes

1. Open a blank MMC by clicking Start, Run. Then type **`mmc`** to open a blank MMC.
2. In your new console, click the File menu and select Add/Remove Snap-in. The Add/Remove Snap-in dialog box opens.
3. Click the Add button to open the Add Standalone Snap-in dialog box.
4. Scroll down the list, select IP Security Monitor, and click the Add button.
5. Select IP Security Policy Management and click the Add button. You are prompted to choose the scope that the snap-in will manage.
6. For this example, choose Local Computer from the Select Computer or Domain page. Notice that you have the option to select the Active Directory domain that this computer is part of, another Active Directory domain, or another computer. Click Finish to complete the addition of the IP Security Policy Management snap-in to your console.
7. Click Close on the Add Standalone Snap-in dialog box.
8. Click OK on the Add/Remove Snap-in dialog box. Your completed IPSec management console is shown.
9. Save your newly created console by clicking File, Save. Enter a suitable name, such as **`IPSec Management Console`**, and click Save. By default, the console is saved in the Administrative Tools folder of the currently logged-in user.

6.2 Examining Kerberos Ticket Information

In this exercise, you download, install, and use the `kerbtray.exe` utility to examine the Kerberos tickets in effect on your server.

Estimated time: 20 minutes

1. Go the Microsoft Downloads website, at www.microsoft.com/downloads, and search for "Windows Server 2003 Resource Kit Tools."
2. Download the Windows Server 2003 Resource Kit Tools to your server.
3. Install the Windows Server 2003 Resource Kit Tools to your server.
4. Click Start, Programs, Windows Resource Kit Tools, Command Shell to open a command shell in the installation directory.

5. Start the `kerbtray.exe` utility by entering the command **`kerbtray.exe`** and pressing Enter.
6. The application starts and appears in your server's tray area, near the clock.
7. Double-click the tray icon to open the Kerberos Tickets dialog box.
8. In the scrolling section, examine the various tickets your session currently has.
9. Use the bottom section to examine the properties of each ticket.

Review Questions

1. What IPSec policies does Windows Server 2003 provide by default?
2. Why is IPSec so important in a routed environment?
3. What is Kerberos used for in Windows Server 2003?
4. You are planning a new IPSec policy for use on your internal network between your Financial subnet and your Accounting subnet. What authentication methods will you have to select from when creating this new policy?
5. What functions does AH provide in IPSec?

Exam Questions

1. You are the network administrator for Joe's Crab Shack, a regional restaurant chain. You have recently begun to implement IPSec to secure communications on the internal network segments. You have just completed the configuration and implementation of the Richmond office network segment. Users in Richmond are now complaining to you that they can connect to their network resources from some computers but not from others. What do you suspect is the most likely cause of this problem?

   ❍ **A.** The computers do not have basic network connectivity.

   ❍ **B.** More than one IPSec policy is in place.

   ❍ **C.** The Domain Controller is not responding.

   ❍ **D.** The Kerberos key distribution center is not responding.

2. You are the network administrator for Widgets and Hammerstein, LLC. Andrea, one of your users, has called you and says that she cannot connect to one of the network servers that requires secured communication. What can you do to quickly verify the IPSec policy in use on that computer?

   ❍ **A.** Use the IP Security Monitor snap-in to see what IPSec policy is in use on the computer.

   ❍ **B.** Use the Network Monitor to see what IPSec policy is in use on the computer.

   ❍ **C.** Use the IP Security Policies snap-in to see what IPSec policy is in use on the computer.

   ❍ **D.** Use the `ipconfig/all` command to see what IPSec policy is in use on the computer.

3. You are the network administrator for Sunny Day, Inc. You are creating a new IPSec policy for your internal network's financial subnet. When creating your new policy, which items can you specify as part of the IP filter? (Choose all that apply.)

❍ **A.** Source IP address

❍ **B.** Destination IP address

❍ **C.** Network protocol

❍ **D.** Operating system

4. From the list of header components given, which one is signed but *not* encrypted in an IP packet with the ESP header inserted in transfer mode?

❍ **A.** IPSec ESP trailer

❍ **B.** Packet data

❍ **C.** IPSec ESP header

❍ **D.** TCP header

5. You are the systems administrator for Herb's Happenings, a public relations firm. While examining the IPSec statistics in the Main Mode node of the IP Security Monitor snap-in, you notice that you have a very low number of IKE Main mode SAs and a very high number of soft associations. What is typically the problem that causes this to happen?

❍ **A.** SAs were not formed with computers because of credentials or permissions mismatches.

❍ **B.** SAs were formed with computers that do not support IPSec or were not capable of negotiating successful IPSec connections.

❍ **C.** SAs were not formed with computers due to Service Pack–level mismatches.

❍ **D.** SAs were formed with computers that do not have a valid domain account in Active Directory.

6. You are a technical architect for Little Faith Enterprises, a venture capital company. You are still training your newly assigned security intern, Allison, about how the Authentication Header (AH) and Encapsulating Security Protocol (ESP) work. When discussing AH, which of the following header fields is responsible for ensuring the integrity of the message?

❍ **A.** Next Header

❍ **B.** Length

❍ **C.** Security Paramters Index (SPI)

❍ **D.** Sequence Number

❍ **E.** Authentication Data

7. You are the systems administrator for Widgets and Hammerstein, LLC. You have been directed by the network manager to secure all communications between servers and workstations in the financial department. All the server and workstations are on a single isolated subnet. What would be the easiest way to ensure that non-IPSec-enabled (and configured) computers could not establish any communications with your servers?

❍ **A.** Create a custom IPSec policy.

❍ **B.** Assign the Client (Respond Only) policy.

❍ **C.** Assign the Server (Request Security) policy.

❍ **D.** Assign the Secure Server (Require Security) policy.

8. From the list of header components given, what is the correct order of headers for an IP packet with the ESP header inserted in transfer mode? (All options will be used and need to be arranged in the correct order to correctly answer this question.)

❍ **A.** IPSec ESP header

❍ **B.** IPSec ESP trailer

❍ **C.** IP header

❍ **D.** Packet data

❍ **E.** IPSec ESP authentication

❍ **F.** TCP header

9. What tool can you use to graphically monitor the Kerberos tickets that a user has in his or her temporary cache?

❍ **A.** `kerbtray.exe`

❍ **B.** `klist.exe`

❍ **C.** IP Security Monitor

❍ **D.** `pathping`

10. You are the network administrator for Herb's Happenings, a public relations firm. You want to create a new IPSec policy for traffic on your private network that provides the strongest secret key possible. In Windows Server 2003, what is the maximum Diffie-Hellman value that can be used?

❍ **A.** 512 bit

❍ **B.** 768 bit

❍ **C.** 1,024 bit

❍ **D.** 2,048 bit

11. From the list of header components given, what is the correct order of headers for an IP packet with the AH header inserted in transfer mode? (All options will be used and must be arranged in the correct order to correctly answer this question.)

- ❍ **A.** Packet data
- ❍ **B.** TCP header
- ❍ **C.** IP header
- ❍ **D.** IPSec AH header

12. From the list of header components given, what is the correct order of headers for an IP packet with the ESP header inserted in tunnel mode? (All options will be used and must be arranged in the correct order to correctly answer this question.)

- ❍ **A.** New IP header
- ❍ **B.** IPSec ESP authentication
- ❍ **C.** TCP header
- ❍ **D.** IPSec ESP trailer
- ❍ **E.** Packet data
- ❍ **F.** IPSec ESP header
- ❍ **G.** Original IP header

13. You are a technical architect for Little Faith Enterprises, a venture capital company. You have recently been assigned a new security intern that will be assisting you over the summer months to implement a company-wide IPSec solution on your networks. In talking with your intern, Allison, you discover that she is a little weak on IPSec and its relevant components, so you decide to teach her about how the Authentication Header (AH) and Encapsulating Security Protocol (ESP) work. When discussing ESP, which of the following header fields is responsible for ensuring that a replay attack will not be successful?

- ❍ **A.** Security Parameters Index (SPI)
- ❍ **B.** Sequence Number
- ❍ **C.** Padding
- ❍ **C.** Padding Length
- ❍ **E.** Next Header

Answers to Review Questions

1. Windows Server 2003 comes with the following three preconfigured IPSec policies, which might or might not meet your needs:

    - **Client (Respond Only)**—This policy requires IPSec-provided security only when another computer requests it. This policy allows the computer to attempt unsecured communications first and switch to IPSec-secured communications if requested. This policy contains the default response rule, which creates dynamic IPSec filters for inbound and outbound traffic based on the requested protocol and port traffic for the communication that is being secured. This policy, which can be used on workstations and servers alike, provides the minimum amount of IPSec security.

    - **Server (Request Security)**—This policy requests security from the other computer and allows unsecured communication with non-IPSec-aware computers. The computer accepts inbound unsecured traffic but always attempts to secure further communications by requesting IPSec security from the sending computer. If the other computer is not IPSec-enabled, the entire communication is allowed to be unsecured. This policy, which can be used on workstations and servers alike, provides a medium level of IPSec security.

    - **Secure Server (Require Security)**—This policy is implemented on computers that require highly secure communications, such as servers transmitting sensitive data. The filters in this policy require all outbound communication to be secured, allowing only the initial inbound communication request to be unsecured. This policy has a rule to require security for all IP traffic, a rule to permit ICMP traffic, and the default response rule to respond to requests for security from other computers. This policy, typically used only on servers, provides the highest level of IPSec security on a network. This policy can also be used on workstation computers, if you want. Non-IPSec-enabled computers cannot establish any communications with computers using this policy.

    You can opt to either use one of the preconfigured policies that comes with Windows Server 2003 or create your own policy. You can also modify the preconfigured policies to suit your needs, if you want. For more information, see the section "Configuring and Implementing IPSec."

2. IPSec provides data integrity between two host IDs. The data and identity are safe and kept from being changed or read by other users through intermediary software. For more information, see the section "Monitoring and Troubleshooting Network Protocol Security."

3. The Kerberos version 5 protocol is used for user authentication in Windows 2000 and newer networks. For more information, see the section "Monitoring and Troubleshooting Kerberos."

4. IPSec on Windows Server 2003 can use Kerberos v5, a digital certificate, or a shared secret (string) for user authentication. For more information, see the section "Planning Security for Data Transmission."

5. The IPSec AH provides three services as part of the IPSec protocol. First (as its name might suggest), AH authenticates the entire packet. Second, it ensures data integrity. Third, it prevents any replaying of the packet by a third party that might be trying to penetrate the IPSec tunnel. One service that AH doesn't provide is payload encryption. AH protects your data from modification, but an attacker who is snooping the network would still be able to read the data. For more information, see the section "Authentication Header (AH)."

Answers to Exam Questions

1. **B.** More often than not when you have some computers that can create IPSec connections and others that cannot, you have more than one IPSec policy in place. If you are intentionally using multiple policies, you need to ensure that you have at least one common authentication and security method between them; otherwise, communications will fail. Basic network connectivity, while always a potential problem, does not appear to be the problem here; thus, answer A is incorrect. The status of the domain controller is not an issue here; thus, answer C is incorrect. The status of the KDC is also not an issue here; thus, answer D is incorrect. For more information, see the section "General IPSec Troubleshooting."

2. **A.** You need to use the IP Security Monitor snap-in to examine what IPSec policy, if any, is currently assigned to the computer. Network Monitor and the IP Security Policies snap-in will not show you what IPSec policy is assigned, and neither will the `ipconfig/all` command; thus, answers B, C, and D are incorrect.

3. **A, B, and C.** You can specify the source IP address, destination IP address, source port, destination port, and network protocol in your IP filters. The operating system is not part of the filters; thus, answer D is incorrect. For more information, see the section "Configuring and Implementing IPSec."

4. **C**. The IPSec ESP header is signed but not encrypted when an IP packet is sent with the ESP header inserted in transfer mode; thus answers A, B, and D are incorrect. The remaining header items listed are all signed and encrypted. For more information, see the section "Understanding the Architecture and Components of IPSec."

5. **B**. When you see a high number of soft associations, this is typically an indication of SAs formed with computers that do not support IPSec or were not capable of negotiating successful IPSec connections; thus answers A, C, and D are incorrect. This problem can be an indication of mismatched security and authentication settings. For more information, see the section "Monitoring IPSec."

6. **E**. The Authentication Data field contains the Integrity Check Value (ICV) used to verify the integrity of the message, which is a calculated hash value; thus, answers A, B, C, and D are incorrect. The receiver calculates the hash value and checks it against the ICV to verify packet integrity. For more information, see the section "Understanding the Architecture and Components of IPSec."

7. **D**. In this case, the easiest way to accomplish the required solution is to assign the Secure Server (Require Security) policy; thus, answers A, B, and C are incorrect. This policy is implemented on computers that require highly secure communications, such as servers transmitting sensitive data. The filters in this policy require all outbound communication to be secured, allowing only the initial inbound communication request to be unsecured. For more information, see the section "Configuring and Implementing IPSec."

8. **C-1, A-2, F-3, D-4, B-5, E-6**. When an IP packet is sent with the ESP header inserted in transfer mode, the packet headers are in the following order: IP header, IPSec ESP header, TCP header, packet data, IPSec ESP trailer, IPSec ESP authentication. For more information, see the section "Understanding the Architecture and Components of IPSec."

9. **A**. `kerbtray.exe`, part of the Windows Server 2003 Resource Kit tools, is used to display the cached Kerberos tickets a user has. `kerbtray.exe` is used from within the Windows GUI. `klist.exe` performs the same function but from the command line. For more information, see the section "Monitoring and Troubleshooting Kerberos."

10. **D.** Windows Server 2003 provides the increased Diffie-Hellman option of 2,048 bits; thus, answers A, B, and C are incorrect. The Diffie-Hellman group is used to determine the length of the base material that is actually used to generate the IPSec secret key. This increased length increases the secret key strength and thus makes it more difficult for an attacker to break. For more information, see the section "Planning Security for Data Transmission."

11. **C-1, D-2, B-3, A-4**. When an IP packet is sent with the AH header inserted in transfer mode, the packet headers are in the following order: IP header, IPSec AH header, TCP header, packet data. For more information, see the section "Understanding the Architecture and Components of IPSec."

12. **A-1, F-2, G-3, C-4, E-5, D-6, B-7**. When an IP packet is sent with the ESP header inserted in tunnel mode, the packet headers are in the following order: new IP header, IPSec ESP header, original IP header, TCP header, packet data, IPSec ESP trailer, IPSec ESP authentication. For more information, see the section "Understanding the Architecture and Components of IPSec."

13. **B**. The Sequence Number field provides the antireplay functionality of ESP; thus, answers A, C, D, and E are incorrect. The sequence number is an incrementally increasing number (starting from 0) that is never allowed to cycle and indicates the packet number. The machine receiving the packet checks this field to verify that the packet has not been received already. If a packet with this number has already been received, the packet is rejected. For more information, see the section "Understanding the Architecture and Components of IPSec."

Suggested Readings and Resources

1. Davies, Joseph, and Thomas Lee. *Microsoft Windows Server 2003 TCP/IP Protocols and Services Technical Reference*. Redmond, WA: Microsoft Press, 2003.

2. Microsoft Corporation. *Microsoft Windows Server 2003 Resource Kit*. Redmond, WA: Microsoft Press, 2003.

3. Microsoft Corporation. *Microsoft Windows Server 2003 Deployment Kit*. Redmond, WA: Microsoft Press, 2003.

4. "Technical Overview of Windows Server 2003 Security Services." www.microsoft.com/windowsserver2003/techinfo/overview/security.mspx.

7

CHAPTER SEVEN

Planning, Implementing, and Troubleshooting Secure Network Access

Continuing on with our examination of methods and means to secure Windows Server 2003, we now move to securing remote and wireless access to your servers and network, including remote administration methods. Secure, however, is a relative term and one that is defined by the business and organizational requirements in place in your organization.

Objectives

Microsoft defines the remote access portion of the "Planning, Implementing, and Maintaining Routing and Remote Access," and the network access portion of the objective and the "Planning and Maintaining Network Security" objective as follows:

Plan secure network administration methods.

- **Create a plan to offer Remote Assistance to client computers.**
- **Plan for remote administration by using Terminal Services.**
- In today's distributed computing world, no longer can administrators easily or efficiently travel to all locations within an organization. The ability to remotely assist users and administer computers in real time gives administrators much more flexibility and offers them a means to better care for their network.

Plan security for wireless networks.

- The rapid and widespread introduction of IEEE 802.11–based wireless networks has caused serious problems for those networks without a solid wireless network security plan. The power and utility of the wireless network also account for its threat and danger. Windows Server 2003 provides new Group Policy–based features that provide a good first step toward mitigating the threats posed by wireless networks.

Plan security for remote access users.

- **Plan remote access policies.**
- **Analyze protocol security requirements.**
- **Plan authentication methods for remote-access clients.**
- Remote access can be a great thing for your users—if planned and implemented properly, including security. To fully secure your remote access solution, you need to understand the authentication methods available, as well as how to configure and implement remote access policies.

Outline

Study Strategies

- Become familiar with the concepts of Remote Assistance and Remote Desktop for Administration. Not only will these two new technologies save you time and trouble in your daily job, but they also are very important on this exam.
- Set up two computers—preferably both Windows Server 2003, but one can be a Windows XP Professional computer—to practice sending and accepting Remote Assistance requests.
- Set up two computers—preferably both Windows Server 2003, but one can be a Windows XP Professional computer—to practice using Remote Desktop for Administration.
- If you have a wireless LAN at your disposal, be sure to create and implement a WLAN security policy.
- Get your hands dirty. The Step by Steps throughout this book provide plenty of directions and exercises, but go beyond these examples and create some of your own. If you can, experiment with each of the objectives to see how they work and why you would use each one.

Introduction

Although we examined the basics of network security in Chapter 1, “Planning, Implementing, and Troubleshooting a TCP/IP Network Infrastructure,” we have much more to talk about in regard to securing your network; that is the topic of this chapter. This chapter, however, is not the end-all when it comes to security or securing your Windows Server 2003 network. Many volumes have been written on this topic, but we seek to examine only a small sampling of the overall subject area in this chapter that is directly related to the objectives for this exam.

Planning Secure Remote Administration Methods

One of the features that Microsoft has been slowly developing since Windows 2000 first appeared is that of built-in remote administrative capabilities. No longer do you have to purchase and install a costly third-party application to provide remote administrative access to your servers and workstations; Windows XP and Windows Server 2003 support it natively, as does the Windows 2000 Server line after you install Terminal Services in Remote Administration mode. Better yet, Windows XP and Windows Server 2003 also include Remote Desktop, which further takes advantage of the *Remote Desktop Protocol (RDP)*, allowing users to connect to a computer remotely as if they were actually using it locally.

In this section, we examine two key parts of the Terminal Services/Remote Desktop Protocol combination: *Remote Assistance* and *Remote Desktop for Administration*. Both are installed by default with an installation of Windows Server 2003; however, both must be manually enabled and configured before use.

Remote Assistance

Objective:

Plan secure network administration methods.

- Create a plan to offer Remote Assistance to client computers.

Remote Assistance, first introduced in Windows XP, provides a built-in mechanism allowing an “Expert” to lend assistance to a “Novice,” whether by request or not. The Expert can be located on the same internal network or even somewhere else on the Internet. Remote Assistance allows the Expert to create a connection to the Novice’s computer, view the desktop, communicate with the Novice, and even take remote control of the Novice’s computer if the Novice allows. Remote Assistance can be performed only on computers running Windows XP or Windows Server 2003—a good reason to consider that desktop upgrade to Windows XP. Before a computer is eligible to receive Remote Assistance, however, it must be enabled either locally or by Group Policy.

Assuming that Group Policy has not been configured from its default setting for Remote Assistance, you can enable it on the local computer by selecting the Allow Remote Assistance Invitations to Be Sent from This Computer option on the Remote tab of the System Properties applet (located in the Control Panel), as shown in Figure 7.1.

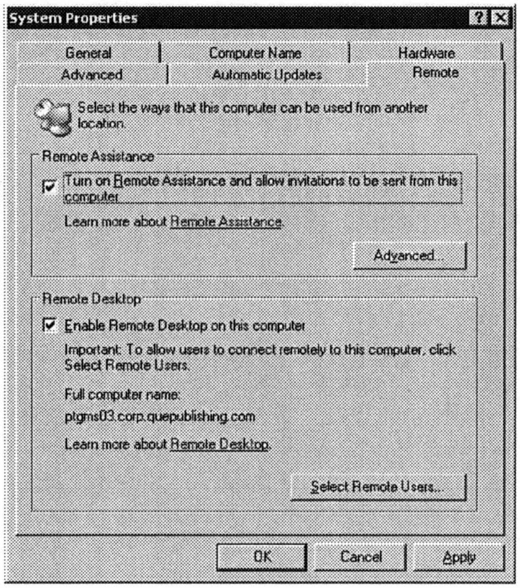

FIGURE 7.1 Remote Assistance must be enabled and configured before it can be used.

Clicking the Advanced button opens the Remote Assistance Settings dialog box, which enables you to further configure Remote Assistance settings. From this dialog box, you have the option to allow the computer to be remotely controlled during the Remote Assistance session; to do so, select the Allow This Computer to Be Controlled Remotely option. You can also configure the length of time that the Remote Assistance requests are valid.

Alternatively, you can configure Group Policy to control the Remote Assistance settings for your entire domain or by specific domains. The settings you need to configure are located in Computer Configuration, Administrative Templates, System, Remote Assistance node, as shown in Figure 7.2. If settings are configured via Group Policy, the option to configure them locally using the System Properties applet is not available. Recall that Group Policy is applied in the following order: local, site, domain, Organizational Unit.

The Solicited Remote Assistance setting shown in Figure 7.2 allows Remote Assistance requests to be sent from the computers that the Group Policy Object (GPO) is applied to. The Offer Remote Assistance setting shown in Figure 7.2 allows Remote Assistance to be offered without a prior request to computers that the GPO is applied to. The user (Novice) still has the option to allow or disallow the Remote Assistance offer.

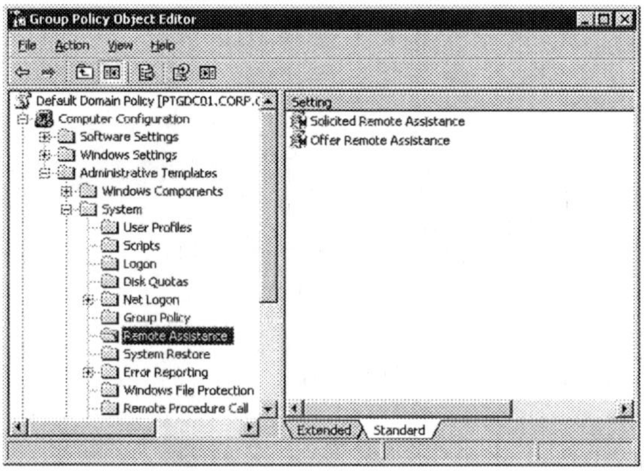

FIGURE 7.2 Remote Assistance can be configured using Group Policy.

EXAM ALERT

Enabling Remote Assistance Be sure that you know and understand the two different ways that Remote Assistance can be enabled and configured.

Configuring Remote Assistance Policies

To configure Remote Assistance policies using Group Policy—always the preferred method—perform the steps outlined in Step by Step 7.1.

STEP BY STEP

7.1 Configuring Remote Assistance via Group Policy

1. Locate the GPO for which you want to configure the Remote Assistance settings.
2. Expand the following nodes: Computer Configuration, Administrative Templates, System, Remote Assistance.
3. Double-click the Solicited Remote Assistance setting to open its Properties dialog box, as shown in Figure 7.3.
4. Select the Enabled radio button.
5. For the Permit Remote Control of This Computer option, select Allow Helpers to Remotely Control the Computer, to ensure that your Experts can fully offer Remote Assistance as needed. The Expert can take control only if the Novice allows it.
6. For the Maximum Ticket Time option, configure a reasonable lifetime for the Remote Assistance request, such as 1 hour. This setting gives the Expert a window in which to respond to the request without creating an overly large security risk.

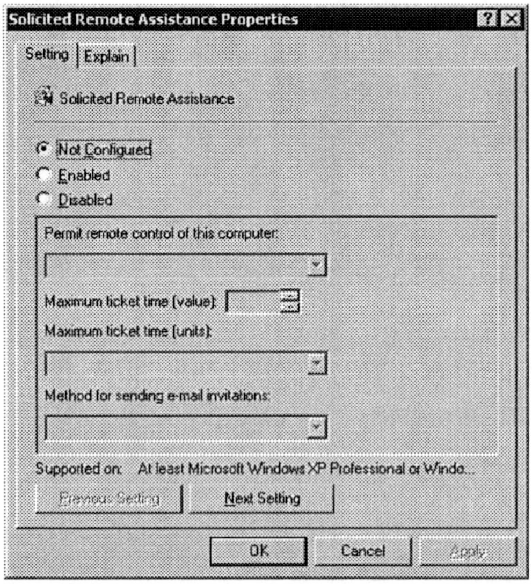

FIGURE 7.3 The Solicited Remote Assistance setting enables the computer's users to request Remote Assistance.

7. For the Method for Sending Email Invitations option, your selection depends on the messaging client in use on your network. The Mailto option configures the Remote Assistance request to be sent as an Internet link and works in virtually all situations. The SMAPI (Simple MAPI) option configures the request to be attached to the message.
8. Click OK to close the Solicited Remote Assistance Properties dialog box.
9. Double-click the Offer Remote Assistance setting to open its Properties dialog box, shown in Figure 7.4.

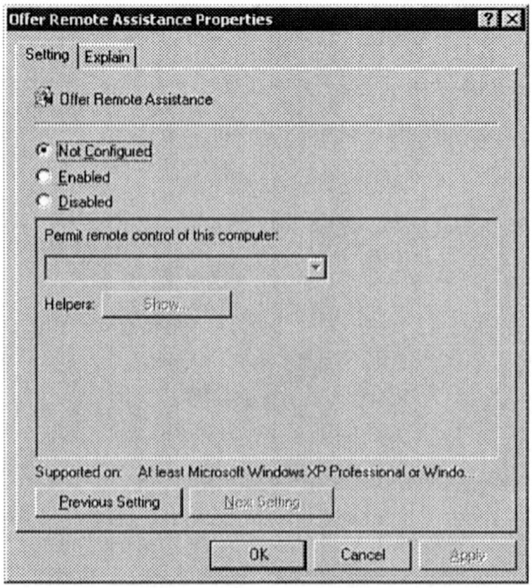

FIGURE 7.4 The Offer Remote Assistance setting enables Experts to offer unsolicited Remote Assistance to users.

10. To allow Experts to offer unsolicited Remote Assistance to users, select the Enabled radio button.
11. For the Permit Remote Control of This Computer option, select Allow Helpers to Remotely Control the Computer, to ensure that your Experts can fully offer Remote Assistance as needed. The Expert can take control only if the Novice allows it.
12. Click the Show button to open the Show Contents dialog box, shown in Figure 7.5.

FIGURE 7.5 You can allow users and groups to offer unsolicited Remote Assistance.

13. To add users and/or groups, click the Add button. You can add only one object at a time, and you must use the following format:

    <Domain Name>\<User Name> or

    <Domain Name>\<Group Name>

14. When you are done adding users and/or groups, click OK to close the Show Contents dialog box.
15. Click OK to close the Offer Remote Assistance Properties dialog box.

Sending and Managing Remote Assistance Requests

Users can request Remote Assistance in three basic ways: Windows Messenger, email (sends a URL), or file (creates a Remote Assistance request file). Note that Windows Messenger is not the same as Microsoft Messenger, although both use similar technologies. You can most easily send Remote Assistance requests by using the Help and Support Center, which you can access by clicking Start, Help and Support. On the main page, click the Remote Assistance link under the Support Tasks column. Figure 7.6 shows the Remote Assistance window.

EXAM ALERT

Using Remote Assistance You use Remote Assistance in the exact same way on your Windows Server 2003 computers as you do on a Windows XP Professional desktop computer.

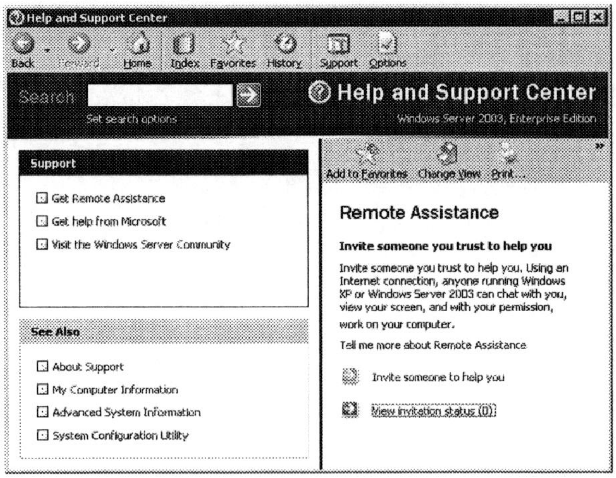

FIGURE 7.6 Remote Assistance requests can be easily sent and managed from within the Help and Support Center.

To send a Remote Assistance request, perform the steps outlined in Step by Step 7.2.

STEP BY STEP

7.2 Sending a Remote Assistance Request

1. Open the Help and Support Center by clicking Start, Help and Support.
2. Click the Remote Assistance link under the Support Tasks column.
3. In the Remote Assistance window, shown in Figure 7.6, click the Invite Someone to Help You link.
4. The most common way to ask for Remote Assistance is to use Windows Messenger because you can easily see who might be available to help you. Note that Windows Messenger is not installed in Windows Server 2003, but you can download it from Microsoft by visiting www.microsoft.com/downloads and searching for "Windows Messenger 5.1."
5. The Remote Assistance window changes, allowing you to pick how to contact the assistant (the Expert). As you can see, Windows Messenger, email, and file methods are available.
6. Selecting a Windows Messenger user and clicking Invite This Person opens the Windows Messenger window on the Expert's computer with the Remote Assistance request, as shown in Figure 7.7. The Expert can then accept or decline the invitation, thus beginning the Remote Assistance session.
7. Alternatively, you can opt to send an email request using a MAPI-compliant messaging application, such as Outlook or Outlook Express, by entering the Expert's first name and clicking Continue.
8. In the next window, you can enter a password and duration for the request to remain valid. Click the Create Email Invitation button to proceed.
9. A new email message opens. You need to enter the correct email address and add any other notes you want before sending the message. The Expert can initiate the Remote Assistance request by clicking the URL in the message, and is then required to download and install an ActiveX applet from the Microsoft website as part of the process.

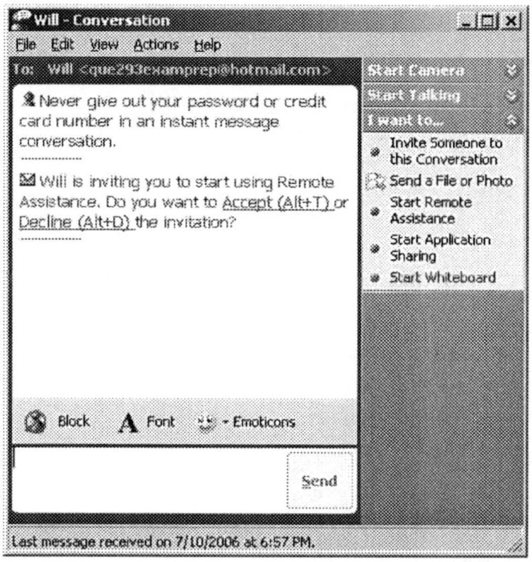

FIGURE 7.7 The Expert receives the Remote Assistance request in his or her Windows Messenger window.

10. Your last option is to create a Remote Assistance file and either give the file to the Expert or place it in a location where the Expert can access it, such as on a file share. You can create the Remote Assistance file by clicking Send Invitation as a File (Advanced). You can configure the name of the Expert, the duration the request should remain valid, and a password as well when creating the saved file. Remote Assistance request saved files have the `*.msrcincident` file extension.

You can view and manage Remote Assistance requests by clicking the View Invitation Status link (*x*), shown previously in Figure 7.6. The *x* represents the number of Remote Assistance requests you have to manage. Clicking this link changes the window to the one shown in Figure 7.8.

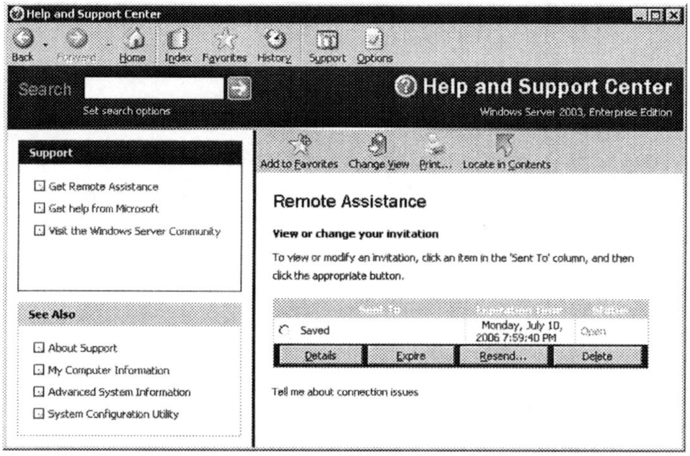

FIGURE 7.8 You can quickly and easily manage all your Remote Assistance requests.

For each Remote Assistance request, the following options are available:

- **Details**—Enables you to view details about the request, including to whom it was sent, when it was sent, when it will expire, what its current status is, and whether it is password protected.
- **Expire**—Enables you to force an open request to expire immediately, regardless of its configured duration.
- **Resend**—Enables you to resend an expired request. Resending expired requests allows you to easily send the same request again without needing to re-enter all the required details.
- **Delete**—Enables you to permanently delete the request.

Using Remote Assistance

Regardless of how the Remote Assistance request is sent, the results are all the same. After the Expert accepts the request, a direct connection is made between the Expert's computer and the Novice's computer. This enables the Expert to communicate directly with the Novice and to see the Novice's desktop in view-only mode, as shown in Figure 7.9.

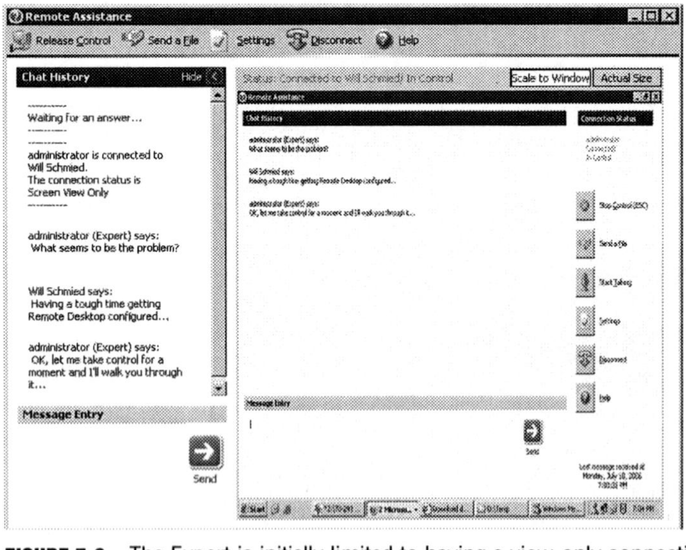

FIGURE 7.9 The Expert is initially limited to having a view-only connection.

The following control buttons are available to the Expert:

- **Take Control**—Sends a request to the Novice to allow the Expert to take control of the Novice's computer.

- **Send a File**—Enables the Expert to transmit a file from the Expert's computer to the Novice's computer. This capability is useful for sending updates and such.
- **Start Talking**—Establishes an audio connection between the Expert and Novice similar to that offered in Windows Messenger or Net Meeting.
- **Settings**—Enables the Expert to configure the Remote Assistance settings for his or her computer.
- **Disconnect**—Terminates the Remote Assistance session and closes the direct connection between the two computers.
- **Help**—Displays Remote Assistance help.

The following control buttons are available to the Novice:

- **Stop Control**—Terminates the Expert's ability to remotely control the computer
- **Send a File**—Enables the Novice to transmit a file from the Novice's computer to the Expert's computer
- **Start Talking**—Establishes an audio connection between the Expert and Novice similar to that offered in Windows Messenger or Net Meeting
- **Settings**—Allows the Novice to configure the Remote Assistance settings for his or her computer
- **Disconnect**—Terminates the Remote Assistance session and closes the direct connection between the two computers
- **Help**—Displays Remote Assistance help

Remote Assistance Security Concerns

Remote Assistance, like all the Terminal Services and Remote Desktop Protocol–based applications, requires that TCP port 3389 be available to make a connection. This raises the question of whether you want to leave this port open on your external firewalls. Logic says no. By closing this port on your external firewalls, you can instantly prevent the largest security risk associated with Remote Assistance: compromise by unauthorized external entities. In most cases, there is no reason why any person physically located outside your protected, private internal network should be tasked with providing Remote Assistance. If this situation arises, consider implementing leased WAN links directly between sites or using permanent VPN connections to give some extra measure of security.

EXAM ALERT

Remote Desktop Protocol Don't forget that all RDP-based applications, including Remote Assistance and Remote Desktop, use TCP port 3389. This might be an important fact on your exam.

But what do you do about the Remote Assistance request itself? The email is sent by default as a standard email message and thus is subject to capture. The Remote Assistance files are simply XML files that are easily taken apart once captured. Email messages can be, and should be, digitally signed and encrypted. If you are using Exchange 2000 or later with Outlook 2000 or later on your network, the fix is easy. If you are not, consider acquiring a personal email certificate or using Pretty Good Privacy (PGP) or some other message encryption and signing utility. The Remote Assistance files should be protected by whatever means are available, including NTFS permissions, EFS encryption, or other third-party methods. Recall that Windows XP and Windows Server 2003 allow for multiple EFS users to have access to the same file.

Remote Desktop for Administration (RDA)

Objective:

Plan secure network administration methods.

- Plan for remote administration by using Terminal Services.

Remote Desktop for Administration, previously referred to as Remote Administration mode in Windows 2000, provides a built-in method to remotely administer and control servers. Provided you have the correct credentials, you can even remotely restart or shut down a server. Of course, you probably ought to warn any users who might be connected to it before doing such!

You can use Remote Desktop for Administration in one of two ways. The first and simplest (although less feature-rich) method is to use the Remote Desktop Connection utility, which you can find by clicking Start, Programs, Accessories, Communications, Remote Desktop Connection. After you click the Options button, the Remote Desktop Connection dialog box opens, as shown in Figure 7.10.

By entering the computer's name or IP address and clicking Connect, you can make a Remote Desktop for Administration connection. You might be required to supply your network credentials to complete the connection and logon process. Figure 7.11 shows what the Remote Desktop connection looks like when not in full-screen mode.

The second method for creating Remote Desktop for Administration connections is to use the new Remote Desktops console. This method offers two features that Windows administrators have been clamoring for since the introduction of Terminal Services:

- **Multiple connection profiles can be created.** You can configure multiple connections in the Remote Desktops console and then switch through them quickly and easily, all within the confines of a single window. The multiple windows required when using the Remote Desktop Connection utility or the Terminal Services client are not required.

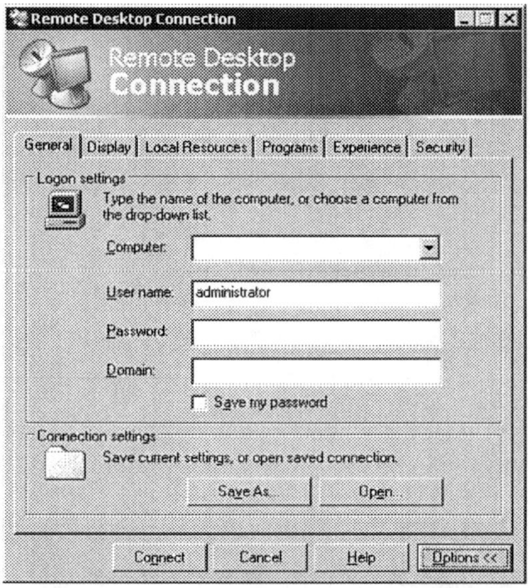

FIGURE 7.10 The Remote Desktop Connection utility enables you to quickly and easily create a connection to a remote computer.

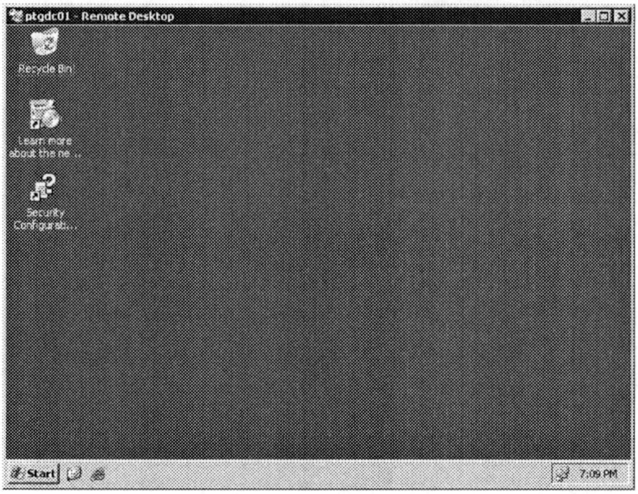

FIGURE 7.11 The Remote Desktop for Administration window can be full screen or smaller, if you like.

- **Connections are made directly to the console session.** In the past, Terminal Services connections could not be made to the console session, preventing many administrators from using Terminal Services for remote administration or prompting the use of third-party applications such as PC Anywhere or VNC. Windows Server 2003, using the Remote Desktops console, now creates connections to the console session, allowing administrators to view messages and pop-ups that are not redirected to any other session. You can also use the `/console` switch on the Remote Desktop Client to create a console connection.

EXAM ALERT

Connecting to the console The ability to connect to the console session using the Remote Desktop Client or the Remote Desktops console is an important new feature to remember. You should keep in mind what the console session enables you to do something that other remote connections do not—receive messages and pop-ups that are displayed only on the console session.

Figure 7.12 shows the Remote Desktops console, with a connection in progress.

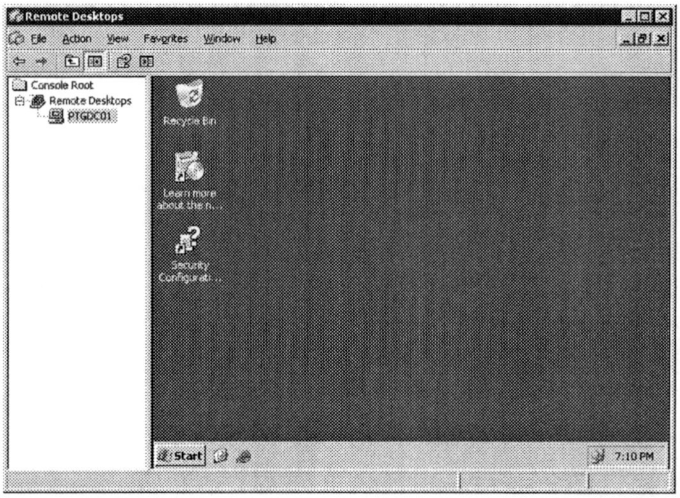

FIGURE 7.12 The Remote Desktops console is the best way to manage multiple servers remotely.

EXAM ALERT

Remote Desktop Web Connection utility It's important to note that the Windows 2000 Terminal Services Web Client is still around in Windows Server 2003—although with a new name and many improvements. It is now known as the Remote Desktop Web Connection utility.

RDA Security and Management Issues

Remote Desktop for Administration, like Terminal Services Administration mode before it, is fairly restrictive in who can use it and how it can be used:

- Only administrators can create Remote Desktop for Administration connections by default; this is a good thing. You want the number of users with this power to be as small as possible, to minimize the risk of an attacker gaining complete control over your network. Access control is handled by virtue of being a Domain Administrator or through membership in the Remote Desktop Users group, which is empty by default.

- Only two nonconsole Remote Desktop sessions can exist on a computer; active and disconnected (but still running) sessions count toward this number. This restriction exists so that the number of concurrent changes being made to a computer is minimized, to prevent configuration errors and conflicts. However, this does present a potential for a denial-of-Service (DoS) attack against a computer—or at least the Remote Desktop portion. In addition to these two connections, one other connection can exist to the server's console session.

EXAM ALERT

Limited connections Remember that you can establish only two regular Remote Desktop connections to a server. You can establish one additional session to a console. Additional sessions cannot be created as long as these limits have been met; this can lead to problems if administrators do not properly end their Remote Assistance sessions by logging out and not just disconnecting.

Because administrators have the capability to create Remote Desktop connections by default, the use of these accounts should be minimized. Administrators should use their administrative accounts only when absolutely required and, even then, should make judicious use of the Run As command. This just makes for good network security sense and is part of the *principle of least privilege*. Using the principle of least privilege, a compromised user account has a smaller impact on the overall security of the network than if you were to blanket-assign to users permissions that they did not need. Ideally, all normal user operations should be carried out in the context of a User account. If additional privileges are required for a specific reason, the administrator can either log in to the network with a special account for the purpose of performing those actions or use the Run As command to perform those actions within the context of the account that has the additional privileges. You also should enforce strong security precautions and account-lockout policies on all accounts that have the capability to connect using Remote Desktop; Chapter 8, "Planning and Implementing Other Network Security Measures," discusses this topic in more detail.

Although the Remote Desktop Connection utility offers the capability to create and save connection configurations on a local computer, this practice should be avoided, if at all possible. Connection configurations are saved to a computer that contain all the Remote Desktop Connection settings in a plain-text file with the file extension of *.RDP. Although the password, if entered, is encoded, it is only a matter of time before an application is written that can quickly decode this information. Even if an attacker does not decode the password, all required information is available to establish the Remote Desktop connection and begin wreaking havoc on your network.

Questions that often arise with Remote Desktop are "What do we do about disconnected sessions?" and "How long should the timeout value be for these disconnected sessions?" There are no hard and fast answers for these questions. Consider the situation in which an administrator has made a Remote Desktop connection to a server and begun the process of applying a service pack. After starting the installation, the administrator disconnects from the server and begins working on another server. Would you really want to impose a timeout limit on this session or manually terminate the session? You must spend some time considering the requirements of your network and the ways you will meet them, to avoid problems down the road.

Specific users can configure session timeout values as granular, so this is an option that you might want to configure. A special shared administrative account that has no timeout values configured on it can be used; when this account is used to create a Remote Desktop connection, all operations can proceed without danger of automatically timing out. This also allows individual administrators to make connections to the server as required to perform other tasks, provided that they log off the server when they are finished. Remember that shutting down or restarting a server from a Remote Desktop session results in that action occurring on the server if the user has the required permissions, so be careful when using the Shut Down Windows dialog box.

Planning Wireless LAN (WLAN) Security

Objective:

Plan security for wireless networks.

It's an inescapable fact of today's computing environment that users want to be connected while on the move. For users, this means the power to move freely about an office or even an entire building without being wired to the wall anymore. For administrators this usually means headaches, heartaches, and visions of hackers silently sifting through the network. Fortunately, the latter doesn't have to be the case.

NOTE

Where do Windows Server 2003 WLAN Policies fit in? Although the Wireless LAN (WLAN) security functionality provided in Windows Server 2003 is in no way intended to replace a dedicated solution available from a company that specializes in WLAN technologies, it is a good start for smaller organizations and a nice addition to existing security measures in larger organizations.

In Windows Server 2003, administrators can now use Group Policy to design and implement security policies to secure 802.11 Wireless LANs. The use of both Wired Equivalent Privacy (WEP) and 802.1x authentication is supported. The Group Policy options that are configured in a GPO and applied to a computer then take precedence over any user-configured settings, thus ensuring that your configuration is applied. You can create policies for three types of Wireless LANs:

- **Access Point (infrastructure)**—The most common type of wireless LAN, the infrastructure mode WLAN, consists of wireless clients communicating directly with wireless Access Points (APs). No direct client-to-client communications exist. This is considered to be the most secure type of WLAN.
- **Computer-to-computer (ad hoc)**—Ad hoc WLANs consist of wireless clients communicating directly with each other without the use of an AP in the middle. This type of communication does not provide a direct path to the wired network.
- **Any available network Access Point preferred**—This option configures the policy to attempt a connection to an Access Point first if one is available. If an AP is not available, the client attempts to create an ad hoc connection, if possible. This method is least preferred and usually most problematic over time.

You can locate the Wireless LAN Group Policy options, shown in Figure 7.13, in the Computer Configuration, Windows Settings, Security Settings node. By default, no policies are defined, meaning that you must create and configure them as your network requires. We examine this process later in this section.

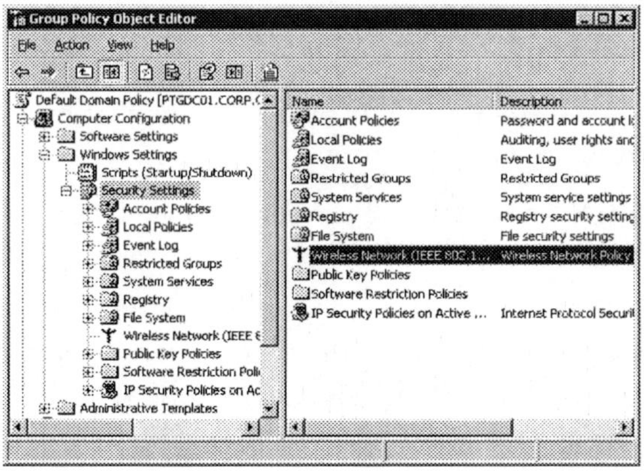

FIGURE 7.13 You can now configure wireless LAN policies for your Windows Server 2003 and Windows XP Professional computers.

Before creating a policy, you should spend some time planning for it first. Wireless LANs are great when implemented and secured properly. Fail to plan properly for the security of your WLAN, and you should just as well plan to fail. When you are preparing to implement WLAN security policies, consider the following key points in regard to authentication issues:

- Your Access Points must support the authentication method that you intend to use, such as 802.1x.
- Your clients and RADIUS servers must all support the same authentication method, such as EAP-TLS or PEAP over 802.1x.

- Computers should always be authenticated. This setting, by default, is enabled.
- If using EAP-TLS (recommended), you should consider allowing the autoenrollment of certificates for users and computers. Autoenrollment makes the process much simpler. Note that you will need a Certificate Authority (CA) in order to use EAP-TLS.

EXAM ALERT

Authentication methods You should be aware of the various authentication methods afforded you in Windows Server 2003, for both wireless and wired networks. This topic is discussed in more detail later in this chapter.

When configuring and implementing WLAN security policies via Group Policy, you need to keep the following points in mind about how they behave:

- Configurations made in Group Policy Objects take precedence over user-configured settings, with the exception of the preferred networks list. The preferred networks lists are merged from the GPO settings and the user-configured settings to form a composite list. When the network list is merged, infrastructure networks always have higher precedence than ad hoc networks. Also, the user can change the configured Wired Equivalent Privacy (WEP) key that is assigned per Group Policy.
- As with all GPOs, nonadministrators cannot remove or disable the policy so that it does not apply to them. This also holds true for administrators.
- When GPO-configured WLAN settings are changed, the client connection is momentarily broken (the client is disassociated) if the new policy takes precedence over the old policy.
- When GPO-configured WLAN settings are removed (when the GPO is deleted or the link is removed), the client is disassociated while the Wireless Configuration service performs a soft reset and clears its cache. When the service restarts, the client reverts to any existing client-configured settings in place.
- When a client is subject to multiple GPOs at various levels that assign WLAN settings, the normal Group Policy processing order applies. The GPO that is closest to the computer object takes precedence and overrides the settings that are assigned to a higher-level Active Directory container.

With your initial planning out of the way, you can begin the process of creating WLAN security policies using Group Policy, as outlined in Step by Step 7.3.

STEP BY STEP

7.3 Configuring a Wireless Network Policy

1. Using either the Group Policy Management Console (GPMC) or Group Policy Editor (GPE), locate the GPO in which you want to create the WLAN security policy.
2. Expand the Computer Configuration, Windows Settings, Security Settings nodes in the GPO to locate the Wireless Network (IEEE 802.11) Policies node. Right-click it and select Create Wireless Network Policy from the context menu to start the Wireless Network Policy Wizard.
3. Click Next to dismiss the opening page of the wizard.
4. Enter a name and description for the new policy on the Wireless Network Policy Name dialog box. Click Next to continue.
5. The Completing the Wireless Network Policy Wizard dialog box appears. Ensure that the Edit Properties option is selected and click Finish to exit the wizard and start configuring the policy's properties.
6. The policy Properties dialog box opens, as seen in Figure 7.14, with the options available as discussed in Table 7.1. Configure your selections as you like per the information in Table 7.1 and switch to the Preferred Networks tab.

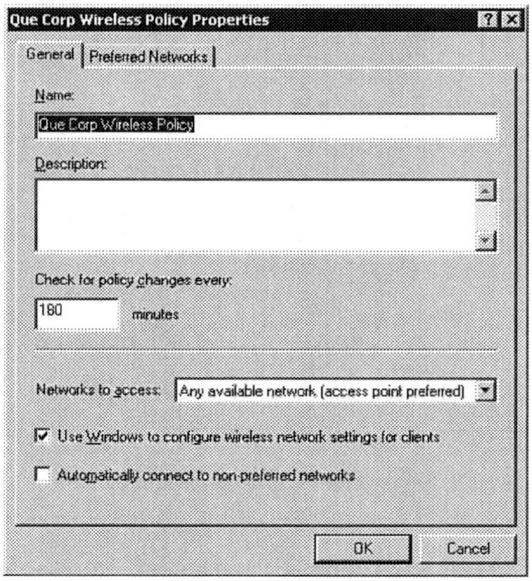

FIGURE 7.14 As usual, you'll need to configure some General properties before continuing.

7. On the Preferred Networks tab, shown in Figure 7.15, click the Add button to open the New Preferred Setting Properties dialog box.

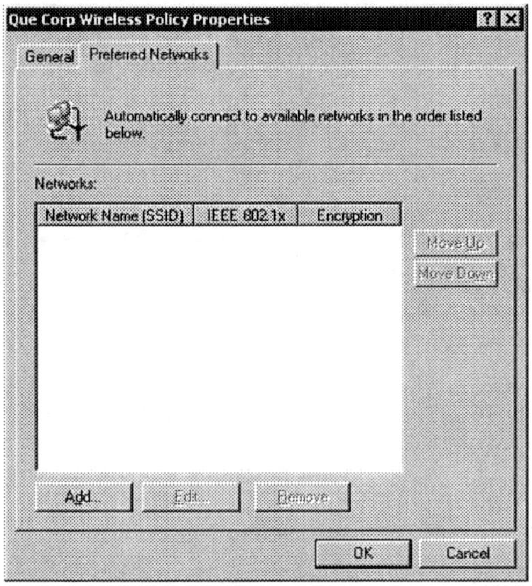

FIGURE 7.15 You need to configure preferred networks for the policy.

8. On the Network Properties tab, shown in Figure 7.16, configure the selections as necessary per the information in Table 7.2. When you are done, switch to the IEEE 802.1x tab.

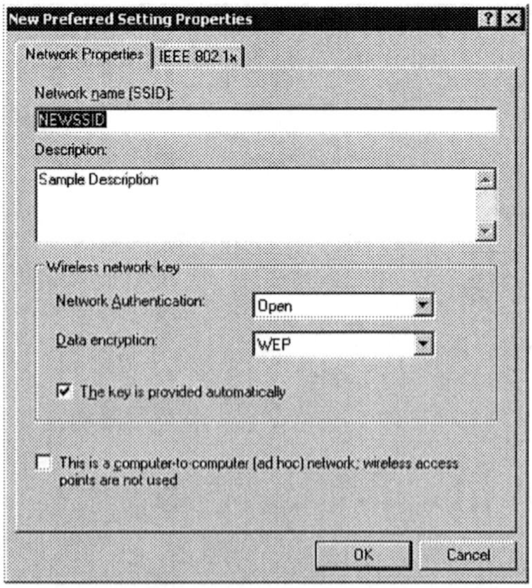

FIGURE 7.16 Creating a new preferred network starts with entering basic configuration items.

9. On the IEEE 802.1x tab, shown in Figure 7.17, configure the selections as necessary per the information in Table 7.3. When you are done, click OK to commit the preferred network to the policy.

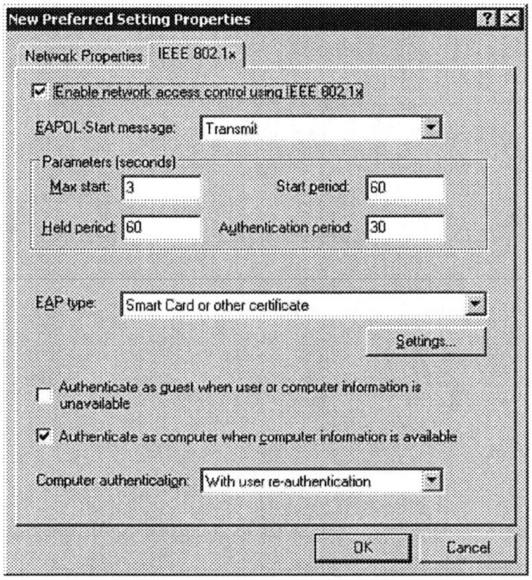

FIGURE 7.17 When using 802.1x authentication, you have several configuration options available to you.

10. Back at the Preferred Networks tab of the policy Properties dialog box, you can add another preferred network, if you want. You can also remove or edit existing preferred network entries, as well as change their relative order by using the Move Up and Move Down buttons.
11. Click OK to close the WLAN policy Properties dialog box.
12. If you want to force Active Directory replication to occur, thus implementing your new WLAN policies, enter the **`gpupdate /target:`*`computer`*** command.

Table 7.1 outlines the configuration options that are available on the General tab of the Wireless LAN Properties dialog box, as discussed in step 6 of the Wireless Network Policy creation process.

TABLE 7.1 Options Available on the General Tab of the WLAN Properties Dialog Box

Option	Description
Name	Enables you to specify a descriptive name for the policy.
Description	Enables you to enter a longer description of the policy.
Check for Policy Changes Every	Configures how often Active Directory should be polled to check for changes to this security policy. The default value is 180 minutes and is acceptable in most instances.

(continues)

TABLE 7.1 *Continued*

Option	Description
Network to Access	Specifies the types of wireless LANs that you want to allow clients to make connections to. You have the following available options: ▶ Any Available Network (Access Point Preferred) ▶ Access Point (Infrastructure) Networks Only ▶ Computer-to-Computer (Ad Hoc) Networks Only
Use Windows to Configure Wireless Network Settings for Clients	Configures whether client settings are automatically configured for a client's 802.11 WLAN connections by the Wireless Configuration service.
Automatically Connect to Nonpreferred networks	Configures whether clients can connect to other 802.11 WLANs for which they are in range.

Table 7.2 outlines the configuration options that are available on the Network Properties tab of the New Preferred Setting Properties dialog box, as discussed in step 8 of the Wireless Network Policy creation process.

TABLE 7.2 Options Available on the Network Properties Tab of the New Preferred Setting Properties Dialog Box

Option	Description
Network Name (SSID)	Specifies the Service Set Identifier (SSID) of the wireless LAN. This value must exactly match the SSID value being used by your Access Points and wireless clients.
Description	Enables you to enter a longer description of the WLAN.
Wireless Network Key (WEP)	Specifies that a WEP key is required for the available options: ▶ Data Encryption (WEP Enabled)—This option specifies that a WEP key is used to encrypt data sent over the WLAN. ▶ Network Authentication (Shared Mode)—This option specifies that a WEP key is used to perform authentication to the WLAN. ▶ The Key Is Provided Automatically—This option specifies that the WEP key is provided automatically to wireless clients by a key server of some sort, typically a RADIUS server.
This Is a Computer-to-Computer (Ad Hoc) Network; Wireless Access Points Are Not Used	When selected, configures this network as an ad hoc network. If not selected, configures this network as an infrastructure network.

Table 7.3 outlines the configuration options that are available on the IEEE 802.1x tab of the New Preferred Setting Properties dialog box, as discussed in step 9 of the Wireless Network Policy creation process.

TABLE 7.3 Options Available on the IEEE 802.1x Tab of the New Preferred Setting Properties Dialog Box

Option	Description
Enable Network Access Control Using IEEE 802.1x	Specifies that 802.1x authentication is to be used when connecting to the WLAN.
EAPOL-Start Message	Specifies how Extensible Authentication Protocol over LAN (EAPOL) start messages are to be transmitted. Options include ► Do Not Transmit ► Transmit (default) ► Transmit Per IEEE 802.1x
Max Start	Default Max Start value is 3 seconds.
Held Period	Default Held period is 60 seconds.
Start Period	Default Start period is 60 seconds.
Authentication Period	Default Authentication period is 30 seconds.
EAP Type	Specifies what EAP type is to be used from the following options: smart card or other certificate and Protected Extensible Authentication Protocol (PEAP). Clicking the Settings button enables you to configure additional options, including the following: ► Using a smart card or certificate on the computer ► Validating server certificates ► Specifying which servers to connect to ► Specifying Trusted Root Certification Authorities ► Viewing certificates ► Selecting and configuring an authentication method
Authenticate as Guest When User or Computer Information Is Unavailable	Specifies that wireless clients are to attempt to authenticate to the WLAN as a guest when user or computer information is not available.
Authenticate as Computer When Computer Information Is Available	Specifies that wireless clients must attempt to authenticate to the WLAN even if a user is not logged on.
Computer Authentication	Specifies how the computer is to authenticate to the WLAN. The following options are available: ► With User Authentication ► With User Reauthentication (default) ► Computer Only

The recommend setting is With User Reauthentication. This setting forces the computer to authenticate before a user is logged on and then performs authentication using the user's credentials when the user logs on. When the user logs off, authentication is performed again using the computer's credentials.

Challenge

Jeff's Jeep Tours is an Australian tour company that provides unique tours of the Australian continent. Jeff's has a central office that is located in Sydney with 20 other smaller remote offices located all over the country. Some of the remote offices have only three or four employees and no IT staff. The IT management responsibility for these offices is shared among all the IT staff in other locations. Jeff's network currently consists of a mixture of Windows 98, Windows NT 4.0 Workstation, and Windows 2000 Professional client computers with Windows 2000 Server and Windows Server 2003 domain controllers and member servers.

The CEO of Jeff's Jeep Tours, Jeff Johnson, has hired you as an outside consultant to plan and implement a solution for a new network that will allow for increased performance, security, and manageability. All workstations will be replaced with new Pentium-class computers. No new servers will be purchased. The Sydney office uses an Active Directory domain with Windows 2000 Server domain controllers. You will be allowed to upgrade all domain controllers as required.

You propose a plan that upgrades all servers to Windows Server 2003 and installs Windows XP Professional on all client workstations. You further propose to raise the domain functional level to Windows Server 2003 and create Group Policies that provide Remote Assistance support for all remote offices that have no onsite IT personnel. You will create a top-level OU named Locations with individual OUs created inside the Locations OU for each remote site. Each client computer will be a member of its respective OU. All user accounts will also be placed in their respective OUs.

Through your discussions with the key stakeholders in this project, you've determined the following additional information:

- The current environment does not provide efficient management or operation.
- The workstation computers will be replaced to allow installation of Windows XP Professional.
- Remote Assistance can be used to remotely assist users as long as the computers on both ends of the connection are Windows XP or Windows Server 2003.

Your task is to implement the new network for Jeff's Jeep Tours.

Try to complete this exercise on your own, listing your conclusions on a sheet of paper. When you have completed the exercise, compare your results to those given here.

By installing Windows XP Professional SP2 on all client computers and placing all computer and user accounts in OUs for their location, you can easily create, configure, and implement Remote Assistance policies that will enable your IT staff to respond to user requests for assistance from any location.

Planning and Implementing Remote Access Security

In this section, we examine the process of planning and implementing security for remote access solutions. In general, if you were to think about overall network security when dealing with a remote access solution, the most important consideration would be that remote access means "remote" sites, users, and so on will be entering your protected core network to access resources needed to perform business. Therefore, you need to consider how to authenticate them and make sure that you are giving access to these critical resources to the right people and that they are logged as doing such so if a problem occurs, it can be traced back to the source.

To implement remote access security, you need to follow a general process similar to this: First, determine what risks and problems you are likely to encounter. Next, choose a solution that fits your business needs (Windows Server 2003 RRAS for this discussion) and then implement the solution. After you have implemented the solution, test it—to try to break it, in effect, looking for weaknesses in its design and implementation. This section focuses on planning and creating secure remote access solutions using remote access policies and the various user-authentication methods available in Windows Server 2003.

Windows Server 2003 provides remote access for both dial-in connections and virtual private network (VPN) connections, and includes a set of features that provide flexibility and security for your remote access solution. If you need to review the basics of implementing and configuring remote access, be sure to see *MCSA/MCSE 70-291 Exam Prep: Implementing, Managing, and Maintaining a Windows Server 2003 Network Infrastructure*, by Will Schmied (Que Publishing, 2007).

Before you go any further with your plan for secure remote access, you should ask yourself the following questions to gain an insight into what security you might need:

- Do all your users require remote access? In the majority of networks, only a small group of users actually needs to have remote access capabilities. Your remote access policies should take this into account and prevent unauthorized users from making remote access connections to your network.
- Of the users who *do* need remote access, do they need differing levels of remote access? You need to plan for this if you have users who require differing levels of remote access.
- Of the users who *do* need remote access, do they need to access network resources or only the resources located on the Remote Access Server? If users do not need to access any internal resources, you can contain them to the Remote Access Server for increased security and accountability.

Remote access enables users with remote computers to create a logical connection to an organization's network or the Internet. In this chapter, we do not look at the specifics of how connections are created (that is the scope of Exam 70-291), but instead at how to authenticate and secure these connections.

Planning Authentication Methods

Objective:

Plan security for remote access users.

- ▶ Analyze protocol security requirements.
- ▶ Plan authentication methods for remote access clients.

To handle network traffic (and to know what to do with it through security), you need to select a protocol to use with your remote access setup in Windows Server 2003. This section highlights your options, which one seems best to use, what differences they have and why, and what you can use if you don't want a high-end security solution. Regardless, you need to know these options for Exam 70-293.

Remote access authentication methods are configured on the Authentication Methods dialog box, shown in Figure 7.18. In this section, we cover EAP, CHAP, MS-CHAP, MS-CHAP v2, SPAP, PAP, and unauthenticated access.

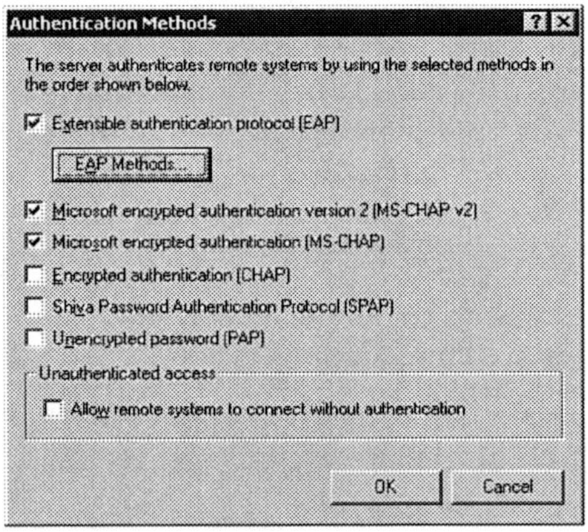

FIGURE 7.18 You can select any number of available remote access authentication methods.

Extensible Authentication Protocol (EAP)

Extensible Authentication Protocol (EAP) is a commonly used protocol on networks today. It is responsible for creating an authentication method in which the authentication scheme to be used is negotiated by the remote access client and the authenticator, which could be either the Remote Access Server or even a RADIUS server. Windows Server 2003 Routing and Remote Access (RRAS) includes support for EAP-TLS by default; TLS stands for *Transport Layer Security*. It could be considered an EAP type, much like the wireless access protocol called LEAP, which is provided by Cisco systems. Many types of EAP exist, although they all perform similar functions, such as authentication; they just use different methods to do so. These are some of the more common forms of EAP:

- **EAP-MD5 CHAP (Extensible Authentication Protocol–Message Digest 5 Challenge Handshake Authentication Protocol)**—This form of EAP uses the same type of CHAP authentication that is explained in the next authentication method, but it wraps the authentication in EAP packets for increased security during transmission.
- **PEAP (Protected Extensible Authentication Protocol)**—This relatively new form of EAP is used in wireless networks.
- **EAP-TLS (Extensible Authentication Protocol–Transport Layer Security)**—This derivative of EAP uses smart cards or digital certificates to perform the authentication.

Challenge Handshake Authentication Protocol (CHAP)

Challenge Handshake Authentication Protocol (CHAP) uses the industry-standard Message Digest 5 (MD5) protocol. MD5 is a hashing scheme that encrypts your data in transit over the remote access network. CHAP is supported by virtually all remote access clients and servers. This protocol uses a user's password to perform authentication; by default, Windows Server 2003 does not allow CHAP to access a user's password. If you plan to use CHAP, you must configure the user's password for CHAP by selecting the Store Passwords Using Reversible Encryption option either on a specific user's account or in Group Policy. After this change has been made, all applicable users must then change their passwords so that they will be stored in a form that CHAP can access.

Microsoft Challenge Handshake Authentication Protocol (MS-CHAP)

MS-CHAP provides one-way authentication of the user to the Remote Access Server and uses a single encryption key for all transmitted and received messages. Windows 95 and Windows NT 3.51 clients cannot make use of the newer, more secure, MS-CHAP Version 2 (discussed next); thus, MS-CHAP is provided in Windows Server 2003 for backward compatibility with these clients.

MS-CHAP Version 2

MS-CHAP Version 2 is a stronger version of the MS-CHAP protocol that provides for mutual authentication by both the user and the server using encrypted passwords. MS-CHAP v2 is the simplest remote access authentication method to employ if all your clients are Windows 98 or newer.

Shiva Password Authentication Protocol (SPAP)

The Shiva Password Authentication Protocol (SPAP) is an authentication protocol originally used by the Shiva LAN Rover line of products. If a Shiva client tries to connect to a Windows Server 2003 Remote Access Server, or a Windows client connects to a Shiva LAN Rover, SPAP must be used. Because Shiva was prominent in the remote access market at one time, support is still included in Windows Server 2003 even though SPAP is extremely insecure. SPAP is susceptible to replay attacks (such attacks occur when data packets are captured in transit, examined, and then replayed to the server to gain access) because the same user password is always sent over the network in the same reversibly encrypted way each time. You should use SPAP only when you absolutely have to.

Password Authentication Protocol (PAP)

The Password Authentication Protocol (PAP) is the weakest authentication method available in Windows Server 2003. PAP sends your credentials in plain text, not encrypted or otherwise protected from compromise. Any network-sniffing tool could pick up a packet with your credentials in it and, by simply looking at the packet, you could log in to a network with someone else's ID. PAP is most commonly used as a method of last resort if a client and server cannot agree on any other method. Even PAP authentication is better than no authentication at all, as discussed next. You should plan to never use sensitive accounts, such as administrative accounts, when PAP is the authentication method in place.

Using Unauthenticated Access

Windows Server 2003 supports the use of Guest access, better known as *unauthorized access*, which allows a connection attempt to be granted without need for credentials. You should avoid the use of unauthenticated access, if at all possible.

EXAM ALERT

Know the methods You absolutely must know the different remote access authentication methods that are available in Windows Server 2003 before test time.

Using Dial-In Properties for Access Control

Even though Windows Server 2003 provides a full array of encrypted authentication methods, you can configure several basic dial-in properties on a user-by-user basis, as shown in Figure 7.19.

You can use the following options on the Dial-In tab to control how remote access connections are made:

- **Remote Access Permission**—This enables to you allow or deny remote access to the user. Alternatively, you can leave the default selection of Control Access through Remote Access Policy. (We discuss remote access policies shortly.)
- **Verify Caller ID**—If you enter a phone number in this area, the Remote Access Server will not accept any calls from any other number.
- **Callback Options**—This option group enables you to specify how callback should be handled for the user. This is both a cost-saving measure and a means of security.

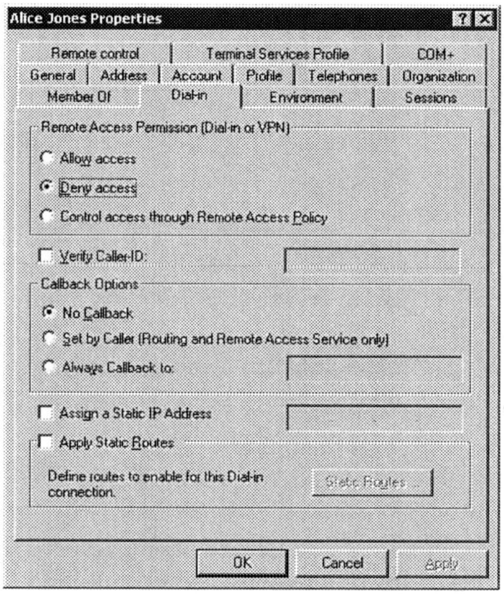

FIGURE 7.19 You can use these basic dial-in properties as your first line of defense.

Now that you've seen the available methods of authenticating remote access, you're ready to start creating remote access policies.

Planning and Creating Remote Access Policies

Objective:

Plan security for remote access users.

- Plan remote access policies.

Remote access policies are a set of conditions and connection settings that give network administrators more flexibility in authorizing connection attempts. They provide both granular and flexible configuration settings for both RAS and VPN connections. This granularity and flexibility unfortunately come at the expense of ease of use: Remote access policies can be very complex, and you need an in-depth understanding of them if you are going to successfully provide secure remote access to your users. With remote access policies, you can grant remote access by individual user account or through the configuration of specific remote access policies.

Windows Server 2003 uses three types of remote access policies to control access:

- **Group policies**—Access can be controlled by group policies created on each Windows Server 2003 Routing and Remote Access Server. This is the simplest method for authenticating users as long as you are using a single server for remote access.

- **Local Internet Authentication Services policies**—These local policies are derived from RADIUS and can be used to define access permissions based on a number of client attributes. This mechanism requires that the Internet Authentication Service be installed on the Windows Server 2003 Remote Access Server. This is typically the best solution if you are planning to add Windows Server 2003 Remote Access Servers and don't want to have to replicate the policies to each new server.
- **Central Internet Authentication Services policies**—A Windows Server 2003 Routing and Remote Access Service server can be configured to use a central Internet Authentication Server (IAS) RADIUS server to provide its policies. This allows multiple Routing and Remote Access dial-up servers to use the same policies without requiring the manual replication of policies and settings. This is the most practical solution for companies deploying multiple Windows Server 2003 Remote Access Servers.

Windows Server 2003 supports two methods for creating a remote access policy: using a wizard to create commonly used remote access policies and a using a custom method that enables you to create less common remote access policies. But before we look at creating a policy, we need to discuss how Windows Server 2003 determines whether to accept a remote access connection.

The first step in establishing a remote access connection is for the client to successfully authenticate to the server. *Authentication* is the verification of user credentials used in the connection attempt. This is typically a user ID and password (unless EAP is used in conjunction with a token or smart card). The client sends its credentials to the server, where they are validated.

After the client has been successfully authenticated, it needs to be authorized to connect. A client that can successfully authenticate but is not authorized will have its connection attempt denied.

The Windows Server 2003 RRAS uses three mechanisms to authorize a connection, depending on the server's authentication configuration:

- **Windows authentication**—If the server is using Windows authentication, the connection is authenticated using the local server's security configuration, and then the dial-in properties of the user account and locally stored remote access policies are used to authorize the connection.
- **Non-IAS RADIUS authentication**—If the server is using non-IAS RADIUS authentication, the credentials of the connection attempt are passed to the RADIUS server for both authentication and authorization. If the connection attempt is both authenticated and authorized, the RADIUS server sends an accept message to the server, and the connection attempt is accepted. If the connection attempt fails to be authenticated or authorized, the RADIUS server sends a reject message to the server, and the connection attempt is rejected.
- **IAS authentication**—If the server is configured to use an IAS server, the IAS server performs authentication through the selected Windows authentication mechanisms and then performs the authorization through the dial-in properties of the user account and remote access policies stored on the IAS server.

Step by Step 7.4 walks you through the creation of a new remote access policy to allow VPN access to anyone in the Domain Users group by using the wizard.

NOTE

Using local authentication for the rest of the Step by Steps To ensure the success of the following Step by Steps, make sure that the authentication method set on the server Properties dialog box Security tab is set to Windows Authentication. Setting up a remote access policy under IAS for centralized policy management works in exactly the same way as setting up the policy locally, but it complicates any testing you might want to do.

STEP BY STEP

7.4 Using the New Remote Access Policy Wizard to Create a VPN Access Policy

1. Log on to Windows Server 2003 by using the Administrator account or another account that has administrator privileges.
2. Open the Routing and Remote Access console by selecting Start, Administrative Tools, Routing and Remote Access.
3. Right-click the Remote Access Policies node in the left pane of the Routing and Remote Access console and select New Remote Access Policy from the menu. The New Remote Access Policy Wizard appears, as shown in Figure 7.20.

FIGURE 7.20 The New Remote Access Policy Wizard is used to create new remote access policies.

4. Click Next to continue. The Policy Configuration Method dialog box of the wizard, shown in Figure 7.21, appears. Select the option Use the Wizard to Set Up a Typical Policy for a Common Scenario. In the Policy Name field, type **Allow Remote Access to Remote Users**. If you are in a complex environment with many remote access policies, you might even need a naming convention for these policies to keep them straight.

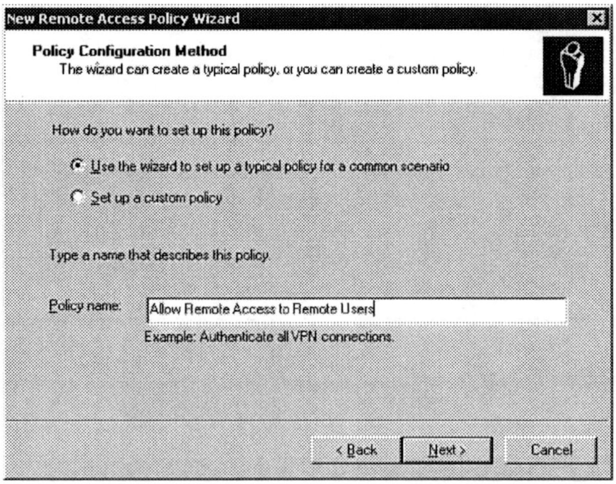

FIGURE 7.21 The Policy Configuration Method dialog box enables you to decide whether to use the wizard or manual configuration to create a remote access policy.

5. Click Next to continue. The Access Method dialog box of the wizard appears, as shown in Figure 7.22. In this case, select VPN. Be aware of the additional options for your information—it is good to know what can be done with this wizard.

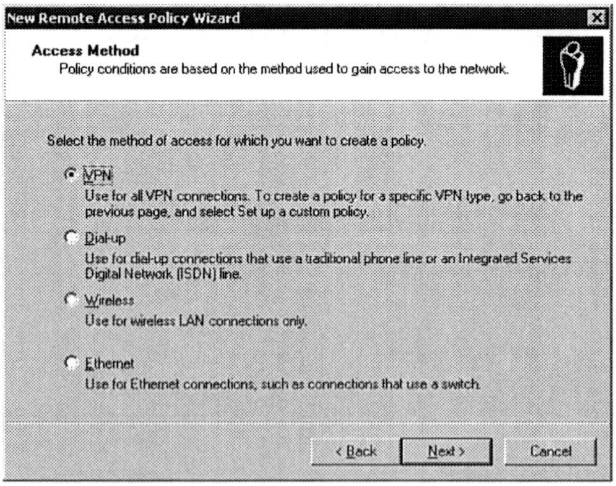

FIGURE 7.22 The Access Method dialog box enables you to select how users will be connecting to the Windows Server 2003 remote access server.

6. Click Next to continue to the User or Group Access dialog box of the wizard. Select the Group option and Click Add to open the Select Groups dialog box, as seen in Figure 7.23. Type **Domain Users** in the Enter the Object Names to Select field. If you click Check Names, the console confirms that the object exists in Active Directory.

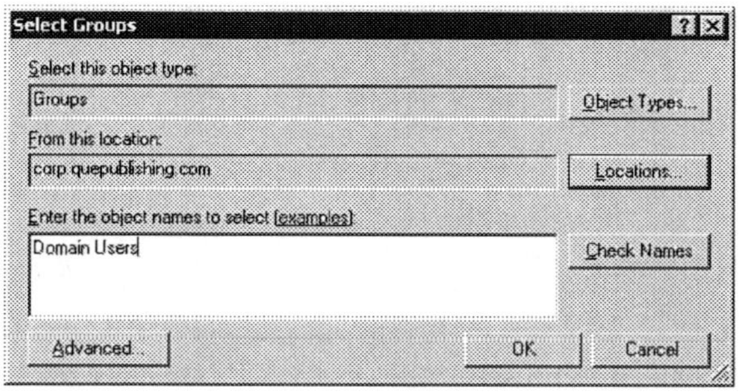

FIGURE 7.23 The Select Groups dialog box enables you to populate the list of groups that will be affected by this policy.

7. Click OK to return to the User or Group Access dialog box, shown in Figure 7.24. Notice that the group you entered in step 6 now appears in the list of groups.

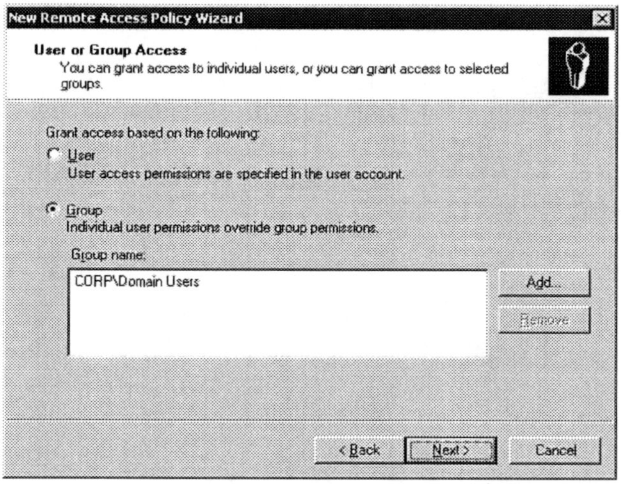

FIGURE 7.24 Any groups added appear in the Group Name field of the User or Group Access dialog box.

8. Click Next to continue. The Authentication Methods dialog box of the wizard appears as shown in Figure 7.25. Notice that the only authentication types allowed are EAP, MS-CHAPv2, and MS-CHAP. To use other authentication types, you need to use a custom remote access policy. Make sure MS-CHAPv2 is selected.

9. Click OK to continue. The Policy Encryption Level dialog box of the wizard appears as shown in Figure 7.26. Because you are dealing with a VPN connection, select Strongest Encryption. If this were a dial-up connection, you would have an additional option—No Encryption.

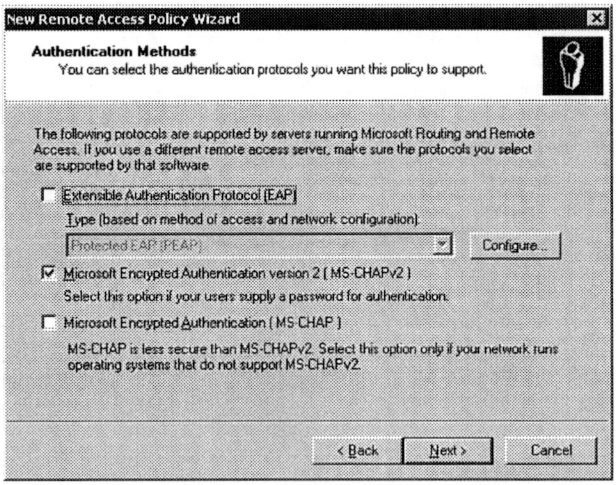

FIGURE 7.25 The Authentication Methods dialog box is used to select which authentication methods will be permitted for accessing the Windows Server 2003 RRAS server by using this remote access policy.

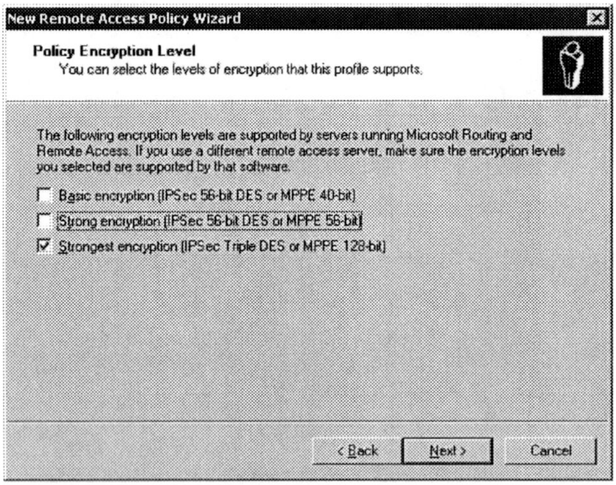

FIGURE 7.26 Windows Server 2003 RRAS supports three different encryption strengths for VPN connections.

10. Click Next to continue. The Completing the New Remote Access Policy Wizard dialog box appears as shown in Figure 7.27.
11. Click Finish to complete the policy creation. Figure 7.28 shows the newly created remote access policy.

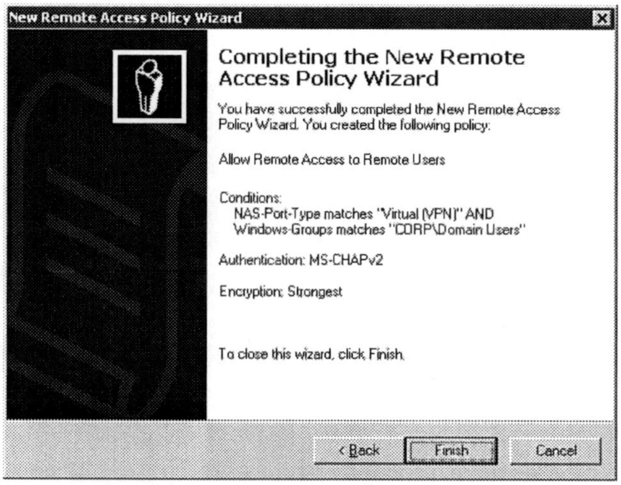

FIGURE 7.27 The Completing the New Remote Access Policy Wizard dialog box summarizes the configuration of the policy.

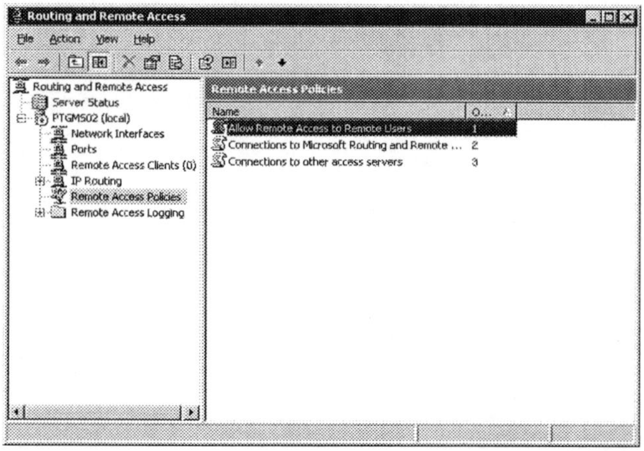

FIGURE 7.28 The Remote Access Policy folder shows all the policies that are in effect on the local server.

Step by Step 7.5 takes you through the process of creating a custom remote access policy that restricts access based on the day of the week and the time of day.

STEP BY STEP

7.5 Using the Routing and Remote Access Console to Create a Custom RRAS Policy to Restrict the Times When Users Are Able to Connect Remotely

1. Log on to Windows Server 2003 by using the Administrator account or another account that has administrator privileges.
2. Open the Routing and Remote Access console by selecting Start, Administrative Tools, Routing and Remote Access.

3. Right-click Remote Access Policies in the left pane and select New Remote Access Policy from the menu. The New Remote Access Policy Wizard appears.
4. Click Next to continue. The Policy Configuration Method dialog box appears. Select the Set Up a Custom Policy option, shown in Figure 7.29. In the Policy Name field, type **Deny Access Based on Time of Day**.

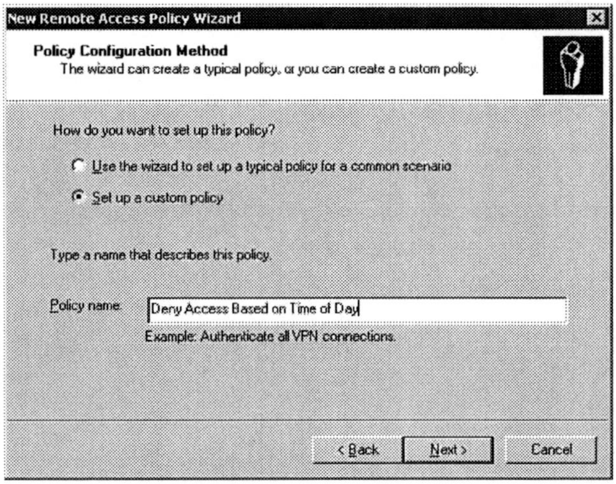

FIGURE 7.29 Selecting the Set Up a Custom Policy option in the Policy Configuration Method dialog box enables you to perform advanced policy creation.

5. Click Next to continue. The Policy Conditions dialog box of the wizard appears as shown in Figure 7.30. You can use this dialog box to add the conditions that need to be matched for the policy to take effect. You have the option to configure multiple conditions, but in this case, select a single condition.

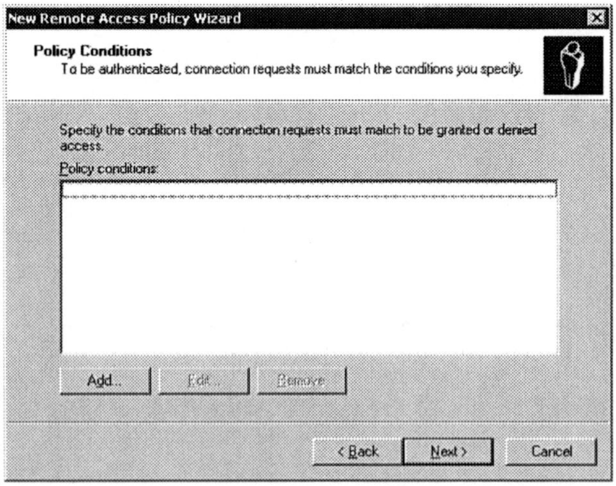

FIGURE 7.30 The Policy Conditions dialog box enables you to select conditions from an extensive list of options.

6. Click the Add button to open the Select Attribute screen, shown in Figure 7.31.

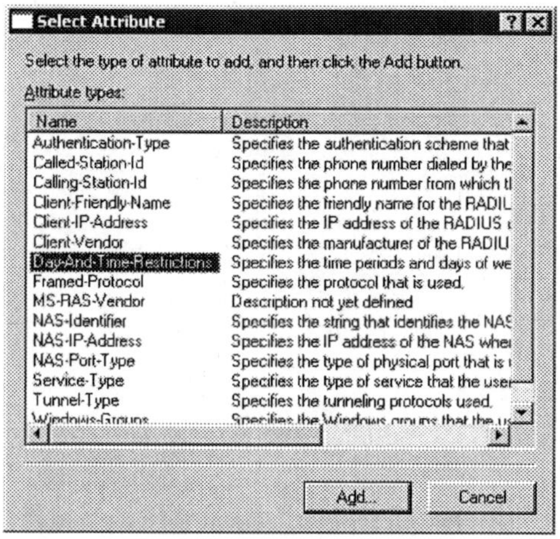

FIGURE 7.31 Windows Server 2003 offers an extensive list of options for setting conditions on a remote access policy.

7. Because you are working on setting time restrictions for remote users, select Day-and-Time Restrictions from the list of conditions. (Later, you should explore the rest of these conditions so that you are familiar with them.) Click the Add button to select this attribute. The Time of Day Constraints screen appears. It is initially blank because the default setting is Denied. Changing the setting to Permitted changes the screen to entirely blue, which indicates permit access. Select the times from 5:00 a.m. until 8:00 p.m. for all days of the week and click the Permit Access radio button. The selected region should turn blue to indicate that access is permitted during that time. The result should look like Figure 7.32.

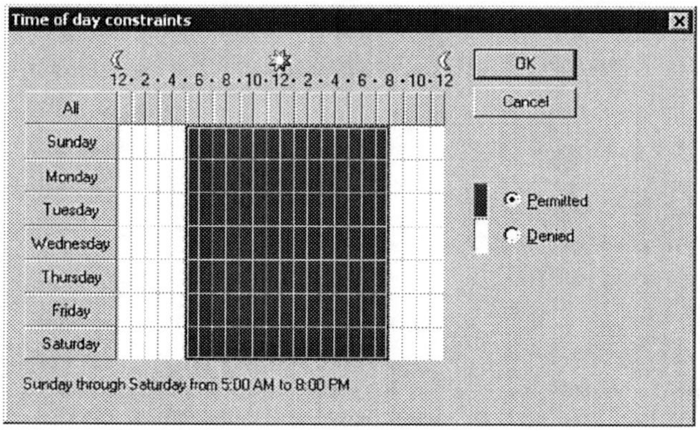

FIGURE 7.32 The time-of-day constraints are some of the most common conditions to be set in a remote access policy.

8. Click OK to continue. The time-of-day restriction appears in the Policy Conditions field of the Policy Conditions dialog box, shown in Figure 7.33.

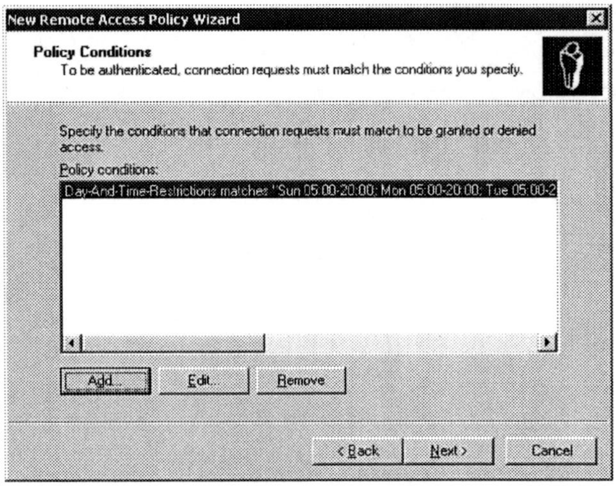

FIGURE 7.33 Any conditions set appear in the Policy Conditions field.

9. Click Next to continue. The Permissions dialog box of the wizard appears as shown in Figure 7.34. Select Grant Remote Access Permission. This enables users to connect to the Windows Server 2003 RRAS server during the permitted times.

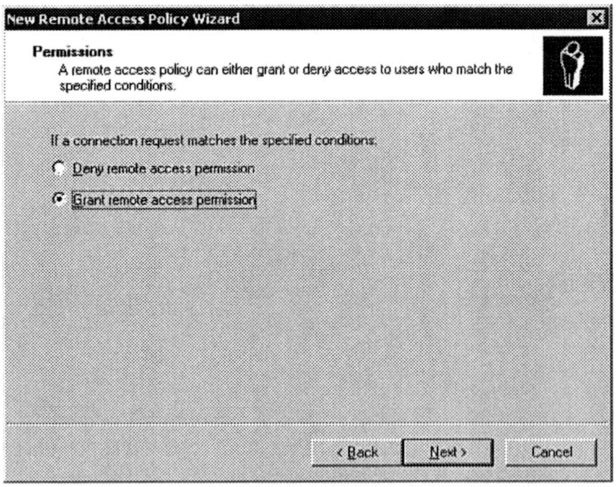

FIGURE 7.34 The Permissions dialog box enables you to configure a policy to accept connections that meet the conditions of the policy or deny them if needed.

10. Click Next to continue. The Profile dialog box of the wizard appears as shown in Figure 7.35.

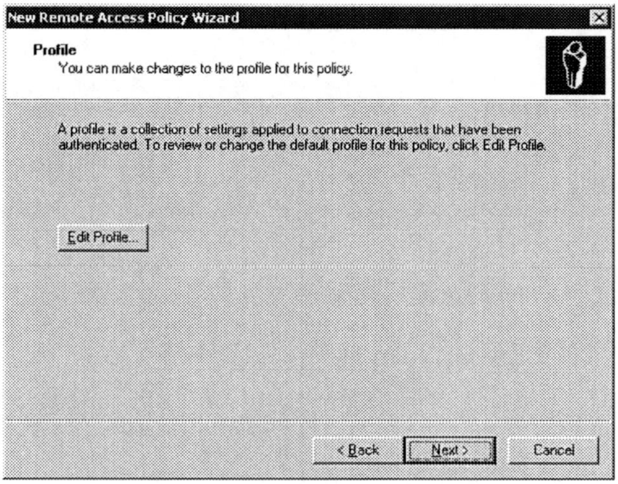

FIGURE 7.35 The Profile dialog box gives you access to the remote access profile, which enables you to further refine the configuration of the remote access policy.

11. Click Edit Profile. The Edit Dial-in Profile dialog box appears as shown in Figure 7.36. Dial-in profiles are discussed in detail in the next section of this chapter.

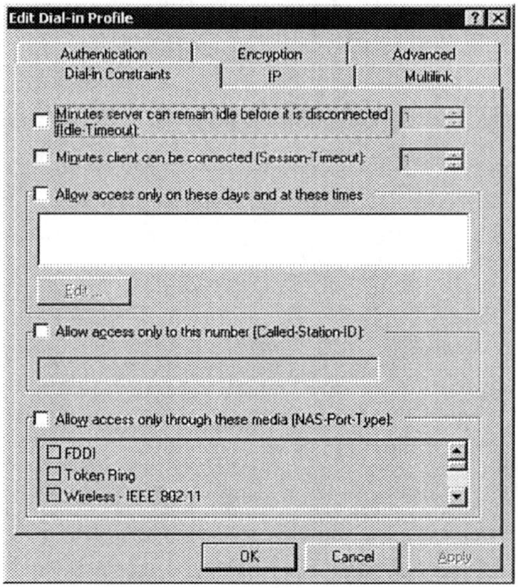

FIGURE 7.36 The Edit Dial-In Profile dialog box enables you to configure a number of parameters that are used to authenticate users.

12. Click OK to return to the Profile dialog box and click Next to continue. The Completing the New Remote Access Policy Wizard dialog box appears.

13. Click Finish to complete the creation of the new remote access policy.

EXAM ALERT

Order matters Remote access policies are applied in the order in which they appear in the remote access policy list. This can sometimes lead to conflicting policies or unintended results, so it is important to understand not only how remote access policies work, but also how the order in which they are applied can affect their results. Keep this in mind when dealing with remote access policies on your Exam 70-293.

Remote Access Profiles

In conjunction with the remote access policy, there is a component known as the *remote access profile*. This profile contains a number of variables that enable you to further refine the parameters of the remote access policy. You can modify a remote access profile during the creation of a remote access policy, as is done in Step by Step 7.5, or you can review or modify a profile for an existing remote access policy by right-clicking the policy in either the Routing and Remote Access console or the Internet Authentication Service console, selecting Properties, and then clicking the Edit Profile button. The Settings dialog box appears as shown in Figure 7.37, and you can use it to add conditions to the policy, edit the profile, or review or change the grant and deny access settings on the policy. Six tabs are available in the Edit Dial-in Profile dialog box; the following sections look at them one at a time.

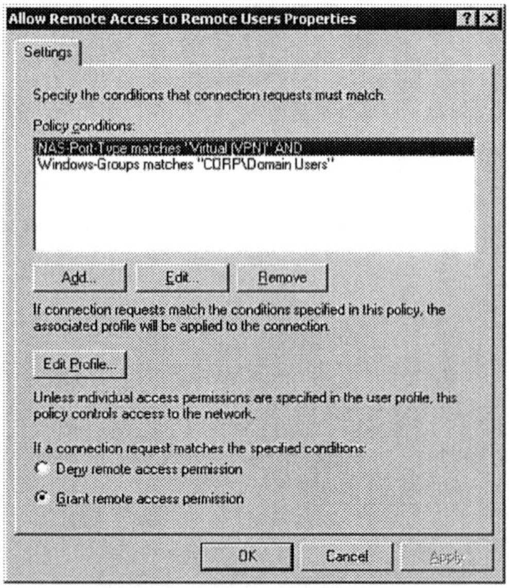

FIGURE 7.37 The Settings tab of the Properties dialog box enables you to refine the configuration of a remote access policy.

The Dial-In Constraints Tab

The parameters that can be configured on the Dial-In Constraints tab of the Edit Dial-In Profile dialog box, shown in Figure 7.38, include the following:

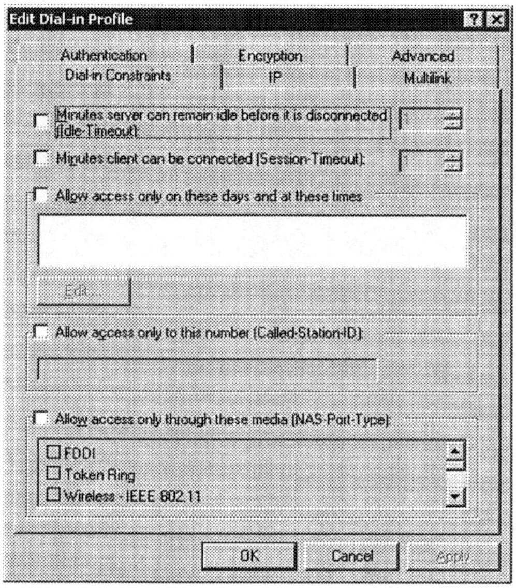

FIGURE 7.38 The Dial-In Constraints tab can be used to restrict how dial-in access can be used.

- **Minutes Server Can Remain Idle Before It Is Disconnected (Idle-Timeout)**—This setting enables you to set the number of minutes of inactivity a user has before the system disconnects the user. This setting can be used to limit toll charges being incurred by an idle system or to protect a network from the vulnerability a connected but idle system presents. This setting can also be used to maximize the availability of ports if the server has a limited number of ports. This prevents idle users from tying up ports that other users might need.
- **Minutes Client Can Be Connected (Session-Timeout)**—This setting enables you to set the total number of minutes a session can last. This can be used to limit toll charges for users who might leave themselves connected for extended periods of time.
- **Allow Access Only on These Days and at These Times**—This setting enables you to place day and time limits on any remote access policy, without needing to make that a condition of the policy.
- **Allow Access Only to This Number (Called-Station-ID)**—This setting is typically used in conjunction with a branch office connection, to ensure that the connection is originating from the appropriate number. This field can contain a phone number or an IP address, so it can be used in conjunction with a site-to-site VPN as well as a branch demand-dial connection.
- **Allow Access Only Through These Media (NAS-Port-Type)**—This parameter enables you to control the types of network media that can be used to connect by using this profile. You might use this to ensure that a VPN connection can be established only by using LAN media and not dial-in lines.

EXAM ALERT

Changing parameters: new wording in Windows Server 2003 Don't get confused with Windows 2000 parameters—the parameters in the Edit Dial-In Profile dialog box have changed subtly in Windows Server 2003. Microsoft has changed the language from "Restrict To" to "Allow Only" terminology. For example, in Windows 2000, the parameter Restrict Dial-In to This Number Only is now Allow Access Only to This Number (Called-Station-ID) in Windows Server 2003. The Called-Station-ID field is the remote access policy condition used to set this parameter.

The IP Tab

The parameters that can be configured on the IP tab of the Edit Dial-In Profile dialog box, shown in Figure 7.39, include the following:

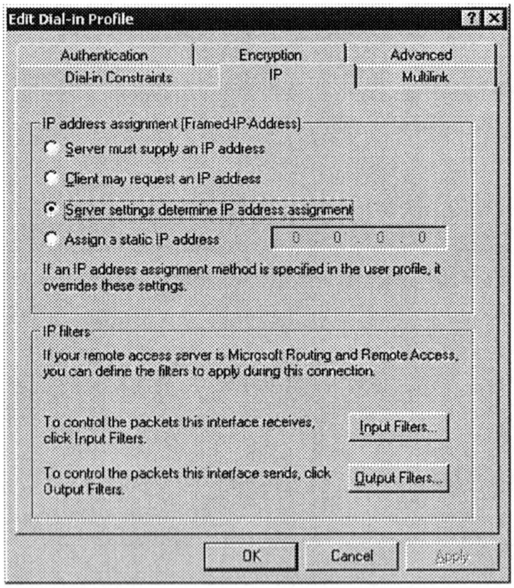

FIGURE 7.39 The IP tab can be used to configure the characteristics of IP for a remote access policy.

- **IP Address Assignment (Framed-IP-Address)**—The options in this section define how users being authorized by this policy will get their IP addresses. This is typically left at the default setting, but you can change the setting to restrict how IP addresses are assigned.
- **IP Filters**—This section enables you to set IP packet filters on the connection. For example, if this connection were being used only for getting web access to your intranet server, you might set an inbound filter for port 80 (HTTP) to access only the intranet server.

The Multilink Tab

The parameters that can be configured on the Multilink tab of the Edit Dial-In Profile dialog, shown in Figure 7.40, include the following:

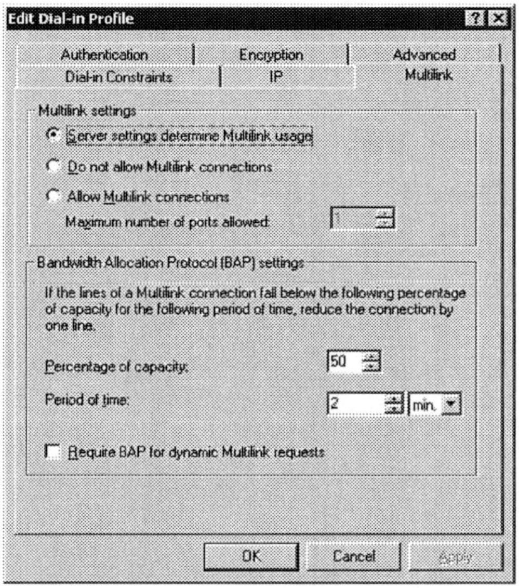

FIGURE 7.40 The Multilink tab can be used to configure the multilink (aggregation of multiple physical connections into a single logical connection) capabilities of Windows Server 2003 RRAS.

- **Multilink Settings**—The settings in this section control how the Multilink protocol can be used with this remote access policy:
  - **Server Settings Determine Multilink Usage**—When this option is selected, the RRAS server settings are used to determine whether Multilink is permitted.
  - **Do Not Allow Multilink Connections**—This setting disables the use of Multilink.
  - **Allow Multilink Connections**—This setting allows a client computer to connect by using multiple ports and can also be used to set the maximum number of ports that can be used.

  Windows 2000 and later operating systems support the use of Multilink—using multiple connections to a single server, which are aggregated to provide additional bandwidth. Although it can improve performance, Multilink can be a very resource-intensive solution. Not only does it tie up multiple ports per user at the server end of the connection, but it also requires multiple modems and phone lines on the user's end. This has largely been phased out as multiple modem lines are replaced by high-speed Internet connections such as cable modem lines and Digital Subscriber Line (DSL).

- **Bandwidth Allocation Protocol (BAP) Settings**—BAP monitors the utilization on a Multilink connection and dynamically reduces the number of connected lines if the user's utilization drops below a certain amount. You use this section to set the utilization percentage and time before dropping one line of the Multilink connection. You can (and should) require the use of BAP with any Multilink connection. BAP can also be configured to request additional bandwidth when utilization reaches a threshold.

The Authentication Tab

These parameters can be configured on the Authentication tab of the Edit Dial-In Profile dialog box, shown in Figure 7.41:

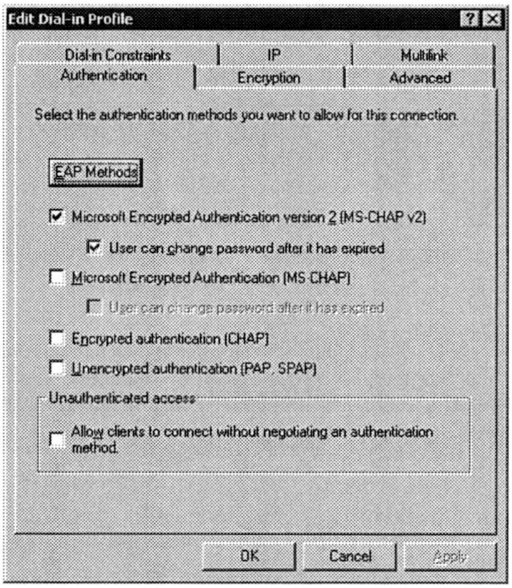

FIGURE 7.41 The Authentication tab enables you to configure the authentication protocols that can be used with this profile.

- **Authentication methods**—You can select what protocols can be used to authenticate a user connecting by using this remote access policy. Whenever possible, you should use MS-CHAPv2 or EAP, which provide the most secure authentication.
- **Unauthenticated Access**—You should never enable unauthenticated access. It essentially allows clients to connect without authenticating first and should never be used as a production option because it bypasses all authentication security. This can be very useful when you're troubleshooting problems because it allows the elimination of authentication as a source of the problems. You just need to be sure to reenable authentication when the problem is resolved.

The Encryption Tab

The Encryption tab of the Edit Dial-In Profile dialog box, shown in Figure 7.42, enables you to select how strong the encryption used by this connection must be. If you are running an entirely Windows 2000 or greater client population, you should permit only the strongest level of encryption. If you have older clients, you might need to permit less strong encryption levels.

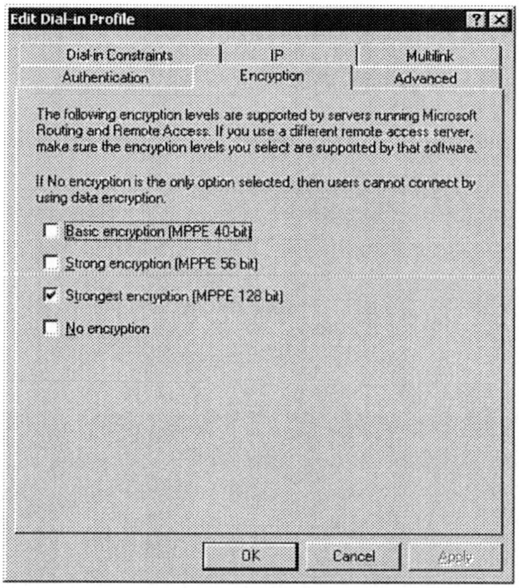

FIGURE 7.42 The Encryption tab is used to specify the permitted encryption strengths for a connection.

The Advanced Tab

The Advanced tab of the Edit Dial-In Profile dialog box, shown in Figure 7.43, enables you to specify additional connection attributes, typically related to RADIUS requirements for a connection. This tab is generally used for only very complex implementations involving centralized RADIUS servers for remote access policy storage.

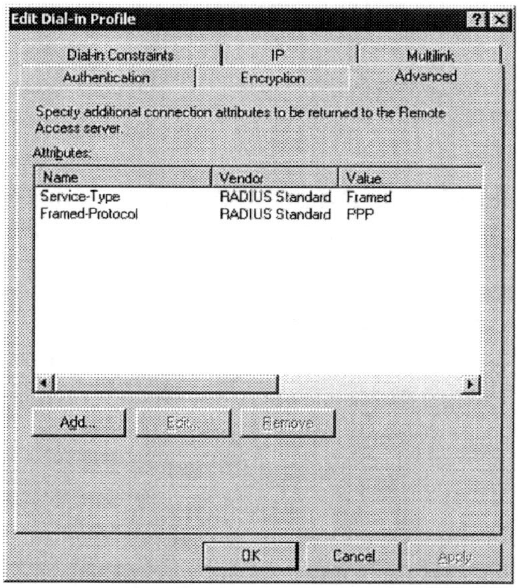

FIGURE 7.43 The Advanced tab is used to specify additional connection attributes to be returned to the remote access server.

Advanced Network Access Configuration: The Network Access Quarantine Control

As you have already seen in this chapter, the normal remote access connections you've worked with have only validated the credentials of the user. However, with the ever-growing threat to computer networks from viruses, spyware, and other unwanted applications, it only makes sense that a truly secure network would be one that controls which computers can remotely connect to it as well. When a user has made a remote access connection with their computer, that computer becomes part of the network (if only temporarily) and thus can spread unwanted malware.

EXAM ALERT

Network Access Quarantine Control This is a very advanced topic and not extremely likely to be found on your Exam 70-293, as evidenced by its omission from the exam objectives. It's anticipated that you will likely not have the required environment to implement Network Access Quarantine Control; thus, we will not be examining it in great enough detail in this book to warrant Step by Step exercises. Our coverage here is limited to an introduction only so that you'll at least be familiar with what it does and how it works.

Network Access Quarantine Control, a new feature introduced with Windows Server 2003, is a means to prevent users who possess valid credentials but are using computers that do not meet the required corporate configuration from making remote access connections. As an example, you might not necessarily want a valid user to connect with an incorrectly configured computer that had any of these problems:

- Missing a Service Pack
- Missing security updates that are more than 1 month old
- Missing up-to-date and active antivirus software
- Missing a software firewall (such as the Windows Firewall) that is operational on the network adapter

If all of your company's computers were internal and never left the building, your job would be easier and you would not need remote access or Network Access Quarantine Control. However, it is more common now than ever for valid network users to connect back to the corporate network from any number of locations, such as from home, from a hotel room via a portable computer, or even from an Internet cafe. To combat the out-of-control problem that keeping all of these computers up to corporate specifications would be, Network Access Quarantine Control delays remote access by your users to your corporate network until the configuration of the computer they are using has been examined and approved. A special script is provided by an administrator to be used in this examination.

When Network Access Quarantine Control is enabled and configured, a remote access user who successfully authenticates is not just dumped onto the network as he or she normally would be. Instead, after the user has been authenticated, the computer is granted IP address (as it normally would be) and then the connection is placed into a quarantine, in which network access is substantially limited. The script that was provided for Network Access Quarantine Control is then run on the remote computer to check its configuration. If the script determines that the remote computer is compliant with the policies in effect, that computer is removed from the quarantine and is provided with normal remote access—as if Network Access Quarantine Control was not in effect. While the computer is in the quarantine, its network access can be restricted by using packet filters to control traffic to or from the computer. Additionally, a time limit can be configured for the quarantine so that the remote computer is automatically disconnected after a set amount of time. If the script determines that the remote computer is not compliant, typically it is written so that the user is directed to an internal web page that provides instructions on how to install the items required to be in compliance.

Although Network Access Quarantine Control does appear to be a security solution, it is not that in the most typical sense. Although it will increase your overall network security, it does not replace all the other security considerations you must give to your network. Network Access Quarantine Control was designed not to stop unauthorized users from making remote connections to your network, but instead to stop otherwise authorized users with noncompliant computers from making remote connections to your network.

To learn more about this advanced remote access topic, visit www.microsoft.com/technet/itsolutions/network/vpn/quarantine.mspx.

Chapter Summary

In this chapter, we examined some of the many options that are available to plan for and maintain more secure remote and wireless access to Windows Server 2003 networks.

Remote Assistance and Remote Desktop for Administration are both Remote Desktop Protocol–based services and can be used to remotely manage a computer. Remote Assistance is typically initiated by a user (the Novice) asking an administrator (the Expert) for help by using Windows Messenger or an email request. A file request can also be used if required. After the Expert has accepted the invitation, he or she can view and even take control of the remote computer if the Novice allows. This provides a means to help the remote user with problems on his or her computer. Remote Desktop for Administration is the replacement for Terminal Services Administration mode in Windows 2000 and does not require an invitation request to be sent. An administrator can initiate a connection to a server and remotely administer the server—even shutting it down or restarting it. Only two concurrent Remote Desktop for Administration connections can be created to any one server.

With the recent rise in popularity and availability of wireless LANs, security issues have begun to occur within organizations using WLANs. Although several vendors create full-featured security solutions for 802.11 wireless networks, Microsoft has also provided a basic security implementation within Windows Server 2003. Using Group Policy, you can configure wireless network policies that can be used to determine what wireless networks your clients can connect to and how the connection must be made with respect to authentication and encryption.

Finally, you learned about Routing and Remote Access, what it does with Windows Server 2003, and how to plan remote access into your network. Remember that Windows Server 2003 supports a large number of authentication protocols, such as EAP, MS-CHAPv2, and PAP. A good understanding of the basic operation and use of each is critical to your successful remote access solution—and test day experience. Remote access is controlled through policies and profiles, and this chapter examined each.

Key Terms

- 802.1x
- CHAP
- Extensible Authentication Protocol (EAP)
- Internet Key Exchange (IKE)
- IPSec
- Microsoft Management Console (MMC)
- MPPE

- MS-CHAP Version 1
- MS-CHAP Version 2
- PAP
- RADIUS
- Remote Assistance
- Remote Desktop for Administration
- Remote Desktop Protocol (RDP)
- RRAS
- SPAP
- TCP/IP
- Terminal Services
- Transport mode
- Tunnel mode
- Wireless LAN (WLAN)

Apply Your Knowledge

In this chapter, you examined the planning and implementation of secure wireless, remote, and remote administrative methods in Windows Server 2003. In the following exercises, you practice some of the concepts and methods discussed in this chapter.

Exercises

7.1 Sending a Remote Assistance Request

In this exercise, you create and send a Remote Assistance request. You need two Windows XP Professional or Windows Server 2003 computers (or one of each) to complete this procedure.

Estimated time: 15 minutes

1. Open the Help and Support Center by clicking Start, Help and Support.
2. Click the Remote Assistance link under the Support Tasks column.
3. In the Remote Assistance window, click the Invite Someone to Help You link.
4. Select a Windows Messenger user and click Invite This Person.

5. To send an email request using your MAPI-compliant messaging application, enter the Expert's first name and click Continue.
6. Supply the password and duration for the Remote Assistance request.
7. Enter the correct email address and add any other notes you want before sending the message.
8. To send the Remote Assistance request using a saved file, click Send Invitation as a File (Advanced).

7.2 Configuring Remote Assistance Group Policy Options

In this exercise, you configure the Group Policy options for Remote Assistance. You should have at least one Windows Server 2003 computer for this procedure.

Estimated time: 20 minutes

1. Locate the GPO for which you want to configure the Remote Assistance settings.
2. Locate the Remote Assistance node.
3. Double-click the Solicited Remote Assistance setting to open its Properties dialog box.
4. Select the Enabled radio button.
5. For the Permit Remote Control of This Computer option, select Allow Helpers to Remotely Control the Computer, to ensure that you can fully offer Remote Assistance as needed. You can take control only if the user allows it.
6. For the Maximum Ticket Time option, configure a reasonable lifetime for the Remote Assistance request, such as 1 hour. This gives you a window in which to respond to the request without creating an overly large security risk.
7. For the Select the Method for Sending Email Invitations option, your selection depends on the messaging client in use on your network. The Mailto option configures the Remote Assistance request to be sent as an Internet link and works in virtually all situations. The SMAPI (Simple MAPI) option configures the request to be attached to the message.
8. Click OK to close the Solicited Remote Assistance Properties dialog box.
9. Double-click the Offer Remote Assistance setting to open its Properties dialog box.
10. To enable you to offer unsolicited Remote Assistance to users, select the Enabled radio button.
11. For the Permit Remote Control of This Computer option, select Allow Helpers to Remotely Control the Computer to ensure that you can fully offer Remote Assistance as needed. You can take control only if the user allows it.
12. Click the Show button to open the Show Contents dialog box.
13. To add users and/or groups, click the Add button. You can add only one object at a time, and you must use the following format:

    <Domain Name>\<User Name> or
    <Domain Name>\<Group Name>
14. Click OK to close the Offer Remote Assistance Properties dialog box.

7.3 Creating a Wireless Network Security Policy

In this exercise, you create a new wireless network security policy. You need at least one Windows Server 2003 computer to complete this process.

Estimated time: 20 minutes

1. Using either the Group Policy Management Console (GPMC) or Group Policy Editor (GPE), locate the GPO in which you want to create the WLAN security policy.
2. Locate the Wireless Network (IEEE 802.11) Policies node. Right-click it; then select Create Wireless Network Policy from the context menu to start the Wireless Network Policy Wizard.
3. Click Next to dismiss the opening page of the wizard.
4. Enter a name and description for the new policy on the Wireless Network Policy Name dialog box. Click Next.
5. The Completing the Wireless Network Policy Wizard dialog box appears. Ensure that the Edit Properties option is selected; then click Finish to exit the wizard and start configuring the policy's properties.
6. The Policy Properties dialog box opens. Configure your selections as you like and switch to the Preferred Networks tab.
7. Click the Add button to open the New Preferred Setting Properties dialog box.
8. On the Network Properties tab, configure the selections as necessary. When you are done, switch to the IEEE 802.1x tab.
9. On the IEEE 802.1x tab, configure the selections as necessary. When you are done, click OK to commit the preferred network to the policy.
10. Back at the Preferred Networks tab of the policy Properties dialog box, you can add another preferred network if you want. You can also remove or edit existing preferred network entries, as well as change their relative order by using the Move Up and Move Down buttons.
11. Click OK to close the WLAN policy Properties dialog box.
12. If you want to force Active Directory replication to occur, thus implementing your new WLAN policies, enter the **`gpupdate /target:`*`computer`*** command.

7.4 Enabling Routing and Remote Access

In this exercise, you enable and perform basic configuration on the Routing and Remote Access Service.

Estimated time: 15 minutes

1. Open the Routing and Remote Access console by choosing Start, Control Panel, Administrative Tools, and then Routing and Remote Access. By default, the local computer is listed as a server.
2. Right-click the server you want to configure and select Configure and Enable Routing and Remote Access. The Routing and Remote Access Server Setup Wizard starts.

3. Click Next to start configuring the Routing and Remote Access Service. The Configuration dialog box opens.
4. Select the Secure Connection Between Two Private Networks option and click Next to continue. The Demand-Dial Connections dialog box opens.
5. In the Demand-Dial Connections dialog box, select No and click Next to continue. The Completing the Routing and Remote Access Server Setup Wizard summary dialog box opens.
6. Click Finish to complete the enabling of routing services.

Review Questions

1. You need to create and implement a plan for your network that will enable you to ensure that users can always receive real-time support for their problems. What new feature of Windows Server 2003 provides this solution for you?
2. You are attempting to connect to one of your Windows Server 2003 computers using the Remote Desktop Connection utility but cannot. What is the most likely reason for this trouble?
3. You are creating a new Wireless Network Security Policy. You need to ensure that your wireless clients can connect only to your Access Points and not directly to each other. What mode should you select?
4. How many concurrent, nonconsole Remote Desktop sessions are possible in Windows Server 2003?
5. What must you do before you can use Windows Messenger to request Remote Assistance on a Windows Server 2003 computer?

Exam Questions

1. Sally is the senior network administrator for Runners Corp. She runs a network of 20 Windows Server 2003 systems, as well as 250 Windows XP Professional clients. Sally needs to set up remote access polices so that clients with proper credentials can access the Remote Access Server and gain access to the internal network to get resources. Sally wants to ensure that all users are secure when connecting via the Internet. Which protocol can users use from a client to connect to and access a Remote Access Server securely?

   ❍ **A.** PAP

   ❍ **B.** SPAP

   ❍ **C.** EAP

   ❍ **D.** OSPF

2. You are the network administrator for Jeff's Jeep Tours, an Australian tour company. You have a central office located in Sydney and 20 other smaller remote offices located all over the country. You have recently completed your rollout of Windows Server 2003 for all servers and Windows XP Professional for all clients in the corporate network. Some of the remote offices have only three or

four employees and no IT staff. The IT management responsibility for these offices is shared among all the IT staff in other locations. When users in remote locations with no IT staff have problems with their Windows XP Professional computers, what feature should they use to get help for their problem?

- ❍ **A.** Terminal Services
- ❍ **B.** Remote Desktop for Administration
- ❍ **C.** Remote Desktop Protocol
- ❍ **D.** Remote Assistance

3. You are the network administrator for Jeff's Jeep Tours, an Australian tour company. You have a central office located in Sydney and 20 other smaller remote offices located all over the country. You have recently completed your rollout of Windows Server 2003 for all servers and Windows XP Professional for all clients in the corporate network. Some of the remote offices have only three or four employees and no IT staff. The IT management responsibility for these offices is shared among all the IT staff in other locations. You need to install a service pack on one of the Windows XP computers located in an office with no IT staff. What feature of Windows Server 2003 will you use?

- ❍ **A.** Terminal Services
- ❍ **B.** Remote Desktop for Administration
- ❍ **C.** Remote Desktop Protocol
- ❍ **D.** Remote Assistance

4. Marshall is the network administrator for QBC Corp. He runs a network of 20 Windows Server 2003 systems on a network backbone, as well as 200 Windows XP Professional clients. Marshall is worried about a single PC that cannot connect to the network. He wants to ensure that all users are secure when connecting via the Internet. Which protocol can users use from a client to connect to and access a Remote Access Server securely, and is the most secure?

- ❍ **A.** PAP
- ❍ **B.** SPAP
- ❍ **C.** CHAP
- ❍ **D.** EAP

5. You are the network administrator for Joe's Crab Shack, a regional restaurant chain. While at a standards-setting meeting in Redmond, Washington, you are informed that one of your newly installed Windows Server 2003 DHCP servers has stopped leasing addresses. Rick, the president of the company, has asked you to make a Remote Desktop for Administration connection to the server via your VPN connection. After you have connected to your internal network via VPN, you attempt to create a Remote Desktop for Administration connection to the affected DHCP server and cannot. The DHCP server is located on the same IP subnet as the VPN server. You can create

Remote Desktop for Administration connections to other Windows Server 2003 computers, however. What is the most likely reason for this problem?

❍ **A.** Remote Desktop is not enabled on the server.

❍ **B.** Your VPN server is not functioning correctly.

❍ **C.** TCP port 3389 is being blocked at your firewall.

❍ **D.** Remote Desktop is not enabled on your portable computer.

6. You are the network administrator for Roger's Rockets, a manufacturer of toy rocket kits. You are preparing to configure a new wireless LAN policy for your network. You want your wireless clients to connect only to Access Points and create no other connections. Which type of network will you configure in the new WLAN security policy?

❍ **A.** Ad hoc

❍ **B.** Infrastructure

❍ **C.** Central

❍ **D.** Core

7. Sally is the senior network administrator for Runners Corp. She runs a network of 20 Windows Server 2003 systems, as well as 250 Windows XP Professional clients. Sally needs to use MS-CHAP Version 1 on her Remote Access Server. She is told that this would not be wise and to use MS-CHAP Version 2 instead. Why would Sally want to use Version 2 over Version 1?

❍ **A.** MS-CHAPv2 enables users to log in and check against a RADIUS server.

❍ **B.** MS-CHAPv2 provides for mutual authentication of both the remote access client and the remote access server for increased connection security.

❍ **C.** MS-CHAPv2 can authenticate as well as encrypt.

❍ **D.** MS-CHAPv2 enables users to send small packets across the network.

8. You are the network administrator for Roger's Rockets, a manufacturer of toy rocket kits. You have configured four different WLAN security policies for your network: one at the domain level, one on the Graphics OU, one on the Engineering OU, and one on the Manufacturing OU, which is a child object inside the Engineering OU. All users and computers in each department are located in the corresponding OU. For a computer located in the Manufacturing OU, which security policy will be implemented?

❍ **A.** The domain WLAN security policy

❍ **B.** The Engineering OU WLAN security policy

❍ **C.** The Graphics OU WLAN security policy

❍ **D.** The Manufacturing OU WLAN security policy

9. You are the network administrator for Roger's Rockets, a manufacturer of toy rocket kits. You have one WLAN security policy in place for your network that is configured in the Default Domain GPO. When you make a change to this WLAN security policy that changes the list of preferred networks, what will any currently connected wireless clients do?

❍ **A.** The client connection will be momentarily broken if the new policy takes precedence over the old policy.

❍ **B.** The client connection will be momentarily broken. When the Wireless Configuration service restarts, the client will revert to any existing client-configured settings in place.

❍ **C.** The client connection will be momentarily broken. When the Wireless Configuration service restarts, the client will revert to the client settings that are configured in the next-higher-level WLAN security policy.

❍ **D.** The client connection will be broken until the radio on the wireless client has been restarted.

10. Marshall is the network administrator for QBC Corp. He runs a network of 20 Windows Server 2003 systems on a network backbone, as well as 200 Windows XP Professional clients. Marshall needs to allow for the delay of a remote access connection attempt to the Remote Access Server until a script runs verifying the identity of the remote access computer. What is the new Windows Server 2003 feature called?

❍ **A.** IIS Lockdown tool

❍ **B.** Network Access Quarantine Control

❍ **C.** `Wscript.exe`

❍ **D.** Remote Access Scripter

11. You are the network administrator for Joe's Crab Shack, a regional restaurant chain. While at a standards-setting meeting in Redmond, Washington, you are informed that one of your newly installed Windows Server 2003 DHCP servers has stopped leasing addresses. Your assistant administrator has verified that there are plenty of unused leases in the current DHCP scope but is unable to determine the cause of the problem. Company policy prohibits the use of any instant-messaging clients within your internal network. How can your assistant get Remote Assistance from you to help troubleshoot the DHCP server?

❍ **A.** Use Emergency Management Services to make the request.

❍ **B.** Use the Recovery Console to make the request.

❍ **C.** Use an email-based request.

❍ **D.** Use MSN Messenger to make the request.

12. You are the network administrator for Roger's Rockets, a manufacturer of toy rocket kits. You have just completed changing the WLAN security policy that is applied to your Engineering OU. You want this policy to be enforced immediately on all clients. What command can you issue to cause Group Policy to replicate immediately?

❍ **A.** `gpupdate /target:`*`user`*

❍ **B.** `secedit /configure`

❍ **C.** `gpupdate /target:`*`computer`*

❍ **D.** `secedit /analyze`

13. You are the network administrator for Joe's Crab Shack, a regional restaurant chain. While at a standards-setting meeting in Redmond, Washington, you are unsuccessfully attempting to initiate a Remote Desktop for Administration session with one of your Windows Server 2003 servers over the Internet. The server has a publicly accessible IP address, but it is located behind your network's external firewall. You can `ping` the server from your location and have verified via telephone conversation with onsite IT staff that Remote Desktop is enabled for this server. Your account is a member of the Domain Admins, Enterprise Admins, and Administrators groups for your Active Directory network. What is the most likely reason for the inability to make the Remote Desktop for Administration connection?

❍ **A.** IIS 6.0 is not installed on the server in question.

❍ **B.** TCP port 3389 is being blocked at the external firewall.

❍ **C.** TCP port 8088 is being blocked at the external firewall.

❍ **D.** Your user account does not have the required permissions to use Remote Desktop for Administration.

14. You are the network administrator for Roger's Rockets, a manufacturer of toy rocket kits. You are creating a new WLAN security policy for the wireless clients located in the Engineering OU. You have one approved 802.11b WLAN in your organization with an SSID of rogrcktint1. From time to time, the Engineering department needs to use a special testing WLAN. The SSID of this testing WLAN changes each time it is implemented. What setting can you configure for the Engineering OU WLAN security policy that will allow these wireless clients to connect to the special testing WLAN when it is available?

❍ **A.** You need to update the WLAN security policy every time the special testing WLAN is available.

❍ **B.** You need to create a new WLAN security policy in the Engineering OU every time the special testing WLAN is available.

❍ **C.** You need to select the Automatically Connect to Nonpreferred Networks option.

❍ **D.** You need to select the Wireless Network Key (WEP) option.

15. You are the network administrator for Jeff's Jeep Tours, an Australian tour company. You are configuring one of your Windows Server 2003 computers so that it will support Remote Desktop for Administration connections. You want two additional nonadministrative personnel to be able to create Remote Desktop connections to the server. To what local group do you need to add their user accounts to allow these users to create Remote Desktop for Administration connections?

    ❍ **A.** HelpServicesGroup

    ❍ **B.** Remote Desktop Users

    ❍ **C.** Network Configuration Operators

    ❍ **D.** Administrators

Answers to Review Questions

1. Users can use Remote Assistance to request help from an Expert with their problems, provided that the computers on both ends of the connection are Windows XP or Windows Server 2003. For more information, see the section "Remote Assistance."

2. The most likely reason you cannot create the connection is that this server already has two existing Remote Desktop connections. For more information, see the section "Remote Desktop for Administration (RDA)."

3. To ensure that wireless clients create connections only to Access Points, select the Access Point (Infrastructure) Networks Only option. For more information, see the section "Planning Wireless LAN (WLAN) Security."

4. You can establish only two regular Remote Desktop connections to a server. You can establish one additional session to a console. Additional sessions cannot be created as long as these limits have been met; this can lead to problems if administrators do not properly end their Remote Assistance sessions by logging out and not just disconnecting. For more information, see the section "RDA Security and Management Issues."

5. You must download Windows Messenger for Windows Server 2003 from Microsoft and install it on the server to enable this method of requesting Remote Assistance. For more information, see the section "Remote Assistance."

Answers to Exam Questions

1. **C.** PAP, SPAP, and OSPF are incorrect; thus, answers A, B, and D are incorrect. EAP is by far the most secure and up-to-date protocol Sally can use, especially because it is not vendor specific and has many extensions, such as EAP-TLS and LEAP. For more information, see the section "Extensible Authentication Protocol (EAP)."

2. **D.** If configured to allow it, Windows XP and Windows Server 2003 computers can send Remote Assistance requests to an Expert asking for help with problems. The Novice requesting the Remote Assistance can choose from Windows Messenger, email, or a file to ask for Remote Assistance

and can control the level of interaction and control the Expert has on the Novice's computer after the Remote Assistance connection has been made. Terminal Services is used in Windows Server 2003 to provide the Terminal Server role, enabling users to make connections to a Terminal Server to execute applications that are not available on their local computer, and does not provide a means for users to get help with problems on their computers; thus, answer A is incorrect. Remote Desktop for Administration is used to create administrative connections to computers and does not require a request to be sent; thus, answer B is incorrect. The Remote Desktop Protocol is used to power Remote Assistance and Remote Desktop for Administration but does not directly provide the solution required; thus, answer C is incorrect. For more information, see the section "Remote Assistance."

3. **B.** The Remote Desktop for Administration feature replaces what was previously known as Remote Administration mode of Terminal Services in Windows 2000 Server. RDA allows for a maximum of two concurrent connections to a server for the purposes of managing and maintaining it. Unlike Remote Assistance, RDA sessions do not start with a user request; an administrator can initiate an RDA connection whenever desired. Terminal Services is used in Windows Server 2003 to provide the Terminal Server role, enabling users to make connections to a Terminal Server to execute applications that are not available on their local computer, and does not provide a means for users to get help with problems on their computers; thus, answer A is incorrect. Remote Desktop for Administration is used to create administrative connections to computers and does not require a request to be sent; thus, answer C is incorrect. Remote Assistance enables a Novice to request help from an Expert if the Novice's computer is configured to allow Remote Assistance; thus, answer D is incorrect. For more information, see the section "Remote Desktop for Administration (RDA)."

4. **D.** PAP, SPAP, and OSPF are incorrect; thus, answers A, B, and C are incorrect. EAP is by far the most secure and up-to-date protocol Marshall can use, especially because it is not vendor specific and has many extensions, such as EAP-TLS and LEAP. For more information, see the section "Extensible Authentication Protocol (EAP)."

5. **A.** Because you can create a connection to your network via the VPN server, the most likely problem is that Remote Desktop is not enabled on this server. The VPN server is obviously functioning correctly because you are able to connect to the network via VPN; thus, answer B is incorrect. Because you are connecting directly to your internal network via a VPN tunnel, the status of the firewall configuration is not an issue; thus, answer C is incorrect. Remote Desktop does not need to be enabled on your portable computer; thus, answer D is incorrect. For more information, see the section "Remote Desktop for Administration (RDA)."

6. **B**. Infrastructure networks are those in which wireless clients create connections only to Access Points. Ad hoc networks are those in which wireless clients can create connections directly to each other without the need for an Access Point; thus, answer A is incorrect. Central and Core are not network types; thus, answers C and D are incorrect. For more information, see the section "Planning Wireless LAN (WLAN) Security."

7. **B.** MS-CHAPv2 provides for mutual authentication of both the remote access client and the remote access server for increased connection security, thus making it more secure and a better choice than MS-CHAPv1. For more information, see the section "Microsoft Challenge Handshake Authorization Protocol (MS-CHAP)."

8. **D.** WLAN security policies are applied using the normal Group Policy processing order; thus, the security policy that is closest to the computer object takes precedence. Consequently, answers A, B, and C are incorrect. For more information, see the section "Planning Wireless LAN (WLAN) Security."

9. **A.** When a WLAN security policy is changed, the client connection will be momentarily broken if the new policy takes precedence over the old policy—that is, if the new policy changes something such as the authentication method; thus, answers B, C, and D are incorrect. For more information, see the section "Planning Wireless LAN (WLAN) Security."

10. **B.** Windows Server 2003 provides a new feature called Network Access Quarantine Control. This feature allows the delay of a remote access connection attempt to the Remote Access Server until a script runs verifying the configuration of the remote access system. The IIS Lockdown tool, `Wscript.exe`, and the Remote Access Scripter either are not valid services or are improper services for this solution; thus, answers A, C, and D are incorrect. For more information, see the section "Advanced Network Access Configuration: The Network Access Quarantine Control."

11. **C.** Of the available options, the only valid one is to create and send an email request for Remote Assistance. The email request will contain a special URL that the Expert can use to initiate the Remote Assistance connection via the Microsoft website. The Expert will need to download and install an ActiveX applet as part of the connection process. Emergency Management Services and the Recovery Console cannot be used to send Remote Assistance requests; thus, answers A and B are incorrect. MSN Messenger is similar to Windows Messenger but cannot be used to send Remote Assistance requests; thus, answer D is incorrect. For more information, see the section "Remote Assistance."

12. **C.** You need to use the `gpupdate /target:`*`computer`* command to immediately cause the computer-configuration portion of Group Policy to refresh and update your changes. Wireless LAN security policies are not kept in the user-configuration portion of Group Policy; thus, answer A is incorrect. The `secedit` command is no longer used to refresh Group Policy in Windows Server 2003; thus, answers B and D are incorrect. For more information, see the section "Planning Wireless LAN (WLAN) Security."

13. **B.** The most likely problem is that your external firewall has been configured to block traffic on TCP port 3389 and is thus preventing Remote Desktop Protocol traffic from crossing the firewall. IIS does not need to be installed to use Remote Desktop for Administration; thus, answer A is incorrect. TCP ports 8088 and 8080 are used by the Web Interface for Remote Administration and are not related to Remote Desktop for Administration; thus, answer C is incorrect. Your account does, in fact, have the required permissions because it is a member of the Enterprise Admins, Domain Admins, and Administrators groups in your domain; thus, answer D is incorrect. For more information, see the section "Remote Desktop for Administration (RDA)."

14. **C.** By creating the WLAN security policy and selecting the Automatically Connect to Nonpreferred Networks option, you can enforce the settings you want (such as those for authentication and so forth) on preferred networks but still allow wireless clients to connect to nonpreferred networks, if required. Under normal circumstances, you might likely not configure this option because it removes some administrative control you would otherwise exercise over what networks wireless

clients can connect to. You don't need to modify the existing WLAN security policy when the special testing WLAN is available; thus, answer A is incorrect. Likewise, you don't need to create a new WLAN security policy; thus, answer B is incorrect. The Wireless Network Key (WEP) option is not related to this issue; thus, answer D is incorrect. For more information, see the section "Planning Wireless LAN (WLAN) Security."

15. **B.** You must add the user accounts for these two users to the local Remote Desktop Users group on the computer. The HelpServicesGroup is used by Remote Assistance connections; thus, answer A is incorrect. The Network Configuration Operators group is allowed to manage the networking properties of a server; thus, answer C is incorrect. You don't need to add these user accounts to the Administrators group to allow them to create Remote Desktop connections to this server; thus, answer D is incorrect. For more information, see the section "Remote Desktop for Administration (RDA)."

Suggested Readings and Resources

1. Davies, Joseph, and Thomas Lee. *Microsoft Windows Server 2003 TCP/IP Protocols and Services Technical Reference*. Redmond, WA: Microsoft Press, 2003.

2. Microsoft Corporation. *Microsoft Windows Server 2003 Resource Kit*. Redmond, WA: Microsoft Press, 2003.

3. Microsoft Corporation. *Microsoft Windows Server 2003 Deployment Kit*. Redmond, WA: Microsoft Press, 2003.

4. "Network Access Quarantine Control." www.microsoft.com/technet/itsolutions/network/vpn/quarantine.mspx.

8

CHAPTER EIGHT

Planning and Implementing Other Network Security Measures

Security is all the rage right now—and rightly so. For many years, security was thought of as something that only certain networks needed. When security was planned for a network, more often than not, it included only a weak solution that the company hoped would keep external intruders out of the network. No longer can networks be exposed to the Internet without a well-thought-out and layered defense plan. In this chapter, we examine a few of the tasks that you can address in your security plan: using digital certificates, using smart cards, auditing, monitoring event logs, and keeping your Windows computers up-to-date with the latest security updates.

Objectives

Microsoft defines the "Planning, Implementing, and Maintaining Security Infrastructure" objectives as follows:

Configure Active Directory directory service for certificate publication.

- Although you do not have to perform any direct configuration of Active Directory to make Certificate Services function, you can configure some advanced tasks, such as certificate autoenrollment for your network's users and computers.

Plan a public key infrastructure (PKI) that uses Certificate Services.

- **Identify the appropriate type of certificate authority to support certificate issuance requirements.**
- **Plan the enrollment and distribution of certificates.**
- **Plan for the use of smart cards for authentication.**
- At the heart of the Windows security solution lies Certificate Services. You use digital certificates every day in Windows Server 2003 without even realizing it. (Have you ever encrypted a file using EFS?) Certificate Services enables you to implement and configure one or more CAs to issue and revoke digital certificates for your network. You might also want to take your security a level further and implement a smart card authentication solution.

Plan a framework for planning and implementing security.

- **Plan for security monitoring.**
- **Plan a change and configuration management framework for security.**
- Being able to just sit back and watch the network run after implementing your security solution would be nice; however, this is not the case. You must maintain a constant watch over your network, examining many different aspects of it to determine what is occurring that should not be. By auditing and examining the event logs, you can quickly get a good idea of what is going on in your network—free, without the purchase of any advanced network-monitoring tools. Also, without a document in place for your organization to manage change and configuration, you will likely find yourself in trouble if an ill-planned configuration change goes awry.

Plan a security update infrastructure. Tools might include Microsoft Baseline Security Analyzer and Microsoft Software Update Services.

- In a perfect world, you would be able to install your server or client operating system and have it be perfect and perfectly secure right out of the box. Although Microsoft has made great progress toward meeting that ideal in Windows Server 2003, it's not quite a reality yet. Part of keeping an operating system secure involves identifying and applying updates as required. The combination of the Microsoft Baseline Security Analyzer (MBSA) and Windows Server Update Services (WSUS) makes this task easier for the Windows Server 2003 network administrator.

Outline

Study Strategies

- Become familiar with the topics presented in this chapter, including Certificate Services, auditing, event logs, WSUS, and MBSA. All these topics will be important as you plan and implement a security solution for your network.
- Get your hands dirty. The Step by Steps throughout this book provide plenty of directions and exercises, but you should go beyond these examples and create some of your own. If you can, experiment with each of the objectives to see how they work and why you would use each one.

Introduction

As you might realize, networks today keep growing and intermingling with other networks. This growth presents a challenge for Microsoft Certified Systems Engineers, in that it increases network exposure to users and other individuals who seek to penetrate its defenses and gain entry. What makes it possible for all these networks to be vulnerable to attack? They share a common protocol.

The common protocol used in the exchange of data is Transmission Control Protocol/Internet Protocol (TCP/IP), as discussed in previous chapters of this book. Data sent via TCP/IP is broken up and sent over various routes to the final destination. Because of the design of TCP/IP, data can be intercepted easily without the sender or the receiver knowing that the data has been intercepted. Certainly, as data passes through networks around the globe, it is susceptible to interception or forgery, and users are often the recipients of data whose content could jeopardize their own data.

We need a way to protect our outgoing data and ensure that our incoming data has not been compromised. We also need a way to verify that people and machines we might communicate with are who they say they are. Enter the *digital certificate*. This chapter introduces the fundamentals of certificates and then discusses installing and configuring CA Services.

Maintaining a secure network is not a one-step or one-day event; it is a daily, ongoing event that requires you to not only implement an initial solution, but also monitor it and massage it over time to ensure that new threats and required changes are being taken into account. Too many times in the past, administrators have tried to treat server and network security as a "set it and forget it" type of thing, but that's just not possible today. To help Windows Server 2003 administrators keep their computers and networks secure, Microsoft has provided a relatively pain-free method of identifying and installing required updates and security fixes through use of the *Microsoft Baseline Security Analyzer (MBSA)* and *Windows Server Update Services (WSUS)*, as well as many other tools we won't get to discuss here.

Of course, as you might have guessed, at the heart of all your security plans must lie a solid plan to not only implement and control security, but also to monitor and manage it. Planning is key in network administration, and Windows Server 2003 networks are no different.

What's New in Windows Server 2003 Certificate Services?

When combined with a Windows XP Professional client computer in a Windows Server 2003 Active Directory–based network, Windows Server 2003 features several enhancements and improvements to Certificate Services. These features will make more sense to you as you work your way through this chapter's discussion of PKI and Certificate Services. Some of the features you will discover are listed next:

- **Version 2 certificate templates**—Version 2 templates extend the range of properties that you can configure from those provided in Version 1 templates. You now can create new certificate templates (an option sorely lacking from Windows 2000), copy existing certificate templates, and supersede certificate templates that are already in use. You need a Window Advanced Server 2003 functioning as the Enterprise Root CA.
- **Integrated and enhanced key recovery**—Windows 2000 Server relied on a Data Recovery Agent (DRA) to decrypt files following the loss or damage of an encryption key. Additionally, the Exchange 2000 Server Key Management Service (KMS) ran on top of Windows 2000 Certificate Services and did not fully integrate. Windows Server 2003 allows the archival and recovery of private keys and enables the administrator to access data encrypted with a lost or damaged private key. Now Key Recovery Agents (KRAs) are used to recover lost or damaged private keys across Windows Server 2003 and Exchange Server 2003.
- **Delta Certificate Revocation Lists**—Windows Server 2003 supports RFC 2459–compliant delta Certificate Revocation Lists (CRLs) that contain only the certificates whose status has changed since the last full (base) CRL was compiled. This results in a much smaller CRL, which can be more frequently published with no adverse effects on the network or client computers. Additionally, this provides more accurate CRLs because of reduced latency periods. In Windows 2000, CRLs were typically published once per week (the default setting). Delta CRLs enable you to publish one or more times daily as required.
- **CA qualified subordination**—Another part of RFC 2459, qualified subordination allows a parent CA to granularly configure what a Subordinate CA is allowed to. Examples include preventing the Subordinate CA from signing a certificate for another Subordinate CA.
- **Common Criteria role separation**—By separating common CA-related tasks over several different levels of administration, you can meet Common Criteria requirements and enhance task delegation. Because roles are separated, no one individual should possess the capability to compromise the services or operation of the CA.
- **Enhanced auditing**—Windows Server 2003 provides for more detailed auditing of Certificate Services by adding two new types of events: access check and system events. System events come from seven critical areas: CA service, backup and restoration, certificate requests, certificate revocations, CA security, key archival and key recovery, and CA configuration.

After your introduction to public key infrastructure (PKI) and the enhancements found in Windows Server 2003 Certificate Services, you are ready to take the first step in implementing a PKI: planning. Remember that if you fail to plan, you must plan to fail—especially when dealing with the sometimes confusing and complex world of PKI.

EXAM ALERT

Delta CRLs The Delta CRL feature of Windows Server 2003 is an important one that you should be aware of.

Planning a Windows Server 2003 Public Key Infrastructure (PKI)

So you want to install a Windows Server PKI on your network to issue and validate digital certificates? Great idea! But what exactly is a PKI, and what is it made up of? Before getting around to the planning and implementing of the often-misunderstood PKI, you should have a good idea of what it is and how it works. After you've perused an introduction to PKI, you can more efficiently plan for, and subsequently implement, your PKI solution.

Introduction to the PKI

To combat the openness of TCP/IP without losing the functionality of the protocol, PKI has been developed in tandem with TCP/IP as a means of offering security for data sent between hosts—on an intranet or on the Internet.

Using encryption, network administrators and security experts can ensure that the data is read only by the intended recipient and that data received has not been tampered with. The analogy of a physical signature and envelopes sealed with wax is an excellent parallel to how PKI is used today. In lieu of your "John Hancock" and sealing wax, you use a digital signature.

A digital signature ensures that the message is from the source it says it's from and that the message hasn't been digitally "steamed open." In addition to digital signatures, you can implement digital identifications—thus, the digital certificate.

Certificates

What exactly is a *digital certificate*? Essentially, it's the electronic version of your passport or employee identification card. It proves that you are who you say you are. This certificate ultimately enables you to access resources and data.

Certificates are issued not only to individuals, but also to organizations, businesses, routers, and other entities as a way of controlling and securing data. A digital certificate contains the following information:

- The user's name
- The user's public key
- Serial number

- Expiration date
- Information on the certificate itself
- Information on the entity (called a certificate authority) that issued the certificate

When secure data is transferred, an electronic seal is inserted into the data through cryptography. When the recipient opens the data, a key verifies that the electronic seal exists and that it has not been tampered with. In addition, the recipient can be assured that the sender of the data is who he says he is.

Traditionally, when you want to send encrypted data to other users, you use your key to encrypt and secure the data. When the recipients want to open the encrypted data, they use their copy of the key to unlock the data. If others without the key intercept the packets, they cannot decrypt the information. This method of security is not really very secure. The problem is that when unauthorized users gain access to the key, they gain access to the data—not unlike discovering your house keys in the outside lock of your door.

Digital certificates, however, use a slightly different method of locking and unlocking the data. With digital certificates, you no longer have to make copies of keys for others to unlock your data. Digital certificates use a private key to lock the data and then a different key, the public key, to unlock the data. No longer is the same key used to lock and unlock data.

With this two-key technology, your private key remains private. No one but the rightful owner should ever have access to it. However, by means of the digital certificate, you can disperse the public key to whoever might need it.

When Dick wants to send a private message to Jane, for example, Dick uses Jane's public key to encrypt the message. No one other than Jane can decrypt the message, but now the private key, Jane's key, is required to unlock the contents. When Jane responds to Dick, she can use Dick's public key to encrypt the response. Dick then uses his own private key to unlock the message.

Certificate Authorities (CAs)

All certificates are issued by a CA, such as VeriSign or one internal to your own network. The CA verifies that the owner of the certificate is who he says he is. A CA is a trusted third party that is responsible for physically verifying the legitimacy of the identity of an individual or organization before issuing a digital certificate. A CA is also responsible for issuing certificates, revoking certificates, and publishing a list of revoked certificates.

With Windows Server 2003, you can use a third-party CA or you can create your own CA through Microsoft's Windows Server 2003 Certificate Services, which offers four distinct types of CAs: Enterprise Root CA, Enterprise Subordinate CA, Standalone Root CA, and Standalone Subordinate CA. We take a closer look at these types of CAs throughout the chapter.

If you elect to create an internal CA for your organization, you need to establish some rules and guidelines to verify that users are employees. You can use Social Security numbers, employee badges, or an even more secure method—smart cards, which enable users to log in and access and send data, such as email and data on a network.

The Enterprise CA

A Windows Server 2003 *Enterprise CA* provides certificates for the internal security of an entire organization, whereas an external CA (such as VeriSign) typically provides security for external security needs. Microsoft provides support for both, and you can mix and match to fit your business needs. It's worth noting, however, that this model is not mandatory—many organizations use an external CA as the root of their PKI and yet others use Windows Server 2003 CAs for external usage.

If users request a certificate in a Windows Server 2003 environment, their user accounts can act as the credentials for the user because they are logged on and recognized in the Active Directory.

A Windows Server 2003 Enterprise CA has five key characteristics:

- The CA server can run on any Windows Server 2003 server in the domain. You should plan for activity, network load, and physical placement of the server for best implementation. Note that you cannot use a Windows Server 2003 Web Edition server as a Certificate Authority.
- Because the CA name is integrated into the certificates it assigns, the name of the server should be determined before implementing CA services.
- The Enterprise CA Authority is integrated into the Active Directory.
- When you've installed an Enterprise CA, a policy module is created. An administrator can edit the policy.
- Because the CA is crucial for the successful implementation of the PKI, it must have a fault-tolerance scheme and a schedule of regular secure backups.

The Standalone CA

Another type of CA that Windows Server 2003 allows you to install is a *Standalone CA*. The Standalone CA doesn't require the interaction of Active Directory, but it can use Active Directory if it's available.

A Standalone CA is useful in issuing certificates and digital signatures, and it supports secure email (S/MIME) and Secure Sockets Layer (SSL) or Transport Layer Security (TLS).

A typical Standalone CA has these key characteristics:

- It doesn't require Active Directory interaction.
- It can be used with extranets.

- It doesn't verify the requests for certificates. (All requests are pending until an administrator approves them.)
- Users requesting a certificate from a Standalone CA must supply all user account information. This information is not required within an Enterprise CA because the user is recognized by the logon account in the Active Directory.
- No certificate templates are used.
- Windows Sever 2003 logon credential certificates are not stored on smart cards. Other certificates can be, however.
- An administrator must distribute the Standalone CA certificate to the Trusted Root Certificate Store.

If Active Directory exists on the network and a Standalone CA can access it, additional options are available:

- If a domain administrator with write access to Active Directory installs the Standalone CA, the standalone is added to the Trusted Root Certification Authorities Certificate Store. In this situation, you must make certain that the default action of pending requests isn't changed to allow the Standalone CA to automatically approve all requests for certificates. Do not change the default action of pending certificate requests on a Standalone CA.
- If a domain administrator group member of the parent domain (or an administrator with write access to Active Directory) installs the Standalone CA, the Standalone CA will publish the certificate and the Certificate Revocation List to Active Directory.

With this brief PKI introduction out of the way, we can now move forward into the planning stages for your Windows Server 2003 PKI implementation.

EXAM ALERT

CA types Ensure that you have a good understanding of the characteristics, abilities, and uses of the four different CA types.

Initial Planning for the PKI

When you are preparing to install a CA, you should start by planning how to configure your PKI. Windows Server 2003 Group Policy can allow you to publish and revoke certificates directly to user accounts. This feature enables you to change a user's digital information and enforce it for accessing and retrieving data. Finally, your PKI scheme should include measures for your enterprise to secure email using S/MIME and SSL and/or TLS.

Before you can install the PKI and your first CA, you need to have a plan that addresses these additional questions:

- What type of CA or CAs do you require?
- How many CAs total will you require?
- How long will certificates be valid for?
- Who will manage the security?
- Will administrative duties be delegated?
- How will the CA be monitored? Who will monitor it?
- What kind of auditing should be in place for the CA?
- Where will the CA be located?
- Will you be using smart cards?

After you've answered these questions and have documented your answers to formulate a plan, you're ready to move into the next stages of planning.

Planning the CA Hierarchies

Windows Server 2003 PKI allows for and encourages a dispersed hierarchy of CAs. Building a tree of CAs allows for scalability with other organizations, internal and external resources, and compatibility with third-party CA implementations.

It might seem to be the ideal solution to have only one CA—at least, in terms of ease of administration. However, this is not a realistic solution, for many reasons, including size and number of domains and physical locations, along with the number of users who must be serviced by the PKI infrastructure. Each CA hierarchy begins with the *Root CA*, and multiple CAs branch from this Root CA in a parent-child relationship. The child CAs are certified by the parent CA all the way back to the Root CA. The parent CAs bind a CA public key to the child CA's identity.

In this parent-child relationship, child CAs are trusted by the parent. That parent is, in turn, trusted by its parent CA, all the way back to the originating Root CA. Also in this model, when an organization trusts a CA by adding its certificate in the Trusted Root Certification Authorities Certificate Store, the organization therefore trusts every Subordinate CA in the hierarchy. If a Subordinate CA has its certificate revoked by the issuing CA, the revoked CA is no longer trustworthy.

Hierarchies serve many purposes. Some of the reasons for creating a CA hierarchy include these:

- **Varying usages**—Certificates can be issued for a number of purposes, such as secure email, SSL, and TSL. Different CAs can be responsible for different areas of security.

- **Politics**—A hierarchy allows various departments within an enterprise to use unique policies.
- **Geography**—In a wide area network (WAN) environment, a different CA might be needed in each physical location to save network resources.
- **Security**—The Root CA requires a very secure environment with fault-tolerant devices. Subordinate CAs do not require the same amount and type of security as the root.
- **Revocation**—Most organizations need to have the capability to revoke individual CAs rather than be forced to revoke an entire enterprise.

As you're planning your hierarchy, remember that a Root CA is a CA from which all Subordinate CAs branch. This CA should be the most secure and should probably be taken offline (in the case of a Standalone CA) after the installation to ensure the security of the originating certificate and keys. Figure 8.1 illustrates how you might have multiple branching CAs in your organization.

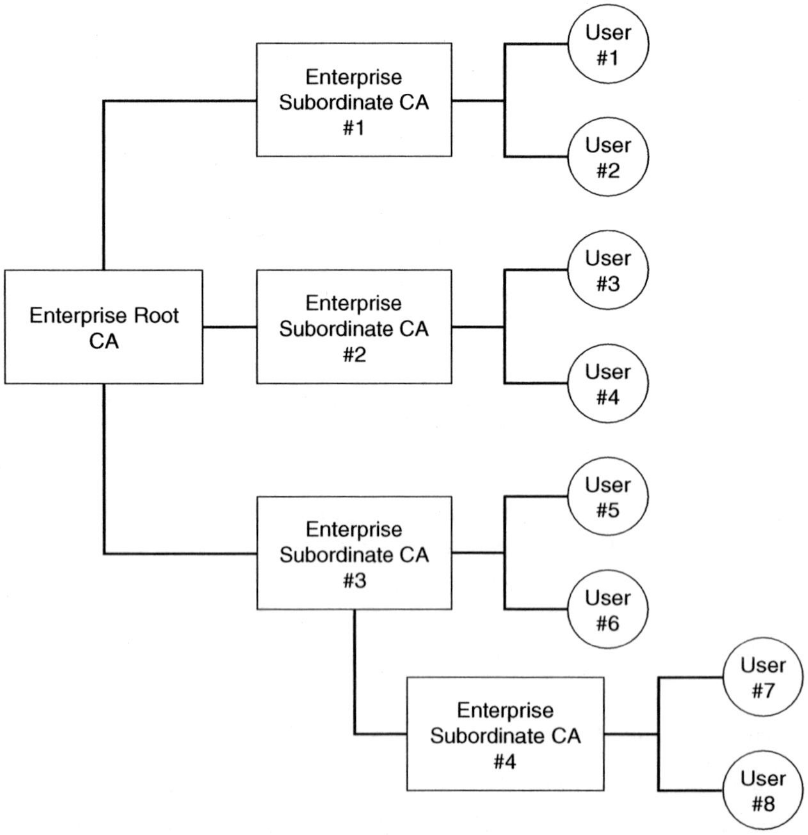

FIGURE 8.1 You can have certificate authorities arranged in any hierarchical order you require.

Planning Certificate Revocation and Renewal

CAs are responsible not only for issuing and signing digital certificates, but also for maintaining an accurate and up-to-date listing of certificates that are no longer valid and thus should not be trusted. This listing of invalid certificates is known as a Certificate Revocation List (CRL) and is itself digitally signed by the issuing CA to verify its authenticity.

When a certificate is issued, it has a set validity period attached to it—typically five years, by default. Under normal circumstances, the certificate can be used for this period of time and ceases to be valid automatically if it is not renewed before the expiration date has been reached. Thus, it is necessary to place on the CRL only certificates that have been revoked early; certificates that have expired (that is, have passed their expiration date) are automatically considered invalid and do not need to be placed on a CRL.

The real decisions that you must make in relation to certificate revocation are, in most cases, limited to determining what circumstances require a certificate revocation and how to publish the CRL. Some organizations might require a certificate to be revoked only when an employee leaves the company, whereas other organizations might require a certificate to be revoked for Acceptable Use Policy (AUP) violations and the like. Also, you might need to change the interval and location to which CRLs are published. You can publish the CRL as often as once per day to any combination of the following locations: Active Directory (the default), a URL for access via a web browser, or a CRL file that can be transported to a different location. The method or methods you choose in your environment will depend on where your users are located in reference to where your CAs are located.

In direct contrast to certificate revocation, certificate renewal is just as important to your PKI implementation. Will you allow certificates to be renewed after their initial validity period has passed? When will you allow certificates to be renewed? How much of their lifetime must have passed before they can be renewed? Will you be using the same key pair for the renewed certificate—allowing users to extend the useable life of their keys—or will you require a new key pair to be created for the renewal—making any previously encrypted information unreadable?

Renewing CAs

In a parent-child relationship between CAs, the parent CA issues a certificate as part of the relationship to designate the child CA. Just like the certificate to a client, the certificate to a Subordinate CA includes a validity period.

When the validity period expires for a CA, its own certificate must be renewed before it can grant any certification requests from client computers. When organizing your PKI, take into account the time a certification in a parent-child relationship should last.

As a safety and security measure, Windows Server 2003 PKI is set up so that a CA cannot issue certificates to requestors that will last beyond its own certificate's expiration date. This measure is handy because it ensures, for example, that a CA scheduled to expire this October cannot issue a certificate that might expire later than October.

Even the Root CA's own certificate will eventually expire. Therefore, certificates that it issues to subordinates are staggered from its own expiration date. In other words, when the Root CA expires, all Subordinate CAs will have expired as well. No Subordinate CAs are valid beyond the date of the originating CA.

Planning Certificate Template Usage

Windows Server 2003 comes with a wide range of preconfigured certificate templates that can be used to issue a variety of digital certificates. Although you do not need to decide which certificate templates to use before you begin your PKI implementation, you need to be aware of the certificate templates that are available and what purpose they serve. Certain applications—Exchange Server, for example—cannot be installed with full functionality unless certain optional certificate templates are made available first. Table 8.1 outlines the certificate templates that are available for use in Windows Server 2003.

TABLE 8.1 The Windows Server 2003 Certificate Templates

Template	Purpose	Issued To	Published to AD?
Administrator	Provides for trust list signing and user authentication	User	Yes
Authenticated Session	Allows the user to authenticate to a web server	User	No
Basic EFS	Allows the user to encrypt data using the Encrypting File System (EFS)	User	Yes
CA Exchange	Provides for key storage areas that are configured for private key archival	Computer	No
CEP Encryption	Allows the computer to act as a registration authority (RA) for Simple Certificate Enrollment Protocol (SCEP) requests	Computer	No
Code Signing	Provides a means of digitally signing software	User	No
Computer	Provides a means for a computer to authenticate itself on the network	Computer	No
Cross-Certification Authority	Used for cross-certification and qualified subordination of CAs	CrossCA	Yes
Directory Email Replication	Provides a means of replicating email within Active Directory	DirEmailRep	Yes
Domain Controller	Acts as a general-purpose certificate used by domain controllers	DirEmailRep	Yes
Domain Controller Authentication	Allows computers and users to authenticate to Active Directory	Computer	No
EFS Recovery Agent	Allows the user to decrypt files that have been encrypted with EFS	User	No
Enrollment Agent	Allows a user to request certificates on behalf of another subject	User	No
Enrollment Agent (Computer)	Allows a computer to request certificates on behalf of another computer subject	Computer	No

TABLE 8.1 *Continued*

Template	Purpose	Issued To	Published to AD?
Exchange Enrollment Agent (Offline Request)	Allows Exchange Server to request certificates on behalf of another subject and supply the subject name in the request	User	No
Exchange Signature Only	Allows the Microsoft Exchange Key Management Service (KMS) to issue certificates to Exchange users for digitally signing email	User	No
Exchange User	Allows the KMS to issue certificates to Exchange users for encrypting email	User	Yes
IPSec	Provides a means for a computer to use IP Security (IPSec) to digitally sign, encrypt, and decrypt network communication	Computer	No
IPSec (Offline Request)	Allows IPSec to digitally sign, encrypt, and decrypt network communication when the subject name is supplied in the request	Computer	No
Key Recovery Agent	Provides a means of recovering private keys that are archived on the certificate authority	KRA	No
RAS and IAS Server	Provides a means for RAS and IAS servers to authenticate their identity to other computers	Computer	No
Root Certification Authority	Allows the Root CA to prove its identity	CA	No
Router (Offline Request)	Allows a router to request a certificate when requested through Simple Certificate Enrollment Protocol (SCEP) from a certificate authority that holds a CEP Encryption certificate	Computer	No
Smart Card Logon	Allows a user to authenticate to the domain using a smart card	User	No
Smart Card User	Provides a means for a user to authenticate and protect email using a smart card	User	Yes
Subordinate Certification Authority	Provides a means to prove the identity of the root certificate authority	CA	No
Trust List Signing	Allows the user to digitally sign a trust list	User	No
User	Provides users a certificate for email, encrypting files, and client authentication to Active Directory	User	Yes
User Signature Only	Provides a means for users to digitally sign data	User	No
Web Server	Allows a web server to prove its identity	Computer	No
Workstation Authentication	Allows client computers to authenticate their identity to servers	Computer	No

EXAM ALERT

Certificate templates Don't worry too much about being tested on all the certificate templates Windows Server 2003 provides. This listing is provided primarily for completeness and as a reference for you to use when configuring a CA solution on your network.

With your basic PKI planning out of the way, you are now ready to move forward into more specific planning and implementation of your PKI solution.

Planning Appropriate Certificate Authority Types

Plan a public key infrastructure (PKI) that uses Certificate Services.

- Identify the appropriate type of certificate authority to support certificate issuance requirements.

What exactly are the certificate requirements for your network? Will you be issuing certificates solely for use on your internal private network, or will you need to issue code-signing certificates used to digitally sign applications that can be downloaded or otherwise distributed? The uses for digital certificates that you have ultimately determine the type of certificate authorities that you need to implement. Just as a note, CA types and certificate uses are directly related: The type of CA you install determines what your users and computers can do.

As a general review, let's examine each of the four basic CA types again briefly as you plan the needs for your network.

Enterprise Root CA

Recall that the Root CA is at the top of the CA chain, as shown previously in Figure 8.1; this holds true for both Enterprise and Standalone hierarchies. The Enterprise Root CA, then, is at the top of an Enterprise—Active Directory—certificate chain and is at the top of the hierarchy. In short, all other CAs trust this Root CA.

The Enterprise Root CA can issue any type of certificate desired, including those for Subordinate CAs, users, and computers. However, it is usually best (and most commonly implemented) to have the Root CA issuing certificates only to its Subordinate CAs; this preserves the hierarchical nature of the certificate chain and specifies a single point that is "all knowing," so to speak.

The Subordinate CAs are then charged with the responsibility of issuing certificates directly to users and computers within the organization. By implementing this parent-child relationship, you can segregate different levels of authority, providing for an overall more robust and secure CA infrastructure.

Because the Enterprise Root CA sits at the top of the certificate chain, it must sign its own certificate, asserting that it is the root of the certificate chain and that all other CAs are to trust it as such.

Enterprise Subordinate CA

The Enterprise Subordinate CA is the child in the parent-child relationship of CAs, as discussed previously. The Enterprise Subordinate CA does require Active Directory to function and can issue certificates to other (lower level) Subordinate CAs, users, and computers, as shown previously in Figure 8.1.

Enterprise Subordinate CAs can be implemented in various locations through the network to provide for increased performance and better load balancing among CAs. You can theoretically have as many Enterprise Subordinate CAs as you want, although practicality dictates that you should have only enough to ensure that all users can connect to a CA that is relatively nearby. Having unnecessary CAs on the network causes a security weakness, in that a compromised CA might lead to further network compromises.

Standalone Root CA

Just as the Enterprise Root CA is at the top of the certificate chain in an Active Directory network, the Standalone Root CA is at the top of the chain in a network that might not be using Active Directory. If Active Directory is available, the Standalone Root CA can make use of it, however. Being independent of Active Directory gives the Standalone Root CA the advantage of being removed physically from the network, thus greatly increasing its security.

You can actually use a Standalone Root CA effectively to increase the security of your network by issuing from it those certificates that are very important, such as those for Subordinate CAs and those used by developers for digitally signing applications for distribution.

Standalone Subordinate CA

The Standalone Subordinate CA behaves similarly to the Enterprise Subordinate CA—with one major difference. The Standalone Subordinate CA does not require the presence of Active Directory. Standalone Subordinate CAs are used to issue certificates directly to users; without Active Directory, you have no reason to issue certificates to computers.

At this time, we need to go above and beyond the objectives for this exam so that you gain the required knowledge. Although you won't explicitly see installing and configuring a CA listed in the objectives, understanding all the points made in the following sections will be very difficult if you haven't seen a CA installed and configured first. To that end, we examine the installation and initial configuration of an Enterprise Root CA in the next section.

Installing and Configuring an Enterprise Root CA

Now that you've reached this point in the chapter, you are really ready to install and perform the basic configuration of your first CA. After you've done this, you can more easily move through the remaining sections of this chapter that relate to PKI. Step by Step 8.1 outlines the process to install an Enterprise Root CA.

NOTE

Internet Information Services (IIS) 6.0 in Windows Server 2003 Unlike IIS 5.0 in Windows 2000 Server, IIS 6.0 is not installed by default in Windows Server 2003, with the exception of Windows Server 2003 Web Edition. If you have not previously manually installed IIS, you need to install it from the Windows Component Wizard under the Application Server option group before you install the Enterprise Root CA.

You should be aware of the fact that you must provide the following information during the installation of your first CA:

- **CA type**—You must indicate the type of CA you will be using.
  - **Enterprise Root CA**—The Enterprise Root CA is the root of all CAs in your hierarchy. Typically, an enterprise has only one. It requires Active Directory. Intermediate Subordinate CAs branch off this server. The Enterprise Root CA can be only a parent.
  - **Enterprise Subordinate CA**—A Subordinate CA must obtain its certificate from a CA higher in the hierarchy. It requires Active Directory. This is the child of another CA. This CA could also be a parent to another CA.
  - **Standalone Root CA**—A Standalone Root CA is like an Enterprise Root CA, except that it does not require Active Directory but can use it if it exists. Often this CA is offline to protect the validity of the originating certificates and keys.
  - **Standalone Subordinate CA**—This CA does not require Active Directory but can use it if Active Directory is available. The Subordinate CA must obtain its certificate from another CA. This is the child in the relationship but can become a parent if it supplies a certificate to another CA.
- **Advanced options**—If you enable advanced options during the CA installation, you must provide the following:
  - **The Cryptographic Service Provider (CSP)**—The CSP enables you to generate the public and private keys.
  - **Key length**—The longer the key, the more secure the key.

- **Hash algorithm**—This computation produces a hash value of some piece of data. The default is Secure Hash Algorithm (SHA)-1, which is a 160-bit hash value.

- **CA name**—You can use just about any character you want. The name you assign the CA will also be the common name (CN) of the CA's distinguished name in Active Directory. Special characters (non–ASCII and ASCII punctuation) are stripped out in a sanitized name. Also remember that Active Directory is limited to 64 characters before it truncates names.
- **Organization**—You must provide the name of your organization as it is known throughout its community.
- **Organizational Unit**—You must indicate the division this CA manages.
- **City and state or province**—You must indicate the city and state or province where the CA is located.
- **Country**—You must indicate the X.500 two-character code for your country.
- **Location of the database**—By default, the database is stored in `\%systemroot%\system32\certlog`.
- **Shared folder**—You can create a shared folder for CA information if the CA is not participating in Active Directory (such as a standalone server).

CAUTION

Changing the CA name After you install Certificate Services on the server, you cannot change its name or domain membership without first removing Certificate Services. This is, of course, for a very good reason: Changing either of these items would destroy the CA hierarchy.

STEP BY STEP

8.1 Installing an Enterprise Root CA

1. Log in to a Windows Server 2003 that is a member of the Active Directory domain with administrative permissions.
2. From the Control Panel, double-click the Add or Remove Programs applet to open the Add or Remove Programs dialog box.
3. Click the Add/Remove Windows Components button located on the left side of the Add or Remove Programs dialog box to open the Windows Components Wizard.
4. Select the Certificate Services option, as shown in Figure 8.2.

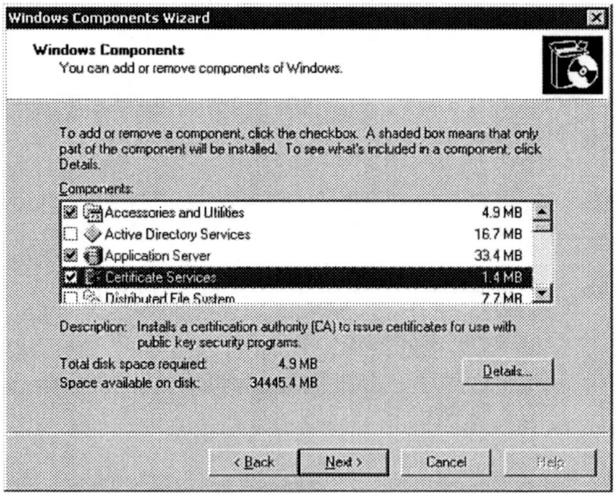

FIGURE 8.2 You need to select the Certificate Services option to install your CA.

5. A warning dialog box, shown in Figure 8.3, informs you that you cannot rename the server after installing Certificate Services on it. Click Yes to continue.

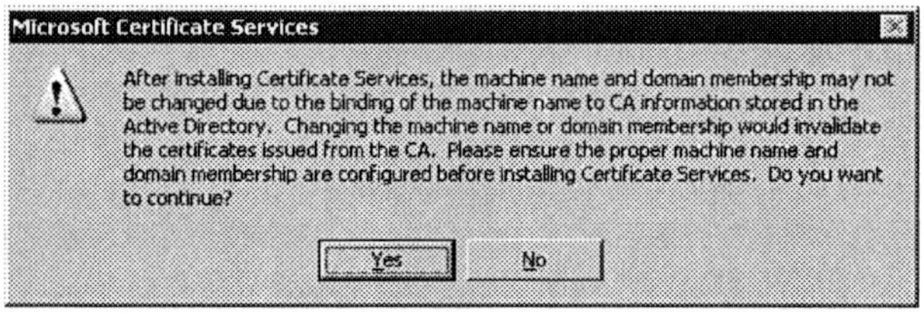

FIGURE 8.3 You cannot rename this server after installing Certificate Services on it.

6. Click Next on the Windows Components Wizard dialog box to start the installation process.
7. In the CA Type dialog box, shown in Figure 8.4, select the type of CA you are installing. For this example, select Enterprise Root CA and click Next to continue. If you want to customize the key pair settings, you can do so by selecting the Use Custom Settings to Generate the Key Pair and CA Certificate option.
8. If you selected to customize your key settings, the Public and Private Key Pair dialog box appears next, as shown in Figure 8.5. You have the opportunity to customize the installation by selecting the CSP and the key length. You can also use and import an existing certificate and key. Selecting the Allow This CSP to Interact with the Desktop option allows system services to interact with the desktop of the user who is currently logged on. Click Next to continue.
9. In the CA Identifying Information dialog box, shown in Figure 8.6, enter the common name of the CA. This name should be descriptive but should not contain any special characters. You also need to configure the Validity period; the default value is five years. After entering your selections, click Next to continue.

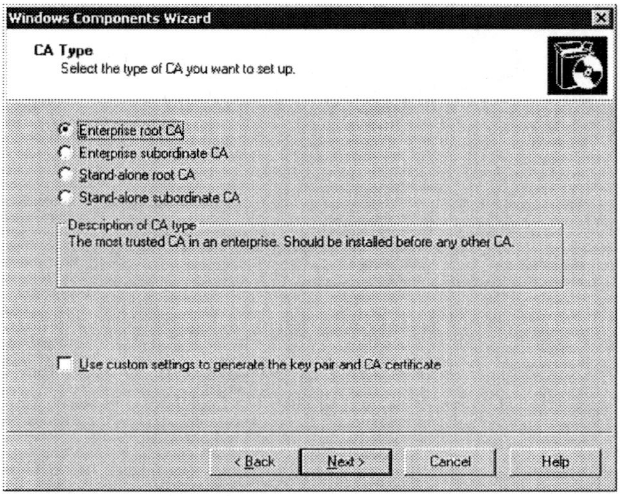

FIGURE 8.4 You must select one of the four available types of CAs.

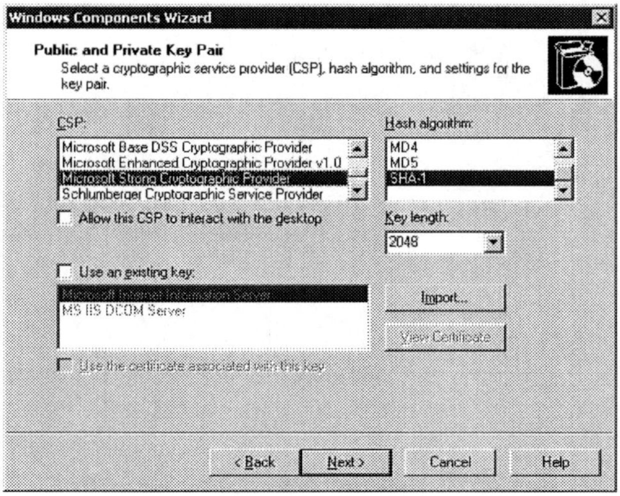

FIGURE 8.5 You can specify custom public and private key pair settings during the installation of the CA.

10. In the Certificate Database Settings dialog box, shown in Figure 8.7, enter the database and log locations or simply use the default selections—usually the best option, in most cases. If you have clients that are not using Active Directory, you might want to specify that the CA maintains a shared folder in which newly created certificates are placed; you can do so by selecting the Store Configuration Information in a Shared Folder option and entering the path of the shared folder. (If you are reinstalling Certificate Services onto a server that has already been a CA, the Preserve Existing Certificate Database option becomes available.) Click Next to continue.

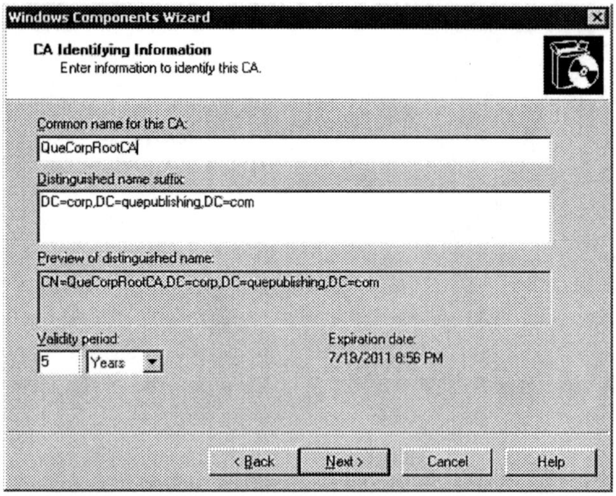

FIGURE 8.6 Your common name should be short and descriptive, to provide for easy identification of the CA.

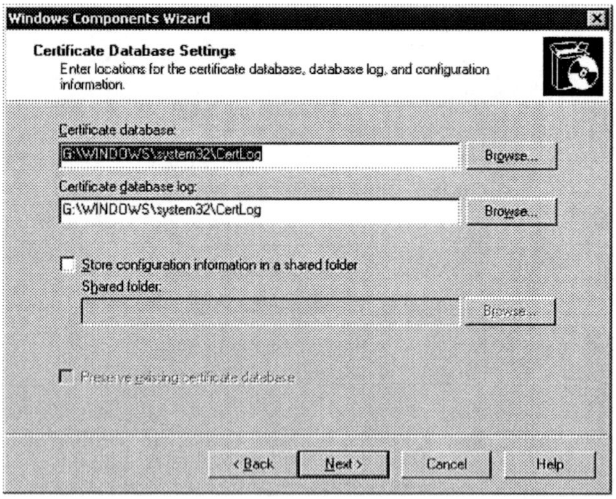

FIGURE 8.7 You can specify the location of the database and log files, if desired.

11. If IIS is running on the server, you are prompted to acknowledge that it will be stopped to perform the configuration of the CA. If IIS is not installed, you are prompted to install it before Web Enrollment can be used. Click Yes to acknowledge the warning.
12. Setup prompts you to enable ASP pages, if not already enabled on the server. Click Yes to enable Active Server Pages so that you can use Web enrollment on your CA.
13. Click Finish to close the Windows Component Wizard. The CA is now ready and available for immediate use.

NOTE

The key to security When creating the Root CA, you also need to ensure a long validity period for the public and private key of this CA by using a long key length as a deterrent to hackers who make brute-force attacks. The longer the key, the longer you can use the private and public keys with confidence that the keys have not been compromised.

Microsoft recommends using a key length of at least 2048 bits. However, there is a trade-off between key length and CA server performance because longer key lengths require more system resources.

With the knowledge of how to install the first CA in hand, you can move forward into configuring Active Directory for certificate publication.

Configuring Active Directory for Certificate Publication

Objective:

Configure Active Directory directory service for certificate publication.

By default, the Enterprise CA automatically publishes all certificates directly into Active Directory. As such, there really is no need for any additional configuration in that regard. However, you can configure two other parts of Certificate Services that deal with the publication of Certificate Revocation Lists (CRLs) and which certificates a user is allowed to submit a new certificate request for.

Recall that a CRL is used to identify all certificates that have been revoked (canceled) before their normal end-of-validity period. The default behavior of an Enterprise Root CA is to publish the CRL to Active Directory—as you might well expect. However, you can perform some modification of the CRL publishing configuration to suit the needs of your network, as outlined in Step by Step 8.2.

STEP BY STEP

8.2 Configuring CRL Publication Properties

1. Select Start, Programs, Administrative Tools, Certification Authority to open your Certification Authority management console.
2. Locate the CA of concern in the CA management console and expand its nodes.
3. Right-click the Revoked Certificates node and select Properties from the context menu.
4. The Revoked Certificates Properties dialog box opens, as shown in Figure 8.8. You can configure the CRL publication interval as well as the Delta CRL publication interval—or disable the use of Delta CRLs completely. Click Apply to set your changes.

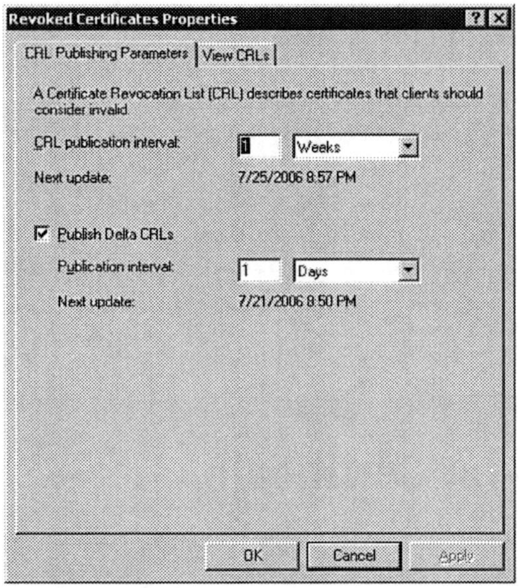

FIGURE 8.8 You can change the default values for CRL publication, if you like.

5. You can view CRLs that have been published by switching to the View CRLs tab, shown in Figure 8.9. You can examine the contents of a specific CRL by selecting it and clicking the View CRL or View Delta CRL buttons, as applicable. When you have finished, click OK to close the Revoked Certificates Properties dialog box.

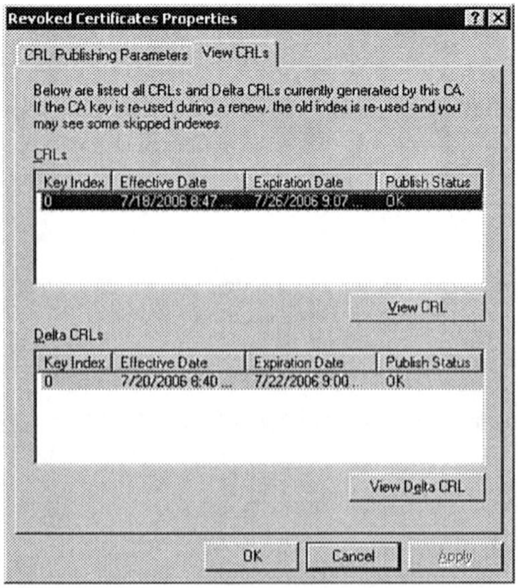

FIGURE 8.9 The Certification Authority management console provides a way to view CRLs.

6. To change the CRL publication location, right-click the CA name and select Properties from the context menu.
7. When the CA Properties dialog box opens, switch to the Extensions tab, shown in Figure 8.10. You can publish to Active Directory, a file system location, and an FTP or HTTP location. Note that not all options are available for each location. After making your configuration change, click OK. You are prompted to stop and restart Certificate Services to make the changes take effect.

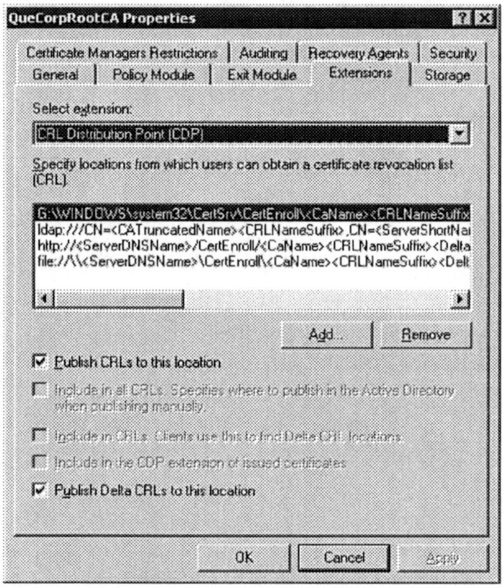

FIGURE 8.10 You can modify the locations to which the CRL is published from the Extensions tab of the CA Properties dialog box.

8. When you've configured the CRL publication schedule and location to your liking, you might want to immediately publish the CRL manually to all CRL Distribution Points (CDPs). To manually publish the CRL, right-click again on the Revoked Certificates folder and select All Tasks, Publish. You are asked what type of CRL you want to publish, as shown in Figure 8.11. Select either a New CRL or a Delta CRL and click OK to publish it as you've previously configured.

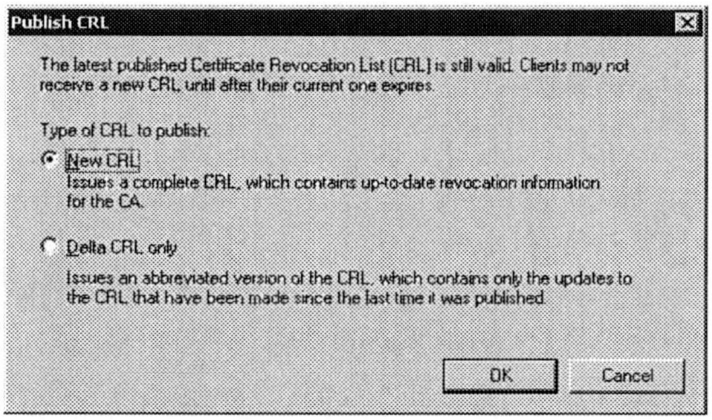

FIGURE 8.11 You can select either a New CRL or a Delta CRL.

EXAM ALERT

Publishing the CRL What would you do after revoking a certificate to ensure that it could no longer be used? You would publish the CRL to all CRL Distribution Points, of course! Be on the lookout for scenarios that require you to revoke certificates because publishing the CRL is the next logical step you should complete.

The only other configuration you might want to undertake in regard to certificate publication involves modifying the default configuration of the allowed certificate templates. You might want to perform the following additional actions from within the Certification Authority management console:

- ▶ Specify the types of certificates that each of your CAs can issue. You do so by deleting or adding (as required) certificate templates in the Certificate Templates node of the CA.
- ▶ Configure the Access Control List (ACL) for each template to limit its use to those users you specifically allow. To request a new certificate using a specific template, the user must have the Enroll permission enabled on the certificate template ACL.

Step by Step 8.3 outlines the process by which you can manage the certificate templates your CA is allowed to issue to your users.

STEP BY STEP

8.3 Managing Certificate Templates Available for Use

1. Open the Certification Authority management console and expand the nodes under your CA.
2. Click the Certificate Templates node, which enables you to examine the certificate templates that are currently available for your CA.
3. To remove a certificate template—and thus prevent that CA from using it to issue new certificates—right-click the certificate template and select Delete from the context menu. Click Yes when prompted to confirm that you really want to remove the certificate template from the CA. Note that the certificate template is not deleted; it's just removed from use at that time.
4. To add a new certificate template that is not currently listed, right-click the Certificate Templates node and select New, Certificate Template to Issue from the context menu.
5. The Enable Certificate Templates dialog box, shown in Figure 8.12, opens, enabling you to select the certificate template you want to make available for use. Select the certificate template and click OK. The selected certificate template now shows up in your Certificate Templates node.

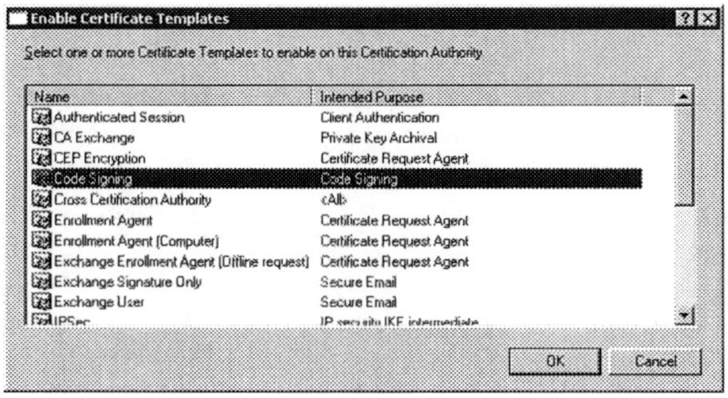

FIGURE 8.12 You can add certificate templates as you require.

6. If you want to configure the ACL for a certificate template, you need to first open the Certificate Templates console by right-clicking the Certificate Templates node and selecting Manage.

7. The Certificate Templates console, new to Windows Server 2003 and shown in Figure 8.13, opens, enabling you to configure the properties of all certificate templates installed on your CA.

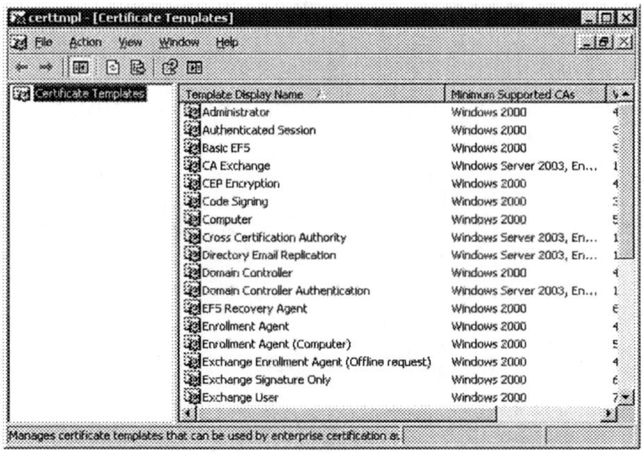

FIGURE 8.13 The Certificate Templates console enables you to manage the properties of your certificate templates from a centralized location.

8. To modify the ACL of a certificate template, right-click it from within the Certificate Templates console and select Properties from the context menu.

9. The certificate template Properties dialog box opens. Switch to the Security tab, shown in Figure 8.14, and select the Allow box for the Enroll permission for your users and groups, as required. Click OK to close the Properties dialog box when you are done.

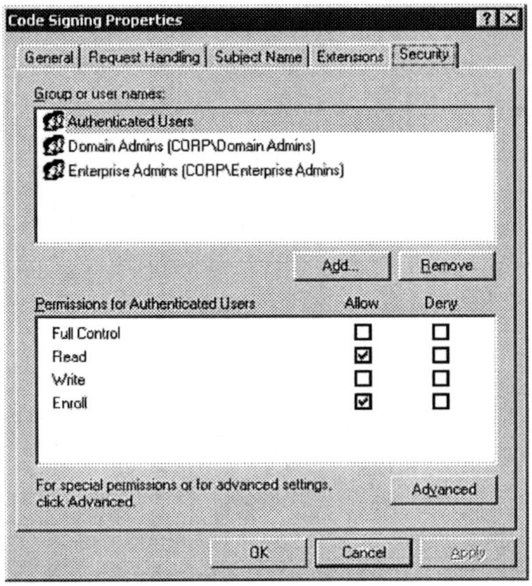

FIGURE 8.14 You can control who can request a certificate using a specific template by configuring the ACL.

With the discussion of CRL publication and certificate template configuration behind us, we move on to certificate enrollment and distribution planning.

Planning Certificate Enrollment and Distribution

Objective:

Plan a public key infrastructure (PKI) that uses Certificate Services.

- Plan the enrollment and distribution of certificates.

With your CA installed and configured, now comes the question of how you will enroll and distribute (install) the newly requested certificates. Depending on the configuration of your network, you can choose from four different certificate enrollment options:

- **Certificate autoenrollment and renewal**—I mentioned at the beginning of this chapter that a Windows Server 2003 Active Directory domain with Windows XP Professional clients provides the most robust Certificate Services model. This is certainly the case when discussing certificate autoenrollment and renewal. Using these features, you can automatically issue certificates that enable PKI-based applications, such as smart card logon, EFS, SSL, and S/MIME, for users and computers within your Active Directory environment. Through a combination of certificate template properties and Group Policy settings, you can opt to enroll computers when they start up and users when they log in to their domain on the network.

- **Certificate Request Wizard/Certificate Renewal Wizard**—Users of Windows 2000, Windows XP, and Windows Server 2003 computers can manually request certificates through the Certificates MMC snap-in. This snap-in can be added to any custom MMC. Alternatively, you can launch the Certificates console by entering **`certmgr.msc`** at the command prompt.
- **Web Enrollment web pages**—You can connect to a CA by entering **`http://`*`CAname`*`/certsrv`** in your browser. By default, the Web Enrollment pages, which consist of ASP and ActiveX controls and thus could be considered dangerous, are installed on a CA. However, you can install these pages on any other Windows Server 2003 computer running IIS that you want. If you're up to it, you can also customize these Web Enrollment pages to suit your specific needs. The Web Enrollment pages provide an easy way to connect clients to your CA without using the Certificates management console. Although Standalone CAs also use the Web Enrollment pages, they cannot provide certificates for smart card logon and for autoenrollment—only Enterprise CAs. Also, when Standalone CAs are used with Web Enrollment pages, the requester must specifically state all required information because Active Directory is not available to provide the information for the certificate template. Windows 2000, Windows XP, and Windows Server 2003 computers support the use of Web Enrollment pages.
- **Smart Card enrollment station**—This is an advanced form of the Web Enrollment pages that enables trusted administrators to request and enroll smart card logon certificates for smart card users on the network. Only Windows XP and Windows Server 2003 computers support this form of enrollment.

Now that you've had a brief introduction to the various means available for your users to request and enroll new certificates, let's examine how the first three are used. Smart cards are discussed in the next section.

Configuring Certificate Autoenrollment and Renewal

As already mentioned, one of the new features of Windows Server 2003 Certificate Services is the concept of autoenrollment for new certificates and automatic renewal for those approved certificates. Through the combination of Version 2 certificate templates and Group Policy settings, Windows XP and Windows Server 2003 computers and their users can automatically request and enroll new and newly renewed certificates at every Group Policy refresh. Group Policy is refreshed during computer startup, during user login, and on a configured refresh interval for the network.

If you've ever been responsible for managing a PKI infrastructure, you can quickly appreciate the value in users and computers being allowed to automatically enroll and renew the most commonly used certificate types, such as those for EFS, SSL, smart cards, and S/MIME. The once daunting task of distributing (also referred to as enrolling or installing) an approved certificate occurs automatically, thus saving the PKI administrator time and effort, as well as cutting down on the number of mistakes and errors made.

Step by Step 8.4 outlines the process to configure Group Policy for autoenrollment.

STEP BY STEP

8.4 Configuring Certificate Autoenrollment

1. On a domain controller or domain workstation running Administration Tools, select Start, Programs, Administrative Tools, Active Directory Users and Computers to open the Active Directory Users and Computers console.
2. Expand the nodes of your Active Directory forest until you locate the specific site, domain, or Organizational Unit (OU) for which you want to configure certificate autoenrollment.
3. Right-click the desired location and select Properties from the context menu.
4. Switch to the Group Policy tab of the Properties dialog box, shown in Figure 8.15.

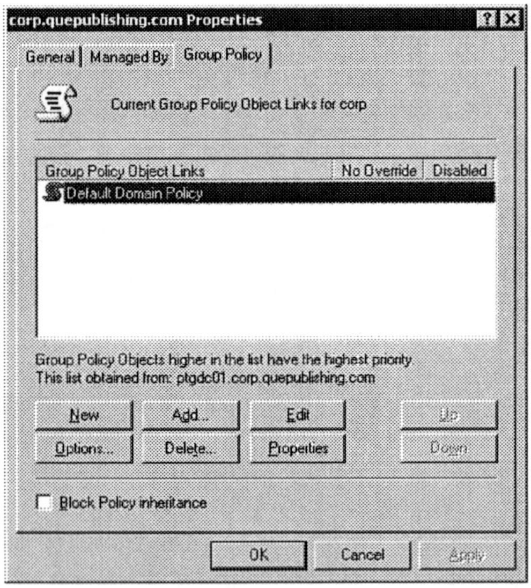

FIGURE 8.15 You need to select the GPO to be edited or create a new one.

5. Either select an existing GPO to be edited for certificate autoenrollment options or create a new one as desired.
6. Within the Group Policy Editor, expand the nodes as follows to configure certificate autoenrollment for computers: Computer Configuration, Windows Settings, Security Settings, Public Key Policies (see Figure 8.16).
7. Double-click the Autoenrollment Settings option and configure computers for autoenrollment as desired, as shown in Figure 8.17.

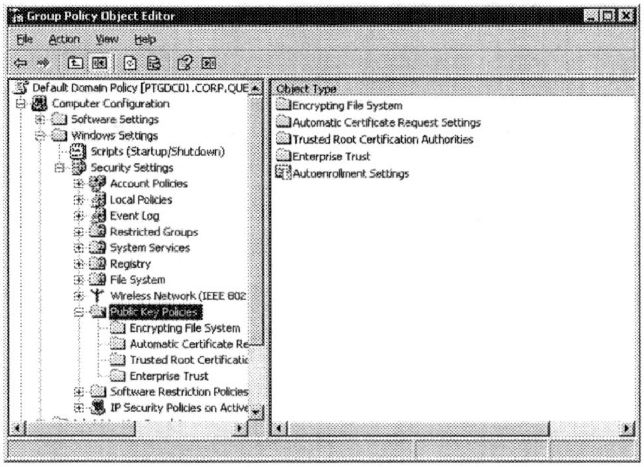

FIGURE 8.16 Certificate autoenrollment settings are located in the Public Key Policies node.

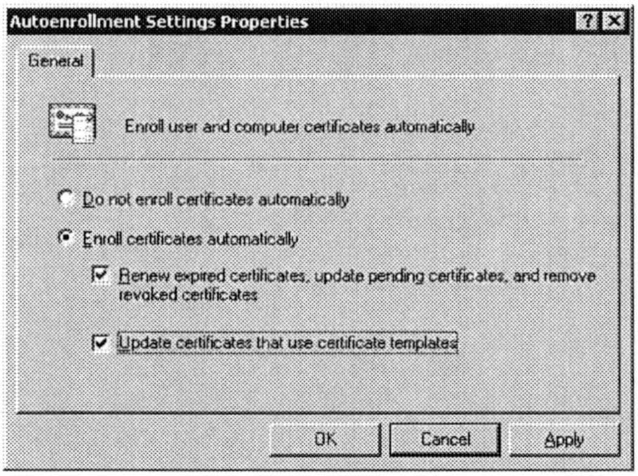

FIGURE 8.17 You need to select the Enroll Certificates Automatically option to enable autoenrollment.

8. Click OK to close the Autoenrollment Settings Properties dialog box.
9. If you want to configure certificate autoenrollment settings for users, do so from the User Configuration\Windows Settings\Security Settings\Public Key Policies node of the Group Policy Editor.

CAUTION

Changes to certificate autoenrollment in SP1 After you apply Windows Server 2003 SP1 to your certification authority, you'll likely quickly notice some issues with autoenrollment by Domain Controllers. The Microsoft Knowledge Base article located at http://support.microsoft.com/kb/903220 provides the required steps you'll need to complete to remedy this issue.

Using the Certificate Request Wizard and Certificate Renewal Wizard

Although not as new and fancy as certificate autoenrollment, the Certificate Request Wizard and Certificate Renewal Wizard are effective ways for Windows 2000 computers (as well as Windows XP and Windows Server 2003 computers) to quickly request and renew certificates. Step by Step 8.5 outlines the use of the Certificate Request Wizard to request a new certificate from the CA.

STEP BY STEP

8.5 Requesting a New Certificate with the Certificate Request Wizard

1. Open the Certificates console, shown in Figure 8.18, by adding it as a snap-in to a custom MMC or by entering **`certmgr.msc`** at the command prompt.

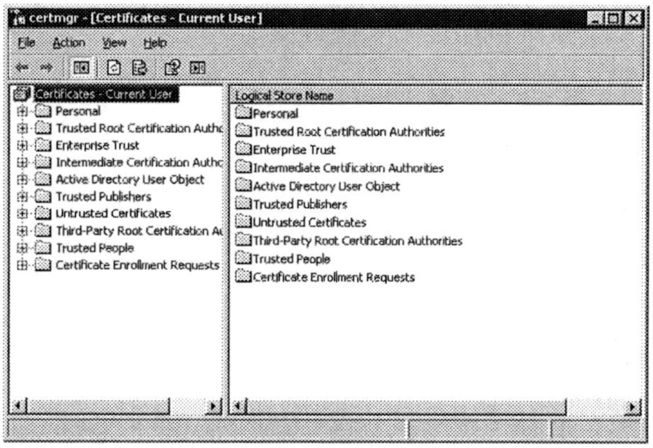

FIGURE 8.18 The Certificate Request Wizard enables you to quickly request a new certificate.

2. Right-click the Personal node and select All Tasks, Request New Certificate to start the Certificate Request Wizard.
3. Click Next to dismiss the opening page of the Certificate Request Wizard.
4. In the Certificate Types dialog box, shown in Figure 8.19, select the type of certificate being requested. You can also configure advanced options, including the CSP to be used, by selecting the Advanced check box. Click Next to continue.
5. In the Certificate Friendly Name and Description dialog box, shown in Figure 8.20, enter a friendly name and description for your certificate to identify it more easily in the future. Click Next to continue.
6. Click Finish on the Completing the Certificate Request Wizard dialog box to complete the process. If your request was approved, you see the dialog box indicating this fact. Click OK to close the dialog box.

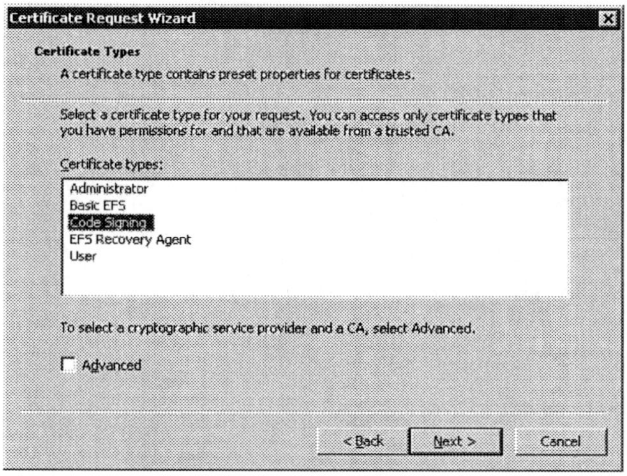

FIGURE 8.19 You are limited in your request by what certificate templates are available.

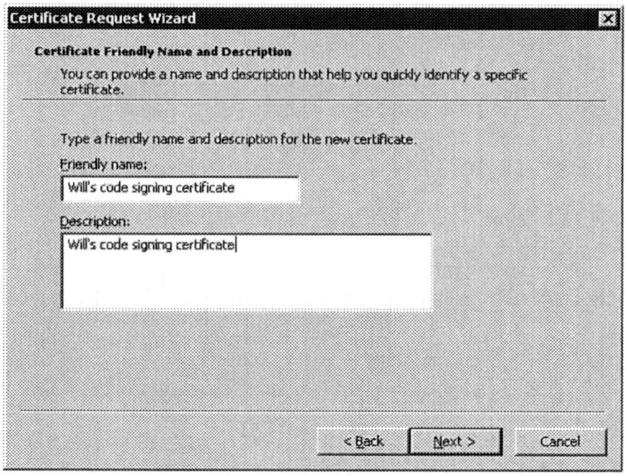

FIGURE 8.20 You should enter a description to help you determine what the certificate is used for.

Using the Web Enrollment Web Pages

As an alternative, and sometimes more useful, means of requesting certificates, you can easily allow your clients to use the Certificate Services Web Enrollment pages. Assuming that you have IIS installed on the CA—which you should do before installing the CA itself—you can use Web Enrollment by connecting to the CA using the local Internet web address http://*CAname*/certsrv in your web browser. It is recommended that you use a current version of Internet Explorer because other browsers or older versions do not always work properly.

Step by Step 8.6 outlines the use of the Web Enrollment pages to request a new certificate from the CA.

STEP BY STEP

8.6 Requesting a New Certificate via Web Enrollment

1. Open a new Internet Explorer window and enter **`http://`*`CAname`*`/certsrv`** in the address bar, where *CAname* represents the name or IP address of your CA, as shown in Figure 8.21. You might be asked to add this IP address to IE's trusted locations. Additionally, you might be prompted to supply your network credentials for authentication.

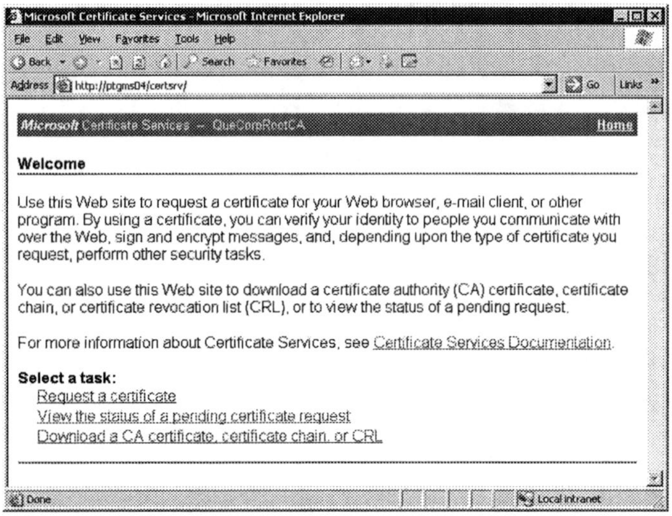

FIGURE 8.21 You can request new certificates, check the status of requests, and download the CRL from the Web Enrollment pages.

2. Click the Request a Certificate Link to request a new certificate. If you want, you also can check the status of a previous certificate request or download the current CRL from this CA.

3. To request a basic user certificate, click the User Certificate link, shown in Figure 8.22. If you want to request any other type of certificate, click the Advanced Certificate Request link. For this example, you want to request a smart card certificate, so click Advanced Certificate Request.

4. On the Advanced Certificate Request page, shown in Figure 8.23, click the Create and Submit a Request to This CA link to continue.

5. On the Advanced Certificate Request page, shown in Figure 8.24, select the type of certificate being requested and configure its properties as you require. After you have configured your certificate request as desired, click the Submit button located at the bottom of the page.

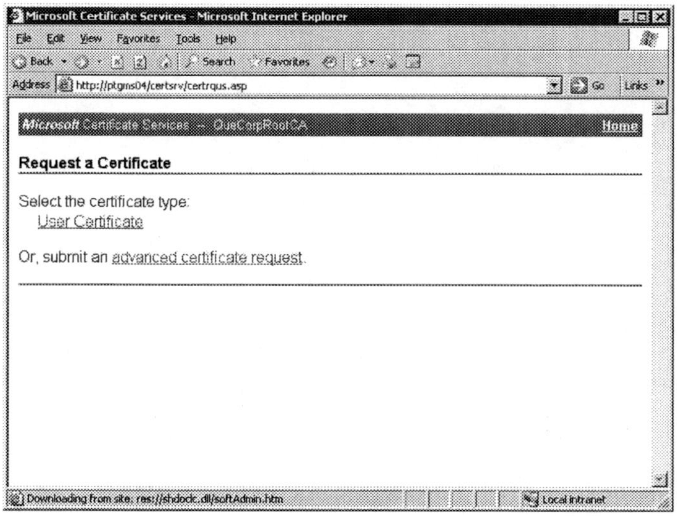

FIGURE 8.22 You need to click the Advanced Certificate Request link to request any certificate type other than a user certificate.

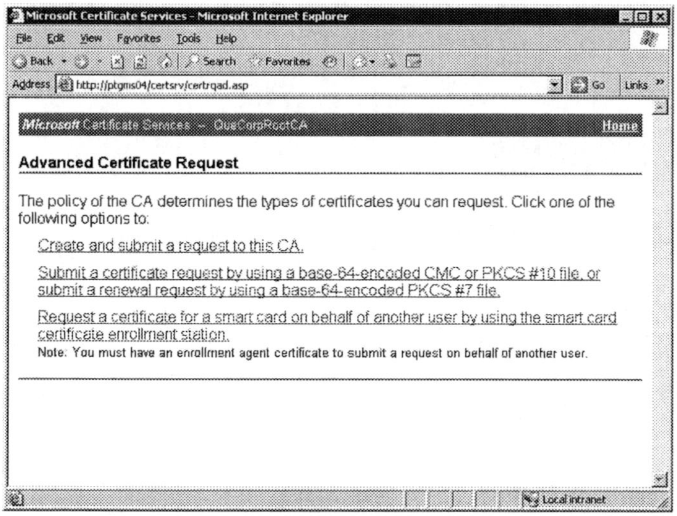

FIGURE 8.23 You have several request options available for your selection.

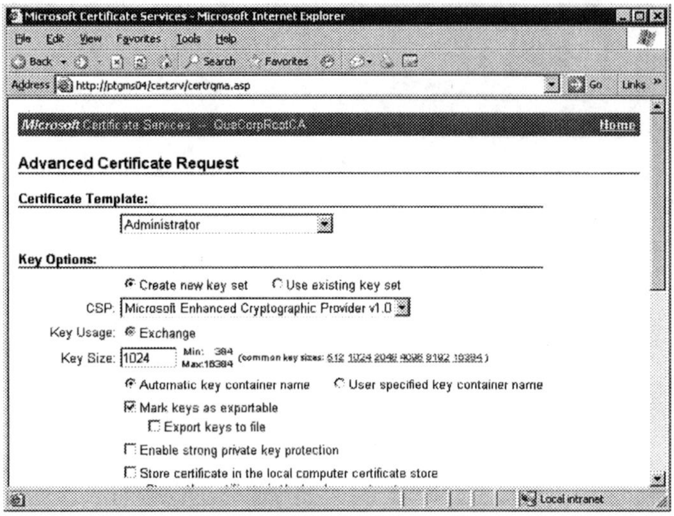

FIGURE 8.24 You can change the key length and several other options using an advanced certificate request.

6. As part of the enhanced security of Windows Server 2003 (and Windows XP), a warning dialog box indicates that a web page is requesting a certificate on your behalf, as shown in Figure 8.25. This is not a problem unless you see this warning while surfing the Internet! Click Yes to allow this certificate to be requested.

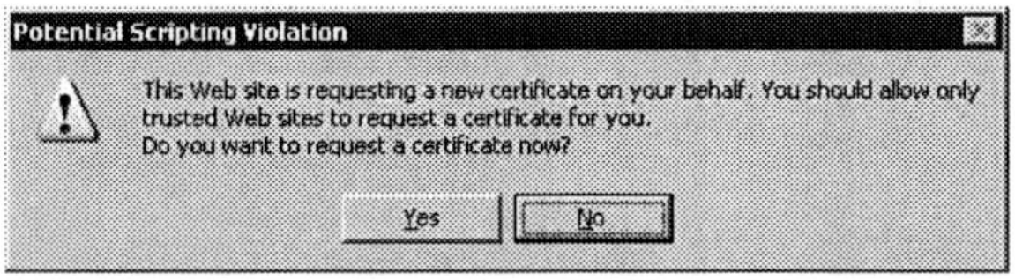

FIGURE 8.25 Windows warns you that a web page is requesting a certificate for you.

7. If the request was successfully approved, you are next presented with the Certificate Issued page, shown in Figure 8.26. Click Install This Certificate to install your new certificate.

8. Again, Windows alerts you that the web page is attempting to perform some action related to a digital certificate, as shown in Figure 8.27. In this case, the web page is attempting to install the certificate for you. Click Yes to allow the certificate to be installed.

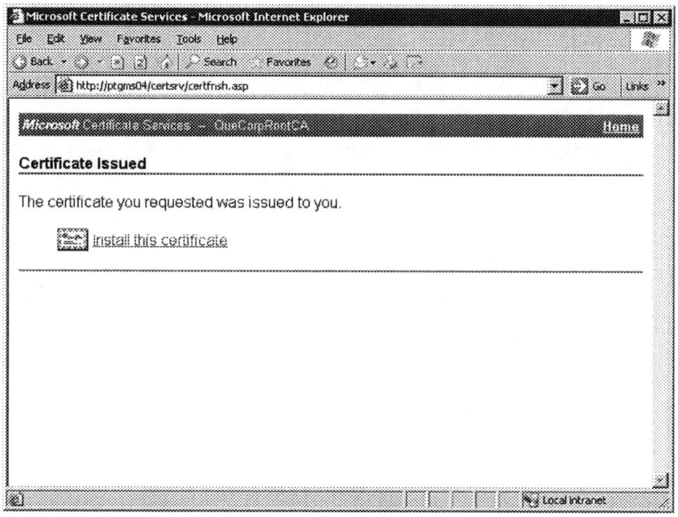

FIGURE 8.26 You are informed immediately of the status of your certificate request.

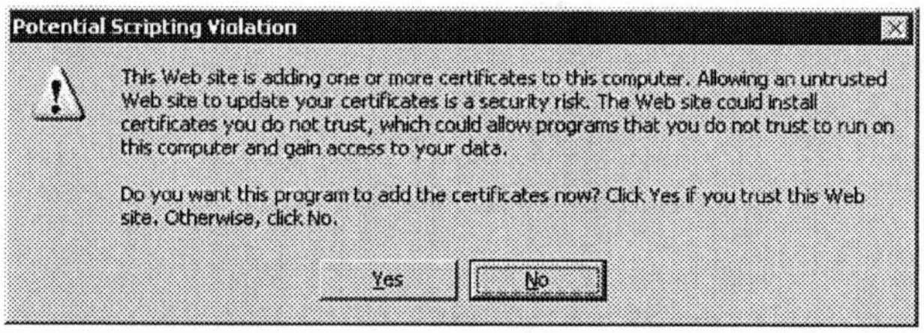

FIGURE 8.27 You are warned again about the web page's interaction with a certificate.

9. Your certificate is now installed, and the Web Enrollment pages will reflect this fact.

Planning a Smart Card Solution

Objective:

Plan a public key infrastructure (PKI) that uses Certificate Services.

- Plan for the use of smart cards for authentication.

Introduced for the first time in Windows 2000, smart cards provided an alternative—and secure—means for user authentication. Smart cards are tamper-resistant hardware tokens that can be used to add another layer of security to the network. Although smart cards might at first be confused with standard credit cards, they have metallic contacts on them instead of the magnetic strip found on a credit card. Smart cards also require specially designed readers that are attached to the computer being used for login.

Smart cards are used to provide the highest level of user authentication available in Windows Server 2003 networks. For maximum security, a user can use a password or PIN to access the digital certificate on the smart card, thus further protecting the user's identity from rogue applications and attackers. Through the use of on-card digital signatures, smart cards can ensure that a user's private key is never exposed. Perhaps the single best feature of smart cards is that they—unlike software-based private keys—can be moved at will from one computer to another with ease. An administrator can prevent smart cards from being used to access the network after a preconfigured number of incorrect login attempts, protecting them further from dictionary attacks—a type of password-guessing attack in which a password is guessed from a list, or dictionary, of common words and phrases.

When implementing a smart card system, you should consider making the following certificate templates available for use. Bear in mind that none of these certificate templates is made available for use by default; you must manually add all of them to the Certificate Templates node of the certificate authority, as discussed earlier in this chapter in the section "Configuring Active Directory for Certificate Publication."

- **Enrollment Agent**—Enables authorized users to request smart card certificates on behalf of other users
- **Smart Card User**—Enables a smart card user to log on to the network and digitally sign email
- **Smartcard Logon**—Enables a smart card user to log on to the network

Smart cards can provide you with a great benefit—if they are implemented properly in your network. As you might have guessed, that means more planning for you! You should consider the following items during your smart card planning:

- Smart card distribution requirements
- Smart card enrollment options
- Smart card user education
- Smart card Group Policy options

Smart Card Distribution Requirements

The most difficult aspect of implementing a new smart card system is determining how smart cards will be distributed. What happens if a user has a lost, damaged, or stolen smart card? What about when common occurrences such as name changes, job changes, or department changes occur? All these issues need to be addressed in your smart card issuance-and-distribution plan. How do you handle these situations for your Windows user accounts? Perhaps you can model your smart card solution in part after your network password solution.

Another critical question that must be answered for smart cards to be a valid solution is how you will ensure that you are giving the correct credentials to the correct person. Will you require users to present validated photo identification such as corporate employee badges or driver's licenses to ensure that users really are who they claim to be? What will you do if you have users who are geographically distant from your location? An ideal solution might be to issue blank smart cards to authorized users and then let them autoenroll (and thus install) the certificate to their smart card. In this way, only the authorized user has access to the smart card and the PIN required to access it. Your smart card distribution solution will be unique to the needs and organization of your company but, in any case, must ensure that the security of the smart card program is maintained at all times.

Although these things might not seem as though they should be part of the distribution planning, you must also ensure that you have adequately planned for public key length values, certificate validity periods, and certificate renewal policies. Be aware, however, that the memory capacity of the smart card you use can dictate the length of the public key; larger, more secure public keys require larger amounts of storage space, as you might imagine.

Smart Card Enrollment Options

As briefly mentioned previously, you need to ensure that you have a method in place to actually enroll the smart card certificates that will be required. You can choose from two basic options when you want to enroll smart card certificates:

- **Use an enrollment agent**—The use of an enrollment agent allows a trusted administrator to process all smart card certificate requests and ensures that smart cards and their certificates are created and installed properly. Although this can be a good thing from a user's point of view, it can quickly become an overwhelming task if too few enrollment agents are designated.
- **Allow self-enrollment by smart card users**—Although using enrollment agents is usually the best (and, by far, the most secure) method to enroll smart cards, in some cases, you might need or want to have users perform this task themselves. If you cannot physically (and safely) distribute fully ready smart cards, you might want to consider issuing blank smart cards and allowing the users to self-enroll. If you think that self-enrollment is completely insecure, recall that you can configure your CA to hold all new requests pending a manual administrative approval, thus giving you a chance to examine and validate the request before allowing the smart card to be enrolled with its certificate.

EXAM ALERT

Smart card enrollment Make sure you understand the basic options available to you related to smart card distribution and user enrollment.

Smart Card User Education

What would any security plan be without a good dose of user education? Smart cards are still a rather esoteric feature in most networks today; therefore, you should take steps to ensure that your users thoroughly understand what a smart card is, how it works, and what it provides for the network. Although this is not an all-inclusive listing, the following points should definitely be in your user-education plan for a new smart card implementation.

NOTE

Form of a smart card Without really thinking about it, you have most likely already been using a smart card in some way. ATM cards, building and parking garage access cards, and other cards with magnetic strips are all just different forms of a smart card.

- Ensure that users understand what special hardware and/or software they need to use their smart cards properly.
- Ensure that users know where to get this hardware and/or software. Additionally, ensure that users know who to contact when they run into problems with their smart cards.
- Ensure that users understand that smart cards need to be protected from scratching, chipping, denting, and other forms of damage on the external chip area. These sorts of damages can prevent the card from being read properly, rendering it unusable.
- Ensure that users understand that the card should not be exposed to temperature extremes, direct sunlight, or magnetic sources—as with any form of magnetic media.
- Ensure that users are instructed not to fold, spindle, or mutilate (yes, I had to say this!) their smart cards. Smart cards are fairly rugged, but they contain several internal components that can be broken by slipping the smart card into a back pocket, using the smart card to open a locked door (yes, this happens), or performing other abusive actions.

Smart Card Group Policy Options

When you are using smart cards for increased security of your network, you can configure several Group Policy options to further enhance the security of your smart card implementation:

- **Interactive Logon: Require Smart Card**—This option, located in the Computer Configuration\Windows Settings\Security Settings\Local Policies\Security Options node of the Group Policy Editor, can be used to prevent users from logging in to the domain by using a standard Windows username and password. Although this setting provides enhanced security, it can leave users without network access if their smart cards become unavailable for any reason. You should apply this policy at the OU level, making each smart card user a member of a domain local group and placing that group within the OU. Mistakenly applying this setting to non–smart card users will have disastrous effects. It's worth noting, however, that you can enable smart card usage on a user by user basis by configuring the Smart card is required for interactive logon option on their user account in Active Directory Users and Computers.

- **Interactive Logon: Smart Card Removal Behavior**—This option, also located in the Security Option node, can be used to define what Windows should do when a smart card is removed from its reader with the user logged in. Possible options include No Action, Lock Workstation, and Force Logoff. This option again presents both benefits and dangers. A user who mistakenly removes her smart card with open documents could well lose any changes made since the document was last saved. On the other hand, for computers located in kiosks or other insecure areas, this setting can greatly increase the security of the computer and your network. This Group Policy setting requires training on your part to ensure that your smart card users understand the consequences of their actions. Again, this setting should be configured on an OU containing only users who have been issued smart cards.
- **Do not allow smart card device redirection**—This option, located in the Computer Configuration\Administrative Templates\Windows Components\Terminal Services\Client/Server data-redirection node of the Group Policy Editor, can be used to prevent users from logging in to a Terminal Server with a smart card. This can increase security and decrease loading on your Terminal Servers.
- **Account Lockout Policy**—The Account Lockout Policy node, located at Computer Configuration\Windows Settings\Security Settings\Account Policies\Account Lockout Policy in the Group Policy Editor, contains three useful Group Policy settings that you can use to enhance both smart card and standard Windows logins. The Account Lockout Threshold setting can be configured to specify how many failed logon attempts should be allowed before that user account is locked out. The Account Lockout Duration setting specifies how long the account is to be locked out (barring an administrator unlocking the account early). The Reset Account Lockout Counter After option specifies how much time must pass before failed logon attempts are no longer counted against the Account Lockout Threshold setting. These policies are typically applied at a high level in your organization, such as the root of a domain, to cause them to apply to all users within the domain.

Challenge

Rockwell Financial Services is a company that deals in all aspects of financial management and investments. It has agents throughout North America that represent various firms for insurance and investments.

These agents use Windows XP Professional on their laptops. From the client's site, agents use the laptop to enter the investment information, and then they commute back to their respective networks and transfer the data to their local SQL Server, which is then transferred to a centralized SQL Server in Chicago.

The company realizes the need for the security of this data, and this is why the agents currently must return to the office to transfer their information. However, the agents are complaining that they are losing valuable time that they could use to visit other clients, and, in some cases, they lose sales because the market fluctuates and opportunities are missed.

Rockwell Financial Services would like to implement a plan that would enable its agents to use the Internet to connect to the central SQL Server and upload the data through a web interface—while securing data. In addition, the company would like to offer services to its clients that would enable the clients to access their account information online.

Through your discussions with the key stakeholders in this project, you've determined the following critical points of this project:

- Agents must be able to securely upload sensitive data over the Internet.
- The solution must enable clients to securely access their own data over the Internet.

Your task is to implement the required solution for Rockwell Financial Services.

Try to complete this exercise on your own, listing your conclusions on a sheet of paper. When you have completed the exercise, compare your results to those given here.

Rockwell Financial Services should install Certificate Services. A hierarchy of CA could start in the central office in Chicago and then be dispersed to a child CA in each geographical location.

Sales reps would be issued a certificate from the local CA. A web presence with a sales front and a SQL interface would be created to support secure uploads of client data over the Internet. In addition, a plan could be developed to secure any data the sales reps saved on their laptops through smart cards or through EFS implementation.

A web presence would be created for clients accessing their personal data. A certificate would be issued by a CA to verify that the clients have access to only their data.

Planning and Implementing a Security Update Infrastructure

Objective:

Plan a security update infrastructure. Tools might include Microsoft Baseline Security Analyzer and Microsoft Software Update Services.

As administrators, we constantly strive to maintain a secure and functional computing environment for our users. In a perfect world, administrators would never have to update an installation of Windows; unfortunately, this is just not the case. Between weaknesses that are inherent to Windows (through coding mistakes or other issues) and the insatiable desire of Black Hats (bad hackers, as opposed to White Hats, which are good hackers) to find new and more devious ways to open up your network like a can of sardines, you will soon have your hands full trying to keep your network's security stance up-to-date with the latest patches and hotfixes.

Realizing that it needed to become more proactive in helping Windows network administrators understand and correct the issues associated with the various security flaws that occur in the Windows operating systems, Microsoft has provided you with several tools that you can use to identify, categorize, and correct security-related issues on your network. The choice of what tool you use really depends on how you want to go about keeping your network updated. The following options are available for you to use in identifying and installing required security updates on your network's computers:

- **Microsoft Baseline Security Analyzer (MBSA)**—MBSA is an enhanced GUI version of the popular command-line `HFNetChk` application that can be used on Windows 2000, Windows XP, and Window Server 2003 computers to look for missing security updates, missing service packs, and weak security configurations in the supported Windows operating systems, Office, IIS, Structured Query Language (SQL) Server, and several other popular Microsoft applications. MBSA does a good job of identifying and categorizing missing updates and security problems that it finds, but it does not provide any direct means of updating required patches. The real strength of MBSA is that it can be used to scan many computers, even remote ones, at a time, providing a quick and easy-to-interpret graphical output.
- **Windows Update**—Windows Update, which has been around since Windows 98 arrived, provides an easy-to-use (although not always accurate) web-based tool for determining the need to install newly available updates on a local computer. Automatic Update works in conjunction with Windows Update where WSUS has not been installed; it provides automatic downloading and installation of required updates.

- **Windows Server Update Services (WSUS)**—Introduced originally as Software Update Services (SUS) for Windows 2000 and improved now as WSUS, this free add-on for Windows networks enables you to provide one or more Windows Update servers that run inside your protected internal network. WSUS enables the administrator to exercise granular control over which updates are installed and which aren't. Only updates that are specifically approved are installed on network computers configured to use an WSUS server for updating. After installing WSUS, you perform all its management and configuration from within your web browser, for ease of administration.
- **Automatic Updates**—Automatic Updates was first introduced with Windows XP SP1 and is actually responsible on the client side for downloading and installing required updates from either the Windows Update web servers or your internal WSUS servers, depending on how it has been configured. The default configuration is to use the Windows Update web servers. Automatic Updates is included in the default installation of Windows Server 2003. To configure Automatic Updates to use an internal WSUS server, you must first install and configure at least one WSUS server and then configure the appropriate Group Policy settings to require clients to use the designated WSUS servers.

Planning for Windows Server Update Services

Although Windows Server 2003 provides native support for Windows Server Update Services, it does not by default include WSUS. You can easily enough acquire the WSUS installation package, however, and begin work configuring and implementing WSUS on a network. But what, really, is WSUS? It is nothing more than a locally controlled and managed Windows Update server. Instead of configuring the Automatic Updates client on your client workstations to download updates directly from the Microsoft Windows Update servers, you can install and configure one or more WSUS servers on your internal network and point your client workstations toward those servers.

As you might imagine, the capability to have your client workstations use an internal server for Windows Update can be a tremendous benefit to you because it means decreased bandwidth use. As important as bandwidth savings might be, there is actually a larger benefit to be realized by implementing a WSUS solution on your internal network: the ability to approve specific updates that are to be installed on your clients. When you use Windows Update, your client computers install any available update that matches their needs, but with WSUS, you can specify which of the available updates are authorized to be pushed to the clients when you are satisfied that the update will pose no problems for the systems. This is a tremendous benefit that often goes unrealized.

As previously implied, WSUS is actually one part of a two-part system. The other part, the Automatic Updates client, runs on the servers and client workstations for which you want to download updates. Computers that are running the Automatic Updates client and that are to be updated by WSUS must meet one of the following requirements:

- Microsoft Windows 2000 Professional with Service Pack 3 (SP3) or Service Pack 4 (SP4)
- Windows 2000 Server with SP3 or SP4, or Windows 2000 Advanced Server with SP3 or SP4
- Microsoft Windows XP Professional with or without Service Pack 1 or Service Pack 2
- Microsoft Windows Server 2003, Standard Edition; Windows Server 2003, Enterprise Edition; Windows Server 2003, Datacenter Edition; or Windows Server 2003, Web Edition

The requirements for installing WSUS on a Windows Server 2003 computer are as follows:

- The system partition of the server must be formatted with the NTFS file system.
- The partition on which you install WSUS must be formatted with the NTFS file system.
- The system partition must have at least 1GB of free space available.
- The partition where you install WSUS must have a minimum of 6GB of free space available; however, it is recommended to have at least 30GB of free space available.
- The partition where WSUS setup installs the Windows SQL Server 2000 Desktop Engine (WMSDE) must have at least 2GB of free space available.
- The server must have Internet Information Services (IIS) 6.0 installed.
- The server must have the Microsoft .NET Framework 1.1 Service Pack 1 for Windows Server 2003 software installed. You can download the .NET Framework 1.1 and .NET Framework 1.1 Service Pack 1 for Windows Server 2003 from MSDN at http://msdn.microsoft.com/netframework/downloads/updates/version1/default.aspx.
- The server must have the Background Intelligent Transfer Service (BITS) 2.0 update installed.

Although it can be a bit of work to get one or more WSUS servers installed, configured, and running smoothly for your network, the benefits can be plentiful—especially if your organization has no budget for expensive third-party patching applications.

WSUS provides the following client-side features:

- **Requires local administrative privileges**—Only users who have local administrative privileges can change the settings of Automatic Updates. This prevents all other users from changing the configuration and possibly preventing required updates from being installed.
- **Requires digital signatures**—Only updates that have a valid Microsoft digital signature can be downloaded and installed.
- **Uses just-in-time validation**—Automatic Updates can determine which of the available updates are required for the computer.
- **Uses minimized bandwidth**—Through the Background Intelligent Transfer Service (BITS), Automatic Updates uses only idle (unused) bandwidth to download available updates, thus preventing the download of updates from slowing other network activities.

- **Safely installs multiple updates simultaneously**—Using the same Windows Update technologies that allow for multiple updates to be installed with only a single restart, Automatic Updates can install multiple updates and request only one restart, thus improving computer availability. This feature works similarly to the way the `QChain` utility was used previously from the command line.

WSUS provides the following server-side features:

- **Local administrative privileges required**—Only users who have local administrative privileges can change the settings of WSUS. This prevents all other users from changing the configuration and possibly preventing required updates from being installed.
- **Digital signatures required**—Only updates that have a valid Microsoft digital signature can be downloaded and installed.
- **Update approval**—Only updates that you have manually approved are made available to your Automatic Updates clients for download and installation. This provides for increased reliability of your network by enabling you to thoroughly test each update in a nonproduction environment before releasing it onto your live network.
- **Update availability**—Because the WSUS server synchronizes with the Windows Update web servers, you always have the most current list of updates available.
- **Remote administration**—SUS is administered from IE 5.5 or higher using either HTTP or HTTPS, allowing for an easy-to-administer interface. You need to install and configure an SSL certificate on the WSUS website before using HTTPS connections.
- **Logging**—A web server running IIS on your network can be specified as the log server and will receive statistics about updates that have been downloaded and whether the updates were installed. These statistics are placed in the log file of the configured web server and can be used to monitor and troubleshoot the performance of WSUS and Automatic Updates.
- **Server synchronization**—You might need to install and configure multiple WSUS servers to meet the needs of your network. WSUS enables you to configure WSUS servers to receive its update packages from another WSUS server, if you choose.
- **Multiple language support**—WSUS can be configured to make available different language versions of updates. To do so, you configure it to download specific language versions.
- **Diversified update hosting**—Depending on the specific needs of your network, you can configure your WSUS servers to download the actual update packages or to have WSUS servers pointing to the Windows Update web servers for the download of approved updates, as required.

The actual process of installing and configuring WSUS and Automatic Updates is covered in Exam 70-291, “Implementing, Managing, and Maintaining a Microsoft Windows Server 2003

Network Infrastructure." Refer to *70-291 Exam Prep: Implementing, Managing, and Maintaining a Windows Server 2003 Network Infrastructure* (Que Publishing, 2006), by Will Schmied, for more information on installing and configuring your WSUS solution.

EXAM ALERT

Know WSUS WSUS is a key part of Microsoft's security update infrastructure. You need to have a very good understanding of what it does, how it works, and how you can configure it to meets your needs and requirements.

Using the Microsoft Baseline Security Analyzer

You can quickly learn to use the Microsoft Baseline Security Analyzer. After downloading the most current version from www.microsoft.com/technet/security/tools/mbsahome.mspx and installing it, you are just a few mouse clicks away from performing security analysis of your network's computers.

When you launch the MBSA utility, you are presented with the option to scan one computer, scan multiple computers, or review previous scan reports, as shown in Figure 8.28.

By clicking the Pick Multiple Computers to Scan link, you can enter the NetBIOS domain name or IP address range that you want scanned, as shown in Figure 8.29.

After the scan has completed, you can see the results of a computer's scan, as shown in Figure 8.30. As you can see, this computer is missing a critical security update that creates a severe risk situation on the computer.

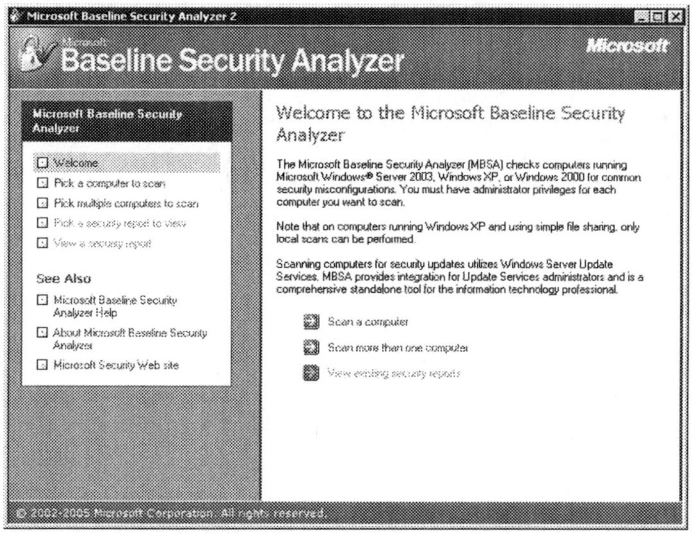

FIGURE 8.28 You can quickly scan multiple computers with just a few clicks of the mouse using MBSA.

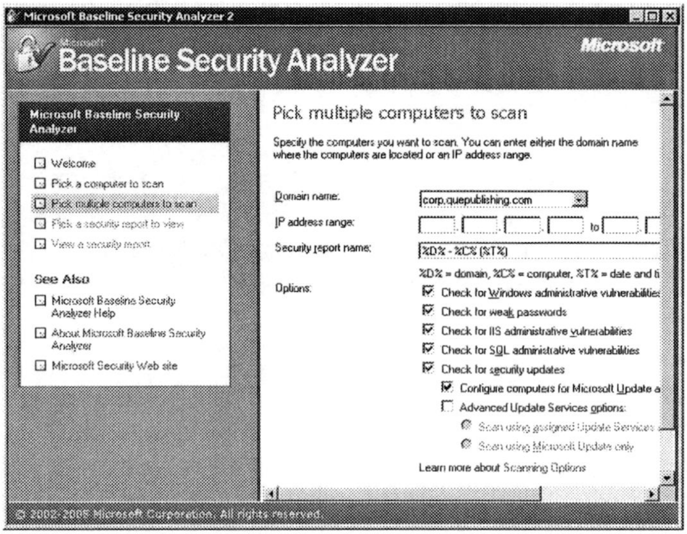

FIGURE 8.29 You can enter an entire domain to scan or scan a specific portion of the network.

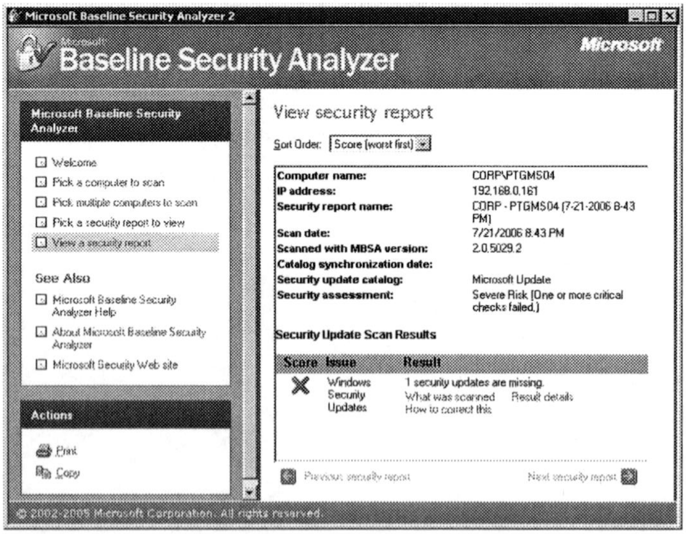

FIGURE 8.30 This computer is at severe risk because of a missing security update.

As mentioned previously, MBSA scans your computers not only for Windows security updates, but also for updates associated with other Microsoft products. MBSA 2.0 (the current version as of this writing) scans for security updates in the following products:

- Microsoft Windows 2000 (Professional and Server versions) with SP3 or SP4
- Microsoft Windows XP Professional

- Microsoft Windows Server 2003 (all versions)
- Microsoft Windows XP and Windows Server 2003 (all versions), 64-bit editions
- Microsoft Windows XP, Embedded Edition
- DirectX
- .NET Framework
- Microsoft Windows Messenger
- Microsoft FrontPage Server Extensions
- Microsoft Windows Media Player 10
- Windows Script 5.1, 5.5, 5.6
- Microsoft Outlook Express
- Microsoft SQL Server 2000 with SP4
- Microsoft Exchange 2000 with SP3
- Microsoft Office XP

Maintaining a Security Update Infrastructure

In newly implemented Windows Server 2003 Active Directory networks, implementing a WSUS solution to download and install approved security updates most likely is your best bet. If you have an existing security update architecture in place, such as Systems Management Server (SMS) or some other third-party solution, you might need to evaluate the benefits and costs of changing to WSUS. If you are relying only on Windows Update or Automatic Updates (without WSUS) to keep your systems up-to-date, you need to seriously look into rolling out WSUS.

One possible scenario for using WSUS and MBSA on your network to monitor and maintain security goes like this: You install and configure one or more WSUS servers on your network, as determined by the number of clients that will be accessing them (each server can handle approximately 15,000 clients) and the geographical dispersion of your network. You configure WSUS to automatically synchronize content nightly when network traffic is at its lowest. You also configure Automatic Updates via a GPO to download, install, and restart computers as required nightly, thus installing any newly approved updates. You also make it a habit to review, test, and approve new security updates one or more times a week to keep your systems up-to-date. Finally, you could run MBSA against your network computers twice monthly to spot-check the effectiveness of WSUS in keeping your computers updated with the patches you have approved.

Planning a Security Framework

As the adage goes, "Fail to plan, plan to fail." Nowhere does this expression ring more true than when you are dealing with network security and change and configuration management. By now, you've undoubtedly performed quite a bit of work on your network in an attempt to increase its security. But you need to ask two questions at this point:

1. How will you determine whether your security implementation is functioning as desired?
2. How will you ensure that the security of your network is not reduced or compromised through changes made to the network?

Although the topics of monitoring and change and configuration management are extensive, we briefly examine both of them here.

Planning for Security Monitoring

Objective:

Plan a framework for planning and implementing security.

- Plan for security monitoring.

Your network is now complete. You've rolled out all your servers and clients, network links are 100% available, and all Group Policy Objects are working properly. Your network is in a Utopian state—or is it? How would you know if things weren't really as good deep down as they appear to be on the surface? If you can't see any problems, does that mean that they do not exist? Unfortunately, no.

You need to include in your administrative plan for the network a strategy to perform routine regular security monitoring of all parts of the network—from the most high-profile server to the seemingly least important client workstation sitting in the lobby kiosk. But how will you go about monitoring security? It can be a big job that only increases exponentially as the number of computers on the network increases. Although you can use (and might want to at a later time) many good third-party products to centrally monitor security for your network, you can do a fair bit of monitoring yourself using only the tools provided within Windows or made available as an add-on download by Microsoft.

First and foremost, before you even start to monitor security, you should strive to always enforce the principle of least privilege for your users. This principle dictates that users are given only the minimum privileges required to perform the specific set of tasks that they have been assigned.

If you use the principle of least privilege, a compromised user account has a smaller impact on the overall security of the network than if you were to blanket-assign to users permissions that they did not need. Ideally, all normal user operations should be carried out in the context of a User account. If additional privileges are required for a specific reason, the administrator can either log in to the network with a special account for the purpose of performing those actions or use the Run As command to perform those actions within the context of the account that has the additional privileges.

After you have completely implemented the principle of least privilege, the task of monitoring network security will be greatly simplified because you can more easily determine what types of events are normal and what types of events are abnormal—indicating a possible security flaw or breach in your network.

The first part of your security-monitoring plan should be to implement a well-thought-out and carefully configured auditing program. Windows Server 2003 enables you to perform auditing of the following areas:

- **Audit Account Logon Events**—This option configures auditing to occur for user logons and logoffs. A successful audit generates an audit entry when a user successfully logs in, and a failed audit generates an entry when a user unsuccessfully attempts to log in.
- **Audit Account Management**—This option configures auditing to occur for each event of account management on a computer. Typical account-management events include creating a user, creating a group, renaming a user, disabling a user account, and setting or changing a password. A success audit generates an audit entry when any account-management event is successful, and a failure audit generates an entry when any account-management event fails.
- **Audit Directory Service Access**—This option configures auditing to occur when a user accesses an Active Directory object that has its own system access control list (SACL). This setting is only for Active Directory objects, such as GPOs, not for file system and Registry objects. A success audit generates an audit entry when a user successfully accesses an Active Directory object that has an SACL specified, and a failure audit generates an entry when an unsuccessful access attempt occurs.
- **Audit Logon Events**—This option configures auditing to occur upon each instance of a user logging on or off a computer. The audit events are generated on domain controllers for domain account activity and on local computers for local account activity. When both the Audit Logon Events and the Audit Account Logon Events options are configured, logons and logoffs that use a domain account generate logon or logoff audit events on the local computer as well as the domain controller. A success audit generates an audit entry when a logon attempt succeeds, and a failure audit generates an audit entry when a logon attempt fails.
- **Audit Object Access**—This option configures auditing to occur upon each user access of an object, such as a file, folder, printer, or Registry key that has its own SACL configured. To configure auditing for object access, you also need to configure auditing specifically on each object for which you want to perform auditing. A success audit generates an audit entry when a user successfully accesses an object, and a failure audit generates an audit entry when a user unsuccessfully attempts to access an object. You can only audit object access for objects stored on NTFS volumes.

- **Audit Policy Change**—This option configures auditing to occur upon every occurrence of changing user rights assignment policies, audit policies, or trust policies. A success audit generates an audit entry when a change to one of these policies is successful, and a failure audit generates an audit entry when a change to one of these policies fails.
- **Audit Privilege Use**—This option configures auditing to occur upon every occurrence of a user exercising a user right. A success audit generates an audit entry when the exercise of a user right succeeds, and a failure audit generates an audit entry when the exercise of a user right fails.
- **Audit Process Tracking**—This option configures auditing to occur for events such as program activation, process exit, handle duplication, and indirect object access. A success audit generates an audit entry when the process being tracked succeeds, and a failure audit generates an audit entry when the process being tracked fails.
- **Audit System Events**—This option configures auditing to occur when certain system events occur, such as computer restarts and shutdowns. A success audit generates an audit entry when a system event is executed successfully, and a failure audit generates an audit entry when a system event is attempted unsuccessfully.

EXAM ALERT

Auditing options You must have a good understanding of these auditing options and the ways they can be used to accomplish the auditing goals set forth.

The second part of your security-monitoring plan should be to collect, filter, and examine the event logs for all network computers in a centralized location. Several third-party applications provide this type of utility, often with many other nice features as well, but you can get good results by using the `EventCombMT` or `DumpEL` utilities. You can download `EventCombMT` by following the link contained in the Microsoft Knowledge Base article located at http://support.microsoft.com/default.aspx?scid=kb;en-us;824209.

Figure 8.31 shows the `EventCombMT` utility after the completion of a log gathering session. Note that text files are created with the output results in tab-delimited format.

You also might want to use the `DumpEL` (Dump Event Log) utility, which is run from the command line and can be scripted for greater power. `DumpEL` provides the same basic functionality as `EventCombMT`, but from the command line. The best way to find `DumpEL` is to search for it at the Microsoft Downloads Center, located at www.microsoft.com/downloads/.

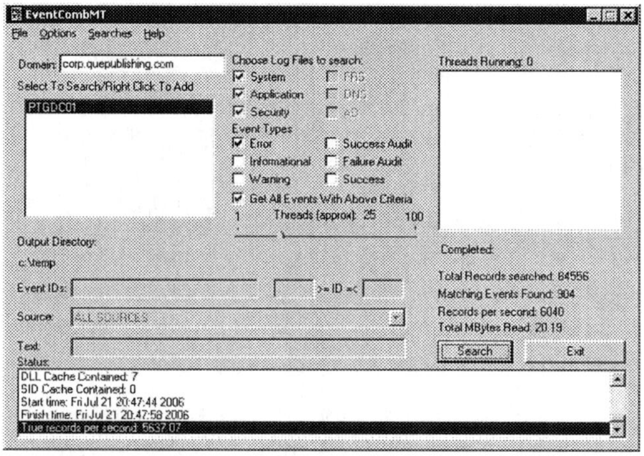

FIGURE 8.31 The `EventCombMT` utility provides a quick, easy, and free method of gathering event logs from the network.

Planning for Change and Configuration Management

Objective:

Plan a framework for planning and implementing security.

- Plan a change and configuration management framework for security.

In today's networking environment, it's fair to say that you can no longer just go off and make changes to the configuration of the network or its computers without having documentation in hand. More often than not, this documentation is two-fold: One set of documents details exactly what you will be doing and how you will back out of it if problems arise. You create the second set of documentation as you work, documenting the new configuration that you have set in place.

The first document—the one outlining exactly what will be done, how it will be done, and what will happen if things do not work out correctly—is in itself derived using yet another document: the change and configuration management policy for your network. You use the change and configuration management policy document to create all future plans for making security and configuration changes on your network. The key point that you must realize—and make all members of your organization realize—that even the smallest change to the network can turn out to be the largest security problem you've ever seen. A good example is a (routine) routing table change that causes PPTP traffic to take the tunnel in one direction and the regular IP subnet on the return path so that only half of the conversation is encrypted.

As you can see from this simple example, even the smallest, most routine administrative tasks can have a large impact on the security and functionality of your network. Thus, you must implement a change-and-control policy that will be used when making any change to the network—whether or not the change appears to be security related. Such a policy should require, at a minimum, the following steps:

1. As the need for change is discovered or recognized, a pending change request is filed. Such requests are reviewed and evaluated at regular intervals.
2. If the change request is approved during the review process, a change order is created. In addition to describing the change and its desired results, the change order should specify staffing, budget, and schedule requirements.
3. When the change order schedule indicates that work to incorporate the requested change is to begin, a change job or work order is enacted. Normally, such changes apply to a copy of the system being changed and do not affect changes to production environments until later in this process. The implementation group must also document its changes and file proposed changes to security policy documents at this time.
4. During the implementation process, module and unit tests make sure the change as implemented meets the requirements of the change as specified. When the implementation team decides the change is complete, it is turned over to a test group for change testing as an external check.
5. If the external testing group agrees that the change meets the specifications, that the change has no adverse effects on overall system behavior or capability, and that the documentation changes properly reflect resulting security policy, change enactment is authorized. Only at this point are changes introduced into a production environment, so only at this point do real, visible changes occur.

NOTE

Take control For more information about security monitoring and change-and-control policies, be sure to see *TICSA Training Guide* (Que Publishing, 2002; ISBN 0789727838), by Mike Chapple, Debra Littlejohn Shinder, and Shawn Porter.

As you can see, this process can become lengthy and time-consuming, but no amount of planning is ever wasted. Fortunately, you do not have to reinvent the wheel to implement a good change-and-configuration-control plan; you can find many high-quality resources both in print and on the Internet. One of the many useful change management–related websites on the Internet is www.change-management.com.

Chapter Summary

As you have seen, proper planning is the single most important key to success when implementing a network security plan. No effective security plan consists of only one security solution; the concept of defense in depth states that multiple, layered security solutions should be implemented to increase network security as much as possible. An example of the defense-in-depth principle is a network that requires a username and password to gain access to the network. To further protect sensitive information, data on file servers is encrypted using EFS. Finally, IPSec is implemented to secure network communications as they cross the network cabling itself.

Digital certificates come into play with many of these security solutions. Digital certificates can be used for smart cards to authenticate and verify the identity of the user, digital certificates are required for the use of EFS, and digital certificates can be used to provide security and authentication for IPSec communications on your network. The scope and type of PKI infrastructure you implement are specified, in large part, by the requirements of your network's users.

Two basic types of CAs are available for use in Windows Server 2003. Enterprise CAs are completely integrated with Active Directory and provide some features not otherwise available in Standalone CAs. Standalone CAs do not require the presence of Active Directory, but if AD is in use, they can make use of it. Standalone CAs can be used to issue certificates and then can be removed from the network to increase their physical security. Each type of CA has two child types: Root and Subordinate. Only one Root CA exists within a PKI implementation; all other CAs are Subordinate (or child) CAs. The Root CA signs its own CA certificate and the CA certificate of all Subordinate CAs directly below it. Subordinate CAs issue and sign certificates for network users, computers, and other Subordinate CAs.

Microsoft introduced Software Update Services in Windows 2000 to provide an easy-to-administer way for network administrators to keep their networks up-to-date with required security updates. SUS has been integrated into Windows Server 2003. Using SUS and Automatic Updates, you can have approved updates automatically installed on client computers on the schedule you have configured. By allowing only administratively approved updates to be installed on client computes, SUS and Automatic Updates help you protect your network from problems that might be caused by required updates that are not compatible with your network or network applications.

When you've planned and implemented a security solution for your network, you need to ensure that your network stays secure. Microsoft has a two-step network security plan: Get Secure, Stay Secure. The Stay Secure portion requires you to maintain security after you have it in place. To maintain security, you need to monitor it. Security monitoring can be accomplished in many ways, but the most common include auditing and event logs. Also, you need to have a functional and well-thought-out change-and-configuration plan in place to prevent mistakes from being made that can compromise the security of your network.

Key Terms

- Auditing
- Automatic Updates
- Certificate
- Certificate Authority
- Certificate Revocation List (CRL)
- Enterprise CA
- EventCombMT
- GPO
- Group Policy Editor
- Microsoft Baseline Security Analyzer (MBSA)
- Principle of least privilege
- Revoked certificate
- Root CA
- Software Update Services (SUS)
- Standalone CA
- Subordinate CA
- Validity period

Apply Your Knowledge

In this chapter, you examined more advanced methods in Windows Server 2003 to get secure and stay secure. In the following exercises, you practice some of the concepts and methods discussed in this chapter.

Exercises

8.1 Creating an Enterprise Root CA

In this exercise, you create an Enterprise Root CA for your network. You need to have a Windows Server 2003 computer that is part of an Active Directory network. If you want to use the Web Enrollment pages, you need to install IIS before installing this CA.

Estimated time: 20 minutes

1. Log in to a Windows Server 2003 that is a member of the Active Directory domain with administrative permissions.
2. Select Start, Settings, Control Panel, Add or Remove Programs to open the Add or Remove Programs dialog box.
3. Click the Add/Remove Windows Components button located on the left side of the Add or Remove Programs dialog box to open the Windows Components Wizard.
4. Select the Certificate Services option.
5. A warning dialog box informs you that you cannot rename the server after installing Certificate Services on it.
6. Click Next on the Windows Components Wizard dialog box to start the installation process.
7. In the CA Type dialog box, select the type of CA you are installing. For this example, select Enterprise Root CA. If you want to customize the key pair settings, you can do so by selecting the Use Custom Settings to Generate the Key Pair and CA Certificate option.
8. If you selected to customize your key settings, the Public and Private Key Pair dialog box appears next. You have the opportunity to customize the installation by selecting the CSP and the key length. You also can use and import an existing certificate and key.
9. In the CA Identifying Information dialog box, enter the common name of the CA. This name should be descriptive but should not contain any special characters. You also need to configure the validity period; the default value is five years.
10. In the Certificate Database Settings dialog box, enter the database and log locations or simply use the default selections—usually the best option, in most cases.
11. If IIS is running on the server, you are prompted to acknowledge that it will be stopped to perform the configuration of the CA. If IIS is not installed, you are prompted to install it before Web Enrollment can be used.
12. Click Finish to close the Windows Component Wizard. The CA is now ready and available for immediate use.

8.2 Configuring CRL Publication Properties

In this exercise, you configure the CRL publication properties of your CA. To complete this exercise, you should first complete Exercise 8.1.

Estimated time: 15 minutes

1. Select Start, Programs, Administrative Tools, Certification Authority to open your Certification Authority management console.
2. Locate the CA of concern in the CA management console and expand its nodes.
3. Right-click the Revoked Certificates node and select Properties from the context menu.
4. The Revoked Certificates Properties dialog box opens. Configure the CRL publication interval and the Delta CRL publication interval, or disable the use of Delta CRLs completely.
5. View those CRLs that have been published by switching to the View CRLs tab.
6. To change the CRL publication location, right-click the CA name and select Properties from the context menu.
7. When the CA Properties dialog box opens, switch to the Extensions tab. You can publish to Active Directory, a file system location, and an FTP or HTTP location.
8. To manually publish the CRL, right-click again on the Revoked Certificates folder and select All Tasks, Publish. You are asked what type of CRL you want to publish.

8.3 Requesting a Certificate with the Certificate Request Wizard

In this exercise, you request a new digital certificate from your CA using the Certificate Request Wizard. You need to complete Exercise 8.1 before attempting this exercise.

Estimated time: 10 minutes

1. Open the Certificates console by adding it as a snap-in to a custom MMC console or by entering **`certmgr.msc`** at the command prompt.
2. Right-click the Personal node and select All Tasks, Request New Certificate to start the Certificate Request Wizard.
3. Click Next to dismiss the opening page of the Certificate Request Wizard.
4. In the Certificate Types dialog box, select the type of certificate being requested. You also can configure advanced options, including the CSP to be used, by selecting the Advanced check box.
5. In the Certificate Friendly Name and Description dialog box, enter a friendly name and description for your certificate to identify more easily in the future.
6. Click Finish on the Completing the Certificate Request Wizard dialog box to complete the process.

8.4 Requesting a Certificate via the Web Enrollment Pages

In this exercise, you request a new digital certificate using the Web Enrollment pages. To complete this exercise, you must first complete Exercise 8.1 and install IIS on your CA.

Estimated time: 10 minutes

1. Open a new Internet Explorer window and enter **`http://`*`CAname`*`/certsrv`** in the address bar, where *CAname* represents the name or IP address of your CA.
2. Click the Request a Certificate link to request a new certificate.
3. To request a basic user certificate, click the User Certificate link. If you want to request any other type of certificate, click the Advanced Certificate Request link.
4. On the Advanced Certificate Request page, click the Create and Submit a Request to This CA link to continue.
5. On the Advanced Certificate Request page, select the type of certificate being requested, and configure its properties as you require. When you have configured your certificate request as desired, click the Submit button located at the bottom of the page.
6. As part of the enhanced security of Windows Server 2003 (and Windows XP), a warning dialog box indicates that a web page is requesting a certificate on your behalf.
7. If the request was successfully approved, you are presented with the Certificate Issued page. Click Install This Certificate to install your new certificate.
8. Again, Windows alerts you that the web page is attempting to perform some action related to a digital certificate.

Review Questions

1. What is a certificate?
2. Why would an organization have a Standalone CA?
3. Why would a CA need to renew its certificate?
4. You are the network administrator of a large campus-wide community college network. Your network consists of computers running every version of Windows from Windows 95 to Windows Server 2003. Is SUS a good solution for your network, to ensure that all computers are up-to-date with the latest security patches?
5. Your CIO has instructed you to implement an WSUS solution for your corporate network. He is concerned, however, about making unsecured connections to the WSUS server. What can be done to provide connection security?

Exam Questions

1. Christopher is the systems administrator for the Heron Woods Resort Cottages company. Heron Woods rents vacation cottages at several locations along the Eastern Shore of Virginia and Maryland. Christopher needs to implement a solution that will keep the Windows Server 2003 and Windows XP Professional computers at all his locations up-to-date with the latest security updates, while at the same time installing only those updates that he has specifically approved. Heron Woods has a main office in Chincoteague, Virginia, connected to the Internet by a fractional T1 line. All other locations are considered remote locations and have a dedicated ISDN link connecting them to the main office. What solution can Christopher implement that will allow him to meet his goals of providing available updates and allowing only approved updates to be installed? Christopher has received authorization from the CEO of Heron Woods to add only the absolute minimum number of additional servers as required to provide the best solution for meeting the requirements.

   ❍ **A.** Christopher should configure all servers and client workstations to connect directly to the Microsoft Windows Update web servers weekly to download and install any new security updates that are required.

   ❍ **B.** Christopher should install an WSUS server at each of his locations, including the remote offices, that is configured to automatically synchronize each night with the Windows Update web servers. Additionally, he should configure Automatic Updates to download and install any new security updates that are required on a nightly basis from the local WSUS server.

   ❍ **C.** Christopher should install an WSUS server at each of his locations, including the remote offices. The WSUS server at the main office should be configured to automatically synchronize each night with the Windows Update web servers. The WSUS servers at each of the remote offices should be configured to synchronize each night using the WSUS server at the main office as its source. Additionally, he should configure Automatic Updates to download and install any new security updates that are required on a nightly basis from the local WSUS server.

   ❍ **D.** Christopher should install an WSUS server at his main office that synchronizes nightly with the Windows Update Web servers. Automatic Updates for all clients, local and remote, should be configured to download and install all approved updates from the main office WSUS server on a nightly basis.

2. Andrea is the systems administrator for Purple Pony Wear, Inc., a leading supplier of novelty clothing items. The Purple Pony network consists of 2 Windows Server 2003 computers and 34 Windows XP Professional client computers, 30 of which are laptops in use in various remote locations by sales personnel. Andrea wants to create and implement a PKI solution so that her users can use smart cards to log on to their laptop computers, thus increasing the security of the laptops and the Purple Pony network. Priscilla, the President of Purple Pony, is concerned about users removing their smart cards from their laptop computers during their sessions and leaving their laptops logged in without being in front of them. Priscilla would like all laptops to be configured to lock the workstation when the smart card is removed so open documents will not be lost. What option does Andrea need to configure to ensure that the desired result is achieved?

- ❍ **A.** Do Not Allow Smart Card Device Redirection
- ❍ **B.** Interactive Logon: Require Smart Card
- ❍ **C.** Account Lockout Policy
- ❍ **D.** Interactive Logon: Smart Card Removal Behavior

3. You are the systems administrator of a Windows Server 2003 Active Directory network. Your company policy states that the network-access attempts of all temporary employees are to be tracked, regardless of what workstation they log on to. What auditing options do you need to configure to ensure that you can track the access of all temporary employees? (Choose two correct options.)

- ❍ **A.** Audit Account Management
- ❍ **B.** Audit Directory Service Access
- ❍ **C.** Audit Logon Events
- ❍ **D.** Audit Privilege Use
- ❍ **E.** Audit System Events
- ❍ **F.** Audit Account Logon Events

4. You are the systems administrator of a large Windows Server 2003 network. Your company is a leading provider of state-of-the-art satellite communications services for customers all over the world. The CIO of your company is very concerned about user account properties being modified by users who should not have administrative permissions. As part of your efforts to determine who might be modifying user account properties, you have decided to implement auditing. What auditing option should you configure to help you determine who is changing the user account properties on your network?

- ❍ **A.** Audit Account Management
- ❍ **B.** Audit Object Access
- ❍ **C.** Audit Logon Events
- ❍ **D.** Audit Privilege Use
- ❍ **E.** Audit System Events
- ❍ **F.** Audit Account Logon Events

5. You are the systems administrator of a large Windows Server 2003 network. Your company is a leading provider of state-of-the-art satellite communications services for customers all over the world. The CIO of your company is very concerned about who is able to access files and folders located in a sensitive folder named Contacts. What auditing option should you configure to help you determine what users on your network are accessing the files and folders located within the Contacts folder?

- ❍ **A.** Audit Account Management
- ❍ **B.** Audit Object Access
- ❍ **C.** Audit Logon Events
- ❍ **D.** Audit Privilege Use
- ❍ **E.** Audit System Events
- ❍ **F.** Audit Account Logon Events

6. You are the systems administrator for Nebuchadnezzar Furnaces. The company's Windows Server 2003 domain consists of domain controllers, 2 member servers, and 765 Windows XP Professional workstations. Every summer, you hire 30 to 40 temporary employees to assist with additional production and sales needs for the upcoming winter season. Each employee is issued a digital certificate for smart card use to allow him or her to securely access the network. The digital certificates have a validity period of two years by default because of the configuration of the CA that has issued them. Allison, your CIO, has told you on more than one occasion that she does not like the idea of having unused digital certificates still active. What should you do to increase your network's level of security?

- ❍ **A.** Change the CSP key length.
- ❍ **B.** Revoke the unused digital certificates.
- ❍ **C.** Lock the user's accounts.
- ❍ **D.** Disable the unused digital certificates.

7. You have just composed and sent an email message to a colleague who is located within a different Windows Server 2003 network than your own. Your email message has been digitally signed using your email certificate. Your Root CA uses a third-party certificate from a trusted third-party organization. What will your colleague need to have available to be able to read your email and verify that it originated from you?

- ❍ **A.** Your private key
- ❍ **B.** Your public key
- ❍ **C.** The third-party CA's private key
- ❍ **D.** The third-party CA's public key

8. You have just received an email message from a colleague who is located within a different Windows Server 2003 network than your own. The email message has been digitally signed by the public key for your email certificate. Her Root CA uses a third-party certificate from a trusted third-party organization. What will you need to have available to you to be able to read her email and verify that it originated from her?

- ❍ **A.** Your private key
- ❍ **B.** Your colleague's public key
- ❍ **C.** The third-party CA's private key
- ❍ **D.** The third-party CA's public key

9. Rick is the systems administrator for Mr. Whippy's Ice Cream. Rick recently installed and configured an Enterprise Root CA for his Windows Server 2003 network on a server named CHOCOLATE. He performed no configuration for this new CA other than what was required during the installation process. When he tries to access the Web Enrollment web pages at http://CHOCOLATE/certsrv, he receives a 404 error from Internet Explorer. What is the most likely cause of this problem?

- ❍ **A.** Rick forgot to start the Certificate Services service following the completion of the installation process.
- ❍ **B.** Rick has not installed Terminal Services on his CA.
- ❍ **C.** Rick has not installed IIS on his CA.
- ❍ **D.** Rick did not create a new CNAME record for the CA.

10. Hannah is the systems administrator for the Wallops Island Rocket Company, Inc. Her network is required to maintain the highest level of security possible without adversely affecting the required operations of its users. For the past 10 weeks, six visiting rocket scientists have been working at her facility on a joint project with another company. Hannah issued each of these users a secure laptop including a smart card—allowing them to securely access and update the rocket systems data stored in the SQL databases. These six visiting users have completed their work and have now left the facility, leaving behind their laptop computers and smart cards as required. Hannah has just completed sanitizing their laptop computers; what should she do next?

- ❍ **A.** Delete the data created by the scientists during their stay.
- ❍ **B.** Degauss the hard drives installed in the laptop computers the scientists were using.
- ❍ **C.** Perform a background check with the FBI, NSA, and NCIS on the scientists.
- ❍ **D.** Revoke the smart card certificates the scientists were issued and immediately publish the CRL to all configured CDPs.

11. Chris is the systems administrator for Island Dreams Tour and Rentals, Inc. She is preparing to implement a smart card solution for her Windows Server 2003 network. All her client computers are Windows XP Professional desktops and laptops. Some users have both a desktop computer and a laptop computer. Chris wants users to be able to use a single smart card at all times, regardless of what computer they are logging in to the network from. Chris does not want users to be able to log on to the network without using their assigned smart cards. What can she configure to enforce this requirement on her users?

- ❍ **A.** Do Not Allow Smart Card Device Redirection
- ❍ **B.** Interactive Logon: Require Smart Card
- ❍ **C.** Account Lockout Policy
- ❍ **D.** Interactive Logon: Smart Card Removal Behavior

12. Jim recently completed a configuration change to one of his network's firewalls. Now multiple users have called the help desk complaining that they can no longer access external resources. What document did Jim most likely not have in hand that could have prevented this problem?

- ❍ **A.** A security-monitoring policy
- ❍ **B.** A firewall-configuration policy
- ❍ **C.** A change-and-configuration-control policy
- ❍ **D.** A user-naming convention policy

13. Kim has requested a new smart card certificate from one of her organization's CAs. Her request was not automatically approved and thus has been placed in a queue for administrative approval. You are the network administrator for the organization where Kim is employed. What must you do to approve her smart card certificate request?

- ❍ **A.** You need to log in using Kim's user account and supply the approval key for her certificate request.
- ❍ **B.** You need to use the Active Directory Users and Computers console to locate the Pending Requests folder.
- ❍ **C.** You need to use the Certificates console to locate the Pending Requests folder.
- ❍ **D.** You need to use the Certification Authorities console to locate the Pending Requests folder.

14. Kim has requested a new smart card certificate from one of her organization's CAs using the Web Enrollment pages. Her request was not automatically approved and thus has been placed in a queue for administrative approval. Kim wants to check on the status of her certificate request to see whether the certificate has been approved for issuance. Where can Kim most easily find this information and install the certificate if her request has been approved?

- ❍ **A.** Active Directory Users and Computers console
- ❍ **B.** Certificates console, Personal Store node
- ❍ **C.** Log on to the CA Web Enrollment pages again
- ❍ **D.** The Certificate Request Wizard

15. Chris is the systems administrator for Seashell Cruises, Ltd. The Seashell network has recently been upgraded from a mixed environment consisting of Windows 98 clients with Windows NT 4.0 Server and Windows 2000 Server servers. All clients now run Windows XP Professional, and all servers now run Windows Server 2003. Some computers were upgraded in place, whereas others were clean installations. Chris has recently been hired by Seashell Cruises and wants to establish the security level of her network using the least administrative effort. She has approximately 200 client workstations and 30 servers spread over two different locations in the same geographic area all on the same IP subnet. What method can Chris use to most easily analyze all her computers and find security problems with them?

   ❍ **A.** Use Windows Update locally on each computer to download and install required security updates

   ❍ **B.** Use Automatic Updates on each computer to download and install required security updates

   ❍ **C.** Install and configure WSUS on one of her servers and configure Automatic Updates on the clients to download and install approved required security updates

   ❍ **D.** Use the MBSA utility to scan her entire subnet to quickly identify security problems and missing security updates on all computers

Answers to Review Questions

1. A certificate is a component that enables you to send and receive secure data over a network. It assures the recipient that you are whom you claim to be, and it assures the sender that the data will reach the recipient without being jeopardized. For more information, see the section "Certificates."

2. Standalone CA is an excellent choice when Active Directory is not present or when you want to manually approve certificate requests. For more information, see the section "The Standalone CA."

3. When a CA is created, it is assigned a certificate. This certificate, like all certificates, is set to expire. When a certificate has expired or is about to expire, an administrator can choose to renew the certificate. For more information, see the section "Renewing CAs."

4. If you have large numbers of pre–Windows 2000 computers (that is, legacy clients), WSUS is probably not the best solution for your updating needs. In this situation, you would most likely want to examine a solution such as SMS or a third-party solution that provides the same type of functionality.

5. You can enable SSL support on the WSUS website and thus require that all connections be SSL secured. For more information, see the section "Planning for Windows Server Update Services."

Answers to Exam Questions

1. **D.** Because WAN link usage is not an issue in this scenario, and because Christopher has received authorization to add only those new servers that are absolutely required, his best option is to install and configure one WSUS server at the main office that synchronizes nightly with the Windows Update web servers. All Automatic Updates clients will then be configured to receive their updates from the home office WSUS server. For more information, see the section "Planning for Windows Server Update Services."

2. **D.** By configuring the Smart Card Removal Behavior option, located in the Computer Configuration\Windows Settings\Security Settings\Local Policies\Security Options node of the Group Policy Editor, for Lock Workstation, Andrea can achieve the desired results. For more information, see the section "Smart Card Group Policy Options."

3. **C, F.** When both the Audit Logon Events and the Audit Account Logon Events options are configured, logons and logoffs that use a domain account generate logon or logoff audit events on the local computer as well as the domain controller. A success audit generates an audit entry when a logon attempt succeeds, and a failure audit generates an audit entry when a logon attempt fails. For more information, see the section "Planning for Security Monitoring."

4. **A.**The Audit Account Management option configures auditing to occur for each event of account management on a computer. Typical account-management events include creating a user, creating a group, renaming a user, disabling a user account, and setting or changing a password. A success audit generates an audit entry when any account-management event is successful, and a failure audit generates an entry when any account-management event fails. For more information, see the section "Planning for Security Monitoring."

5. **B.** The Audit Object Access option configures auditing to occur upon each user access of an object, such as a file, folder, printer, or Registry key that has its own SACL configured. To configure auditing for object access, you also need to configure auditing specifically on each object for which you want to perform auditing. A success audit generates an audit entry when a user successfully accesses an object, and a failure audit generates an audit entry when a user unsuccessfully attempts to access an object. For more information, see the section "Planning for Security Monitoring."

6. **B.** In this scenario, the best option for increasing security is to revoke any unused certificates and immediately publish the CRL to all CDPs. For more information, see the section "Configuring Active Directory for Certificate Publication."

7. **B.** All that is necessary to read the email and verify that it came from you is your public key, which can be safely transferred to anyone you want. Your private key should never be given out. If your colleague were to install the third-party CA's root certificate, he would thus be able to verify the entire certificate chain for your digital certificate. For more information, see the section "Certificates."

8. **A.** In this scenario, because the email has been signed with your public key, you need to have access to your private key, which should not be any problem. Your private key can be used to verify messages signed with your public key and can be used to verify messages that can be decrypted with your public key. For more information, see the section "Certificates."

9. **C.** To use the Certificate Services Web Enrollment pages, Rick must ensure that IIS is installed and configured properly to allow ASP pages to function properly. For best results, Rick should have installed IIS before installing the CA. For more information, see the section "Installing and Configuring an Enterprise Root CA."

10. **D.** Hannah should revoke the smart card certificates and immediately publish the CRL next. After doing so, she should also delete any unused user accounts that might have been created for the scientists' use during their visit to Hannah's facility. For more information, see the section "Configuring Active Directory for Certificate Publication."

11. **B.** By configuring the Interactive Logon: Require Smart Card Group Policy setting, Chris can ensure that all her users are required to log on to the network using their smart cards. Smart cards are used to provide the highest level of user authentication available in Windows Server 2003 networks. A user uses a password or PIN to access the digital certificate on the smart card, thus protecting the user's identity from rogue applications and attackers. Through the use of on-card digital signatures, smart cards can ensure that a user's private key is never exposed. Perhaps the single best feature of smart cards is that they—unlike software-based private keys—can be moved at will from one computer to another with ease. You can prevent smart cards from being used to access the network after a preconfigured number of incorrect login attempts, protecting them further from dictionary attacks—a type of password-guessing attack in which a password is guessed from a dictionary or list of common words and phrases. For more information, see the section "Smart Card Group Policy Options."

12. **C.** Had Jim used a change-and-configuration-control policy along with an approved change request, he most likely would not have created the problem he did as a result of his configuration change on the firewall. For more information, see the section "Planning for Change and Configuration Management."

13. **D.** Queued certificates are located in the Pending Requests folder of the Certification Authorities console. You can find and issue this certificate for Kim from this location. For more information, see the section "Installing and Configuring an Enterprise Root CA."

14. **C.**The easiest way for Kim to check on the status of her requested certificate is to go back to the CA from which she requested it via its Web Enrollment pages. If the certificate request has been approved, she also can install the certificate from that location. For more information, see the section "Using the Web Enrollment Web Pages."

15. **D.** Chris wants to only determine the security status of her network at this time, not install any updates. Using the MBSA utility is the best option because she can configure a single scan of all computers located on her subnet. When MBSA has completed the scan, she can examine each computer's results separately from the others, quickly determining what areas of their security configuration are weak and determining what security updates are missing on each computer. For more information, see the section "Planning for Windows Server Update Services."

Suggested Readings and Resources

1. WSUS home page. www.microsoft.com/windowsserversystem/updateservices/.
2. *Microsoft Windows Server 2003 Administrator's Companion.* Redmond, WA: Microsoft Press, 2003.
3. *Microsoft Windows Server 2003 PKI and Certificate Security.* Redmond, WA: Microsoft Press, 2003.
4. Windows Server 2003 online help: "Auditing Security Events" and "Security Configuration Manager." http://technet2.microsoft.com/WindowsServer/en/library.
5. Microsoft Windows Server 2003 Deployment Kit. "Designing a Managed Environment" and "Designing and Deploying Directory and Security Services." www.microsoft.com/windowsserver2003/techinfo/reskit/deploykit.mspx.
6. Certificate Autoenrollment in Windows Server 2003, http://www.microsoft.com/technet/prodtechnol/windowsserver2003/technologies/security/autoenro.mspx.

9

CHAPTER NINE

Monitoring and Maintaining Server Availability

This chapter helps you learn and master some of the more common concepts associated with implementing and maintaining availability of servers through such administrative tasks as performance monitoring, log monitoring, and backups. Highly available server solutions, such as clustering and network load balancing, will be discussed next in Chapter 10, "Planning, Implementing, and Maintaining Highly Available Servers."

Objectives

Microsoft has the following objectives for the routine administrative portion of the "Planning, Implementing, and Maintaining Server Availability" unit:

Identify system bottlenecks, including memory, processor, disk, and network-related bottlenecks.

- **Identify system bottlenecks by using System Monitor.**
- Examining the inner workings of the operating system can provide an administrator with some valuable insight on how and when future problems might occur. System Monitor can provide information that, if used properly, can help avoid costly downtime or performance degradation on servers and client machines.

Plan a backup and recovery strategy.

- **Identify appropriate backup types. Methods can include the backup types full, incremental, and differential.**
- **Plan a backup strategy that uses volume shadow copy.**
- **Plan system recovery that uses Automated System Recovery (ASR).**
- Regardless of how much planning and effort you put into keeping your servers running smoothly, disaster might still strike. Being familiar with the use and options of the Windows Backup Utility is a critical part of a disaster-recovery plan in Windows Server 2003.

Outline

Study Strategies

- The key points to understand in this chapter revolve around the various means of disaster prevention and recovery available to you as an administrator. It is important to have a good grasp on ways you can identify and troubleshoot performance issues that affect your computers.
- It is important to understand how the Performance console is set up and what its component parts are. Know how to create a system monitor, create counter and trace logs, and configure alerts. Know specifically the main counters associated with the processor, memory, network, and disk objects, as outlined in this chapter. You won't likely be tested specifically on counters, but you should be aware of them anyway.
- As they pertain to data backup and recovery, know how Windows Backup and Restore work, how to invoke them, and how the scheduler works. You also need to have a thorough understanding of Automated System Recovery (ASR) and volume shadow copy.
- Get your hands dirty. The Step by Steps throughout this book provide plenty of directions and exercises, but you should go beyond these examples and create some of your own. If you can, experiment with each of the topics we discuss in this chapter to see how they work and why you would use each one.

Introduction

Troubleshooting is something we all wish we'd never have to do, but more often than not, we find ourselves doing it. Knowing how to properly troubleshoot and perform repairs on servers and client computers is critical for an administrator and is a task that should not be taken lightly. Knowing how to look ahead to identify problems before they occur is even more important. Unfortunately, identifying impending problems is a fine art learned over time with practice and patience.

During the course of this chapter, we look at methods to recover servers if disaster strikes (despite your best efforts) and at means of identifying and correcting problems before they occur. A good understanding of these two areas will go a long way toward making your life as an administrator a happier one.

Monitoring System Performance for Bottlenecks

Objective:

Identify system bottlenecks, including memory, processor, disk, and network-related bottlenecks.

- Identify system bottlenecks by using System Monitor.

Administering a Windows Server 2003 network is not simply about making sure that people have access to resources and that information is secure. The question administrators ask themselves is not just "Is it running?" but also "Is it running well?" Of course, "well" is relative and can't really be quantified outside your individual context.

This section examines the assessment of server performance using System Monitor, a tool located within the Performance console. In addition, it discusses some tips on how to tune your server before problems occur and which devices should be monitored when they do.

Periodic monitoring of your Windows Server 2003 network is important to the process of optimization. Monitoring helps overcome the feeling-based assessment of your users. For example, by comparing current network performance against a previously established baseline, you have more information than the anecdotal "The network is slow today!" on which to base your actions. By gathering current information and comparing it against established norms for your systems (a *baseline*), you can detect bottlenecks, identify those system components that are slowing server performance, and fix them before they become a problem to your users.

Although the actual procedure for creating a baseline is outlined later in this section, it is important to discuss the concept of a baseline here because it is the first thing you will do in practice—even if it is not the first concept that is presented here. A *baseline* is an established norm for the operation of your server as determined by normal load. This baseline can then be used as a basis of comparison for future performance to see whether repairable problems exist. As the configuration of your server changes (when, for example, a processor is added or RAM is added), new baselines are established to reflect the new expected performance.

The importance of establishing a baseline before beginning to monitor performance can't be overstated. Although there are some guidelines on what absolute performance numbers indicate, as you compare current performance against past performance (the baseline), you will really be able to evaluate how well current demand is being met and whether you require more resources on your server. In addition, it is imperative that a baseline be established before problems begin to occur. If users are already beginning to complain, "The network is slow," it is too late to establish a baseline because the statistics gathered will include whatever performance factors are contributing to the dissatisfaction.

At a minimum, you must perform periodic monitoring on the following areas of your Windows Server 2003 computers: the hard disk(s), processor(s), memory, and network adapter(s). Regardless of which type of services the server is providing, these four areas interact to make your server efficient (thereby appearing fast) or inefficient. The actual speed or efficiency of each of the components varies in importance, depending on the application. In some applications, memory is more important than processor speed or availability; in other applications, disk speed and availability are more important than fast network access.

The Performance Console

Recognizing the need to be able to monitor the performance (and thus the health) of servers and client computers, Microsoft built the Performance console into Windows Server 2003. Whether you are looking for real-time graphical views or a log you can peruse at your convenience, the Performance console can provide the type of data you need to evaluate performance and recommend system modification, if necessary.

Monitoring performance begins with the collection of data. The Performance console, shown in Figure 9.1, gives you various methods of working with data, although all methods use the same means of collecting data. Data collected by the Performance console is broken down into objects, counters, and instances. An *object* is the software or device being monitored, such as the memory or a processor. A *counter* is a specific statistic for an object. Memory has a counter called Available Bytes, and a processor has a counter called % Processor Time. An *instance* is the specific occurrence of an object you are watching; in a multiprocessor server with two processors, you have three instances: `0`, `1`, and `_Total`.

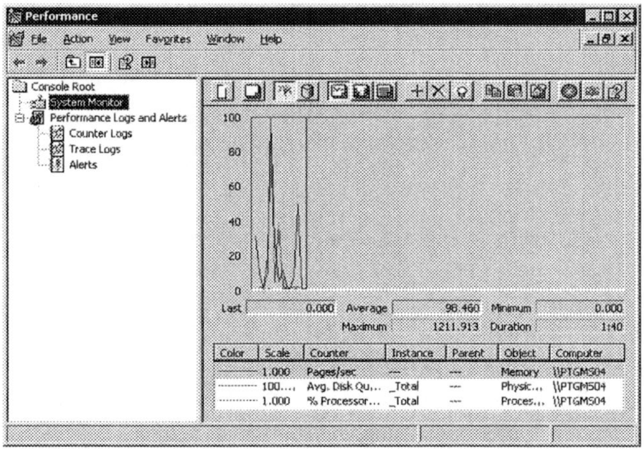

FIGURE 9.1 The Performance console consists of four different tools.

The primary difference between using System Monitor and counter logs or trace logs is that you typically watch performance real-time in System Monitor (or playback saved logs), whereas you use counter logs and trace logs to record data for later analysis. Alerts function in real time by providing you with alerts when a user-defined threshold is exceeded. Counter logs, trace logs, and alerts are beyond the scope of Exam 70-293; if you want to learn more about them, however, be sure to see the Windows Server TechCenter located at http://technet2.microsoft.com/windowsserver/en/default.mspx.

Introduction to System Monitor

You can access System Monitor from the Administrative Tools folder by selecting Start, Programs, Administrative Tools, Performance. When you initially open the Performance console, it looks like the console shown previously in Figure 9.1. System Monitor enables you to view statistical data either live or from a saved log. You can view the data in three formats: graph, histogram, or report. Graph data is displayed as a line graph, histograms are displayed as bar graphs, and text-based reports show the current numerical information available from the statistics.

The basic use of System Monitor is straightforward. You decide which object/instance/counter combinations you want to display and then configure the monitor accordingly. At that point, information begins to appear. You can also change the properties of the monitor to display information in different ways.

The best way to become familiar with the System Monitor is to start using it. Step by Step 9.1 lets you do just that by configuring monitoring for some network counters.

STEP BY STEP

9.1 Using System Monitor

1. Select Start, Programs, Administrative Tools, Performance to open the Performance console.
2. Click the System Monitor node.
3. To add counter items to System Monitor, click the + icon on the toolbar, as shown in Figure 9.2.

FIGURE 9.2 To start adding counter items, you need to click the + icon on the toolbar.

4. The Add Counters dialog box, shown in Figure 9.3, opens, enabling you to begin adding counters.

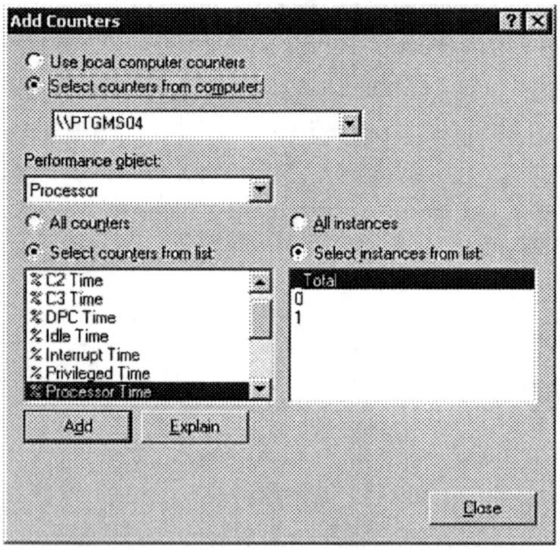

FIGURE 9.3 You can add counters to begin monitoring the processor statistics.

5. Select Network Interface from the Performance Object drop-down list box. This brings up the list of counters that relate to network interfaces and are available for selection. If you need to know what a counter means, select the counter and click the Explain button.
6. Be sure that you are adding counters for the correct network interface in your server and not for the loopback interface by selecting the Select Instances from This List option and then selecting the correct network interface, as shown in Figure 9.4.
7. When you have decided what counter you want to monitor, click Add. You can add multiple counters either by selecting each counter and clicking Add or by holding down the Ctrl key while you select all the counters you want to monitor and then clicking Add.
8. Click Close when you are finished. Your counters are now actively graphed, like those shown in Figure 9.5.

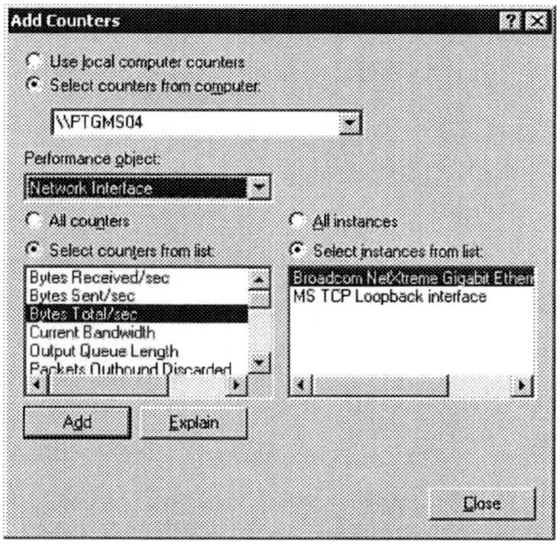

FIGURE 9.4 Make sure you are adding the counters for the correct instance when multiple instances exist.

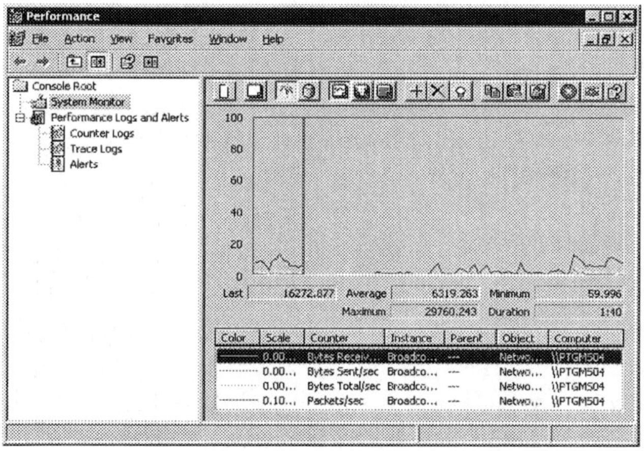

FIGURE 9.5 You can monitor the selected network interface statistics in real time.

Working with Counters

Now that you've seen how System Monitor works from a high level, let's dig in a little and examine the basic building block of performance monitoring: *counters*. Figure 9.6 shows a typical Add Counters dialog box. At the top of the dialog box is a set of radio buttons with which you can obtain statistics from the local machine or a remote machine. This feature is useful when you want to monitor a computer in a location that is not within reasonable physical distance from you. Under the radio buttons is a pull-down list naming the performance objects that can be monitored. Which performance objects are available depends on the features (and applications) you have installed on your server. Also, some counters come with specific applications. These performance counters enable you to monitor statistics relating to that application from the Performance console.

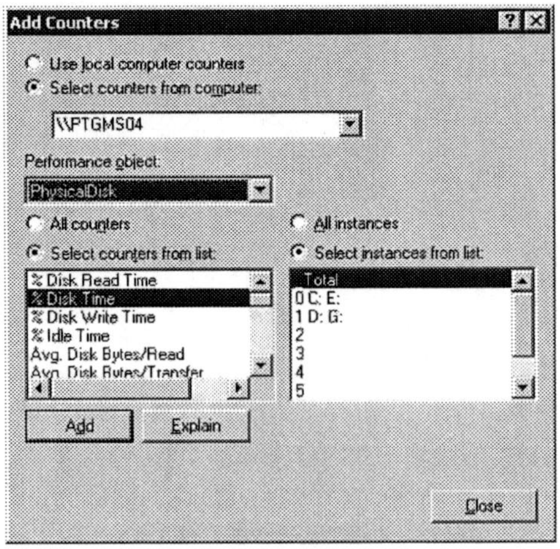

FIGURE 9.6 The Add Counters dialog box contains many options you need to understand.

Under the performance object is a list of counters. When applied to a specific instance of an object, counters are what you are really after, and the object just narrows your search. The counters are the actual statistical information you want to monitor. Each object has its own set of counters from which you can choose. Counters enable you to move from the abstract concept of an object to the concrete events that reflect that object's activity. For example, if you choose to monitor the processor, you can watch for the average processor time and how much time the processor spent doing nonidle activity. In addition, you could watch for %user time (time spent executing user application processes) versus %privileged time (time spent executing system processes).

To the right of the counter list is the instances list. If applicable, instances enumerate the physical objects that fall under the specific object class you have chosen. In some cases, the instances list is not applicable. For example, no instances list is available with memory. In cases in which the instances list is applicable, you see multiple instance variables (refer to Figure 9.4). One variable represents the average of all the instances, and the rest of the variables represent the values for the first physical object (numbers 0, 1, and so on). For example, if you have two processors in your server, you see (and can choose from) three instance variables: `_Total`, `0`, and `1`. This way, you can watch each processor individually and watch them as a collective unit.

Using System Monitor to Discover Bottlenecks

Every chain, regardless of its strength, has its weakest link. When pulled hard enough, some point gives before all the others. Your server is similar to a chain. When it's under stress, some component cannot keep up with the others. This results in a degradation of overall performance. The weak link in the server is referred to as a *bottleneck* because it's the component that slows everything else. As an administrator responsible for ensuring efficient operation of a Windows Server 2003 computer, you need to determine the following two things:

- Which component is causing the bottleneck?
- Is the stress on the server typical enough that action is warranted either now or in the future?

As was mentioned previously, under normal operation, only four system components typically affect system performance: memory, processors, disks, and network adapters. Therefore, you should monitor the counters that tell you the most about how those four components affect system performance. The information from these counters is critical because you can determine the answer to the two diagnostic questions listed here.

The biggest monitoring problem is not collecting the data, but interpreting it. Not only is it difficult to determine what a specific value for a particular counter means, but it is also difficult to determine what that value means in the context of other counters. The biggest difficulty is that no subsystem (disk, network, processor, or memory) exists in isolation. As a result, weaknesses in one might show up as weaknesses in another. Unless you take them all into consideration, you might end up adding another processor when all you need is more RAM.

Understanding how the subsystems interact is important to understanding the significance of the counter values that are recorded. For example, if you detect that your processor is constantly running at 90%, you might be tempted to purchase a faster processor (or another processor if you have a system board that can accommodate more than one). However, it is important to look at memory utilization and disk utilization as well because the problem could be originating there instead. If you do not have enough memory, the processor must swap pages to the disk frequently. This page swapping results in high memory utilization, high disk utilization, and higher processor utilization. By purchasing more RAM, you could alleviate all these problems.

This one example illustrates how no one piece of information is enough to analyze your performance problems or your solution. You must monitor the server as a whole unit by putting together the counters from a variety of objects. Only then can you see the big picture and solve problems that might arise.

The recommended method of monitoring is to use a counter log, which captures data over a period of time. This type of monitoring helps you eliminate questions of whether the current stress on the server is typical. If you log over a period of a week or a month and consistently see a certain component under excessive load, you can be sure the stress is typical.

Baselining Servers

As we've already discussed, monitoring the present operation of your servers and network presents you with only half of the picture. You need to create a baseline of the server performance that you can use to compare against future performance statistics to locate problematic areas. If you create baselines on servers, you can compare the present-day performance to a known value. This comparison can be very useful when you're troubleshooting, and it also aids when you are modifying configurations.

TIP

Creating a monitoring station Most administrators recommend that you not perform performance monitoring locally from the server on which you are attempting to monitor and collect data. When you run System Monitor directly on a server, you can skew the results because, of course, the actual act of monitoring consumes system resources. It's generally better to run System Monitor on a workstation pointed at the server you want to monitor (in addition to being able to monitor multiple servers from a single console).

A baseline is a set of typical readings that define "normal" for your servers, client computers, or network under various operating conditions, such as no load, moderate load, and heavy load. Of course, what is normal is obviously open to interpretation, but you could say that normal is a server providing users with what they want in a time frame that they think is reasonable. By creating baselines early on, you have something that you can later look back at and compare current server operating conditions to. If your system is already to the point that you are seeing system degradation, it is really too late to establish a baseline.

To establish a baseline, you pick a time (or duration of time) that represents typical user interaction with the server. Then you create a log of important counters for the duration you have determined. Table 9.1 summarizes some of the more commonly used (and recommended) counters. For a complete reference to these counters, see www.microsoft.com/technet/prodtechnol/windowsserver2003/proddocs/deployguide/counters1_lkxw.asp.

TABLE 9.1 Counters to Monitor for Baselining and Bottleneck Troubleshooting

Server Component	Recommended Counters
Memory	Memory\Page Faults/sec Memory\Page Reads/sec Memory\Page Writes/sec Memory\Pages Input/sec Memory\Pages Output/sec Memory\Available Bytes Memory\Pool Nonpaged Bytes Process\Page Faults/sec Process\Working Set Process\Private Bytes Process\Page File Bytes
Processor	Processor\% Processor Time System\Processor Queue Length Process\% Privileged Time Process\% Processor Time Process\% User Time Process\Priority Base Thread\% Privileged Time

TABLE 9.1 *Continued*

Server Component	Recommended Counters
Processor	Thread\% Processor Time Thread\% User Time Thread\Context Switches/sec Thread\Priority Base Thread\Priority Current Thread\Thread State
Disk	PhysicalDisk\% Disk Time PhysicalDisk\Avg. Disk Queue Length PhysicalDisk\Current Disk Queue Length PhysicalDisk\Avg. Disk Sec/Read PhysicalDisk\Avg. Disk Sec/Write PhysicalDisk\Disk Read Bytes/sec PhysicalDisk\Disk Write Bytes/sec PhysicalDisk\Avg. Disk Bytes/Write PhysicalDisk\Disk Reads/sec PhysicalDisk\Disk Writes/sec LogicalDisk\% Disk Time LogicalDisk\Avg. Disk Queue Length LogicalDisk\Current Disk Queue Length LogicalDisk\Avg. Disk Sec/Read LogicalDisk\Avg. Disk Sec/Write LogicalDisk\Disk Read Bytes/sec LogicalDisk\Disk Write Bytes/sec LogicalDisk\Avg. Disk Bytes/Write LogicalDisk\Disk Reads/sec LogicalDisk\Disk Writes/sec
Network	Network Interface\Bytes Total/sec Network Interface\Bytes Sent/sec Network Interface\Bytes Received/sec TCPv4\Segments Received/sec TCPv4\Segments Sent/sec TCPv4\Frames Sent/sec TCPv4\Frames Received/sec Server\Bytes Total/sec Server\Bytes Received/sec Server\Bytes Transmitted/sec

The log you create should be stored in a safe place to ensure that you can refer to it in the future. Every time you perform a major hardware upgrade (such as increasing RAM or adding a processor), you should create a new set of baselines and consider deleting the old ones.

Which actual counters you want to monitor are based on the particular applications running on your server and the requirements you have for the server. Although Table 9.1 gives some recommendations, you might want to watch other objects as well if you have specific applications installed.

EXAM ALERT

Don't be tricked! When taking Exam 70-293, carefully read each question—especially those that deal with performance monitoring—to ensure that you select the correct answer. You might find several very similar answers presented, but only one of them is correct.

Creating Baseline Counter Logs

To create a baseline, you create a counter log from the Counter Logs option of the Performance Logs and Alerts node of the Performance console. Step by Step 9.2 outlines the creation of a counter log.

STEP BY STEP

9.2 Creating and Using a Baseline Counter Log

1. Select Start, Program, Administrative Tools, Performance to open the Performance console.
2. Expand the Performance Logs and Alerts node and click the Counter Logs entry, as shown in Figure 9.7.

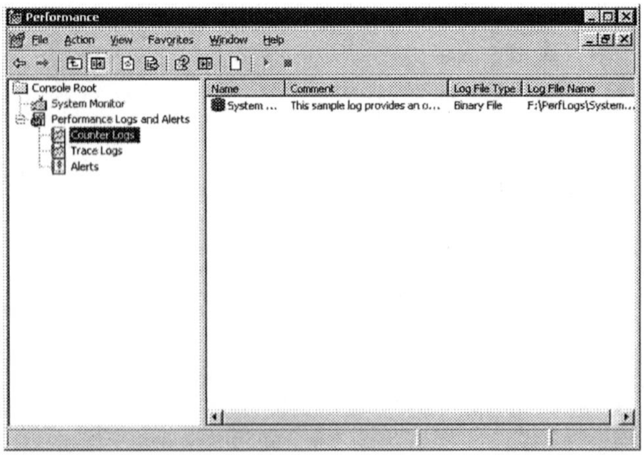

FIGURE 9.7 A counter log is created to keep baseline (historical) statistics about performance.

3. To add a new counter log, right-click the Counter Logs entry and select New Log Settings from the context menu.
4. Enter the name of the new counter log, as shown in Figure 9.8, and click OK. The Network Adapter Performance dialog box appears (see Figure 9.9).

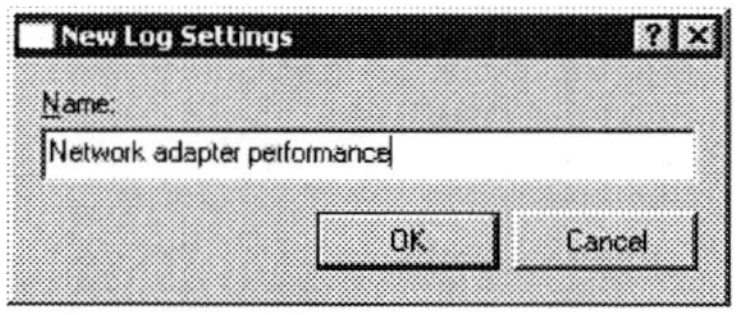

FIGURE 9.8 You should enter a descriptive name for the new counter log.

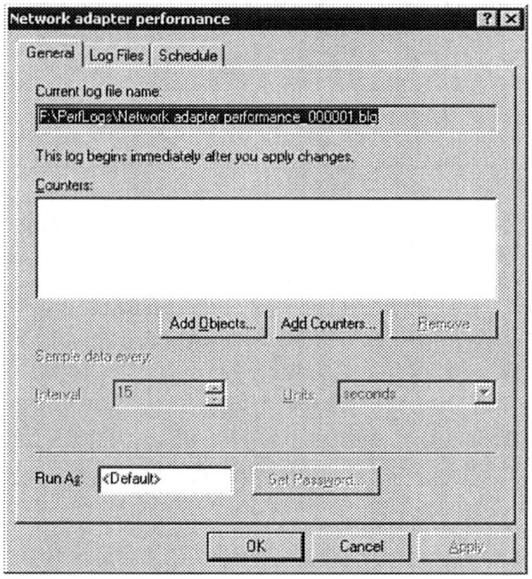

FIGURE 9.9 You must configure objects or counters on the new counter log before proceeding.

5. Configure new entire objects to be monitored by clicking the Add Objects button to open the Add Objects dialog box (see Figure 9.10). Alternatively, add individual counters by clicking the Add Counters button to open the Add Counters dialog box (see Figure 9.11). Add the objects or counters you want to the counter log. Only the counters you add will be available for viewing later.

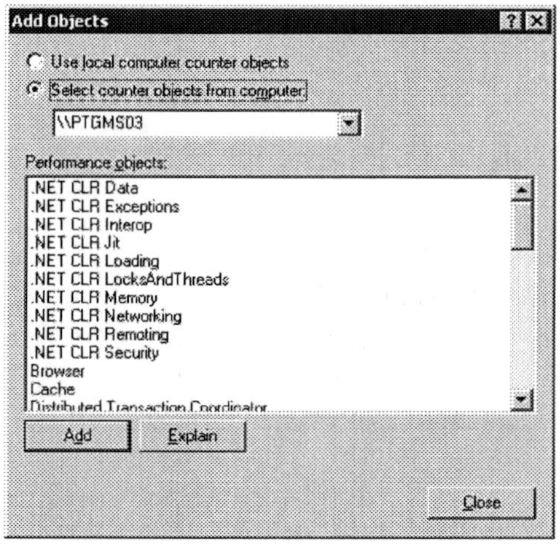

FIGURE 9.10 You can add entire objects to the counter log, if desired.

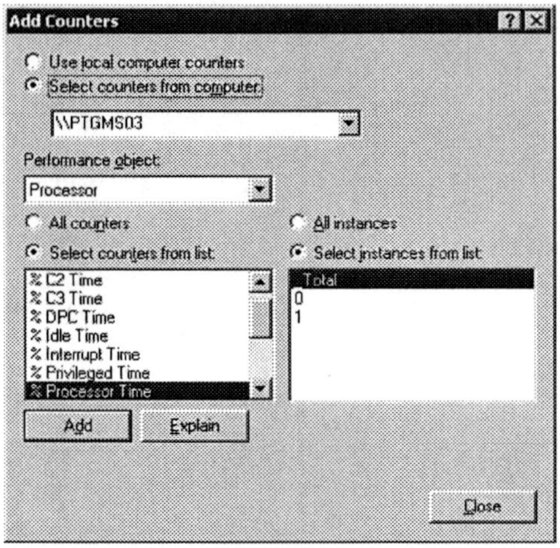

FIGURE 9.11 You can add specific individual counters to the counter log, if desired.

6. After you have added some objects or counters, you can configure the options for sampling interval. The default is every 15 seconds, meaning that while the counter log is running, data will be collected from the computers being monitored every 15 seconds. The sampling interval has a trade-off associated with it: Smaller intervals mean larger, more accurate log files; larger intervals result in smaller, less accurate log files. In addition, the smaller the sampling interval, the more resources performance monitoring consumes. You can also configure the account to be used to run the counter log.

7. On the Log Files tab of the Network Adapter Performance dialog box, shown in Figure 9.12, select the type of log file to be created, as well as the numbering system to be used. The default settings are Binary File and nnnnn. The available options are explained after this Step by Step in Tables 9.2 and 9.3. In addition, you can enter a comment that will help identify the counter log.

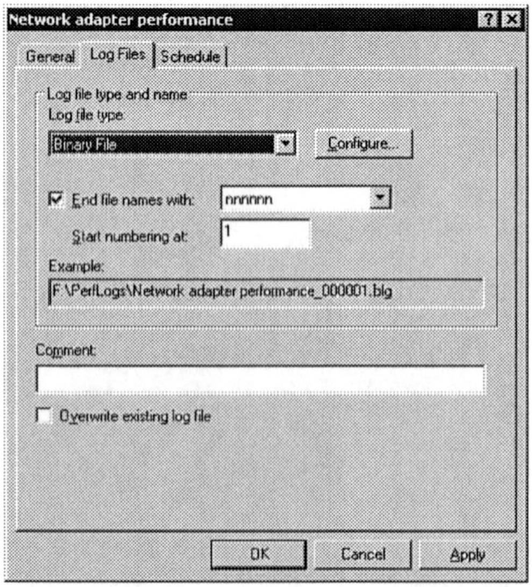

FIGURE 9.12 You can use the Log Files tab to configure how the log is to be saved.

8. Click the Configure button to open the Configure Log Files dialog box, shown in Figure 9.13. From here you can change the path of the log file and its maximum allowed size. In some cases, it would be a wise idea to place the log file on a different volume than the boot partition. Click OK after you make your changes.

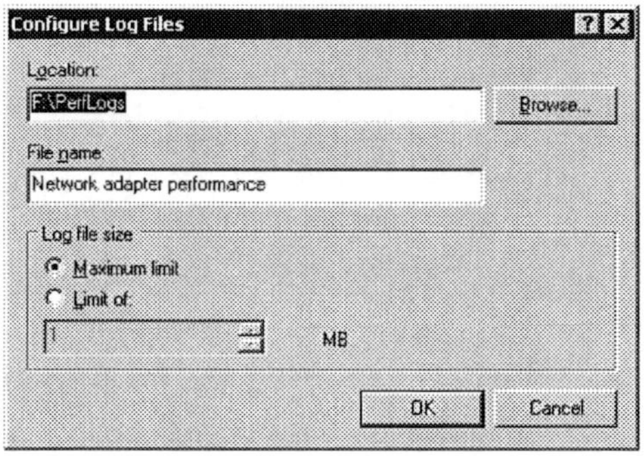

FIGURE 9.13 You can use the Configure Log Files dialog box to configure the maximum log file size and its path.

9. On the Schedule tab of the Network Adapter Performance dialog box, shown in Figure 9.14, you can configure how and when the counter log is to run. Typically, you will run it manually, although you might opt to have it run automatically at a configured time. Some suggested times might be for two hours in the morning when users come to work and log in, for an hour during the middle of the day and for an hour at the end of the day. Your environment will ultimately dictate when and how much logging you perform.

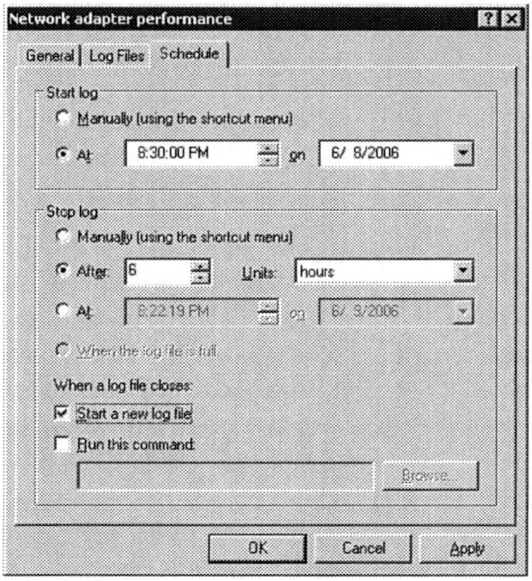

FIGURE 9.14 The counter log can be configured to start and stop automatically, if desired.

10. After you make all your configurations, click OK to save the counter log settings. Back at the Counter Logs node, shown previously in Figure 9.15, select the new counter log object and start it by clicking the Start (right arrow) button in the menu. If you configured the counter log to start automatically, as shown in Figure 9.14, it will start at the configured time and run as configured, as you can see in Figure 9.15.

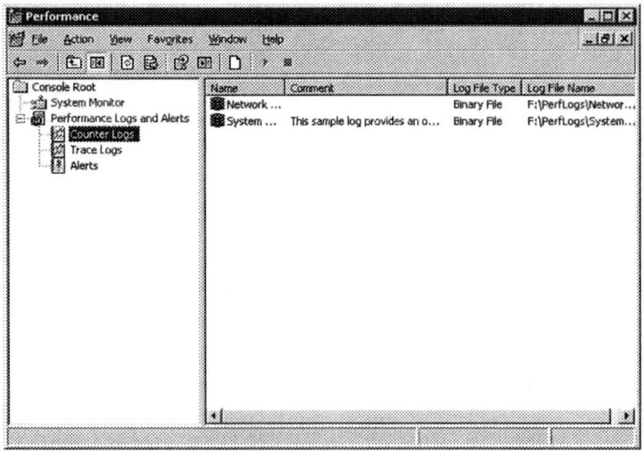

FIGURE 9.15 The counter log automatically starts if you configured it with a start time.

11. When the counter log has run for some time (or for its scheduled time), click the square Stop icon to stop it.

12. Click the System Monitor node to switch back to System Monitor. Click the database icon to open a log file, as shown in Figure 9.16. The System Monitor Properties dialog box opens, showing the Source tab (see Figure 9.17).

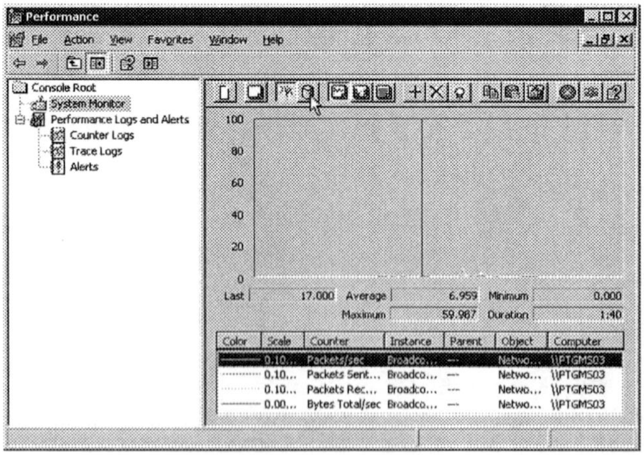

FIGURE 9.16 You need to load the counter log file into System Monitor to examine it.

13. Select the Log Files radio button and click the Add button to locate and add the counter log file.

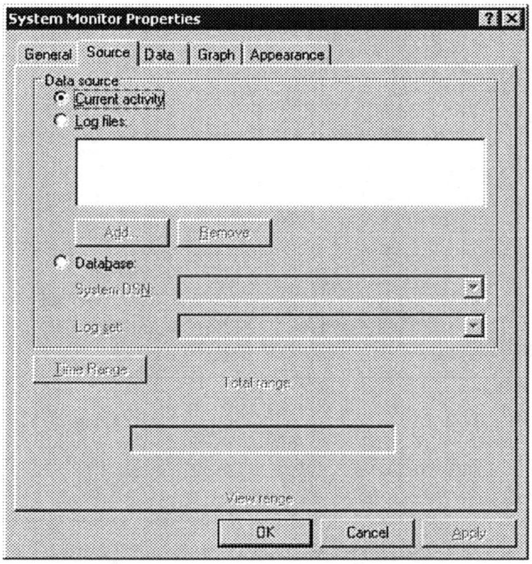

FIGURE 9.17 You can add one or more counter logs to System Monitor.

14. Switch to the Data tab, shown in Figure 9.18, and ensure that all counters for which you are interested in seeing data are added. You will see data displayed only for counters that are selected here.

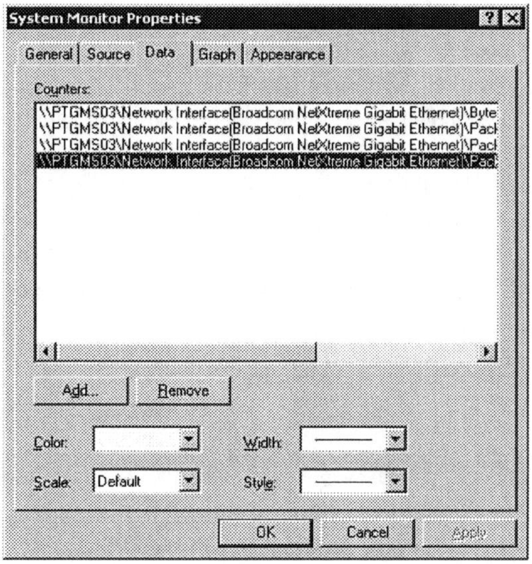

FIGURE 9.18 You need to ensure that all counters have been added for viewing.

15. The counter log data is displayed in System Monitor, as shown in Figure 9.19. If you need to display only a certain portion of the data, you can do so by configuring the Time Range option on the Source tab of the System Monitor Properties dialog box (refer to Figure 9.17).

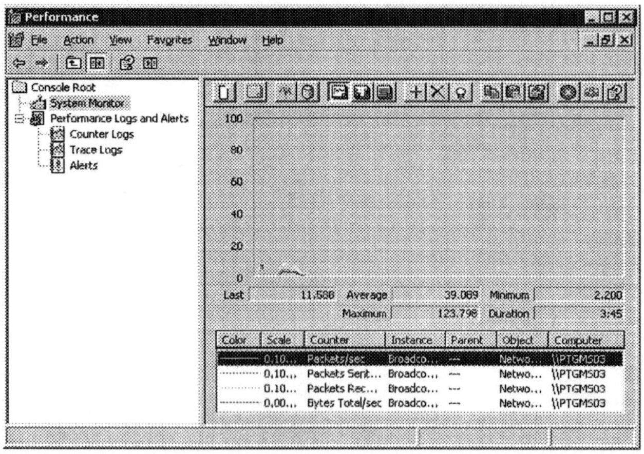

FIGURE 9.19 After you make the correct configurations, you can examine the historical counter log data.

Table 9.2 details the available counter log file format options you have to choose from.

TABLE 9.2 Counter Log File Format Options

Option	Description
Text File (Comma Delimited)	This option defines a comma-delimited log file (with a .csv extension).
Text File (Tab Delimited)	This option defines a tab-delimited log file (with a .tsv extension).
Binary File	This option defines a sequential, binary-format log file (with a .blg extension). You should use this file format if you want to be able to record data instances that are intermittent—that is, stopping and resuming after the log has begun running. Only binary file formats can accommodate instances that are not persistent throughout the duration of the log.
Binary Circular File	This option defines a circular, binary-format log file (with a .blg extension). You should use this file format to continuously record data to the same log file, overwriting previous records with new data when the file reaches its maximum size.

Table 9.3 details the available counter log numbering options you have to choose from.

TABLE 9.3 Counter Log Numbering Systems

System	Example
nnnnnn	`Network Adapter Performance_000007.blg`
mmddhh	`Network Adapter Performance_042011.blg`
mmddhhmm	`Network Adapter Performance_04201126.blg`
yyyyddd	`Network Adapter Performance_2003111.blg`
yyyymm	`Network Adapter Performance_200304.blg`
yyyymmdd	`Network Adapter Performance_20030420.blg`
yyyymmddhh	`Network Adapter Performance_2003042011.blg`

Daily Monitoring for Usage

On a daily basis, you might not want to monitor the full group of counters that were listed previously in Table 9.1. The counters in Table 9.4 present a smaller and, thus, easier-to-manage group of counters that you might consider monitoring on a daily basis to get a quick snapshot of your system and network performance.

TABLE 9.4 Counters to Monitor on a Daily Basis

Server Component	Recommended Counters
Memory	Memory\Available Bytes Memory\Cache Bytes Memory\Pages/sec Memory\Page reads/sec Memory\Pool Paged Bytes Memory\Pool Nonpaged Bytes
Processor	Processor\% Processor Time (all instances) System\Processor Queue Length (all instances) Processor\Interrupts/sec
Disk	Physical Disk\Disk Reads/sec Physical Disk\Disk Writes/sec Logical Disk\% Free Space Logical Disk\% Disk Time Physical Disk\Current Disk Queue Length (all instances) Physical Disk\Split IO/sec
Network	Network Interface\Bytes total/sec

As they pertain to Table 9.4, the following are descriptions of the counters:

- **Physical Disk\Disk Reads/sec**—The number of disk reads that occur per second. This value is a measure of the read activity on the disk. The transfer rate of the hard drive being used determines what values you should be looking for here, so check the vendor's supplied documentation. In general, Ultra Wide SCSI disks can handle about 50–70 I/O operations per second.
- **Physical Disk\Disk Writes/sec**—The number of disk writes that occur per second. This value is a measure of the write activity on the disk. The same guidelines apply for this counter as for the Physical Disk\Disk Reads/sec counter.
- **Logical Disk\% Free Space**—The ratio of free space to total disk space on a logical drive. This value is a measurement of remaining capacity on your logical drives. You generally should track this value for each logical drive. To prevent excessive fragmentation, you should not allow the value here to drop below 15%.

- **Logical Disk\% Disk Time**—The ratio of busy time to the total elapsed time. This value represents the percentage the disk is servicing read or write requests. You generally should track this value for each physical drive. If one drive is being used a lot more than another, it might be time to balance the content between the drives. The lower this number, the greater the capacity a disk has to do additional work. This value should typically not exceed 90%.
- **Physical Disk\Current Disk Queue Length**—The average number of read and write requests that are waiting in queue. Optimally, this number should be no more than 2 because a larger number means the disk is a bottleneck; it is incapable of servicing the requests placed on it.
- **Physical Disk\Split IO/sec**—The rate at which the operating system divides I/O requests to the disk into multiple requests. A split I/O request might occur if the program requests data in a size that is too large to fit into a single request or if the disk is fragmented. Factors that influence the size of an I/O request can include application design, the file system, or drivers. A high rate of split I/O might not, in itself, represent a problem. However, on single-disk systems, a high rate for this counter tends to indicate disk fragmentation.
- **Memory\Available Bytes**—The total amount of physical memory available to processes running on the computer. This number's significance varies as the amount of memory in the computer varies, but if this number is less than 4MB, you generally have a memory deficiency.
- **Memory\Cache Bytes**—The amount of cache memory available to processes running on the computer. This counter indicates growth or shrinking of the cache. The value includes not only the size of the cache, but also the size of the paged pool and the amount of pageable driver and kernel code. Lower values indicate a problem, although there is no agreed-upon standard value.
- **Memory\Pages/sec**—The number of hard page faults occurring per second. A hard page fault occurs when data or code is not in memory and must be retrieved from the hard drive. Each time this happens, disk activity is required and the process is temporarily halted (because disk access is momentarily slower than RAM access). A bottleneck in memory is likely when this number is 20 or greater.
- **Memory\Page reads/sec**—The number of times the disk needed to be read to resolve a hard page fault. Unlike Memory\Pages/sec, this counter is not an indicator of the quantity of data being retrieved, but rather the number of times the disk had to be consulted. This counter can give a general feeling of a memory bottleneck, whereas Memory\Pages/sec gives a more quantifiable value to the bottleneck.
- **Memory\Pool Paged Bytes**—The number of bytes of memory taken up by system tasks that can be swapped out to disk, if needed. Although this counter is not a direct indicator of a memory bottleneck, if the number of Pool Paged Bytes is large, it can indicate a lot of system processes. If this number is a significant percentage of total memory, you might need to increase RAM to allow for these tasks to remain in RAM instead of being swapped out.

- **Memory\Pool Nonpaged Bytes**—The number of bytes of memory taken up by system tasks that can't be swapped out to disk. This figure can indicate a bottleneck in memory, especially if the figure is a significant percentage of the total amount of RAM. Because these processes can't be swapped out, they continue to take up RAM for as long as they are running.
- **Network Interface\Bytes Total/sec**—An indication of the total throughput of the network interface. This figure can be used for general capacity planning and does not necessarily indicate a network bottleneck.
- **Processor\% Processor Time**—The amount of time the processor spends executing nonidle threads. This figure is an indication of how busy the processor is. The processor for a single-processor system should not exceed 75% capacity for a significant period of time. The processors in a multiple-processor system should not exceed 50% for a significant period of time. High processor utilization can be an indication of processor bottlenecks, but it could also indicate lack of memory.
- **System\Processor Queue Length**—The number of processes that are ready but waiting to be serviced by the processor(s). There is a single queue for all processors, even in a multiprocessor environment. A sustained queue of more than 2 generally indicates processor congestion.
- **Processor\Interrupts/sec**—The number of hardware requests the processor is servicing per second. This is not necessarily an indicator of system health, but, when compared against the baseline, it can help to determine hardware problems. Hardware problems are sometimes indicated by a device dramatically increasing the number of interrupts it sends.

System Monitor Tips and Tricks

Microsoft provides some helpful tips and tricks that you should keep in mind when working with the Performance console to solve performance-related problems. Through careful analysis of data, you might be able to determine problems with the network that are not otherwise seen, such as excessive demands on resources that result in bottlenecks—and, therefore, slow network performance to the degree that users begin to notice that something is wrong.

TIP

Saving time by saving your configuration No one wants to reinvent the wheel. This holds true when you are configuring System Monitor with a set of counters. You can save a good amount of time and effort by setting up System Monitor with the counters and options you want on one server and then saving the configuration file and distributing that file to each of your other servers instead of re-creating the configuration each time.

The following are some of the most common causes of bottlenecks that you might encounter while troubleshooting your network:

- The current level of provided resources is inadequate, thus requiring additional or upgraded resources to be added to the network.
- The available resources are not utilized evenly, thus requiring some form of load balancing to be implemented.
- An available resource is malfunctioning or stopped and needs to be repaired or restarted.
- An available resource is incorrectly configured, thus requiring a configuration correction.

TIP

Making changes equals making a new baseline Every time you change the hardware or software configuration of a server you need to create a new baseline on it.

When you have identified a problem, you should take care to avoid creating new problems while correcting the old one. You should make one change at a time to avoid masking the impact of changes. After each change, you should perform additional monitoring to determine the result and the effect of the change and reevaluate the status and condition of the previously identified problem(s). In addition, you can compare the performance of applications that are run over the network to their performance when run locally to determine how the network is affecting performance.

EXAM ALERT

Don't forget about the Task Manager Even though the Task Manager is a very simple tool, don't underestimate its usefulness. You can quickly launch the Task Manager to get a real-time look at network utilization (and process performance) without having to open System Monitor and configure counters.

With our discussion of performance monitoring and baselining out of the way, let's move forward and examine the second topic of this chapter: disaster recovery operations.

Challenge

You have installed a new custom-developed program that runs continuously in the background as a Windows service. You and a number of remote users who are accessing data on your system use this program. When you first install it, you run the Performance console on your system to establish a baseline of performance during normal working conditions. A few days later, your system becomes sluggish and noticeably slower in all functions. You reboot your system, and it appears to be working normally

(continues)

(continued)

again. A few days later, the same performance problems occur. You run the Performance console and discover that the amount of available memory has dropped to almost 0 and the paging file is very active.

Through your investigation into this problem, you've determined the following facts:

- The system has just had a new application installed.
- The application runs continuously as a service to local and remote users.
- After several days of continuous running, the system performance degrades.
- Rebooting the system temporarily solves the problem. However, it eventually returns.
- Available memory is consumed and paging activity increases.

Your task is to determine the source of the problem and correct it.

Try to complete this exercise on your own, listing your conclusions on a sheet of paper. When you have completed the exercise, compare your results to those given here.

When dealing with performance problems, you must remember that almost everything is interrelated. Memory problems can cause disk activity, which can manifest itself as a processor bottleneck. In this case, because the problem was apparently solved when the system was restarted, the problem is likely related to consumption of a resource rather than an elevated rate of activity. When the problem occurred again days later, the Performance console showed a higher-than-expected paging activity and almost no available memory. That combination would normally indicate a system that is underconfigured in memory for the process running. Because this situation did not exist when the new application was brought online, the conclusion is that the new background service leaks memory. In this situation, memory acquired by the service during normal processing is not returned to the system. Over time, the amount of working memory assigned to the service would exceed the amount available, and Windows would begin to page to meet the needs of its normal workload. The recommendation is to send the new service back to the developers for analysis.

Planning Backup and Recovery Operations

Disasters happen. They are an administrator's worst nightmare, but they don't have to be. Even if you have the best hardware and most fault-tolerant design, nothing can replace a solid backup and restoration plan. The Backup Utility provided in Windows Server 2003, `ntbackup.exe`, is actually a "lite" version of the commercially available third-party product from Veritas Software (now part of Symantec). Although its capability is limited, the included Backup Utility, when used properly, can provide you with all the functionality you should need for small networks or workgroups. If you have a larger network, you might want to place some serious thought into acquiring an enterprise backup solution, such as Backup Exec.

You should keep in mind the following general points when working with Windows Backup:

- You can back up locally to either a file or a tape drive, or across the network to a share.
- You can back up files from either the local machine or remote computers, provided that you have access to the files you want to back up on the remote computer. The limitation of backing up a computer remotely is that System State information cannot be saved.
- To perform a backup, you must have Read access to the files or the user right of Backup and Restore Files, which is granted by default to Administrators and Backup Operators.
- Special permissions are granted the Administrators and Backup Operators groups to access all files for the purposes of doing backups. Even if members of these groups cannot access the data as users, they can back it up.

The Backup Utility in Windows Server 2003 has undergone some changes from its predecessor in Windows 2000 Server. No longer will you be creating an Emergency Repair Disk (ERD); it has been replaced by the new and improved Automated System Recovery (ASR) function. Windows Server 2003 also introduces volume shadow copy in the Backup Utility. Each of these new functions is explained in more detail in the following section.

New Windows Server 2003 Backup Features

When you use the volume shadow copy, a copy of the original file is created instantly at the time you initiate the backup. Data is then subsequently backed up to the backup media from this shadow copy instead of the original files. This new technology provides a means of backing up open files that were in use at the time the backup was initiated. When you use volume shadow copy, files that would normally be skipped during the backup are instead backed up in their current state (at the time of the shadow copy creation) and thus appear closed on the backup media. Any applications that are running during the backup process can continue to run. When the backup completes, the shadow copy is deleted. The volume shadow copy feature requires the NTFS file system to be in use and can be disabled, if desired.

Another new use of the volume shadow copy feature is to create "snapshots" of shared network folders that can be used to roll back to a previous version of a file; this topic is discussed later in the "Using Volume Shadow Copy" section of this chapter.

NOTE

Limitations on disabling volume shadow copy You cannot disable the volume shadow copy option when performing a backup of the System State data.

Automated System Recovery (ASR) is an advanced restoration option of the Backup Utility that can be used to restore your system if other disaster-recovery methods fail or are not available for use. Using ASR, you can restore the operating system to a previous state, which enables you to start Window Server 2003 if other methods do not work. You should always consider ASR your last resort for recovery, after Safe Mode, the Recovery Console, and Last Known Good Configuration (LKGC). You should make a point to keep your ASR media up-to-date as you make configuration changes to your computer. This is recommended to minimize the amount of recovery required if you ever need to use ASR. To use the ASR Wizard to create a set of ASR media, you only need to click on the Automated System Recovery Wizard button on the main page of the Backup tool, which we examine later in this section.

Backup Methods and Media Rotation

Objective:

Plan a backup and recovery strategy.

- Identify appropriate backup types. Methods can include the backup types full, incremental, and differential.

Windows Server 2003 supports the following five backup methods:

- **Normal (full) backup**—Copies all selected files and marks each file as having been backed up (the archive attribute is cleared). Only the most recent copy of the backup file is required to perform restoration.
- **Incremental backup**—Copies only those files created or changed since the last normal or incremental backup; the archive attribute is then cleared. Using normal and incremental backups, you require the last normal backup and all incremental backups to be able to perform restoration.
- **Differential backup**—Copies files created or changed since the last normal (full) or incremental backup; the archive attribute is not cleared in this case. Using normal and differential backups, you need the last normal backup and the last differential backup to be able to perform restoration.
- **Copy backup**—Copies all selected files but does not mark each file as having been backed up (the archive attribute is not cleared). Copy backups have no effect on any other type of backup operation.
- **Daily backup**—Copies all selected files that have been modified the day the daily backup is performed; the archive attribute is not cleared in this case. Using normal and daily backups, you require the last normal backup and all daily backups to be able to perform restoration.

TIP

The archive bit The archive bit is a file attribute that is used to denote the file's backup status. If the archive bit is set, the file is eligible for backup using a normal, daily, incremental, or differential backup. If the archive bit is not set, these backup types skip the file because this signifies that the file has not been modified since the last backup. Normal and incremental backups clear the archive bit, making the file ineligible for backup again until the file has been subsequently modified.

As you might guess, the true secret to effectively planning and implementing a viable backup plan is *media rotation*. When thinking about media rotation, you must consider two basic requirements:

- **Media lifetime**—Most backup systems use some sort of magnetic tape media. Although these tapes are very durable in most cases, they do not last forever. A good backup plan must take into account media lifetime and seek to spread wear and tear evenly over multiple tapes to increase both the lifetime of the tapes and the reliability of the tapes, in case they be needed to perform a restoration. A media-rotation system makes this happen by preventing overly high use of one tape over another.
- **Data availability**—If time were not a concern, you could just perform a full backup each night, but in large networks with large amounts of critical data, performing such backups could likely take many, many hours and reduce network performance during working hours. To this end, a good backup plan includes some combination of full, incremental, daily, and differential backups. For a restoration to be successful, you must have all the correct tapes available and restore the data from them in the correct order. Using a well-documented media-rotation system helps you ensure that this happens.

So with these points in mind, let's examine two of the more common media-rotation systems in use today.

Five-Tape Rotation Method

As the name implies, the five-tape media-rotation method uses five different tapes—one for each day of the normal workweek. Typically, these tapes would be labeled as follows: Monday, Tuesday, Wednesday, Thursday, Friday. To start this rotation, you need to perform a full backup of all data. When you complete this backup, you can perform a daily, differential, or incremental backup on the first four days of the week. On Friday of every week, you perform a full backup again. Table 9.5 outlines how the five-tape rotation method could be used with differential backups during the week.

TABLE 9.5 The Simple Five-Tape Rotation Method

Sunday	Monday	Tuesday	Wednesday	Thursday	Friday	Saturday
	1 Differential	2 Differential	3 Differential	4 Differential	5 Full	6
7	8 Differential	9 Differential	10 Differential	11 Differential	12 Full	13
14	15 Differential	16 Differential	17 Differential	18 Differential	19 Full	20
21	22 Differential	23 Differential	24 Differential	25 Differential	26 Full	27
28	29 Differential	30 Differential	31 Differential			

As you can see, the five-tape rotation system could easily be expanded to six or seven tapes if your business needs require backups to be performed on the weekend days as well. However many tapes you use, you should always have the last one of the week set as the full backup, with each day before it being either a daily, differential, or incremental backup.

The major advantage of the five-tape rotation system is that it requires only five backup tapes. This advantage, however, comes at the cost of providing the backup history for only the past week. You can mitigate this limitation to some degree, however, by expanding to a 10-tape rotation, thus providing two weeks of backup history. Expanding to 10 tapes also has the advantage of longer media lifetime and generally more reliable media.

Daily, Weekly, Monthly Rotation Method

The daily, weekly, monthly rotation method is perhaps the most popular one in use today, and it provides a fairly easy method to make backup histories available for an entire year at a time. This availability does come at a cost, however: The system requires at least 20 backup tapes to be available. As with the five-tape rotation method, to start a new rotation, you should create a full backup of the data. As this method's name implies, three different types of tapes are made using the system:

- **Daily**—These tapes are used Monday, Tuesday, Wednesday, and Thursday to perform daily, differential, or incremental backups. The daily tapes require four backup tapes to be available.
- **Weekly**—These tapes are used on the last Friday of each week of the month—except for the last Friday of the month—to perform full backups. The weekly tapes require four backup tapes to be available for months that have five Fridays.
- **Monthly**—These tapes are used on the last Friday of every month to perform a full backup. The monthly tapes require 12 backup tapes to be available.

Table 9.6 outlines how the daily, weekly, monthly rotation method could be used.

TABLE 9.6 The Daily, Weekly, Monthly Rotation Method

Sunday	Monday	Tuesday	Wednesday	Thursday	Friday	Saturday
	1 Differential	2 Differential	3 Differential	4 Differential	5 Weekly Full #1	6
7	8 Differential	9 Differential	10 Differential	11 Differential	12 Weekly Full #2	13
14	15 Differential	16 Differential	17 Differential	18 Differential	19 Weekly Full #3	20
21	22 Differential	23 Differential	24 Differential	25 Differential	26 Monthly Full	27
28	29 Differential	30 Differential	31 Differential			

The daily, weekly, monthly rotation method is a middle-of-the-road solution that provides good recoverability and also minimizes wear and tear on backup tapes.

Using Windows Backup

Objective:

Plan a backup and recovery strategy.

Using the Backup Utility consists of three distinct processes: creating one or more backup configurations, scheduling backups to occur automatically, and performing restorations. Each of these processes is examined in the following sections.

Creating Backup Job Configurations

The Windows Backup Utility enables you to easily create a backup configuration. The basic steps to create the configuration are outlined in Step by Step 9.3, although your options and decisions will vary depending on how your system and backup media devices are configured.

STEP BY STEP

9.3 Creating a New Backup Configuration

1. Open the Backup or Restore Wizard, shown in Figure 9.20, by selecting Start, Programs, Accessories, System Tools, Backup.

FIGURE 9.20 The Backup or Restore Wizard can be used in place of Advanced mode.

2. Click the Advanced Mode link to switch to Advanced mode of the Backup Utility, as shown in Figure 9.21.

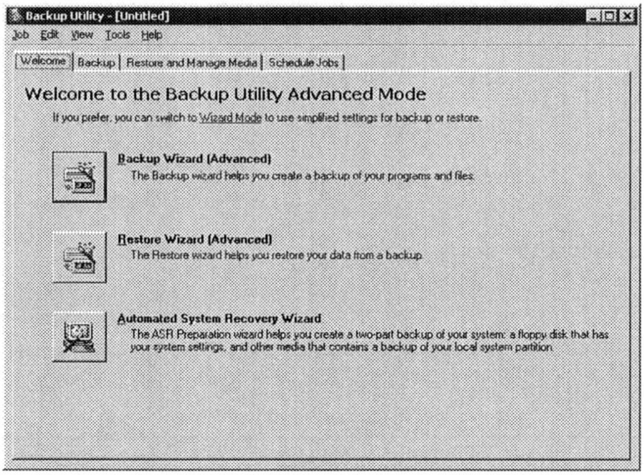

FIGURE 9.21 The Backup Utility Advanced mode provides you with all the tools you need to create and schedule backups.

3. Start the Backup Wizard by clicking the Backup Wizard (Advanced) button from the main page of the Backup Utility.
4. Click Next to dismiss the opening page of the wizard.
5. In the What to Back Up dialog box, shown in Figure 9.22, select the scope of the backup. Click Next to continue. If you choose to back up selected files and folders, proceed to step 6; otherwise, skip to step 7.

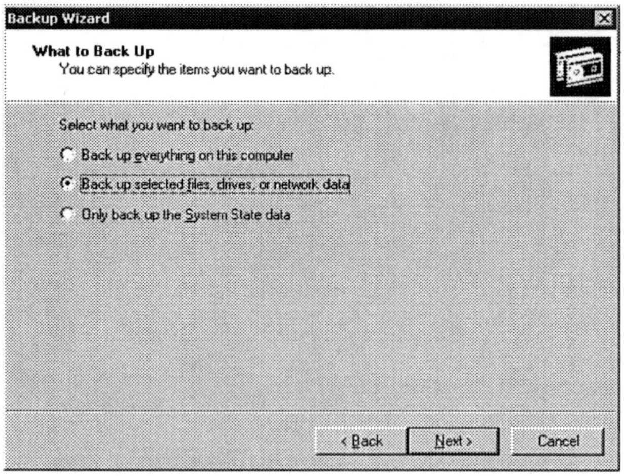

FIGURE 9.22 You need to select the scope of the backup that is to be performed.

NOTE

System State data The System State data contains information that is critical to the proper startup and operation of your Windows Server 2003 Active Directory structure. The following items are included in the System State data:

- Registry
- COM+ class-registration database
- Critical boot and system files
- System files that are protected by Windows File Protection
- Certificate Services database, if the server is a Certificate Authority
- Active Directory service, if the server is a domain controller
- SYSVOL directory, if the server is a domain controller
- Cluster service information, if the server is a member of a cluster
- IIS metadirectory, if IIS is installed on the server

6. In the Items to Back Up dialog box, shown in Figure 9.23, select the files and folders to back up. Click Next to continue.
7. In the Backup Type, Destination, and Name dialog box, shown in Figure 9.24, choose the location to save the backup file, using the Browse button, if necessary, and enter the filename for the backup file. Click Next to continue.

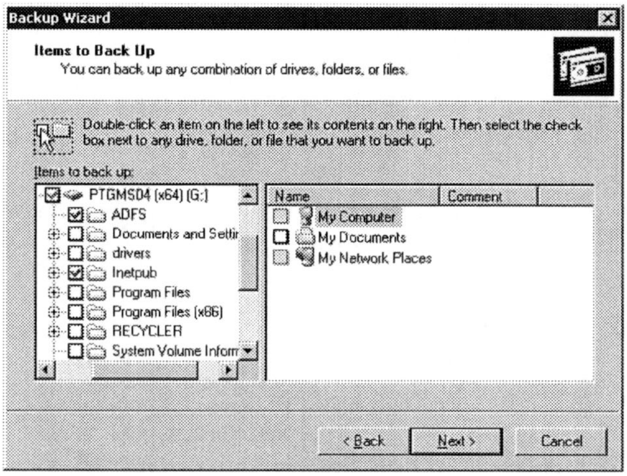

FIGURE 9.23 You can select entire volumes, folders, or specific files to be backed up.

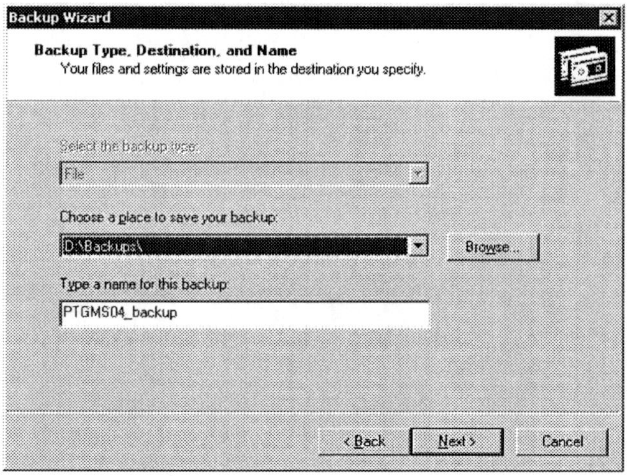

FIGURE 9.24 You should provide a filename for the backup file that describes its purpose or contents.

8. The Completing the Backup Wizard dialog box appears, as shown in Figure 9.25. To configure advanced options, including scheduling and disabling volume shadow copy, click Advanced and proceed to step 9. If you want to perform this backup immediately, click Finish.

9. In the Type of Backup dialog box, shown in Figure 9.26, select the type of backup you want. The default selection is Normal. Click Next to continue.

FIGURE 9.25 You need to configure the Advanced options to schedule the backup to occur later.

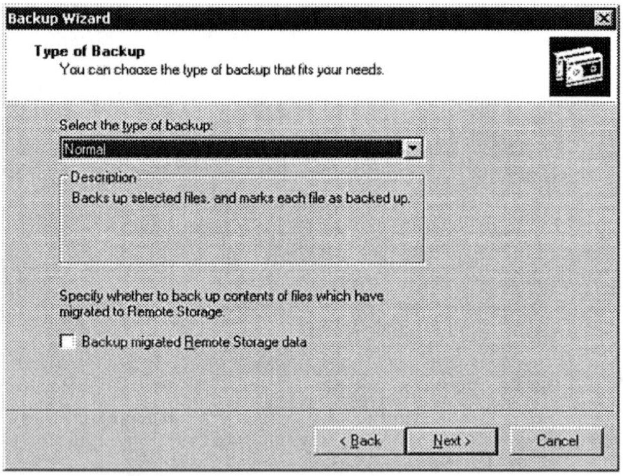

FIGURE 9.26 By default, all backups are configured as Normal; you can choose from any of the five types previously discussed.

10. In the How to Back Up dialog box, shown in Figure 9.27, you can select options to verify data, enable hardware compression (if supported by your backup device), and disable volume shadow copy. Data verification and hardware compression are usually desirable options. You should not disable the volume shadow copy unless you have a specific reason to do so. After making your selections, click Next to continue.

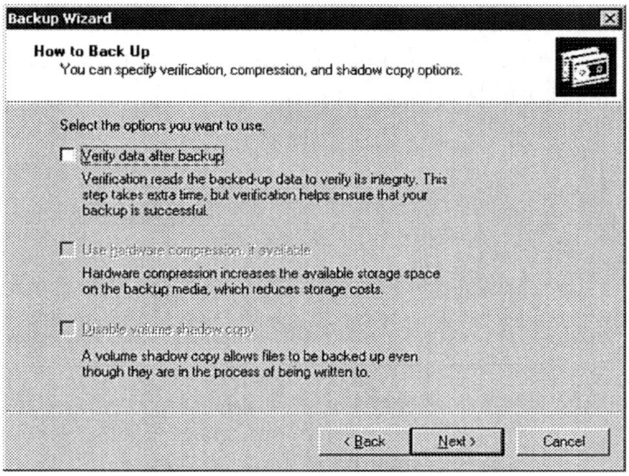

FIGURE 9.27 You should not disable the volume shadow copy without a valid reason to do so.

11. In the Backup Options dialog box, shown in Figure 9.28, you need to select whether to append existing backup data on your media or to replace it. In most cases, you simply overwrite the old data each night—especially if you are using one of the media-rotation methods discussed previously in this section. After making your selections, click Next to continue.

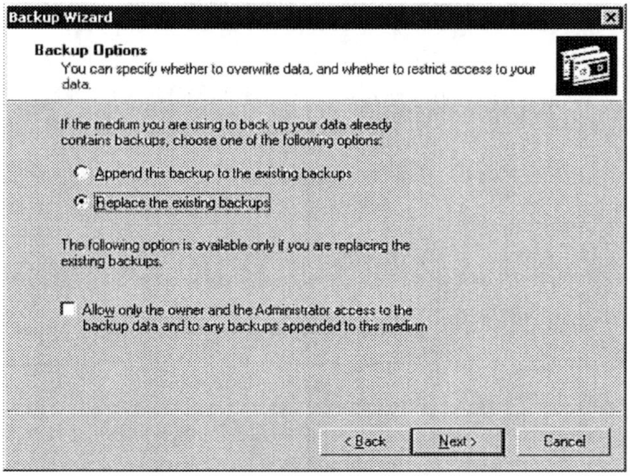

FIGURE 9.28 In most cases, you should overwrite any existing data on the backup media.

12. In the When to Back Up dialog box, shown in Figure 9.29, you need to configure the data and time that you want to perform this backup job. Using the Set Schedule button enables you to configure the scheduling options for the backup; alternatively, you can run the backup immediately by leaving the Now radio button selected. After making your selections, click Next to continue.

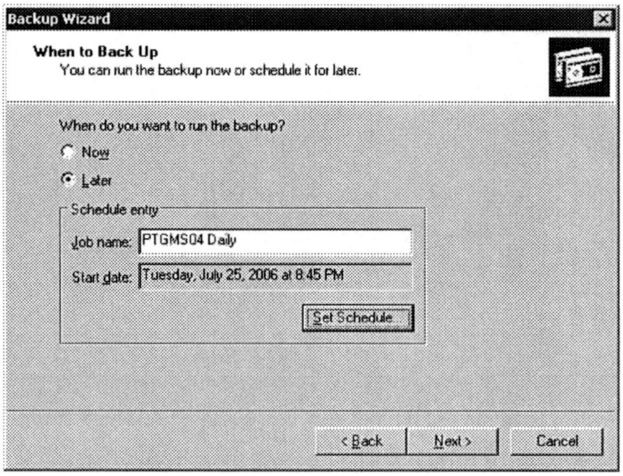

FIGURE 9.29 You can schedule backups to occur when your network will not be adversely affected.

13. If you selected Now, click Finish to complete the Backup Wizard and start the backup. If you selected Later, you are prompted for the username and password of a domain user account authorized to perform backups. Click Finish to complete the Backup Wizard; the backup will run at the date and time you selected.

Additionally, you can choose to create a backup configuration manually; however, you still make all the same decisions as when using the Backup Wizard.

Scheduling Backup Jobs

Managing a backup schedule is easy in Windows Server 2003. In the Backup Utility, simply switch to the Schedule Jobs tab, shown in Figure 9.30. Each day on the calendar shows what type of backup is scheduled for that day. Holding the cursor over a backup displays the backup name. You can edit the backup properties, including rescheduling the backup, by clicking it. You can also create new backup configurations by clicking the Add Job button.

TIP

Scheduling backup jobs Many administrators disable the Windows Task Scheduler because it is commonly seen as an unneeded service and, thus, a security risk. If you want to schedule backup jobs using the Windows Backup Utility, you must not disable the Windows Task Scheduler.

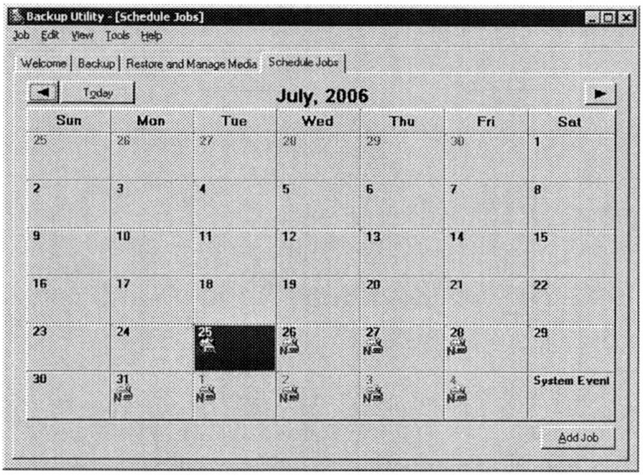

FIGURE 9.30 Using the Schedule Jobs tab, you can quickly determine what backup jobs are scheduled.

Performing Restorations Using Windows Backup

If the day actually comes that you need to put your backup system to the test, the actual process of performing the restoration is relatively easy in Windows Server 2003—as long as you are ready for the task. The basic steps to perform a restoration are outlined in Step by Step 9.4, although your options and decisions will vary depending on how your system and backup media devices are configured.

STEP BY STEP

9.4 Performing Data Restoration

1. Open the Backup or Restore Wizard by selecting Start, Programs, Accessories, System Tools, Backup.
2. Click the Advanced Mode link to switch to Advanced mode of the Backup Utility, as shown previously in Figure 9.21.
3. Start the Restore Wizard by clicking the Restore Wizard (Advanced) button from the main page of the Backup Utility.
4. Click Next to dismiss the opening page of the wizard.
5. In the What to Restore dialog box, shown in Figure 9.31, select the media and files that are to be restored. If your choice of media is not listed, click the Browse button to locate it. After making your selections, click Next to continue.
6. The Completing the Restore Wizard dialog box appears, as shown in Figure 9.32. To configure advanced options, including where to restore the files to and what to do with existing files found in the restoration location, click Advanced and proceed to step 7. If you want to perform this restoration immediately, click Finish.

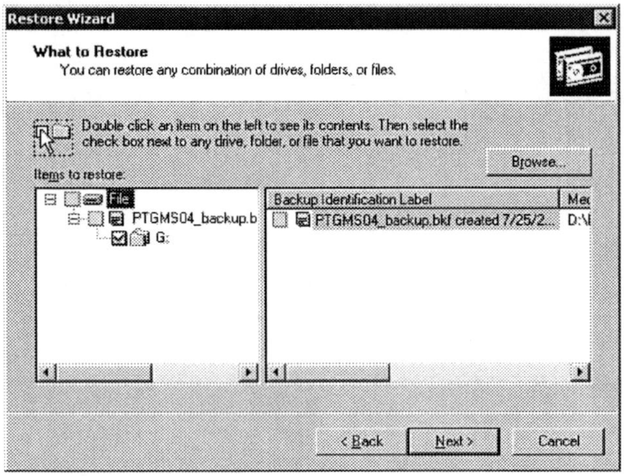

FIGURE 9.31 You can select to restore only certain parts of the backup file, if you want.

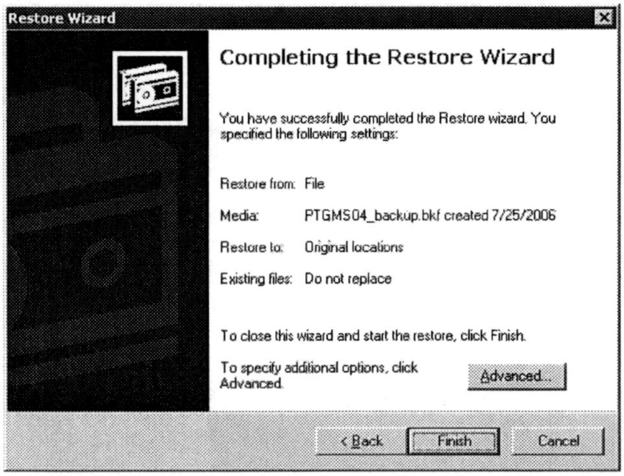

FIGURE 9.32 You need to configure the Advanced options to be able to restore the files to a different location than where they were originally located.

7. In the Where to Restore dialog box, shown in Figure 9.33, select the restoration location for the folders and files from the drop-down. Click Next to continue.
8. In the How to Restore dialog box, shown in Figure 9.34, decide what is to occur if existing files are found in the restoration location. Click Next to continue.
9. In the Advanced Restore Options dialog box, shown in Figure 9.35, you can select from several advanced restoration options, as explained in the list following this procedure. The available options are determined by the data that has been backed up, the type of hardware installed in your server, and the role of the server. After making your selections, click Next to continue.

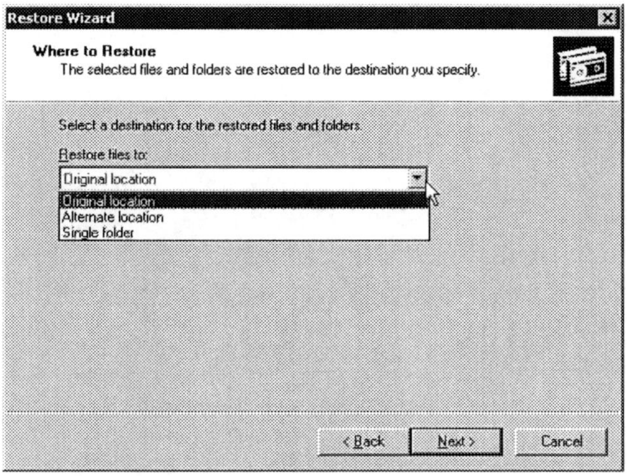

FIGURE 9.33 You can restore the files to the same or a different location, if you want.

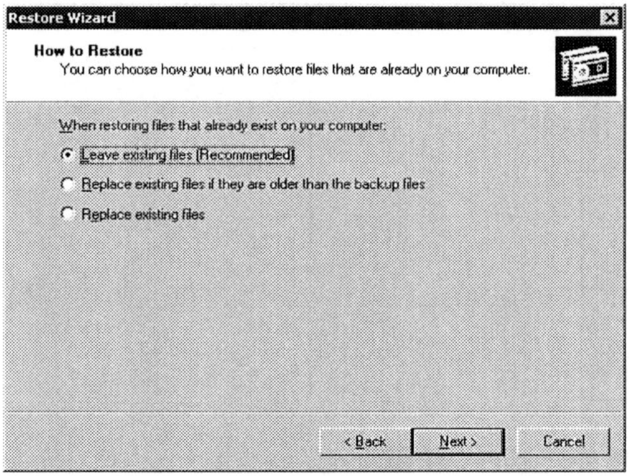

FIGURE 9.34 In most cases, you should leave existing files or replace older files during the restoration process.

10. Click Finish to start the restoration.

11. The Restore Progress dialog box appears, informing you of the restoration's status. When the restoration is complete, you see results similar to those shown in Figure 9.36.

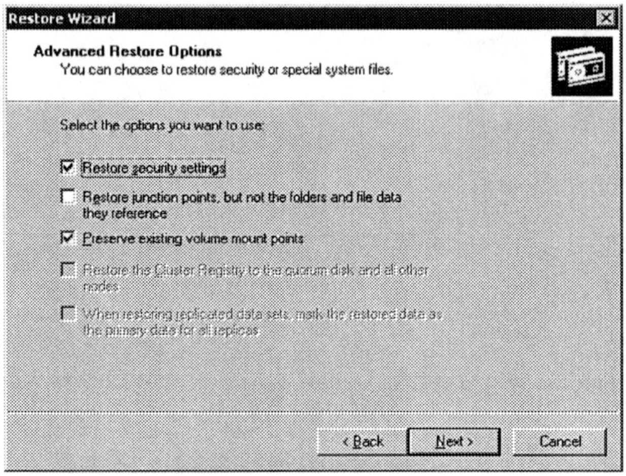

FIGURE 9.35 The Advanced Restore Options dialog box features several high-level configuration options.

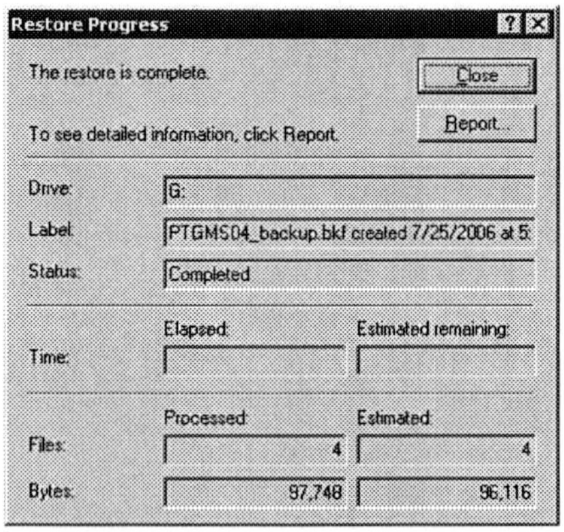

FIGURE 9.36 In the Restore Progress dialog box, you can determine the status of your restoration process.

The Advanced Restore Options are as follows:

- **Restore Security Settings**—This option restores security settings for each file and folder; these settings include permissions, auditing entries, and ownership information. This option is available only for data that was backed up from an NTFS-formatted volume.
- **Restore Junction Points, and Restore File and Folder Data Under Junction Points to the Original Location**—This option restores all junction points to your hard disks, as well as the data that the junction points point to. If you are restoring a mounted drive and you want to restore the data that is on the mounted drive, you must select this check box. If you do not select this check box, you restore only the folder containing the mounted drive.

- **Restore Junction Points, but Not the Folders and File Data They Reference**—This option restores junction points only to your hard drive. This option does not restore any folders or file data that reference the junction points.
- **When Restoring Replicated Data Sets, Mark the Restored Data as the Primary Data for All Replicas**—This option performs a restoration and ensures that the restored File Replication Service (FRS) data is replicated to other configured servers.
- **Restore the Cluster Registry to the Quorum Disk and All Other Nodes**—This option ensures that the cluster quorum database is restored and is also replicated on all nodes in the cluster.
- **Preserve Existing Volume Mount Points**—This option prevents the restore operation from writing over any volume mount points you have created on the partition or volume you are restoring data to.
- **Restore Removable Storage Database**—This option restores the Removable Storage database and deletes the existing Removable Storage database. If you are not using Removable Storage to manage storage media, you do not need to select this option.

NOTE

Form of a junction point A *junction point* is a physical location on a hard disk that points to data at another location on your hard disk or another storage device. Junction points are created when you create a mounted drive.

With the discussion of the Windows Backup Utility behind us, we now move forward and examine a new feature in Windows Server 2003: Automated System Recovery.

Using Automated System Recovery

Objective:

Plan a backup and recovery strategy.

- Plan system recovery that uses Automated System Recovery (ASR).

Although making regular backups is an important task to accomplish, they are of no use to you if a server suffers a critical failure that prevents it from starting normally. Although you can use the `ntbackup.exe` command to create backups from the command line, you cannot perform restorations from the command line—a serious limitation if you are unable to start a Windows Server 2003 computer normally.

CAUTION

Keeping ASR up-to-date For an ASR recovery to be effective, you must keep it up-to-date. You should create a new ASR set after any configuration change to the server. You should also create a new ASR set on a regular schedule—just as you would with a normal backup set.

As discussed previously, you can use ASR to restore the operating system to a previous state, enabling you to start Window Server 2003 if other methods do not work. You should always consider ASR your last resort for recovery, after Safe Mode, the Recovery Console, and Last Known Good Configuration (LKGC).

ASR is a two-part process that uses a startup floppy disk to boot the Windows Server 2003 computer and a backup file (that must be accessible during ASR restoration) containing the System State, system services, and all disks associated with the operating system components. The startup disk contains information about the backup, the disk configurations, and the way the restoration is to be accomplished.

To create a new ASR set, perform the steps outlined in Step by Step 9.5.

STEP BY STEP

9.5 Creating an Automated System Recovery Set

1. Place a blank, formatted 1.44MB 3.5-inch floppy disk in your server's floppy drive.
2. Open the Backup or Restore Wizard by selecting Start, Programs, Accessories, System Tools, Backup.
3. Click the Advanced Mode link to switch to Advanced mode of the Backup Utility.
4. Start the Automated System Recovery Preparation Wizard by clicking the Automated System Recovery Wizard button on the main page of the Backup Utility.
5. Click Next to dismiss the opening page of the wizard.
6. In the Backup Destination dialog box, shown in Figure 9.37, provide the path and filename of the backup file to be created. Click Next to continue.

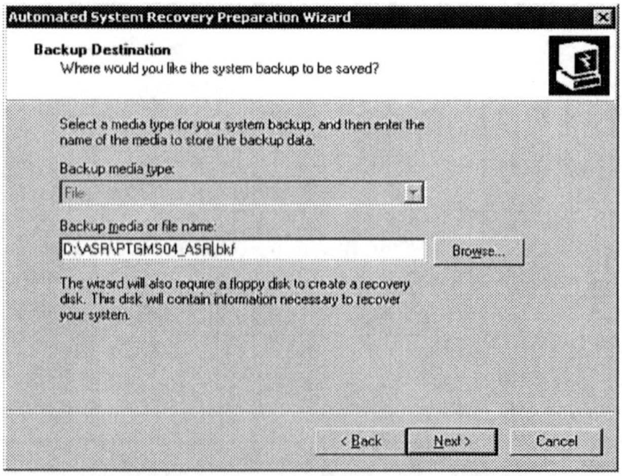

FIGURE 9.37 ASR creates a backup file and startup floppy disk.

7. Click Finish to close the wizard and start the ASR set-creation process.
8. Ensure that the blank, formatted floppy disk is inserted in your server's floppy drive when prompted. Click OK to create the startup floppy disk.

To perform an ASR recovery—after all other available methods to start the server normally have failed—you need to perform the steps listed in Step by Step 9.6. However, before starting the procedure, you need to locate the following items and have them readily available to you:

- The correct (up-to-date) ASR startup floppy disk.
- The correct (up-to-date) ASR backup media.
- The original Windows Server 2003 installation CD-ROM you used to install the server.
- Special drivers required for any mass storage controllers located in your server that are not available on the Windows Server 2003 CD-ROM; they also need to be available on floppy disk.

STEP BY STEP

9.6 Performing Automated System Recovery

1. Power on the server to be recovered using ASR.
2. Insert your original Windows Server 2003 CD into the CD-ROM drive.
3. When prompted to start from the CD-ROM, press the appropriate key.
4. If you need a special mass storage driver, press F6 when prompted to install it.
5. Press F2 when prompted to initiate an ASR recovery.
6. Insert the ASR startup floppy disk.
7. Follow the directions that are displayed.
8. If you need a special mass storage driver, press F6 when prompted to install it after the server restarts.
9. Follow the directions that are displayed.

That's all there is to using ASR. Remember, however, that ASR is your last option and should not be used without attempting all other available methods to start the server.

Using Volume Shadow Copy

Objective:

Plan a backup and recovery strategy.

- Plan a backup strategy that uses volume shadow copy.

As you've already seen, the volume shadow copy is another new backup feature available in Windows Server 2003. The usefulness of volume shadow copies, however, extends beyond your ability to use Windows Backup to create backups of open files; this feature also provides you with a way to archive copies of data over time, enabling users to locate and restore a specific file if they want. When the necessary configuration has been completed and the required software has been installed, users can view the volume shadow copies of shared network folders, including any previous versions in existence. Users can then copy any or all of the older files, enabling them to effectively restore a backup copy of the files from an earlier time.

As you might imagine, volume shadow copies can provide a number of benefits to your network users—the least of which is the ability to restore an older version if the current version of a file becomes corrupt or is deleted beyond recovery. You also can compare different versions of files to see what changes have occurred over time.

Files contained in a volume shadow copy are read-only while archived, preventing them from being modified and thus nullifying the benefits of the volume shadow copy. After a file has been extracted from a volume shadow copy archive, it can be modified or moved to any location desired for editing.

Shadow copies are disabled by default but can be enabled and configured from the Shared Folders node of the Computer Management console, shown in Figure 9.38.

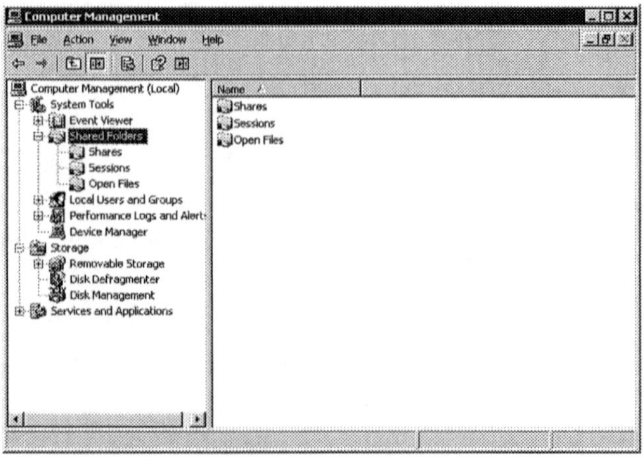

FIGURE 9.38 Volume shadow copies are managed from the Computer Management console.

Windows Server 2003 allows for only 64 volume shadow copies of a specific shared folder. When this limit is reached, the oldest copy is deleted to make room for a newer copy. Before your network clients can take advantage of this technology, they must have the Volume Shadow Client software installed. The client software is available on your Windows Server 2003 computer in the %systemroot%\system32\clients\twclient\ folder.

Step by Step 9.7 outlines the basic process to enable and configure volume shadow copies for a volume on your Windows Server 2003 computer.

STEP BY STEP

9.7 Enabling and Configuring Volume Shadow Copies

1. Open the Computer Management console by selecting Start, Programs, Administrative Tools, Computer Management.
2. Expand the System Tools node and locate the Shared Folders node.
3. Right-click the Shared Folders node and select All Tasks, Configure Shadow Copies.
4. The Shadow Copies dialog box opens, as shown in Figure 9.39. This dialog box displays a listing of all available volumes for which you can enable shadow copies.

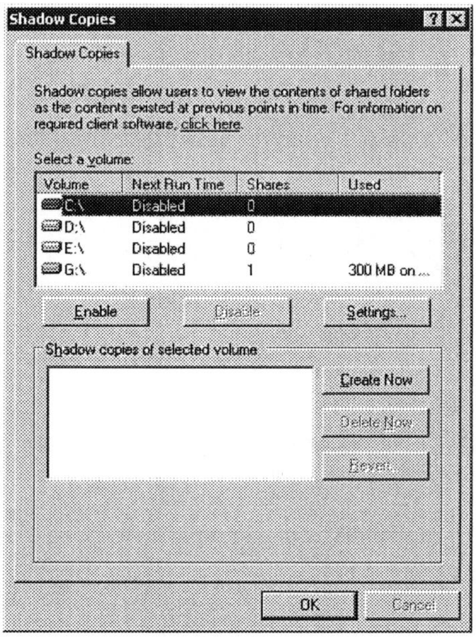

FIGURE 9.39 Shadow copies are disabled by default for all volumes.

5. Select the volume for which you want to enable shadow copies and click the Enable button.
6. You are prompted with a dialog box asking for confirmation that you actually want to enable shadow copies for this volume. Click Yes to continue.

7. After some time, the shadow copy is completed and appears in the lower half of the Shadow Copies dialog box, shown in Figure 9.40.

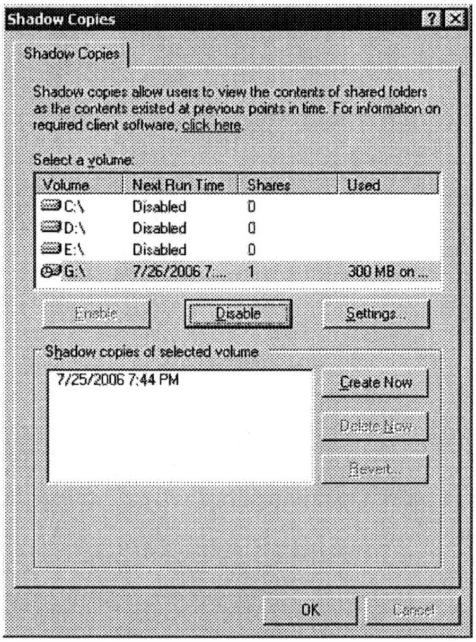

FIGURE 9.40 You can quickly view recent shadow copies that have been created.

8. If you want to change the default configuration settings, click the Settings button on the Shadow Copies dialog box. The Settings dialog box opens, as shown in Figure 9.41.

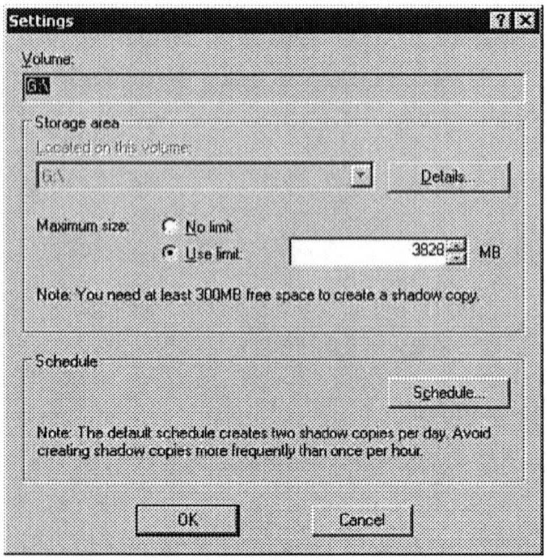

FIGURE 9.41 You need to configure at least 100MB of space for volume shadow copies.

9. In the Settings dialog box, you can change the location where the shadow copies are to be stored, as well as the amount of space you want to allot to them. To configure the schedule for volume shadow copies, click the Schedule button. The Schedule dialog box opens, as shown in Figure 9.42.

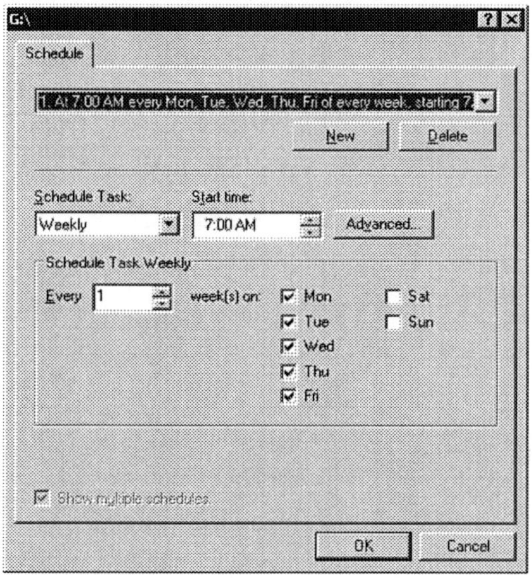

FIGURE 9.42 You can create a custom shadow copy schedule to fit your needs.

10. The default schedule creates volume shadow copies twice daily at 7 a.m. and 12 p.m. You can modify the existing schedules or delete them and create new ones as you like.

11. Click OK three times to close all the shadow copies configuration dialog boxes.

After you've configured volume shadow copies, Windows Server 2003 computers and client computers with the Volume Shadow Client software installed can view the shadow copies available for a shared network folder. You first need to locate the shared network folder, shown in Figure 9.43, using My Network Places.

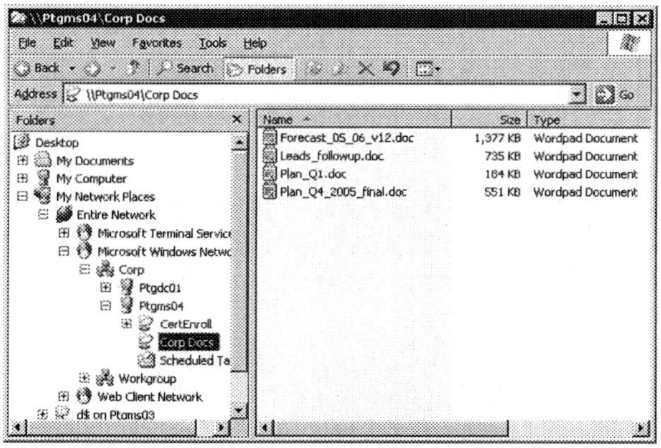

FIGURE 9.43 You can take advantage of the shadow copies only over the network.

Right-clicking the shared folder and selecting Properties from the context menu displays a new tab on the Properties dialog box—the Previous Versions tab, shown in Figure 9.44.

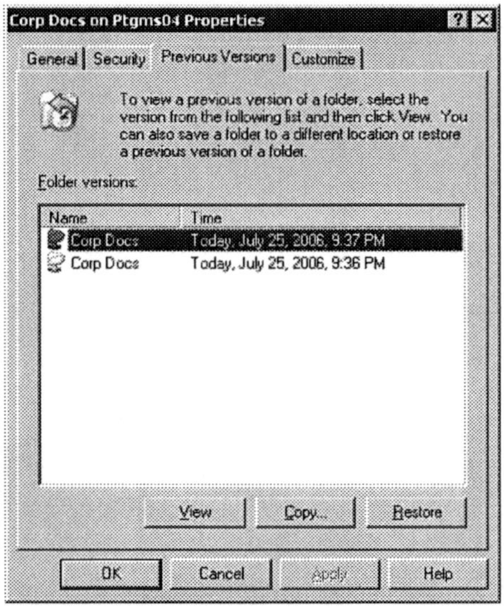

FIGURE 9.44 The Previous Versions tab displays all previous versions of the folder.

By selecting a previous version and clicking the View button, you can open a new Windows Explorer window displaying the previous version's contents, as shown in Figure 9.45. If you want to restore a single file or multiple files, you can simply drag them out of this location. You can also restore the entire folder by selecting it and clicking the Restore button on the Previous Versions tab. To restore the previous version of the entire folder to a different location, select the previous version and click the Copy button on the Previous Versions tab.

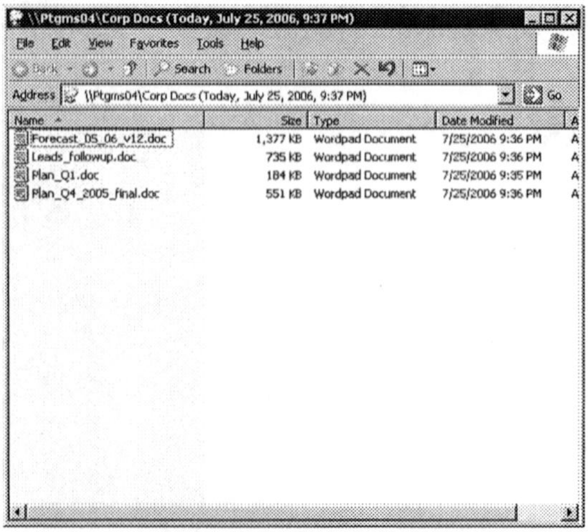

FIGURE 9.45 The Previous Versions tab displays all previous versions of the folder.

Chapter Summary

This chapter covered perhaps two of the most important day-to-day activities you will be faced with as an administrator: ensuring server performance and providing disaster recovery.

Ensuring performance (and health) of servers and client computers involves using the Performance console (System Monitor, Counter Logs, Trace Logs, and Alerts), the Event Viewer, and also the Task Manager. Data gathered from these sources can be used to identify, troubleshoot, and correct problem areas.

Even with the best-laid highly available server plans, disaster can and will strike when you can least afford it. Only by having a well-designed and adequate backup and restoration plan will your network live again without days of downtime. Several widely accepted backup methods and media-rotation systems are available; however, you can opt to create a customized solution that fits the unique needs of your organization. Whatever solution you end up with, you must ensure that all responsible persons are aware of its requirements and that it is tested routinely to validate its process and check for required updates and corrections.

Remember, server reliability begins with you and your good planning.

Key Terms

- Automated System Restore
- Backup
- Baseline
- Bottleneck
- Copy backup
- Counter
- Counter log
- Daily backup
- Differential backup
- Incremental backup
- Normal backup
- `ntbackup.exe`
- Performance console
- Restoration
- Volume shadow copy

Apply Your Knowledge

In this chapter, you examined performance-monitoring and data-backup methods in Windows Server 2003. In the following exercises, you practice some of the concepts and methods discussed in this chapter.

Exercises

9.1 Creating a Baseline Counter Log

In this exercise, you use the Performance console to create a baseline counter log. You then can use the baseline as a comparison point for future performance monitoring.

Estimated time: 30 minutes

1. Open the Performance console.
2. Expand the Performance Logs and Alerts node and click the Counter Logs entry.
3. Create a new counter log and name it **`BASLINELOG1`**.
4. Add entire objects or specific counters as you like. For this example, add the Packets Sent/sec, Packets Received/sec, and Packets Received Errors counters.
5. Leave the default data-collection rate and account settings as is.
6. Configure the type of log file to be used as binary. Choose the numbering system of your choice.
7. Leave the default schedule of manual activation as is.
8. Click OK to save the counter log settings.
9. Allow the counter log to run for approximately 20 minutes and then stop it.
10. Switch to the System Monitor node and click the database icon to open the counter log for viewing.
11. Click the Add button to locate and add the counter log file.
12. On the Data tab, ensure that you have configured all the same counters to be displayed as you used in the counter log itself. Click OK. The counter log data is displayed in System Monitor.

9.2 Monitoring Performance

In this exercise, you monitor the current performance characteristics of a computer's network adapter.

Estimated time: 15 minutes

1. Open the Performance console.
2. Click System Monitor.

3. Click the + icon to open the Add Counters dialog box. Add the counters you want to monitor on your computer, such as Packets Sent/sec, Packets Received/sec, and Packets Received Errors.

4. Click Close when you are finished. Watch the configured counters for 10 minutes while performing various activities that require network transfer to and from your computer.

9.3 Configuring a New Backup Job

In this exercise, you configure a new backup job to be run on your Windows Server 2003 computer.

Estimated time: 20 minutes

1. Open the Backup or Restore Wizard.
2. Click the Advanced Mode link to switch to Advanced mode of the Backup Utility.
3. Start the Backup Wizard.
4. Click Next to dismiss the opening page of the wizard.
5. In the What to Back Up dialog box, select the scope of the backup. If you choose to back up selected files and folders, proceed to step 6; otherwise, skip to step 7.
6. In the Items to Back Up dialog box, select the files and folders to back up.
7. In the Backup Type, Destination, and Name dialog box, choose the location to save the backup file, using the Browse button, if necessary, and enter the filename for the backup file.
8. To configure advanced options, including scheduling and disabling volume shadow copy, click Advanced and proceed to step 9. If you want to perform this backup immediately, click Finish.
9. In the Type of Backup dialog box, select the type of backup you want.
10. In the How to Back Up dialog box, select to verify data, enable hardware compression (if supported by your backup device), or disable volume shadow copy.
11. In the Backup Options dialog box, select whether to overwrite existing backup data on your media or overwrite it.
12. In the When to Back Up dialog box, configure the date and time that you want to perform this backup job.
13. If you selected Now, click Finish to complete the Backup Wizard and start the backup. If you selected Later, you are prompted for the username and password of a domain user account authorized to perform backups.

9.4 Enabling and Configuring Volume Shadow Copy

In this exercise, you enable and configure the volume shadow copy feature on your Windows Server 2003 computer.

Estimated time: 15 minutes

1. Open the Computer Management console.
2. Expand the System Tools node and locate the Shared Folders node.
3. Right-click the Shared Folders node and select All Tasks, Configure Shadow Copies.
4. Select the volume for which you want to enable shadow copies and click the Enable button.
5. Click the Settings button on the Shadow Copies dialog box.
6. Change the location where the shadow copies are to be stored, as well as the amount of space you want to allot to them.
7. Click the Schedule button.
8. Configure the volume shadow copy schedule as required.

Review Questions

1. What is a baseline, and why is it important to create one?
2. You have enabled the volume shadow copies on your file server using the default settings. When you try to locate a version of a file that is 42 days old, you cannot. Why is this so?
3. You create backups on Monday, Tuesday, Wednesday, and Thursday nights using differential backup. On Friday night, you perform a full backup. If you need to perform a restoration on Thursday morning, which tapes do you need?
4. Besides enabling you to create previous versions of files and folders, what other feature does the volume shadow copy provide in Windows Server 2003?
5. In general, when should you create baselines for your servers?

Exam Questions

1. Christopher needs to back up the contents of a data folder on his server, but he does not have a tape drive. What other media can he use with Windows Backup?

   ❍ **A.** CD-ROM

   ❍ **B.** Floppy disk

   ❍ **C.** Text dump

   ❍ **D.** No other media can be used

2. You are the third-shift systems administrator for Bob's Bull Riding College. You have just completed the installation and configuration of a new Windows Server 2003 file server. What should you do on this new computer over the next day or so to provide troubleshooting guidance in the future, in case network traffic problems occur?

❍ **A.** Remove all unnecessary protocols from the server's network adapters.

❍ **B.** Create a baseline counter log that documents what the server's performance was like at the time it was placed on the network.

❍ **C.** Check the event logs to ensure that no abnormal events occurred when the computer was joined to the network.

❍ **D.** Configure and implement IPSec to secure network traffic to and from the file server.

3. You are creating a disaster-recovery plan for your organization. You have decided to implement the Daily, Weekly, Monthly media-rotation method to provide a good mix of backup history and backup media wear. Your plan has been approved by management and implemented for use on the network. After three months, you perform a comprehensive review of the disaster-recovery plan and determine that it does not provide an adequate solution to protect critical operating system files. What additional information should you ensure is backed up when your backup files are created?

❍ **A.** `SYSVOL` directory

❍ **B.** C:\

❍ **C.** System State

❍ **D.** All files and folders on all volumes on all servers

4. You are trying to monitor the performance statistics of your Windows Server 2003 computer's network interface. You have only one network interface installed in the computer. After you have selected the desired counters from the Network Interface object and returned to the System Monitor, you see no performance statistics displayed for the selected counters, even though you have been accessing Internet websites and transferring files across the network. What is the most likely cause of this problem?

❍ **A.** The network interface is disabled.

❍ **B.** The network interface does not support System Monitor.

❍ **C.** You have selected the internal loopback network interface.

❍ **D.** You did not click Add to add the counters to be monitored.

5. You have enabled and configured volume shadow copies on one of your Windows Server 2003 file servers. The file server has a shared folder named Financial that is located at `C:\FinanceDocs`. You have deployed the Previous Versions Client to all your Windows XP Professional workstations. When you attempt to confirm that your configuration is functioning correctly by viewing the properties of the `Financial` share in Windows Explorer on your server, there is no Previous Versions tab. What is the most likely problem?

- ❍ **A.** You forgot to install the client software on the server.
- ❍ **B.** The client software was installed prior to enabling the shadow copies.
- ❍ **C.** The Previous Versions tab is available only when viewing the folder over the network using My Network Places.
- ❍ **D.** The shared folder is empty.

6. You have recently completed the configuration of a baseline counter log that you will use to collect data about the performance of a new server you have just placed on the network. You configured a maximum log file size of 1MB. You let the counter log run for approximately six hours before stopping it. When you look at the data you have collected, you see only a fraction of this total time displayed—the last 45 minutes or so that you had the counter log catching data. What is the most likely reason for this problem?

- ❍ **A.** There has not been enough activity to generate more data than this.
- ❍ **B.** You configured the file type as binary.
- ❍ **C.** You configured the file type as binary circular.
- ❍ **D.** The computer was experiencing operating system instability problems that prevented the collection of more data.

7. Deanna needs to back up critical data on her server. However, she does not have enough DAT tapes to back up everything on her server. She wants to make sure that, in addition to the user data she is backing up, she backs up the Registry on her server. What should Deanna select in addition to those data files she wants to back up?

- ❍ **A.** C:
- ❍ **B.** System State
- ❍ **C.** My Documents
- ❍ **D.** My Computer

8. You are configuring a counter log that is to run automatically each day and collect information about the performance of the network interface installed in your file server. Which of the following log-numbering systems would most likely make the resulting counter logs easy to track back to the date and time they were created?

- ❍ **A.** *nnnnnn*
- ❍ **B.** *yyyymm*
- ❍ **C.** *mmddhhmm*
- ❍ **D.** *yyyymmddhh*

9. You are preparing to enable and configure volume shadow copies on one of your Windows Server 2003 file servers. All shared folders are located on Volume C of the file server. Volume C on the server has 85MB of free space available. How much space will be used by volume shadow copies?

   ❍ **A.** 850KB

   ❍ **B.** 8.5MB

   ❍ **C.** 42.5MB

   ❍ **D.** 0MB

10. Christopher wants to determine whether his server is short of memory. Under light load, users get good response. However, as load increases, so does the lack of responsiveness. Which of the following counters will aid him in determining whether memory is the bottleneck in his system? Select all correct answers.

   ❍ **A.** Memory\Pages/sec

   ❍ **B.** Paging File\% Usage

   ❍ **C.** Processor\Interrupts/sec

   ❍ **D.** Network Segment\% Net Utilization

11. Andrea is preparing a disaster-recovery plan for her company. She asks you which backup option backs up only the files that have not been marked as archived and then sets the archive bit for all files that are backed up. What should you tell her?

   ❍ **A.** Daily backups act this way.

   ❍ **B.** Normal backups act this way.

   ❍ **C.** Copy backups act this way.

   ❍ **D.** Differential backups act this way.

   ❍ **E.** Incremental backups act this way.

12. Christopher is assisting Andrea with preparations for disaster recovery. He asks you which backup option requires only one media device for the entire backup and sets the archive bit to indicate that the data has been backed up. What should you tell him?

   ❍ **A.** Daily backups act this way.

   ❍ **B.** Normal backups act this way.

   ❍ **C.** Copy backups act this way.

   ❍ **D.** Differential backups act this way.

   ❍ **E.** Incremental backups act this way.

13. Austin wants to monitor how much of the paging file is being used. He opens System Monitor and starts to add the counter for this, but he is unsure which one to add. Which counter should you tell him to add to monitor the paging file usage?

   ❍ **A.** Paging File\Pages/sec

   ❍ **B.** Memory\Pages/sec

   ❍ **C.** Paging File\% Usage

   ❍ **D.** Memory\% Paging File

14. Hannah is trying to determine what could be causing her disk access to slow over time. She opens System Monitor and starts to add counters to help her diagnose this situation, but she is unsure what to add. Which counter should you tell her to add to help her diagnose problems with her hard-drive access speed? (Select all that apply.)

   ❍ **A.** Physical Disk\Disk Reads/sec

   ❍ **B.** Logical Disk\% Free Space

   ❍ **C.** Physical Disk\Split IO/sec

   ❍ **D.** Network Interface\Bytes Total/sec

15. You are creating a disaster-recovery plan for your organization. You have decided to implement the Daily, Weekly, Monthly media-rotation method to provide a good mix of backup history and backup media wear. Your plan has been approved by management and implemented for use on the network. After three months, you perform a comprehensive review of the disaster-recovery plan and determine that it does not provide an adequate solution in case the server cannot be started normally. What feature of Windows Server 2003 can you take advantage of to close this gap in your disaster-recovery plan?

   ❍ **A.** Volume shadow copy

   ❍ **B.** Automated System Recovery

   ❍ **C.** Automatic Updates

   ❍ **D.** Safe Mode

Answers to Review Questions

1. A baseline is a set of performance readings taken at a specific time and used to reference future readings to identify changes in performance. For more information, see the section "Baselining Servers."

2. By default, volume shadow copies create a shadow copy twice daily. Volume shadow copies can maintain only 64 previous versions, for a total of 32 days in the default configuration. For more information, see the section, "Using Volume Shadow Copy."

3. You need the full backup tape from the previous Friday night and the differential backup tape from Wednesday night. For more information, see the section "Backup Methods and Media Rotation."

4. Volume shadow copies also enable you to back up files that are open at the time of the backup. This way, file servers can be backed up without forcing users to close all open files. Open files are backed up in a closed state as they are at that point in time. For more information, see the section "New Windows Server 2003 Backup Features."

5. You should create a baseline when a new server is placed in operation, after each hardware change, and after each software or application modification. For more information, see the section "Baselining Servers."

Answers to Exam Questions

1. **B.** In addition to tape drives, Windows Backup can store to any local or network drive. Of the given choices, only the floppy disk is a valid choice. For more information, see the section "Planning Backup and Recovery Operations."

2. **B.** The best thing for you to do at this time is to configure a counter log that collects information about the performance of the server over the next day or so to use as a baseline for future troubleshooting efforts. This baseline log should contain counters for any pertinent objects that you will likely want to monitor and troubleshoot later, including network, memory, and other objects. You also should consider creating a document that lists all applications and services that are running on the server. This document can be helpful later when you are trying to determine what might be causing changes in performance over time. For more information, see the section "Baselining Servers."

3. **C.** You can select to have the System State information backed up to provide recovery protection for all critical operating system files, including those that are required to properly start and operate the operating system. The System State consists of the following items:

    - Registry
    - COM+ class-registration database
    - Critical boot and system files
    - System files that are protected by Windows File Protection
    - Certificate Services database, if the server is a Certificate Authority
    - Active Directory directory service, if the server is a domain controller
    - SYSVOL directory, if the server is a domain controller
    - Cluster service information, if the server is a member of a cluster
    - IIS metadirectory, if IIS is installed on the server

For more information, see the section "Creating Backup Job Configurations."

4. **C.** The most likely reason for this problem is that you have mistakenly selected the internal loopback interface instead of the actual network interface that the computer is using. By default, the loopback interface is selected if the name of the network interface starts with a letter after *l*. For more information, see the section "Introduction to System Monitor."

5. **C.** The Previous Versions tab is available in the Properties dialog box only when the share is accessed over the network or locally using the My Network Places folder. For more information, see the section "Using Volume Shadow Copy."

6. **C.** Configuring the counter log file format as binary circular causes the log file to overwrite older information when it has reached its maximum allowed size. For more information, see the section "Baselining Servers."

7. **B.** To back up (and, hence, recover) the Registry, you must back up the System State information for a local server. For more information, see the section "Creating Backup Job Configurations."

8. **D.** The *yyyymmddhh* log-numbering format provides the easiest method of determining the data and time each counter log was created. For more information, see the section "Baselining Servers."

9. **D.** Volume shadow copies require at least 100MB of free space on the volume; therefore, you cannot enable volume shadow copies on this file server. For more information, see the section "Using Volume Shadow Copy."

10. **A, B.** Pages/sec shows how many times per second the server has to go to the hard drive to recover information it thought ought to be in memory but has been swapped out because of a shortage of memory. % Usage of the paging file can be an indicator of low memory because, if it constantly decreases as applications run, the amount of RAM is not sufficient to fill the demand on the server, which causes the paging file to be increased in size. For more information, see the section "Daily Monitoring for Usage."

11. **E.** Incremental backups look to see the current status of the archive bit before backing up data. If the archive bit is False, an incremental backup skips the file because it has been backed up. If the archive bit is True, an incremental backup saves the file and sets its archive bit to False. If Andrea changes a file and then runs two incremental backups in a row, only the first backs up the file. The second encounters the False archive bit set by the first incremental backup and skips the file. For more information, see the section "Backup Methods and Media Rotation."

12. **B.** Normal backups (sometimes called full backups) save all files, regardless of the state of the archive bit. While saving the files, normal backups set the archive bit to False to indicate that the files have been backed up. This means that if Christopher were to do two normal backups in a row, both would save all the data, and both would set the archive bits to False. For more information, see the section "Daily Monitoring for Usage."

13. **C.** Paging File\% Usage is the ratio of the amount of paging file being used to the total size of the paging file. A high number is desired here because it indicates that the paging file is sized correctly for the system. If this number is low, either the paging file has been set too large (and, therefore, is consuming more disk space than is necessary) or the paging file has been recently resized. For more information, see the section "Daily Monitoring for Usage."

14. **B, C.** In this case, given the counter options listed, these two choices are the best options. With these two counters, Hannah can troubleshoot low disk space and fragmentation issues. Logical Disk\% Free Space is the ratio of free space total disk space on a logical drive, which is a measurement of remaining capacity on your logical drives. Hannah usually should track this for each logical drive. To prevent excessive fragmentation, the value here should not be allowed to drop below 10%. Physical Disk\Split IO/sec reports the rate at which the operating system divides I/O requests to the disk into multiple requests. A split I/O request might occur if the program requests data in a size that is too large to fit into a single request or if the disk is fragmented. Factors that influence the size of an I/O request can include application design, the file system, and drivers. A high rate of split I/O might not, in itself, represent a problem. However, on single-disk systems, a high rate for this counter tends to indicate disk fragmentation. For more information, see the section "Daily Monitoring for Usage."

15. **B.** The Automated System Restore (ASR) feature is new in Windows Server 2003 and provides a means of restoring a server, in case all other methods fail or are not available for use. You should consider ASR as a last option and use it only after Safe Mode, Recovery Console, and the Last Known Good Configuration (LKGC) have failed. The ASR set consists of a startup floppy disk and a standard Windows Backup file. In addition to these two items, you need your original Windows Server 2003 installation CD-ROM and any mass storage device drivers (on floppy disk) to perform an ASR recovery action. For more information, see the section "Using Automated System Recovery."

Suggested Readings and Resources

1. Storage Services Technology Center. www.microsoft.com/windowsserver2003/technologies/storage/default.mspx.

2. Microsoft Corporation. *Microsoft Windows Server 2003 Deployment Kit*. Redmond, WA: Microsoft Press, 2003.

3. Stanek, William R. *Windows Server 2003 Administrator's Pocket Consultant*. Redmond, WA: Microsoft Press, 2003.

10

CHAPTER TEN

Planning, Implementing, and Maintaining Highly Available Servers

High availability has become something of a buzzword in the past few years in the IT sector. People were striving for many years before that to achieve "five nines," or 99.999% server uptime. Microsoft makes it easier than ever to achieve this goal with the Network Load Balancing and Clustering services provided in Windows Server 2003.

Objectives

Microsoft has the following objectives for the high availability portion of the "Planning, Implementing, and Maintaining Server Availability" unit:

Plan services for high availability.

- **Plan a high availability solution that uses clustering services.**
- **Plan a high availability solution that uses network load balancing.**
- High availability solutions are becoming more popular and more critical in today's Internet-based economy. It is important to understand and be able to work with the highly available solutions provided with Windows Server 2003.

Implement a cluster server.

- After finishing your plan for a high availability cluster solution, you need to successfully implement and manage it.

Monitor network load balancing. Tools might include the Network Load Balancing Monitor Microsoft Management Console (MMC) snap-in and the WLBS cluster control utility.

- Network load balancing (NLB) typically can be counted on to function with little to no administrative action required. However, you do need to perform routine monitoring on your NLB clusters to ensure that they are operating properly. Windows Server 2003 contains several useful utilities that you can use to monitor NLB.

Recover from cluster node failure.

- Clusters are implemented to minimize the adverse effects of failure. The capability to quickly and effectively recover from the failure of one or more cluster nodes is a key part of the overall high availability solution.

Outline

Study Strategies

- For many people, the concept of high availability servers is a new one. It is important to get a good grasp of the concepts presented in this chapter, including high availability, clustering, network load balancing, failover, and failback.
- Ensure that you understand the specific requirements, benefits, and costs associated with high availability solutions that use clustering or network load balancing.
- Get your hands dirty. The Step by Steps throughout this book provide plenty of directions and exercises, but you should go beyond these examples and create some of your own. If you can, experiment with each of the topics we discuss in this chapter to see how they work and why you would use each one.

Introduction

What's all the buzz about high availability? Why is everyone so intent on achieving the Utopia of high server availability: five nines? It really all comes down to one thing: economics. The economics of today's "always on, always in use" world demand that critical services and servers be available 100% of the time. In the absence of perfection, which no one has delivered yet, the bar for high availability solutions has been set at five nines: 99.999% uptime. What exactly does that equate to, though?

Five nines availability enables you to have critical services offline for 5.25 minutes per year! That's an unbelievably low number, no matter how you look at it. But that's the goal of high availability solutions. Of course, 5 minutes per year is barely enough time to apply a hot fix, much less a service pack. The answer to this problem: high availability server solutions.

When discussing high availability solutions, you can look at the problem in two distinctly different ways: from hardware and software perspectives. Windows Server 2003 provides you with two types of software-based high availability: clustering and network load balancing. Each is discussed in detail in the following sections.

Designing for High Availability

When it comes to creating high availability solutions, your design plans should not start at the operating system itself—in this case, Windows Server 2003 SP1 or R2. To create true high availability server solutions, you need to start with your hardware first. An important first step in creating high availability solutions is purchasing and using high-quality hardware components from reputable first-tier vendors such as IBM or HP. You also need to consider other issues, such as power supply, power conditioning, and environmental conditioning.

Uninterruptible Power Supplies

You might look silly if you go through all the work to create and implement a high availability solution only to have it crippled by a power failure. *Uninterruptible power supplies (UPSs)* can help prevent this problem. Not only do UPSs provide a backup source of power during power outage, but many of the better UPSs also provide *power conditioning*. Power conditioning extends the life of sensitive electronic components by removing voltage spikes, voltage dips (brownouts), and line noise.

During a power outage, UPSs automatically switch over to battery mode, providing additional time to safely—and gracefully—shut down servers and other infrastructure hardware, such as switches, routers, and firewalls. It is important to closely follow the recommendations of the UPS manufacturer when connecting devices to the UPS so that it is not overloaded during a power outage condition, resulting in reduced battery operation time. Many UPS manufacturers also provide software that can be installed on critical servers to monitor the battery condition in the UPS and perform actions such as run scripts or shut down servers as the battery capacity decreases. This graceful securing of servers greatly increases your chances of recovering quickly from the casualty situation.

Fault-Tolerant Storage Systems

Storage systems—hard drives, in common vernacular—are a key part of any high availability system. Fault-tolerant disk systems can be created in one of two basic ways: either by using third-party hardware solutions or by using dynamic disks within Windows Server 2003. Either way, you should create a Redundant Array of Inexpensive Disks (RAID). Several variations on RAID exist, as discussed in the following paragraphs.

The basic premise of a RAID array is that you can use two or more relatively inexpensive hard drives to create a robust and redundant storage system that can withstand the failure of a disk and still provide disk access. Many hard drives used in RAID arrays are hot-swappable, meaning that they can be pulled and inserted into a server while it remains powered on. As you might expect, this feature can greatly increase server and service uptime by enabling you to replace the failed member of an array without having to shut down the server first.

Although they are not all-inclusive, the following are two of the more common forms of RAID in use today:

- **RAID-1**—Data is written to one disk and then mirrored in its entirety to the second disk. RAID-1 mirror sets use two identical disks, called mirror volumes. The disks should be the same size. If one disk fails, the system can continue to operate using the remaining disk. Depending on which disk fails, you might experience startup problems and might need to use a boot disk containing an edited version of the `boot.ini` file that points toward the remaining mirror disk. No parity information is created when using a mirror set. RAID-1 sets are commonly used for the system/boot partition in servers.
- **RAID-5**—The entire block of data is written to one data disk. The parity information for data blocks in the same rank is written to the parity disk. RAID-5 requires at least three hard drives of equal size to implement. The total capacity of a RAID-5 array is equal to $(N-1) \times C$, where N is the total number of disks and C is the capacity of one disk.

Figure 10.1 depicts a RAID-1 array graphically.

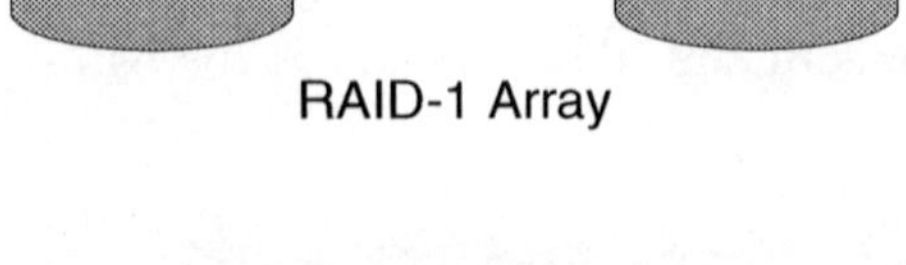

FIGURE 10.1 The RAID-1 array offers the least amount of fault tolerance.

Figure 10.2 depicts a RAID-5 array graphically.

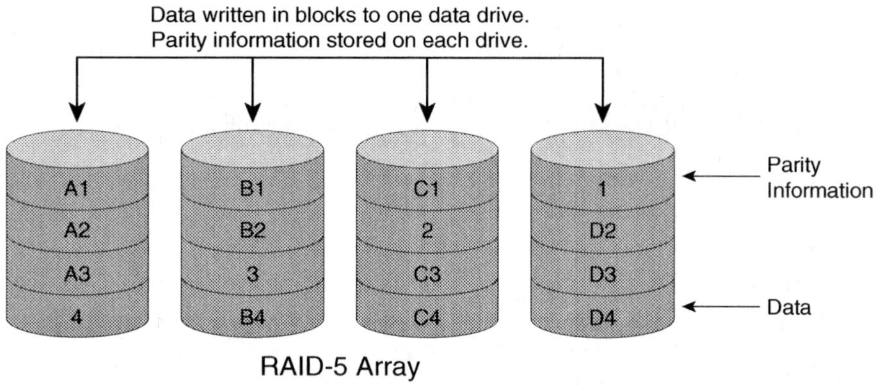

FIGURE 10.2 The RAID-5 array creates a higher level of fault tolerance because of the parity stripe.

When deciding between using hardware-based RAID and software-based RAID (Windows Server 2003), you should give serious consideration to using hardware-based solutions. When you use a hardware-based RAID solution, you gain decreased headaches as well as increased performance and configurability over software-based RAID. The general problem with software-based (Windows-based) RAID solutions is that you must first reinstall and restore the operating system before you can ever get to restoring data from the RAID set—something you won't have to face if using hardware-based RAID solutions. In addition, when you remove the responsibility for managing the RAID array from Windows Server 2003, the operating system will perform better overall. Also, hardware-based RAID arrays are not limited by the available options and requirements of Windows Server 2003. This gives you greater design flexibility and easier recovery if disaster strikes.

Redundant Networking Infrastructure

You should consider making your network infrastructure fault-tolerant. This is usually accomplished by creating redundant routes for traffic to travel over. Also, you can use load-balanced or standby infrastructure hardware. Although load balancing and failover are discussed in great detail later in this chapter, a brief description is suitable here. Load-balanced devices divide the total load between two or more devices: If one fails, the remaining "living" devices pick up the load and distribute it evenly among themselves. Standby, or failover, devices kick into action after the primary device experiences a failure condition; thus, the load is transferred to a new device entirely.

Many infrastructure devices have been designed with redundancy in mind. Vendors such as Cisco have been designing and perfecting redundancy features in their network infrastructure devices for years now. Options such as dual or even triple power supplies and the capability to configure redundancy via the Internetwork Operating System (IOS) itself ensure that these devices are no longer a single point of failure (SPOF).

Planning High Availability Solutions

As briefly mentioned previously, Windows Server 2003 provides support for two different types of high availability, or clustering, technologies. Of course, the capability to implement high availability solutions does not come without a price. In the case of Windows Server 2003, you must be using either the Enterprise or Datacenter Server versions to have this capability available to you. In this section we first examine the types of clustering provided in Windows Server 2003. Next, we present key terms and operational modes that will be of importance to you as you plan and implement clustering solutions. Finally, we implement and manage clusters and network load balancing using Windows Server 2003.

High Availability Solutions

Clustering is accomplished when you assemble a group of independent servers into one large collective entity that is accessed as if it were a single system. Incoming requests for service can be evenly distributed across multiple cluster members or can be handled by one specific cluster member.

The *Microsoft Cluster Service (MSCS)* in Windows Server 2003 provides high availability fault-tolerant systems through *failover*. When one of the cluster members (nodes) cannot respond to client requests, the remaining cluster members respond by distributing the load among themselves, thus responding to all existing and new connections and requests for service. In this way, clients see little, if any, disruption in the service the cluster provides. Cluster nodes are kept aware of the status of other cluster nodes and their services through the use of *heartbeats*. A heartbeat is used to keep track of the status of each node and also to send updates in the configuration of the cluster. Clustering is most commonly used for database applications such as Exchange Server or SQL Server, file servers, print servers, or network services such as DHCP servers. Windows Server 2003 supports up to eight nodes in a cluster.

Windows Server 2003 also provides *network load balancing (NLB)*, in which all incoming connection requests are distributed using a mathematical algorithm to members of NLB cluster. NLB clustering is best used when clients can connect to any server in the cluster, such as websites, Terminal Services servers, and VPN servers. You can configure the way the client interacts with the NLB cluster as well, such as allowing the client to use multiple NLB cluster members during a single connection (acceptable for websites) or forcing the client to use the same cluster member for the entire connection period (a necessity for VPN and Terminal Services servers). Windows Server 2003 NLB clusters can contain as many as 32 nodes.

NOTE

Combining clustering and network load balancing Although you can use both clustering and NLB in your final design, such as in the case of an e-commerce site that uses NLB for front-end web servers and clustering for back-end SQL servers, you cannot use both technologies on the same server.

Now that we've discussed clustering technologies provided in Windows Server 2003, let's look at some of the key clustering terminology and operational modes.

High Availability Terminology

A good understanding of the following MSCS and NLB clustering terminology is key to successfully implementing and managing any clustered solution. Although the following list of terms is not all-inclusive, it represents some of the more important ones you should understand before attempting to implement any high availability solution.

- **Cluster**—A group of two or more independent servers that operate together and are viewed and accessed as a single resource.
- **Cluster resource**—A network application service, or hardware device (such as network adapters and storage systems) that is defined and managed by the cluster service.
- **Cluster resource group**—The resources contained within a cluster. Cluster resource groups are used as failover units within a cluster; when a cluster resource group fails and the cluster service cannot automatically restart it, the entire cluster resource group is placed in an offline status and failed over to another node.
- **Cluster virtual server**—A cluster resource group that has a network name and IP address assigned to it. Cluster virtual servers are thus accessible by their NetBIOS name, DNS name, and IP address.
- **Convergence**—The process by which NLB clustering hosts determine a new, stable state among themselves and elect a new default host after the failure of one or more cluster nodes. During convergence, the total load on the NLB cluster is redistributed among all cluster nodes that share traffic handling on specific ports, as determined by their port rules.
- **Heartbeat**—A network communication sent among individual cluster nodes at intervals of no more than 500ms, used to determine the status of all cluster nodes.
- **Failback**—The process of a cluster group moving back to the preferred node after the preferred node has resumed cluster membership. For failback to occur, it must be configured for the cluster group, including the failback threshold and selection of the preferred node.

- **Failover**—The process of a cluster group moving from the currently active node to another still functioning node in the cluster group. Failover typically occurs when the active node becomes unresponsive for any reason and cannot be recovered within the configured failure threshold.
- **Node**—An individual server within a cluster.
- **Quorum disk**—The disk drive that contains the definitive cluster-configuration data. Clustering with MSCS requires the use of a quorum disk and requires continuous access to the data contained within the quorum disk. The quorum disk contains vital data about the nodes participating in the cluster, the applications and services defined within the cluster resource group, and the status of each node and cluster resource. The quorum disk is typically located on a shared storage device, either a Fibre Channel storage area network (SAN) or a shared SCSI array.

EXAM ALERT

Clustering terminology Although you must understand the clustering terms presented here to be able to implement and support cluster solutions, you should not expect to be directly tested on them on exam day.

With the discussion of key clustering terminology now behind us, we can safely move forward and begin to plan for and implement high availability solutions. Because network load balancing clusters are the simpler of the two types to understand, deploy, and support, we start our discussion with them.

Planning and Implementing NLB Clusters

Objective:

Plan services for high availability.

- Plan a high availability solution that uses network load balancing.

Objective:

Implement a cluster server.

As discussed previously, the NLB cluster is most often used to create distributed fault-tolerant solutions for applications such as websites, VPN servers, and Terminal Services servers. NLB clusters consist of between 2 and 32 nodes, each of which must contain the exact same applications and content. Because NLB clusters do not replicate content among the member nodes, using applications that require users to save data locally on the node is not a good idea. In this instance, you would need to implement a clustered server environment on the back end, such as an SQL Server cluster.

TIP

Replicating information across NLB clusters Although it is beyond the capabilities of the normal NLB service, Application Center 2000 can be used to create NLB clusters that replicate from a master node to all other member nodes, thus ensuring that changes made to the master node are kept current on all other member nodes.

The most critical part of deploying an NLB cluster is determining the operational mode that is to be used and also the port rules that will be required. To plan for these items, you must know and understand what types of applications or services will be running on the NLB cluster. Certain applications, such as an e-commerce application, make extensive use of cookies during and between client connections. If the NLB cluster is configured to allow multiple requests during the same session to be sent to more than one server, the client could experience application failures because the expected cookie would be missing from the other NLB cluster members. We discuss port rules, filtering mode, affinity, and cluster operation modes in the following sections. When you understand these key NLB concepts, you will be ready to start implementing an NLB clustered solution in your organization.

Port Rules

When a network load balancing cluster is created, port rules are used to determine what types of traffic are to be load-balanced across the cluster nodes. Within the port rule is the additional option to configure *port rule filtering*, which determines how the traffic will be load-balanced across each of the cluster nodes.

In an NLB cluster, every cluster node can answer for the cluster's IP address; thus, every cluster node receives all inbound traffic by default. When each node receives the inbound request, it either responds to the requesting client or drops the packet if the client has an existing session in progress with another node. If no port rule is configured to specifically define how traffic on the specific port is to be handled, the request is passed off to the cluster node with the lowest configured priority. This can result in decreased performance by the whole NLB cluster if the traffic is not meant to be or cannot be load-balanced.

Port rules enable you to change this behavior in a deliberate and controlled fashion. Think of port rules as the network load balancing equivalent of a firewall rule set. When you configure port rules to allow traffic on the specific ports you require to reach the NLB cluster and configure an additional rule to drop all packets that do not meet any other port rules, you can greatly improve the performance of the NLB cluster by permitting it to drop all packets that are not allowed to be load-balanced. From an administrative and security standpoint, port rules allow for easier monitoring of the server because of the limited number of ports that must be monitored.

Filtering Mode and Affinity

As mentioned briefly in the previous section, you can configure how NLB clusters load-balance traffic across cluster nodes; this action is referred to as *filtering*. By configuring filtering, you can specify whether only one node or multiple nodes within the NLB cluster are allowed to respond to multiple requests from the same client during a single session (connection).

The three filtering modes are as follows:

- **Single Host**—When this filtering mode is configured, all traffic that meets the port rule criteria is sent to a specific cluster node. The Single Host filter might be used in a website that has only one SSL server; thus, the port rule for TCP port 443 would specify that all traffic on this port must be directed to that one node.
- **Disable Port Range**—This filtering mode instructs the cluster nodes to ignore and drop all traffic on the configured ports without any further action. This type of filtering can be used to prevent ports and port ranges from being load-balanced.
- **Multiple Host**—The default filtering method, Multiple Host, specifies that all active nodes in the cluster are allowed to handle traffic. When Multiple Host filtering is enabled, the host affinity must be configured. *Affinity* determines how clients interact with the cluster nodes and varies depending on the requirements of the applications that the cluster is providing. Three types of affinities can be configured as follows:
    - **None**—This affinity type sends an inbound client request to all nodes within the cluster. This type of affinity results in increased speed but is suitable only for providing static content to clients, such as static websites and FTP downloads. Typically, no cookies are generated by the applications running on the clusters that are configured for this type of affinity.
    - **Class C**—This affinity type causes all inbound client requests from a particular Class C address space to a specific cluster node. This type of affinity allows a user's state to be maintained but can be overloaded or fooled if all client requests are passed through a single firewall or proxy server.
    - **Single**—This affinity type maintains all client requests on the same node for the duration of the session (connection). This type of affinity provides the best support for maintaining user state data and is often used when applications are running on the cluster that generates cookies.

EXAM ALERT

Affinity During the exam, pay attention to questions dealing with web applications that use cookies and other means of maintaining user session state. These are your keys to determining the required affinity type.

NLB Cluster Operation Mode

The mathematical algorithm used by network load balancing sends inbound traffic to every host in the NLB cluster. The inbound client requests can be distributed to the NLB cluster nodes through one of two methods: *unicast* or *multicast*. Although both methods send the inbound client requests to all hosts by sending them to the media access control (MAC) address of the cluster, they go about it in different ways.

When you use the *unicast* method, all cluster nodes share an identical unicast MAC address. To do so, NLB overwrites the original MAC address of the cluster network adapter with the unicast MAC address that is assigned to all the cluster nodes. When you use the *multicast* method, each cluster node retains its original MAC address of the cluster network adapter. The cluster network adapter is then assigned an additional multicast MAC address, which all the nodes in the cluster share. Inbound client requests can then be sent to all cluster nodes by using the multicast MAC address.

The unicast method is usually preferred for NLB clusters unless each cluster node has only one network adapter installed in it. Recall that in any clustering arrangement, all nodes must be capable of communicating not only with the clients, but also among themselves. Recall that NLB modifies the MAC address of the cluster network adapter when unicast is used; thus, the cluster nodes cannot communicate among themselves. If only one network adapter is installed in each cluster node, you need to use the multicast method.

Switch Port Flooding

As discussed previously, the mathematical algorithm used by network load balancing sends inbound traffic to every host in the NLB cluster. It does so by preventing the switch that the NLB cluster nodes are attached to from ever associating the NLB cluster's MAC address with a specific port on the switch. However, this leads to the unwanted side effect of switch port flooding, where the switch floods all its ports with all packets inbound to the NLB cluster.

Switch port flooding is both a waste of valuable network resources and a nuisance to you when implementing NLB clusters. In Windows 2000, you need to place all nodes of an NLB cluster on a dedicated switch or on a dedicated VLAN within the switch to get around the problems of switch port flooding. A new feature in Windows Server 2003, however, prevents switch port flooding from occurring.

Internet Group Management Protocol (IGMP) support has been provided in Windows Server 2003 network load balancing to prevent flooding from occurring on switch ports that do not have an NLB cluster node attached to them. With this feature, non-NLB cluster nodes do not ever see inbound traffic that is intended for the NLB cluster. At the same time, all NLB cluster nodes continue to receive all inbound traffic, thus meeting the requirements of the NLB algorithm. IGMP support is available only when multicast mode is configured for the NLB cluster—which presents its own set of benefits and drawbacks. As an alternative, you can use the dedicated switch or VLAN methods to eliminate switch port flooding with the NLB cluster in unicast mode; unicast mode does not present the same drawbacks associated with multicast mode.

At this point, you are ready to move forward and create an NLB cluster. After creating your NLB cluster, you can then join additional cluster nodes to it and begin managing the NLB cluster.

Creating an NLB Cluster

By now, you've received a good introduction to network load balancing and some of its key parts. However, you still might not have a good idea of exactly what an NLB cluster solution might look like. Figure 10.3 shows a four-node NLB cluster arrangement.

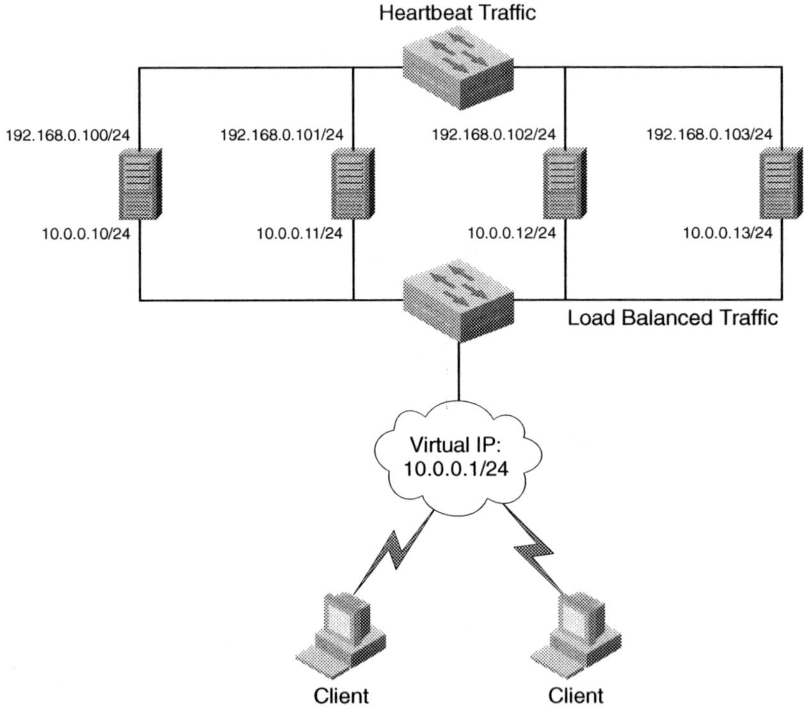

FIGURE 10.3 This four-node NLB cluster provides high availability websites.

Any good implementation needs a good plan. To successfully implement your NLB cluster, you need to identify the key parameters that require you to have information ready ahead of time. They are broken down into two major parts: *cluster parameters* and *cluster host parameters*. We examine each in turn in the following paragraphs.

The following parameters are of interest when planning for the entire cluster:

- **Cluster virtual IP address**—You must determine the virtual IP (VIP) address that will be assigned to represent the entire cluster. This IP address must be in the same IP subnet as the IP addresses assigned to the cluster network adapters on all cluster hosts. Also, these IP addresses should be in different IP subnets than the IP addresses chosen for the administrative IP addresses. In the example shown in Figure 10.3, the cluster VIP is 10.0.0.1/24, whereas the individual cluster network adapter IP addresses for the four nodes are 10.0.0.10/24 10.0.0.13/24.

- **Cluster FQDN**—A fully qualified domain name (FQDN) must be assigned to the cluster, just as with any host on the network. This FQDN will be registered in DNS and allow clients to access the cluster as one unit. You also need to designate an FQDN for each application and service that you are running on the cluster because clients will access their FQDNs.
- **Cluster operation mode**—You must choose between unicast or multicast mode for distributing inbound client requests, as discussed previously in the "NLB Cluster Operation Mode" section.
- **Cluster remote control settings**—By default, remote administration of the cluster using `nlb.exe` is disabled. To maintain the highest level of security for your NLB cluster, you should specify that all remote administration is to be performed using the Network Load Balancing Manager. Also, you should specify that all cluster administration must be done only from specified computers that are within your trusted and secured internal network, to prevent compromise of cluster administrative control.

The following parameters are of interest when planning for each of the cluster nodes:

- **Cluster host priority**—Each cluster node is identified by a unique host priority number ranging from 1 to 32. During cluster convergence, the remaining cluster node with the lowest numeric host priority triggers the end of convergence and becomes the default host. No two cluster nodes can have the same host priority assignment. It's worth mentioning that you have a maximum of 32 nodes in your cluster and that the priority of each node acts as a "ranking" system, indicating the order in which you want the cluster nodes to become the default host during failure situations.
- **Administrative (private) IP address**—These IP addresses are assigned to each non-load-balanced network adapter and should all be in the same IP subnet. These IP addresses should also be in a different IP subnet than the IP addresses chosen for the cluster IP addresses so that load-balanced and administrative traffic is completely separated, thus providing increased security for the administrative traffic.
- **Cluster (public) IP address**—These IP addresses are assigned to each cluster network adapter and must be in the same IP subnet as the cluster VIP. These IP addresses should also be in a different IP subnet than the IP addresses chosen for the administrative IP addresses.
- **Initial host state**—A Windows Server 2003 server configured to be an NLB cluster node starts the NLB service very early in the operating system startup process and joins the NLB cluster. If this occurs before clustered services and applications are started and

available on the cluster node, clients might experience service disruptions. You need to specify whether cluster nodes will automatically start the NLB service and join the NLB cluster upon operating system load or whether the NLB service will be manually started at some later time.

With the required information in hand, you are now ready to create an NLB cluster and join additional nodes to the cluster. Step by Step 10.1 outlines the steps required to create a new NLB cluster.

NOTE

Using two network adapters is best When implementing either an NLB solution or a MSCS cluster, you should have two network adapters installed in each cluster node. All the discussion and examples that follow assume that you have two network adapters installed in your cluster nodes. In addition, all network adapters that are in use should be (preferably) identical in make and model (or at least the same for all public adapters and the same for all private adapters); this results in easier maintenance and upkeep because you have only one set of drivers to keep up-to-date. If you cannot use identical network adapters across the cluster, you should use the same speed adapters (such as 10/100 or 100/1000), to minimize potential bottlenecks.

STEP BY STEP

10.1 Creating a New NLB Cluster

1. Open the Network Connections window by selecting Start, Settings, Network Connections. The Network Connections window opens, displaying all configured connections on the computer.
2. Double-click the network adapter that you will be using as the administrative (private) network adapter to open the network adapter Status dialog box.
3. Click the Properties button to open the dialog box in Figure 10.4.
4. On the General tab, select Internet Protocol (TCP/IP) and then click Properties. The Internet Protocol (TCP/IP) Properties dialog box opens, as shown in Figure 10.5.
5. Enter the IP address and subnet mask to be used for the administrative interface. In most cases, these interfaces are connected only to each other, as in Figure 10.3, and thus do not require a default gateway or DNS server. You can configure this information if required, however.
6. Click Close to close the Local Area Connection Properties dialog box.

NOTE

Configuring TCP/IP properties If you need a refresher on configuring TCP/IP properties, check out the *70-291 Exam Prep: Implementing, Managing, and Maintaining a Microsoft Windows Server 2003 Network Infrastructure* (Que Publishing, 2006; ISBN 0789736497).

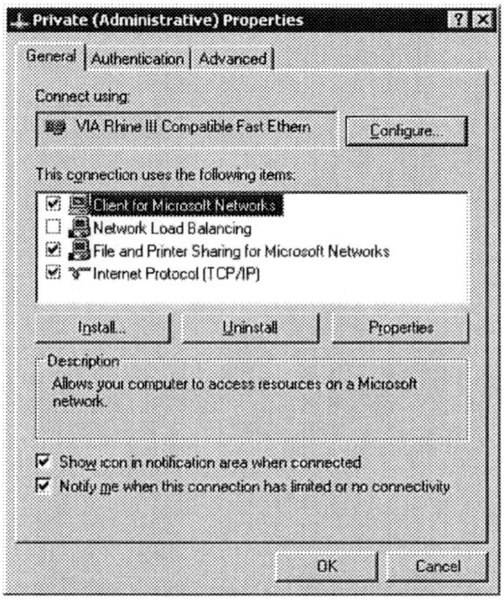

FIGURE 10.4 The network adapter dialog box enables you to configure network connection properties.

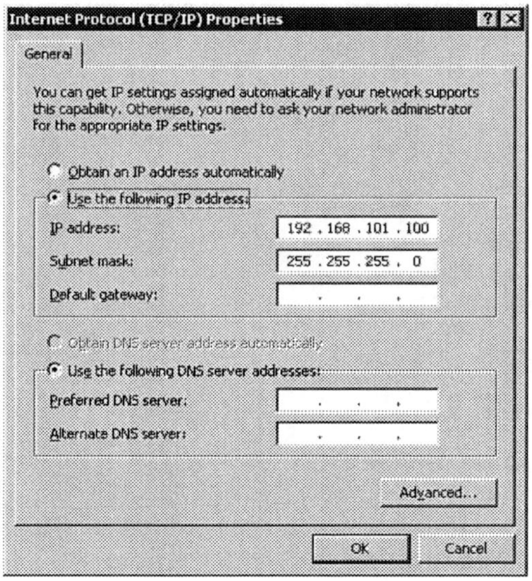

FIGURE 10.5 The Internet Protocol (TCP/IP) Properties dialog box enables you to configure TCP/IP settings for a network connection.

7. Configure the load-balancing adapter, if not already done, by performing steps 2–6 again for the load-balancing adapter. Recall that this network adapter will typically be on a different subnet than the administrative adapter.

8. Open the Network Load Balancing Manager, shown in Figure 10.6, by selecting Start, Programs, Administrative Tools, Network Load Balancing Manager.

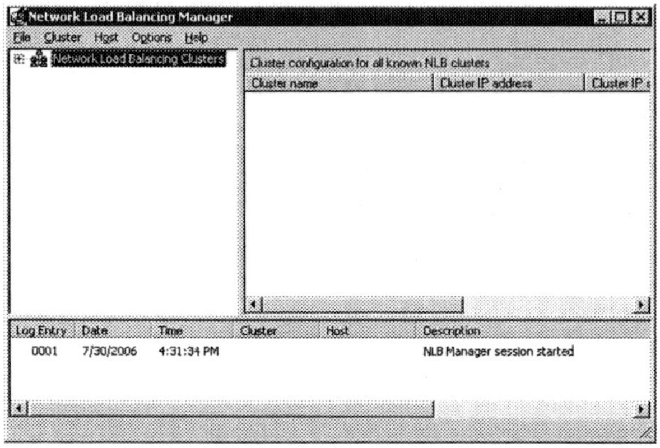

FIGURE 10.6 The Network Load Balancing Manager enables you to perform all administrative actions on NLB clusters.

9. Right-click Network Load Balancing Clusters and select New Cluster from the context menu. The Cluster Parameters dialog box appears, as shown in Figure 10.7.

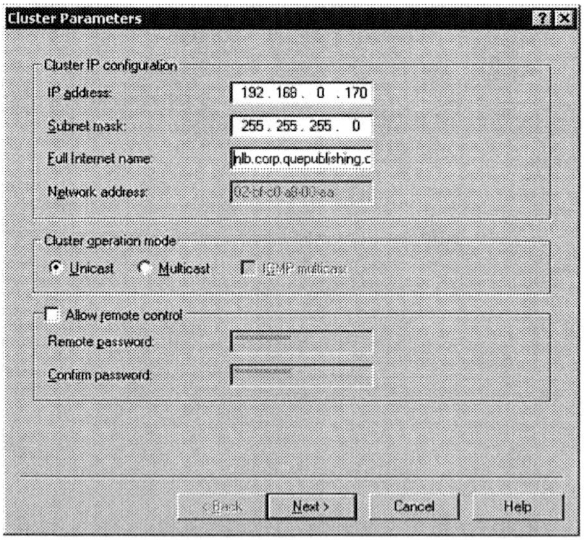

FIGURE 10.7 The Cluster Parameters dialog box enables you to create a new NLB cluster.

10. Enter the cluster's IP address, subnet mask, and cluster domain name. The IP address configured here is the cluster's virtual IP (VIP) address. Configure the cluster for unicast or multicast as desired. You can also configure IGMP multicast and remote control as desired. Click Next to continue.

11. In the Cluster IP Addresses dialog box, shown in Figure 10.8, enter any additional virtual IP addresses using the Add button. Click Next when you are ready to continue.

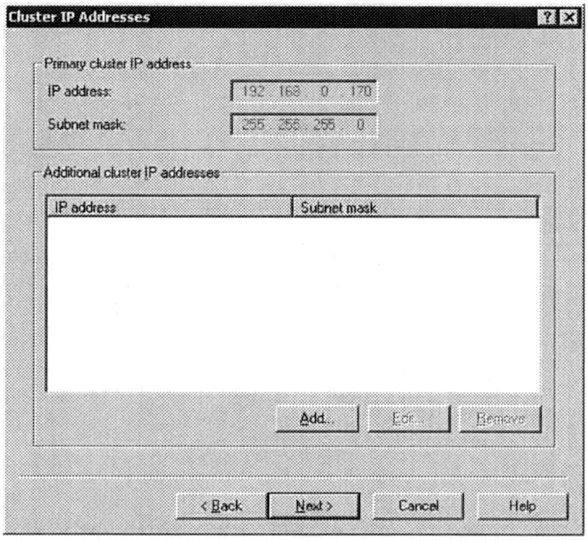

FIGURE 10.8 You can enter multiple virtual IP addresses as required by your services and applications.

12. In the Port Rules dialog box, shown in Figure 10.9, configure any port rules that are appropriate for your NLB cluster installation. Clicking the Add button opens the Add/Edit Port Rule dialog box, shown in Figure 10.10.

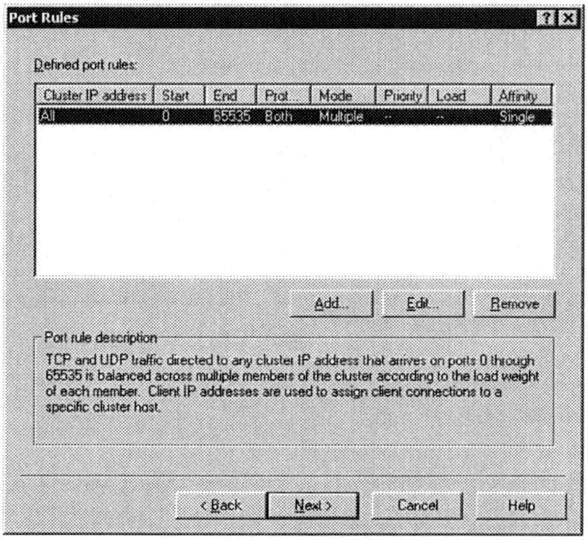

FIGURE 10.9 Port rules are used to quickly filter traffic from being load-balanced by the NLB cluster.

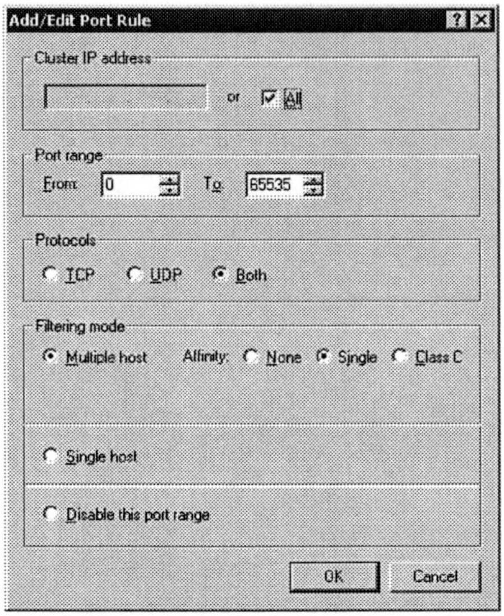

FIGURE 10.10 You can use port rules to allow or disallow traffic types and configure how the traffic is to be load-balanced.

13. Configure your port rules as discussed previously in the "Port Rules" and "NLB Cluster Operation Mode" sections of this chapter. Click OK to accept the new port rule. Click Next to continue creating the NLB cluster.

14. In the Connect dialog box, shown in Figure 10.11, type the name of the first cluster node and click the Connect button. After a brief period, all available network adapters are displayed in the bottom half of the dialog box. Select the network adapter that is to be used for load balancing and click Next to continue.

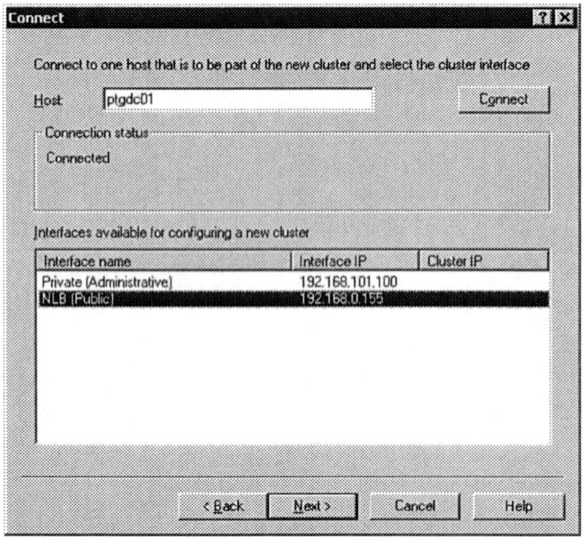

FIGURE 10.11 You need to select the proper network adapter to use as the load-balancing adapter.

15. In the Host Parameters dialog box, shown in Figure 10.12, configure the host priority, cluster node dedicated IP address and subnet mask, and the initial state of the cluster node. The dedicated IP address is that of the cluster network adapter itself; it must be unique and in the same subnet as the cluster VIP. After entering all required information, click Finish to complete the NLB cluster creation process.

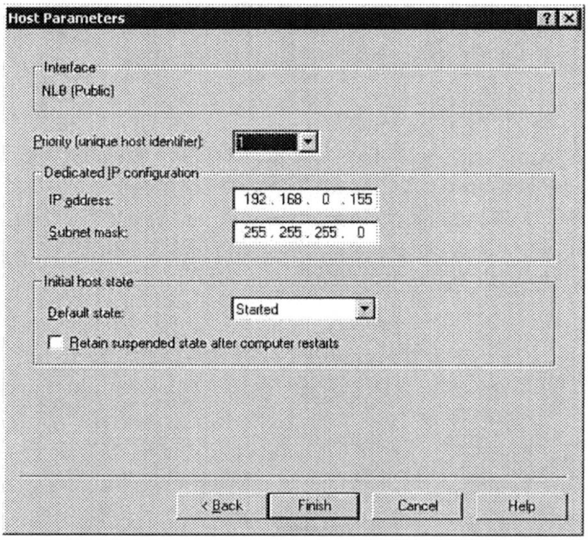

FIGURE 10.12 The Host Parameters dialog box contains critical configuration items that identify the specific cluster node.

16. After a brief period of time, you can see the newly created and fully converged cluster displayed in the Network Load Balancing Manager, as shown in Figure 10.13.

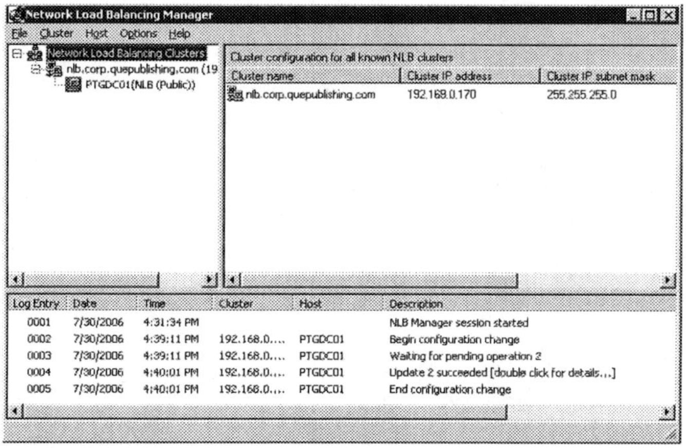

FIGURE 10.13 After a brief delay, the newly created NLB cluster shows up and is fully converged.

Of course, after you have created the NLB cluster, you need to add one or more cluster nodes to it. Step by Step 10.2 outlines the required steps to add nodes to the NLB cluster.

STEP BY STEP

10.2 Adding Cluster Nodes to the NLB Cluster

1. From the cluster node where the NLB cluster was created, open the Network Load Balancing Manager.
2. If the Network Load Balancing Manager does not display the cluster, connect to it by right-clicking Network Load Balancing Clusters and select Connect to Existing from the context menu.
3. Right-click the NLB cluster and select Add Host to Cluster from the context menu.
4. In the Connect dialog box, shown in Figure 10.14, type the name of the additional cluster node and click the Connect button. After a brief period, all available network adapters are displayed in the bottom half of the dialog box. Select the network adapter that is to be used for load balancing and click Next to continue.

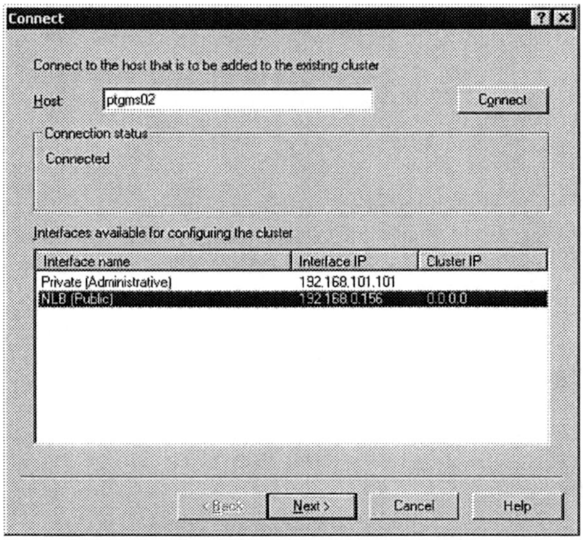

FIGURE 10.14 Ensure that you select the proper network adapter to use as the load-balancing adapter.

5. In the Host Parameters dialog box, shown in Figure 10.15, configure the host priority, the cluster node dedicated IP address and subnet mask, and the initial state of the cluster node. The dedicated IP address is that of the cluster network adapter itself; it must be unique and in the same subnet as the cluster VIP. After entering all required information, click Finish to complete the NLB cluster-creation process.
6. After a brief period of time, you can see the updated and fully converged cluster displayed in the Network Load Balancing Manager, as shown in Figure 10.16.

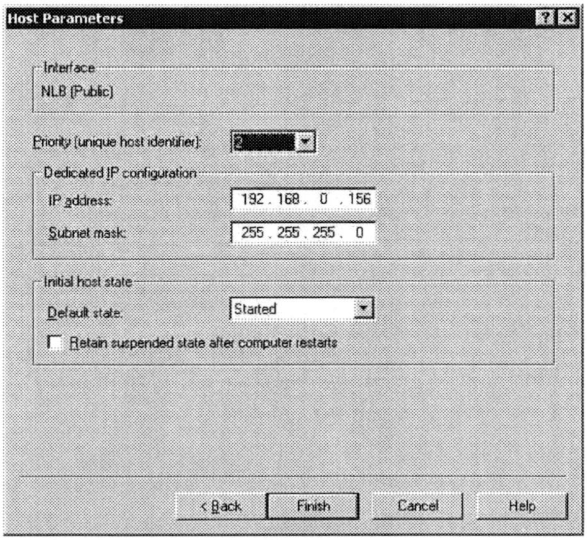

FIGURE 10.15 The Host Parameters dialog box contains critical configuration items that identify the specific cluster node.

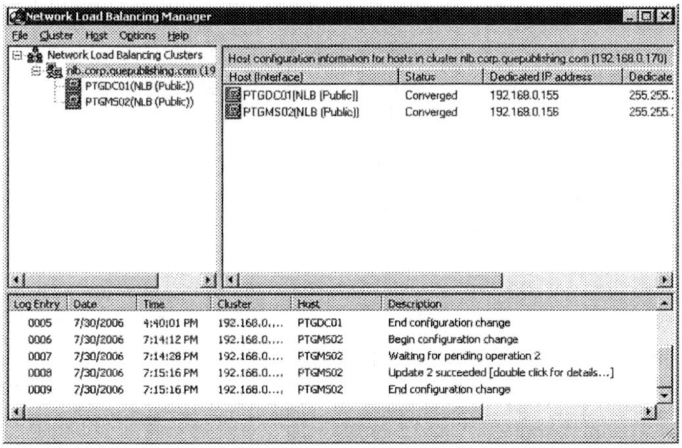

FIGURE 10.16 After a brief delay, the updated NLB cluster is fully converged.

NOTE

Using the Network Load Balancing Manager Although it is possible to configure NLB settings directly on a network adapter using its Properties dialog box, you should not do so. The advantages to using the NLB Manager include not having to manually duplicate settings among all hosts in the cluster. You also avoid the potential for problems and unpredictable results that often occur when attempting to manage NLB settings manually.

With the discussion of creating NLB clusters behind us, we now move forward and examine MSCS clusters—commonly just referred to as *clusters*.

Planning and Implementing MSCS Clusters

Objective:

Plan services for high availability.

- Plan a high availability solution that uses clustering services.

Objective:

Implement a cluster server.

I made the statement earlier in this chapter that NLB clusters were the "simpler of the two types to understand, deploy, and support." This is very much a true statement. As you saw, NLB clusters require no special hardware. In fact, the only real additional requirement above meeting those to install Windows Server 2003 is that each NLB cluster should have two network adapters installed. The services and applications installed on the NLB cluster might have additional requirements, but, for the most part, NLB clusters are less expensive and easier to implement and maintain.

However, clustering has its advantages—especially when uninterrupted access to data and services is a "must have." Typical situations in which you can expect to deploy clusters are in support of Exchange Server, SQL Server, file shares, and printer shares—all services that businesses, clients, and users demand 24/7 access to.

So what's the difference between clustering and network load balancing. As you saw previously in Figure 10.3, NLB uses a group of between 2 and 32 servers to distribute inbound requests among them in a fashion that permits the maximum amount of loading with the minimum amount of downtime. Each NLB cluster node contains an exact copy of the static and dynamic content that every other NLB cluster node has; in this way, it doesn't matter which NLB cluster node receives the inbound request, except in the case of host affinity where cookies are involved. The NLB cluster nodes use heartbeats to keep aware of the status of all nodes.

Clustering, on the other hand, uses a group of between two and eight servers that all share a common storage device. Recall that a cluster resource is an application, service, or hardware device that is defined and managed by the cluster service. The cluster service (MSCS) monitors these cluster resources to ensure that they are operating properly. When a problem occurs with a cluster resource, MSCS attempts to correct the problem on the same cluster node. If the problem cannot be corrected—such as a service that cannot be successfully restarted—the cluster service fails the resource, takes the cluster group offline, moves it to another cluster node, and restarts the cluster group. MSCS clusters also use heartbeats to determine the operational status of other nodes in the cluster.

Two clustering modes exist:

- **Active/Passive**—One node in the cluster is online providing services. The other nodes in the cluster are online but do not provide any services or applications to clients. If the active node fails, the cluster groups that were running on that node are failed over to the passive node. The passive node then changes its state to active and begins to service client requests. The passive nodes cannot be used for any other purpose during normal operations because they must remain available for a failover situation. All nodes should be configured identically to ensure that when failover occurs, no performance loss is experienced.
- **Active/Active**—One instance of the clustered service or application runs on each node in the cluster. If a failure of a node occurs, that instance is transferred to one of the running nodes. Although this clustering mode enables you to use all cluster nodes to service client requests, it can cause significant performance degradation if the cluster was already operating a very high load at the time of the failure.

You must choose one of three available cluster models when planning for your new cluster. They are discussed in the next section.

Cluster Models

Three distinctly different cluster models exist for configuring your new cluster. You must choose one of the three models at the beginning of your cluster planning because the chosen model dictates the storage requirements of your new cluster. The three models are presented in the following sections in order of increasing complexity—and cost.

Single-Node Cluster

The single-node cluster model, shown in Figure 10.17, has only one cluster node. The cluster node can make use of local storage or an external shared storage device. If local storage is used, the local disk is configured as the cluster storage device. This storage device is known as a *Local Quorum resource*. A Local Quorum resource does not make use of failover and is most commonly used as a way to organize network resources in a single network location for administrative and user convenience. This model is also useful for developing and testing cluster-aware applications.

Despite its limited capabilities, this model offers the administrator some advantages at a relatively low entry cost:

- The cluster service can automatically restart services and applications that might not be capable of automatically restarting themselves after a failure. This capability can be used to increase the reliability of network services and applications.

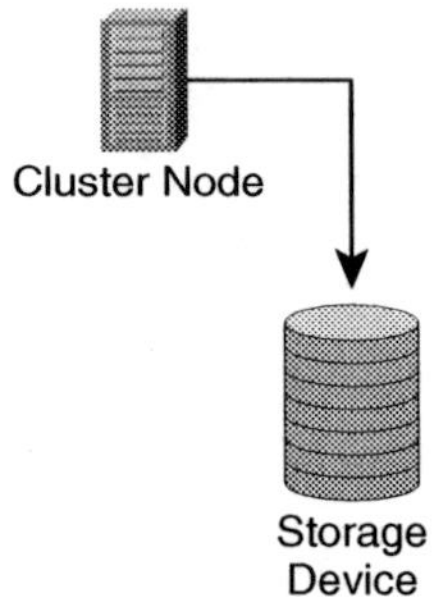

FIGURE 10.17 The single-node cluster can be used to increase service reliability and also to prestage cluster resource groups.

- The single node can be clustered with additional nodes in the future, preserving the resource groups that you have already created. You need to merely join the additional nodes to the cluster and configure the failover and move policies for the resource groups to ready the newly added nodes.

TIP

Creating single-node clusters The New Server Cluster Wizard creates the single-node cluster using a Local Quorum resource by default if the cluster node is not connected to a shared storage device.

Single-Quorum Cluster

The single-quorum cluster model, shown in Figure 10.18, has two or more cluster nodes that are configured so that each node is attached to the shared storage device. All cluster-configuration data is stored on a single-cluster storage device. All cluster nodes have access to the quorum data, but only one cluster node owns the quorum disk resource at any given time.

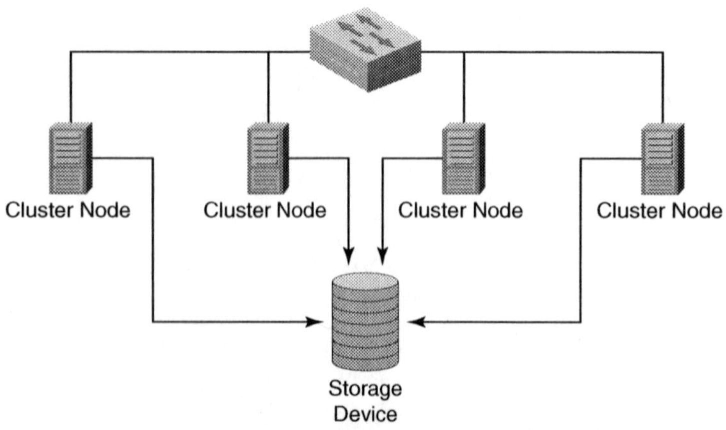

FIGURE 10.18 The single-quorum cluster shares one cluster-storage device among all cluster nodes.

Majority Node Set Cluster

The majority node set cluster model, shown in Figure 10.19, has two or more cluster nodes that are configured in such a way that the nodes might or might not be attached to one or more cluster storage devices. Cluster-configuration data is stored on multiple disks across the entire cluster, and the cluster service is responsible for ensuring that this data is kept consistent across all the disks. All quorum traffic travels in an unencrypted form over the network using server message block (SMB) file shares. This model provides the advantage of being capable of locating cluster nodes in two geographically different locations because they do not all need to be physically attached to the shared cluster storage device.

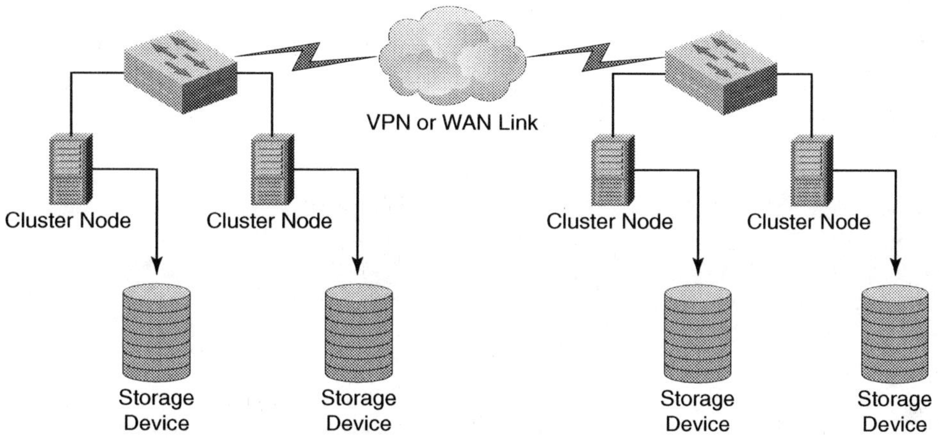

FIGURE 10.19 The majority node set cluster model is a high-level clustering solution that allows for geographically dispersed cluster nodes.

Even if all cluster nodes are not located in the same physical location, they all appear as a single entity to clients. The majority node set cluster model provides the following advantages over the other clustering models:

- Clusters can be created without cluster disks. This capability is useful when you need to make available applications that can fail over but you have another means of replicating data among the storage devices.
- If a local quorum disk becomes unavailable for some reason, it can be taken offline while the rest of the cluster remains available to service client requests.

However, you must abide by some requirements when implementing majority node set clusters to ensure that they are successful:

- A maximum of two sites can be used.
- The cluster nodes at either site must be capable of communicating with each other with less than a 500ms response time for the heartbeat messages to accurately indicate the correct status of the cluster nodes.
- A high-speed, high-quality WAN or VPN link must be established between sites so that the cluster's IP address appears the same to all clients, regardless of their location on the network.
- Only the cluster quorum information is replicated between the cluster storage devices. You must provide a proven effective means of replicating other data between the cluster storage devices.

EXAM ALERT

Don't look for majority node quorums Although this is a new technology in Windows Server 2003, you should not expect to see questions dealing with this technology on the exam. Majority node quorums are high-level hardware-dependent solutions that will be provided as a complete package from an OEM.

The primary disadvantage to this clustering model is that if a certain number of nodes fail, the cluster loses its quorum and it then fails. Table 10.1 shows the maximum number of cluster nodes that can fail before the cluster itself fails.

TABLE 10.1 Number of Failed Nodes to Fail the Majority Node Set Cluster

Number of Nodes in the Cluster	Number of Nodes to Cause the Cluster to Fail
1	0
2	0
3	1
4	1
5	2
6	2
7	3
8	3

As shown in Table 10.1, the majority node cluster set remains operational as long as more than half of the initial cluster nodes remain available.

CAUTION

Using majority node set clusters Majority node set clusters most likely will be the clustering solution of the future because of their capability to geographically separate cluster nodes, thus further increasing the reliability and redundancy of your clustering solution. However, Microsoft currently recommends that you implement majority node set clustering only in specific instances and only with close support from your original equipment manufacturer (OEM), independent software vendor (ISV), or independent hardware vendor (IHV).

Now that you have seen the three cluster models available in Windows Server 2003, you should consider choosing the operation mode that your cluster will use if it is a single-quorum cluster or a majority node set cluster. The next section discusses cluster operation modes.

Cluster Operation Modes

You can choose from four basic cluster operation modes when using a single-quorum cluster or a majority node set cluster. These operation modes are specified by defining the cluster failover policies accordingly, as discussed in the next section. Following are the four basic cluster operation modes:

- **Failover Pair**—This mode of operation is configured by allowing applications to fail over between only two specific cluster nodes. Only the two desired nodes should be placed in the possible owner list for the service of concern.
- **Hot-standby (N+I)**—This mode of operation enables you to reduce expenses and overhead associated with dedicated failover pairs by consolidating the spare node for each failover pair into a single node. This provides a single cluster node that is capable of taking over the applications from any active node in the event of a failover. Hot-standby is often referred to as Active/Passive, as discussed previously in this chapter. Hot-standby is achieved through a combination of using the preferred owners list and using the possible owners list. The preferred node is configured as the node that will run the application or service under normal conditions in the preferred owners list; the spare (hot-standby) node is configured in the possible owners list.
- **Failover Ring**—This mode of operation has each node in the cluster running an instance of the application or service. If a node fails, the application or service on the failed node is moved to the next node in the sequence. The failover ring mode is achieved by using the preferred owner list to define the order of failover for a given resource group. This order should start on a different node on each node in the cluster.

- **Random**—This mode of operation enables the cluster to determine which node will be failed over to randomly. You define the random failover mode by configuring an empty preferred owner list for each resource group.

Now that we've introduced failover, let's examine cluster failover policies; this is the topic of the next section.

Cluster Failover Policies

Although the actual configuration of failover and failback policies is discussed later in this chapter, it is important at this time to discuss them briefly to properly acquaint you with their use and function. Each resource group within the cluster has a prioritized listing of the nodes that are supposed to act as its host.

You can configure failover policies for each resource group to define exactly how each group will behave when a failover occurs. You must configure these three settings:

- **Preferred nodes**—An internal prioritized list indicates available nodes for resource group failovers and failbacks. Ideally, all nodes in the cluster are in this list, in the order of priority you designate.
- **Failover timing**—The resource can be configured for immediate failover if the resource fails, or the cluster service can be configured to try to restart the resource a specified number of times before failover actually occurs. The failover threshold value should be equal to or less than the number of nodes in the cluster.
- **Failback timing**—Failback can be configured to occur as soon as the preferred node is available or during a specified period of the time, such as when peak load is at its lowest, to minimize service disruptions.

Creating a Cluster

Now that you have a good introduction to what clustering is and how it works, you are ready to create the cluster and install the first node in the cluster. As with the NLB cluster, you should do a bit of preparation before actually starting the configuration process, to ensure that your cluster is created successfully.

Any good implementation needs a good plan. To successfully implement your MSCS cluster, you need to determine and document the following pieces of information:

- All services and applications that will be deployed on the cluster.
- Failover and failback policies for each service or application that is to be deployed.
- The quorum model to be used.
- The configuration and operating procedures for the shared storage devices to be used.
- All hardware, to ensure that it is listed on the Hardware Compatibility List (HCL). MSCS clusters have higher hardware requirements than NLB clusters.
- The clustering and administrative IP address and subnet information, including the cluster IP address itself.
- The cluster name. This should be no more than 15 characters long so that it complies with NetBIOS naming requirements.

After you've configured and prepared your servers and shared storage device, you are ready to move forward with the creation of the MSCS cluster. Any installation and configuration required for the shared storage device must be completed in accordance with the manufacturers' or vendors' specifications to ensure successful deployment.

Step by Step 10.3 shows how to create a new MSCS cluster.

NOTE

Creating a cluster Step by Steps 10.3 and 10.4 use an external shared storage device with two Windows Server 2003 R2 computers. You will not be able to complete these procedures if you don't have this type of setup. However, you can follow the steps and create a local quorum cluster (as seen in Figure 10.29) if your server has two or volumes in it, one of which is formatted as NTFS and is not currently being used by anything else.

If you can get your hands on a used SCSI storage array, such as a Dell PowerVault 210S (or equivalent) and two LSI Logic MegaRAID SCSI 320-1 RAID cards (or equivalent), you can re-create this exact clustering configuration yourself. If not, try to create the local quorum cluster so you'll at least have that much hands-on experience with this more high-level topic.

Whatever you end up doing, be sure that you understand the concepts and definitions that we've discussed relating to both NLB and MSCS clustering—that knowledge will be vital when you take your exam!

STEP BY STEP

10.3 Creating a New MSCS Cluster

1. Open the Active Directory Users and Computers console and create a domain user account to be used by the MSCS service. Configure the password to never expire. Later during the cluster creation process, this user account will be given Local Administrator privileges on all cluster nodes and will also be delegated cluster-related user rights in the domain, including the Add Computer Accounts to the Domain user right. Figure 10.20 shows an example of how your summary page might look after creating the domain user account.

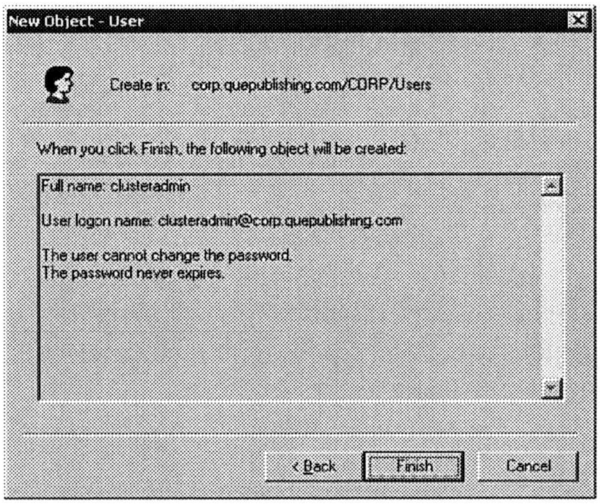

FIGURE 10.20 Ensure that the cluster service domain user account's password is set to never expire.

2. Ensure that the load-balancing and administrative network adapters on the first cluster node are configured correctly, as discussed previously and in Step by Step 10.1.

3. Open the Cluster Administrator by selecting Start, Programs, Administrative Tools, Cluster Administrator. You should be prompted with the Open Connection to Cluster dialog box, shown in Figure 10.21. If not, click File, Open Connection. Select Create New Cluster and click OK to continue.

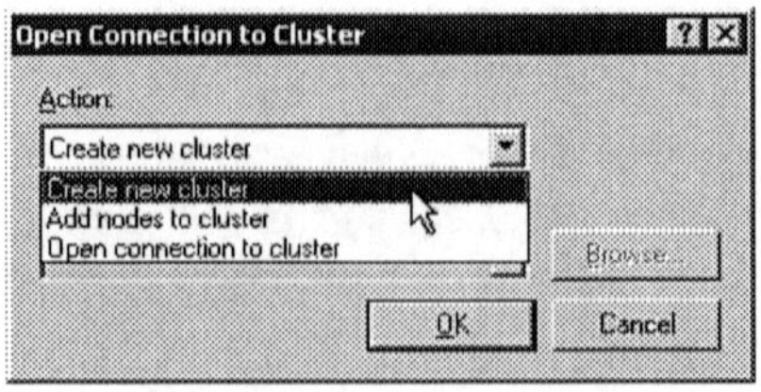

FIGURE 10.21 You need to create a new cluster because you don't already have an existing one to open.

4. Click Next to dismiss the opening dialog box of the New Cluster Creation Wizard.

5. In the Cluster Name and Domain dialog box, shown in Figure 10.22, select the cluster domain from the drop-down list. Enter the cluster name in the space provided. Click Next to continue.

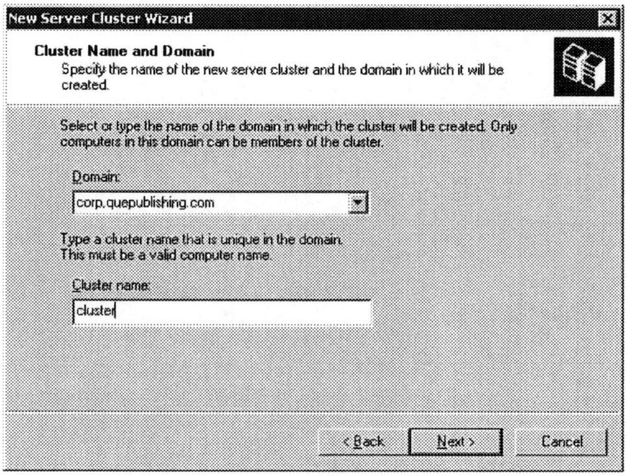

FIGURE 10.22 Only computers that are members of the selected domain can join the cluster.

6. In the Select Computer dialog box, shown in Figure 10.23, select the computer that will be the first node in the new cluster. Click Next to continue.

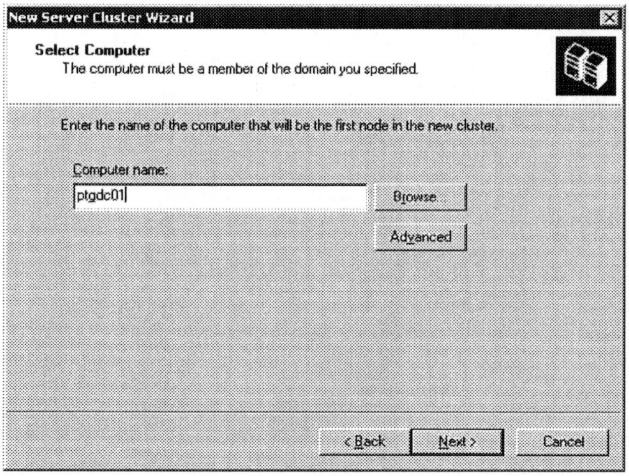

FIGURE 10.23 Enter or browse to the name of the first node of the cluster.

7. The Analyzing Configuration dialog box, shown in Figure 10.24, appears and runs for a short period of time. You can continue with caution as long as no errors or warnings occur. You can examine the log file by clicking the View Log button. The log file is shown in Figure 10.25; notice that a local quorum is being created in this cluster. Click Next to continue when you are done viewing the output.

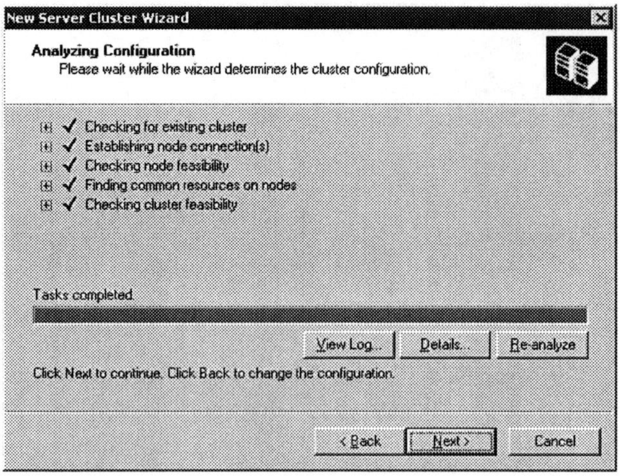

FIGURE 10.24 The Analyzing Cluster process alerts you to any show-stoppers encountered with your selected node.

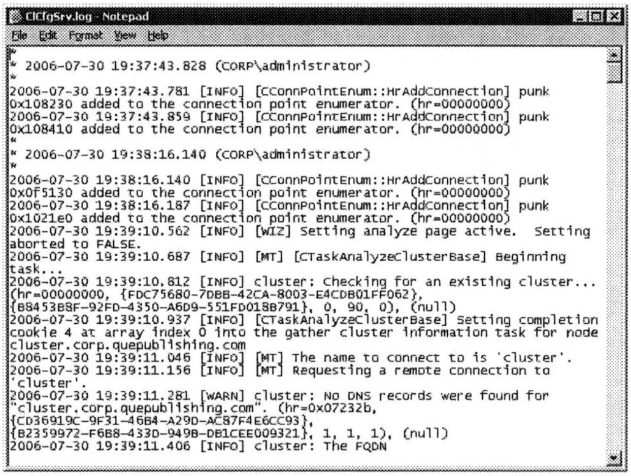

FIGURE 10.25 Because the log file is very detailed, it can yield some useful information.

8. In the IP Address dialog box, shown in Figure 10.26, enter the IP address that is being assigned to the cluster. Click Next to continue.

9. In the Cluster Service Account dialog box, shown in Figure 10.27, enter the proper credentials for the cluster domain user account you created previously. Click Next to continue.

10. In the Proposed Cluster Configuration dialog box, shown in Figure 10.28, you can review the cluster configuration before continuing. Clicking the Quorum button enables you to change the type of quorum being used, as shown in Figure 10.29. When done, click Next to continue.

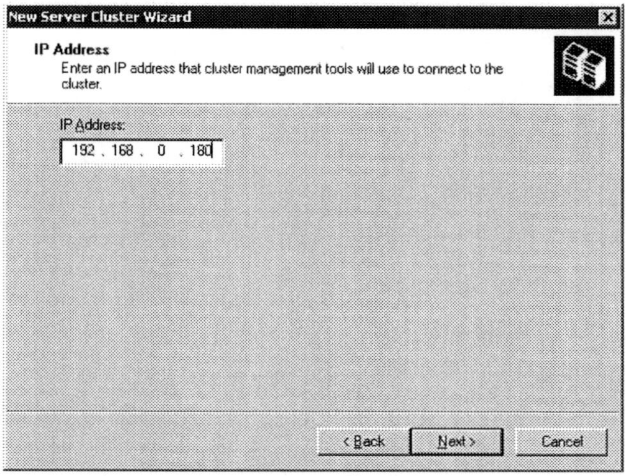

FIGURE 10.26 Ensure that the IP address entered here is correct and in the same IP subnet as the IP addresses configured for the clustering network adapter.

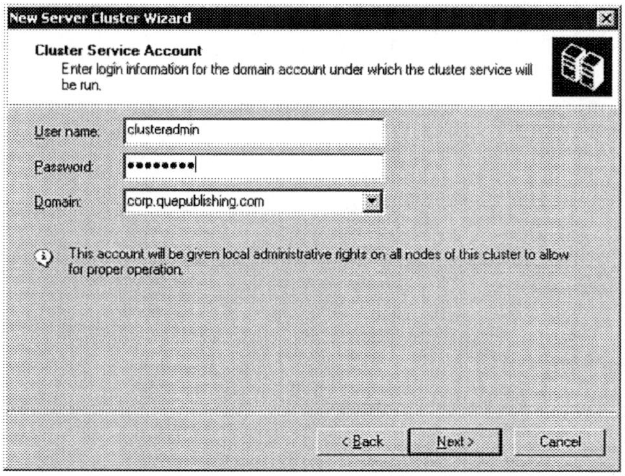

FIGURE 10.27 You need to supply the cluster domain user account name and password to continue the cluster-creation process.

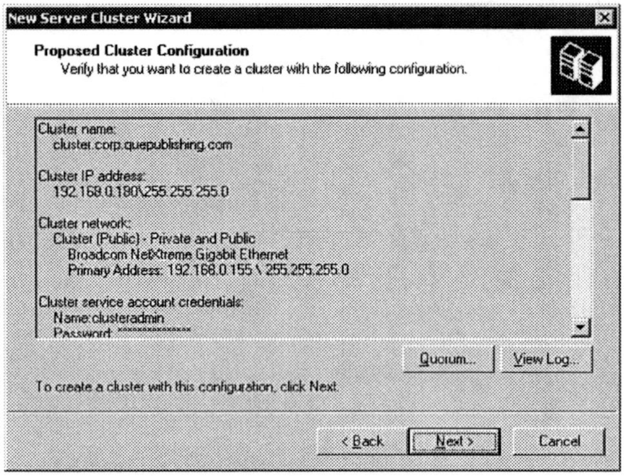

FIGURE 10.28 You can review the selected cluster configuration before creating it.

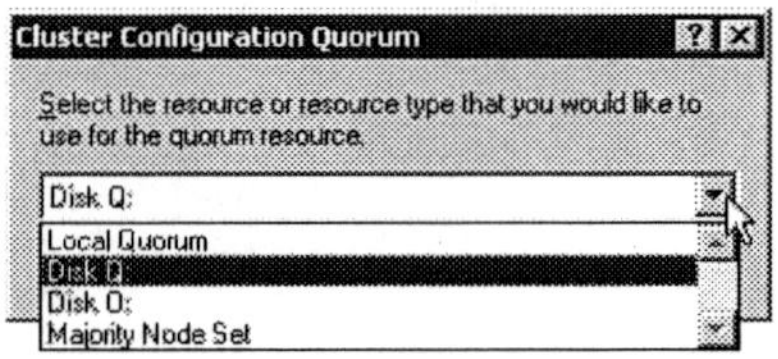

FIGURE 10.29 You can change the quorum type by selecting one of the available options, if desired.

11. If all goes well—and, of course, it will—you should see results in the Creating the Cluster dialog box, like those shown in Figure 10.30. Click Next to continue.

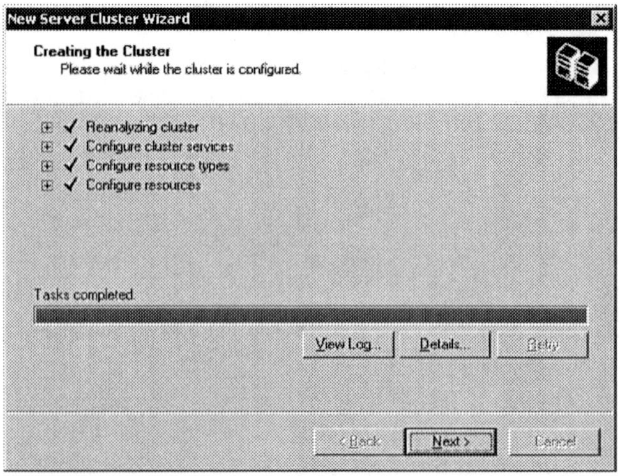

FIGURE 10.30 The Creating the Cluster dialog box informs you of the status of cluster creation.

12. Click Finish to complete the Create New Cluster Wizard.

13. Your new cluster appears in the Cluster Administrator, as shown in Figure 10.31.

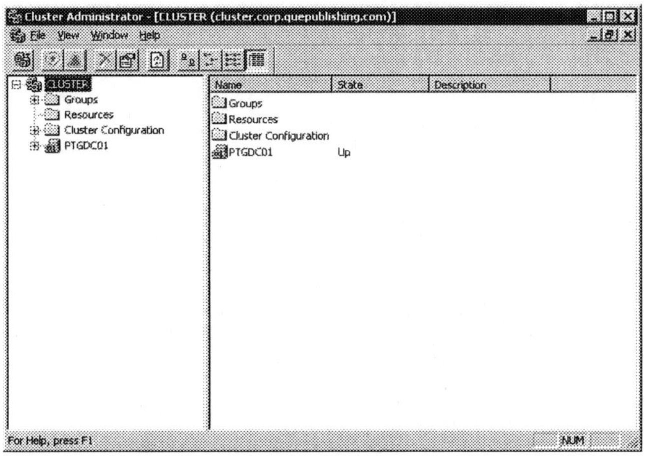

FIGURE 10.31 The Cluster Administrator shows your new cluster now.

Congratulations, you just created your first cluster! One thing you should change immediately, however, is the operational mode of the cluster node network adapters. By default, both the cluster and administrative network adapters are configured to pass both types of traffic; this is undesirable and should be corrected as soon as possible. To correct this setting, locate the Networks node of the Cluster Administrator, as shown in Figure 10.32. Right-click each adapter to open its properties dialog box, shown in Figure 10.33. Configure the adapter according to its role in the cluster.

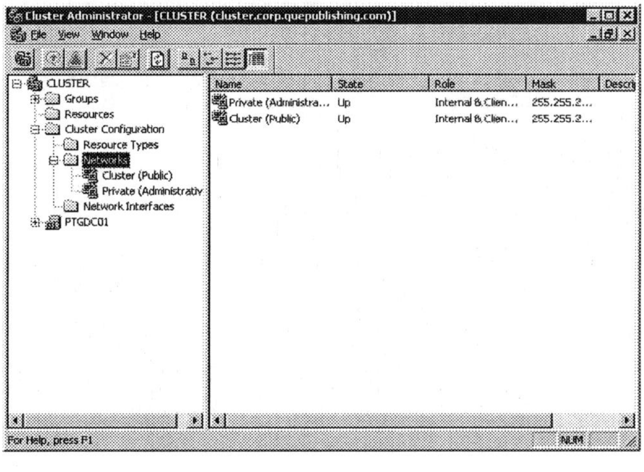

FIGURE 10.32 You should change the network adapter operational mode as soon as possible.

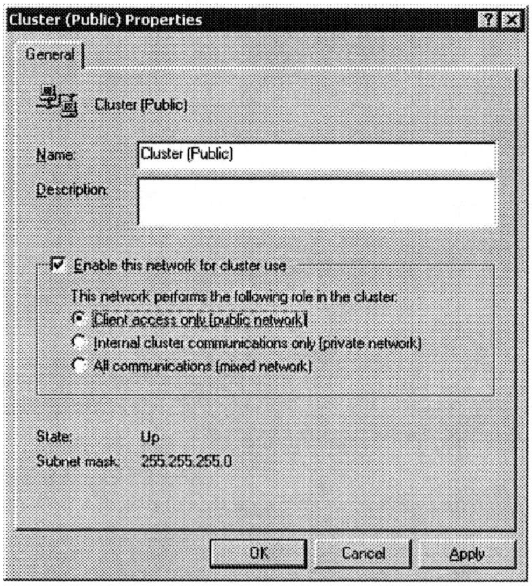

FIGURE 10.33 Select Client Access Only for the cluster network adapter.

Be sure to also configure the administrative (private) network for internal cluster communications only.

You are now ready to add a second node to your new cluster. Step by Step 10.4 outlines this procedure.

STEP BY STEP

10.4 Adding a Node to an MSCS Cluster

1. Ensure that the load-balancing and administrative network adapters on the new cluster node are configured correctly, as discussed previously and in Step by Step 10.1.
2. Open the Cluster Administrator. If the cluster does not appear in the Cluster Administrator, click File, Open Connection and supply the required information to connect to the cluster.
3. Right-click the cluster name in the Cluster Administrator and select New, Node from the context menu.
4. Click Next to dismiss the opening dialog box of the Add Nodes Wizard.
5. In the Select Computers dialog box, shown in Figure 10.34, enter the computer names that are to be joined to the cluster.
6. The Analyzing Configuration dialog box appears for the new node(s), providing information about their suitability to join the cluster. Click Next to continue.
7. In the Cluster Service Account dialog box, enter the correct password for the cluster service account. Click Next to continue.

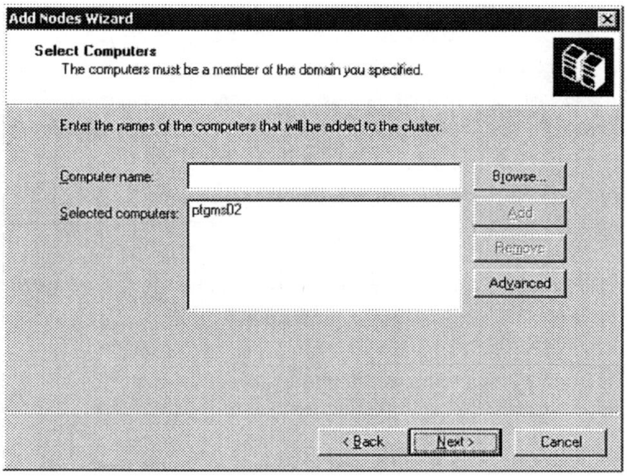

FIGURE 10.34 You can have up to eight nodes in a Windows Server 2003 cluster.

8. In the Proposed Cluster Configuration dialog box, you can review the cluster configuration before continuing. Click Next to continue.
9. The Adding Nodes to the Cluster dialog box appears, detailing the status of the node addition. Click Next to continue.
10. Click Finish to complete the Add Nodes Wizard.
11. Your new cluster node appears in the Cluster Administrator, as shown in Figure 10.35.

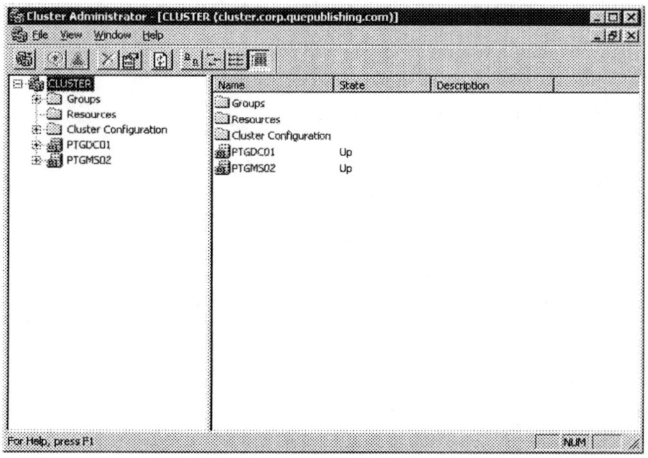

FIGURE 10.35 The Cluster Administrator displays the newly added cluster node.

Now that you know how to create MSCS clusters, let's move forward and examine monitoring and managing your high availability solutions.

NOTE

Clustering, beyond the basics Although you've created and configured a two-node cluster, you still have a lot more work to do before this cluster could actually provide a highly available service or application resource to your network. What you do after this point depends on the service or application you want to provide.

If you want to provide a clustered DHCP implementation, for example, you must create a new network name resource, a new IP address resource, and a new disk resource, and then create the DHCP service resource, all within a cluster resource group. If you want to create an Exchange Server 2003 cluster, you must install Exchange Server 2003 on each cluster node; then create a new network name resource, a new IP address resource, and one or more new disk resources; and then create the Exchange Virtual Servers—for each node that would be actively running Exchange Server 2003.

The point to take away here is that creating and configuring the cluster itself (which can be a challenge, depending on the hardware you have to work with) is just the beginning of creating a highly available service or application resource.

Challenge

You have been hired by the Think Pink Bicycle Company to implement a Windows Server 2003–powered solution for its Internet e-commerce website.

Think Pink has two teams of developers working to create the Active Server Pages (ASP)–based application that will run the front end of the website and also on the SQL database that will serve as the back end of the website.

Customers will be able to browse the catalog and add items to their shopping carts without being signed into the website, but they must sign in before starting the order process. Customers will have the option to sign in to their accounts at any time they like. Cookies will be used with the shopping cart and also to maintain customers' information as they move around the website.

The CEO of Think Pink has emphasized to you on several occasions that the overall customer experience while using the new website is of prime importance to him. You are to ensure that the website is available as much of the time as possible and also to ensure that the customer shopping experience is as smooth and flawless as possible.

Through your discussions with key stakeholders, you've determined the following key points of concern:

- A high availability solution will be required to ensure that the website remains up and available to customers as much of the time as possible.
- This typical N-tier high availability solution will require a network load-balancing front end and an MSCS clustering back end.
- The NLB cluster should be configured to maintain client session state when multiple client requests are sent during a single session.

Your task is to create and implement the required solution for the Think Pink Bicycle Company.

(continues)

(continued)

Try to complete this exercise on your own, listing your conclusions on a sheet of paper. When you have completed the exercise, compare your results to those given here.

You will implement an N-tier (two-layered) solution with at least two (preferably four or more) web servers running in an NLB cluster. The cluster should be configured for Multiple Host with the Single affinity to ensure that the client session state information in the cookies is accurately maintained over the course of the client session.

The back end should use at least two (preferably four or more) SQL servers in an MSCS cluster. The cluster should be configured using a single quorum or majority node set cluster (if supported by the vendor).

Each server being used in this solution should have two network adapters installed. The load-balancing network adapters in the NLB cluster should be configured in unicast mode, for best results. The network adapters in the MSCS cluster should be configured appropriately so that only clustering traffic crosses the clustering adapter and administrative traffic crosses the administration adapter.

Monitoring and Managing High Availability Solutions

After you have planned and implemented your new high availability server solution, you need to perform routine monitoring and management tasks on it to keep it operating correctly. For the most part, high availability solutions are prone to the same sorts of problems that plague regular servers: hardware failures, service stoppages, data corruption, and so on. Recall that the purpose of implementing a high availability solution is not to prevent these sorts of events from occurring (although it would be nice), but instead to minimize the impact of these occurrences on the client experience.

In this section, we examine the process to recover from the failure of a cluster node, as well as some of the tools that can be used to monitor network load-balancing implementations.

Recovering from Failed Cluster Nodes

Objective:

Recover from cluster node failure.

If you've done all your planning and implementing up to now, you are ready for the day when something happens to render one of your cluster nodes inoperable. As mentioned previously, high availability servers are still subject to the same sorts of problems and failures that plague any server; the difference is that because you have implemented a high availability solution, your clients will continue to have access to the required applications and services and should not, under most circumstances, even notice that something terrible has happened behind the scenes.

It's a nice feeling knowing that even if disaster strikes, your clients can carry on as if nothing ever happened. However, you cannot afford to rest on your laurels when disaster does strike; you need to get that failed cluster node back online and in the cluster in short order. How you do this depends exactly on what the problem at hand is.

In most cases, when an MSCS cluster node has failed, you need to either rebuild it (hardware failure) or restore it (software failure or corruption) from an earlier backup set. In either case, you need to first evict the node from the cluster. To evict a node from a cluster, open the Cluster Administrator and connect to the cluster in question. Locate the node to be evicted (see Figure 10.36) and right-click it. From the context menu, select Evict Node. Before the node is actually evicted, Windows will ask you if this is really your intention; click Yes to carry out the eviction process. Note that you cannot evict a node where the Cluster Service is still running.

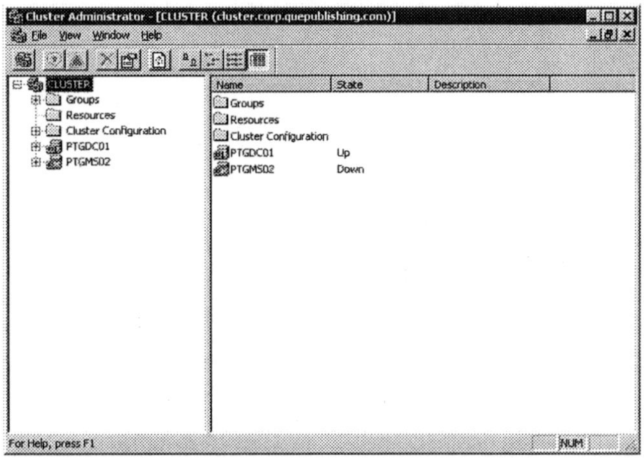

FIGURE 10.36 A failed node will be clearly evident in the Cluster Administrator.

EXAM ALERT

Evicting nodes You can practice evicting nodes by first stopping the cluster service from the context menu. After this is done, the node can be evicted as discussed previously.

Evicting the last remaining node in the MSCS cluster removes the entire cluster itself, so be careful not to do so unless this is your intention. The eviction process is fairly abrupt, but it poses no problem to an already failed node because it is no longer providing service to clients.

After the cluster node has been evicted, you can rebuild it or perform a restoration on it, as required. If you need to rebuild the cluster node, you must ensure that its configuration matches exactly that of the node it is replacing. IP address, local driver letters, computer name, and domain membership are all critical to being able to successfully join the newly created node to the cluster. If you need to perform a restoration from a previous backup set, you can perform this as discussed in Chapter 9, "Monitoring and Maintaining Server Availability."

In a worst-case scenario in which you cannot evict a cluster node that is still operating but is experiencing problems with the Cluster Service, you can initiate manual removal of the Cluster Service from the node by issuing the command `cluster node nodename /forcecleanup` from the command line, as shown in Figure 10.37.

FIGURE 10.37 If nothing else works to evict the cluster node, you can initiate manual removal of the Cluster Service.

After a cluster node has failed, you should also monitor the remaining cluster nodes to ensure that they are not adversely affected or overloaded as a result. This situation can easily occur when Active/Active clustering is being used. Chapter 9 discusses monitoring server performance in Windows Server 2003. Finally, after a cluster node has failed, you should make sure that any failovers that were configured to occur have occurred properly. If they have not already properly occurred, you need to manually move the resource group (see Figure 10.38) by right-clicking it and selecting Move Group.

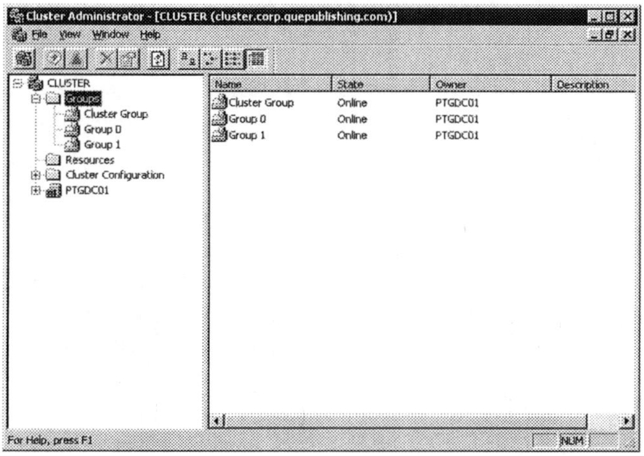

FIGURE 10.38 You might have to manually move a resource group if the failover has not occurred properly for some reason.

Monitoring Network Load Balancing

Objective:

Monitor network load balancing. Tools might include the Network Load Balancing Monitor Microsoft Management Console (MMC) snap-in and the WLBS cluster control utility.

When it comes to monitoring your NLB clusters, there is really not a whole lot to do. As a standard administrative practice, you should perform basic performance monitoring on each of your NLB cluster nodes. You should monitor the following items:

- CPU
- Disk
- Memory
- Network
- Service- or application-specific items, as required

Using the Performance console to monitor and baseline servers is discussed at length in Chapter 6, “Planning, Implementing, and Troubleshooting Network Security Using IPSec,” and is not discussed here.

However, you can also perform some monitoring of your NLB cluster and NLB cluster hosts from the command line using the `wlbs.exe` command. For those of you screaming out that the Windows Load Balancing Service was retired with Windows NT 4.0, you are correct; Microsoft has kept the *WLBS* acronym around for good measure. In reality, `wlbs.exe` and `nlb.exe` are identical in every way; therefore, we discuss `nlb.exe`.

TIP

Using `nlb.exe` remotely The strength of the `nlb.exe` command is that it can be used to manage NLB clusters and cluster nodes remotely across a LAN or WAN, if desired. To run the `nlb.exe` command from a remote computer, you must enable remote control for the NLB cluster.

Enabling remote control presents security risks to the NLB cluster, such as data tampering, denial of service (DoS), and unintentional data disclosure to attackers. Remote control should be used only from a trusted computer inside the same firewall as the NLB cluster or, if outside the firewall, over a VPN.

If you choose to enable remote control despite the risks associated with it, you should take steps to protect the NLB cluster from attack as a result. The default User Datagram Protocol (UDP) control ports for the cluster, 1717 and 2504 at the cluster VIP, should be protected by a firewall. Also, you must ensure that you have configured a strong remote control password.

The `nlb.exe` command has the following basic context:

```
nlb <command> [/PASSW [<password>]] [/PORT <port>]
```

You can find a complete listing of all available NLB commands in the Windows Server 2003 Help and Support Center by searching for "nlb.exe" or looking online at http://technet2.microsoft.com/windowsserver/en/default.mspx.

From a monitoring point of view, we focus only on the commands outlined in Table 10.2.

TABLE 10.2 The `nlb.exe` Monitoring-Specific Commands

Command	Description
`query`	Displays the current cluster state and the list of host priorities for the current members of the cluster. This command can be targeted at a specific cluster, a specific cluster on a specific host, all clusters on the local computer, or all computers that are part of a cluster. The possible states are Unknown, Converging, Draining, and Converged.
`queryport`	Displays information about a given port rule. The command returns the following information: ▶ Whether the specified port rule was found ▶ The current state of the specified port rule ▶ The number of packets accepted and dropped on the specified port rule
`display`	Displays extensive information about the current NLB parameters, cluster state, and past cluster activity.
`params`	Displays information about the current NLB configuration.
`ip2mac`	Displays the MAC address that corresponds to the specified cluster name or IP address. If multicast support is enabled, the multicast media access control address is used by network load balancing for cluster operations. Otherwise, the unicast media access control address is used.

Figure 10.39 shows the output of the `nlb display` command on the NLB cluster we created previously in Step by Steps 10.1 and 10.2.

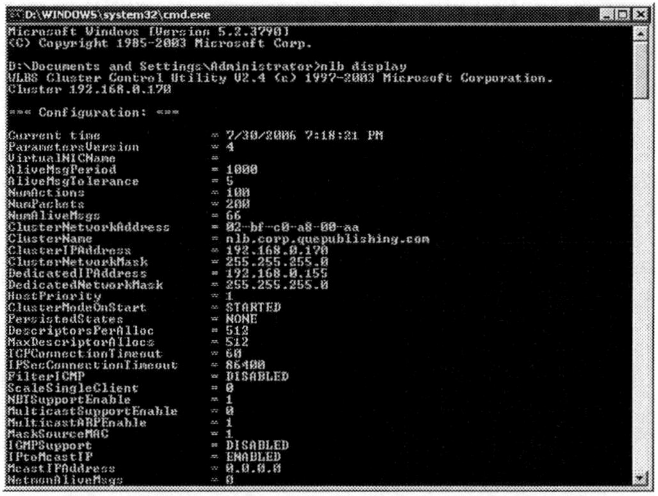

FIGURE 10.39 The `nlb.exe` command is useful to monitoring and troubleshooting NLB clusters.

Chapter Summary

Server reliability is an important item in today's computer-driven world. It seems that everything from the large plasma displays in Times Square to many automatic teller machines are driven by Windows-powered servers. Being able to keep your Windows Server 2003 solution up and running as much of the time as possible is not only expected, but demanded.

It's a fact of life, however, that nothing is ever perfect. Hardware fails, software stops functioning properly, systems become unavailable. In this chapter, we examined an area of server reliability that most administrators have only heard about in passing: high availability solutions.

Businesses want high availability servers to be up and operating 99.999% of the time; that's just more than 5 minutes a year of allowable downtime. For an ordinary server solution, having so little downtime would be impossible; just applying regular hot fixes and service packs takes longer than this. However, by using network load balancing and MSCS clustering, you can create high availability server solutions from multiple servers.

In the end, server reliability begins with you and your good planning.

Key Terms

- Affinity
- Cluster
- Cluster resource
- Cluster resource group
- Cluster virtual server
- Clustering
- Convergence
- Heartbeat
- Failback
- Failover
- Network load balancing
- Node
- Port rules
- Quorum disk

Apply Your Knowledge

In this chapter, you examined how to create highly available server solutions in Windows Server 2003. In the following exercises, you practice some of the concepts and methods discussed in this chapter.

Exercises

10.1 Creating a New NLB Cluster

In this exercise, you create a new network load balancing cluster. You will need a Windows Server 2003 Enterprise computer to complete this exercise.

Estimated time: 20 minutes

1. Open the Network Connections window.
2. Configure the IP address and subnet mask for the load-balancing and administrative network adapters on the first NLB cluster node.
3. Open the Network Load Balancing Manager.
4. Right-click Network Load Balancing Clusters and select New Cluster from the context menu.
5. Enter the cluster's IP address, subnet mask, and cluster domain name. Configure the cluster for unicast or multicast as desired. You can also configure IGMP multicast and remote control as desired. Click Next to continue.
6. In the Cluster IP Addresses dialog box, enter any additional virtual IP addresses using the Add button.
7. In the Port Rules dialog box, configure any port rules that are appropriate for your NLB cluster installation.
8. Configure your port rules as required.
9. In the Connect dialog box, type the name of the first cluster node and click the Connect button. Select the network adapter that is to be used for load balancing.
10. In the Host Parameters dialog box, configure the host priority, cluster node dedicated IP address and subnet mask, and initial state of the cluster node.

10.2 Adding Nodes to an Existing NLB Cluster

In this exercise, you add a node to an existing NLB cluster. You need to complete Exercise 10.1 before attempting this one.

Estimated time: 15 minutes

1. On the server that is to be added to the NLB cluster, open the Network Connections.
2. Open the network adapter Status dialog box for the network adapter that will be used for load balancing.

3. Click the Properties button to open the network adapter Properties dialog box.
4. Install the Network Load Balancing service.
5. From the cluster node where the NLB cluster was created, open the Network Load Balancing Manager.
6. If the Network Load Balancing Manager does not display the cluster, connect to it.
7. Right-click the NLB cluster and select Add Host to Cluster from the context menu.
8. In the Connect dialog box, type the name of the additional cluster node and click the Connect button. Select the network adapter that is to be used for load balancing.
9. In the Host Parameters dialog box, configure the host priority, cluster node dedicated IP address and subnet mask, and initial state of the cluster node.

10.3 Creating an MSCS Cluster

In this exercise, you create a new MSCS cluster. You need a Windows Server 2003 Enterprise computer that is part of an Active Directory domain to accomplish this exercise.

Estimated time: 20 minutes

1. Create a domain user account to be used by the MSCS service. Configure the password to never expire.
2. Ensure that the load-balancing and administrative network adapters on the first cluster node are configured correctly.
3. Open the Cluster Administrator. You should be prompted with the Open Connection to Cluster dialog box. If not, click File, Open Connection. Select Create New Cluster and click OK.
4. Click Next to dismiss the opening dialog box of the New Cluster Creation Wizard.
5. In the Cluster Name and Domain dialog box, select the cluster domain from the drop-down list. Enter the cluster name in the space provided.
6. In the Select Computer dialog box, select the computer that will be the first node in the new cluster.
7. The Analyzing Configuration dialog box appears and runs for a short period of time.
8. In the IP Address dialog box, enter the IP address that is being assigned to the cluster.
9. In the Cluster Service Account dialog box, enter the proper credentials for the cluster domain user account you created previously.
10. In the Proposed Cluster Configuration dialog box, review the cluster configuration before continuing. Change the quorum type if desired.

10.4 Adding a Node to an Existing MSCS Cluster

In this exercise, you add a node to an existing MSCS cluster. Before starting this exercise, you need to complete Exercise 10.3 and have a second computer that is part of the same domain as in Exercise 10.3.

Estimated time: 15 minutes

1. Ensure that the load-balancing and administrative network adapters on the new cluster node are configured correctly.
2. Open the Cluster Administrator. If the cluster does not appear in the Cluster Administrator, click File, Open Connection and supply the required information to connect to the cluster.
3. Right-click the cluster name in the Cluster Administrator and select New, Node from the context menu.
4. Click Next to dismiss the opening dialog box of the Add Nodes Wizard.
5. In the Select Computers dialog box, enter the computer names that are to be joined to the cluster.
6. The Analyzing Configuration dialog box appears for the new node(s), providing information about their suitability to join the cluster.
7. In the Cluster Service Account dialog box, enter the correct password for the cluster service account.
8. In the Proposed Cluster Configuration dialog box, you can review the cluster configuration before continuing.
9. The Adding Nodes to the Cluster dialog box appears, detailing the status of the node addition.
10. Click Finish to complete the Add Nodes Wizard.

Review Questions

1. What is network load balancing?
2. What does convergence mean?
3. What desirable function do port rules provide?
4. What ports must be made available for NLB remote control to work?
5. What is the difference between load balancing and clustering?

Exam Questions

1. Andrea is your newly hired assistant systems administrator. She has been asking you recently about high availability solutions using Windows Server 2003. She tells you that she has heard of the phrase "five nines" but doesn't understand what it means. What is the correct meaning of the phrase "five nines"?

- ❍ **A.** “Five nines” means that servers must be up for at least 99,999 minutes per year.
- ❍ **B.** “Five nines” means that servers cannot ever have 99.999% CPU utilization.
- ❍ **C.** “Five nines” means that servers must be up for at least 99.999% of the time per year.
- ❍ **D.** “Five nines” means that all servers must have a minimum of five 90GB hard drives.

2. Austin is interviewing for the position of assistant server reliability administrator in your organization. You are asking Austin questions during the technical proficiency portion of his interview. You have asked Austin what types of high availability solutions Windows Server 2003 provides. What two correct answers should Austin provide you?

- ❍ **A.** Network load balancing
- ❍ **B.** Windows File Protection
- ❍ **C.** Clustering
- ❍ **D.** Redundant power supplies

3. When discussing the process of convergence, what are you referring to?

- ❍ **A.** A network communication sent among individual cluster nodes at intervals of no more than 500ms that is used to determine the status of all cluster nodes.
- ❍ **B.** The process of a cluster group moving back to the preferred node after the preferred node has resumed cluster membership.
- ❍ **C.** The process by which NLB clustering hosts determine a new, stable state among themselves and elect a new default host after the failure of one or more cluster nodes.
- ❍ **D.** The process of a cluster group moving from the currently active node to another still-functioning node in the cluster group.

4. You are preparing to implement a network load balancing solution for your organization’s e-commerce website. You will be load-balancing six Windows Server 2003 computers running IIS on the front end, with four Windows Server 2003 computers in a cluster on the back end providing access to an SQL Server 2000 database. You are using the unicast cluster operation mode. In what two ways can you prevent switch port flooding from occurring on the NLB cluster?

- ❍ **A.** Configure IGMP multicast support for the NLB cluster.
- ❍ **B.** Place the NLB cluster nodes on a dedicated switch.
- ❍ **C.** Place the NLB cluster nodes on a dedicated VLAN.
- ❍ **D.** Configure single affinity for the NLB cluster.

5. You are preparing to implement a network load balancing solution for your organization’s e-commerce website. You will be load-balancing six Windows Server 2003 computers running IIS on the front end, with four Windows Server 2003 computers in a cluster on the back end providing access to an SQL Server 2000 database. You are trying to decide which clustering mode to use for your back-end servers. What two clustering modes exist?

- ❍ **A.** Active/Passive
- ❍ **B.** Passive/Active
- ❍ **C.** Passive/Passive
- ❍ **D.** Active/Active

6. You are preparing to implement a network load balancing solution for your organization's e-commerce website. You will be load-balancing six Windows Server 2003 computers running IIS on the front end, with four Windows Server 2003 computers in a cluster on the back end providing access to an SQL Server 2000 database. Which of the following cluster models is not available in Windows Server 2003?

- ❍ **A.** Single-node cluster
- ❍ **B.** Multiple-quorum cluster
- ❍ **C.** Single-quorum cluster
- ❍ **D.** Majority node set cluster

7. You are preparing to implement a network load balancing solution for your organization's e-commerce website. You will be load-balancing six Windows Server 2003 computers running IIS on the front end, with four Windows Server 2003 computers in a cluster on the back end providing access to an SQL Server 2000 database. Your e-commerce application makes heavy use of cookies to maintain user session state information during the active connection. Which type of filtering mode should you configure to ensure that clients receive the best possible overall service during their connection period?

- ❍ **A.** Single Host
- ❍ **B.** Disable Port Range
- ❍ **C.** Multiple Host
- ❍ **D.** Allow Port Range

8. You are preparing to implement a network load balancing solution for your organization's e-commerce website. You will be load-balancing six Windows Server 2003 computers running IIS on the front end, with four Windows Server 2003 computers in a cluster on the back end providing access to an SQL Server 2000 database. Your e-commerce application makes heavy use of cookies to maintain user session state information during the active connection. Which type of affinity should you configure to ensure that clients receive the best possible overall service during their connection period?

❍ **A.** None

❍ **B.** Class C

❍ **C.** Multiple

❍ **D.** Single

9. You are preparing to implement a network load balancing solution for your organization's e-commerce website. You will be load-balancing six Windows Server 2003 computers running IIS on the front end, with four Windows Server 2003 computers in a cluster on the back end providing access to an SQL Server 2000 database. You are using the unicast cluster operation mode. Which of the following statements are true about the load-balancing adapters installed in your network load balancing servers? (Choose two correct answers.)

❍ **A.** All cluster nodes share an identical unicast MAC address.

❍ **B.** All cluster nodes retain their original MAC address. The load-balancing adapters are also assigned an additional multicast MAC address.

❍ **C.** If a network load balancing server is using the unicast operational mode and has only one network adapter installed, it will be incapable of communicating with the other nodes in the network load balancing cluster.

❍ **D.** Inbound client requests are sent to all cluster nodes using the multicast MAC address.

10. You are preparing to implement a network load balancing solution for your organization's e-commerce website. You will be load-balancing six Windows Server 2003 computers running IIS on the front end, with four Windows Server 2003 computers in a cluster on the back end providing access to an SQL Server 2000 database. You are using the unicast cluster operation mode. How many total IP addresses will you need to assign for the network load balancing portion of the solution?

❍ **A.** 1

❍ **B.** 6

❍ **C.** 7

❍ **D.** 12

11. Chris is creating a new cluster. She has nearly all the required information written down so that she can enter it during the creation process, but she is missing for the user account that is to be used. What user account should Chris use during the cluster-creation process as the cluster service account?

❍ **A.** The built-in local Administrator account

❍ **B.** An account that is a member of the Domain Admins group

❍ **C.** An account that is a member of the Enterprise Admins group

❍ **D.** A user account that is configured for the password to never expire

12. Jeff wants to use the `nlb.exe` command to manage his NLB cluster from his desktop computer. What must Jeff do before he will able to manage the NLB cluster from his desktop computer?

- ❍ **A.** Ensure that he is a member of the Enterprise Admins group
- ❍ **B.** Enable remote control on the NLB cluster
- ❍ **C.** Disable remote control on the NLB cluster
- ❍ **D.** Configure the required port rules on the NLB cluster

13. Dave is a senior systems administrator in a large Windows Server 2003 Active Directory network. He is responsible for managing and maintaining his company's server clusters. On Monday morning during his normal monitoring cycle, he notices that one of the cluster nodes in his Exchange Server cluster has stopped responding to client requests because the Cluster Service is not running. What is the first step that Dave should perform to begin the recovery process on this failed node?

- ❍ **A.** Initiate an ASR restoration
- ❍ **B.** Evict the node from the cluster
- ❍ **C.** Initiate Windows Backup restoration
- ❍ **D.** Add a new node to the cluster

14. Rick has just completed the planning and configuration of a new NLB cluster that is to be used as the front end of an Internet website. All the cluster nodes are connected to the same switch on the core network. After several days, Rick has noticed an exceptionally high amount of traffic on the switch that he cannot explain. What might be the cause of this excessive traffic?

- ❍ **A.** The switch is unmanaged and, therefore, cannot map the MAC address to the IP address correctly for the servers attached to it.
- ❍ **B.** The switch is experiencing port flooding.
- ❍ **C.** The switch has an incorrectly configured VLAN on it.
- ❍ **D.** The cluster node network adapters are configured for half-duplex operation.

15. Rick has just completed the planning and configuration of a new NLB cluster that is to be used as the front end of an Internet website. All the cluster nodes are connected to the same switch on the core network. After several days, Rick has received complaints from users stating that their shopping carts sometimes lose the contents as they move around the website. What is the most likely reason for this problem?

- ❍ **A.** The client affinity is misconfigured.
- ❍ **B.** The port rules are misconfigured.
- ❍ **C.** The operational mode is misconfigured.
- ❍ **D.** The host priorities are misconfigured.

Answers to Review Questions

1. Network load balancing distributes all incoming connection requests using a mathematical algorithm to members of the NLB cluster. For more information, see the section "High Availability Solutions."

2. Convergence is the process by which NLB clustering hosts determine a new, stable state among themselves and elect a new default host after the failure of one or more cluster nodes. For more information, see the section "High Availability Terminology."

3. Port rules can be used to allow traffic only on specific ports to be load-balanced. If you configure explicit allow rules for specific ports and an explicit deny rule dropping all other traffic, only the desired traffic will be load-balanced. For more information, see the section "Port Rules."

4. The default UDP control ports are 1717 and 2504 at the cluster VIP. For more information, see the section "Monitoring Network Load Balancing."

5. Network load balancing distributes all incoming connection requests using a mathematical algorithm to members of the NLB cluster. Clustering allows several independent servers to act and appear as a single entity to clients. For more information, see the section "High Availability Solutions."

Answers to Exam Questions

1. **C.** The phrase "five nines" refers to server (or service/application) availability and means that the server must be available for client requests at least 99.999% of the time; this equates to only 5.25 minutes of downtime per year. For more information, see the section "Introduction."

2. **A, C.** Windows Server 2003 provides network load balancing and MSCS clustering services to create high availability server solutions. For more information, see the section "High Availability Solutions."

3. **C.** Convergence is the process by which NLB clustering hosts determine a new, stable state among themselves and elect a new default host after the failure of one or more cluster nodes. For more information, see the section "High Availability Terminology."

4. **B, C.** If the multicast operation mode is configured, you can use the new IGMP multicast support function. Because unicast is being used in this case, you have the option of placing the NLB cluster nodes on a dedicated switch or VLAN to eliminate switch port flooding. For more information, see the section "NLB Cluster Operation Mode."

5. **A, D.** You can select either Active/Passive or Active/Active clustering mode. Active/Passive has one node in the cluster online and providing services. All other nodes are online and in a standby state, ready to assume the services if the active node fails. Active/Active has an instance of the clustered service running on all nodes in the cluster. If a node fails, the service instance is transferred to one of the remaining operational nodes. For more information, see the section "Planning and Implementing MSCS Clusters."

6. **B.** Windows Server 2003 supports the single-node cluster, single-quorum cluster, and majority node set cluster models. No multiple-quorum cluster model exists. For more information, see the section "Cluster Models."

7. **C.** By using the multiple host filtering mode, you allow all cluster nodes to handle client traffic. When multiple host filtering mode is configured, you can also configure a client affinity setting. Client affinity determines how cluster nodes will handle repeated client requests during the same session. For more information, see the section "Filtering Mode and Affinity."

8. **D.** By configuring the single affinity setting, you maintain all client requests on the same node for the duration of the session. Single affinity provides the best support for maintaining user state data and is often used when applications that are running on the cluster generate cookies. For more information, see the section "Filtering Mode and Affinity."

9. **A, C.** Unicast mode should be used only when the network load balancing servers have two network adapters installed. If only one network adapter is installed, the cluster nodes will not be capable of communicating with each other. When unicast mode is used, all cluster nodes are assigned an identical unicast MAC address that overwrites the MAC address of the load-balancing adapter. For more information, see the section "NLB Cluster Operation Mode."

10. **C.** You must assign a total of seven IP addresses for the network load balancing portion of this solution. Each load-balancing network adapter in the front-end IIS servers requires a dedicated IP address, such as 10.0.25.11–10.0.25.16. Also, the entire network load balancing cluster is assigned a virtual IP (VIP) address, such as 10.0.25.10. For more information, see the section "Creating an NLB Cluster."

11. **D.** Chris should use an ordinary domain user account that has been configured to never have its password expire. During the cluster-creation process, this user account will be given Local Administrator privileges on all cluster nodes and will also be delegated cluster-related user rights in the domain, including the Add Computer Accounts to the Domain user right. For more information, see the section "Creating a Cluster."

12. **B.** Before the `nlb.exe` command can be used to remotely manage an NLB cluster over a LAN or WAN, remote control must be enabled on the NLB cluster. For more information, see the section "Monitoring Network Load Balancing."

13. **B.** Dave must first evict the failed node from the cluster before he can begin any recovery operation on the node. For more information, see the section "Recovering from Failed Cluster Nodes."

14. **B.** The most likely reason for the excessive amount of traffic on the switch is switch port flooding. The mathematical algorithm used by network load balancing sends inbound traffic to every host in the NLB cluster. It does so by preventing the switch that the NLB cluster nodes are attached to from ever associating the NLB cluster's MAC address with a specific port on the switch. However, this leads to the unwanted side effect of switch port flooding, in which the switch floods all its ports with all packets inbound to the NLB cluster. For more information, see the section "NLB Cluster Operation Mode."

15. **A.** Rick's problem is most likely that the client affinity is misconfigured. The affinity should be configured for single affinity. This affinity type maintains all client requests on the same node for the duration of the session (connection). This type of affinity provides the best support for the maintaining of user state data and is often used when applications are running on the cluster that generates cookies. For more information, see the section "Filtering Mode and Affinity."

Suggested Readings and Resources

1. Windows Server 2003 Deployment Kit: Planning Server Deployments. http://go.microsoft.com/fwlink/?LinkId=15309.
2. Clustering Services Technology Center. www.microsoft.com/windowsserver2003/technologies/clustering/default.mspx.

PART II

Final Review

Fast Facts

Practice Exam

Practice Exam Answers

Fast Facts

Planning and Maintaining a Microsoft Windows Server 2003 Network Infrastructure

Now that you've finished reading this book and working through the exercises, you're ready for the exam. This section of the book is intended to be used as you're sitting in the testing center parking lot doing your "final cram" before you head in the door.

Organized by chapter, this section of the book is not only a summary, but it is also a concentrated review of the most important points. If you know and are comfortable with the content and concepts presented here, the odds are good that you are truly prepared for Exam 70-293, "Planning and Maintaining a Microsoft Windows Server 2003 Network Infrastructure."

Planning, Implementing, and Troubleshooting a TCP/IP Network Infrastructure

The Transmission Control Protocol/Internet Protocol (TCP/IP) maps to both the Open System Interconnect (OSI) and DoD (Department of Defense) models, but it maps more closely with the DoD model because the Department of Defense was the original creator and user of this protocol. In Table 1, you can see where TCP and IP map to the DoD model as well as some other common protocols in use on typical local area networks.

TABLE 1 Viewing the DoD Model with TCP/IP Mapped to It

Process and Application Layer	SMTP (Email-Based Protocol)
Host to Host Layer	TCP
Internet Layer	IP
Network Access Layer	Ethernet

TCP/IP is the basic communication language or protocol of the Internet. Many other protocols are available out there, some of which you might be familiar with, such as AppleTalk, IPX/SPX, even SNA. All these protocols have been displaced by TCP/IP, however. Because most networks today are connected to the Internet somehow, using only TCP/IP makes more sense.

TCP/IP is responsible for creating and keeping communications among all network-connected devices that need to communicate with each other. Without the need for communication, TCP/IP would serve no true purpose, but because the whole purpose of a network is to share resources, TCP/IP is the medium that provides such communication. Couple this need for communication with some form of physical topology (cabling or wireless), and you have a network.

An IP address is a 32-bit number that denotes a node or host on a network. The number, which resembles 10.1.1.1/24, is a unique host on a single network. If you have two nodes, numbered 10.1.1.1 and 10.1.1.2, they can communicate if they are connected to the same network segment and no other outstanding issues stop communication.

An IP address is broken down into two specific parts: the network identifier and host identifier. Let's look at the following IP address to understand it better:

IP address: 10.1.1.1

Subnet mask: 255.255.255.0

You need to break down this number into binary bits to truly see what we mean by masking. First, consider the fact that you have a 32-bit address written in decimal format. If you want to see the subnet mask 255.255.255.0 in binary, you have to change the format from decimal to binary, or base 2 numbering, as follows:

255.255.255.0 = 11111111.11111111.11111111.00000000

Remember, binary uses only 1s and 0s, either on or off. No other numbers are used, so you can see how the network is masked. All 1s in the network portion denotes the actual network you are working on. This leaves the host portion (the 0s at the end) available for assignment. This way, any device can know what network it's on—or, better, what subnet. Because we've used 24 1s here, we denote the IP address as 10.1.1.0/24. Using this form of notation is an easier way to show a subnet mask assignment. If you see /30, for example, the address appears like this in binary:

11111111.11111111.11111111.11111100

Public IP addressing uses three major spaces: Classes A, B, and C. There are also two more classes: Class D, which is used for multicast-based networks, and Class E, which is still experimental. Class A is for very large networks, Class B is for medium-size networks, and Class C is used for networks that have no more than a couple hundred nodes. Table 2 shows public ranges.

TABLE 2 Viewing IP Address Classes

Class	Range
Class A	1–126
Class B	128–191
Class C	192–223

Notice that 127 is not listed in the address range. The IP address 127.0.0.0 is reserved for loopback networks and testing. 127.0.0.1 is also located in the `HOSTS` file, which enables you to test the IP connectivity of your own machine. If you use the command **`ping loopback`** (which is the host name located in the `HOSTS` file), you can resolve to 127.0.0.1, and you should see a reply. This way, you know that TCP/IP is configured properly—at least, on your own system.

Although the private IP address ranges shown in Table 3 fall within Class A, B, and C public IP addresses, note that private IP addresses are not routable on the Internet by design (and by default) and should never be seen outside an internal network.

TABLE 3 Viewing Private IP Classes

Class	Range
Class A	10.0.0.0–10.255.255.255
Class B	172.16.0.0–172.31.255.255
Class C	192.168.0.0–192.168.255.255

When implementing a new network, you should know what you want the network to look like before you even contemplate ordering gear to populate it. This step is important because you must consider many factors before implementation. These factors include the following:

- Do you want redundancy and high availability?
- Do you want security?
- Where will the application flows be generated from?
- How do you stop bottlenecks from occurring or contain them?

IPX/SPX, which stands for Internetwork Packet Exchange/Sequence Packet Exchange, is similar to TCP/IP. You can think of IP mapping to IPX and TCP mapping to SPX. These protocols perform similar operations. IPX/SPX was originally created and used extensively by Novell with its NetWare platform of network operating systems. Although IPX/SPX was a great protocol, TCP/IP became the protocol of the Internet. To avoid missing out on the Internet revolution, all NOS vendors chose to develop TCP/IP into all their solutions moving forward, leaving in other protocols such as IPX/SPX only for backward compatibility. Novell NetWare version 5.0 was the first version to be shipped with a real version of TCP/IP, whereas the older versions of NetWare (versions 4.x and before) used add-on packs.

Systems Network Architecture (SNA) is an old but still widely used protocol. Developed by IBM, SNA is a protocol suite that runs on most mainframes used today. Microsoft professionals who know only Microsoft might be shocked to learn that in today's networks they most likely will be confronted with some form of mainframe and might also be responsible for network connectivity to it.

Another old protocol, the Network Basic Input/Output System (NetBIOS) is a session-layer communications service used by client and server applications in IBM-based Token Ring and PC LAN Ethernet-based networks. NetBIOS is really just a way for application programming interface–based communications to take place. This means that higher-level services can run over lower-level protocols such as IP. This process is known as NetBIOS over TCP/IP (NBT). The NetBIOS service contains three main sections: the name, session, and datagram services.

To connect your LAN to the Internet, you need to plan for the following

- What type of connection do you want? What media, what technology?
- How much bandwidth do you need to provide?

- What hardware will you use?
- Will security be involved?
- Who provides DNS?
- Will you be doing Network Address Translation?
- Where does Windows Server 2003 fit into network connectivity?

When troubleshooting client-based TCP/IP problems, you must develop a good troubleshooting methodology; otherwise, you will be wasting your time.

If you cannot make a client resolve names properly because its client-side DNS cache is either corrupted or not updated to a change already made on the DNS server, you can easily flush out that information by using one of the following commands:

- **`ipconfig/flushdns`**—This command purges the DNS Resolver cache.
- **`ipconfig/displaydns`**—This command displays the contents of the DNS Resolver cache.
- **`ipconfig/registerdns`**—This command refreshes all DHCP leases and reregisters DNS names.

You can use Network Monitor to capture packets on a network. From these packets, you can troubleshoot network problems, discern how busy a network load is, and predict how the network will grow.

Network Monitor is made up of two primary components:

- **Network Monitor**—Network Monitor is the tool you use to capture packets sent to and from this server. The version of Network Monitor that is included with Windows Server 2003 records only packets sent to and from this server and the LAN.
- **Network Monitor driver**—The Network Monitor driver is installed automatically when you install Network Monitor on a server. However, you might want to install just the Network Monitor driver for remote computers to be monitored through the full version of Network Monitor that is included with Systems Management Server (SMS). If you install the Network Monitor driver on additional computers, you should make a point to install it only once per subnet.

Sometimes you might encounter network problems that Network Monitor doesn't help troubleshoot. Recall that the version of Network Monitor included in Windows Server 2003 can be used only to capture network traffic going to or from the server it is being run on. Although many very capable third-party network sniffers are available for use, Exam 70-293 is not concerned with their use. Therefore, for the exam, you need to know how to use System Monitor to monitor the statistics associated with network interfaces.

The following counters are listed under the Network Interface performance object:

- **Bytes Received/Sec**—This counter measures the rate at which bytes, including framing characters, are received over each network adapter. This counter is a subset of the Bytes Total/Sec counter.
- **Bytes Sent/Sec**—This counter measures the rate at which bytes, including framing characters, are sent over each network adapter. This counter is a subset of the Bytes Total/Sec counter.
- **Bytes Total/Sec**—This counter measures the rate at which bytes, including framing characters, are sent and received over each network adapter.
- **Current Bandwidth**—This counter measures an estimate of the current bandwidth of the network interface, in bits per second.
- **Output Queue Length**—This counter measures the length of the output packet queue (in packets). If this counter is greater than 2, there are delays, and you should find and eliminate the bottleneck, if possible.
- **Packets Outbound Discarded**—This counter measures the number of outbound packets that were chosen to be discarded even though no errors had been detected to prevent transmission. One possible reason for discarding packets could be to free up buffer space.
- **Packets Outbound Errors**—This counter measures the number of outbound packets that could not be transmitted because of errors.
- **Packets Received Discarded**—This counter measures the number of inbound packets that were chosen to be discarded, even though no errors had been detected to prevent their delivery to a higher-layer protocol. One possible reason for discarding packets could be to free up buffer space.
- **Packets Received Errors**—This counter measures the number of inbound packets that contained errors that prevented them from being deliverable to a higher-layer protocol.
- **Packets Received Non-Unicast/Sec**—This counter measures the rate at which non-unicast packets are delivered to a higher-layer protocol.
- **Packets Received Unicast/Sec**—This counter measures the rate at which unicast packets are delivered to a higher-layer protocol.
- **Packets Received Unknown**—This counter measures the number of packets received through the interface that were discarded because of an unknown or unsupported protocol.

- **Packets Received/Sec**—This counter measures the rate at which packets are received on the network interface.
- **Packets Sent Unicast/Sec**—This counter measures the rate at which packets are requested to be transmitted to subnet-unicast addresses by higher-layer protocols.
- **Packets Sent/Sec**—This counter measures the rate at which packets are sent on the network interface.
- **Packets/Sec**—This counter measures the rate at which packets are sent and received on the network interface.

Planning and Troubleshooting TCP/IP Routing

Routing is the process of sending data from one network to another network.

A static routing environment is one in which all routing entries in a routing table are entered manually. In other words, if you want the router to know that the destination for all traffic is not local to the subnet that the router is connected to, you must manually enter the route into the router's table so it can be used.

You create a dynamic routing table with a routing protocol such as Routing Information Protocol (RIP) or Open Shortest Path First (OSPF). Understanding the routing table first is key to understanding the protocol because the protocol is responsible for building the table for you from information it is configured to learn. In other words, if you turn on RIP, the router builds a table from information it learns from other routers that are adjacent to it.

Routing tables are used to compute the next hop for a packet. Remember that a routing table must have two fields: the IP prefix and the next-hop address, which also needs to be valid. The router the packet is leaving and going to must be capable of reaching this valid address. You must be connected; otherwise, the router will not work. Finally, if you do not have a match (a packet comes in and does not have a routing table entry match), the packet is discarded and you will most likely get an Internet Control Message Protocol (ICMP) notification that the destination host was unreachable.

Following are some pros and cons of the different routing types:

- Static routing is tedious. You must know exactly what you want to do because any mistake causes the router to either not work properly or make routing errors.
- You might want to implement static routing if you have only a few routes to maintain. Remember, each time a packet enters the router, the router needs to process it, so tables that are very long can cause the router to take longer to make a routing decision;

this could slow down your network. When you use dynamic routing protocols, it is possible to have a router learn as many as hundreds of routes, depending on network size.

- Static routes are more secure because only a few required routes are in the table, so no one can see too much information. In this case, if the router is compromised by an attacker, he or she cannot glean too much information from your compromised router. The attacker might know only a default route back to the core network, for example, whereas if the attacker compromises a core router with 300 networks in the table, he or she can map your whole network from that one router.
- Dynamic routing is easy to configure and, once configured, is easy to maintain. If changes are made to the network, more than likely the routers will learn the changes, and they can quickly establish convergence on the network. Convergence occurs when all routers know all other routers on the network and the topology is accurate.
- Dynamic routing is becoming more secure as more routing protocols provide ways to encrypt and authenticate updates between peers. However, configuring dynamic routes requires that the administrator have a greater level of knowledge and experience than when configuring static routes.

A link-state routing protocol ensures that each router on the network maintains a map of the network. For example, say one of your WAN links has a problem that results in two routers losing contact with each other. Both can (through the routing protocol) adjust for this loss of the link between them because they are programmed to do so. When your router link fails, it is programmed to sense the loss of carrier on the line and then, through the routing protocol, send updates to the other routers adjacent to them so that they all know that the link is down and the IP subnet that they maintained is no longer available for destination packets on the wire. When a network link changes state (up to down, or vice versa), a notification called a link-state advertisement (LSA) is flooded throughout the network. Routers all over the network address this change and make sure that their routing tables are adjusted accordingly. Another configurable option of link-state protocols is that they can use something other than hop count to determine their path through the network. Link-state protocols can also determine that going over more routers might be quicker if the available bandwidth is higher instead of choosing the shortest path deemed solely on how many routers away the destination is.

Distance-vector protocols are easy to configure and maintain but are not as reliable or efficient as link-state protocols. Distance-vector protocols (such as RIP) allow for simple design and easy maintenance, but your bandwidth might suffer as a result. A distance-vector protocol lets every router that is configured to use it inform every other adjacent router of its entire routing table. This means that each router on the network gets a full routing table from each neighboring router. These tables are used to create a metric based on hop count. Each router knows how far it is to another subnet in the network so that when incoming packets (when the router strips the header and reads the destination address) are read, the router will know the quickest way to get the packet there.

RIP is a distance-vector routing protocol. Following are some details about RIP:

- RIP is limited to 15 router hops, with 16 hops being infinity. What does this mean? Picture a LAN with a PC that needs to communicate with a server on another LAN that is 15 routers away. The routers keep a list of which subnets are no more than 15 routers away, and if you try to expand the network past the 16th router, communications do not happen. Remember, you have a 15-hop minimum between networks, and the 16th is deemed infinity.

- RIP has problems with subnetted networks. RIP was created and deployed before networks were subnetted to the degree that they are today, and because they have no direct support for RIP, your networks cannot support it. It really comes down to the information that the routers send to each other and what that packet contains. If the routing update does not contain a field in the packet to allow for subnetted networks, it does not carry over the information you might need it to. In other words, the RIP protocol is configured to look at the prefix of the IP address in the routing update and know whether it's A, B, or C, and nothing more. If you subnet, your subnet will not be supported because RIP understands only that if a packet with an IP address of 10.0.0.1 comes in, it's automatically assigned a subnet of 255.0.0.0, even if you have it subnetted down to 255.255.255.0.

- RIP is bandwidth intensive, and although that isn't a problem on most networks, a smaller network with WAN links that are set small (such as Frame Relay links set with a 32KB committed information rate) could feel the effect of constant broadcasts every 30 seconds, especially if the routing table is large. If the routing table is too large, more than one update could be sent every 30 seconds, making it even more bandwidth intensive. For Exam 70-293, remember that, by default, RIP broadcasts to its neighbors every 30 seconds lists of networks and subnets it can reach.

- RIP is not very secure. RIP contains no security features or configurable parameters to make it secure. Other protocols used today have configurable parameters to make them more secure; however, RIP does not contain any solution to make it secure by default.

RIP2, or RIP version 2, was created for RIP users to overcome problems with security. This version adds an option for authentication to the RIP packet, adds support for subnetted networks, and allows for variable-length subnetted networks to be passed through routing updates.

Open Shortest Path First (OSPF) is a link state–based nonproprietary routing protocol. Following are some details about OSPF:

- OSPF is highly scalable. You will be hard-pressed to build (or support) a network large enough to outdo OSPF. OSPF was designed to work in very large networks, and it works very well. It does not have a hop-count restriction as RIP does. With OSPF's use of areas and a subdivided domain, the design possibilities are almost seemingly infinite.
- With RIP, you cannot use subnetted networks; with OSPF, you can.
- With OSPF, your bandwidth is spared. With RIP, an entire routing table is broadcast from every router on the network every 30 seconds. With OSPF (in stable environments that do not suffer from many changes), packets (called hello packets) are sent out intermittently to verify links between adjacent routers. This way, less bandwidth is used, and a major update check is performed only every 30 minutes.

OSPF divides the network (what it considers a routing domain) into areas. An area is a subdivision of the entire network and is given a label. Area 0 (zero) is considered the backbone of an OSPF network. If your network is small enough, you can set up the entire network to use Area 0, which is very important. For example, if the network becomes more subdivided (say you have three areas, including Area 0), you would need to know that if all traffic must travel between areas, the packets are first routed to the backbone, or Area 0. When you plan a network this way, the design keeps subnets consolidated to areas, thus reducing the size of the link-state database that is updated on every router in an OSPF network. This keeps your OSPF network running optimally.

Following is some other important information to remember about OSPF:

- OSPF sends out hello packets to each adjacent router connected to the network. OSPF uses hello packets to verify that the network is always ready to work as advertised. These hellos are sent out of every router interface every 10 seconds but are so small in size that they do not affect your available bandwidth.
- Link-state advertisements provide other functionality, such as providing a solution for a scenario in which a router does not hear from its neighboring router for more than 40 seconds. The router then sends out LSAs marking the other router as down so that all the other routers can adjust their tables with the change.
- Hellos can be adjusted. A hello has a timer value that, when configured properly throughout the OSPF network, allows proper and accurate communications to take place. It is important to know that if a hello timer is misconfigured (not all timers are identical), problems can occur. Make sure that when you plan an OSPF network, you ensure that all the hello timers match. They must all be consistent across all routers on a network segment.
- Because LSAs age, it is important to get a refreshed routing table (or database) from a neighboring router, just in case anything has changed. If nothing has changed on a particular router for 30 minutes, the router flushes its information and seeks an updated

database from its adjacent routers. This means that the network reconverges every 30 minutes—a far cry from the forced reconvergence in a RIP network every 30 seconds!

Three forms of traffic traverse a network:

- **Unicast**—When a single node on the network sends data to its destination node under one single packet, it knows where the destination node is and gets the data to it. Remember *uni* as being a single transmission.
- **Broadcast**—Broadcasting (think of the word *broad*) occurs when the destination is not known or cannot be found, and that node (which needs to find the destination node) sends out packets to all nodes on the network segment to see whether it can find its destination node. This process is conducive to increased traffic, collisions on hubbed networks, and so on. Broadcasts are at times a necessary evil, but most of the time you should prevent them from happening often or control their number. Basically, broadcast traffic adds overhead to your network (bandwidth utilization) and its devices (processing packets they don't need to look at).
- **Multicast**—Multicast is the happy medium but still can cause problems. A multicast transmission is based on a group. In simple terms, think of 20 nodes on a network, 5 of which need to communicate at all times and 15 of which do not need to ever know what the other 5 are doing. Say these nodes are OSPF routers. OSPF routers send out updates to each other via a multicast, so you might ask, "What about devices that do not need to know this information?" If you use a multicast address, such as 224.0.0.5 (the all-OSPF routers multicast address) for OSPF-based networks, only those devices listen for transmissions from other nodes using this service. This reduces the problems caused by broadcast traffic and enables you to cause one sender to get information to multiple (group) nodes without that message going to every node on the network. Consequently, multicasting is good, but as with any other technology, it can cause problems as well or require an advanced level of administration to make it work properly.

Considering multicast routing is very important because your network must be capable of building packet-distribution trees that allow sources to send packets to all receivers. These trees are meant to make certain that each packet on the network exists one time only and is found only on a specific network. If this limitation did not exist, you would have problems with IP multicast routing. Also, multicast routing, which is the propagation of multicast listening information, is provided by multicast routing protocols such as Distance Vector Multicast Routing Protocol (DVMRP) and Multicast Open Shortest Path First (MOSPF), which is an extension to OSPF that allows it to support IP multicasting. Such protocols ease manual configuration of VPN- and OSPF-based networks and are becoming the standard for these types of networks.

The Internet Group Management Protocol (IGMP) is an Internet protocol that allows nodes that are configured to use it to communicate as a group instead of individually. IGMP allows a node to report its multicast group membership (the group to which it is assigned) to adjacent routers. Multicasting allows a node to send data to many other nodes that have also identified themselves as being part of that group. This cuts down on broadcast traffic and bandwidth consumption. IGMP is detailed in RFC 2236.

Planning, Implementing, and Troubleshooting DHCP

DHCP was the Internet community's answer to the problem of dynamically distributing IP addresses. Here's how a client computer gets an address:

1. The client computer broadcasts a `DHCPDISCOVER` message that is intended for the DHCP server(s) on the network. If a router sits between the DHCP server and the client, it needs to be configured with the IP address of the DHCP server. It also needs to be configured to forward BOOTP.
2. Each DHCP server that receives the `DHCPDISCOVER` message responds with a DHCP offer message, which includes an IP address that is appropriate for the subnet where the client computer is attached. The DHCP server determines the appropriate address by looking at the source subnet for the broadcast `DHCPDISCOVER` message.
3. The client computer considers the offer messages and selects one (usually the first offer it receives). It sends a request (`DHCPREQUEST`) to use the address to the DHCP server that originated the offer. If there are multiple DHCP servers, they need to be carefully configured. It is very easy to inadvertently configure servers so that they conflict; therefore, it is important that if you have multiple DHCP servers on a network, they should not have the capability to offer duplicate IP addresses. Because DHCP servers do not communicate with one another, they have no way of telling whether an address has already been issued by another DHCP server.
4. The DHCP server acknowledges the request and grants the client computer a lease to use the address.
5. The client computer uses the IP address to bind to the network. If the IP address is associated with any configuration parameters, the parameters are incorporated into the client computer's TCP/IP configuration.
6. When 50% of the configured lease time has elapsed, the client sends another `DHCPREQUEST` message to the DHCP server that granted its lease, asking to renew and extend its current lease.

7. If the DHCP server is reachable, it responds with a `DHCPACK` message to the client, renewing and extending the DHCP lease as requested.

8. If the DHCP server is not reachable, the client continues trying to reach it until 87.5% of the lease time has elapsed. At that point, the client attempts to renew its lease with any DHCP server that responds. If this is unsuccessful, the client starts the process of acquiring a new DHCP lease.

DHCP is not a new service in Windows Server 2003, but it has undergone some changes from both Windows 2000 and Windows NT 4.0. The following list summarizes some of the major changes between DHCP in Windows NT 4.0 (and Windows 2000 Server as well) and Windows Server 2003:

- **DHCP integration in DNS**—DHCP servers in a Windows Server 2003 environment can trigger dynamic updates in the DNS database for all clients to which it leases IP addresses. Windows 2000 and newer clients can automatically update their DNS records if they are authorized to do so. Legacy clients can have their records updated by the DHCP server if it is authorized to do so.

- **Rogue DHCP server detection**—Unauthorized, or *rogue*, DHCP servers can cause a wide variety of problems, including a denial of service (DoS) to clients. To prevent such problems, Windows Server 2003 requires an administrator to authorize DHCP servers before they can start to service client requests. In this way, only those DHCP servers that have been authorized can provide DHCP leases to clients. You must be an enterprise administrator to authorize a DHCP server.

- **Superscope and multicast scope support**—Superscopes enable you to group several standard DHCP scopes into a single administrative group without causing any service disruption to network clients. Multicast scopes enable you to lease Class D IP addresses to clients for participation in multicast transmissions. These include streaming video and audio transmissions.

- **Local security groups for DHCP management**—Two new local administrative security groups are created when the DHCP service is installed: DHCP Users and DHCP Administrators.

- **Improved monitoring and reporting**—Windows Server 2003 provides a full set of performance-monitoring counters that can be used to monitor DHCP server performance.

- **Custom DHCP option classes**—User- and vendor-specified option classes can be used to distribute specific options to the clients that need them.

When planning for your DHCP implementation using Windows Server 2003, you'll need to consider some basic items. They include, but are not limited to, the following:

- What type of infrastructure does your organization have? Is it centralized, distributed, or mixed?
- Will you be using one of the DHCP server distribution rules on your network? The common ones are 50/50, 70/30, and 80/20. The type of network you have will help determine the type of server distribution you'll want.
- Will you be using clustered or standby DHCP servers?
- What, if any, DHCP reservations will you need to configure to support your environments unique needs?
- What types of DHCP options will you need to configure? You can configure options at multiple levels.

A scope is a range of IP addresses that is available for dynamic assignment to hosts on a given subnet. The scope for a particular subnet is determined by the network address of the broadcast DHCP request. In addition to address information, a scope can include a set of configuration parameters to be assigned to client computers when the address is assigned. This list of configuration parameters can include DNS servers, WINS servers, default gateways, the subnet mask, a NetBIOS scope ID, IP routing information, and WINS proxy information.

A supernetted network is a network that has multiple network addresses or subnets running on the same segment. This configuration is common in a network environment with more than 254 hosts on a subnet and in an environment in which certain hosts need to be isolated from the rest of the logical network for security or routing reasons. Superscopes support a local multinet or a multinet that is located across a router and configured to use the BOOTP forwarder service.

Windows Server 2003 makes use of the concept of a multicast scope. The DHCP service has been extended to allow the assignment of multicast addresses in addition to unicast (single-computer) addresses. MADCAP (Multicast Address Dynamic Client Allocation Protocol) is an IETF standard (RFC 2730) that defines multicast address allocation.

You can configure DHCP options at four different levels for each DHCP server:

- **Server**—DHCP options that are applied, by default, to all scopes on the DHCP server.
- **Scope**—DHCP options that are applied only to the specific scope on the DHCP server. When a scope option conflicts with a server option, the scope option wins and that value is made a part of the scope. If the conflicting scope option is later removed, the server option once again becomes effective in the scope.

- **Class**—DHCP options that are applied only to clients identified as members of specified user or vendor classes.
- **Reservation**—DHCP options that are applied only to a specific computer.

Table 4 presents some of the more common DHCP scope options.

TABLE 4 DHCP Scope Options

Code	Option Name	Option Description
2	Time Offset	Specifies the offset of the client's subnet in seconds from UTC
3	Router	Specifies a list of IP addresses for routers on the client's subnet
4	Time Server	Specifies a list of RFC 868 time servers available to the client
5	Name Servers	Specifies a list of name servers available to the client
6	DNS Servers	Specifies a list of DNS servers available to the client
9	LPR Servers	Specifies a list of RFC 1179 line printer servers available to the client
15	DNS Domain Name	Specifies the domain name that the client should use when resolving host names via DNS
27	All Subnets Are Local	Specifies whether the client can assume that all subnets of the IP network to which the client is connected use the same MTU as the subnet of the network to which the client is directly connected
28	Broadcast Address	Specifies the broadcast address in use on the client's subnet
44	WINS/NBNS Servers	Specifies a list of RFC 1001/1002 NBNS servers, listed in order of preference
46	WINS/NBT Node Type	Allows NetBT clients, which can be configured as described in RFC 1001/1002
47	NetBIOS Scope ID	Specifies the NetBT scope parameter for the client, as specified in RFC 1001/1002

Table 5 shows Microsoft-specific DHCP options.

TABLE 5 Microsoft-Specific DHCP Options

Code	Option Name	Option Description
1	Microsoft Disable NetBIOS	This option can be used to selectively enable or disable NetBT for DHCP-enabled computers running Windows.
2	Microsoft Release DHCP Lease on Shutdown	This option can be used to control whether DHCP-enabled computers running Windows send a release for their current DHCP lease to the DHCP server when shutdown occurs.
3	Microsoft Default Router Metric Base	This value is a specified router metric base to be used for all default gateway routes.

When you provide DHCP using Windows Server 2003, you can take advantage of the tight integration between DHCP and DNS, and thereby ensure that all clients are automatically registered in DNS. You can configure the following settings for DNS integration:

- Dynamically Update DNS A and PTR Records Only If Requested by the DHCP Clients
- Always Dynamically Update DNS A and PTR Records
- Discard A and PTR Records When Lease Is Deleted
- Dynamically Update DNS A and PTR Records for DHCP Clients That Do Not Request Automatic Updates

You can set up a DHCP relay agent in three basic configurations:

- The first involves entering the IP address or addresses of the DHCP server(s) into the router itself, instructing it to pass DHCP messages to a specified IP address for action.
- The second method involves using the Windows Server 2003 Routing and Remote Access (RRAS) component as a router (in place of a hardware-based router) and configuring the DHCP relay agent within it.
- The third solution uses a Windows Server 2003 computer located on a subnet without a DHCP server to act as a DHCP relay agent. This option requires the use of the RRAS components, but it does not involve the creation or configuration of a router, as would be the case with the second solution. What's important to understand is that the server providing the DHCP relay agent service does not have to be dedicated to that purpose; it could be a file server, a print server, or any other type of Windows Server 2003 (or Windows 2000 Server) server on that subnet.

Planning and Implementing a Name Resolution Infrastructure

In the domain name system (DNS), containers called domains hold the information. The hierarchy starts with a root container, called the root domain. The root domain doesn't have a name, so it is typically represented by a single period. The root domain contains pointers to all top-level domains (TLDs), which are directly below the root domain. They are also sometimes called first-level domains. Lower-level domains are second-level, third-level, and so on. Every domain name has a suffix that indicates which TLD domain it belongs to. There are only a limited number of such domains, as defined by Request for Comments (RFC) 1591. Following are some of the more common TLDs:

- **.COM**—Intended for commercial entities, but it has become the overwhelming favorite top-level domain (example: area51partners.com)
- **.EDU**—Intended for higher-education institutions, such as four-year colleges and universities (example: berkeley.edu)
- **.GOV**—Intended for use by agencies of the U.S. federal government (example: whitehouse.gov)
- **.MIL**—Intended for use by agencies of the U.S. military (example: af.mil)
- **.NET**—Intended for use by network providers and organizations dedicated to the Internet, such as Internet service providers (example: ibm.net)
- **.ORG**—Intended for nonprofit or noncommercial establishments, such as professional groups, charities, and other such organizations (example: stjude.org)

DNS is used to translate a host name to an IP address. The fully qualified domain name (FQDN) typically looks something like the following:

```
filesvr042.accounting.quepublishing.corp
```

This is known as the host's FQDN because it lists the host's precise location in the DNS hierarchy. The DNS name in the example represents the host FILESVR042 in the subdomain ACCOUNTING (this is frequently a department or division in a company), which is in the subdomain QUEPUBLISHING (this is frequently the name of the company or organization that has registered the domain), which is in the TLD .CORP (which is an internal TLD).

Following are some questions you should ask yourself when planning your namespace needs:

- **Is your DNS namespace to be used for internal purposes only?** If so, you can use characters that are not typically used in DNS names, such as those outside the RFC 1123 standards. An example might be bigcorp.local.
- **Is your DNS namespace to be used on the Internet as well?** If you are currently using a corporate DNS namespace on the Internet, or think that you might at any point in the future, you should register your own domain name and conform to Internet naming standards.
- **Will you be implementing Active Directory?** The design and implementation of Active Directory on your network play a critical role in determining how domains should be created and nested within each other.

You need to consider the following three basic options when planning the DNS namespace you will be using:

- **Use an existing DNS namespace**—This option uses the same namespace for both the internal (corporate network) and external (Internet) portions of your network. If your domain name is `bigcorp.com`, you would use this for both internal and external use. Although this method is the easiest and provides simple access to both internal and external resources, it poses additional administrative requirements because an administrator must ensure that the appropriate records are being stored on the internal and external DNS servers as a security precaution.
- **Use a delegated DNS namespace**—This option uses a delegated domain of the public namespace. If your domain name is `bigcorp.com`, you might consider using `corp.bigcorp.com` for the internal namespace. When you use this option, the `corp.bigcorp.com` domain becomes the root of the Active Directory forest and domain structure. Internal clients should be allowed to resolve external namespace addresses; however, external clients should not. Using a delegated DNS namespace provides a namespace that is easy to understand and remember, and that fits in nicely with the existing registered domain name. All internal domain data is isolated in the domain or domain tree, thus requiring its own DNS server for the delegated internal domain. The downside to delegated namespaces is that this adds length to the total FQDN.
- **Use a unique DNS namespace**—This option uses a completely separate but related domain name for your internal namespace. As an example, if you are using `bigcorp.com` for your external namespace, you might use `bigcorp.net` for your internal namespace. This configuration provides the advantage of improving security by isolating the two namespaces from each other. Additionally, the administrative burden is relatively low because zone transfers do not need to be performed between the two namespaces, and the existing DNS namespace remains unchanged. In addition, this configuration prevents internal resources from being exposed directly to the Internet.

When creating DNS namespaces that are several levels deep, you must keep in mind some general DNS restrictions, as outlined in Table 6.

TABLE 6 DNS Name Restrictions

Restriction	Standard DNS	DNS in Windows Server 2003 (and Windows 2000)
Characters	Supports RFC 1123, which permits A to Z, a to z, 0 to 9, and the hyphen (–)	Supports several different configurations: RFC 1123 standard, as well as support for RFCs 2181 and the character set specified in RFC 2044.
FQDN length	Permits 63 bytes per label and 255 bytes for an FQDN	Permits 63 bytes per label and 255 bytes for an FQDN. Domain controllers are limited to 155 bytes for an FQDN.

Although it is typically abbreviated in the world of DNS, a zone is actually a *zone of authority*, which means that it contains the complete information on some part of a domain namespace. In other words, it is a subset or root of that portion of namespace. The nameserver is considered to have authority for that zone, and it can respond to any requests for name resolution from that zone. So when you look at the DNS name `www.quepublishing.com`, `quepublishing.com` is a DNS zone within the `.com` hierarchy. The `www` denotes the DNS record of a host contained within the `quepublishing.com` zone.

This conceptual representation of a zone also has a physical counterpart: All the information relating to a particular zone is stored in a physical file known as the *zone database file*, or more commonly the *zone file*, that can be found at `%systemroot%\system32\dns` for zones that are not stored in Active Directory. The following types of zones are supported by Windows Server 2003:

- **Standard primary**—A standard primary zone holds a master copy of a zone and can replicate it to all configured secondary zones in standard text format. Any changes that must be made to the zone are made on the copy stored on the primary.
- **Standard secondary**—A standard secondary zone holds a read-only copy of the zone information in standard text format. Secondary zones are created to increase performance and resilience of the DNS configuration. Information is transferred from the primary zone to the secondary zones.
- **Active Directory–integrated**—Active Directory–integrated zones are available only on Windows 2000 Server and Windows Server 2003 DNS servers in an Active Directory domain. The zone information is contained within the Active Directory database and is replicated using Active Directory replication. Active Directory–integrated zones provide an increased level of replication flexibility as well as security. Active Directory–integrated zones also operate in a multimaster arrangement because they are hosted within Active Directory itself; this way, any DNS server (domain controller) hosting the Active Directory–integrated zone can update the zone data.
- **Stub**—Microsoft introduced support for stub zones for the first time in Windows Server 2003. A stub zone contains only those resource records that are necessary to identify the authoritative DNS servers for that zone. Those resource records include name server (NS), Start of Authority (SOA), and possibly glue host (A) records. (Glue host records provide A record pointers to ensure that the master zone has the correct name server information for the stub zone.)

When you are using a standard primary/standard secondary DNS zone implementation, the following points are of concern:

- A single DNS server is the master, holding the only writeable copy of the DNS zone file.
- Zone transfers can be conducted using either incremental or full zone transfer.
- This implementation is made fully compatible with BIND DNS servers by using the standard DNS zone-transfer methods in place.

When you are using an Active Directory–integrated DNS zone implementation, the following points are of concern:

- A multimaster arrangement allows any DNS server to make updates to the zone file.
- Zone data is replicated with Active Directory data.
- Increased security is provided on the zone file.
- Redundancy is provided for DNS dynamic update.
- The administrator can adjust replication scope. Additionally, the zone file can be replicated to a standard secondary DNS server—a common practice for DNS servers placed on screened subnets.
- This implementation appears to be a standard primary zone to a BIND DNS server, thus allowing the use of BIND DNS servers as standard secondary zone servers.

Table 7 compares Active Directory–integrated zones and standard DNS zones.

TABLE 7 DNS Zone Type Comparison

DNS Feature	Standard DNS Zones	Active Directory–Integrated Zones
Complies with IETF specifications	Yes	Yes
Uses Active Directory for replication	No	Yes
Increases availability by providing a multimaster arrangement	No	Yes
Allows for zone updates after the failure of a single DNS server	No	Yes
Supports incremental zone transfers	Yes	Yes

Regardless of whether you create standard or Active Directory–integrated DNS zones, you should be aware of the benefits of also using standard secondary zones. Following are some of the benefits you can realize by placing secondary zones on your network:

- Adding standard secondary zone servers increases the redundancy of the zone by providing name resolution even if the primary zone server is unresponsive.
- When remote locations are connected to the core network over WAN links, secondary zone servers can greatly reduce costs and network traffic. By placing standard secondary zones in these remote locations or in locations with a high number of clients, you can improve overall network performance.
- Standard secondary zone servers reduce the load on the primary servers by distributing name-resolution requests among more DNS servers.

Unlike WINS, which allows for a push/pull arrangement, zone transfers always originate with the secondary server polling the primary zone at the configured interval. They do so by checking the zone version number on the primary server to see whether it has changed in comparison to the version number on the secondary server. If the zone version number on the primary server has been incremented, a zone transfer is required and will be performed. If the secondary zone supports incremental zone transfers (which Windows Server 2003 does), the secondary zone pulls (from the primary zone) only the changes made to resource records for each incremental zone version—meaning that a resource record could potentially be updated one or more times in a single zone transfer. When you use incremental zone transfers, network traffic is reduced and zone transfer speed is increased.

Windows Server 2003 supports two zone transfer types for standard zones: full zone transfers and incremental zone transfers. You might also see them abbreviated as AXFR and IXFR, respectively. A full zone transfer causes the entire zone data file to be transferred, which is a large user of both bandwidth and time. Older, and some non-Microsoft, DNS servers will always require a full zone transfer to be performed—for example, when using Windows NT 4.0 DNS servers. Most newer DNS servers will offer support for incremental zone transfers.

Active Directory–integrated DNS zones replicate data among all domain controllers, allowing any domain controller to modify the zone file and replicate the changes to the rest of the domain controllers. This form of replication is known as multimaster replication because multiple DNS servers are allowed to update the zone data—domain controllers that are running the DNS service, in this case. Replication occurs on a per-property basis, meaning that only the relevant changes are replicated. Active Directory–integrated zones replicate only the final result of multiple changes to a resource record, unlike standard zones, which transfer the changes to a resource record that occurred in each zone version number.

In a TCP/IP network, a DNS resolver is any system that has been configured with one or more DNS server IP addresses and that performs queries against these DNS servers. The DNS resolver is part of the DNS Client service, which is automatically installed when Windows is installed. The resolver can request one of two types of queries from a DNS server: recursive or iterative.

A *recursive query* is a DNS query that is sent to a DNS server from a DNS resolver asking the DNS server to provide a complete answer to the query, or an error stating that it cannot provide the information. If the DNS server is also configured as a forwarder, the query can be forwarded directly to another DNS server. If the query is for a name outside the local DNS server's zone of authority, it performs an iterative query against a root DNS server, which then responds with the IP address of the DNS server whose zone of authority includes the desired IP top-level domain. Additional iterative queries are then performed until the name is resolved into its IP address or an error is produced.

An *iterative query* is a DNS query that is sent by a DNS server to another DNS server in an effort to perform name resolution. Consider the example of a workstation (DNS resolver) in the `bigcorp.com` domain that wants to communicate with a web server located in the `smallcorp.com` domain.

A *DNS forwarder* is a DNS server that accepts forwarded recursive lookups from another DNS server and then resolves the request for that DNS server. This capability can be useful if you do not have local copies of your internal DNS zone and want to have your local DNS server forward DNS queries to a central DNS server that is authoritative for your internal DNS zone. Caching-only servers make good DNS forwarders. If the DNS forwarder does not receive a valid resolution from the server that it forwards the request to, it attempts to resolve the client request itself.

A *DNS slave server* is a DNS forwarder server that does not try to resolve a resolution request if it doesn't receive a valid response to its forwarded DNS request. You typically see this type of DNS server implemented in conjunction with a secure Internet connection.

A new feature in Windows Server 2003, *conditional forwarding*, enables administrators to direct DNS requests to other DNS servers based on domain. Previous versions of Microsoft DNS supported only one forwarder, so if forwarding were enabled, all requests would be sent to a single server. This feature is used frequently when you want requests made to the internal network to be forwarded to a master DNS server that stores internal DNS zones but have resolution requests that are made to Internet domains be sent to the Internet using the standard resolution process.

A common implementation of DNS forwarders in a Windows Server 2003 network has one specific DNS server being allowed to make queries to DNS servers outside the firewall. This implementation allows the firewall to be configured to allow DNS traffic only from this specific DNS server to leave the protected network, and allows only valid replies to the DNS server to enter the protected network. Through this approach, all other DNS traffic—both inbound and outbound—can be dropped at the firewall, adding to the overall security of the network and the DNS service.

Configuring DNS security can be divided into the following five general areas of concern:

- Dynamic updates
- Active Directory DNS permissions
- Zone transfer security
- DNS server properties
- DNS Security (DNSSEC)

Dynamic updates occur when a DHCP server or a DNS client computer automatically updates the applicable DNS resource records when a DHCP lease is granted (or expires). Three types of dynamic updates exist in Windows Server 2003, each with its own security specifics.

Secure dynamic updates are available when Active Directory–integrated zones are in use. Using secure dynamic update, the DNS zone information is stored in Active Directory and thus is protected using Active Directory security features. When a zone has been created as or converted to an Active Directory–integrated zone, Access Control List (ACL) entries can be used to specify which users, computers, and groups can make changes to a zone or a specific record.

If the zone is integrated with Active Directory, the Discretionary Access Control List (DACL) for the zone can be used to configure the permissions for the users and groups that might change or control the data in the DNS zone. Table 8 lists the default group and user permissions for Active Directory–integrated DNS zones. These default values can be modified to suit your particular needs.

TABLE 8 Default Group and User Permissions on Active Directory–Integrated DNS Zones

Group or User	Permissions
Administrators	Allow: Read, Write, Create All Child Objects, Special Permissions
Authenticated Users	Allow: Create All Child Objects
Creator Owner	Allow: Special Permissions
DnsAdmins	Allow: Full Control, Read, Write, Create All Child Objects, Delete Child Objects, Special Permissions
Domain Admins	Allow: Full Control, Read, Write, Create All Child Objects, Delete Child Objects
Enterprise Admins	Allow: Full Control, Read, Write, Create All Child Objects, Delete Child Objects
Enterprise Domain Controllers	Allow: Full Control, Read, Write, Create All Child Objects, Delete Child Objects, Special Permissions
Everyone	Allow: Read, Special Permissions
Pre–Windows 2000 Compatible Access	Allow: Special Permissions
System	Allow: Full Control, Read, Write, Create All Child Objects, Delete Child Objects

By default, Windows Server 2003 DNS performs zone transfers only with the DNS servers that are listed in a zone's Name Server (NS) resource records. Even though this configuration is fairly secure, you should consider changing this setting to allow zone transfers to be carried out only with specific IP addresses that you have explicitly configured.

If you must perform zone transfers across an untrusted network, you should consider implementing and using a virtual private network (VPN) tunnel between the two DNS servers. Encrypted zone information traveling inside the tunnel is safe from prying eyes, thus providing an uncompromised zone transfer. When using a VPN tunnel for zone transfer data, you should use the strongest possible level of encryption and authentication supported by both sides of the tunnel.

By default, Windows Server 2003 DNS servers use a secure response option that eliminates the addition of unrelated resource records that are included in a referral answer to the cache. The server typically caches any names in referral answers, thus expediting the resolution of subsequent DNS queries. However, when this feature is in use, the server can determine whether the referred name is polluting or insecure and discard it. The server thus determines whether to cache the name offered in the referral, depending on whether it is part of the exact DNS domain tree for which the original name query was made. As an example, a query made for `sales.bigcorp.com` with a referral answer of `smallcorp.net` would not get cached.

It's a fact of life that many organizations already have existing DNS solutions in place, such as UNIX BIND. In some cases, these existing BIND servers might not meet the DNS requirements of Active Directory. Table 9 outlines the features of some of the more common versions of BIND in use.

TABLE 9 Features of Various BIND Versions

BIND Version	Features
4.9.4	Support for fast zone transfers
4.9.6	Support for SRV resource records
8.1.2	Support for dynamic DNS (DDNS)
8.2.1	Support for incremental zone transfer (IXFR) between DNS servers
8.2.2	Full support for all Active Directory features

If you are dealing with other DNS systems, you have two basic choices of implementation:

- Upgrade existing DNS systems to meet the DNS requirements of Active Directory. For BIND, versions 8.1.2 and later are sufficient.
- Migrate existing DNS zones to Windows Server 2003 DNS.

Although it is recommended that you use only Windows Server 2003 DNS servers to ensure full support for Active Directory, you can use any DNS system that meets the following specifications:

- Support for SRV (Service) resource records
- Dynamic updates per RFC 2136

If you have UNIX BIND servers in your DNS infrastructure, you should consider placing them as secondaries instead of primaries. By default, Windows Server 2003 DNS servers use a fast zone transfer format whereby compression is used and multiple records can be sent in a single TCP message. BIND versions 4.9.4 and later support fast zone transfers. If you are using an earlier version of BIND or another third-party DNS system that does not support fast zone transfers, you must disable fast zone transfers. When you select the BIND Secondaries option, fast zone transfers are disabled for that server. You also should configure your zones to not transfer WINS-related information during zone transfers to these secondary servers.

In most environments that rely on WINS for name resolution for legacy systems, it is important to ensure that more than one WINS server exists so that you provide redundancy and availability. To ensure that each server has a current copy of the database, you need to configure replication between your WINS servers. You can configure the following types of replication for the WINS service:

- **Pull replication**—In pull replication, your server pulls the database from the replication partner. A pull replication is time based and occurs at the time you have configured. You can decide whether to establish a persistent connection for replication, and you can set the start time and interval for replication.
- **Push replication**—In push replication, your server pushes its database to the replication partner. A push replication is event driven, and the number of database updates determines when the event occurs. You can decide whether to use a persistent connection for push activities, and you can set the number of changes in version ID before replication.
- **Replication partner type**—The partner type can be push, pull, or push/pull, depending on your requirements. (In push/pull replication, database replication can occur using either method—push or pull.)

Microsoft TCP/IP uses NetBIOS over TCP/IP (NetBT), as specified in RFC 1001 and 1002, to support the NetBIOS client and server programs in the local area network (LAN) and wide area network (WAN) environments. Before we look at the specifics of NetBIOS name resolution, let's briefly review how computers communicate on the network. This review should help you understand how the different NetBIOS modes work and why some are preferable to others.

Computers can use two ways to communicate on a network:

- Through broadcast messages, which every computer receives
- Through directed messages, which are sent to a specific computer

Although networks can be organized using a mixture of node types, Microsoft recommends against doing so. B-node client computers ignore P-node directed messages, and P-node client computers ignore B-node broadcasts. Therefore, it is conceivable that two client computers could separately be established with the same NetBIOS name. If WINS is enabled on a Windows 2000 or XP computer, the system uses H-node by default. Without WINS, the system uses B-node by default. Non-WINS client computers can access WINS through a WINS proxy, which is a WINS-enabled computer that listens to name query broadcasts and then queries the WINS server on behalf of the requesting client computer.

The actual configuration of a computer to use `LMHOSTS` for NetBIOS name resolution is not done by using the WINS console or a Group Policy Object, as you might expect. Instead, you must actually configure it computer by computer by setting the options available to you on the WINS tab of the Advanced TCP/IP Settings dialog box.

Planning and Implementing Server Roles and Server Security

Role-based security is implemented by using a layered approach to security; the most general security settings are applied at the highest level and grow increasingly restrictive as you go deeper into the organizational structure of the domain. Through the use of the preconfigured security templates included with Windows Server 2003, combined with careful planning and attentive administration of the network, you can implement a role-based security solution.

Windows Server 2003 comes with a complete set of preconfigured security templates that you can use to quickly apply standardized security settings to a single computer, an Organizational Unit (OU), or a domain, if desired. In addition to these preconfigured security templates, Microsoft has made available security templates that you can use to enforce specific security settings on Windows Server 2003 computers, depending on their assigned roles.

OUs, sometimes thought of as nothing more than an organizational tool to "clean up" the visual appearance of Active Directory, are actually among the most powerful tools for planning, implementing, and maintaining a secure network environment. OUs offer an easy way to segment users and other security principals—specifically, computers, in this instance—for the purpose of creating and enforcing administrative boundaries. By nesting OUs within each other, each with its own specific Group Policy Object (GPO), you can quickly piece together the overall security solution for your network.

You can identify the default security settings on a newly installed Windows Server 2003 member server through a variety of different means, such as the Local Group Policy console, the Local Security Policy console, or the Resultant Set of Policy (RSoP) snap-in.

A security template is little more than a specially formatted flat text file that can be read by the Security Configuration Manager tools. These preconfigured templates have the extension `.inf` and can be located in the `%systemroot%\security\templates` folder on your Windows Server 2003 computer. You can use the Security Configuration and Analysis console, the `secedit.exe` tool, or the Local Security Policy console to apply these templates to a local computer. You can apply templates to an OU or domain by importing them into the Security Settings section of the applicable Group Policy using the Group Policy Editor. You also can use these preconfigured templates to baseline an unknown system against a known set of configuration settings by using the Security Configuration and Analysis console or the `secedit.exe` tool.

Table 10 details the preconfigured security templates that ship with Windows Server 2003.

TABLE 10 The Preconfigured Security Templates in Windows Server 2003

Template (Filename)	Description
Default (`Setup security.inf`)	This template is created during the installation of Windows on the computer. This template varies from one computer to the next, depending on whether the installation was performed as a clean installation or an upgrade. `Setup security.inf` represents the default security settings that a computer started with and thus can be used to reset portions of security as required. This template can be applied to both workstations and member servers, but not to domain controllers (DCs). Also it should never be applied via Group Policy because of the large amount of data it contains. Applying this template via Group Policy could result in performance degradations.
Default DC (`DC security.inf`)	This template is automatically created when a member server is promoted to a DC. It represents the file, Registry, and system service default security settings for that DC, and can be used later to reset those areas to their default configurations.
Compatible (`compatws.inf`)	The Compatible workstation/member server template provides a means of allowing members of the Users group to run applications that do not conform to the Windows Logo Program for Windows 2000 and above. Applications that were written for Windows NT 4.0 do not use the same security model that Windows 2000 and above applications use. Applications that do conform to the Windows Logo Program can be successfully run by members of the Users group without any further modifications required, in most cases. For applications that do not conform, there are two basic choices: You can make the users members of the Power Users group or relax the default permissions of the Users group. The Compatible template solves this problem by changing the default file and Registry permissions that are granted to the Users group to allow them to run most applications that are not part of the Windows Logo Program. As a side effect of applying this template, all users are removed from the Power Users group because the basic assumption is that the template is being applied to prevent the need for that group. This template should not be applied to DCs, so you need to be sure not to import it into the Default Domain Policy or the Default Domain Controller Policy.
Secure (`securews.inf` and `securedc.inf`)	The Secure templates are the first ones to actually begin the process of locking down the computer to which they are applied. Two different Secure templates exist: `securews.inf`, which is for workstations and member servers, and `securedc.inf`, which is for DCs only. The Secure templates prevent the use of the LAN Manager (LM) authentication protocol. Windows 9x clients need to have Active Directory Client Extensions installed to enable NT LAN Manager

(continues)

TABLE 10 *Continued*

Template (Filename)	Description
	Version 2 (NTLMv2). Only when NTLMv2 is enabled on these legacy clients can they communicate with Windows 2000 and above clients and servers using these templates. These templates also impose additional restrictions on anonymous users. Such restrictions include preventing them from enumerating account and share information. The secure templates also enable Server Message Block (SMB) signing on the server side. By default, SMB signing is enabled on client computers. If you apply this template, SMB packet signing will always be negotiated between clients and servers.
Highly Secure (`hisecws.inf` and `hisecdc.inf`)	The Highly Secure templates impose further restrictions on the computers to which they are applied. Whereas the Secure templates require at least NTLM authentication, the Highly Secure templates require NTLMv2 authentication. The Secure templates enable SMB packet signing, and the Highly Secure templates require SMB packet signing. In addition to the various extra security restrictions that the Highly Secure templates impose, these templates make several changes to group membership and the login process. All members of the Power Users group are removed from this group. In addition, only members of the Domain Admins group and the local administrative account are allowed to be members of the local Administrators group. When the Highly Secure templates are used, it is assumed that only Windows Logo Program–compliant applications are in use. Therefore, no provision is in place for users to use noncompliant applications because the Compatible template is not needed and the Power Users group has no members. Members of the Users group are able to use applications that comply with the Windows Logo Program. In addition, members of the Administrators group can use any application they want.
System Root (`rootsec.inf`)	This template defines the root permissions for the root of the system volume. If these permissions are changed, you can reapply them using this template. In addition, you can modify this template to apply the same permissions to other volumes. Explicitly configured permissions are not overwritten on child objects when you use this template.
No Terminal Server Use SID (`notssid.inf`)	This template is used on servers that are not running Terminal Services to remove all unnecessary Terminal Services security identifiers (SIDs) from the file system and Registry. However, this does not increase the security of the server.
Internet Explorer SACL (`iesacls.inf`)	This template is used to enable auditing on Registry keys that Internet Explorer uses. By default, the keys in question are set to allow the built-in Everyone group Full Control. By enabling this auditing, changes can be tracked if users (or the applications they use within Internet Explorer) attempt to modify the settings of any of these keys.

All the preconfigured security templates are incremental, meaning that they have been designed to be applied to computers that use the default security settings. These templates do not implement the default security settings before applying their security settings.

The Security Configuration Manager tools are to be used to design, test, and implement these (and other) security templates. The components of the Security Configuration Manager include the following:

- The Security Configuration and Analysis snap-in
- The Security Templates snap-in
- Group Policy security extensions
- The `secedit.exe` command

The Security Configuration and Analysis snap-in is an important tool in any administrator's security template toolbox. By using the Security Configuration and Analysis snap-in, you can create, configure, test, and implement security template settings for a local computer. Therein lies its one real weakness: You can use it to work only with the settings of a local computer. However, you can find ways to work around this limitation by using the other tools that are at your disposal, including `secedit.exe` and the security extensions to Group Policy.

The Security Configuration and Analysis snap-in can be used in two basic modes, as its name suggests: configuration and analysis—although not necessarily in that order. When you're using the Security Configuration and Analysis snap-in to analyze the current system security configuration, no changes are ever made to the computer being analyzed. The administrator simply selects a security template to compare the computer against (either a preconfigured template or a custom-created template). The settings from the template are loaded into a database and then compared to the settings currently implemented on the computer. It is possible to import multiple templates into this database, thus merging their settings into one conglomerate database. In addition, you can specify that existing database settings are to be cleared before another template is imported into the database. When the desired security templates have been loaded into the database, any number of analysis actions can be performed, both by the Security Configuration and Analysis snap-in and by the `secedit.exe` command.

After the database has been populated and an analysis scan has been initiated, the Security Configuration and Analysis snap-in examines every configurable Group Policy option and then reports back to you the results of the analysis scan. Each setting is marked with an icon that denotes one of several possible outcomes, such as that the settings are the same, the settings are different, or the settings do not apply. Table 11 outlines the possible icons that you might see and what they indicate.

TABLE 11 The Preconfigured Security Template Icons in Windows Server 2003

Icon	Description
Red circle with white X	The item is defined in the analysis database and on the computer but does not match the currently configured setting.
Green check mark	The item is defined in the analysis database and on the computer, and matches the currently configured setting.
Question mark	The item is not defined in the analysis database and was not examined on the computer.
Exclamation point	The item is defined in the analysis database but not on the computer.
No special icon	The item is not defined in the analysis database or the computer.

You can analyze and configure several areas by using the Security Configuration and Analysis snap-in:

- **Account Policies**—This node contains items that control user accounts. In Windows NT 4.0, these items are managed from the User Manager for Domains. This node has two subnodes: Password Policy and Account Lockout Policy. The Password Policy node deals with account password-related items, such as minimum length and maximum age. The Account Lockout Policy node contains options for configuring account lockout durations and lockout reset options.
- **Local Policies**—This node contains policies that are applied to the local machine. It has three subnodes: Audit Policy, User Rights Assignment, and Security Options. The Audit Policy node is relatively self-explanatory: It offers options for configuring and implementing various auditing options. The User Rights Assignment node contains miscellaneous options that deal with user rights, such as the ability to log in to a computer across the network. The Security Options node contains many other options—such as the option to set a login banner or allow the system to be shut down without being logged in first—that previously could be edited only in the Windows NT 4.0 Registry or by using System Policies.
- **Event Log**—This node contains options that enable you to configure the behavior and security of the event log. In this node, for example, you can include maximum log sizes and disallow guest access to the event logs.
- **Restricted Groups**—This node enables you to permanently configure which users are allowed to be members of specific groups. For example, company policy might provide the capability to perform server backups to a specific group of administrators. If another user who is not otherwise authorized with these privileges is added to this group and not removed after he or she has performed the intended function, you have created a security problem because the user has more rights than normally authorized. By using the Restricted Groups node, you can reset group membership to the intended membership.

- **System Services**—This node enables you to configure the behavior and security assignments associated with all system services running on the computer. Options include defining that a service is to start automatically or be disabled. In addition, you can configure the user accounts that are to have access to each service.
- **Registry**—This node enables you to configure access restrictions that specify who is allowed to configure or change individual Registry keys or entire hives. This option does not provide you with the means of creating or modifying Registry keys, however; that must still be done by using the Registry Editor.
- **File System**—This node enables you to set folder and file NTFS permissions. This capability is especially handy if you need to reset the permissions on a large number of folders or files.

The Security Templates snap-in might at first seem to have no real purpose. However, this is not the case. You can use this snap-in to modify existing templates or create new ones from scratch without the danger of accidentally applying the template to the computer or GPO.

You can easily and quickly import security templates into GPOs by using the Group Policy Editor to configure large portions of your network with the settings contained in the security template. You should apply the most generic settings at the domain level and then, at the OU level, apply specific settings that pertain to the computers in that OU; this is the cornerstone of role-based network security.

You can use `secedit` to perform the same functions as the Security Configuration and Analysis snap-in, plus a couple of additional functions not found in the snap-in. The `secedit` command has the following top-level switches available for use:

- **`/analyze`**—This option enables you to analyze the security settings of a computer by comparing them against the baseline settings in a database.
- **`/configure`**—This option enables you to configure the security settings of the local computer by applying the settings contained in a database.
- **`/export`**—This option enables you to export the settings configured in a database to a security template `.inf` file.
- **`/import`**—This option enables you to import the settings configured in a security template `.inf` file into a database. If you will be applying multiple security templates to a database, you should use this option before performing the analysis or configuration.
- **`/validate`**—This option validates the syntax of a security template to ensure that it is correct before you import the template into a database for analysis or configuration.
- **`/GenerateRollback`**—This option enables you to create a rollback template that can be used to reset the security configuration to the values it had before the security template was applied.

Of the available options, you will most often use the `/analyze` and `/configure` switches.

Security policies (via security templates and GPOs) are typically applied at the three following hierarchical levels to create role-based security:

- **Domain**—The most common security requirements, such as password and account lockout policies, are applied at the domain level. These policies are applied to all computers—servers and workstations alike—within the domain.
- **Baseline**—This policy contains security configuration items that apply to all member servers, such as auditing policies and user rights assignments.
- **Role-specific**—To address the specific security needs of each specific server role, member servers are divided into role-based groups using OUs and have specific, individual security policies applied to them.

Planning, Implementing, and Troubleshooting Network Security Using IPSec

The following are the standard features of the Windows Server 2003 IPSec implementation:

- IPSec in Windows Server 2003 is policy based. Thus, it cannot be configured without an IPSec policy being in place. The IPSec policy enables an administrator to more easily apply settings to groups of objects, such as computers or users.
- IPSec on Windows Server 2003 can use Kerberos v5, a digital certificate, or a shared secret (string) for user authentication.
- IPSec mutually authenticates computers before any data is exchanged.
- IPSec establishes a security association (SA) between the two host computers involved in the data transfer. An SA is the collection of a policy and keys, which define the rules for security settings.
- IPSec encrypts data using Data Encryption Standard (DES) or Triple DES (3DES).
- IPSec uses the MD5 or SHA1 algorithm for data hashing.
- IPSec is invisible to users. IPSec operates at the network level of the Open System Interconnet (OSI) model; therefore, users and applications do not directly interact with the protocol. After an IPSec tunnel has been created, users can connect to applications and services as if they were on the local network and not on the other side of a public network.

The IPSec Authentication Header (AH) provides three services as part of the IPSec protocol. First (as its name might suggest), AH authenticates the entire packet. Second, it ensures data integrity. Third, it prevents any replaying of the packet by a third party who might be trying to penetrate the IPSec tunnel. One service AH doesn't provide is payload encryption. AH protects your data from modification, but an attacker who is snooping the network would still be able to read the data. To prevent the modification of the data, AH uses two hashing algorithms to "sign" the packet for integrity:

- The Message Digest 5 (MD5) algorithm applies the hashing function to the data in four passes.
- The Secure Hash Algorithm 1 (SHA-1) is closely modeled after MD5. SHA-1 uses 79 32-bit constants during the computation of the hash value, which results in a 160-bit key. Because SHA-1 has a longer key length, it is considered more secure than MD5.

Encapsulating Security Protocol (ESP) provides confidentiality in addition to authentication, integrity, and antireplay. This portion of the IPSec protocol encrypts the data contents of the packet. The format of the ESP varies, depending on the type and mode of encryption being used. ESP can be used alone or in combination with AH.

Policies enable you to quickly and easily configure IPSec based on the settings required within your organization. Windows Server 2003 comes with the following three preconfigured IPSec policies that might may or might not meet your needs:

- **Client (Respond Only)**—This policy requires IPSec-provided security only when another computer requests it. This policy allows the computer to attempt unsecured communications first and switch to IPSec-secured communications if requested. This policy contains the default response rule, which creates dynamic IPSec filters for inbound and outbound traffic. The filters are based on the requested protocol and the port traffic for the communication that is being secured. This policy, which can be used on workstations and servers alike, provides the minimum amount of IPSec security.
- **Server (Request Security)**—This policy requests security from the other computer and allows unsecured communication with computers that are not IPSec-aware. The computer accepts inbound unsecured traffic but always attempts to secure further communications by requesting IPSec security from the sending computer. If the other computer is not IPSec-enabled, the entire communication is allowed to be unsecured. This policy, which can be used on workstations and servers alike, provides a medium level of IPSec security. If desired, you can opt to use this policy on a workstation computer as well.
- **Secure Server (Require Security)**—This policy is implemented on computers that require highly secure communications. These computers include servers transmitting sensitive data. The filters in this policy require all outbound communication to be

secured, allowing only the initial inbound communication request to be unsecured. This policy has a rule to require security for all IP traffic, a rule to permit ICMP traffic, and the default response rule to respond to requests for security from other computers. This policy, typically used only on servers, provides the highest level of IPSec security on a network. This policy can also be used on workstation computers, if you want. Computers that are not IPSec-enabled cannot establish any communications with computers using this policy. This policy can also be used on a workstation, if desired.

Filter actions define the type of security and methods by which security is established. The default methods are Permit, Block, and Negotiate Security. The Permit option passes the traffic without the requirement for security. This action is appropriate if you never want to secure traffic to which a rule applies. The Block action silently blocks all traffic from computers specified in the IP filter list. The Negotiate Security action specifies that the computer is to use a list of security methods to negotiate the appropriate security for the communication.

The IP Security Monitor snap-in is divided into three major areas: the Active Policy node, the Main Mode node, and the Quick Mode node. Table 12 explains each of the information items shown in the Active Policy node of the IP Security Monitor snap-in. The Active Policy is the IPSec policy that is currently in effect on the computer.

TABLE 12 Active Policy Node Items

Item	Description
Policy Name	Specifies the name of the active IPSec policy.
Description	Describes the active IPSec policy.
Policy Last Modified	Provides the date and the time that the active IPSec policy was modified.
Policy Store	Provides the storage location for the active IPSec policy. For a local policy, it reads Local Store, and for a domain policy, it reads Domain Store.
Policy Path	Applies only to domain policies and provides the LDAP path to the active IPSec policy.
Organizational Unit	Applies only to domain policies and lists the organizational unit to which the GPO is applied.
Group Policy Object Name	Applies only to domain policies and lists the GPO to which the active IPSec policy is applied.

Table 13 explains each of the information items shown in the Statistics folder in the Main Mode node of the IP Security Monitor snap-in. The Main Mode SA, also known as the ISAKMP SA, is used to protect the IPSec security negotiations.

TABLE 13 Main Mode (Internet Key Exchange) Statistics

Statistic	Description
Active Acquire	Specifies a request by the IPSec policy to have IKE perform a task. This number includes all outstanding and queued requests and is typically 1. Under heavy loading, this number increases.
Active Receive	Displays the number of IKE messages that have been received and are queued for processing.
Acquire Failures	Displays the number of times that an acquire has failed.
Receive Failures	Displays the number of times that errors have occurred in receiving IKE messages.
Send Failures	Displays the number of times that errors have occurred in sending IKE messages.
Acquire Heap Size	Displays the number of entries in the acquire heap, which stores active acquires. This number increases with heavy loading and decreases as the heap is cleared.
Receive Heap Size	Displays the number of entries in the IKE receive buffers for incoming IKE messages.
Authentication Failures	Displays the total number of identity authentication failures that have occurred during Main Mode negotiation. This is a very useful indicator to determine whether the authentication methods match between two computers attempting communications.
Negotiation Failures	Displays the total number of negotiation failures that occurred during Main Mode or Quick Mode negotiation. This is a useful statistic to determine whether security and/or authentication methods match between two computers attempting communications.
Invalid Cookies Received	Specifies a value contained in a received IKE message that is used by IKE to find the state of an active Main Mode. If a cookie in a received IKE message cannot be matched with an active Main Mode, it is invalid.
Total Acquire	Displays the total number of requests submitted by IKE to the IPSec driver to establish an SA for securing traffic.
Total Get SPI	Displays the total number of requests submitted by IKE to the IPSec driver to obtain a unique Security Parameters Index (SPI).
Key Additions	Displays the number of outbound Quick Mode SAs added by IKE to the IPSec driver.
Key Updates	Displays the number of inbound Quick Mode SAs added by IKE to the IPSec driver.
Get SPI Failures	Displays the number of requests submitted by IKE to the IPSec driver to obtain a unique SPI that have failed.
Key Addition Failures	Displays the number of outbound Quick Mode SA addition requests submitted by IKE to the IPSec driver that have failed.
Key Update Failures	Displays the number of inbound Quick Mode SA addition requests submitted by IKE to the IPSec driver that have failed.
ISADB List Size	Displays the number of Main Mode state entries, including negotiated Main Modes, Main Modes in progress, and Main Modes that have failed and have not yet been deleted.
Connection List Size	Displays the number of Quick Mode state entries. This number indicates the load placed on the computer.

(continues)

TABLE 13 *Continued*

Statistic	Description
IKE Main Mode	Displays the total number of successful SAs created during Main Mode negotiations.
IKE Quick Mode	Displays the total number of successful SAs created during Quick Mode negotiations. There are typically multiple Quick Mode SAs created for each Main Mode SA; thus, this value might not necessarily match that of the Main Mode.
Soft Associations	Displays the total number of negotiations that resulted in the use of unsecured traffic (also known as *soft SAs*). Typically, this is an indication of SAs formed with computers that do not support IPSec or could not negotiate successful IPSec connections. This can be an indication of mismatched security and authentication settings.
Invalid Packets Received	Displays the number of received IKE messages that were invalid. Most commonly, invalid IKE messages are a result of retransmitted IKE messages or unmatched shared keys between the communicating computers.

Table 14 explains each of the information items shown in the Statistics folder in the Quick Mode node of the IP Security Monitor snap-in. The Quick Mode SAs, also known as the IPSec SAs, are security associations that have been created to protect the data sent between computers communicating securely using IPSec.

TABLE 14 Quick Mode (IPSec) Statistics

Statistic	Description
Active Security Associations	Displays the number of active IPSec SAs.
Offloaded Security Associations	Displays the number of active IPSec SAs that have been offloaded to hardware.
Pending Key Operations	Displays the number of IPSec key operations that are in progress.
Key Additions	Displays the total number of successful IPSec SA negotiations.
Key Deletions	Displays the number of key deletions for IPSec SAs.
Re-Keys	Displays the number of rekey operations for IPSec SAs.
Active Tunnels	Displays the number of active IPSec tunnels.
Bad SPI Packets	Displays the total number of packets for which the SPI was incorrect. SPIs are used to match inbound packets with SAs. If the SPI is incorrect, the inbound SA might have expired. If rekeying intervals are set very short, this number is likely to increase rapidly. Under normal conditions, a bad SPI packet does not mean that IPSec is failing because SAs expire normally.
Packets Not Decrypted	Displays the total number of packets that were not decrypted successfully. This might indicate that a packet has arrived for which the SA has previously expired. When the SA expires, the session key used to decrypt packets is removed. By itself, this does not indicate that IPSec is failing.
Packets Not Authenticated	Displays the total number of packets for which data could not be verified, meaning that the integrity hash verification failed. Most commonly, this is a result of an expired SA.

TABLE 14 *Continued*

Statistic	Description
Packets with Replay Detection	Displays the total number of packets that contained a valid Sequence Number field.
Confidential Bytes Sent	Displays the total number of bytes sent using the ESP protocol.
Confidential Bytes Received	Displays the total number of bytes received using the ESP protocol.
Authenticated Bytes Sent	Displays the total number of bytes sent using the AH protocol.
Authenticated Bytes Received	Displays the total number of bytes received using the AH protocol.
Transport Bytes Sent	Displays the total number of bytes sent using IPSec transport mode.
Transport Bytes Received	Displays the total number of bytes received using IPSec transport mode.
Bytes Sent in Tunnels	Displays the total number of bytes sent using IPSec tunnel mode.
Bytes Received in Tunnels	Displays the total number of bytes received using IPSec tunnel mode.
Offloaded Bytes Sent	Displays the total number of bytes sent using hardware offload.
Offloaded Bytes Received	Displays the total number of bytes received using hardware offload.

Configuring the IP Security Monitor hasn't changed much since Windows 2000, except that the IP Security Monitor is now an MMC snap-in. You can open the IP Security Monitor properties for any server listed in the IP Security Monitor node by right-clicking it and selecting Properties from the context menu. You have the option to change the refresh interval for the display of the IP Security Monitor statistics and to decide whether you want to enable DNS name resolution, which comes into play when you're examining the SAs that are formed.

If you have problems with IPSec, you should first verify that any routers or firewalls that traffic might be passing through are configured to support IPSec traffic. You need to allow the following traffic:

- Protocol ID 50 and 51 or ESP and AH traffic
- UDP port 500 for IPSec negotiation traffic

Some other basic problems and troubleshooting tips for them are outlined here:

- **You are not able to establish any communications with a computer**—In this case, you should first verify that basic network connectivity exists between the computers in question by using the `ping` command. You should also ensure that all required network services, such as DHCP and DNS, are operating properly for both computers.
- **You are not able to establish any communications with a computer**—A computer might have been removed from the domain. Whatever the cause, IPSec communications will fail.
- **Communications are occurring, but not as expected**—You need to ensure that you have the correct (and compatible) IPSec policies assigned on both computers.

- **No hard associations are being formed**—If there are currently soft associations in place, a hard association will not be formed. You need to completely stop all communications between the computers for approximately 5–10 minutes to allow the soft associations to time out. The easiest way to do this is to disable the network connection. After you have allowed the soft association to time out, you should check to see that a hard association has been formed. If a hard association still has not been formed, you need to examine the IPSec policy to verify that unsecured communications are not allowed.
- **IPSec communications are failing after you configure a digital certificate for authentication**—You must make sure that the required digital certificate is installed on the computers that are attempting to communicate by using that IPSec policy. This can also be a result of specifying an incorrect Certificate Authority (CA).
- **Some computers can create IPSec connections and some cannot**—This is most likely caused by not having the same IPSec policy applied to all the computers. If you are intentionally using different policies, you need to ensure that they share at least one common authentication and security method.

You should also be aware that IPSec-related problems can be found in the security log. You can view IKE events (negotiation successes and negotiation failures) by enabling success and/or failure auditing for the Audit Logon Events audit policy for the domain or the local computer. The IKE event category is also used for the auditing of user logon events in other services, but you can disable this by editing the Registry.

When success and/or failure auditing for the Audit Logon Events audit policy is enabled, IPSec records the success and/or failure of each Main Mode and Quick Mode negotiation. The establishment and termination of each negotiation is logged as a separate event, for easier analysis and troubleshooting. Be aware, however, that when you enable audit logon events, the security log will likely quickly fill up with IKE events unless you opt to disable auditing of those events through Registry editing.

Although no default tools provided in Windows Server 2003 enable you to monitor and manipulate Kerberos tickets, two *Windows Server 2003 Resource Kit* tools are available:

- **`kerbtray.exe`**—You can use the `kerbtray.exe` utility to view cached Kerberos tickets for the current computer from within the Windows GUI.
- **`klist.exe`**—The `klist.exe` utility is a command-line tool that is similar to `kerbtray.exe`. `klist.exe` enables you to view and delete cached Kerberos tickets.

You can download the *Windows Server 2003 Resource Kit* tools from www.microsoft.com/downloads if you search for "Windows Server 2003 Resource Kit Tools."

Often when policies are applied on multiple levels, results can conflict. Using the RSoP snap-in can help you to easily determine where the problem lies and the precedence (processing order) of the policies involved. RSoP can be used in one of two modes:

- **Planning mode**—This mode enables you to simulate the effect of policy settings that you want to apply to a computer and user.
- **Logging Mode**—This mode enables you to determine the existing policy settings for a computer and user who is currently logged on.

Planning, Implementing, and Troubleshooting Secure Network Access

When you want to access a network remotely, you must provide credentials. If you did not, security would not exist, and anyone could freely enter your network and exploit it. Based on this fact, you could say that Windows Server 2003 handles network access authorization based on account dial-in properties as well as remote access policies. Remote access polices are sets of rules (applied in an order) that define how incoming requests for authentication are handled—either accepted or rejected. Each policy is made up of profile settings and a remote access permissions setting.

Windows Server 2003 includes a new feature called Network Access Quarantine Control. This feature allows the delay of a remote access connection attempt to the Remote Access Server (RAS) until a script that verifies the configuration of the remote access computer runs. The connection attempt goes into quarantine until verified. The actual process is as follows: When a remote computer attempts to connect to the Remote Access Server, the computer is assigned an IP address to participate on the network. Then the user credentials are verified and authenticated, but the connection stays in quarantine until the remote computer is verified against the script. A script runs, and after it is completed, the server hosting quarantine releases the connection from quarantine after this information is verified. Network Access Quarantine Control is one of the newest features of Remote Access Security provided by default with Windows Server 2003.

Windows Server 2003 also provides Secure User Authentication. This means that security is obtained from the encrypted user credentials that are exchanged when you try to connect to a system. This can be done via the Point-to-Point Protocol (PPP) and its authentication-based protocols such as Extensible Authentication Protocol (EAP), Challenge Handshake Authentication Protocol (CHAP), and others. You can configure your Windows Server 2003 Remote Access Server to require specific secure authentication methods. The connection attempt is denied if the authentication credentials are not met.

EAP is a commonly used protocol on networks today; it is good at authenticating. EAP is responsible for creating an authentication method in which the authentication scheme to be used is negotiated by the remote access client and the authenticator, which could be either the Remote Access Server or even a RADIUS server. Windows Server 2003 Routing and Remote Access (RRAS) includes support for EAP-TLS by default; TLS stands for Transport Layer Security. It could be considered an EAP type, much like the wireless access protocol called LEAP, provided by Cisco systems. Many types of EAP exist, although they all perform similar functions, such as authentication; they just use different methods to do so.

Microsoft Challenge Handshake Authentication Protocol (MS-CHAP) is a nonreversible, encrypted password authentication protocol. MS-CHAP allows you to use Microsoft Point-to-Point Encryption (MPPE), which enables you to encrypt the data as well.

Version 2 of the MS-CHAP protocol provides stronger security for remote access connection attempts to your Remote Access Server. MS-CHAP Version 2 solves a major issue with the cryptographically weak LAN Manager encoding used for backward compatibility and password changes because backward compatibility is no longer supported. This way, you don't have problems with crypto-based attacks on your networks that might break your security posture. For reasons such as this, you should opt to use Version 2 over Version 1.

Version 2 also solves other problems with Version 1; for example, Version 2 stops one-way authentication, which allows masquerading attacks on your Remote Access Server. Because two-way authentication is not available with Version 1, such attacks are possible because the client that is trying to connect to a network remotely does not know whether it is dialing into the company's Remote Access Server or perhaps another server used for malicious intent. Again, you should use Version 2 instead of Version 1. MS-CHAP v2 provides two-way authentication, which is also called mutual authentication.

Challenge Handshake Authentication Protocol (CHAP) uses the industry-standard Message Digest 5 (MD5) protocol. MD5 is a hashing scheme that encrypts your data in transit over the remote access network. CHAP does not allow you to change passwords during the authentication process, which could be a major issue and one of the major reasons you would not want to include CHAP as part of your network.

The Shiva Password Authentication Protocol (SPAP) is an authentication protocol provided by a Shiva LAN Rover. If a Shiva client tries to connect to a Windows Server 2003 Remote Access Server, or a Windows client (such as XP) connects to a Shiva LAN Rover, SPAP is used. Because Shiva was prominent in the remote access market at one time, it is wise to include this support. Because PAP is used for cross-platform connectivity, it is not as secure as CHAP or even MS-CHAP. SPAP is even open to replay attacks (such attacks occur when data packets are captured in transit, examined, and then replayed to the server to gain access) because the same user password is always sent over the network in the same reversibly encrypted way each time. You should use SPAP only when you absolutely have to.

Remote Assistance, first introduced in Windows XP, provides a built-in mechanism allowing an "Expert" to lend assistance to a "Novice," whether or not by request. The Expert can be located on the same internal network or even somewhere else on the Internet. Remote Assistance allows the Expert to create a connection to the Novice's computer, view the desktop, communicate with the Novice, and even take remote control of the Novice's computer if the Novice allows. Remote Assistance can be performed only on computers running Windows XP or Windows Server 2003—a good reason to consider that desktop upgrade to Windows XP. Before a computer is eligible to receive Remote Assistance, however, it must be enabled either locally or by Group Policy.

Users can request Remote Assistance in three basic ways: Windows Messenger, email (sends a URL), or file (creates a Remote Assistance request file). Note that Windows Messenger is not the same as Microsoft Messenger, although both use similar technologies. You can most easily send Remote Assistance requests by using the Help and Support Center, which you can access by clicking Start, Help and Support.

Remote Assistance, like all the Terminal Services and Remote Desktop Protocol–based applications, requires that TCP port 3389 be available to make a connection.

Remote Desktop for Administration, previously referred to as Remote Administration mode in Windows 2000, provides a built-in method to remotely administer and control servers. Provided you have the correct credentials, you can even remotely restart or shut down a server. Of course, you probably ought to warn any users who might be connected to it before doing so!

You can use Remote Desktop for Administration in one of two ways. The first and simplest (although less feature-rich) method is to use the Remote Desktop Connection utility, which you can find by clicking Start, Programs, Accessories, Communications, Remote Desktop Connection.

The second method for creating Remote Desktop for Administration connections is to use the new Remote Desktops Microsoft Management Console (MMC). This method offers two features that Windows administrators have been clamoring for since the introduction of Terminal Services:

- **Multiple connection profiles can be created**—You can configure multiple connections in the Remote Desktops MMC and then switch through them quickly and easily, all within the confines of a single window. The multiple windows required when using the Remote Desktop Connection utility or the Terminal Services client are not required.
- **Connections are made directly to the console session**—In the past, Terminal Services connections could not be made to the console session, preventing many administrators from using Terminal Services for remote administration or causing the use of third-party applications such as PC Anywhere or VNC. Using the Remote

Desktops console, Windows Server 2003 now creates connections to the console session, enabling administrators to view messages and pop-ups that are not redirected to any other session. There is no other way in Windows Server 2003 to connect to the existing console session and see these messages.

Remote Desktop for Administration, like Terminal Services Administration mode before it, is fairly restrictive in who can use it and how it can be used:

- Only administrators can create Remote Desktop for Administration connections, by default. This is a good thing. You want the number of users with this power to be as small as possible, to minimize the risk of an attacker gaining complete control over your network. Access control is handled through membership in the Remote Desktop Users group.
- Only two Remote Desktop sessions can exist on a computer, *and both* active and disconnected (but still running) sessions count toward this number. This restriction exists so that the number of concurrent changes being made to a computer is minimized, to prevent configuration errors and conflicts. However, this presents potential for a denial-of-service (DoS) attack against a computer—or, at least, the Remote Desktop portion.

In Windows Server 2003, administrators can now use Group Policy to design and implement security policies to secure 802.11 Wireless LANs. The use of both Wired Equivalent Privacy (WEP) and 802.1x authentication is supported. The Group Policy options that are configured in a GPO and applied to a computer then take precedence over any user-configured settings, thus ensuring that your configuration is applied. You can create policies for three types of wireless LANs:

- **Access point (infrastructure)**—The most common type of wireless LAN, the infrastructure mode WLAN, consists of wireless clients communicating directly with wireless access points (APs). No direct client-to-client communications exist. This is considered to be the most secure type of WLAN.
- **Computer-to-computer (ad hoc)**—Ad hoc WLANs consist of wireless clients communicating directly with each other, without the use of an AP in the middle. This type of communication does not provide a direct path to the wired network.
- **Any available network access point preferred**—This option configures the policy to attempt a connection to an access point first, if one is available. If an AP is not available, the client attempts to create an ad hoc connection, if possible. This method is least preferred and usually most problematic over time.

Planning and Implementing Other Network Security Measures

When combined with a Windows XP Professional client computer in a Windows Server 2003 Active Directory–based network, Windows Server 2003 features several enhancements and improvements to Certificate Services.

- **Version 2 certificate templates**—Version 2 templates extend the range of properties that you can configure from those provided in Version 1 templates. You now can create new certificate templates (an option sorely lacking from Windows 2000), copy existing certificate templates, and supersede certificate templates that are already in use. You need a Window Advanced Server 2003 functioning as the Enterprise Root CA.
- **Integrated and enhanced key recovery**—Windows 2000 Server relied on a Data Recovery Agent (DRA) to decrypt files following the loss or damage of an encryption key. Additionally, the Exchange 2000 Server Key Management Service (KMS) ran on top of Windows 2000 Certificate Services and did not fully integrate. Windows Server 2003 allows the archival and recovery of private keys, and enables the administrator to access data encrypted with a lost or damaged private key. Now Key Recovery Agents (KRAs) are used to recover lost or damaged private keys across Windows Server 2003 and Exchange Server 2003.
- **Delta Certificate Revocation Lists**—Windows Server 2003 supports RFC 2459–compliant Delta Certificate Revocation Lists (CRLs) that contain only the certificates whose status has changed since the last full (base) CRL was compiled. This results in a much smaller CRL, which can be more frequently published with no adverse effects on the network or client computers. Additionally, this provides more accurate CRLs because of reduced latency periods. In Windows 2000, CRLs were typically published once per week (the default setting). Delta CRLs enable you to publish one or more times daily, as required.
- **CA qualified subordination**—Another part of RFC 2459, qualified subordination allows a parent CA to granularly configure what a subordinate CA is allowed to do. Examples include preventing the subordinate CA from signing a certificate for another subordinate CA.
- **Common Criteria role separation**—By separating common CA-related tasks over several different levels of administration, you can meet Common Criteria requirements and enhance task delegation. Because roles are separated, no one individual should possess the ability to compromise the services or operation of the CA.
- **Enhanced auditing**—Windows Server 2003 provides for more detailed auditing of Certificate Services by adding two new types of events: access check and system events.

System events come from seven critical areas: CA service, backup and restoration, certificate requests, certificate revocations, CA security, key archival and key recovery, and CA configuration.

A Windows Server 2003 Enterprise CA has five key characteristics:

- The CA server can run on any Windows Server 2003 server in the domain. You should plan for activity, network load, and physical placement of the server for best implementation.
- Because the CA name is integrated into the certificates it assigns, the name of the server should be determined before implementing CA services.
- The Enterprise CA Authority is integrated into the Active Directory.
- When you've installed an Enterprise CA, a policy module is created. An administrator can edit the policy.
- Because the CA is crucial for the successful implementation of the PKI, it must have a fault-tolerance scheme and a schedule of regular secure backups.

A typical Standalone CA has these key characteristics:

- It doesn't require Active Directory interaction.
- It can be used with extranets.
- It doesn't verify the requests for certificates. (All requests are pending until an administrator approves them.)
- Users requesting a certificate from a Standalone CA must supply all user account information. This information is not required within an Enterprise CA because the user is recognized by the logon account in the Active Directory.
- No certificate templates are used.
- Windows Sever 2003 logon credential certificates are not stored on smart cards. Other certificates can be, however.
- An administrator must distribute the Standalone CA certificate to the Trusted Root Certificate Store.

If Active Directory exists on the network and a Standalone CA can access it, additional options are available:

- If a domain administrator with write access to Active Directory installs the Standalone CA, the standalone is added to the Trusted Root Certification Authorities Certificate

Store. In this situation, you must make certain that the default action of pending requests isn't changed to allow the Standalone CA to automatically approve all requests for certificates. Do not change the default action of pending certificate requests on a Standalone CA.

- If a domain administrator group member of the parent domain (or an administrator with write access to Active Directory) installs the Standalone CA, the Standalone CA will publish the certificate and the Certificate Revocation list to Active Directory.

Windows Server 2003 PKI allows for and encourages a dispersed hierarchy of CAs. Building a tree of CAs allows for scalability with other organizations, internal and external resources, and compatibility with third-party CA implementations.

Ideally (for ease of administration), an enterprise would have one CA; this is not usually a reality, however. Each CA hierarchy begins with the Root CA, and multiple CAs branch from this Root CA in a parent-child relationship. The child CAs are certified by the parent CA all the way back to the Root CA. The parent CAs bind a CA public key to the child CA's identity.

In this parent-child relationship, child CAs are trusted by the parent. That parent is, in turn, trusted by its parent CA, all the way back to the originating Root CA. Also in this model, when an organization trusts a CA by adding its certificate in the Trusted Root Certification Authorities Certificate Store, the organization therefore trusts every Subordinate CA in the hierarchy. If a Subordinate CA has its certificate revoked by the issuing CA, the revoked CA is no longer trustworthy.

CAs are responsible not only for issuing and signing digital certificates, but also for maintaining an accurate and up-to-date listing of those certificates that are no longer valid and thus should not be trusted. This listing of invalid certificates is known as a Certificate Revocation List (CRL) and is itself digitally signed by the issuing CA to verify its authenticity.

When a certificate is issued, it has a set validity period attached to it, typically 1 year, by default. Under normal circumstances, the certificate can be used for this period of time and ceases to be valid automatically if it is not be renewed before the expiration date has been reached. Thus, it is necessary to place on the CRL only certificates that have been revoked early; certificates that have expired (that is, have passed their expiration date) are automatically considered invalid and do not need to be placed on a CRL.

In a parent-child relationship between CAs, the parent CA issues a certificate as part of the relationship to designate the child CA. Just like the certificate to a client, the certificate to a Subordinate CA includes a validity period.

When the validity period expires for a CA, its own certificate must be renewed before it can grant any certification requests from client computers. When organizing your PKI, take into account the time a certification in a parent-child relationship should last.

As a safety and security measure, Windows Server 2003 PKI is set up so that a CA cannot issue certificates to requestors that will last beyond its own certificate's expiration date. This measure is handy because it ensures, for example, that a CA scheduled to expire this October cannot issue a certificate that might expire later than October.

Even the Root CA's own certificate will eventually expire. Therefore, certificates that it issues to subordinates will be staggered from its own expiration date. In other words, when the Root CA expires, all Subordinate CAs will have expired as well. No Subordinate CAs are valid beyond the date of the originating CA.

Depending on the configuration of your network, you can choose from four different certificate enrollment options:

- **Certificate autoenrollment and renewal**—A Windows Server 2003 Active Directory domain with Windows XP Professional clients provides the most robust Certificate Services model. This is certainly the case when discussing certificate autoenrollment and renewal. Using these features, you can automatically issue certificates that enable PKI-based applications, such as smart card logon, EFS, SSL, and S/MIME, to users and computers within your Active Directory environment. Through a combination of certificate template properties and Group Policy settings, you can opt to enroll computers when they start up and users when they log in to their domain on the network.
- **Certificate Request Wizard/Certificate Renewal Wizard**—Users of Windows 2000, Windows XP, and Windows Server 2003 computers can manually request certificates through the Certificates MMC snap-in. This snap-in can be added to any custom MMC. Alternatively, you can launch the Certificates management console by entering **`certmgr.msc`** at the command prompt.
- **Web Enrollment web pages**—You can connect to a CA by entering **`http://`*`CAname`*`/certsrv`** in your browser. By default, the Web Enrollment pages, which consist of ASP and ActiveX controls and thus could be considered dangerous, are installed on a CA. However, you can install these pages on any other Windows Server 2003 computer running IIS that you want. If you're up to it, you can also customize these Web Enrollment pages to suit your specific needs. The Web Enrollment pages provide an easy way to connect clients to your CA without using the Certificates management console. Although Standalone CAs also use the Web Enrollment pages, they cannot provide certificates for smart card logon and for autoenrollment—only Enterprise CAs. Also, when Standalone CAs are used with Web Enrollment pages, the requester must specify all required information because Active Directory is not available to provide the information for the certificate template. Windows 2000, Windows XP, and Windows Server 2003 computers support the use of the Web Enrollment pages.
- **Smart Card enrollment station**—This is an advanced form of the Web Enrollment pages that allows trusted administrators to request and enroll smart card logon certificates for smart card users on the network. Only Windows XP and Windows Server 2003 computers support this form of enrollment.

You can choose from two basic options when you want to enroll smart card certificates:

- **Use an enrollment agent**—The use of an enrollment agent allows a trusted administrator to process all smart card certificate requests and ensures that smart cards and their certificates are created and installed properly. Although this can be a good thing from a user's point of view, it can quickly become an overwhelming task if too few enrollment agents are designated. The other disadvantage of using enrollment agents becomes apparent if one of the enrollment agents is later deemed to be untrustworthy. What do you do with all the smart cards that agent previously enrolled?
- **Allow self-enrollment by smart card users**—Although using enrollment agents is usually the best (and by far the most secure) method of enrolling smart cards, in some cases you might need or want to have users perform this task themselves. If you cannot physically (and safely) distribute fully ready smart cards, you might want to consider issuing blank smart cards and allowing the user to self-enroll. If you think that self-enrollment is completely insecure, recall that you can configure your CA to hold all new requests pending a manual administrative approval, thus giving you a chance to examine and validate the request before allowing the smart card to be enrolled with its certificate.

When you use smart cards for increased security of your network, you can configure several Group Policy options to further enhance the security of your smart card implementation:

- **Interactive Logon: Require Smart Card**—This option, located in the Computer Configuration\Windows Settings\Security Settings\Local Policies\Security Options node of the Group Policy Editor, can be used to prevent users from logging in to the domain by using a standard Windows username and password. Although this setting provides enhanced security, it can leave users without network access if their smart cards become unavailable for any reason. You should apply this policy at the OU level, making each smart card user a member of a domain local group and placing that group within the OU. Mistakenly applying this setting to non–smart card users will have disastrous effects.
- **Interactive Logon: Smart Card Removal Behavior**—This option, also located in the Security Option node, can be used to define what Windows should do when a smart card is removed from its reader with the user logged in. Possible options include No Action, Lock Workstation, and Force Logoff. This option again presents both benefits and dangers. A user who mistakenly removes her smart card with open documents could well lose any changes made since the document was last saved. On the other hand, for computers located in kiosks or other insecure areas, this setting can greatly increase the security of the computer and your network. This Group Policy setting requires training on your part to ensure that your smart card users understand the consequences of their actions. Again, this setting should be configured on an OU containing only those users who have been issued smart cards.

- **Do Not Allow Smart Card Device Redirection**—This option, located in the Computer Configuration\Administrative Templates\Windows Components\Terminal Services\Client/Server data redirection node of the Group Policy Editor, can be used to prevent users from logging in to a Terminal Server with a smart card. This can increase security and decrease loading on your Terminal Servers.
- **Account Lockout Policy**—The Account Lockout Policy node, located at Computer Configuration\Windows Settings\Security Settings\Account Policies\Account Lockout Policy in the Group Policy Editor, contains three useful Group Policy settings that you can use to enhance both smart card and standard Windows login. The Account Lockout Threshold setting can be configured to specify how many failed logon attempts should be allowed before that user account is locked out. The Account Lockout Duration setting specifies how long the account is to be locked out (barring an administrator's unlocking the account early). The Reset Account Lockout Counter After option specifies how much time must pass before failed logon attempts are no longer counted against the Account Lockout Threshold setting. These policies are typically applied at a high level in your organization, such as the root of a domain, to cause them to apply to all users within the domain.

Windows Server 2003 enables you to perform auditing of the following areas:

- **Audit Account Logon Events**—This option configures auditing to occur for user logons and logoffs. A successful audit generates an audit entry when a user successfully logs in, and a failed audit generates an entry when a user unsuccessfully attempts to log in.
- **Audit Account Management**—This option configures auditing to occur for each event of account management on a computer. Typical account-management events include creating a user, creating a group, renaming a user, disabling a user account, and setting or changing a password. A success audit generates an audit entry when any account-management event is successful, and a failure audit generates an entry when any account-management event fails.
- **Audit Directory Service Access**—This option configures auditing to occur when a user accesses an Active Directory object that has its own system access control list (SACL). This setting is only for Active Directory objects, such as GPOs, not for file system and Registry objects. A success audit generates an audit entry when a user successfully accesses an Active Directory object that has an SACL specified, and a failure audit generates an entry when an unsuccessful access attempt occurs.
- **Audit Logon Events**—This option configures auditing to occur upon each instance of a user logging on to or off a computer. The audit events are generated on domain controllers for domain account activity and on local computers for local account activity. When both the Audit Logon Events and the Audit Account Logon Events options are

configured, logons and logoffs that use a domain account generate logon or logoff audit events on the local computer as well as the domain controller. A success audit generates an audit entry when a logon attempt succeeds, and a failure audit generates an audit entry when a logon attempt fails.

- **Audit Object Access**—This option configures auditing to occur upon each user access of an object, such as a file, folder, printer, or Registry key that has its own SACL configured. To configure auditing for object access, you also need to configure auditing specifically on each object you want to perform auditing on. A success audit generates an audit entry when a user successfully accesses an object, and a failure audit generates an audit entry when a user unsuccessfully attempts to access an object.
- **Audit Policy Change**—This option configures auditing to occur upon every occurrence of changing user rights assignment policies, audit policies, or trust policies. A success audit generates an audit entry when a change to one of these policies is successful, and a failure audit generates an audit entry when a change to one of these policies fails.
- **Audit Privilege Use**—This option configures auditing to occur upon every occurrence of a user exercising a user right. A success audit generates an audit entry when the exercise of a user right succeeds, and a failure audit generates an audit entry when the exercise of a user right fails.
- **Audit Process Tracking**—This option configures auditing to occur for events such as program activation, process exit, handle duplication, and indirect object access. A success audit generates an audit entry when the process being tracked succeeds, and a failure audit generates an audit entry when the process being tracked fails.
- **Audit System Events**—This option configures auditing to occur when certain system events occur, such as computer restarts and shutdowns. A success audit generates an audit entry when a system event is executed successfully, and a failure audit generates an audit entry when a system event is attempted unsuccessfully.

Although Windows Server 2003 provides native support for the Windows Server Update Service (WSUS) and the older Server Update Service (SUS), it does not by default include WSUS. It's easy enough, however, to acquire the WSUS installation package and get to work configuring and implementing WSUS on a network. But what, really, is WSUS? WSUS is nothing more than a locally controlled and managed Windows Update server. Instead of allowing the Automatic Updates client on your client workstations and servers to download updates directly from the Microsoft Windows Update servers, you can install and configure one or more WSUS servers on your internal network and point your client workstations and servers toward those WSUS servers.

As you might imagine, the capability to have your client workstations use an internal server for Windows Update can be a tremendous benefit to you because it means decreased bandwidth usage. As important as bandwidth savings might be, there is actually a larger benefit to be realized by implementing a WSUS solution on your internal network: the ability to approve specific updates that are to be installed on your clients. When you use Windows Update, your client computers install any available update that matches their needs, but with WSUS, you can specify which of the available updates are authorized to be pushed to the clients when you are satisfied that the update will pose no problems for the systems. This is a tremendous benefit that often goes unrealized.

The requirements to install WSUS on a Windows Server 2003 computer are as follows:

- The system partition of the server must be formatted with the NTFS file system.
- The partition on which you install WSUS must be formatted with the NTFS file system.
- The system partition must have at least 1GB of free space available.
- The partition where you install WSUS must have a minimum of 6GB of free space available; however, for best results, it is recommended that the partition being used have at least 30GB of free space available.
- The partition where WSUS setup installs the Windows SQL Server 2000 Desktop Engine (WMSDE) must have at least 2GB of free space available.
- The server must have Internet Information Services (IIS) 6.0 installed.
- The server must have the Microsoft .NET Framework 1.1 SP1 for Windows Server 2003 software installed.
- The server must have the Background Intelligent Transfer Service (BITS) 2.0 update installed.

Clients to be updated by WSUS must fall into one of the following groups:

- Microsoft Windows 2000 Professional with SP3 or SP4.
- Windows 2000 Server with SP3 or SP4, or Windows 2000 Advanced Server with SP3 or SP4.
- Microsoft Windows XP Professional, with or without SP1 or SP2.
- Microsoft Windows Server 2003, Standard Edition; Windows Server 2003, Enterprise Edition; Windows Server 2003, Datacenter Edition; or Windows Server 2003, Web Edition.

Monitoring and Maintaining Server Availability

Periodic monitoring of your Windows Server 2003 network is important to the process of optimization. Monitoring helps to overcome the feeling-based assessment of your users. For example, by comparing current network performance against a previously established baseline, you have more information than the anecdotal "The network is slow today!" on which to base your actions. By gathering current information and comparing it against established norms for your systems (a baseline), you can detect bottlenecks, identify system components that are slowing down server performance, and fix them before they become a problem to your users.

The importance of establishing a baseline before you begin to monitor performance can't be overstated. Although there are some guidelines as to what absolute performance numbers indicate, only if you compare current performance against past performance (the baseline) can you really evaluate how well current demand is being met and whether you require more resources on your server. In addition, it is imperative that a baseline be established before problems begin to occur. If users are already beginning to complain, "The network is slow," it is too late to establish a baseline because the statistics gathered will include whatever performance factors are contributing to the dissatisfaction.

A baseline is a set of typical readings that define "normal" for your servers, client computers, or network under various operating conditions, such as no load, moderate load, and heavy load. Of course, what is normal is obviously open to interpretation, but you could say that "normal is a server providing users with what they want in a time frame that they think is reasonable. By creating baselines early on, you have something that you can later look back at and compare current server operating conditions to. If your system is already to the point that you are seeing system degradation, it is really too late to establish a baseline. To establish a baseline, you pick a time (or duration of time) that represents typical user interaction with the server. Then you create a log of important counters for the duration you have determined.

At a minimum, you must perform periodic monitoring on the following areas of your Windows Server 2003 computers: the hard disk(s), processor(s), memory, and network adapter(s). Regardless of which type of services the server is providing, these four areas interact to make your server efficient (thereby appearing fast) or inefficient. The actual speed or efficiency of each of the components varies in importance, depending on the application. In some applications, memory is more important than processor speed or availability; in other applications, disk speed and availability are more important than fast network access.

Recognizing the need to be able to monitor the performance (and thus the health) of servers and client computers, Microsoft built the Performance Monitor into Windows Server 2003. Whether you are looking for real-time graphical views or a log you can peruse at your convenience, the Performance Monitor can provide the type of data you need to evaluate performance and recommend system modification, if necessary.

The counters in Table 15 present an easy to manage group of counters that you might consider monitoring on a daily basis to get a quick snapshot of your system and network performance.

TABLE 15 Counters to Monitor on a Daily Basis

Server Component	Recommended Counters
Memory	Memory\Available Bytes Memory\Cache Bytes Memory\Pages/Sec Memory\Page reads/Sec Memory\Pool Paged Bytes Memory\Pool Nonpaged Bytes
Processor	Processor\% Processor Time (all instances) System\Processor Queue Length (all instances) Processor\Interrupts/Sec
Disk	Physical Disk\Disk Reads/Sec Physical Disk\Disk Writes/Sec Logical Disk\% Free Space Logical Disk\% Disk Time Physical Disk\Current Disk Queue Length (all instances) Physical Disk\Split IO/Sec
Network	Network Interface\Bytes total/Sec

The following are some of the most common causes of bottlenecks that you might encounter while troubleshooting your network:

- The current level of provided resources is inadequate, thus requiring additional or upgraded resources to be added to the network.
- The available resources are not utilized evenly, thus requiring some form of load balancing to be implemented.
- An available resource is malfunctioning or stopped and needs to be repaired or restarted.
- An available resource is incorrectly configured, thus requiring a configuration correction.

After you have identified a problem, you should take care to avoid creating new problems while correcting the old one. You should make one change at a time to avoid masking the impact of changes. After each change, you should perform additional monitoring to determine the result and the effect of the change, and reevaluate the status and condition of the previously identified problem(s). In addition, you can compare the performance of applications that are run over the network to their performance when run locally to determine how the network is affecting performance.

You should keep in mind the following general points when working with Windows Backup:

- You can back up to either a file or a tape drive.
- You can back up files from either the local machine or remote computers, provided that you have access to the files you want to back up on the remote computer. The limitation of backing up a computer remotely is that system state information cannot be saved.
- To perform a backup, you must have Read access to the files or the user right of Backup and Restore Files, which is granted by default to Administrators and Backup Operators.
- Special permissions are granted to the Administrators and Backup Operators groups to access all files for the purposes of doing backups. Even if members of these groups cannot access the data as users, they can back it up.

When you use the volume shadow copy, a copy of the original volume is created instantly at the time you initiate the backup. Data is then subsequently backed up to the backup media from this shadow copy instead of the original files. This new technology provides a means of backing up open files that were in use at the time of the backup being initiated. When you use volume shadow copy, files that would normally be skipped during the backup are backed up in their current state (at the time of the shadow copy creation) and thus appear closed on the backup media. Any applications that are running during the backup process can continue to run during the backup process. When the backup completes, the shadow copy is deleted. The volume shadow copy feature requires the NTFS file system to be in use and can be disabled if you want. Another new use of the volume shadow copy feature is to create "snapshots" of shared network folders that can be used to roll back to a previous version of a file.

Automated System Recovery (ASR) is an advanced restoration option of the backup utility that you can use to restore your system if other disaster-recovery methods fail or are not available for use. Using ASR, you can restore the operating system to a previous state, which allows you to start Windows Server 2003 if other methods do not work. You should always consider ASR your last resort for recovery, after Safe Mode, the Recovery Console, and Last Known Good Configuration (LKGC). You should make a point to keep your ASR media up-to-date as you make configuration changes to your computer, to minimize the amount of recovery required if you ever need to use ASR.

ASR is a two-part process that uses a startup floppy disk to boot the Windows Server 2003 computer and a backup file (that must be accessible during ASR restoration) containing the system state, system services, and all disks associated with the operating system components. The startup disk contains information about the backup, the disk configurations, and the way the restoration is to be accomplished.

You should perform an ASR recovery only after all other available methods to start the server normally have failed. However, before starting the procedure, you need to locate the following items and have them readily available to you:

- The correct (up-to-date) ASR startup floppy disk
- The correct (up-to-date) ASR backup media
- The original Windows Server 2003 installation CD-ROM
- Special drivers required for any mass storage controllers located in your server that are not available on the Windows Server 2003 CD-ROM; they also need to be available on floppy disk

The usefulness of volume shadow copies is not limited to its use within Windows Backup to create backups of open files; this feature also provides you with a way to archive copies of data over time, allowing users to locate and restore a specific file, if they want. After the necessary configuration has been completed and the required software installed, users can view the volume shadow copies of shared network folders, including any previous versions in existence. Users can then copy any or all of the older files, allowing them to effectively restore a backup copy of the files from an earlier time.

As you might imagine, volume shadow copies can provide a number of benefits to your network users—the least of which is the ability to restore an older version if the current version of a file becomes corrupt or be deleted beyond recovery. You also can compare different versions of files to see what changes have occurred over time.

Files contained in a volume shadow copy are read-only while archived, preventing them from being modified and thus nullifying the benefits of the volume shadow copy. After a file has been extracted from a volume shadow copy archive, it can be modified or moved to any location desired for editing. Shadow copies are disabled by default but can be enabled and configured from the Shared Folders node of the Computer Management console.

Windows Server 2003 allows for only 64 volume shadow copies of a specific shared folder. When this limit is reached, the oldest copy is deleted to make room for a newer copy. Before your network clients can take advantage of this technology, they must have the Volume Shadow Client software installed. The client software is available on your Windows Server 2003 computer in the `%systemroot%\system32\clients\twclient\` folder.

After you've configured volume shadow copies, Windows Server 2003 computers and client computers with the Volume Shadow Client software installed can view the shadow copies available for a shared network folder.

Windows Server 2003 supports the following five backup methods:

- **Normal (full) backup**—This method copies all selected files and marks each file as having been backed up (the archive attribute is cleared). Only the most recent copy of the backup file is required to perform restoration.
- **Incremental backup**—This method copies only files that have been created or changed since the last normal or incremental backup; the archive attribute is then cleared. Using normal and incremental backups, you need the last normal backup and all incremental backups to be able to perform restoration.
- **Copy backup**—This method copies all selected files but does not mark each file as having been backed up (the archive attribute is not cleared). Copy backups have no effect on any other type of backup operation.
- **Daily backup**—This method copies all selected files that have been modified the day the daily backup is performed; the archive attribute is not cleared, in this case. Using normal and daily backups, you need the last normal backup and all daily backups to be able to perform restoration.
- **Differential backup**—This method copies files that have been created or changed since the last normal (full) or incremental backup; the archive attribute is not cleared, in this case. Using normal and differential backups, you need the last normal backup and the last differential backup to be able to perform restoration.

The System State data contains information that is critical to the proper startup and operation of your Windows Server 2003 computer. The following items are included in the System State data:

- Registry
- COM+ class registration database
- Critical boot and system files
- System files that are protected by Windows File Protection
- Certificate Services database, if the server is a Certificate Authority
- Active Directory directory service, if the server is a domain controller
- `SYSVOL` directory, if the server is a domain controller
- Cluster service information, if the server is a member of a cluster
- IIS metadirectory, if IIS is installed on the server

Planning, Implementing, and Maintaining Highly Available Servers

When we discuss highly available solutions, we can look at the problem in two distinctly different ways: *hardware* and *software*. Windows Server 2003 provides two types of software-based high availability: *clustering* and *network load balancing (NLB)*.

Clustering is accomplished when you put a group of independent servers into one large collective entity that is accessed as if it were a single system. Incoming requests for service can be evenly distributed across multiple cluster members or can be handled by one specific cluster member.

The Microsoft Cluster Service (MSCS) in Windows Server 2003 provides highly available fault-tolerant systems through *failover*. When one of the cluster members (nodes) cannot respond to client requests, the remaining cluster members respond by distributing the load among themselves, thus responding to all existing and new connections and requests for service. In this way, clients see little, if any, disruption in the service being provided by the cluster. Cluster nodes are kept aware of the status of other cluster nodes and their services through the use of heartbeats. A heartbeat keeps track of the status of each node and also sends updates in the configuration of the cluster. Clustering is most commonly used for database, messaging, and file/print servers. Windows Server 2003 supports up to eight nodes in a cluster.

Windows Server 2003 also provides *network load balancing (NLB)*, in which all incoming connection requests are distributed to members of an NLB cluster using a mathematical algorithm. NLB clustering is best used in situations in which clients can connect to any server in the cluster, such as websites, Terminal Services servers, and VPN servers. You can configure how the client interacts with the NLB cluster as well, such as allowing the client to use multiple NLB cluster members during a single connection (acceptable for websites) or forcing the client to use the same cluster member for the entire connection period (a necessity for VPN and Terminal Services servers). Windows Server 2003 NLB clusters can contain as many as 32 nodes.

Although you can use both clustering and NLB in your final design, such as in the case of an e-commerce site that uses NLB for front-end web servers and clustering for back-end SQL servers, you cannot use both technologies on the same server.

When a network load-balancing cluster is created, port rules are used to determine what type of traffic is to be load-balanced across the cluster nodes. Within the port rule is the additional option to configure *port rule filtering*, which determines how the traffic will be load-balanced across each of the cluster nodes.

In an NLB cluster, every cluster node can answer for the cluster's IP address; thus, every cluster node receives all inbound traffic, by default. When each node receives the inbound request, it either responds to the requesting client or drops the packet if the client has an existing session in progress with another node. If no port rule is configured to specifically define how traffic on the specific port is to be handled, the request is passed to the cluster node with the lowest configured priority. This can result in decreased performance by the NLB cluster as a whole if the traffic is not meant to be or cannot be load-balanced.

Port rules enable you to change this behavior in a deliberate and controlled fashion. Think of port rules as the network load-balancing equivalent of a firewall rule set. When you configure port rules to allow traffic on the specific ports you require to reach the NLB cluster and configure an additional rule to drop all packets that do not meet any other port rules, you can greatly improve the performance of the NLB cluster by allowing it to drop all packets that are not allowed to be load-balanced. From an administrative and security standpoint, port rules allow for easier server monitoring because of the limited number of ports that must be monitored.

You can configure how NLB clusters load-balance traffic across cluster nodes; this process is referred to as *filtering*. By configuring filtering, you can specify whether only one node or multiple nodes within the NLB cluster are allowed to respond to multiple requests from the same client during a single session (connection). The three filtering modes are as follows:

- **Single Host**—When this filtering mode is configured, all traffic that meets the port rule criteria is sent to a specific cluster node. The Single Host filter might be used in a website that has only one SSL server; thus, the port rule for TCP port 443 would specify that all traffic on this port must be directed to that one node.
- **Disable Port Range**—This filtering mode instructs the cluster nodes to ignore and drop all traffic on the configured ports without any further action. This type of filtering can be used to prevent ports and port ranges from being load-balanced.
- **Multiple Host**—The default filtering method, Multiple Host, specifies that all active nodes in the cluster are allowed to handle traffic. When Multiple Host filtering is enabled, the host affinity must be configured. Affinity determines how clients interact with the cluster nodes and varies depending on the requirements of the applications that the cluster is providing. The following three types of affinities can be configured:
    - **None**—This affinity type sends an inbound client request to all nodes within the cluster. This type of affinity results in increased speed but is suitable only for providing static content to clients, such as static websites and FTP downloads. Typically, no cookies are generated by the applications running on the clusters that are configured for this type of affinity.
    - **Class C**—This affinity type causes all inbound client requests from a particular Class C address space to go to a specific cluster node. This type of affinity allows a user's state to be maintained but can be overloaded or fooled if all client requests are passed through a single firewall or proxy server.

- **Single**—This affinity type maintains all client requests on the same node for the duration of the session (connection). This type of affinity provides the best support for maintaining user state data and is often used when applications are running on the cluster that generates cookies.

The mathematical algorithm used by network load-balancing sends inbound traffic to every host in the NLB cluster. The inbound client requests can be distributed to the NLB cluster nodes through one of two methods: unicast or multicast. Although both methods send the inbound client requests to all hosts by sending them to the Media Access Control (MAC) address of the cluster, they go about it in different ways.

When you use the *unicast* method, all cluster nodes share an identical unicast MAC address. To do so, NLB overwrites the original MAC address of the cluster network adapter with the unicast MAC address that is assigned to all the cluster nodes. When you use the *multicast* method, each cluster node retains its original MAC address of the cluster network adapter. The cluster network adapter is then assigned an additional multicast MAC address, which all the nodes in the cluster share. Inbound client requests can then be sent to all cluster nodes by using the multicast MAC address.

The unicast method is usually preferred for NLB clusters unless each cluster node has only one network adapter installed in it. Recall that in any clustering arrangement, all nodes must be capable of communicating not only with the clients, but also among themselves. Recall that NLB modifies the MAC address of the cluster network adapter when unicast is used; thus, the cluster nodes cannot communicate among themselves. If only one network adapter is installed in each cluster node, you need to use the multicast method.

NLB uses a group of between 2 and 32 servers to distribute inbound requests among them in a fashion that permits the maximum amount of loading with a minimal amount of downtime. Each NLB cluster node contains an exact copy of the static and dynamic content that every other NLB cluster node has; in this way, it doesn't matter which NLB cluster node receives the inbound request, except in the case of host affinity where cookies are involved. The NLB cluster nodes use heartbeats to keep aware of the status of all nodes.

Clustering, on the other hand, uses a group of between two and eight servers that all share a common storage device. Recall that a cluster resource is an application, service, or hardware device that is defined and managed by the cluster service. The cluster service (MSCS) monitors these cluster resources to ensure that they are operating properly. When a problem occurs with a cluster resource, MSCS attempts to correct the problem on the same cluster node. If the problem cannot be corrected—such as a service that cannot be successfully restarted—the cluster service fails the resource, takes the cluster group offline, moves it to another cluster node, and restarts the cluster group. MSCS clusters also use heartbeats to determine the operational status of other nodes in the cluster.

Two clustering modes exist:

- **Active/Passive**—One node in the cluster is online providing services. The other nodes in the cluster are online but do not provide any services or applications to clients. If the active node fails, the cluster groups that were running on that node are failed over to the passive node. The passive node then changes its state to active and begins to service client requests. The passive nodes cannot be used for any other purpose during normal operations because they must remain available for a failover situation. All nodes should be configured identically to ensure that when failover occurs, no performance loss is experienced.
- **Active/Active**—One instance of the clustered service or application runs on each node in the cluster. If a failure of a node occurs, that instance is transferred to one of the running nodes. Although this clustering mode enables you to make use of all cluster nodes to service client requests, it can cause significant performance degradation if the cluster was already operating at a very high load at the time of the failure.

Each resource group within the cluster has a prioritized listing of the nodes that are supposed to act as its host.

You can configure failover policies for each resource group to define exactly how each group behaves when a failover occurs. You must configure the following three settings:

- **Preferred nodes**—This involves an internal prioritized list of available nodes for resource group failovers and failbacks. Ideally, all nodes in the cluster are in this list, in the order of priority you designate.
- **Failover timing**—The resource can be configured for immediate failover if the resource fails, or the cluster service can be configured to try to restart the resource a specified number of times before failover actually occurs. The failover threshold value should be equal to or less than the number of nodes in the cluster.
- **Failback timing**—Failback can be configured to occur as soon as the preferred node is available or during a specified period of time, such as when peak load is at its lowest, to minimize service disruptions.

Practice Exam

Prep Planning and Maintaining a Microsoft Windows Server 2003 Network Infrastructure

This practice exam consists of 68 questions that are meant to help you assess what you have learned from this *Exam Prep*. It also includes questions that are representative of what you should expect on the actual exam. You will find that the questions here are mostly multiple choice. Some of the question forms that you might see on the actual exam, such as those that appear with simulations, are difficult or impossible to implement in book form because of the limitations of pencil-and-paper testing. Still, this practice exam should help you find out how well you understood the material presented in this *Exam Prep* and give you some experience with Microsoft-style questions.

When you take the exam, you should treat it as you would the real exam. Time yourself (about 90–120 minutes for this number of questions), answer each question carefully, and mark the questions you want to go back and double-check. The answers and their explanations appear at the end of the practice exam.

After you have taken this exam, you should follow up with Que Certification's exclusive MeasureUp test engine that accompanies this book. For more information, see Appendix A, "Accessing Your Free MeasureUp Practice Test," and Appendix B, "MeasureUp's Product Features."

Exam Questions

1. You are the systems administrator for Gus Gus Gas Stations, Inc. You need to implement a more secure network environment across all servers, both domain controllers and member servers. What security templates could you use to provide a higher level of security for these servers and still leave room to increase security again, if desired? (Choose two correct answers.)

    ❍ **A.** `securews.inf`

    ❍ **B.** `hisecws.inf`

    ❍ **C.** `hisecdc.inf`

    ❍ **D.** `securedc.inf`

    ❍ **E.** `compatws.inf`

2. Marshall is the systems administrator for QBC Corp. He runs a network of 20 Windows Server 2003 systems on a network backbone, as well as 200 Windows XP Professional clients. Marshall is asked about using an IP address for a local LAN, whether an IP address is needed, as well as whether a MAC address is needed. Marshall claims that he can assign an IP address but not a MAC address. Why not?

    ❍ **A.** He needs only an IP address, not a MAC address.

    ❍ **B.** MAC addresses are not assigned; by default, they come burned into the network device.

    ❍ **C.** MAC addresses work on top of physical IP addresses.

    ❍ **D.** Neither IP addresses nor MAC addresses are needed if Marshall has the DNS name.

3. You are a network consultant and have been hired by Carmen's Clown College, Inc. You have been given the task of designing a unique DNS namespace for Carmen's new Windows Server 2003 network. Carmen's already owns the clowncollege.com domain, and the company's ISP is hosting its website. Which of the following options represents the best unique DNS namespace?

    ❍ **A.** clowncollege.net

    ❍ **B.** corp.clowncollege.com

    ❍ **C.** clowncollege.corp.com

    ❍ **D.** clowncollege.com.corp

4. You are the systems administrator for QBC Corp. The company has a network of 25 Windows Server 2003 systems on a network backbone, as well as 300 Windows XP Professional clients. You need to test the connectivity of a remote site that is currently four router hops away. You are experiencing a lot of latency. What is the appropriate plan of action to take to solve this issue?

- ❍ **A.** Go from router to router and look at the routing table metrics. If any say 1 or more, you need to deal with a routing issue.
- ❍ **B.** Use a standard `ping`, see how long it takes to get to the target host, and then calculate the time difference between hops.
- ❍ **C.** Use `netsh` in the `routing>` prompt and send a `ping` to the host; then calculate the time it takes to get there.
- ❍ **D.** Use `pathping` to trace the route to the destination and then look at the calculations of latency times in milliseconds on each hop through the network. Find the problem link.

5. Which of the following gives the best description of clustering?

- ❍ **A.** Clustering distributes all incoming client connection requests to its nodes via a mathematical algorithm.
- ❍ **B.** Clustering distributes all incoming client connection requests to its nodes via a round-robin system.
- ❍ **C.** Clustering allows multiple nodes to appear as a single system to clients.
- ❍ **D.** Clustering allows multiple CPUs to be used in a server.

6. You are the systems administrator for Tom's Travel, an international travel agency. You have been directed to create a backup plan that will ensure that all data on your file server is backed up every night, regardless of when the last modification was made to the data. Which of these backup types would meet your requirements?

- ❍ **A.** Incremental
- ❍ **B.** Supplemental
- ❍ **C.** Normal
- ❍ **D.** Differential

7. You are the systems administrator for Roger's Rockets, a manufacturer of toy rocket kits. You want to require that all wireless clients have the correct WEP key to authenticate to your wireless LAN. What setting do you need to select in your WLAN security policy?

- ❍ **A.** Data Encryption (WEP Enabled)
- ❍ **B.** Network authentication (Shared Mode)
- ❍ **C.** The Key Is Provided to Me Automatically
- ❍ **D.** Transmit per IEEE 802.1x

8. You are the systems administrator for Flagston Enterprises. The company's Windows Server 2003 network consists of 8 domain controllers, 4 member servers, and 7,592 Windows XP Professional workstations. You have created a plan to implement a CA. You report to your supervisor that the first CA will be a root CA. Your plans then call for an intermediary CA. Your supervisors want to know why an additional CA is required. Of the following, which is a valid reason for adding an intermediary CA?

❍ **A.** All enterprise CAs require intermediary CAs to communicate with other CAs.

❍ **B.** The intermediary CA would be secured and taken offline, whereas the root CA would remain online to issue certificates to certificate requestors.

❍ **C.** The root CA would be secured and taken offline, whereas the intermediary CA would remain online to issue certificates to certificate requestors.

❍ **D.** The intermediary CA would handle all communication between the subordinate CAs and the root CA.

9. You are the administrator of a large Windows Server 2003 Active Directory network. Your network consists of 1,500 Windows Server 2003 servers spread out over 150 Organizational Units, with approximately 10 servers each. You have just finished creating a customized security template that specifies the Account Policy and Auditing settings that are required for specific departments by your organization's corporate policy. What is the best way for you to apply this template to only the Sales, Marketing, Production, and Engineering OUs?

❍ **A.** Import the security template at the domain level into a Group Policy Object.

❍ **B.** Import the security template into each required Organizational Unit using a Group Policy Object.

❍ **C.** Script the `secedit.exe` command to apply the security template to the required computers.

❍ **D.** Manually apply the security template to each of the computers.

10. You are the systems administrator for the ShoeBox Shoe company. The corporation is running a routed network with a centrally located Windows Server 2003 DHCP server. The server can issue addresses to users on the local segment but cannot issue addresses to any sites across a router. What is the most probable cause of this problem?

❍ **A.** The DHCP forwarder service is not enabled on the DHCP server.

❍ **B.** The BOOTP forwarder service is not enabled on the DHCP server.

❍ **C.** The DHCP forwarder service is not enabled on the routers.

❍ **D.** The BOOTP forwarder service is not enabled on the routers.

11. Helper Hal is a leading manufacturer of household goods. The CIO of Helper Hal has hired you to design a new DNS namespace for an upcoming Windows Server 2003 deployment. Helper Hal already owns the helperhal.com domain name. Helper Hal's corporate offices are in England, and satellite offices are located in the United States, Canada, India, Germany, and Japan. The corporate office contains five departments: Sales, Production, Support, Facilities, and Finance. Each satellite office has only Sales and Support departments. Which of the following FQDNs for a client named `FILESVR042` in the Production department represents the best designed DNS namespace?

- ❍ **A.** filesvr042.production.helperhal.com
- ❍ **B.** filesvr042.uk.helperhal.com
- ❍ **C.** filesvr042.production.uk.helperhal.com
- ❍ **D.** filesvr042.helperhal.com

12. Pete is the systems administrator for RDT, Inc. He runs a network of 25 Windows Server 2003 systems on a network backbone, as well as 300 Windows XP Professional clients. Pete wants to be able to set up a Windows Server 2003 server as a router using the RRAS console and needs to be able to connect up to three different network segments, which are 10.1.1.0 /24, 10.1.2.0 /24, and 10.1.3.0 /24. To do so, Pete needs to build the server as a trihomed unit. He connects three links and sets up the Routing Information Protocol. For some reason, one of the users on the 10.1.1.0 /24 network segment cannot communicate with a system on the 10.1.2.0 /24 segment. What could be the potential problem?

- ❍ **A.** The routing table does not accurately show the route to the destination subnet in question. Pete needs to use the `route add` command to verify.
- ❍ **B.** The routing table does not accurately show the route to the destination subnet in question. Pete needs to use the `route change` command to verify.
- ❍ **C.** The routing table does not accurately show the route to the destination subnet in question. Pete needs to use the `route check` command to verify.
- ❍ **D.** The routing table does not accurately show the route to the destination subnet in question. Pete needs to use the `route print` command to verify.

13. Which of the following gives the best description of network load balancing?

- ❍ **A.** Network load balancing distributes all incoming client connection requests to its nodes via a mathematical algorithm.
- ❍ **B.** Network load balancing distributes all incoming client connection requests to its nodes via a round-robin system.
- ❍ **C.** Network load balancing allows multiple nodes to appear as a single system to clients.
- ❍ **D.** Network load balancing allows multiple CPUs to be used in a server.

14. You are the systems administrator for Tom's Travel, an international travel agency. You have been directed to create a backup plan that will ensure your company's critical data is backed up nightly. Your plan must minimize the time that is required each night to perform the backups. Your plan also should require the minimum amount of time and number of tapes possible during the restoration process. What combination of backup types should you use? (Choose two correct answers.)

- ❍ **A.** Copy
- ❍ **B.** Incremental
- ❍ **C.** Normal
- ❍ **D.** Daily
- ❍ **E.** Differential

15. You are the systems administrator for Jeff's Jeep Tours, an Australian tour company. While assisting one of your remote office users via Remote Assistance with a configuration issue on the user's computer, you have tried unsuccessfully to take control of the user's computer. Why are you not able to take control? (Select two correct answers.)

- ❍ **A.** Your computer is not configured to allow it to initiate remote control sessions.
- ❍ **B.** The remote computer is not configured to allow it to be controlled remotely.
- ❍ **C.** A firewall is in place blocking the request.
- ❍ **D.** The novice is not allowing you to take control of his computer.

16. You are the systems administrator for Fast Sloth Enterprises. After increasing the security of your network client computers, you need to implement an auditing system to keep track of times computers are restarted and shut down. Which of the following options should you configure to track these events?

- ❍ **A.** Audit Process Tracking
- ❍ **B.** Audit System Events
- ❍ **C.** Audit Object Access
- ❍ **D.** Audit Privilege Use

17. You are the systems administrator of the Gidgets Widgets, LLC, corporate network. You have instructed Andrea, your assistant administrator, to configure file access auditing for all files in the `CorpDocs` folder on your file server. Where will Andrea find the auditing options in the Group Policy Editor?

- ❍ **A.** Account Policies
- ❍ **B.** Local Policies
- ❍ **C.** Restricted Groups
- ❍ **D.** File System

18. Sally is the senior systems administrator for Runners Corp. She runs a network of 20 Windows Server 2003 systems, as well as 1,250 Windows XP Professional clients. Sally needs to connect a server to the network. She has been given an IP address of 172.16.1.100 with a subnet mask of

255.255.255.0. She enters the IP address information given and tries to `ping` a server on a remote subnet. The IP address she is trying to `ping` is 172.16.2.100. What could the problem be?

- ❍ **A.** Sally needs to change her IP address to 172.16.2.101.
- ❍ **B.** Sally needs to add the default gateway address to the server.
- ❍ **C.** Sally needs to `ping` localhost to see whether she has IP connectivity.
- ❍ **D.** Sally has done nothing wrong; the problem is most likely with the host at 172.16.2.100.

19. You are planning a new DNS namespace for Lou's Loghomes, Inc. Security and redundancy are important factors in your design. Which of the following zone types should you choose to ensure the highest level of security and most redundancy possible?

- ❍ **A.** Standard primary
- ❍ **B.** Standard secondary
- ❍ **C.** Stub
- ❍ **D.** Active Directory–integrated

20. You are the systems administrator for QBC Corp. The company has a network of 25 Windows Server 2003 systems on a network backbone, as well as 2,300 Windows XP Professional clients. You want to use a tool that can capture packets sent to and from a server. You decide to use Network Monitor, so you try to capture traffic from a remote server. Why are you failing to do so? (Choose only one answer.)

- ❍ **A.** You need to use System Monitor; it tells you what packets are traversing the LAN.
- ❍ **B.** Network Monitor is available only on Windows 2000; Network Analyzer is available on Windows Server 2003.
- ❍ **C.** Network Monitor is for system processes only; it does not pick up network packets.
- ❍ **D.** The version of Network Monitor included with Windows Server 2003 records only packets sent to and from this server and the LAN.

21. When discussing the process of convergence, what are you referring to?

- ❍ **A.** A network communication sent among individual cluster nodes at intervals of no more than 500ms that is used to determine the status of all cluster nodes.
- ❍ **B.** The process of a cluster group moving back to the preferred node after the preferred node has resumed cluster membership.
- ❍ **C.** The process by which NLB clustering hosts determine a new, stable state among themselves and elect a new default host after the failure of one or more cluster nodes.
- ❍ **D.** The process of a cluster group moving from the currently active node to another still-functioning node in the cluster group.

22. You are the systems administrator for Tom's Travel, an international travel agency. You are currently performing backups using your approved corporate backup plan. The plan calls for a normal backup to be made every Saturday night and differential backups to be made on Monday through Friday nights. On Thursday morning, your file server crashes and must be rebuilt with a clean installation of Windows Server 2003. In what order should you use the backup tapes you have?

- ❍ **A.** Friday, Monday, Thursday, Saturday
- ❍ **B.** Tuesday, Monday, Friday
- ❍ **C.** Saturday, Wednesday
- ❍ **D.** Monday, Tuesday, Wednesday, Saturday
- ❍ **E.** Saturday, Wednesday, Tuesday, Monday

23. You are the systems administrator for Roger's Rockets, a manufacturer of toy rocket kits. You are configuring a new WLAN security policy for the wireless clients that are located in your Accounting OU. You want to provide the maximum level of security for your WLAN by requiring that all computers authenticate to the WLAN upon creating their wireless connection. You want the computer to authenticate using its computer account. You are using a RADIUS server to handle authentication, and the authentication database is Active Directory. What setting do you need to configure in the WLAN security policy?

- ❍ **A.** Authenticate As Guest When User or Computer Information Is Unavailable
- ❍ **B.** Transmit Per IEEE 802.1x
- ❍ **C.** Data Encryption (WEP Enabled)
- ❍ **D.** Authenticate As Computer When Computer Information Is Available

24. Andrea is the systems administrator for the Think Pink Bike Company. She has recently finished implementing an auditing solution for her Windows Server 2003 network. Andrea wants to track unauthorized access attempts to the company network. After 2 weeks, she has not found any authorized access attempts, even though she tried password-guessing several users' accounts just this morning. What is the most likely reason for the problem that Andrea is experiencing?

- ❍ **A.** Andrea has not configured success audits for the Audit Account Logon events option.
- ❍ **B.** Andrea has not configured failure audits for the Audit Account Management option.
- ❍ **C.** Andrea has not configured failure audits for the Audit Logon events.
- ❍ **D.** Andrea has not configured success audits for the Audit Policy Change option.

25. You are the systems administrator for Good Faith Enterprises, LLC. You want to increase the security of your client workstations, which are all Windows XP Professional computers, without causing any adverse effect on network communications between computers. You have already completed this same configuration action on all your domain controllers and member servers. Which security template should you use to accomplish your goal?

- ❍ **A.** `securews.inf`
- ❍ **B.** `securedc.inf`
- ❍ **C.** `compatws.inf`
- ❍ **D.** `hisecws.inf`

26. You are the systems administrator for QBC Corp. The company has a network of 25 Windows Server 2003 systems on a network backbone, as well as 1,300 Windows XP Professional clients. You are asked to connect a server to the network. You are given an IP address of 192.168.5.10/16 and a default gateway of 192.168.5.1. You set up the server and connect it to the network via a network cable. After testing all connectivity, you still cannot access resources on the network. The network you are attaching to is 192.168.5.0/24. What do you think the problem is?

- ❍ **A.** You were given the incorrect IP address.
- ❍ **B.** You were given the incorrect default gateway.
- ❍ **C.** You were given the incorrect subnet mask.
- ❍ **D.** You must have a routing issue; there is nothing wrong with this configuration.

27. A DNS resolver performs a recursive query against its local DNS server asking it to provide the IP address for the host www.quepublishing.com. Assuming that the local DNS server is not authoritative for the quepublishing.com domain, does not have the answer in its local cache, and is configured for forwarding, what will happen next?

- ❍ **A.** The local name server will return an error to the DNS resolver stating that it could not resolve the name as requested.
- ❍ **B.** A root name server will make an iterative query to determine the IP address of the quepublishing.com domain.
- ❍ **C.** A root name server will make an iterative query to determine the IP address of the host www.quepublishing.com.
- ❍ **D.** The local DNS server will make an iterative query to a root name server to determine the IP address of the host www.quepublishing.com.

28. Sally is the senior systems administrator for Runners Corp. Sally runs a network of 20 Windows Server 2003 systems, as well as 2,250 Windows XP Professional clients. Sally would like to implement a new remote access feature called Network Access Quarantine Control on the Windows Server 2003 system. What does this new feature do?

- ❍ **A.** The remote access sender's connection attempt goes into quarantine until verified.
- ❍ **B.** The quarantine holds viruses trying to access your RAS server.
- ❍ **C.** Network quarantine is a central repository that enables you to store antivirus updates deployed to your server.
- ❍ **D.** This new feature enables you to set up a repository where you can store executables that are grabbed from users attempting to connect to your RAS server.

29. In regard to a network load-balancing cluster, what desirable function do port rules provide?

❍ **A.** They can be used to allow traffic only on specific ports to be load-balanced, dropping all other traffic.

❍ **B.** They assign a unique numerical identifier to each cluster node.

❍ **C.** They specify the IP address where the network load-balancing cluster can be accessed.

❍ **D.** They specify the IP subnet on which the administrative network adapter is to be located.

30. You are the systems administrator for Jorge's Gyms, a health club company. You have been directed to create a backup plan that will back up all data on the Financial department's file servers. The data must be backed up even if it is currently in use by a user. You need to minimize the impact of the backup on user operations. How should you configure the backup plan?

❍ **A.** Configure a backup job that backs up data in Remote Storage.

❍ **B.** Configure a backup job that compresses data to save space.

❍ **C.** Configure a backup job that verifies data after the backup is complete.

❍ **D.** Configure a backup job that uses the volume shadow copy.

31. You are the systems administrator for Jeff's Jeep Tours, an Australian tour company. A user in one of your remote locations has sent you an email request for remote assistance, but it expired before you were able to assist the user with her problem. You have called the user on the telephone and informed her of the problem with the expired request. You need to have this request answered. What is the easiest way to handle this situation?

❍ **A.** Have the user create a new request and send it to you.

❍ **B.** Have the user extend the lifetime of the initial request.

❍ **C.** Have the user delete the expired request, causing it to be re-created anew.

❍ **D.** Have the user resend the expired request to you again.

32. You are the administrator of a very large multinational organization. You are getting some error messages from the DHCP server. What counter in the Performance Console would display the number of DHCPOFFER messages sent per second by the DHCP server to a client computer?

❍ **A.** Offers/Sec

❍ **B.** Discovers/Sec

❍ **C.** Acks/Sec

❍ **D.** DHCPAcks/Sec

33. You are an assistant systems administrator for the Nimbus Flying Broom corporation. You are responsible for 575 Windows XP Professional workstations and 5 Windows Server 2003 member server computers. You have been directed to perform a security analysis on each computer, comparing its settings to those contained in the `hisecws.inf` template. How you can accomplish your assigned task with the least amount of administrative effort and fewest number of trips to remote computers?

- ❍ **A.** The only way to perform this analysis is to physically visit each computer and use the Security Configuration and Analysis snap-in.
- ❍ **B.** You can create a script that runs Security Configuration and Analysis on each computer, collecting the results in a central location for later viewing.
- ❍ **C.** You can create a script that runs the `secedit /analyze` command on each computer, collecting the results in a central location for later viewing.
- ❍ **D.** You can analyze remote computers from the Security Configuration and Analysis snap-in by targeting the desired computer.

34. Sally is the senior systems administrator for Runners Corp. She runs a network of 200 Windows Server 2003 systems, as well as 7,500 Windows XP Professional clients. Sally needs to connect her LAN to the Internet. She is running a large network that has a private addressing scheme of 10.1.0.0/16. To connect the Internet, Sally must set up what technology on the Internet firewall to get on to the public range of 12.1.1.0?

- ❍ **A.** IPSec
- ❍ **B.** NAT
- ❍ **C.** RIP
- ❍ **D.** BGP

35. What new feature of Windows Server 2003's DNS service enables you to configure multiple DNS forwarders, depending on the destination domain?

- ❍ **A.** DNS forwarder
- ❍ **B.** DNS resolver
- ❍ **C.** Conditional forwarding
- ❍ **D.** Recursion

36. Pete is the systems administrator for RDT, Inc. He runs a network of 25 Windows Server 2003 systems on a network backbone, as well as 2,300 Windows XP Professional clients. Pete has a problem with a remote site (10.10.2.0) from his campus network. None of the users from a remote site company can access his Exchange server (10.10.1.10) in the core network he is responsible for. Pete needs to determine whether this is a problem with the Exchange server or something else. What is the best troubleshooting step Pete should take?

- ❍ **A.** Pete should have the remote users `ping` his default gateway. If he receives a response, it must be the users' problem.

❍ **B.** Pete should have the remote users `ping` his default gateway. If there is no response, it must be the Exchange server's problem.

❍ **C.** Pete should do a `tracert` to the Exchange server and see what path it takes, and then `ping` the server to see if it replies.

❍ **D.** Pete should `ping` 10.10.1.10, `ping` 10.10.2.1 (default gateway), and then have a remote user `ping` 10.10.1.1 (default gateway).

37. You are preparing to implement a network load-balancing solution for your company's website. You will be load-balancing six Windows Server 2003 computers running IIS. Employees and customers using the FTP protocol use the IIS servers only to upload and download files. What type of affinity should you configure to ensure that clients receive the best overall possible service during their connection period?

❍ **A.** None

❍ **B.** Class C

❍ **C.** Multiple

❍ **D.** Single

38. You are the systems administrator for Jorge's Gyms, a health club company. You have enabled volume shadow copy on your Financial department file server using the default configuration. With these settings, how many days' worth of historical data will be available to your users?

❍ **A.** 14

❍ **B.** 21

❍ **C.** 28

❍ **D.** 32

❍ **E.** 45

39. You are the systems administrator for Herb's Happenings, a public relations firm. You are preparing to create a new IPSec policy that will be used to secure all internal network traffic. What available user authentication methods does IPSec in Windows Server 2003 offer? (Choose all that apply.)

❍ **A.** NTLM v2

❍ **B.** Kerberos v5

❍ **C.** EFS

❍ **D.** Digital certificate

❍ **E.** Shared secret

❍ **F.** WEP

40. You are the systems administrator for the Wing Walkers, Inc., corporate network. You are configuring WSUS for your network's client computers, which are all running Windows XP Professional SP2. You want all client computers to automatically download from your SUS server and install any required updates each night at 11:30 p.m. After the updates have been installed, you want the client computers to restart so that the updates can fully install and the computers will be ready for work the next morning. What must you do to ensure that updates will be installed each night and the computers will be restarted after the updates are installed? (Choose all that apply.)

❍ **A.** You must configure the Automatic Updates client options on each of your Windows XP Professional SP2 client computers to download and install updates nightly.

❍ **B.** You must set the Configure Automatic Updates option in Group Policy to Enabled and set option 4. You then need to configure a schedule for nightly updates at 11:30 p.m.

❍ **C.** You must set the No Auto-Restart for Scheduled Automatic Updates Installations option in Group Policy to Disabled.

❍ **D.** You must set the Specify Intranet Microsoft Update Server Location option in Group Policy to Enabled and enter the URL of your WSUS server.

41. You are the systems administrator for Fast Sloth Enterprises. You need to increase the security of your Windows XP Professional client computers and Windows Server 2003 servers. Which security template should you apply to your workstations to ensure that they have the most secure configuration?

❍ **A.** `securews.inf`

❍ **B.** `hisecdc.inf`

❍ **C.** `hisecws.inf`

❍ **D.** `rootsec.inf`

42. Pete is the systems administrator for RDT, Inc. He runs a network of 25 Windows Server 2003 systems on a network backbone, as well as 2,300 Windows XP Professional clients. Pete has to connect all his internal clients to the Internet, but he has only one public IP address. He also needs to accelerate the speed of Internet access while at the same time minimizing impact on the Internet bandwidth. What device should he use on his network?

❍ **A.** A layer 4 router

❍ **B.** A SNA server

❍ **C.** A load balancer

❍ **D.** A proxy server

43. You are concerned about the security of your organization's private internal network. As such, you have configured the firewall to allow traffic only on UDP and TCP ports 53 from one IP address: 192.168.100.133. Your firewall creates dynamic response rules that will allow valid return traffic back to the DNS server if it is a response to traffic originating from the DNS server. Your internal network contains four internal DNS servers, and your network users must be able to perform external name resolution regardless of which DNS server their query is sent to. What should you to do ensure that only the DNS server with IP address 192.168.100.133 makes external DNS queries?

- ❍ **A.** Configure the other three DNS servers to forward name-resolution requests for all domains other than the internal namespace to the DNS server with IP address 192.168.100.133. This server will then perform name resolution by using Internet DNS servers.
- ❍ **B.** Disable the other three DNS servers to prevent them from providing name-resolution services.
- ❍ **C.** Configure all four internal DNS servers to be forwarders to an external DNS server.
- ❍ **D.** Configure all client computers to use the DNS server with IP address 192.168.100.133 as the primary DNS server.

44. You are the systems administrator for QBC Corp. The company has a network of 25 Windows Server 2003 systems on a network backbone, as well as 3,300 Windows XP Professional clients. You have a problem with a remote server that does not seem to show up in one of your MMCs. You need to access this server, so you try to `ping` it but get no response. What is your next step? (Choose the best answer.)

- ❍ **A.** Try running a `tracert` to the remote server.
- ❍ **B.** Try using the `netsh` command with a `routing>` prompt and `ping` to the remote server.
- ❍ **C.** Try using the `arp -a` command to the remote server.
- ❍ **D.** Try using the `ipconfig /check` command on the remote server.

45. You are preparing to implement a network load-balancing solution for your company's website. You will be load-balancing six Windows Server 2003 computers running IIS. Why would you want to ensure that each server has two network adapters installed for this type of solution?

- ❍ **A.** To allow for double the load-balanced traffic
- ❍ **B.** To separate the load-balanced traffic from the administrative traffic
- ❍ **C.** To provide extra redundancy in case an adapter fails
- ❍ **D.** To allow a multicast MAC address to be used

46. You are the systems administrator for Jorge's Gyms, a health club company. You have enabled volume shadow copy on your Financial department's file server using the default configuration. When you try to look at the previous versions of the shared folder locally at the file server using Windows Explorer, you do not have the Previous Versions tab on the share Properties dialog box. What is the reason for this problem?

❍ **A.** You did not install the Previous Versions Client on the server.

❍ **B.** The volume shadow copy has run out of free space on the disk.

❍ **C.** The volume shadow copy service has stopped.

❍ **D.** You can view shadow copies only over the network using My Network Places.

47. You are the systems administrator for Jeff's Jeep Tours, an Australian tour company. You need to connect to the console session of one of your Windows Server 2003 computers to perform some configuration actions. What tool does Windows Server 2003 provide that enables you to do this?

❍ **A.** The Remote Desktops console

❍ **B.** The Web Interface for Remote Administration

❍ **C.** The Remote Desktop Connection web utility

❍ **D.** The Remote Desktop Connection utility

48. Austin is the systems administrator for Captain Bob's Ocean Fantasies, a retailer specializing in hard-to-find ocean-related collectible items. As part of his smart card solution, Austin has decided to limit the number of incorrect logon attempts that users can make within a specified amount of time. Where, within the Group Policy Editor, would Austin be able to locate the settings that he needs to configure?

❍ **A.** Computer Configuration\Windows Settings\Security Settings\Account Policies\Account Lockout Policy

❍ **B.** Computer Configuration\Windows Settings\Security Settings\Local Policies\Security Options

❍ **C.** Computer Configuration\Administrative Templates\Windows Components\Terminal Services\Client/Server Data Redirection

❍ **D.** Computer Configuration\Windows Settings\Security Settings\Public Key Policies

49. Hannah is the systems administrator for Think Pink Bicycles, Inc. She is attempting to configure the Engineering Organizational Unit in her Windows Server 2003 network with the `securews.inf` template. There are 30 member file and print servers in this OU, along with approximately 1,500 Windows XP Professional workstations. Which of the following methods of applying the `securews.inf` template would be the most administratively efficient?

❍ **A.** Using the Security Configuration and Analysis snap-in

❍ **B.** Using the `secedit.exe` command

❍ **C.** Using Group Policy

❍ **D.** Using the Domain Controller Security Policy console

50. Marshall is the systems administrator for QBC Corp. He runs a network of 20 Windows Server 2003 systems on a network backbone, as well as 1,200 Windows XP Professional clients. Marshall is asked to protect his network from Internet-based attacks. He needs to put in a device that will help him to secure his network from attack. What device would you recommend that Marshall install?

❍ **A.** NIC

❍ **B.** IPSec client

❍ **C.** Network Monitor

❍ **D.** Firewall

51. Andrea is an administrator for Carmine's Circus Clowns, Inc. She was just recently hired after the last administrator, oddly enough, ran off to join the circus. Carmine's network includes two domain controllers and three member servers providing file, print, and backup/restoration services. Carmine, the president of the company, has instructed Andrea to implement a more secure configuration on all five Windows Server 2003 servers. Andrea has decided to use the secure templates but is not sure what the current configuration is on each server because the last administrator did not keep any records. What is the best way for Andrea to go about configuring these servers with the secure templates?

❍ **A.** Andrea should apply the default security template from one of her member servers to all five servers and then apply the `securews.inf` and `securedc.inf` templates to them.

❍ **B.** Andrea should apply the default security template found on each computer to that specific computer. After doing this, she should apply the `securews.inf` template to her domain controllers and the `securedc.inf` template to her member servers.

❍ **C.** Andrea should reinstall Windows Server 2003 on all five servers and re-create the domain. After doing this, she should apply the `securews.inf` and `securedc.inf` templates to her servers.

❍ **D.** Andrea should apply the default security template found on each computer to that specific computer. After doing this, she should apply the `securedc.inf` template to her domain controllers and the `securews.inf` template to her member servers.

52. Sally is the senior systems administrator for Runners Corp. She runs a network of 20 Windows Server 2003 systems, as well as 2,250 Windows XP Professional clients. Sally needs to deploy a multicasting solution that allows all multicast traffic to pass through her network and to the MBone, which is the multicast backbone on the Internet. How can Sally set up her Windows Server 2003 system to make sure that it can participate in the forwarding of multicast traffic?

❍ **A.** Set up ICMP routing

❍ **B.** Set up IGMP routing

❍ **C.** Set up OSPF routing

❍ **D.** Set up RIP routing

53. You are the systems administrator for QBC Corp. The company has a network of 25 Windows Server 2003 systems on a network backbone, as well as 1,300 Windows XP Professional clients. You have a problem with a router a few hops away because it does not seem to be passing traffic past it. What tool can you use to troubleshoot with?

❍ **A.** Use `Trace Route`.

❍ **B.** Use `Traceroute`.

❍ **C.** Use `Tracert`.

❍ **D.** Use `Trace`.

54. You are the systems administrator for Jorge's Gyms, a health club company. You have enabled volume shadow copy on your Financial department's file server using the default configuration. When you try to look at the previous versions of the shared folder from one of your Windows XP Professional workstations using My Network Places, you do not see the Previous Versions tab on the share Properties dialog box. What is the reason for this problem?

❍ **A.** You did not install the Previous Versions Client on the client.

❍ **B.** The volume shadow copy has run out of free space on the disk.

❍ **C.** The volume shadow copy service has stopped.

❍ **D.** You can view shadow copies only over the network using My Network Places.

55. You are the systems administrator for Herb's Happenings, a public relations firm. You are preparing to create a new IPSec policy that will be used to secure all internal network traffic. What available data-encryption methods does IPSec in Windows Server 2003 offer? (Choose all that apply.)

❍ **A.** DES

❍ **B.** SHA1

❍ **C.** MD5

❍ **D.** AES

❍ **E.** 3DES

56. Austin is the systems administrator for Captain Bob's Ocean Fantasies, a retailer specializing in hard-to-find ocean-related collectible items. Captain Bob's network currently has about 500 remote traveling users who connect to the network via Terminal Services using their smart cards for authentication. A new change in company policy requires that remote users will no longer be able to make Terminal Services connections to the network, but instead can create and use VPN tunnels to one of the available RRAS servers. In addition to announcing this policy change, what can Austin do to ensure that his remote smart card users do not make Terminal Services connections?

❍ **A.** Interactive logon: Require smart card

❍ **B.** Interactive logon: Smart card removal behavior

❍ **C.** Do not allow smart card device redirection

❍ **D.** Account lockout policy

57. You have just completed an analysis of a computer using the Security Configuration and Analysis snap-in. When you examine the results, you notice several items that have an X icon next to them. What does this icon indicate?

❍ **A.** The item is not defined in the analysis database and was not examined on the computer.

❍ **B.** The item is defined in the analysis database and on the computer, and matches the currently configured setting.

❍ **C.** The item is defined in the analysis database but not on the computer.

❍ **D.** The item is defined in the analysis database and on the computer, but does not match the current configured setting.

58. You are the systems administrator for QBC Corp. The company has a network of 25 Windows Server 2003 systems on a network backbone, as well as 1,300 Windows XP Professional clients. You need to set up a new Windows Server 2003 system on your network. You are given an IP address, a subnet mask, and a default gateway. Your IP address is 10.0.1.10 /8, and the default gateway is 10.0.1.1. You are trying to connect to and `ping` the default gateway but are not able to. You analyze the router and find that it has the IP configured as 10.0.1.1 /24 on the Ethernet port. What do you think the problem is?

❍ **A.** Bad IP address assignment

❍ **B.** Bad default gateway assignment

❍ **C.** Bad Ethernet port assignment

❍ **D.** Bad subnet mask assignment

59. You are in the process of creating a customized security solution for your network's computers. You want to edit the `securedc.inf` template in a text editor. Where can you find the preconfigured security templates?

❍ **A.** `%systemroot%\system32\security`

❍ **B.** `%systemroot%\security\templates`

❍ **C.** `WINNT\security\templates`

❍ **D.** `%systemroot%\system32\templates`

60. Andrea is the systems administrator of the Beachside Entertainment Group, Incorporated, network. Beachside owns and operates several miniature golf centers in resort destinations. Andrea is preparing to implement a smart card solution for use by all Beachside Entertainment employees because their computers are often lacking in other forms of security, such as physical security.

Beachside has locations in 5 Eastern states with a total of 17 offices, including the corporate offices in Chincoteague, Virginia. Andrea has decided to use self-enrollment for her smart card users. Which of the following items must Andrea take into consideration for her self-enrollment plan to work effectively and securely? (Choose two correct answers.)

❍ **A.** Andrea must ensure that all required users get a blank smart card.

❍ **B.** Andrea should configure her CAs not to automatically issue smart card user certificates when requested.

❍ **C.** Andrea must ensure that all required users get a ready-to-use smart card.

❍ **D.** Andrea must ensure that only trusted users are tasked with the job of performing the smart card certificate enrollments.

❍ **E.** Andrea must ensure that she has selected enough enrollment agents to perform the smart card enrollments for users without becoming overburdened.

61. You are the systems administrator for Herb's Happenings, a public relations firm. You are preparing to create a new IPSec policy that will be used to secure all international network traffic. You need to configure this new IPSec policy so that the computers at each end of the connection will communicate with each other and agree on the security parameters that are to be used. What filter action do you need to configure to ensure this behavior occurs?

❍ **A.** Permit

❍ **B.** Block

❍ **C.** Negotiate

❍ **D.** Open

62. You are the systems administrator for Herb's Happenings, a public relations firm. You have decided to use one of the preconfigured IPSec policies that come in Windows Server 2003 to secure network traffic on your international network. Which of the following policies are included with Windows Server 2003? (Choose all that apply.)

❍ **A.** Client (Respond Only)

❍ **B.** Client (Request Security)

❍ **C.** Client (Require Security)

❍ **D.** Server (Respond Only)

❍ **E.** Server (Request Security)

❍ **F.** Server (Require Security)

❍ **G.** Secure Server (Respond Only)

❍ **H.** Secure Server (Request Security)

❍ **I.** Secure Server (Require Security)

63. You are the systems administrator for Herb's Happenings, a public relations firm. You are preparing to create a new IPSec policy that will be used to secure all internal network traffic. What available data hashing methods does IPSec in Windows Server 2003 offer? (Choose all that apply.)

❍ **A.** DES

❍ **B.** SHA1

❍ **C.** MD5

❍ **D.** AES

❍ **E.** 3DES

64. You are the systems administrator for Nebuchadnezzar Furnaces. The company's Windows Server 2003 domain consists of 4 domain controllers, 14 member servers, and 765 Windows XP Professional workstations. Daniel, your supervisor, reports to you that he suspects that Sam is still accessing the network through the Internet, although he was fired from the company 12 days ago. He asks you to resolve the matter so that Sam cannot access the network remotely. What two actions can you perform that would ensure that Sam can no longer use his digital certificate to access the network?

❍ **A.** Delete Sam's previously assigned certificate.

❍ **B.** Revoke Sam's previously assigned certificate.

❍ **C.** Force Sam's certificate to expire early.

❍ **D.** Publish the CRL.

65. You are the systems administrator for Phil's Fillup Stations, Inc. Your CIO has tasked you with increasing the security of all member servers on your network. After examining the security settings configured in the Secure and Highly Secure templates, you have decided that neither one of them completely meets your requirements. You must configure the required settings as efficiently and safely as possible. Which of the following represent the two best available options that you could choose to configure your servers as required? (Choose two correct answers.)

❍ **A.** Create a new (empty) security template and configure the settings you need in it.

❍ **B.** Modify the `securews.inf` security template, changing and adding options as needed.

❍ **C.** Configure the member server settings from the Local Security Policy console on each member server.

❍ **D.** Configure the security settings you need directly into a Group Policy Object linked to the OU containing the member servers.

66. You are the systems administrator for JMS Technologies, and you are trying to determine what settings (in addition to an IP address with your DHCP server) can be assigned to client computers running Windows XP Professional. What settings can be assigned? (Choose two.)

❍ **A.** The IP address of the DNS server

❍ **B.** The IP address of the DHCP server

❍ **C.** The IP address of the file server

❍ **D.** The IP address of the default gateway

❍ **E.** The IP address of the Active Directory domain controller

67. A Windows XP Professional client computer will receive a DHCPACK broadcast message from the DHCP server after which of the following events?

❍ **A.** When the client computer first requests an IP address

❍ **B.** After successfully receiving or renewing a TCP/IP address from the DHCP server

❍ **C.** When a DHCP server offers it a lease

❍ **D.** When the client computer sends a request to use a lease it was offered

68. You are the systems administrator for Giant Snowblowers, LLC. Your organization has always used statically assigned IP address on all computers, including workstations. As part of your migration plan to Windows Server 2003 from Windows NT 4.0, you have been given permission to move to DHCP. Your organization has a central corporate headquarters in Mississippi and several manufacturing, distribution, sales, and repair locations scattered throughout North America, Europe, and Asia. All of your locations are connected to the corporate headquarters through WAN links or by persistent VPN connections over the Internet. You will have at least one Windows Server 2003 computer at each location to provide file and print services. Some larger locations will also get a domain controller and other member servers, as required. You need to design a DHCP solution that is the best fit for your network. Which of the following solutions would you choose to ensure that DHCP is provided at every location in your organization but that prevents DHCP broadcast traffic from crossing your WAN links and VPN connections during normal operations?

❍ **A.** At the corporate headquarters in Mississippi, install and configure DHCP on two Windows Server 2003 servers. Create and configure scopes for all subnets in all locations in your organization using the 50/50 rule.

❍ **B.** At each remote location, install and configure DHCP on your Windows Server 2003 file and print server. Create and configure the scopes for all subnets in that location so that they provide 20% of the IP addresses available. At the corporate headquarters in Mississippi, install and configure DHCP on two Windows Server 2003 servers. Create and configure the scopes for all subnets in all locations so that they provide 80% of the IP addresses available.

❍ **C.** At each remote location, install and configure DHCP on your Windows Server 2003 file and print server. Create and configure the scopes for all subnets in that location so that they provide 50% of the IP addresses available. At the corporate headquarters in Mississippi, install and configure DHCP on two Windows Server 2003 servers. Create and configure the scopes for all subnets in all locations so that they provide 50% of the IP addresses available.

❍ **D.** At each remote location, install and configure DHCP on your Windows Server 2003 file and print server. Create and configure the scopes for all subnets in that location so that they provide 80% of the IP addresses available. At the corporate headquarters in Mississippi, install and configure DHCP on two Windows Server 2003 servers. Create and configure the scopes for all subnets in all locations so that they provide 20% of the IP addresses available.

Answers to Practice Exam

Answers and Explanations

1. **A, D.** By using the Secure templates (`securews.inf` for member servers and workstations and `securedc.inf` for domain controllers), you can increase the baseline security of your servers and still allow for increasing security later (if you want) by using the Highly Secure templates. If you applied the high-security templates right away, you'd have no way to increase security later using the built-in templates; thus, answers B and C are incorrect. Using the `compatws.inf` template actually lowers the security level; thus, answer E is incorrect. For more information, see Chapter 5.

2. **B.** MAC addresses are not assigned; by default, they come burned into the network device. A physical address is a 48-bit alphanumeric number that denotes the host's physical address. Also called a Media Access Control (MAC) address, the physical address is unique to the device it is assigned to; thus, answers A, C, and D are incorrect. For instance, your PC has a MAC address of 00-08-74-97-0B-26; this is unique to that one device's NIC card. For more information, see Chapter 1.

3. **A.** The clowncollege.net namespace represents a unique DNS namespace. clowncollege.net would thus become the root of the Active Directory forest and domain structure. Unique DNS namespaces should typically be similar to the original namespace—in this case, clowncollege.com. Many organizations might choose answer B for their design, but although this is not wrong, it does not provide the most unique namespace; thus, answer B is incorrect. Using the namespace listed in answer C would require the purchase of another domain name to be safe; thus, answer C is incorrect. The namespace listed in answer D doesn't make sense for this organization; thus, answer D is incorrect. For more information, see Chapter 4.

4. **D.** Use `pathping` to trace the route to the destination and then look at the calculations of latency times in milliseconds on each hop through the network. Then find the problem link. Looking at the routing tables on each router might be required later, but this is definitely not the first place you should start your troubleshooting; thus, answer A is incorrect. Although you could calculate the time between hops if you wanted, it would not be accurate, nor is it required because using `pathping` will provide the information you need; thus, answer B is incorrect. You would not use the `netsh` command in this instance; thus, answer C is incorrect. For more information, see Chapter 2.

5. **C.** Clustering is accomplished when you group independent servers into one collective entity that is accessed as if it were a single system. Network load balancing distributes all incoming client connection requests to its nodes via a mathematical algorithm; thus, answer A is incorrect. No clustering solution provided by Microsoft uses a round-robin method; thus, answer B is incorrect. A server architecture that supports symmetric multiprocessing allows multiple CPUs to be used in a server, not clustering; thus, answer D is incorrect. For more information, see Chapter 10.

6. **C.** A normal backup ensures that all selected data is backed up and sets the archive bit, indicating that the data has been backed up. Normal backups are typically used in combination with incremental or differential backups. Incremental and differential backups do not back up all data every night; thus, answers A and D are incorrect. There is no supplemental backup type; thus, answer B is incorrect. For more information, see Chapter 9.

7. **B.** To use WEP to perform WLAN authentication, you need to select the Network Authentication (Shared Mode) option. The Data Encryption (WEP Enabled) option specifies that WEP is to be used to encrypt data placed on the WLAN; thus, answer A is incorrect. The option titled The Key Is Provided to Me Automatically specifies that the key is dynamically assigned from a key server, such as a RADIUS server; thus, answer C is incorrect. The Transmit per IEEE 802.1x option is used to configure how the EAPOL-start message is sent and has nothing to do with WEP; thus, answer D is incorrect. For more information, see Chapter 7.

8. **C.** Creating an intermediary CA allows the root CA to be taken offline and secured. The intermediary server would then issue certificates to other CAs. An intermediary CA is not required to allow enterprise CAs to communicate with clients or other CAs; thus, answers A and D are incorrect. It would make no sense to take the intermediary CA offline and leave the root CA online; thus, answer B is incorrect. For more information, see Chapter 8.

9. **B.** The best way to apply the settings to only those computers that require them is to import the template into a Group Policy Object associated with each OU that requires the settings. Importing the security template into the domain-level GPO would apply the settings to all computers in the domain, most likely with unwanted side effects; thus, answer A is incorrect. Performing either procedure manually would not be the most efficient or accurate method; thus, answers C and D are incorrect. For more information, see Chapter 5.

10. **D**. Before the IP addresses can cross over the router, you need to enable the BOOTP forwarder; thus, answer C is incorrect. There is no such thing as a DHCP forwarder or BOOTP forwarder on a DHCP server; thus, answers A and B are incorrect. For more information, see Chapter 3.

11. **C.** The FQDN filesvr042.production.uk.helperhal.com represents the best designed DNS namespace. This FQDN enables you to quickly and accurately determine the location of the host within the network. Also, this DNS namespace is designed intelligently by using countries as the second-level domains and departments as the third-level domains; thus, answers A, B, and D are incorrect. Alternatively, the helperhal.com domain could be delegated to create a corp.helperhal.com domain, with the countries becoming third-level domains and the departments becoming fourth-level domains. For more information, see Chapter 4.

12. **D.** The routing table does not accurately show the route to the destination subnet in question; Pete should use the `route print` command to verify. All other answers are incorrect. Starting troubleshooting with the `route add` or `route change` commands will not be helpful; thus,

answers A and B are incorrect. There is `route check` command; thus, answer C is incorrect. For more information, see Chapter 2.

13. **A.** Network load balancing distributes all incoming connection requests using a mathematical algorithm to members of the NLB cluster. No clustering solution provided by Microsoft uses a round-robin method; thus, answer B is incorrect. Clustering is accomplished when you group independent servers into one collective entity that is accessed as if it were a single system; thus, answer C is incorrect. A server architecture that supports symmetric multiprocessing allows multiple CPUs to be used in a server, not clustering; thus, answer D is incorrect. For more information, see Chapter 10.

14. **C, E.** You should perform a normal backup once a week during nonworking hours to set the initial state for the critical data that is being backed up. Each night, a differential backup should be run to back up all the data that has been modified since that last normal backup. Although differential backups take slightly longer to perform each night than daily backups, they provide the benefit of a two-tape restoration using the last normal backup and the last differential backup. Using a copy backup will not change the archive bit setting on the files, thus causing the next differential to back up all data; therefore, answer A is correct. Using an incremental backup backs up only changes since the last normal or incremental backup, resulting in the need for more than two tapes for restoration; thus, answer B is incorrect. The daily backup also requires more tapes to be used for restoration; thus, answer D is incorrect. For more information, see Chapter 9.

15. **B, D.** Of the given options, the most likely problems are that the Novice is not allowing you to take control or the remote computer is not configured to allow you to take remote control. Your local computer is not an issue in the case of not being able to take remote control of an existing Remote Assistance session; thus, answer A is incorrect. Because you already have an existing Remote Assistance connection, the firewall is not the source of your problem; thus, answer C is incorrect. For more information, see Chapter 7.

16. **B.** The Audit System Events option configures auditing for certain system events, such as computer restarts and shutdowns. The Audit Process Tracking option configures auditing for events such as program activation, process exit, handle duplication, and indirect object access; thus, answer A is incorrect. The Audit Object Access option configures auditing to occur upon each user access of an object, such as a file, folder, printer, or Registry key that has its own SACL configured; thus, answer C is incorrect. The Audit Privilege Use option configures auditing to occur upon every occurrence of a user exercising a user right; thus, answer D is incorrect. For more information, see Chapter 8.

17. **B.** The Local Policies node of the Group Policy Editor contains three subnodes: Audit Policy, User Rights Assignment, and Security Options. The Audit Policy subnode is the place where Andrea can find the auditing items she needs to configure; thus, answers A, C, and D are all incorrect. For more information, see Chapter 5.

18. **B.** Sally needs to add the default gateway address to the server. The IP address of the closest router on your network segment that can route you either off that segment or to another segment on the network is your default gateway. This makes a routing decision for you to a remote site, which is what Sally needed to make happen. If Sally enters the gateway address, the packets sent to 172.16.2.0 will be sent to the router, which will then forward the request to that host. Without a gateway address, the packet destined for the remote LAN will not be sent anywhere; thus, answers A, C, and D are all incorrect. For more information, see Chapter 1.

19. D. Active Directory–integrated DNS zones store the zone data within the Active Directory database itself, thus allowing for greatly increased security, manageability, and redundancy; thus, answers A, B, and C are incorrect. When Active Directory–integrated zones are used, all DNS servers operate in a multimaster arrangement, allowing any DNS server to make changes to the zone data. If you have multiple DNS servers that are allowed to manage the zone data, dynamic updates are also more redundant because the failure of a single DNS server will not prevent dynamic updates from occurring. For more information, see Chapter 4.

20. D. Network Monitor is the tool you use to capture packets sent to and from this server; thus, answers A and B are incorrect. The version of Network Monitor included with Windows Server 2003 records only packets sent to and from this server and the LAN. Network Monitor is not used for monitoring processes—the Performance console is; thus, answer C is incorrect. For more information, see Chapter 2.

21. C. Convergence is the process by which NLB clustering hosts determine a new, stable state among themselves and elect a new default host after the failure of one or more cluster nodes. The heartbeat is a network communication sent among individual cluster nodes at intervals of no more than 500ms that is used to determine the status of all cluster nodes; thus, answer A is incorrect. Failback is the process of a cluster group moving back to the preferred node after the preferred node has resumed cluster membership; thus, answer B is incorrect. Failover is the process of a cluster group moving from the currently active node to another still-functioning node in the cluster group; thus, Answer D is incorrect. For more information, see Chapter 10.

22. C. To perform the restoration, you first need to use your last normal backup (the Saturday tape) and then your last differential backup (the Wednesday tape). Since the Saturday tape is a complete backup up to that point in time and the Wednesday tape is a complete backup from the last normal backup to that point in time, no other tapes would be required; thus, answers A, B, D, and E are incorrect. For more information, see Chapter 9.

23. D. Selecting the Authenticate As Computer When Computer Information Is Available option forces the computer to authenticate itself to the network as soon as the wireless network connection is made. If the computer cannot authenticate, no authentication is performed. The Authenticate as Guest When User or Computer Information Is Unavailable option allows the computer to authenticate using the Guest account if it cannot authenticate using its computer account; thus, answer A is incorrect. The Transmit per IEEE 802.1x option is used to configure how the EAPOL-start message is sent and has nothing to do with WEP; thus, answer B is incorrect. The Data Encryption (WEP Enabled) option specifies that WEP is to be used to encrypt data placed on the WLAN; thus, answer C is incorrect. For more information, see Chapter 7.

24. C. To track failed logon attempts, Andrea needs to configure failure auditing to occur for the Audit Logon Events option. The Audit Account Logon events option configures auditing to occur for user logons and logoffs; thus, answer A is incorrect. The Audit Account Management option configures auditing to occur for each event of account management on a computer; thus, answer B is incorrect. The Audit Policy Change option configures auditing to occur upon every occurrence of changing user rights assignment policies, audit policies, or trust policies; thus, answer D is incorrect. For more information, see Chapter 8.

25. **A.** By applying the Secure template, `securews.inf`, you can increase the security of the client workstations without adversely affecting network communications. The `securedc.inf` template is for domain controllers; thus, answer B is incorrect. The `compatws.inf` template actually lowers security settings; thus, answer C is incorrect. The `hisecws.inf` template will likely cause some problem on your network; thus, answer D is incorrect. For more information, see Chapter 5.

26. **C.** The subnet mask is the other 32-bit set of numbers you place with an IP address to denote where the network starts and ends and the host-based addressing starts and ends. In other words, if you have a 10.1.1.0 /24 network, this really means you have a subnet mask of 255.255.255.0 assigned to the 10.1.1.0 IP address network; thus, answers A, B, and D are incorrect. The network is 10.1.1 (24 bits mask it with 255.255.255.0), and the last octet, which is simply a zero, is assignable to hosts. For more information, see Chapter 1.

27. **D.** If the local DNS server is not authoritative for the requested domain and does not have the answer in its local cache, it will perform an iterative query to a root name server if it is configured as a forwarder; thus, answers A, B, and C are incorrect. The root name server will likely not know the IP address of the host but will be able to provide the local DNS server with the IP address of another DNS server that is authoritative for the quepublishing.com domain. This DNS server then can provide the requested name-resolution service for the local DNS server. For more information, see Chapter 4.

28. **A.** The connection attempt goes into quarantine until verified. Here's the actual process: When a remote computer attempts to connect to the Remote Access Server, the computer is assigned an IP address with which to participate on the network. Then the user credentials are verified and authenticated, but the connection stays in quarantine until the remote computer is verified against the script. A script runs, and when it is completed, the server hosting quarantine releases the connection from quarantine after this information is verified; thus, answers B, C, and D are incorrect. This is just one of the newest features of Remote Access Security provided by default with Windows Server 2003. For more information, see Chapter 7.

29. **A.** Port rules can be used to allow traffic only on specific ports to be load-balanced. If you configure explicit allow rules for specific ports and an explicit deny rule dropping all other traffic, only the desired traffic will be load-balanced; thus, answers B, C, and D are incorrect. For more information, see Chapter 10.

30. **D.** By using the volume shadow copy feature of Windows Backup, you can back up all files—even the ones that are open and in use at the time of the backup. Open files are backed up in a closed state as of the time of the backup. This enables you to back up open files without closing them for the backup, as previously required; thus, answers A, B, and C are incorrect. For more information, see Chapter 9.

31. **D.** The easiest way to allow an expired request to be answered is to resend it. This way, some of the information that was originally entered can be saved from the expired request. Creating a new request is not the easiest way to solve this problem; thus, answer A is incorrect. When a request has expired, it can be only deleted or resent; thus, answer B is incorrect. Deleting the request does not cause it be automatically re-created; thus, answer C is incorrect. For more information, see Chapter 7.

32. **A**. The performance counter that counts the number of `DHCPOFFER` messages sent per second by the DHCP server to a client computer is Offers/Sec. The Discovers/Sec counter monitors the number of `DHCPDISCOVER` messages received per second by the server; thus, answer B incorrect. The Acks/Sec counter monitors the number of `DHCPACK` messages sent per second by the DHCP server to client computers; thus, answer C is incorrect. DHCPAcks/Sec is not a real counter; thus, answer D is incorrect. For more information, see Chapter 3.

33. **C.** The easiest way to accomplish this task is to create a script that runs the `secedit/analyze` command on the computers and collects the results in a central network location. For more information, see Chapter 5.

34. **B.** Network Address Translation (NAT) turns one IP address into another, and the device that performs this NAT keeps a table of which IP addresses given from the NAT pool map to the one that was distributed. For more information, see Chapter 1.

35. **C.** A new feature in Windows Server 2003, conditional forwarding, enables you to configure a DNS forwarder with multiple forwarding IP addresses. As an example, you could have all name-resolution requests for the bigcorp.com domain sent to one IP address and all other name requests sent to a second, completely different IP address. This way, you can provide for both internal and external name resolution from within the internal network. For more information, see Chapter 4.

36. **D.** Pete should `ping` 10.10.1.10, `ping` 10.10.2.1 (default gateway), and then have a remote user `ping` 10.10.1.1 (default gateway). For more information, see Chapter 2.

37. **A.** Setting the affinity setting to None results in an inbound client request being sent to all nodes within the cluster. This type of affinity results in increased speed but is suitable only for providing static content to clients, such as static websites and FTP downloads. Typically, no cookies are generated by the applications running on the cluster that is configured for this type of affinity. For more information, see Chapter 10.

38. **D.** When enabled with its default settings, volume shadow copy creates a shadow copy twice daily. Volume shadow copy is limited to a maximum of 64 copies; thus, the maximum number of days to retrieve the historical data is 32 days. For more information, see Chapter 9.

39. **B, D, E.** The Windows Server 2003 IPSec implementation can use Kerberos v5, digital certificates, or shared secrets to perform user authentication. NTLM v2 is used for network authentication with Windows 2000 and Windows Server 2003; thus, answer A is incorrect. The Encrypting File System (EFS) is used to encrypt files and folders to add extra security to them; thus, answer C is incorrect. WEP is used as both an encryption and an authentication method on wireless LANs; thus, answer F is incorrect. For more information, see Chapter 6.

40. **B, C, D.** For WSUS to operate, the WSUS server must be provided to the Automatic Updates client computers via the Specify Intranet Microsoft Update Server Location Group Policy option; thus, answer A is incorrect. In addition, you need to configure the schedule by using the Configure Automatic Updates option and configure for restarting by using the No Auto-Restart for Scheduled Automatic Updates Installations option. For more information, see Chapter 8.

41. **C.** Of the given choices, the `hisecws.inf` template will provide the most secure configuration to your Windows XP Professional clients. For more information, see Chapter 5.

42. **D.** A proxy server is a server-based application that serves as a go-between for the internal LAN clients and the public Internet. If you do not want all your internal hosts accessing the Internet and perhaps exposing all the internal IP addressing information to the world, you could put in a proxy server to act as the middleman when searching the Internet. A proxy server also caches the pages so that Internet response seems faster to internal clients. For more information, see Chapter 1.

43. **A.** If you configure the other three internal DNS servers to forward name-resolution queries to the DNS server with IP address 192.168.100.133, only that one specific DNS server will make external DNS queries. For more information, see Chapter 4.

44. **A.** You should try a `Tracert` to the remote server. For more information, see Chapter 2.

45. **B.** The reason for, and advantage of, having two network adapters installed in any cluster host is that this setup enables you to separate the load-balanced traffic from the administrative traffic by placing the adapters in different IP subnets. This increases security of the administrative traffic by not exposing it to the load-balanced front end and also improves the performance of the host by allowing more load-balanced traffic to be passed over its front-end load-balancing network adapter. For more information, see Chapter 10.

46. **D.** Shadow copies can be viewed only when connecting to the shared folder over the network using My Network Places or locally on the server using My Network Places. On a Windows Server 2003 computer, you do not need to install the Previous Versions Client software to view shadow copies. For more information, see Chapter 9.

47. **A.** The Remote Desktops console can be used to connect to the console session if it is configured correctly. When you are creating the new connection, ensure that you select the Connect to Console option. The Web Interface for Remote Administration, the Remote Desktop Web utility, and the Remote Desktop Connection utility do not provide access to the console session on a remote server; thus, answers B, C, and D are incorrect. For more information, see Chapter 7.

48. **A.** The Account Lockout Policy node contains three items that can be used to limit the number of incorrect logon attempts over a specified amount of time; thus, answers B, C, and D are incorrect. The Account Lockout Threshold setting can be configured to specify how many failed logon attempts should be allowed before that user account is locked out. The Account Lockout Duration setting specifies how long the account is to be locked out (barring an administrator unlocking the account early). The Reset Account Lockout Counter After option specifies how much time must pass before failed logon attempts are no longer counted against the Account Lockout Threshold setting. These policies are typically applied at a high level in the organization, such as the root of a domain, to cause them to apply to all users within the domain. For more information, see Chapter 8.

49. **C.** Although, in a sense, all the answers will produce some or all the results that Hannah needs, only by using Group Policy can Hannah quickly, accurately, and efficiently apply the `securews.inf` template to all the computers (member servers and workstations alike) located in the Engineering OU. To apply these settings to the computers located in the Engineering OU, Hannah needs to import the `securews.inf` template into an existing or new Group Policy Object. For more information, see Chapter 5.

50. **D.** A firewall is a device that protects the internal network from the external Internet, WAN, business partner, or anything else you want to protect against. There are many different kinds, but you

will be responsible for only the most basic information listed here for the exam. Make sure that you understand what a firewall is because exam questions might have the term added into the scenario, but you need to know little other than that. For more information, see Chapter 1.

51. **D.** If Andrea does not know what the current security configuration is, she should apply the default security template to the computer. Each computer has its own default security template that is created at the time of Windows Server 2003 installation for workstations and member servers, and at the time of promotion for domain controllers. Andrea should not apply the default security template from one computer to any other computer. After the security configuration is reset back to a known state by using the default template, the secure templates can be successfully applied to create the desired level of security. Recall that security templates are incremental and only build on the security configuration already configured; they do not reset the computer's security configuration to the default settings before making any changes. For more information, see Chapter 5.

52. **B.** Sally should set up IGMP routing so that her server can forward multicast traffic up- and downstream to other multicast routers on the network. Windows Server 2003 does not support a multicast routing protocol—only a forwarding service. For more information, see Chapter 2.

53. **C.** If you want to troubleshoot remote problems on a multihop network, you need to use `tracert`. This tool can find latency and network holes that span more than a couple of router hops. For more information, see Chapter 2.

54. **A.** For your clients to be capable of viewing and working with shadow copies, you need to install the Previous Versions Client software. For more information, see Chapter 9.

55. **A, E.** The Windows Server 2003 IPSec implementation uses DES and 3DES for data encryption. The Windows Server 2003 IPSec implementation uses SHA1 and MD5 for data hashing; thus, answers B and C are incorrect. Advanced Encryption Standard (AES) is not used in IPSec; thus, answer D is incorrect. For more information, see Chapter 6.

56. **C.** The quickest way to configure Captain Bob's network to prevent smart cards from being used to log in to Terminal Services servers is to configure the Do Not Allow Smart Card Device Redirection option, located in the Computer Configuration\Administrative Templates\Windows Components\Terminal Services\Client/Server data redirection node of the Group Policy Editor; thus answers A, B, and D are incorrect. For more information, see Chapter 8.

57. **D.** An X icon next to an item in the Security Configuration and Analysis results indicates that the item is present in both the database and the computer but does not match the current configured setting. For more information, see Chapter 5.

58. **D.** The subnet mask is the other 32-bit set of numbers you place with an IP address to denote where the network starts and ends and the host-based addressing starts and ends. In other words, if you have a 10.1.1.0/24 network, this really means you have a subnet mask of 255.255.255.0 assigned to the 10.1.1.0 IP address network. The network is 10.1.1 (24 bits mask it with 255.255.255.0), and the last octet, which is simply a zero, is assignable to hosts. For more information, see Chapter 1.

59. **B.** You can locate the preconfigured security templates in the `%systemroot%\security\templates` folder. For a clean installation of Windows Server 2003 on volume C of a computer, this would be `C:\windows\security\templates`. For more information, see Chapter 5.

60. **A, B.** For Andrea to make her smart card self-enrollment solution work efficiently and securely, she needs to ensure that all required users get a blank smart card. To increase the security of the solution, Andrea should configure her CAs so that they do not issue smart card user certificates automatically, but instead place them into the Pending Requests folder awaiting manual administrative approval. Andrea should also take time to properly educate her users in the procedures to be followed to request a smart card certificate and to enroll the approved certificate. Also, all users will require training on the proper use, storage, and handling of their smart cards to prevent loss or damage; thus, answers C, D, and E are incorrect. For more information, see Chapter 8.

61. **C.** If Negotiate Security Action is selected, both computers must agree on the security parameters to be used, meaning that they both must support at least one common set of security parameters from those in the list. The list entries are processed in order of preference from top to bottom. The first security method shared by both computers is used. The Permit option passes the traffic without the requirement for security; thus, answer A is incorrect. This action is appropriate if you never want to secure traffic to which a rule applies. The Block Action silently blocks all traffic from computers specified in the IP filter list; thus, answer B is incorrect. There is no Open filter action; thus, answer D is incorrect. For more information, see Chapter 6.

62. **A, E, I.** The three preconfigured IPSec policies in Windows Server 2003 are Client (Respond Only), Server (Request Security), and Secure Server (Require Security); thus, answers B, C, D, F, G, and H are incorrect. For more information, see Chapter 6.

63. **B, C.** The Windows Server 2003 IPSec implementation uses SHA1 and MD5 for data hashing. The Windows Server 2003 IPSec implementation uses DES and 3DES for data encryption; thus, answers A and E are incorrect. Advanced Encryption Standard (AES) is not used in IPSec; thus, answer D is incorrect. For more information, see Chapter 6.

64. **B, D.** You should revoke Sam's certificate to prevent him from accessing any network resources. After the certificate has been revoked, you should publish the CRL to all CRL Distribution Points to ensure that all locations have the most up-to-date CRL. For more information, see Chapter 8.

65. **A, B.** Although all four of these options can be used to achieve the desired results, the creation of a new security template and the modification of an existing security template represent the best options available. You can opt to configure the settings using the Local Security Policy console, but this approach requires that you make the same changes on all member servers. You could also make the changes directly in Group Policy, but this approach does not give you the opportunity to test your configuration in a lab environment, thus locating problems before they have a chance to occur on the production network. For more information, see Chapter 5.

66. **A, D.** The DHCP server's primary function is to assign a unique IP address to the requesting client computers. DHCP servers can also be used to assign the IP address of the DNS server, the default gateway, the WINS server, and various other options. The IP address of the DHCP server is certainly unknown to the client when it does its broadcast to search for a DHCP server; thus, answer B is incorrect. You cannot pass file server IP address information to clients via DHCP; thus, answer C is incorrect. Active Directory–aware clients (such as Windows XP and Windows 2000) will query DNS for the service record of the domain controller that should service them; thus, answer E is incorrect. For more information, see Chapter 3.

67. **B**. The client computer will receive a DHCPACK message after successfully receiving or renewing a TCP/IP address from the DHCP server. When the client computer first requests an IP address, it issues a DHCPDISCOVER message to find a DHCP server; thus, answer A is incorrect. It then receives a DHCPOFFER message from each DHCP server; thus, answer C is incorrect. It sends a request (DHCPREQUEST) to use the address to the DHCP server that originated the offer; thus, answer D is incorrect. For more information, see Chapter 3.

68. **D**. At each remote location, install and configure DHCP on your Windows Server 2003 file and print server. Create and configure the scopes for all subnets in that location so that they provide 80% of the IP addresses available. At the corporate headquarters in Mississippi, install and configure DHCP on two Windows Server 2003 servers. Create and configure the scopes for all subnets in all locations so that they provide 20% of the IP addresses available. Answer A is incorrect because it does not meet the requirements of minimizing DHCP broadcast traffic on WAN links and VPN connections. Answer B is incorrect because it has the 80% configured at the corporate headquarters instead of at the location itself. When you have DHCP servers in distributed environment, you will not typically use the 50/50 rule; thus, answer C is incorrect. For more information, see Chapter 3.

PART III

Appendixes

APPENDIX A

Accessing Your Free MeasureUp Practice Test

This Exam Prep book features exclusive access to MeasureUp's practice questions. MeasureUp is a Microsoft Certified Practice Test Provider.

To access your free practice questions:

1. Retrieve your unique registration key on the inside of the back cover of this book.
2. Go to http://www.measureup.com.
3. Create a free MeasureUp account or log in to your existing account.
4. On the Learning Locker toolbar, click Register Products.
5. Read and consent to the license agreement by clicking the check box below the license agreement.
6. Type your registration key number in the Key box. Do not remove any dashes or substitute any numbers.
7. Click Register.
8. Click the Learning Locker button to display your Personal Test Locker.
9. Click the Practice Test link and follow the instructions to start your test, or click the Learning Locker tab to return to your Leaning Locker.

For more details about MeasureUp's product features, see Appendix B, "MeasureUp's Product Features."

APPENDIX B

MeasureUp's Product Features

Since 1997, MeasureUp has helped more than one million IT professionals achieve certifications from the industry's leading vendors. Created by content developers certified in their areas and with real-world experience, MeasureUp practice tests feature comprehensive questions (some with performance-based simulations, when simulations are relevant to a particular exam), detailed explanations, and complete score reporting. As a Microsoft Certified Practice Test Provider, MeasureUp's practice tests are the closest you can get to the certification exams!

Multiple Testing Modes

MeasureUp practice tests are available in Study, Certification, Custom, Missed Question, and Non-Duplicate question modes.

Study Mode

Tests administered in Study Mode allow you to request the correct answer(s) and explanation for each question during the test. These tests are not timed. You can modify the testing environment *during* the test by clicking the Options button.

Certification Mode

Tests administered in Certification Mode closely simulate the actual testing environment you will encounter when taking a certification exam. These tests do not allow you to request the answer(s) or explanation for each question until after the exam.

Custom Mode

Custom Mode allows you to specify your preferred testing environment. Use this mode to specify the objectives you want to include in your test, the timer length, and other test properties. You can also modify the testing environment *during* the test by clicking the Options button.

Missed Question Mode

Missed Question Mode allows you to take a test containing only the questions you missed previously.

Non-Duplicate Mode

Non-Duplicate Mode allows you to take a test containing only questions not displayed previously.

Question Types

The practice question types simulate the real exam experience and include the following:

- Create a tree
- Select and place
- Drop and connect
- Build list
- Reorder list
- Build and reorder list
- Single hotspot
- Multiple hotspots
- Live screen
- Command line
- Hot area
- Fill in the blank

Random Questions and Order of Answers

This feature helps you learn the material without memorizing questions and answers. Each time you take a practice test, the questions and answers appear in a different randomized order.

Detailed Explanations of Correct and Incorrect Answers

You'll receive automatic feedback on all correct and incorrect answers. The detailed answer explanations are a superb learning tool in their own right.

Attention to Exam Objectives

MeasureUp practice tests are designed to appropriately balance the questions over each technical area covered by a specific exam.

Technical Support

If you encounter problems with the MeasureUp test engine on the CD-ROM, you can contact MeasureUp at 678-356-5050 or email support@measureup.com. Technical support hours are from 8 a.m. to 5 p.m. EST Monday through Friday. Additionally, you'll find Frequently Asked Questions (FAQs) at www.measureup.com.

If you'd like to purchase additional MeasureUp products, telephone 678-356-5050 or 800-649-1MUP (1687), or visit www.measureup.com.

Glossary

Numbers and Symbols

802.1x An IEEE standard that provides for port-based access control and, thus, authentication for both wired and wireless networks. 802.1x uses the physical characteristics of a switched LAN to authenticate devices (and users) that are attached to each switch port and to disallow access from that port if the user or device cannot be successfully authenticated.

3DES (Triple Data Encryption Standard) A more secure variant of the DES standard that encrypts data by using three different 56-bit keys in succession. 3DES thus extends the DES key to 168 bits, providing approximately 6.2×10^{57} different keys.

%systemroot% A universal reference to the directory in which the Windows system files are installed. Typically, `%systemroot%` is `C:\Winnt` or `C:\Windows`. By default, clean installations of Windows Server 2003 use the `Windows` directory. If multiple copies of Windows are installed in a multiboot system, each copy has its own `%systemroot%` directory.

A

Active Directory The directory services included with Windows Server 2003. Based on the DNS hierarchy, Active Directory provides a domain-based directory service for organizing all the objects and services in a Windows Server 2003 network.

Active Directory–integrated zone A DNS zone file that is stored within the Active Directory data and replicated among other domain controllers running DNS as configured instead of being stored in a normal DNS text file.

Active Directory Users and Computers A Microsoft Management Console provided in Windows 2000 and Windows Server 2003 Active Directory domains that can be used to administer Active Directory objects.

affinity The method used by network load balancing to associate client requests with hosts in the NLB cluster.

AH (authentication header) A protocol in the IPSec suite that is used to authenticate IP traffic. The AH is inserted into the original IP packet immediately after the IP header.

application data partition A new directory partition type in Windows Server 2003 that can be used to store application-specific information in a separate partition that replicates only with the domain controllers that require this information. A common use of such partitions in Windows Server 2003 is for replication of Active Directory–integrated DNS zones.

auditing The process of logging information about network activities such as user logins, system shutdowns, and file access.

authentication The process of verifying a user's identity on a network.

Automated System Restore (ASR) The replacement for the Windows 2000 Emergency Repair Disk in which a boot floppy and a backup file can be used to restore a system to working order.

Automatic Updates The client side of the WSUS solution. Automatic Updates can be configured to work with the Microsoft Windows Update web servers or with internal WSUS servers.

B

B-node (broadcast node) A NetBIOS name–resolution method that relies exclusively on broadcast messages and is the oldest NetBIOS name–resolution mode. A host needing to resolve a name request sends a message to every host within earshot, requesting the address associated with a host name.

backup To make a reliable copy of critical data so that it can be recovered (restored) later in case of emergency or casualty.

baseline A set of collected data that is representative of the normal or beginning performance statistics. You can compare the current performance statistics against a baseline to troubleshoot problems.

BOOTP (Bootstrap Protocol) An Internet protocol that enables a diskless workstation to discover its own IP address from a BOOTP server. BOOTP is still used to allow DHCP requests and responses to traverse a routed network.

bottleneck A situation resulting from the incapability of a computer system to meet or keep up with the demands placed on it.

C

certificate A credential that is used to authenticate the origin, identity, and purpose of the public half of a public/private key pair. A certificate ensures that the data sent and received is kept secure.

Certificate Authority (CA) A service that issues digital certificates to users and computers. Additionally, CAs maintain a current list of revoked certificates that are no longer considered valid.

Certificate Revocation List (CRL) A list maintained by Certificate Authorities that identifies all certificates that are no longer valid but have not yet reached their configured expiration date. Clients validating a certificate can check the CRL to determine whether a presented certificate is still valid.

change management The planning and implementation processes by which changes are proposed within an organization.

CHAP (Challenge Handshake Authentication Protocol) An encrypted authentication scheme in which an unencrypted password is not sent over the network. CHAP is defined in RFC 1994 and is supported by RRAS to allow legacy and non-Windows clients to dial in and authenticate to a Windows Server 2003 Remote Access Server.

child domain A Windows Active Directory domain that exists directly beneath a parent domain in a tree hierarchy.

Class A network The largest of the classes of IP networks. There are 126 Class A networks, each capable of addressing up to 16,777,214 hosts. Class A networks have a first octet between 1 to 126, with a default subnet mask of 255.0.0.0.

Class B network The second-largest class of IP networks. There are 16,384 Class B networks, each capable of addressing up to 65,534 hosts. Class B networks have a first octet between 128 and 191, with a default subnet mask of 255.255.0.0.

Class C network The smallest class of IP networks. There are 2,097,152 Class C networks, each capable of addressing up to 254 hosts. Class C networks have a first octet between 192 and 223, with a default subnet mask of 255.255.255.0.

classless interdomain routing (CIDR) A more efficient IP address–management system than the original class-based system of Class A, B, and C networks. CIDR is typically used by routers and gateways located on the Internet backbone for routing packets across the Internet. CIDR allows any number of contiguous bits in the IP address to be used at the network ID, resulting in more IP addresses becoming available.

cluster A group of two or more independent servers that operate together and are viewed and accessed as a single resource. Also referred to as *clustering*.

cluster resource A network application, service, or hardware device (such as a network adapter or storage system) that is defined and managed by the cluster service.

cluster resource group A defined set of resources contained within a cluster. Cluster resource groups are used as failover units within a cluster. When a cluster resource group fails and cannot be automatically restarted by the cluster service, the entire cluster resource group is placed in an offline status and failed over to another node.

cluster virtual server A cluster resource group that has a network name and IP address assigned to it. Cluster virtual servers are accessible by their NetBIOS name, DNS name, or IP address.

clustering See *cluster*.

Compatible security template A security template that provides a means of allowing members of the Users group to run applications that do not conform to the Windows Logo Program by modifying the default file and Registry permissions that are granted to the Users group.

conditional forwarding A new feature in Windows Server 2003 DNS that enables administrators to direct DNS requests to other DNS servers based on domain. Also known as *intelligent forwarding*.

convergence The process by which NLB clustering hosts determine a new, stable state among themselves and elect a new default host after the failure of one or more cluster nodes. During convergence, the total load on the NLB cluster is redistributed among all cluster nodes that share traffic handling on specific ports, as determined by their port rules.

copy backup A type of backup operation that copies all selected files but does not mark each file as having been backed up (the archive attribute is not cleared). Copy backups have no effect on any other type of backup operation.

counter Part of an object in the System Monitor that can have usage and performance statistics measured.

counter log A log that can be created by using the Performance console for later viewing and comparison against current performance statistics.

CRL distribution point (CDP) A location to which Certificate Revocation Lists are published.

D

daily backup A type of backup operation that copies all selected files that have been modified the day the daily backup is performed; the archive attribute is not cleared in this case. Using normal and daily backups, you need the last normal backup and all daily backups to be able to perform restoration.

dcpromo The command-line command that is issued to start the process of promoting a member server to a domain controller.

Default DC security template A security template that is automatically created when a member server is promoted to DC. It represents the file, Registry, and system service default security settings for that DC and can be used later to reset those areas to their default configurations.

default gateway The configured router on a TCP/IP–enabled system that allows all packets destined for a remote network to be forwarded out of the local network. If a packet is bound for a remote network but no route is specified, the packet is sent to the default gateway address. Also known as the *default router*.

Default security template A security template that is created during the installation of Windows on a computer. This template varies from one computer to the next, depending on whether the installation was performed as a clean installation or an upgrade. This template represents the default security settings that a computer started with and, thus, can be used to reset portions of security, as required.

delegation of control The process by which you can grant nonadministrative users some responsibility for some portion of Active Directory, such as delegating the ability to change users' passwords or add computers to the domain.

DES (Data Encryption Standard) A symmetric encryption scheme that requires the sender and the receiver to know the secret key. DES uses a 56-bit key that provides approximately 7.2×10^{16} different key combinations.

DHCP client Any computer that has DHCP settings enabled and is requesting addresses from a DHCP server.

DHCP exclusion A range of IP addresses that are excluded from being leased to DHCP clients in a configured scope.

DHCP lease An IP address and corresponding TCP/IP configuration that is passed from a DHCP server to a requesting DHCP client.

DHCP reservation An IP address that is given by a DHCP server that never changes.

DHCP server A server that provides the automatic assignment and management of IP addresses to network clients.

differential backup A type of backup operation that copies files created or changed since the last normal (full) or incremental backup and clears the archive attribute. Using normal and differential backups, you need the last normal backup and the last differential backup to be able to perform restoration.

Discretionary Access Control List (DACL) An internal list that is attached to files and folders on NTFS-formatted volumes that is configured to specify the level of permissions that are to be allowed for different users and groups.

distance-vector routing A type of routing that calculates the best path in an OSPF environment.

DNS forwarder A DNS server that has been configured to forward to another DNS server name-resolution queries it cannot answer.

DNS resolver Any computer that has been configured with one or more DNS server IP addresses and that performs queries against these DNS servers.

DNS Security (DNSSEC) A public key infrastructure–based system in which authentication and data integrity can be provided to DNS resolvers as discussed in RFC 2535. Digital signatures are used and encrypted with private keys. These digital signatures can then be authenticated by DNSSEC-aware resolvers by using the corresponding public key. The required digital signature and public keys are added to the DNS zone in the form of resource records.

DNS slave server A DNS forwarder server that does not try to resolve a resolution request if it doesn't receive a valid response to its forwarded DNS request.

domain A container in the DNS name hierarchy or the network Organizational Unit for Windows Server 2003 networks.

domain controller (DC) A server that holds a writeable copy of the Active Directory data and manages information contained within the Active Directory database.

Domain controllers also function as NS servers when Active Directory–integrated zones are used. The Kerberos Key Distribution Center (KDC) is located on every domain controller as well.

domain name system (DNS) A service that dynamically provides name- and address-resolution services in a TCP/IP environment.

DumpEL A command line–based utility that can be used to quickly collect and search event logs. This tool is found in the Windows Server 2003 Resource Kit.

Dynamic Host Configuration Protocol (DHCP) A standards-based method of automatically assigning and configuring IP addresses for DHCP clients.

E

EAP (Extensible Authentication Protocol) An extension to the Point-to-Point Protocol (PPP), as specified in RFC 2284, that provides a means for the primary authentication method to be negotiated during the initiation of the PPP session.

encryption A mechanism for securing data in which data is translated into a secret code that can be read only with the correct key to translate the secret code back to the original data.

Enterprise Certificate Authority The first Certification Authority (CA) in a branch of CAs. It is responsible for assigning certificates to intermediary CAs and other subordinate CAs.

ESP (Encapsulating Security Protocol) A protocol that is used in the IPSec suite to handle data encryption. ESP is usually used with AH to provide the maximum level of security and integrity for data transmitted in IPSec transmissions. ESP uses DES encryption by default, but it can be configured to use 3DES.

EventCombMT A GUI-based utility that can be used to quickly collect and search event logs. This tool is found in the Windows Server 2003 Resource Kit.

exterior gateway protocol (EGP) The original exterior protocol, which is used to exchange routing information between networks that do not share a common administration.

F

failback The process of moving a cluster group (either manually or automatically) back to the preferred node after the preferred node has resumed cluster membership. For failback to occur, it must be configured for the cluster group, including the failback threshold and selection of the preferred node.

failover The process of a cluster group moving from the currently active node to a designated, functioning node in the cluster group. Failover typically occurs when the active node becomes unresponsive (for any reason) and cannot be recovered within the configured failure threshold period.

firewall A device that protects the internal network from the external Internet, WAN, business partner, or anything else you want to protect against.

forest The logical structure that contains all domains in the Active Directory model.

forest and domain functional levels Levels of functionality for Active Directory forests and Active Directory domains that determine what unique features they can possess, such as the capability to remain forests and domains that are configured for Windows Server 2003 mode.

forest root The first domain created within an Active Directory forest.

fully qualified domain name (FQDN) The complete DNS name of a host, including the host name and all domains that connect the host to the root domain. The FQDN is typically expressed without a trailing period, with the root domain assumed.

G

GPO (Group Policy Object) A collection of security and configuration settings that are applied to a container in an Active Directory domain.

Group Policy Editor A subset of the Active Directory Users and Computers console that allows the editing of Group Policy Objects.

Group Policy Management Console (GPMC) A free add-on for managing Windows Server 2003 Active Directory Group Policy Objects that provides a simplified, consolidated interface to manage all domains in a single location.

H

H-node (hybrid node) A hybrid NetBIOS name–resolution mode that favors the use of WINS for NetBIOS name resolution.

heartbeat A network communication sent among individual cluster nodes at intervals of no more than 500ms, used to determine the status of all cluster nodes.

Highly Secure security template A security template that imposes further restrictions on computers it is applied to. Whereas the Secure templates require at least NTLM authentication, the Highly Secure templates require NTLMv2 authentication.

I

IGMP proxy mode The mode used to configure a router that has two or more interfaces with different settings on different interfaces. One interface acts as a proxy multicast host that sends IGMP membership reports on one of its interfaces.

IGMP routing mode The mode in which you can set Windows Server 2003 to listen for IGMP Membership Report packets, as well as to track group membership.

incremental backup A type of backup operation that copies only those files created or changed since the last normal or incremental backup; the archive attribute is then cleared. Using normal and incremental backups, you need the last normal backup and all incremental backups to be able to perform restoration.

interior gateway protocol (IGP) A protocol that is used to pass routing information for routing networks that are under a common network administration.

Internet Control Message Protocol (ICMP) A protocol in the TCP/IP suite of protocols that is used for testing connectivity.

Internet Group Management Protocol (IGMP) One of the core protocols in the TCP/IP suite; a routing protocol that is used as part of multicasting.

Internet Key Exchange (IKE) An encryption scheme that allows disparate VPN servers to share encryption key information and make the IPSec protocol practical in today's environment.

Internet Protocol (IP) The portion of the TCP/IP protocol suite that is used to provide packet routing.

IP address The 32-bit binary address that is used to identify a TCP/IP host's network and host ID. IPv6 IP addresses are 128 bits in length.

IP Security (IPSec) A Layer 3 TCP/IP protocol that provides end-to-end security for data in transit.

`ipconfig` A command line–based tool that enables you to view and modify the TCP/IP properties of installed network adapters. Some if its uses include releasing and renewing DHCP leases, as well as clearing the local DNS resolver cache.

ISAKMP/Oakley (Internet Security Association and Key Management Protocol/Oakley) A protocol that is used to share a public key between sender and receiver of a secure connection. ISAKMP/Oakley allows the receiving system to retrieve a public key and then authenticate the sender using digital certificates.

iterative query A DNS query sent from a DNS server to one or more DNS servers in search of the DNS server that is authoritative for the name being sought.

K

Kerberos v5 An identity-based security protocol based on Internet security standards used by Windows Server 2003 to authenticate users.

kerbtray.exe A GUI-based Kerberos monitoring utility that can be used to display the currently cached tickets.

klist.exe The command-line equivalent of the kerbtray.exe utility. klist.exe can also be used to purge currently cached Kerberos tickets.

L

LAN manager HOSTS (LMHOSTS) A file modeled after the TCP/IP `HOSTS` file and used to provide a static NetBIOS name to IP address resolution in a Windows environment. The `HOSTS` file was originally used for name resolution in a TCP/IP network environment. As the `HOSTS` file was replaced by DNS, the `LMHOSTS` file was replaced by WINS.

Layer 2 Tunneling Protocol (L2TP) A VPN protocol that is created by combining the Point-to-Point Tunneling Protocol (PPTP) and Layer 2 Forwarding (L2F) tunneling protocols. L2TP is used as the transport protocol in the Windows Server 2003 VPN service in conjunction with IPSec.

leaf The end object in a hierarchical tree structure.

link state An operation used by dynamic routing protocols to test the condition of a connection (link) between routers. OSPF is a link-state protocol.

link-state routing Dynamic routing that tests the condition of a connection (link) between routers. OSPF is a link-state protocol.

LSA (link-state advertisement) A notification that is flooded throughout the network when a network link changes state (up to down, or vice versa).

M

Main Mode The first phase of the IKE two-phase operation to establish a secure communication channel. During this phase, the two computers establish a secure, authenticated channel called the Phase I (Main Mode) SA.

M-node (modified node) A hybrid NetBIOS name–resolution mode that first attempts to resolve NetBIOS names using the B-node mechanism. If that fails, an attempt is made to use P-node name resolution. M-node was the first hybrid mode put into operation, but it has the disadvantage of favoring B-node operation, which is associated with high levels of broadcast traffic.

Microsoft Baseline Security Analyzer (MBSA) A utility that can be used to scan computers on a network looking for missing security updates and weak security configurations either from the command line or from within the GUI.

Microsoft Management Console (MMC) A Microsoft Windows framework used for hosting administrative tools.

Microsoft Point-to-Point Encryption (MPPE) A data-encryption method used for PPP-based connections or PPTP VPN connections. MPPE supports strong (128-bit key) and standard (40-bit key) encryption.

MS-CHAP (Microsoft Challenge Authentication Protocol) A Microsoft-specific variation of the CHAP authentication protocol. MS-CHAP is more secure than CHAP and comes in two variations: MS-CHAPv1 and MS-CHAPv2. MS-CHAPv1 supports one-way authentication and is used by Windows NT 4.0. MS-CHAPv2 is used with Windows 2000 or later and supports mutual authentication.

multicast scope A range of IP multicast addresses in the range 224.0.0.0 to 239.254.255.255. Multicast addresses in this range can be prevented from propagating in either direction (send or receive) through the use of scope-based multicast boundaries.

multicasting A method of sending a series of packets to a group of computers instead of to a single computer or all computers on a network. IGMP support is required to use multicasting.

multilink A capability included in Windows Server 2003 that allows the aggregating of multiple modem connections.

N

nbtstat A command-line utility that enables you to verify the current connections over the NBT protocol. It also enables you to check and load the NetBIOS name cache.

NetBIOS name The computer name for NetBIOS networking. This name can be 16 characters long: 15 provide the host name, and the 16th represents the service registering the name.

NetBIOS name cache A list of system NetBIOS names that a host has resolved or that have been preloaded from the LMHOSTS file.

NetBIOS node type The node type that determines the order of name resolution for NetBIOS names. There are four types: B-node, P-node, M-node, and H-node.

NetBIOS over TCP/IP (NBT or NetBT) The name given to the process of running NetBIOS network services over TCP/IP.

netsh A command-line tool used on Windows 2000 and 2003 systems for configuring and troubleshooting networking-based issues.

Network Address Translation (NAT) A process by which private IP addresses are mapped to public IP addresses, and vice versa. The device that performs this NAT keeps a table of which IP addresses given from the NAT pool map to the one that was distributed.

Network Basic Input/Output System (NetBIOS) An application-layer networking protocol that works at the application, presentation, and session layers of the OSI model. Legacy Microsoft networking used NetBIOS as the default application-layer protocol.

network interface card (NIC) A device installed into a PC or other host device to allow it to have a MAC address and be assigned an IP address. This device connects you to the network. Also referred to as a *network adapter*.

network load balancing A way to provide highly available solutions in which all incoming connection requests are distributed using a mathematical algorithm to members of an NLB cluster. NLB clustering is best used when clients can connect to any server in the cluster, such as websites, Terminal Services servers, and VPN servers.

node In regard to clustering, an individual server within a cluster. In regard to networking, a device that communicates on a network and is identified by a unique address. In hierarchies, a node is a container that contains other containers and data.

normal backup A type of backup operation that copies all selected files and marks each file as having been backed up (the archive attribute is cleared). Only the most recent copy of the backup file is required to perform restoration.

ntbackup.exe The command-line version of the Windows Backup Utility.

O

Open Shortest Path First (OSPF) A routing protocol that allows routers to share their routing information, making them dynamic routers.

Organizational Unit (OU) A container that provides for the logical grouping of objects within Active Directory for ease of administration and configuration.

P

P-node (point-to-point node) A NetBIOS name–resolution method that relies on WINS servers for NetBIOS name resolution. Client computers register themselves with a WINS server when they come on the network.

packet The basic unit of information that is transmitted over a network. Packets are also known as frames, datagrams, and cells.

PAP (Password Authentication Protocol) A clear-text authentication scheme that provides no security for information passed over the connection. PAP is defined in RFC 1334.

parent domain The domain that has one or more child domains under it that share the same DNS namespace.

`pathping` A command-line tool that provides the equivalent of the `tracert` command by enabling you to identify which routers are in the path the packets are taking. `pathping` also acts as the equivalent of the `ping` command by sending `ping` requests to all the routers over a specified time period and then computing statistics based on the packets returned from each router. `pathping` displays the number of packets lost at each router or link, enabling you to determine which routers and links (subnets) might be causes of connectivity troubles.

Performance console A preconfigured Microsoft Management Console that contains the System Monitor as well as Performance Logs and Alerts.

physical address (MAC address) A 48-bit alphanumeric number, such as 00-08-74-97-0B-26, that denotes the host's physical address. Also called a Media Access Control (MAC) address, the physical address is unique to the device to which it is assigned.

ping A command-line utility that is used to troubleshoot TCP/IP problems. `ping` sends a packet with data, asking the remote system to echo the packet to the sender.

Point-to-Point Tunneling Protocol (PPTP) A protocol that is used by Microsoft and others to create VPNs.

port rules A configuration that is used to determine what types of traffic are to be load-balanced across the cluster nodes.

primary DNS server The name server that contains the master copy of a zone file. Also called a *primary master*.

primary master See *primary DNS server*.

primary zone A DNS zone that contains the master copies of resource records for a domain.

principle of least privilege An administrative principle that states that users are given only the minimum privileges required to perform the specific set of tasks they have been assigned.

private IP address An IP address range reserved for private (non-Internet-connected) networks. There are private address ranges in the Class A, Class B, and Class C address blocks.

proxy server A server-based application that serves as a go-between for the internal LAN clients and the public Internet. A proxy server also caches the pages so that Internet response seems faster to internal clients.

public IP address An IP address for use on the Internet or a private network that must be assigned via an organization or ISP so that no duplicates exist.

pull replication The act of replicating a copy of the WINS database from a WINS replication partner by pulling data from the partner's database to the local database.

push replication The act of replicating a copy of the WINS database to a WINS replication partner by pushing data from the partner's database to the local database.

push/pull replication The act of replicating a copy of the WINS database to a WINS replication partner by allowing the replication partners to push and/or pull.

Q

quick mode The second phase of the IKE two-phase operation to establish a secure communication channel. During this phase, the two computers establish the rules for communication called the Phase II (Quick Mode) SA. During the second phase, a new shared key is created for use. After the Phase II SA is in place, IPSec secured communications can occur.

quorum disk The disk drive that contains the definitive cluster-configuration data. Clustering with MSCS requires the use of a quorum disk and requires continuous access to the data contained within the quorum disk. The quorum disk contains vital data about the nodes participating in the cluster, the applications and services defined within the cluster resource group, and the status of each node and cluster resource. The quorum disk is typically located on a shared storage device.

R

RADIUS (Remote Access Dial-In User Service) An industry-standard security protocol that is used to authenticate client connections.

recursive query A DNS query that is used to request an authoritative answer or an answer indicating that there is no resolution for a DNS lookup.

registered IP address Any block of addresses registered with Internet Assigned Numbers Authority (IANA).

Remote Assistance A Remote Desktop Protocol–based service in Windows XP and Windows Server 2003 that allows a Novice to ask for and receive help from an Expert over a TCP/IP network connection.

Remote Desktop for Administration A Remote Desktop Protocol–based service that allows administrators to remotely connect to and administer Windows XP and Windows Server 2003 computers. Remote Desktop for Administration replaces Terminal Services Administration mode in Windows 2000.

Remote Desktop Protocol A terminal communications protocol based on the industry standard T.120 multichannel conferencing protocol.

replication partner A server in a WINS architecture that sends or receives a copy of the WINS database from another WINS server.

resource record A data record in a DNS zone. Many types of resource records are available. For example, an address resource record is the data record that describes the address-to-name relationship for a host.

restoration The process of replacing or recreating data on a computer using a set of backup media.

Resultant Set of Policies (RSoP) An MMC snap-in that enables you to determine how various Group Policies are applied to an object.

reverse lookup In DNS, an IP address–to–name resolution.

revoked certificate A digital certificate that has been taken out of use before its configured end of lifetime. Certificates can be revoked for any number of reasons, including loss of keys or employee termination.

RFC (Request for Comments) A document that is used to make notes about the Internet and Internet technologies. RFCs are typically used as the official way to introduce a new Internet standard.

role-based security The process of configuring network security for hardware and users based on the role they play in the network.

root In a hierarchy, the container that holds all other containers.

Root Certificate Authority (CA) A Certificate Authority that forms the top of the CA hierarchy.

route (routing table) utility A utility that enables you to view and modify the routing table on a Windows computer.

router A system or device that forwards or drops packets between networks, based on the entries in its routing table.

Routing and Remote Access Services (RRAS) A service that allows for remote connection to a server.

Routing Information Protocol (RIP) A protocol that dynamic routers use to share their routing tables. Similar to the OSPF and BGP protocols, RIP is an older, less efficient routing protocol.

routing protocol A type of protocol that is used by dynamic routers to share their routing tables with other routers.

routing table A table that describes routing decisions that a host can make. Minimum entries in the routing table include routes to each local network and a default route.

routing table (route) utility A utility that enables you to view and modify the routing table on a Windows computer.

S

secedit.exe The command-line equivalent of the Security Configuration and Analysis snap-in.

secondary DNS server A server that provides name resolution for a zone but cannot be used to modify the zone. It contains a read-only copy of the zone file. Also known as a *secondary master*.

secure dynamic update A secure method used by Active Directory–integrated zones that allows DHCP to automatically update DNS when leases are granted and expired by the DHCP server.

Secure security template A security template that increases the level of security configured on a computer it is applied to, above the default configuration. Secure templates prevent the use of the LAN Manager (LM) authentication protocol. Windows 9*x* clients need to have Active Directory Client Extensions installed to enable NTLMv2 to allow them to communicate with Windows 2000 and later clients and servers using these templates. These templates also impose additional restrictions on anonymous users, such as preventing them from enumerating account and sharing information.

Security Configuration and Analysis snap-in An MMC snap-in that is used to configure, analyze, and implement security templates on a local computer. It can be used to create templates that are imported into GPOs for application to larger groups of computers.

security log A log that is found in the Event Viewer and that contains auditing entries.

security template A text file that contains settings that configure the security settings of the computer or computers to which it is applied. Several preconfigured security templates come with Windows Server 2003, and you can edit and create your own custom ones as required.

Security Templates snap-in An MMC snap-in that can be used to safely create and modify security templates without danger of accidentally applying them to the local computer or the network.

site A well-connected TCP/IP subnet.

snap-in A tool that you can add to the MMC.

SPAP (Shiva Password Authentication Protocol) An encrypted password-authentication protocol that was introduced for Shiva remote access servers.

split horizon A mechanism that is used with RIP to prevent routing loops.

split horizon with poison reverse A mechanism that broadcasts routes with an infinite routing metric.

Standalone CA A Certificate Authority that can be used with or without Active Directory. Certificate requests are set to Pending until an administrator approves the request.

standard primary zone A DNS zone file that holds the master writeable copy of a zone and can transfer it to all configured secondary zones.

standard secondary zone A DNS zone file that holds a read-only copy of the zone file and is used to provide increased reliability and performance.

Start of Authority (SOA) record In a DNS zone file, a record that is used to provide the zone parameters to all the DNS servers for the zone. The SOA record also provides the name of the primary server and the person in charge of the domain.

stub zone A new DNS zone type in Windows Server 2003 that contains only the required resource records that are needed to identify the authoritative DNS servers for another zone.

subnet A subdivision of a TCP/IP internetwork that communicates with other subnets through routers.

subnet mask In TCP/IP, a mask that is used to determine what subnet an IP address belongs to. A subnet mask enables a host or a router to determine which portion of an IP address is the network ID and which is the host ID. The host can then use this information to determine whether to send a packet to a host on the local network or to a router.

subordinate CA Typically the lowest level in a Certificate Authority hierarchy. Subordinate CAs issue certificates directly to users and network hosts.

suffix A domain extension that indicates the root domain. For example, `.com` is a domain suffix.

supernetted network A network that has multiple network addresses or subnets running on the same segment.

superscope A grouping of scopes that are used to support multinetted IP subnets on the same physical network.

T

Terminal Services An RDP-based service offered by Windows NT, Windows 2000, and Windows Server 2003 servers, allowing thin clients to connect to the server and use applications stored on the server.

top-level domain (TLD) A domain that exists directly underneath the root domain.

`tracert` A command-line utility that traces the route that packets travel between the local host and the destination host, and displays it to the screen.

Transmission Control Protocol/Internet Protocol (TCP/IP) The suite of communications protocols used to connect hosts on the Internet.

transport mode The use of IPSec not in a tunnel (with two configured endpoints). Commonly used on a private network between two hosts.

tree A logical group of Windows Server 2003 domains that share a common DNS namespace.

tunnel mode The use of IPSec in a mode where two endpoints have been configured to create a tunnel, such as when a VPN tunnel is created.

U

unicast address A TCP/IP address that is used for host-to-host communications. Unicast addresses are the most commonly used types of TCP/IP addresses.

Universal Naming Convention (UNC) A naming convention that is used to define a resource on a Windows Server 2003 server network. A share named `DOCS` on the server `SERVER1` could be accessed using the UNC path `\\SERVER1\DOCS`.

user logon name Commonly referred to as the pre–Windows 2000 logon name, such as `will`.

user principal name (UPN) The full DNS domain name of an Active Directory user account, such as `will@corp.mcseworld.com`.

V

validity period The length of time a digital certificate is valid.

virtual private network (VPN) A mechanism for providing secure, private communications, using a public network (such as the Internet) as the transport method. VPNs use a combination of encryption and authentication technologies to ensure data integrity and security.

volume shadow copy A new feature in Windows Server 2003 that provides distinctly different functions. The first function allows the Windows Backup Utility (or `ntbackup` from the command line) to back up open files as if they were closed. The second feature provides a means of creating and storing up to 64 historical versions of files located within a network share.

W

Windows 2000 mixed mode The mode that allows Windows NT 4.0 domain controllers to exist and function within a Windows 2003 domain. This is the default setting when Active Directory is installed, although it can be changed to native mode.

Windows 2000 native mode The mode in which all domain controllers in a domain have been upgraded to Windows 2003 and there are no longer any NT 4.0 domain controllers. An administrator explicitly puts Active Directory into native mode, at which time it cannot be returned to mixed mode without removing and reinstalling Active Directory.

Windows 2003 functional level The highest functional level of either the domain or the forest in Windows 2003. This functional level implements all the new features of Windows 2003 Active Directory.

Windows Internet Naming Service (WINS) A service that runs on a Windows Server 2003 server to provide NetBIOS name resolution. When you use WINS, name resolution is performed using directed transmissions, resulting in a reduction in broadcast traffic and the capability to find systems on different subnets. WINS replaces the `LMHOSTS` file in a fashion similar to the way DNS replaced the `HOSTS` file.

wireless LAN (WLAN) A local area network that uses one of the 802.11 standards, such as 802.11b or 802.11a.

workgroup A grouping of computers and resources that use a decentralized authentication and management system.

WSUS (Windows Server Update Services) An add-on service for Windows 2000 and Windows Server 2003 networks that provides the functionality of a Windows Update web server on the internal network. WSUS enables you to select which available updates are authorized for distribution to network clients, thus ensuring that only the updates you have tested and approved are installed.

Z

zone A domain for which a DNS server is authoritative.

zone transfer The process of copying DNS resource records from a primary zone to a secondary zone.

Index

Numbers

A

B

C

D

E

F

I

J–K

L

M

N

P

Q

R

S

T

U

V

W

X–Y–Z